PENGUIN BOOKS

ROBERTSON DAVIES: MAN OF MYTH

Judith Skelton Grant is a well-known authority on Davies' work. Her *Robertson Davies: A Consideration of His Writing* appeared in 1978, and she has edited two collections of his journalism, *The Enthusiasms of Robertson Davies* (1979) and *Robertson Davies: the Well-Tempered Critic: One Man's View of Theatre and Letters in Canada* (1981). She is married with two sons and lives in Toronto.

D1627146

Bronzino's *An Allegory*, Davies' favourite painting.

ROBERTSON DAVIES
MAN *of* MYTH

Judith Skelton Grant

PENGUIN BOOKS

PENGUIN BOOKS
Published by the Penguin Group
Penguin Books Canada Ltd, 10 Alcorn Avenue, Toronto, Ontario, Canada
M4V 3B2
Penguin Books Ltd, 27 Wrights Lane, London W8 5TZ, England
Viking Penguin, a division of Penguin Books USA Inc., 375 Hudson
Street, New York, New York 10014, U.S.A.
Penguin Books Australia Ltd, Ringwood, Victoria, Australia
Penguin Books (NZ) Ltd, 182-190 Wairau Road, Auckland 10, New
Zealand

Penguin Books Ltd, Registered Offices: Harmondsworth, Middlesex,
England

First published in Viking by Penguin Books Canada Limited, 1994

10 9 8 7 6 5 4 3 2 1

Copyright © Judith Skelton Grant, 1994

Manufactured in Canada

Canadian Cataloguing in Publication Data

Grant, Judith Skelton, 1941-
    Robertson Davies: man of myth

Includes bibliographical references.
ISBN 0-14-011452-1

1. Davies, Robertson, 1913-   - Biography.   2. Authors, Canadian
(English) - 20th century - Biography.* I. Title.

PS8507.A67Z64 1994   C813'.54   C94-931858-2
PR9199.3.D3Z64 1994

"This book is bound
"Repkover" to lay
flat when opened".

In memory of my father

Acknowledgments

Robertson Davies' life now spans eighty-one years. While he was growing up, his father, Rupert, a newspaper owner and editor, moved the family from the village of Thamesville to the town of Renfrew and later the city of Kingston, all in Ontario. Davies was educated at Upper Canada College in Toronto, Queen's University in Kingston and Balliol College in Oxford. A brief career as an actor was followed by more than twenty years as a journalist (he was both a columnist and editor of the *Peterborough Examiner*), and for another twenty years he was master of Canada's first graduate college and a professor of drama at the University of Toronto. Getting the measure of these contexts and activities would have kept any conscientious biographer busy for years. Davies' vigorous involvement in Canadian theatre, and the novels that are the ultimate focus of this literary biography, stretched my work to over a decade.

Inevitably, some things must remain unsaid about a person who is still productive, vigorous and engaged with life. Friends and enemies alike may consider it appropriate to be less than frank, while the law of libel provides a limit of its own on what can be said about the living. Some records may be off-limits—in this case, certain of Davies' diaries remained closed to me. But in compensation there are tremendously valuable resources, in particular the number of individuals who may be interviewed, that make it possible to capture the tone and nuance of a life more intimately. And it is here that I would like to acknowledge a multitude of debts to those who took the time to gather their thoughts about Davies. Chief among them is Davies himself, who brought great energy and liveliness to our almost seventy interviews between 1981 and 1993 and kept me on my mettle. Davies' wife, Brenda, his brother Arthur L. Davies and his daughters Miranda, Jennifer Surridge and Rosamond Cunnington all gave me the benefit of thoughtful commentary and suffered my intrusion on their privacy with remarkable grace.

At almost every stage I discovered a surprising number of people who had been aware of Davies, had watched him and had considered what they saw. Even for the years in Renfrew from 1919 to 1925, a number could tell me about him and about the town that he experienced—Allie Clements McCallum (his teacher for "Primer"), John G. McNab and John A. M. Austin (classmates at the North Ward school), Babe Dewey Stacey (a contemporary), Lillian Handford and John Ferrier (neighbours), Isobel Ferrier (resident in the town from 1927 to 1934 and from 1972 to the present), D. W. McCuaig (editor of the Renfrew *Advance*, 1951-70, and of the *Mercury*, 1970-78) and D. W. Stewart. For the three years when Davies attended Victoria School and the Kingston Collegiate Institute, Jackson Telgmann, a classmate, offered an account of his capacities as a young actor, both on and off the stage. Sydney Hermant, Donald Ryerson, Arnold Smith (contemporaries at Upper Canada College) and Alison Grant Ignatieff (the daughter of UCC's headmaster) recalled UCC and the colourful Davies they knew there between 1928 and 1932. For 1932-35, when Davies was a student at Queen's University in Kingston, Donald Ryerson recalled working with him on several theatrical projects, Eleanor A. Sweezey described her dates with him, and James Conacher told me about the experience of being tutored by him and of acting under his direction. Contemporaries in the Oxford years—Horace W. Davenport, Kenneth Garlick, Douglas V. LePan, J. Max Patrick, Philip John Stead and, off the record, Edward Heath—painted vivid word portraits of the Davies who became an "*Isis* Idol" in 1937. And for the two years when Davies pursued a theatrical career in England, as an actor, teacher of drama and dramaturge, Philip John Stead (a flat-mate), Birgitta Rydbeck Heyman (a student at the Old Vic's drama school) and Brenda Davies (the Old Vic's assistant stage manager, Davies' fiancée and bride) provided glimpses of Davies as he first set out to work.

For the long period in Peterborough, Ontario, it was a matter of selecting key observers, since the whole town appeared to have opinions. Many people have helped me to envision Davies in his role as editor of the *Examiner*—associate editors Thomas J. Allen and Ralph Hancox, the paper's accountant Margaret Rodney McCauley, reporters Douglas Vaisey, Ray Timson and James English, general manager W. L. Garner and his wife Edith and columnist Christopher Gledhill. Others spoke with great warmth and appreciation of the Davieses' intense involvement in the town's theatrical life—John Hooper and Tom Allen about the Coventry Nativity Play; John Londerville, Fern Rahmel, Musa and Gertrude Cox about the Peterborough Little Theatre; William Needles, David Gardner, Amelia Hall, Herbert Whittaker, Gwen Brown about summer theatre in Peterborough and elsewhere. Local friends like Elizabeth Breyfogle, Dr. Thomas and Sheila Currier, Valerie and Robert B. Porter, Scott Young shared reminiscences, as did friends from elsewhere who visited during this period—Grant Macdonald, Clair Stewart, Joan McInnes, Gordon Roper, Arnold Edinborough. A number of residents of the Peterborough area during the 1940s and '50s—notably, Margaret Heideman, Ralph Honey, Mrs. David R. Howat, Ellen Macdonald, Mrs. Ken Morris—helped to fill out the picture.

Dama and Alf Bell, John Hayes, Bruce Swerdfager and Tanya Moiseiwitsch gave me their characterizations of Davies' contribution to the Stratford Festival. Donald Davis described his early enthusiasm for Davies' plays and told me how Davies came to write for the Crest Theatre. And Jack Merigold, Bruce Swerdfager and Amelia Hall contributed their recollections of the trying road tour and New York debacle of Davies' play *Love and Libel.*

As was the case in Peterborough, I had to be selective from many witnesses to Davies' twenty or so years at the University of

Toronto and Massey College. Those who helped plan and build the college, or who knew it as members of the staff, almost unanimously conveyed a tremendous admiration for Davies in their assessments—Ron Thom, Hart Massey, Claude Bissell, Gordon Roper, Tanya Moiseiwitsch; Colin Friesen, Douglas Lochhead, Moira Whalon. This was also the line taken by the senior Fellows I interviewed—Claude Bissell, Robert Finch, J. N. Patterson Hume, John Leyerle, Ann Saddlemyer; and that pursued by the college's singers and musicians—Giles Bryant, Joyce Wry, Derek Holman. Those who had been junior Fellows during the Davies years at Massey presented a wider spectrum of views—Ian Alexander, Peter Brigg, James Carley, Beth Gilbert, Jeffrey M. Heath, Michael Laine, Ira Levine, William Stoneman, Lorie Waisberg, Faith E. Wallis. I also benefited from the comments of observers like Betty Lee and W. A. C. Dobson's son Iain, who knew the college in other capacities.

Professors Ann Saddlemyer, Gordon Roper, J. R. de J. Jackson and John M. Robson, and Davies' students Ian Alexander, David Blostein, Daniel Bratton, Peter Brigg, Ramsay Derry, David Gardner and Jeffrey M. Heath all supplied useful insights into the man they knew as a colleague and teacher.

The editors who handled Davies' writing at Clarke, Irwin, Viking, Macmillan of Canada and McClelland and Stewart—R. W. W. Robertson, Elisabeth Sifton, Ramsay Derry and Douglas Gibson—described their working relationships with him with great warmth and frankness.

There was a massive volume of manuscript and print resources to work with. Often these were in private hands, or in places not organized for research, and it was necessary for many people to put themselves out if I were to gain access to this material. Uniformly they did so, showing great kindness. Davies himself spent a great deal of time rooting through cupboards to find family records, scrapbooks, diaries, early poems and the like. I owe a very special debt to his secretary, Moira Whalon, who until the late 1980s had many of his literary papers in her care— notably the successive drafts of plays and novels, of speeches and articles. She still maintains voluminous correspondence files. Not only did she go out of her way to make it possible for me to absorb all of this material, she was extraordinarily helpful and accurate in pinning down facts and details. Several private individuals went to considerable trouble to make their collections of letters available to me—Donald Ryerson, Eleanor A. Sweezey, Horace W. Davenport, Arnold Edinborough, Ralph Hancox, Tanya Moiseiwitsch, Gordon Roper, Domini Blythe. David Gardner and Amelia Hall lent me their theatrical scrapbooks. Heather and Robin Jackson, Jay Macpherson and Sue Howson provided friendly assistance and tracked down elusive materials in far-off places. Dr. Richard C. Davis gave me access to the miscellany of "Daviesiana" that he has been gathering for several years. Institutions opened their files—Upper Canada College, the Book Society of Canada (which held Clarke, Irwin's editorial files for a time), Macmillan of Canada and Viking in New York.

Many papers and relevant material have now been deposited in one public collection or another. I am especially grateful to Anne Goddard and Grace Hyam of the Manuscript Division of the National Archives of Canada, who smoothed my way for weeks at a time after Davies deposited his literary papers there. Similarly Desmond Neill and Marie Korey, librarians at the Robertson Davies Library in Massey College, helped me frequently, and with tremendous efficiency, over the years. I also made heavy use of the resources of the National Library in Ottawa, the Metropolitan Reference Library in Toronto, the Archives of Ontario, the John P. Robarts Research Library, the Thomas Fisher Rare Book Library (both at the University of Toronto), the Mill Memorial Library at McMaster University in Hamilton, the Bodleian Library in Oxford.

Support for the actual writing of the biography came in several forms, and for all of it I am deeply grateful. As I got started, the Social Sciences and Humanities Research Council of Canada gave me a stipend for one year and a modest amount of expense money for excursions to Thamesville, Renfrew, Kingston, Oxford, Peterborough and New York, and, for a time, for secretarial help in transcribing the tapes of interviews. In the late 1980s, the Ontario Arts Council gave me two small grants that covered the cost of research trips to the National Archives in Ottawa. For several years the John P. Robarts Library gave me access, without charge, to the full range of its research and inter-library loan facilities. And for the last few years, Massey College has kindly sustained these privileges. Once I began the actual writing, I had the help of several readers. My mother-in-law, Margaret Grant, and my mother, Margaret Skelton, provided the perspective of contemporaries on a life that spanned roughly the same years as their own. For a number of years Ramsay Derry served as my editor, a role he played with great tact. He taught me a great deal about effective writing, and our discussions were one of the delightful elements of this project. Recently, Catherine Marjoribanks has run a fresh and astute eye over the whole. My sister-in-law, Grace Westcott, kindly read the manuscript from a lawyer's perspective. Robertson and Brenda Davies and Moira Whalon, who all read a near-final draft, rescued me from various mistakes. And my husband, John Grant, maintained a penetrating, companionable, critical, helpful interest throughout.

Contents

Chapter 1

THAMESVILLE: 1913-19

I can recall, at a very early age, standing transfixed before a peony, feeling myself drawn into its gorgeous colour; I know I was very young at the time, for the peony and I were about the same height. But the important thing is that I can still do this, with sight and sound, when I choose, so it is very easy for me to go on a trip—which I believe is the expression now for this sort of experience.

—*Marchbanks' Almanack*, 1967

DR. VON HALLER: What is the earliest recollection you can honestly vouch for?

MYSELF: Oh, that's easy. I was standing in my grandmother's garden, in warm sunlight, looking into a deep red peony. As I recall it, I wasn't much taller than the peony. It was a moment of very great—perhaps I shouldn't say happiness, because it was really an intense absorption. The whole world, the whole of life, and I myself, became a warm, rich peony-red.

DR. VON HALLER: Have you ever tried to recapture that feeling?

MYSELF: Never.

—*The Manticore*, 1972

1

It was in a garden that Francis Cornish first became truly aware of himself as a creature observing a world apart from himself. He was almost three years old, and he was looking deep into a splendid red peony…. It was a significant moment, for it was Francis's first conscious encounter with beauty—beauty that was to be the delight, the torment, and the bitterness of his life….

It was his mother's garden….

—*What's Bred in the Bone*, 1985

IN AN IMPORTANT sense, Robertson Davies was born, not on August 28, 1913, but on the day when the first traces were laid down in his memory. His first recollection is of an encounter with a deep-red peony in his mother's garden, shortly before his third birthday. Peony-height himself, fascinated by the flower's colour, he looked into its heart, and it became the whole of the world to him.

He used this experience three times in his work, in the passages quoted above from *Marchbanks' Almanack*, *The Manticore* and *What's Bred in the Bone*, each time bringing out different details and tailoring his recollection to serve the fictional situation. Memory is in fact a key element in the imaginative constructs that delight and astonish Davies' audiences. He has a richer contact with his past than most of us can manage, and when he chooses to open himself up to it, no veil softens its impact. His parents, long dead now, remain vigorously present in his thoughts, speaking in their own voices and with their own characteristic turns of phrase. Davies once said, only partly in jest, that he hears "hard words" from his mother almost every day of his life, as she tells him, in the way of mothers, to "brace up and clean up and brush up and smarten up."

His earliest memories are centred in the small white house in the southwestern Ontario village of Thamesville, where he was born and lived until May 1919, three months before he turned six. The surrounding country is flat, rich farmland. Like the cities of London to the northeast and Chatham to the southwest, Thamesville lies in the valley of the Thames River, which flows toward Lake St. Clair and Detroit.

Like most houses in the little village of eight hundred, the

Davies home was of frame construction, heated by "baseburners" or stoves in each room. Every spring the stoves had to be taken out, the piping taken down and cleaned and the holes in the wall covered with ornamental plates. In the autumn the procedure was reversed. The main floor contained three principal rooms: the parlour, approached through an archway from the front hall, the combination dining and living room behind another arch and beyond that the kitchen. A small room off the dining area served as his father's study. One of the three upstairs bedrooms was shared by his parents, Rupert and Florence, and a second by his two brothers, Fred and Arthur, eleven and ten years older than he. Davies' own bedroom was the smallest, and it faced west, so he could see the sun setting when he was in bed. On the left side of the front of the house was a verandah, and near it his mother's garden, with its peonies, and a large lilac bush in which he had a secret hiding place. At the back were a woodshed, a second lawn, a trellised grapevine, a garage and a clean privy. (Florence was obsessed with the need for clean privies. She retained a man to come and clean it out every month, "which was regarded as sanitation gone mad in Thamesville.")

The emotional temperature of the household swung widely and unpredictably. Davies recalls Rupert's "appalling black moods which were terrifying—utterly terrifying." When Rupert and Florence disagreed, they never argued in front of the children; instead, a frigid silence descended between them for as much as two weeks at a time. On the other hand, when things were amicable between them they could be extremely amusing, and mealtimes could become absolutely hilarious. When their joint mood was running high, Davies would find himself roused out of bed in the middle of the night, brought downstairs, swaddled in blankets, filled full of cocoa and biscuits and invited to share whatever "high old jinks were going on." He now says wryly, "All Welshmen are manic depressives," but as a child he had to tread warily.

Reading aloud to him, the youngest child, was a family activity that lasted considerably past the time when he could do it himself. Florence read to him at bedtime, and she read to amuse him when he was sick. She chose animal stories—Ruskin's *The King of the Golden River*, Grimms' fairy-tales, Kingsley's *The Water Babies*. (Her affection for *The Water Babies* did not rub off on Davies, who hated "bloody old Mrs. Be-Done-By-As-You-Did," but he remembers that she stopped once at the passage where Kingsley attacks the Welsh as "a pack of crooks and sneaks" and said, "Now you're not to pay attention to any of that because you know your father is Welsh. This is just nonsense.") His brothers read him the funny papers—"Mutt and Jeff," "Maggie and Jiggs," "Bringing Up Father," "The Toonerville Trolley"—and he loved them for their excitement, slang and violence. His father read to him too—Kingsley's *The Heroes*, Hawthorne's *Tanglewood Tales*, Barham's *The Ingoldsby Legends*, Bible stories. Rupert particularly relished the more terrifying tales and may not have been aware of the extent of the reactions they aroused in his son. Davies so feared the minotaur in the *Tanglewood Tales* that he was frightened to go to bed. "Nell Cook!! A Legend of the 'Dark Entry'" in *The Ingoldsby Legends*, with its cook who prepared a poisoned pie, was another that left a mark. Rupert told him too of Spring-heeled Jack, a Welsh bandit who lurked behind hedges. When travellers came along a country lane at night "he'd give a gigantic spring right over the hedge onto their shoulders and stab them to death and rob them" before bounding away. Stories like these, and the manner of their telling, fired Davies' imagination and initiated in him a lifelong fascination with myth, as well as an addiction to ghost stories.

Like many children, Davies told himself stories as he fell asleep. But unlike most children who grow up to be writers, he did not commit his stories to paper once he learned to read and write. Instead he continued in the oral tradition until he was about eighteen, making up and telling stories to himself in bed at night, imposing on himself a rule all the while that they had to be "something that could happen."

Music was always in the air in the Elizabeth Street house. Rupert, Florence and Arthur sang; Florence played the piano, Rupert the flute, Arthur the cornet. Rupert directed the St. James Presbyterian Church choir, and Florence sang in it and played for practices. Davies himself soon learned to sing nursery rhymes and children's songs. He often fell asleep at night to music rising from the rooms below as the choir practised pieces like Kjerulf's "Last night the nightingale woke me / Last night when all was still" and Sir Joseph Barnby's "Sweet and Low." Often his father would sing for his own amusement, or for visiting friends, songs like "Knock'd 'em in the Old Kent Road," accompanied by his mother at the piano.

During the day Davies often listened to records on the family Victrola, one of the first in Thamesville, an affair with a crank but no trumpet. He can still hear the distinctive sound of the early records, which were seemingly capable of doing justice only to contraltos. On one of them Nellie Melba rendered "Home Sweet Home" and Tosti's "Good-Bye" in "a thin, cold voice which uttered the notes, though not in any recognizable form the words." But Schumann-Heink, Louise Homer and Clara Butt sounded to him "like kine lowing in rich pastures," and Harry Lauder's hearty laugh came through clearly in "Stop Your Tickling, Jock." (Years later, after Davies had learned much more about Tosti's "Good-Bye"—about its composer, singer, words, librettist and the repertoire to which it belonged—he used it as a touchstone piece in *A Mixture of Frailties*. Later still he introduced a recording of Harry Lauder's jolly song as a macabre accompaniment to the murder in *The Rebel Angels*.)

Sometimes his mother put on a record in the morning, took her little son by the hand and danced to "The Jolly Coppersmith," or taught him the heel-toe opening of "The Opera Polka" or the steps of the schottische. (Perhaps it would be more accurate to say that she tried to teach him to dance; he has never been good at it.) When the extended Davies family gathered in nearby Brantford at Christmas, everyone sang favourite pieces. Rupert and his brother Percy, for example, tenor and bass respectively, selected old-fashioned songs like "The Moon Hath Raised Her Lamp" from Sir Julius Benedict's 1863 opera *The Lily of Killarney*.

Both Rupert and Florence were avid theatre-goers. Several times a year, Florence and one of her friends would take a day trip to Detroit, where many touring companies played, to see such actors as Mrs. Minnie Maddern Fiske, Billie Burke, Otis Skinner, Ida van Cortland and Johnston Forbes-Robertson. On her return she would describe their performances in detail. When business took Rupert to Toronto, he visited the theatre too, recounting the experience on his return "vividly and with obvious keen relish." He often measured the actors' performances against those of Henry Irving as Mathias in *The Bells* and Shylock in *The Merchant of Venice*, which he had seen in Toronto at the turn of the century. As Shakespeare was another of Rupert's yardsticks, Davies soon came to think that his plays must represent "the very pinnacle of theatre experience."

Inevitably both of his parents belonged to the local amateur dramatic society. In May of 1918 Rupert played a part in Martha Morton's *A Bachelor's Romance*, and the four-year-old Davies was keenly aware that he was going to see his father on stage pretending to be someone else. Also, during the afternoon he had seen his mother making up the "medicine" his father was to take in the play—from cold tea—and it delighted him to be in on the secret that it wasn't really medicine at all!

Rupert hung theatrical pictures on the walls of his little study. Two were of Henry Irving—one a reproduction of a pencil sketch and the other of an illustration by Cyrus Cuneo depicting Irving's first entrance in *The Bells*, the inn door thrown open, standing in his furs, the snow beating down, with an expression on his face so intense as to be transfixing. Also there were pictures of William Faversham and his wife, the beautiful Julie Opp, playing Marc Antony and Portia in Shakespeare's *Julius Caesar*. Davies can still describe them, to his mind "far more interesting, more awesome and noble, than any genuine Roman could possibly have been." In the study he pored over the family copy of Shakespeare, illustrated as it was with portraits of actors in costume and character, and fixed those pictures too in his mind for life. As an adult, he became a collector of theatrical books and memorabilia and acquired his own copy of Cuneo's portrait of Irving.

Both Rupert and Florence were hypochondriacs. In their household, ailments provided the sufferer with a certain stature. Rupert was indeed prone to indigestion, and Florence's stomach had never recovered from the bichloride of mercury that the untrained son of a chemist had given her by mistake some years before. But they went to extremes, always trying out odd regimens or taking some unpleasant mixture. Davies recalls that Rupert "chewed forests of slippery elm" and once almost killed himself by consuming the liquid acquired by cooking a large number of onions in their own juice. Fred had a more serious medical problem, the result of a schoolyard scuffle. He suffered from recurrent attacks of pain in the side. On these occasions he would be put to bed and cossetted with hot-water bottles by his mother and helpful neighbours. After one particularly severe session in 1918, a specialist was brought in from London, and he, according to Arthur, "tapped Fred's abdomen and drew off a large quantity of fluid, which ordinarily would have passed through his kidneys." A kidney had indeed been severely damaged, and after several more years of these unpleasant attacks it was removed.

Both Rupert and Florence were great believers in purgation (an obsession many of their contemporaries shared, judging by the advertisements of the period). Davies recalls that until he and his brothers were about ten years old they were regularly dosed on Friday nights with "some sort of nasty stuff…which gathered all the evil in you," followed by a big glass of Epsom salts on Saturday morning "to drive it out." If that proved ineffective, their parents enlisted the further aid of "Dr. Tyrrell's Domestic Internal Bath," a device they employed regularly on themselves as

Tyrrell's J. B. L. Cascade

An Appliance for the Administration of the Internal Bath

88-422 The rubber bottle holds about 3 qts. and the lower illustration shows the appliance ready for use as an internal bath.

The patient sits on the bottle which has a pipette (controlled by a faucet) that passes into the rectum, the patient's own weight forcing the water into the bowel and flushing out the descending colon. It is suitable for both sexes and can be used as hot water bottle or fountain syringe when needed as such. Complete with small tin of J. B. L. Antiseptic Tonic, Rectal Soap, Book on Health, also fittings and tubing.
Price, delivered. **12.00**

88-423. Extra supply of J. B. L. Antiseptic Tonic, for using in the Cascade… **1.04**

The T. Eaton Co., *Fall and Winter Catalogue*, 1919-20, page 441.

well. As described in *The Manticore*, "It was a rubber bag of a disagreeable gray colour, on the upper side of which was fixed a hollow spike of some hard, black composition. It was filled with warm water until it was fat and ugly; I was impaled on the spike, which had been greased with Vaseline; a control stopcock was turned, and my bodily weight was supposed to force the water up inside me to seek out the offending substances. I was not quite heavy enough, so Netty helped by pushing downward on my shoulders." As a boy Davies did not enjoy any of this, but he did not question his parents' judgment either.

For Rupert and Florence, conversation was both a skill and an art. Davies later came to realize how much his parents preferred vivid, highly coloured language to flat-footed fact. Both of them were gifted mimics, and his mother, a descendant of a pioneer family, spoke with an "old Ontario precision of pronunciation and grammar and use of language which made some of the things that she said very well-pointed and fine-honed and sharp." She could "cut you up with a fine blade if she decided to do so." Davies didn't consciously appreciate her skill until he was a student at Queen's University in Kingston, Ontario, and one of his professors, Wilhelmina Gordon, remarked on it. The Canadian poet Douglas V. LePan, who met Florence in 1936, remembers her "as having a very nice old-fashioned country turn of phrase with very considerable pungency," although he does not recall her as eloquent. Many of her metaphors reflected the period when horses were a part of daily life. She would speak of people who "kicked right over the traces" or who were "old roarers," of "a hack" and of the need to "wait for the pole horse." She read widely, primarily in history and novels, liked the Brontes, Thackeray (but not Dickens), Victor Hugo, Mary Webb and later Sinclair Lewis. She used quotations frequently, particularly from her favourite books, *Elmer Gantry* and *Babbitt.* Like Rupert she was an irreverent quoter of the Bible, and like him she took particular pleasure in its references to vomit: "He hath swallowed down riches, and he shall vomit them up again: God shall cast them out of his belly" (Job 20:15), "As a dog returneth to his vomit, so a fool returned to his folly" (Proverbs 26:11), "The dog is turned to his own vomit again; and the sow that was washed

to her wallowing in the mire" (2 Peter 2:22). Both she and
Rupert enjoyed referring to the fate of the Philistines who were
smitten with "emerods in their secret parts" (I Samuel 5:9). Irony
was her prevailing mode. Davies recalls, "If you said, 'Mother,
am I supposed to do this, that or the other?' she would say,
'What do you suppose?' She never said, 'Yes' or 'No.'"

Rupert, the more voluble of the two, was also of a far more
positive cast of mind. Like Florence, he read widely. He had a
lively and extensive vocabulary, a broad emotional range and an
ear for quotation. One of Davies' earliest memories, probably
from Christmas 1916, is of his father laughing uproariously at
Stephen Leacock's *Nonsense Novels*. That book "took a firm grip
on our household and parts of it passed into that special language which strongly knit families tend to develop. I think I
heard about Guido the Gimlet of Ghent before I knew the name
of the Kaiser, who was another celebrated character of that day.
The techniques of disguise used by The Great Detective were
known to me long before I understood why they were funny."
Like Florence, Rupert loved to poke fun at those who used language less expertly than himself. He would come home and say:
"And who do you think is visiting beneath the parental roof this
week-end?" tickled with the pretentiousness of the social
columns in the weekly newspapers he was reading. Florence,
trained as a secretary, mocked the style of conventional business
letters: "Your esteemed favour of even date to hand and contents
noted." They loved to recall the minister who had opened his
prayers with "Oh Lord, take Thou a live coal from off Thine
altar and touch my lips." Both of them, sitting in the congregation, had silently hoped that He would do just that.

By the time Davies was five, he realized that his parents
expected him to speak "properly," by which they meant gram-
matically. They were quick to correct him, and their own clarity
of expression also helped to convince him that "there was only
one word which would express a particular shade of meaning."
He found it "a delight to find that word. It need not be an elegant word, or a long word, but it had to be the right word."
Since his parents "would not permit a misquotation, even from a
nursery rhyme, if it violated the laws of metre," he soon gained a

working knowledge of the rhythms of poetry. He discovered the pleasures of a shared literacy in an incident that happened when he was about five. "Two electricians were working in my parents' house, and I was watching the one who was busy in the cellar. His boss, who was upstairs, shouted: 'Sam, Sam,' and Sam, who was standing by me, shouted back, 'Speak, Lord, for thy servant heareth.' Then they laughed, and I laughed too, because we all knew the passage from First Samuel, Chapter Three, and because Sam knew what to answer when he was called from a mysterious upper region." (Sam West, the village atheist, was a regular writer of letters to the *Thamesville Herald* and a friend with whom his father discussed politics. He figures briefly in *Fifth Business* under his own name and is also one of the originals of the character Sam North in Davies' play *The Voice of the People*.)

Davies' grasp of village life owed much to his parents', especially his father's, vigorous participation in it. As the owner and editor of the *Herald*, Rupert knew much more about local happenings than he could print, and a good deal of what he didn't print became mealtime fare. (Coupled with his parents' enthusiasm for theatrical doings, this whetted in Davies a lifelong appetite for information about the world behind the scenes.) Rupert was also not only leader of the Presbyterian Church choir and a member of the Amateur Dramatic Society but a teacher in the Presbyterian Sunday school, a member of the Board of Education (later its chairman), foreman of the coroner's juries and a keen member of the lawn-bowling club. And it was he who arranged to bring two musical events to the village, the Hambourg Trio and Madame Hughes' Welsh Choir. Florence, of course, belonged to the choir and the Dramatic Society also, and she was a member of the most important women's group in town, the Thamesville Art and Music Club. As a pair they went to card parties in the winter months, and in the summer they went to see the sulky racing at the fairgrounds.

The neighbourhood was filled with strange and interesting characters. A "witch" lived next door, her house almost overgrown by shrubs and bushes. Davies was not alone in his impression of the elderly and eccentric Miss Patience Minchell; his brothers too, at his age, had been convinced that she was a witch.

And on the other side lived the Harpers. When Annie Harper died, the old man was so grief-stricken that he tried to drown himself in the well, but the situation quickly became absurd as he got stuck on the way down. As Davies' mother helped to haul him out he cried, "I want to go to Annie. I want to go to Annie."

On the other side of the street was a rather grand house, where mad Aunt Ellen Mcfarlane, a relative of the village's founding family, the Fergusons, lived with her keeper. From time to time she would get out and tumble into the middle of the road, where she would throw dust in the air and shout "Christian men come and help me!" until the neighbours, Davies' mother among them, would come and help her back into the house. Also across the street lived the Albertson family. In the mornings Davies would watch the tiny wife levering her fat husband "Albie" out of bed and into a chair with an elaborate system of pulleys and hoists so that she could make the bed. The Davieses and their friends were convinced that Albertson was faking his illness both to tyrannize over his wife and to avoid life's responsibilities. Much later, when he had read Freud, Davies speculated that he had witnessed an instance of hysterical illness.

Around the corner lived two Irish old maids. One was a schoolteacher, the other taught music. Davies knew that his mother had once helped get one of the Miss Causgroves down off the roof, where she'd been sitting making bird noises (because she was menopausal, he was later told). Another house he visited belonged to Mr. Cryderman, the village clerk and auctioneer. He was aware that Cryderman's wife was dying of cancer and that he had taken a mistress, who was a dwarf and the most hideous woman in Thamesville. This woman offended people like Davies' mother by confiding her intention to have Mrs. Cryderman's seal jacket cut down for herself once the woman had died. Davies was especially drawn to the Crydermans' because of their remarkable dog, which could pretend to smoke a pencil. There were no more than one or two children his age in the neighbourhood, so he played with only one on a regular basis, a little girl with whom he pretended to take long imaginary journeys sitting in the buggy in her family's barn.

As a child Davies was unusually observant. Even after the family had moved away from Thamesville, he continued to file away what he heard about the villagers—how this one had had to leave town to have her illegitimate baby, how that one had been sent to the Kingston Penitentiary "for copulating...with one of his daughters." Fifty years later, his memories, richly transmuted, made their way into the novel *Fifth Business* and so captured and defined for many readers the essence of Ontario village life in the second decade of the century. Here is how he used what he knew about Thamesville's citizens in Milo Papple's salty recapitulation of what had happened in the village of Deptford while Dunstan Ramsay was away during the First World War:

> Jeez the war's made a difference in this little old burg. Unsettled. You know what I mean? Lots of changes. Two fires—bad ones—and Harry Henderson sold his store. But I guess I mean changes in people. Young kids in trouble a lot. And Jerry Cullen—you remember him?—sent to the penitentiary. His daughter squealed on him. Said he was always at her. She was just a kid, mind you. But the cream of it was, I don't think Jerry ever really knew what he done wrong. I think he thought everybody was like that. He was always kinda stupid.... And then two bastards, a juicy self-induced abortion, several jiltings, an old maid gone foolish in menopause, a goitre of such proportions as to make all previous local goitres seem like warts, which Dr. McCausland was treating in Bowles Corners. The prurient, the humiliating, and the macabre were Milo's principal areas of enthusiasm, and we explored them all.

Of course, in Davies' hands such details simply serve as background to the miraculous and marvellous things that give Dunstan's life direction and compelling interest and that underpin the development of the book. Davies himself remembers far more than he was ever able to use.

Thamesville was small enough that a boy of five could get to know its physical layout for himself and acquire his own feel for the way things fit together. He could walk to most places, or trundle on his wagon, and he could get an occasional ride with

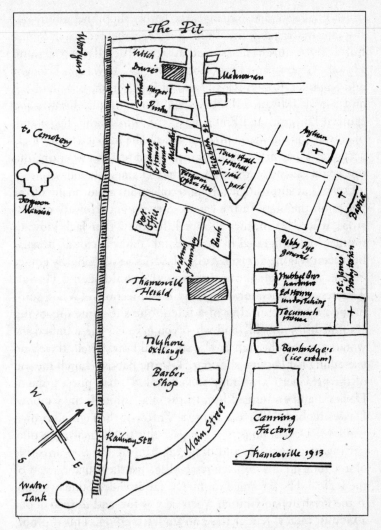

the milkman or the breadman, making leisurely horse-drawn deliveries to almost every house in the village. Almost seventy years later, having made only one brief return visit in the interim, Davies drew me a map locating the gravel pit once used by the Grand Trunk Railway, the cemetery, the three-storey brick mansion of the Ferguson family and the Ferguson Opera House, the town hall (which encompassed the fire hall and jail and had a small park in front of it), the post office, the bank, the *Herald* office, the telephone exchange, the barber shop, the railway station and water tank, the canning factory, the Tecumseh House hotel, five churches, assorted stores (officially Stewart and Howat's Grocery and Dry Goods Store, D. A. Watson Druggist and Stationer, Robert Pye's House of Satisfaction, E. S. Hubbell and Sons Hardware, Ed. Henry and Co. Furniture Dealers and Funeral Directors and Embalmers, and Wm. Bambridge's) and, of course, the houses on his own street. The map is astonishingly accurate. There are simplifications, and a few minor errors, but one could easily use it to walk around Thamesville today.

Davies has surprisingly strong recollections about many of the places on the map. In the case of Stewart and Howat's general store, where his mother shopped, he knew that Jack Howat's mother had emigrated from Scotland "under a cloud" because her infant was illegitimate. At Bambridge's he occasionally got ice cream. At the telephone exchange he could see Lu Howat, Thamesville's operator, plugging in connections. (When summoned by the cranking of a telephone she came on saying "Numbah? Numbah?" and when you gave her the number, she would put you through or else she would say, "Well, there's no use calling her because she's out.") At the Baptist church the son of the preacher ("a whining snivelling kid") had put a stone in Davies' hand and urged him to throw it through the window. Davies replied: "You're a Baptist. Throw it through your own window." Davies, no patsy, later gave this troublemaker his due, getting into a scuffle and dragging him by the feet until his blouse rode up, his stomach scraped against the rough cement of the walk and he screamed for mercy. He attended Sunday school at the Presbyterian Church when he was five and learned about a God of mercy, tenderness and understanding. This did not, however, completely vanquish his earlier conception of God as a menacing giant, with fixed, glaring eyes and coal-black hair and beard, rather like a Russian icon.

Davies had intimate knowledge of one of Thamesville's more important institutions, the *Herald*. The newspaper had three employees—Jumper Thurston, Nell Manning and Nan Purdon—but it was basically his father's show, with Florence, Fred and Arthur helping out. Rupert played all the parts:

reporter, compositor, editor, business manager, printer. Davies remembers his father writing reports and editorials right at the typesetting machine. His mother helped with the accounting, set type by hand, proof-read, folded papers, kept the subscription lists, did some reporting and writing and prepared the copies for the mail using a brass labeller. Fred and Arthur, for fifty cents a week, went to the office before eight every morning, swept the place out and got the fire started. They also worked after school. Fred gradually became an expert mechanic and learned to run the various presses, and Arthur did odd jobs like folding papers, putting away "reglet," replacing "furniture," washing presses and running errands.

Davies, as a little boy, was absolutely forbidden to go near the gravel pit and the creek that ran beside it, half a block from the house. The pit was a haunt of tramps, full of scraggly bushes and pools of standing water. He remembers its edge as a frightening cliff. (Had he been older and taller it would have appeared much less daunting. Although the pit is extensive, it is quite shallow. The older children played in it, and in the winter, once its two large pools had frozen, the villagers skated there.) He was also warned to keep clear of the canning factory, which was built on piles, because the Thames River flooded in the spring. In the shadows under the factory tramps slept and Indians like George Stonefish from the nearby reservation lay drunk, moaning and groaning and smelling "like big rice puddings." He was aware that the Indians drank, not liquor (which they were not allowed to buy) but cases of vanilla extract sold to them by Jack Howat. Howat was a leading elder of the Presbyterian Church, and Davies knew that although the town thought the Indians' behaviour disgraceful, nobody thought any the less of Howat. Another place to avoid was the Tecumseh House hotel, the haunt of Jim Mcfarlane, Aunt Ellen Mcfarlane's nephew. Jim was the fag-end of the once powerful Ferguson family, and as he slouched in front of the hotel, chair tilted against the wall, he made offensive remarks about the women who passed in the street.

Thamesville's finest building stood at the intersection where Elizabeth Street meets the main thoroughfare. It was built of brick and was known as the Ferguson Block. On the main floor, in addition to several stores, was the office of John Coutts ("Barrister, Solicitor, and Notary Public"). Coutts was the father of Dermot Coutts, who later became a successful lawyer in Chatham. (Davies knew Dermot only as a schoolmate of his brothers, but he based the character Diarmuid Mahaffey in *The Manticore* on him. Dermot recognized the portrait when he read the book.)

Above the stores and offices was the town's chief place of assembly, the Ferguson Opera House. This was Davies' first theatre, and he remembers the building, the stage and its roller curtain very clearly. Though the little opera house seated only four hundred, it had indoor and outdoor scenery, which moved in tracks. It was here that Rupert staged his two musical events, and here too that he directed the massed Protestant choirs of the village at a Sunday evening Temperance meeting. It was in the Ferguson Opera House that Davies saw his father perform in *A Bachelor's Romance* and observed him in blackface singing "The Dark Town Strutters' Ball" in a minstrel show, and here too that he gave his own first public performance. His accounts of the latter event are typically sharp in detail. Thus, in 1937 he told an interviewer at Oxford that he "made his first appearance on any stage at the age of four as an Israelite child in an opera called 'Queen Esther.'" In 1954, his *alter ego* Samuel Marchbanks described the occasion at greater length: "He first appeared in public at the age of three in the Ferguson Opera House, Thamesville, as an Israelite child in an opera called *Queen Esther*; he was one of a chorus of children in bathrobes and turbans who hailed the victorious Mordecai in a spirited number in which the words 'We triumph, we triumph' were repeated with typical operatic persistence." Some years later he wrote in his theatre notebook: "In this same opera house I made my first appearance on any stage as an Israelite child in the chorus of an opera called *Queen Esther*. We sang in praise of Mordecai—

Dum-de-dum, and Mordecai great shall be!
We triumph, we triumph, our people are free!

Just before our great moment the curtain rose, taking with it the wig of The Beggar [Dr. Mackilwraith]." The pages of the *Herald* reveal that the Thamesville Choral Society performed the sacred cantata *Queen Esther* on March 28, 1919, when Davies was five. "Bobbie Davies" is listed as one of twelve "Jewish Boys."

The First World War touched every aspect of village life. Davies heard the songs popular in the war, including "The Rose that Blows in No-Man's Land," whose concluding lines he would quote frequently in years to come:

> Mid the war's great curse
> Stands the Red Cross Nurse
> She's the Rose of No Man's Land!

When he was taken to see the famous Marks Brothers (not the Marx Brothers) perform at the Ferguson Opera House, he was struck, not by the play but by the figure of May A. Bell Marks, appearing before the curtain as Britannia at the "act-wait" (intermission). Wearing a Roman helmet, wrapped in a Union Jack, and carrying a trident, she sang "Rule Britannia," and invited the audience to join her in the chorus. She was accompanied, as were many of the acts that visited Thamesville, by the ghastly local Snarey orchestra —Mrs. Snarey playing the violin, "old Snarey" on piano, and "some minor Snarey" on the drums. On Sundays, as Davies listened to Jack Howat, as the Sunday school superintendent, praying "long and loud and extemporaneously," he knew that "If he prayed particularly for our boys in the rest camps, [his son] Dick was in one of the rest camps. If he prayed for those who were prisoners, Dick was a prisoner. And if he prayed for those who were in peril of their lives, Dick was going over the top." Occasionally the war came right to Thamesville. Mrs. Purdon, a neighbour, showed him shell casings which her enlisted son had sent home, and in his own house he watched Roy Kain, the Anglican parson, briefly home on leave, demonstrating how to put a gas mask on quickly. Making a couple of rapid movements he suddenly appeared "with a great trunk coming out of his face and goggle eyes."

Davies pored over the ferocious newspaper caricatures of the Kaiser, the Crown Prince and Hindenburg, including the dark images of Louis Raemaekers, the Dutch editorial cartoonist. One drawing particularly horrified him—"a picture of Germans in a Belgian village and one of them had an infant pierced right through the rump with a bayonet and was holding it high above his head." He was aware that shipments were always being sent to the men overseas. Even he was called upon to make a modest contribution. When the canning factory needed extra hands, it was felt to be patriotic to help out. And so "it was to defeat the Huns that I, three years old and rising four, was snipping beans on our front verandah one sunny afternoon in the summer of 1917." As he snipped, he listened to his mother and a friend talking about German atrocities. After a few moments he put down his scissors, slipped around to the back of the house, lined up several blocks of wood from the woodshed and, naming each one for a town figure—the Presbyterian minister and his wife, the mayor, the magistrate, the policeman, their family doctor—

> With the axe I chopped the law, religion and science. The axe was heavy, and I suppose anyone who had discovered me would have seen a child pecking ineffectively at a few billets of wood, in some danger of hacking his own toes. But to me it was a German massacre; I was a German—a Hun—and I was enjoying myself thoroughly. I experienced a few moments of pure, unrestrained feeling. When I had exhausted my blood-lust I threw the corpses back in the woodshed (an orderliness the Germans might have admired had been imposed upon me in my earliest days) and replaced the axe. I felt much, much better. I snipped no more beans.

Davies tells this story, as he tells the one about his vengeance on the Baptist minister's son, because, like Dunstan Ramsay in *Fifth Business*, he believes that "A boy is a man in miniature, and though he may sometimes exhibit notable virtue, as well as characteristics that seem to be charming because they are childlike, he is also schemer, self-seeker, traitor, Judas, crook, and villain—in short, a man."

The war gave a special character to the rumour and suspicion

that were endemic in village life. Strangers were thought to be
German spies, and it was suspected that the Germans had plans
to poison the village waterworks or to sabotage the canning factory. When Spanish influenza, an epidemic that killed twenty
million people across the world in 1918, struck the village in the
fall, it was blamed on the Huns. Davies knew some of those who
succumbed, among them the Anglican cleric who had ministered
to the afflicted at the Niagara militia encampment, and his wife,
who had worked among the sick in Thamesville. Both stuck in
his mind as people of goodness and character. He also remembers that his father turned the *Herald*'s column rules so that the
front page was lined in black, a giant death notice.

Davies witnessed and remembers the celebrations at the war's
end in astonishing detail. Rupert's accounts in the *Herald* (which
were inaccessible to Davies when he wrote *Fifth Business*, because
the *Herald* was not microfilmed until 1980) stand as a tribute
not just to the accuracy of Davies' recollection but to the
alchemy by which his imagination transformed it into Deptford's
triumphal welcome to Dunstan Ramsay on his return from the
Great War.

At three p.m. on Armistice Day, Thamesville mounted a bang-
up parade:

> First came the Victory Loan committees headed by the
> honour flag with its nine crowns, each man carrying sand-
> wich boards made of Victory Loan posters. Then came the
> band, part from town and part from Moraviantown, under
> the leadership of Joe Jacobs. Next came automobiles driven
> by Mrs. Wallace, Mr. Simpkins, Miss Bateman and Harry
> Grooms, carrying the widows and families, and the moth-
> ers of Thamesville's fallen heroes. Following were: The
> members of the village council; the school children mar-
> shalled by Dr. Boyd and Rev. Whalen; platoons represent-
> ing different allied nations; Soldiers' Service Society in
> uniform of Red Cross nurses, in charge of the president,
> Miss Edna Unsworth; the Red Cross ladies headed by a big
> banner, "Peace," and also including a streamer made of sol-
> diers' sox; the Canning Factory staff headed by Messrs

Fraser and Watts; citizens on foot; citizens carrying flags; and numerous floats, including an effigy of the Kaiser; agriculture, with Miss Margaret Langford and Mr. F. McMillan as farmerette and farmer; Misses Gertrude Johnson and Mary Langford as "Young America." The representative groups of the allied countries were splendid, and for the short time in which they were prepared, very creditable. M. Trudell as Marshal Foch was gotten up in a uniform gay with the tri-colors, and was followed by the Boy Scouts. E. H. Mills and Miss Wanless Evans headed the Belgian delegation, and their costumes of red, black and yellow were very gay and lent color to the parade. Another platoon worthy of special notice was that of the British Empire, in charge of Ed. Henry, with John Hardy as "John Bull," in the traditional red swallowtail coat and white breeches, with vest of Union Jack, and high top boots. He was accompanied by Miss Grace Mead as "Britannia," and Corporal Mead, who has just returned from the front, representing His Majesty's active forces.

There followed brief descriptions of several other groups and of the many automobiles at the end of the parade, an exhaustive listing of the procession's route and a brief report of the concluding short program in the main square, with its "medley of songs," prayer and four "short addresses." According to Arthur, Davies and his father walked in the parade. That evening there was a torchlight parade and an open-air service of thanksgiving before "The Kaiser and Crown Prince were both burnt in effigy at the flagpole, and some fireworks were let off."

But this was not the end of the celebrations. As the soldiers gradually returned, the villagers welcomed them in special evenings at the Ferguson Opera House. The ceremony for "Six of Our Returned Men" (including Dick Howat) on Monday, March 10, 1919, may be typical (although the full flavour of the occasion is not easy to grasp, since the *Herald* devoted most of its report to the speeches). The evening included singing by Miss Milton and Mr. Hetherington, a recitation by Mrs. Lodge, music by the Burwell Orchestra of Wabash and a piper. There were long speeches eulogizing the contribution that each had made, and finally each of them was given "a handsome gold watch with suitable engraving on the inside of the back of the case."

One soldier not so honoured was the Delaware Indian sniper George Stonefish. The lapse, vigorously condemned over dinner at the house on Elizabeth Street, went unmentioned in the *Herald*. Rupert was liberal for the time in his attitude toward Canada's natives, and he had given Stonefish's letters from the front equal billing with those of the more acceptable local hero, Dick Howat, quoting both verbatim on the front page; but he knew he would not last long as editor of the village paper if he challenged the majority more directly. Fifty years later, writing *Fifth Business*, Davies did not feel similarly constrained. Though he did not turn the town's bigotry into a cause, he made sure that it was part of the record.

Chapter 2

FAMILY HISTORY

———————•———————

"Have you a name?"

"Indeed I have, master," says the boy. "Poor as I am I am not so poor that I have no name. I am Gwylim ap Sion ap Emrys ap Dafydd ap Owain ap Hywel ap Rhodri ap Rhydderch ap Gryffyd."

"Good lad," says the traveller. "You know your pedigree even to the ninth degree. And do you know your cousinship, as well?"

"To the ninth degree also," says the boy....

—*Murther and Walking Spirits*, 1991

AFTER DAVIES AND his family had left Thamesville for Renfrew, and later when they lived in Kingston, Florence and Rupert often turned the conversation to events of earlier days—"threshing old straw," as they called it.

One of the things that Davies learned in this way was the manner of his birth. The *Herald*'s announcement of his arrival was very brief:

> Born—On Thursday, August 28th, to
> Mr. and Mrs. W. R. Davies, a son.

But from his parents he learned that he was born in a bed, at home, as was usual at the time. Having been delivered at about seven or eight in the morning by the local G.P., whom he recalls as Dr. George K. Fraser, he was put in the care of Mrs. Craik, an Irish nurse. He was dressed in an unconventionally short night-dress, since his mother held the advanced belief that babies ought to be able to kick their feet, and "within two hours I was out on the lawn being photographed." His precocity was probably not quite so remarkable as this, since the snapshot of Rupert Davies holding a small bundle and waving a finger at it includes Fred and Arthur, who had been sent off to visit their grandmother in Brantford, and who only returned home when their father fetched them on the Sunday three days later. Arthur recalls being taken upstairs with his brother to view the baby. He and Fred, only thirteen months apart in age, "got along fine together and we didn't need anybody else," and were confirmed in their view by the sight of "this red, wrinkled little thing [which] looked frightful to us."

Davies as a baby was unusually frail, and, contrary to usual practice, even though it seemed likely that he would not survive, he was not immediately baptized. When the christening did take place, he was named "William Robertson Davies." (William Robertson was the given name of Rupert's younger brother, who had died of tuberculosis at twenty-five, less than two years before, and who had in turn been named after *his* maternal grandfather, William Robertson.) The baby's health did not improve for quite a while, and at six months he weighed less than he had at birth, because milk disagreed with him. Through all this time, he was, as he delights in saying, "Despaired Of." But then it was discovered that he could tolerate Horlicks Malted Milk, and he began to grow and gain weight. There were still setbacks; before he was one, he had scarlet fever, which has left him slightly deaf. He considers that this has forced him to pay special heed "to what people are saying and the way they speak and what their speech tells you" and "to work at" hearing music.

His unenthusiastic brothers got stuck with a certain amount of baby-minding and bottle-giving (which involved tasting the special milk to "make sure it was okay," a chore Arthur particularly disliked). As the story goes, they would find ingenious ways to dissociate themselves from walking the baby—such as leaving the carriage in the charge of the little girls who hung around the town hall while they themselves played baseball, or parking it while they earned pocket money husking corn or snipping beans on the big outdoor platform at the canning factory. Arthur recollects that "We took the baby out in the stroller and, I don't know where we located the garter snake but [we found one] some place, and gave it to the baby to play with. And our mother came along...and discovered this. And, of course, she had an aversion to snakes anyway, and nearly threw a fit!"

Rupert and Florence Davies were both deeply interested in family history. Rupert was heavily smitten by nostalgia for Wales, the country he had left as a lad of fifteen. He had learned his mother's stories at her knee, and later, after arriving in Canada, he absorbed the tales of his Uncle John Robertson on summer Sunday mornings, sitting on the verandah of Robertson's home outside Brantford. Florence, for her part, took great pride in her pioneer heritage and loved to talk about her many relatives. After the family moved from Thamesville to the remote town of Renfrew, northwest of Ottawa, bouts of asthma and bronchitis confined her to bed for longer and longer periods and her interest in the past intensified, at the expense of the present.

It was in Thamesville that Davies began to hear the stories and anecdotes that made his parents' interests his. His father's tales came mainly at mealtime, but his mother's would reach the corner of his ear while she chatted with her mother and sisters. In contrast to Arthur, who didn't pay much attention, Davies was fascinated and entertained. There is more than a grain of truth in the reflections in a column Davies wrote early in 1947 under the pseudonym Samuel Marchbanks:

> The usual post-holiday relapse, during which everybody sits about, recalling the Good Old Days. I am, generally speaking, better at this than anybody else, for I am not bothered by details of chronology, and tend to regard as my own reminiscences which have been imparted to me by

the Ancients of my tribe. Thus I frequently tell people about how I taught Disraeli to play croquet, because my Great-Uncle Hengist did so, and I also have a good story about how I sent Sir John A. Macdonald his first brief, though I have a hazy notion that it was my second cousin Bloodgood Marchbanks, who did it. Thus I embody in myself the whole Marchbanks Tradition, and possess what anthropologists call Racial Memory.

As he grew older he realized that the stories were a key to understanding his parents, and himself as well. Over the years Davies has made occasional authorial use of one or another detail from this trove, and in his 1991 novel *Murther and Walking Spirits*, he has rifled it from top to bottom.

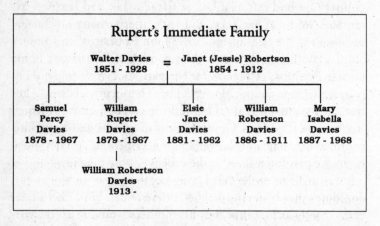

Rupert's Immediate Family

Walter Davies = Janet (Jessie) Robertson
1851 - 1928   1854 - 1912

| Samuel Percy Davies 1878 - 1967 | William Rupert Davies 1879 - 1967 | Elsie Janet Davies 1881 - 1962 | William Robertson Davies 1886 - 1911 | Mary Isabella Davies 1887 - 1968 |

William Robertson Davies 1913 -

Davies' father Rupert was born on September 12, 1879, in Welshpool, Montgomeryshire, Wales. William Rupert Davies was the second of the five children of Walter Davies and Janet (Jessie) Robertson. They lived in very modest quarters above the family tailor shop. His mother had the help of a general servant by the name of Liz Duckett, who "lived in" but also spent time every day at a house she shared with her common-law husband, Jack the Jockey. The Davies home was united and happy, owing particularly to Jessie, evidently a woman of exceptional qualities. A woman of strong faith, she inspired powerful love in those around her, certainly in her second son.

Reading was a major family pastime. Both parents read widely—they liked poetry, especially Byron; they enjoyed Mrs. Humphrey Ward's *Robert Elsmere*, a Methodist novel; they shared the interest of the time in accounts of exploration. There were lots of magazines and papers for the children. And music was in the air, as it would later be in Rupert's household. Rupert and his older brother Percy sang in the Wesleyan Methodist choir, and Rupert also sang in the boys' treble section of the local "Choral" or "Harmonic" society. The family was sufficiently puritanical in outlook to be uncomfortable with the theatre, and so Rupert saw only one play in those years, the morally acceptable *Uncle Tom's Cabin*. But he was interested enough in plays to remember the names of several that came to Welshpool, from their advertisements alone. He also attended the best school in town, the Oldford Grammar School.

In *Far-Off Fields*, the book of family and personal history he completed in 1962, Rupert recalls himself and his brothers and sisters on holidays at Aberdovey, "equipped with a pair of canvas shoes with rubber soles—which, in those days, were called sand shoes for some reason or other—a penny tin pail with a painted outside, a wooden spade and a penny shrimp net." With equal ease he evokes a slightly older self, taking a horse called Dick out to pasture. A good bareback rider, he "could stick on old Dick no matter how fast he went down the canal lane, with nothing but a one-rope halter to hang on to," and they enjoyed "many a surreptitious gallop around the field."

Like Thamesville, Welshpool was small enough to be intimately known. And Rupert, as Davies once said of him, was "unceasingly curious about people," with "the real journalist's flair for people and what was characteristic about them." At the time, many of the poorer citizens of Welshpool, like the Davieses' servant Liz Duckett, lived up "shuts," or narrow blind alleys. As many as twelve or fifteen families lived in the crowded, ill-lit tenements on each of these alleys, served by a common privy, in unimaginable stench and squalor. Though he was warned off by his parents, Rupert's lively curiosity carried him to the shuts again and again to visit the skinners and poachers, the tinsmiths and tinkers. Monday, "fair day" in Welshpool, was

especially marvellous for him, since he loved to watch the coun-
tryfolk who came to town. Townspeople were named for their
trades (Bill the Post or Jack the Jockey), but country people were
referred to by the names of their properties instead of their family names. Davies, listening to his father's tales, thought Wales
must be a magical country and its people almost legendary.

The dark shadow over this otherwise idyllic period was the
gradual failure of his father's tailor shop. Walter Davies' talents
did not include business acumen. When the agricultural depression of the early 1890s slowed his customers' payments and
financial difficulties descended, he didn't have what it took to
stay on his feet. Recalling this period in *Far-Off Fields*, Rupert
says: "I knew a lot about this situation. I was going to the
Grammar School, and many times I had to eat a hurried dinner
and make calls on some of our 'slow poke' debtors to try to collect enough to meet a cheque in the bank that day from a whole-
sale house. My recollection is that somehow or other we used to
meet the cheques, and thus appease the wrath of the bank manager of whom I was sore afraid. However, it was not easy." This
passage, like many in the book, modifies fact to protect family
sensibility; in person and in private, Rupert was blunter. What
actually happened on market days, as he told Davies, was that he
would "see somebody going by and he'd dash out and follow the
man who was passing and say: 'Mr. Walter Davies would like to
speak to you, Sir. Perhaps you could do something about your
account.' And then quite probably the man would come back
and do something about it. But then Walter would scold him.
'Rupert, how could you do that? How could you go out and dun
him in the street?'" Even as a boy Rupert was far tougher than
his father. And he had a clear-eyed apprehension of the grim
consequences of failing to pursue creditors.

By 1894, Walter Davies' business affairs had sunk so low that
when John Robertson and his wife Polly wrote from Brantford,
Ontario (they had emigrated there in 1891) to encourage Walter
and Jessie to bring their family to Canada, the decision was made
to send the two oldest boys, Percy and Rupert. Walter booked
them on the S.S. *Vancouver*, which sailed from Liverpool on
September 13, one day after Rupert's fifteenth birthday. He had

paid for accommodation in a third-class, four-berth cabin, but before it sailed, the ship went on to another dock and picked up hundreds of southern Europeans. The boys found themselves herded with twenty-two other men into quarters so cramped that they had to sleep in their clothes, with no chance to change until they reached Brantford twelve days later. The food was terrible, too. Each of the boys had a golden sovereign sewn into his clothes, but neither dared to spend it, and so they just used a few shillings, chiefly on two bottles of ginger ale, which helped to settle their stomachs. Rupert never forgot the experience, and it undoubtedly strengthened the ambition in him to make good. But he bounced back quickly. He was homesick for two days, then found that "the weather was good, the sea smooth and nearly everybody friendly and in good humour, so we did not fare too badly." As planned, their aunt and uncle met them at the end of the connecting train trip.

In Brantford, Rupert was immediately plunged into the world of work. He had tried tailoring one summer, and served as errand boy for an ironmonger another. He had been tempted to take a seven-year apprenticeship in printing with the *County Times* in Welshpool, having been interested in newspaper work since he had started a short-lived newspaper called "The Oldford Chronicle" with his sister Elsie, but he gave it up when he found that he would earn nothing for the first six years. Now Canada provided him with another chance to learn the newspaper trade.

The day after he reached Brantford, he was hired by T. H. Preston of the *Expositor*, and he started the next day. With his strict Wesleyan Methodist background, he was appalled to find that he was expected to steal fruit at the market for the journeyman printers over the lunch hour. The foul language and drunkenness of the composing room revolted him, too. But he quickly realized that the situation could have been worse. At least beer was not allowed on the premises! So he settled down to his apprenticeship, which was to last four years. He started as a printer's devil, which meant doing the sweeping, collecting the mail, scrubbing the iron urinals with lye and running errands for the older men, like Scotty and Beak Campbell. After eight months he was put to setting the patent medicine advertisements for Saturday's edition, and so he learned to set and distribute type. This allowed him to earn extra money (five cents a thousand ems) by putting away or "dissing" used type for the journeymen. "But," as he recalled years later, "woe betide the poor apprentice who had been careless in his 'dissing' and who had dropped e's in the d box or a's in the r box, or made other similar errors." With his concern for the proprieties, Rupert included none of the colourful language of the shop-floor in his account of the experience in *Far-Off Fields*, nor in the article he later wrote on the turn-of-the-century newspaper trade. But Davies' short television play *Brothers in the Black Art*, aired in 1974, draws frankly on Rupert's oral reminiscences:

> SCOTTY: God damn and blast your bloody-fuckin' arsehole! You do that again and I'll *kill* ya, you little Welsh bugger!
>
> HILO: What's going on here?
>
> SCOTTY: He's fouled the font, Hilo! Lookit—I put my hand into the L-box and what do I get? A Christer, for God's sake! A bloody Christer! He dissed this frame, and he done it.
>
> HILO: Show me…Griffiths, did you distribute this type?
>
> GRIFFITHS: Yes sir. I'm very sorry, Mr. Pike.
>
> HILO: You'd better be sorry. If you hope to be a printer, Griffiths, you'd better learn now that clean distribution is what every journeyman expects—and gets—from an apprentice. You see this piece of type?
>
> SCOTTY: Yeah, a Christer! A Christer in the L-box! Jeeze!
>
> HILO: Scotty, I won't have the Lord's name taken in vain in this shop. What is the proper name for this piece?
>
> SCOTTY: Not a Christer? Well, lemme see—I guess I shoulda called it a dog's cock.
>
> HILO: No, not a dog's cock, either. Griffiths, what is this piece called?
>
> GRIFFITHS: A point of exclamation, Mr. Pike?

Rupert stayed at the *Expositor* for five years, four of them as an apprentice. During this time, eager to learn something of literature, he attended night school and discovered a liking for Tennyson and Swinburne. He then moved to the *Courier*, as a journeyman, and worked in its job printing room under the foreman, Gordon Forsythe, for over a year. Like Davies' character Gordon Fortye in the play, Forsythe sported a waxed moustache and pince-nez, directed the Citizens' Band and played the flute.

Rupert made good friends among his workmates, read voraciously, developed a keen love of theatre and met life with exuberance. He and his friends loved Stephen Phillips' blank verse plays (as do Davies' characters Griff, Phil and Jesse in *Brothers in the Black Art*), and they would shout lines at each other while riding their bicycles from Brantford to the town of Paris on a Saturday afternoon. As a tailor's son, Rupert took great pleasure in dressing well. Arrayed for special occasions in morning coat, blue shirt, fancy vest with white edgings, gates-ajar collar and blue polka dot bow-tie, Rupert looked very like Griff in his courting best. For the rest of his life he regularly wore two clean shirts a day and fussed about his collars, and wore spats while they were in vogue. His sons later called him Queen Elizabeth, because Elizabeth I was reputed never to have worn the same dress twice.

Rupert's mother's people came from the south of Scotland. Her parents, William Robertson and Elizabeth Marchbank, had lived in Dumfries for the first few years of their marriage, and their first three children were born there. They then moved south to Dudley, in the English Midlands, where William established a thriving business in the "Scotch trade," in which packmen sold door-to-door from a central warehouse. In this case the merchandise was woollen and linen cloth, and the customers were the farmers of the district. Seven more children, including Jessie, were born in Dudley. In 1861, William bought Upper Brynelen, a farm about two miles from Llanfair-Caereinion in Wales, and arranged to have a house built there for his family. When he died in 1863 after a horse kicked and fell on him, his wife settled up their affairs in Dudley, and in 1867 she brought her children to the new house.

The Robertsons Rupert knew especially well were those of his mother's generation. In *Far-Off Fields* they appear relatively

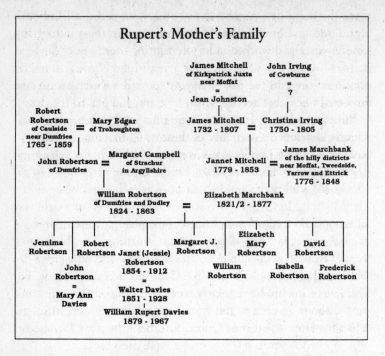

briefly, as one generation of "The Scholarly Robertsons." For Davies, however, these great-aunts and uncles are larger-than-life figures, struck sharply into his imagination by his father's tales, and their personalities and lives are vigorously present in his mind, even though he met them only briefly or not at all. In a 1954 *Saturday Night* article, he reflected: "My great-aunt Isobel Robertson read three books every day for the last twenty-five years of her life, and I am cast in her mould." In Bonn in 1964, he noted in his travel diary: "See something of the town & think of Great Aunt Jemima Robertson who was a governess there so long ago." Speaking to a graduating class of nurses in 1965, he recalled that the British soldiers in the First World War used to change the lines of "The Rose that Blows in No-Man's Land" from "Mid the war's great curse / Stands the Red Cross nurse" to "The War's great Curse / Was the Red Cross nurse." He observed that "this fixed itself in my mind, because a great-aunt of mine was the matron of a large military hospital in England, and she was feared as a disciplinarian. Soldiers who had never flinched in battle or when inspected by Lord Kitchener quailed like school-boys under the eye of Miss Robertson. She was old enough to have known nurses who had known Miss Nightingale herself. She was part of the Great War's Curse. But I never knew her; I just heard legends of her extraordinary ferocity. She always inspected her wards accompanied by a huge dog. I believe dogs are now discouraged as nurses' companions." The following year there is another peep at this same Miss Robertson, in Davies' travel diary: "in Church we sat in the v. pew where Aunt Jemima Robertson sat 70 yrs. ago, when she was setting her cap at Hawkins the curate, who was High Church."

Rupert's father's family story is more dramatic, combining huge swings of fortune with religious conviction and political intrigue. Rupert traced this line back to Thomas Davies, who came to Welshpool about 1800 from the village of Meifod, or from the hills nearby, probably to serve an apprenticeship and then to work in a trade. One of the tales from this time tickled Rupert because it always got a rise out of his sister Elsie (and Davies got

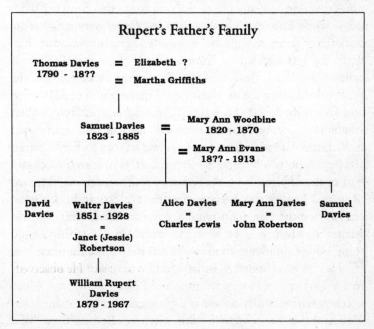

Rupert's Father's Family

Thomas Davies 1790 - 18?? = Elizabeth ?
= Martha Griffiths

Samuel Davies 1823 - 1885 = Mary Ann Woodbine 1820 - 1870
= Mary Ann Evans 18?? - 1913

David Davies
Walter Davies 1851 - 1928 = Janet (Jessie) Robertson
Alice Davies = Charles Lewis
Mary Ann Davies = John Robertson
Samuel Davies

William Rupert Davies 1879 - 1967

a character out of it for one of his stories in *High Spirits*). The ancestor in question was a shepherd who "always had a New Testament in his pocket and sat out on the hills watching the sheep and reading the New Testament for years on end." He never washed his feet. Instead, "He rubbed them with mutton fat and wore very, very heavy hand-knitted socks that were impregnated with mutton fat and then great big boots because, when you are sitting out in the pasture with the sheep, you would get terrible colds in the head if you got your feet wet, so you took care your feet didn't get wet." Davies found Elsie's reaction as priceless as the shepherd himself: "'Oh, Rupert, I'm sure it couldn't have been that way,' and, you know, practically eating her own chin with disapproval."

Thomas sired a large brood, among them Davies' great-grand-father Samuel. Samuel Davies was married twice, first to Mary Ann Woodbine of Wells, in Somerset, who was the mother of his children, and then to Mary Ann Evans. The latter had herself been married twice before, the second time to Thomas Evans, keeper of the Angel Inn in Welshpool. In *Far-Off Fields*, Rupert notes that one consequence of this union was that Samuel Davies came to be known to his cronies as "Angel Sam." What he doesn't say there, though he mentioned it to his son, was that, while she was married to Thomas Evans, Mary Ann Evans was called Mary Evans the Angel. This nickname became one of the germs of the story about Maria Ann Dymock in *The Manticore*, and Davies made use of it again in *Murther and Walking Spirits*.

Samuel Davies built up an extensive tailoring business centred in Welshpool, first on Berriew Street and later at 25 Broad Street. (Rupert, who was born at 25 Broad Street, managed to obtain part of an old beam from the building with the date 1738 carved in it, and Davies now keeps it over the window in his Caledon study.) Samuel also acquired extensive farming interests, and when the railway was put through north Wales, he made a good thing out of supplying food to the workers. His prominence in local affairs was confirmed by his election as mayor of Welshpool in 1877—the first Nonconformist and Liberal to manage this in a town whose politics were dominated by the Anglican, Conservative Earl of Powis. But when he died suddenly of a heart attack in 1885, his financial affairs collapsed like a house of cards.

Walter Davies, Rupert's father and Davies' grandfather, was one of the numerous children born to Samuel Davies and his first wife, relatively few of whom—David, Walter, Alice, Mary Ann (Polly) and Samuel—survived to adulthood. Like his father, Walter was a Wesleyan Methodist and a keen Liberal. He was deeply involved in the election of 1880, at which a Liberal won Montgomeryshire after nearly a hundred years of Conservative representation, by the narrow majority of 2,232 to 2,041. He had been one of the group who persuaded Stuart Rendel, a wealthy ironmaster from the north of England, to contest the seat. When it proved impossible to keep election posters up for more than twenty-four hours, he and his brothers-in-law, John Robertson and Charlie Lewis (a painter by trade), their faces blackened, dressed in old clothes, painted "Vote for Rendel" slogans in white and bright-red paint on the sidewalks of the main streets of Welshpool late one Sunday night so that country people coming into town for fair day on Monday morning would see them.

Davies used the election and what he knew about the political situation in Welshpool as background for the action of his play *A Jig for the Gypsy* and again in *Murther and Walking Spirits*. He was aware, for instance, that during the hard-fought elections of the 1880s and '90s the local Liberals, without their candidate's knowledge, would try to get fortune-tellers to make public predictions, thus influencing the vote, even though such dodges sat uncomfortably with their professed principles as students of Ruskin and Carlyle. He knew that an Anglican vicar in Welshpool, a man by the name of Grimaldi Jones, had used his influence on behalf of the Tories, declaring from the pulpit how his flock should vote. He knew, too, that although the Liberals continued to win Montgomeryshire by narrow majorities, it took real courage to be a Liberal in Welshpool. Walter Davies had once been threatened with violence when he proposed to act as outside scrutineer, and Jessie was once surrounded by shouting Tory hoodlums in the street on voting day.

Davies also knew how the "Castle" (that is, the Earl of Powis) exercised its influence during and between elections. In spite of changes wrought by the nineteenth-century reform bills, the Castle still controlled many votes. The Earl's agent made it clear that his tenants should either vote Conservative or move on. And since the Castle was a great and important patron in the region, it was no small matter to a tailor like Walter Davies that none of the Earl's custom came his way, the making of servants' liveries being an important source of work. It was less serious, though galling, that the flow of largesse from gentry to commoner also failed to reach the Walter Davies family. Davies made effective use of a specific instance of this in *A Jig for the Gypsy*, where he gave one of his Aunt Elsie's childhood memories to the character Bronwen: "I know you will think me silly, but every year when the pheasant-shooting season comes around, the Earl's shandry drives through the town and it's a pair of birds here, and another pair there, for all the Tories. But never a pair for us."

Walter Davies' life was ruined because he buried his talent in order to please his mother—the first of several instances of misguided loyalty in the family that pushed Davies to see the destructiveness of self-abnegation. A fine student, Walter had his sights set on a career in the civil service, but when he was eighteen, his mother sent for him on her deathbed and asked him to give up his studies to enter the business with his father. He gave his promise, and he kept it. But his father's death and business failure forced him early in 1886 to move his half of the business and his wife Jessie and their children to a smaller shop on Berriew Street. Then, in 1895, the family followed Percy and Rupert to Canada. Thus, during the final years of his apprenticeship and the beginning of his career as a printer, Rupert was once again surrounded by his parents and sisters and brothers.

In March of 1900, Rupert, now twenty, moved from Brantford to Toronto, attracted in part by the fact that Sir Henry Irving was performing there at the time. He successfully sat the difficult qualifying examination for the Typographical Union. (He remained a keen supporter of the union all his life, and felt greatly honoured at his retirement in 1951 when the staff of the *Kingston Whig-Standard* presented him with a golden printer's rule, an award given by printers only to printers.)

In the autumn, when a fire at his place of employment suddenly threw him out of work, Rupert seized the opportunity to better himself. He moved to New York and for the next few months maintained a feverish pace. He worked as a printer at several presses and magazines, often putting in several nights of overtime in a week, and in his remaining evenings he tried his hand at freelance writing. He sold squibs, paragraphs, light verse and a number of stories, including "Dashing Dolly Darrington, or Manacled at the Major's." He did well at his last place of employment, where he earned $25 a week and overtime, compared to the $7 he had been making with the *Courier*. But the drunkenness of his co-workers was a constant trial for a man raised in a Temperance household, and his attempt to burn the candle at both ends quickly brought him to the point of nervous exhaustion. Early in 1901 he returned to Brantford, put himself in the care of his doctor for a month and spent a couple of weeks on a farm. He never went back to New York. In his printed reminiscences he says: "There was no enthusiasm in the family for my return to New York," but when Davies pressed him, he admitted, "I wanted my mother."

That spring he worked as a typesetter in Toronto for several months, then returned to Brantford to work for one of the local papers. It was a period when he needed a new and positive element in his life, for not only had his attempt at making something of himself as a printer and journalist come to nothing, but the woman with whom he had fallen in love had jilted him. Into this vacuum came Florence McKay. She shared his enthusiasm for theatre, music and books. She had maturity and a strong sense of self-worth, and a keen intelligence that held tremendous appeal for Rupert, a man impatient with fools of either sex. (Later, he couldn't help tormenting "silly women," and Davies recalls such giving way to tears in their house because his father "just pestered them and crossed them up and bullied them until they couldn't stand it any more.") They met in the Congregational Church choir, the church Rupert had joined when he first arrived in Canada because his aunt and uncle were members. One can imagine them singing duets as they courted, he a tenor, she a contralto, while she played the piano.

Florence's family history defined her as strongly as Rupert's legacy of loss and failure determined him. On her mother's side, one line of descent goes back to Jacob Langs, who arrived in North America in 1750 and settled in Pennsylvania. Although Langs' country of origin is not known, Davies' mother thought of it as Dutch, and Davies takes the same line. Jacob Langs' son, also Jacob Langs, emigrated to Canada perhaps as early as 1807, certainly by 1810, settling in Brant County, Ontario, in a locality that soon became known as Langford. One of the children of this Jacob Langs was Davies' great-grandfather John Langs.

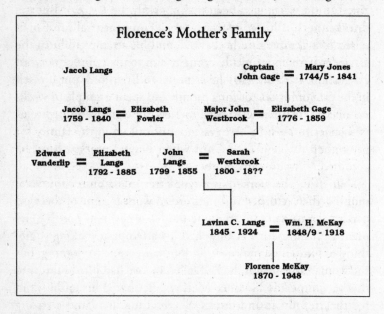

Florence's Mother's Family

Jacob Langs

Jacob Langs 1759 - 1840 = Elizabeth Fowler

Captain John Gage = Mary Jones 1744/5 - 1841

Major John Westbrook = Elizabeth Gage 1776 - 1859

Edward Vanderlip = Elizabeth Langs 1792 - 1885

John Langs 1799 - 1855 = Sarah Westbrook 1800 - 18??

Lavina C. Langs 1845 - 1924 = Wm. H. McKay 1848/9 - 1918

Florence McKay 1870 - 1948

Florence's other maternal line descends from Captain John Gage and his wife Mary Jones, who lived in or near Greenbush, a village on the Hudson River opposite Albany, New York. The Captain died fighting on the British side in the American War of Independence, and in about 1790 his widow, Mary Jones Gage, made a difficult journey with her two children and possibly two brothers, by canoe, or perhaps by horse, from Greenbush to Stoney Creek, just east of the present-day city of Hamilton, Ontario. There she homesteaded on land granted to her as a United Empire Loyalist.

It was on her farm that the half-hour Battle of Stoney Creek, one of the determining events of the War of 1812, took place on the night of June 5-6, 1813, turning the tide against the American invaders on the Niagara frontier. Like his mother before him, Davies takes pride in his family's association with that moment of Canadian history, and in its involvement "in the only war that has ever been waged on Canadian soil in defence of the country." Some of his forbears fought in this war, and a number died. The old farmhouse at Stoney Creek is now a museum, and Davies regrets that the hand-lettered family tree that can be seen there, prepared several years before his birth, does not include him.

Mary Gage's daughter Elizabeth married John Westbrook and settled with him on Fairchild's Creek in Brant County. Their daughter Sarah married John Langs, thus becoming Davies' great-grandmother. Davies' mother passed down a surprising number of this great-grandmother's opinions and turns of speech to Davies, for whom they are a treasured window on a world long gone. In 1943, in an article on the now-forgotten nine-teenth-century Canadian poet J. R. Ramsay, he quoted his great-grandmother's astute judgment: "He was a half-cut schoolmaster and a quarter-cut poet." In 1955, in an essay about proverbial sayings, he wrote of his mother's family:

> [they] possessed many, curiously phrased, which still linger in my mind with a flavor of Upper Canada not long after the war of 1812. My great-grandmother (born in 1800) used to pronounce weightily on a bad match, "She (or less often he) has taken her pig to a poor market." Even as a child I felt that there was something disagreeable, though probably wise, about summing up all the charm and beauty and eagerness of a young bride in the likeness of a pig. That is why I dislike proverbs. There is about so many of them an ugly, brutish cynicism which sounds like wisdom, but is in fact a life-denying, nay-saying clout over the ear.
>
> Of course there were others, the full meaning of which is dark to me even today. From the same source I inherit this: "He looks as pleased as if he had cut a dead dog in two

with a dull knife." There is a macabre gleefullness about
this which is not unpleasing. And "Contrary as a hog on
ice" is good, though not so mysterious as "Bow-legged as a
hog going to war."

In 1958 he used several phrases in *A Mixture of Frailties* that
belong to his great-grandmother's time, though not necessarily
her personally, as part of the colourful speech of Ma Gall and her
tribe—"there; let 'em eat till they're pukin' sick," "slopdolly
housekeeping," "she's got a butt-end on her like a bumble-bee"
and "independent as a hog on ice." And in 1988 he dipped into
his tribal inheritance again for the Old Ontario Loyalist expressions that flavour Simon Darcourt's discourse in *The Lyre of
Orpheus*—"as tight as the bark to a tree," "it all depends whose
ox is gored," "threshing old straw" and so on. Florence used these
expressions herself, but in such a way as to make it clear that they
originated not with her but with her forbears. They figure again
in the speech of the characters that are based on her ancestors in
Murther and Walking Spirits.

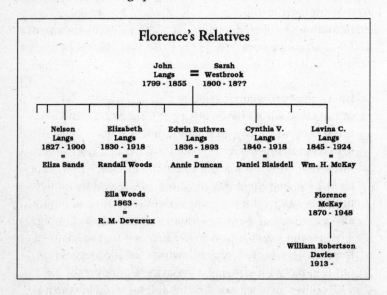

Florence's Relatives

John Langs 1799 - 1855 = Sarah Westbrook 1800 - 18??

Nelson Langs 1827 - 1900	Elizabeth Langs 1830 - 1918	Edwin Ruthven Langs 1836 - 1893	Cynthia V. Langs 1840 - 1918	Lavina C. Langs 1845 - 1924
= Eliza Sands	= Randall Woods	= Annie Duncan	= Daniel Blaisdell	= Wm. H. McKay

Ella Woods 1863 - = R. M. Devereux

Florence McKay 1870 - 1948

William Robertson Davies 1913 -

Florence's stories of the lives of John Langs, Sarah Westbrook
and their children included references to two servants named

Angeline and Emmeline, who were drawn from a fairly large local population of runaway slaves. They also suggested to Davies that many settlers were starved for mental stimulation, a perception that underlies his play *At My Heart's Core*. He came to think of the pioneers as a "grim lot" who "suspected joy; they suspected any unforeseen good fortune; they suspected strangers, and they were suspicious of just about everything." While recognizing that they were courageous and enduring, he suggests that they were not easy to live with. One such was his mother's Uncle Nelson—as his mother-in-law Granny Sands had cause to know. His "idea of a merry joke was to come in with the buggy whip and say, 'Now, Granny, I'm going to touch you up a bit. Let's see you dance, Granny, let's see it!' ...And he'd flick the whip around though never touching the old girl, but as if it were a great lark."

Florence not only led Davies to see the pioneers as intellectually starved, grim and capable of cruelty; she also emphasized to him those elements in their lives that bordered on the grotesque and macabre. She told him a tale, for instance, about a Devereux forbear nicknamed "Bug" who had had the misfortune to have an insect fly into a cut in his face that he had made while shaving with a straight razor. The wound healed over, but then "it swelled and swelled and swelled and swelled and swelled until finally it burst itself open and a noxious creature came out of it." She told him another story about "Fat" Devereux who would gorge himself so horribly that "he had to be greased with turkey fat and laid in front of the open fire because he might burst. And when he died, which he did before he was twenty, he had to be buried in an upright piano box because there was no coffin that would contain him."

The youngest of Sarah Westbrook's and John Langs' eleven children was Lavina, Davies' maternal grandmother. He remembers her in old age as severe in appearance, with white lace at her neck, black skirts to her feet, high-buttoned boots, many rings with turquoise stones on her fingers, earrings and lots of jet "clanking and clinking around." He also remembers his horror as a small child when, waking from a nightmare one night, he came upon her being undressed by his mother and his aunts in front of the fire in the living room. And "it was as though one had seen God. I rushed away screaming. I had seen what I ought not to see." The final scene in Lavina Langs' life, as described to Davies by his mother, inspired Ma Gall's delusory wanderings as she approached death in *A Mixture of Frailties*: she died, "as I understand many women of that generation did, with a great kind of delirious fear that she was in a bawdy house and that negroes were taking after her. You know, the two prime fears— black people and sex."

Lavina married William H. McKay, a moody man, prone to furious tempers, about whom very little is known. From one or two hints, Davies suspects that McKay's forbears were among the many Highland Scots whose leaders took their crofts from them and, for a fee of a pound a head, handed them over to the British government, which shipped them from the northern tip of Scotland to the shores of James Bay. Many of them died, and the survivors made their way arduously, on foot, hundreds of miles south to settlements in Manitoba and Ontario. Certainly this grandfather looked like the stereotypical Highlander—"gaunt, tall, dark, severe."

McKay was subject to asthma, and his doctor brother-in-law dosed him for it with morphia, later giving him prescriptions so that he could treat himself. As a result he became addicted to the drug and under its influence would abuse and frighten his wife and daughters, sometimes going so far as to chase his wife around the house with a carving knife. He was a builder, and inevitably his business suffered, as did his marriage. He and Lavina separated, and, once his addiction had ruined him completely, he ended his days in the Brantford home for indigents.

Four daughters were born to the fraught marriage of William H. McKay and Lavina Langs, of whom the eldest was Davies' mother, Florence. She was born on August 31, 1870, in the village of Langford. One of her earliest recollections was of wandering off at the age of four and discovering a blacksmith shop. Having hung around long enough to absorb some rough language, she used it later in her mother's hearing and was given a "furious whaling" as a result, with no explanation of what she had done wrong. She and several cousins were similarly treated on another occasion of equal innocence. Fascinated by a family funeral, the children dressed in the best clothes they could find, set up a box as a coffin and marched solemnly around it. When the adult mourners discovered them, they were "whaled royally" for making a mock of death.

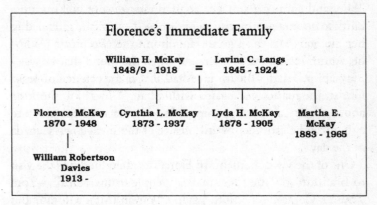

Florence's Immediate Family

William H. McKay 1848/9 - 1918 **=** Lavina C. Langs 1845 - 1924

Florence McKay 1870 - 1948   Cynthia L. McKay 1873 - 1937   Lyda H. McKay 1878 - 1905   Martha E. McKay 1883 - 1965

William Robertson Davies 1913 -

The unbending, unimaginative, unsympathetic rectitude of her parents appears never to have relaxed through all the years Florence lived at home. When she was seventeen or so, for example, she had her tonsils removed under ether at the doctor's office. On the way home, as Davies tells the story, she "felt faint and clutched a fence and looked awful. A woman came out and said, 'Won't you come in, dear?' sat her down on the verandah, brought her a cool drink and sent for her father to bring her home. Her father came and gave her the absolute devil, because she had *dared* to feel faint outside the house of a woman called Kate Lake who was known to keep a bawdy house. That was *Kate Lake* who gave her that drink and she should be *ashamed*. Not one word of pity. Pity was an unknown word!"

Whatever the rigidities of the McKay home, it at least appears to have taken a positive view of the arts and entertainment. There are no stories of confrontation over reading, music, theatre or dancing, and Florence grew up to enjoy all of them. But the Methodist church she attended was not so open-minded. When Florence was eighteen or nineteen, the minister named her and three other girls one Sunday and preached against them for going to a dance. Unrepentant, she joined the more liberal Congregational Church instead. (Her sister Cynthia also broke with the Methodists, though her departure was precipitated not by dancing but by music. She was an accomplished pianist.) Other families in their circle took a less liberal view of the arts than the McKays. Davies tells a story about his mother in which "She, and some girls of her acquaintance, were making up a party to go to a nearby city to see a play. One of the girls said to her mother: 'Ma, can I go to Hamilton to see *Ben Hur?*' 'Who's he, Annie?' asked the mother, and when she found that he was a play-actor, letting on to have had direct experience of Jesus Christ, the matter was closed with a bang." In 1979, speaking about theatrical touring companies, Davies used the story to epitomize the attitude toward theatre of the small-town Canada of the day.

One of the vivid moments of Florence's childhood was the visit to Brantford of "the four smallest people in the world"—Tom Thumb, Commodore Nutt, Lavinia Warren (Mrs. Thumb) and Elfin Minnie Warren. She got to shake hands with "the eminent Thumb, who, at thirty-one inches, was roughly her own size." Another was the sight of the daughters of Chief Johnson (the poetess Pauline Johnson among them) riding into Brantford in sumptuous velvet riding habits, the skirts lined with red silk.

Florence enjoyed school and completed high school at a time when that was rare, even for men. She studied the curriculum of the day—history, geography, English, Latin and mathematics—and this, according to Davies, gave her "a sense of the ancient world and classic modes of thought; a training in reasoning and logic; a sense of the past and of the world at large; and a sense of poetry and the world of the imagination." She did well at her studies, retained what she learned and continued to be interested in education for the rest of her life.

By the time she finished high school, her father's affairs had reached such a pass that she had to go to work to help keep the family afloat financially (as did her sisters in their turn). She trained at secretarial school in Brantford (and used Pitman's shorthand all her life for things like shopping lists), then held secretarial jobs for a number of years with various business concerns in Brantford. There was a certain amount of harassment in the workplace then as now. Among other things, "It meant naughty men went down to Tremaine's Chocolate Works and got a lot of yellow soap covered with chocolate and offered it around among the girls in the office." When the girls bit into the soap, the men would laugh uproariously. Florence particularly liked working for a man by the name of Frank Yeigh. He was a keen amateur bee-keeper, and from him she absorbed surprising facts about bees. Like her, he had Dutch forbears, and he would say: "Now, Miss Florence, you know, we Dutch must stick together."

Once Florence and Rupert Davies revealed that they intended to marry, the McKays made their disapproval felt. Her salary was needed. Her mother wanted her support in coping with her father. Her sisters faced a dismal future of trying to carry the burden of both parents themselves. Nonetheless, Rupert and Florence were married on October 16, 1901, in the McKays' front parlour. Thomas L. Kiernan was the officiating clergyman; Malcolm Robertson (John's son and Rupert's cousin) and Cynthia McKay (Florence's sister) served as witnesses. The McKays were sufficiently angered at this act of defiance that they barely spoke to Florence for two years afterward.

For the first ten years or so of their married life, Rupert and Florence pulled together very well, enjoying a pleasant social life, taking on challenges together, successfully balancing his extroverted, energetic, enthusiastic approach to life with her introverted, sardonic one. They took pleasure in a highly articulate and sharp-tongued manner of discourse. As was expected of women of her class and generation, Florence McKay left her job at the time of her marriage, although she had considerable aptitude for business and little for housework or cooking, and Davies is probably right in speculating that she would have been much happier if she had been able to continue working. In the event, she quickly had to adjust to the duties of motherhood. Frederic Rupert McKay was born on June 10, 1902, and Arthur Llewellyn came into the world on August 18, 1903. The next child, a girl, was stillborn. As we have seen, their fourth and last, William Robertson, did not make his appearance until August 28, 1913. Such free time as Florence had she gave to church work and to a number of activities she enjoyed—embroidery, needlepoint, crocheting, reading, gardening, playing the piano, singing and play-going.

For his part, Rupert supported his young family as a typesetter, alternating between the *Courier* and the *Expositor* in Brantford until 1906. Since he was not mechanically skilled, one of the machines, a temperamental Style B Linotype, almost ran him into the ground. Near breakdown again, he resigned, but luckily, before he had worked out his notice, he was able to obtain a position more appropriate to his temperament, as foreman of the *Ingersoll Chronicle*. But ambition was eating at him, and in 1907 he decided to try his hand at running a weekly newspaper. He selected the *Thamesville Herald* from several possibilities and rented it for $300 a year. The gamble was tremendous, since he had only $378 to his name—indeed, he would not have made it through the first three months had Jack Howat not come to his rescue with a loan of $50. But with Florence's abilities and efficiency assisting him, he made a go of it. On April 2 the following year he bought the paper, and by April 29, 1919 when Ross V. McGuire bought it from him, he had increased his capital to $5,500.

By then, however, his and Florence's partnership had been irrecoverably injured. Rupert had discovered, after they moved to Thamesville, that she had substantially misled him about her age. During their courtship, Rupert's father had warned him that she was much older than he, but she had told him otherwise, and Rupert believed her. On the marriage register itself she admitted to being twenty-seven to Rupert's twenty-two, but not until he came to print a family history written by one of her cousins did he learn that she was fully nine years his senior. According to Davies, "he never forgave that." (He may also have nursed a sense of entrapment over the years: the horse which was said to have precipitated Fred's birth, eight months after the wedding, by stampeding onto a Brantford sidewalk may not actually have deserved the credit.)

Davies can understand why his mother had not been frank with Rupert about her age. He suspects that her lie reflected "a pitiful kind of terror in my mother's heart that she would lose him." "It may have been the work of a moment. He may have said: 'How old are you?' And she'd said: 'Oh, about your age.'" Florence may well have felt insecure about her chances of holding the much younger Rupert. Nonetheless, Davies' sympathy in this matter lies with his father, who had suffered "a very wrongful thing." He feels, too, that he is the worse for having been the child of a woman who, at forty-three, was past the usual age for childbearing. And Rupert comes in for some resentment as well: Davies feels that he was raised by "parents who were more like grandparents and whose attitudes were more than a parental generation away." This may be exaggerated, but it is true that by the time he was six or seven, Florence's health had begun to fail sufficiently that she was taking to her bed for weeks at a time. Although Rupert was only thirty-three when Davies was born, Davies argues that his father "took on an immensely ancient persona in his middle years. He got younger as he grew older." Certainly the ambitious young Rupert was preoccupied by the difficulties of entrepreneurship, worked long hours and aspired to higher social and political circles. Later, when he had made a great deal of money, had been made a senator and was full of honours for his achievements in Canada and Wales, he did relax and take life more easily.

Davies has also from time to time, part seriously, blamed his recurrent respiratory ailments on his mother's age. He suspects too that he was "an unintentional child," that he wasn't "a wildly welcome child," though not "ill-used or anything like that." Also, he considers that the stillborn child between Arthur and himself had made his parents "fearful of another child, and I think I was kind of a nuisance for them."

A diary entry from 1966, eighteen years after Florence's death, makes clear how powerfully Davies felt at that time about his mother's age, and reveals his father's continuing preoccupation with the subject as well:

My deep buried anxiety manifests itself in dreams of loss, of rejection, of love denied. At Leighton WRD [Rupert] reminded me once again that my mother was 43 when I was born; I had not the nerve to ask him whose fault that was? But I have sometimes wondered if my fearful & life-denying mother hated me in the womb & marked me for life? She cd. have done it: a v. strong character, devoted to negative ends. Dutiful as a mother, but not loving. Sometimes I think this early struggle is the key to my character, both its strength & weakness, & its sudden descents into despair.

Despite the serious strains between his parents, in Davies' opinion there was never any question of abandoning the marriage. For many years Florence had supported Rupert in his initiatives, and, although he eventually took extended holidays without her from time to time, the two presented a united front to the outside world, whatever the extent of their private estrangement.

Writing as Samuel Marchbanks, Davies once summed up his origins with commendable brevity:

> He is, like myself, a Canadian of mixed antecedents. On his mother's side he may claim a Canadian ancestry dating from the American Revolution, when his forebears came to this country. They were principally of Dutch stock, with dashes of English and French. Why they chose to be U.E. Loyalists is not known. Presumably they had their reasons, and the kindly thing is to suppose that they were good ones.
>
> On his father's side he is Welsh, with a small dash of Scotch—say about two ounces.

As a boy listening to his father's stories about Wales, or to his mother's stories about her North American pioneer ancestors, Davies felt pulled in contrary directions. What was he? and where did he belong? Accepting that he was a Canadian, and understanding what that meant, took him some considerable time.

Chapter 3

RENFREW: 1919-25

To begin, when Francis was born there, Blairlogie was not the
Jumping-Off Place, and would have strongly resented any such
suggestion. It thought of itself as a thriving town, and for its
inhabitants the navel of the universe. It knew itself to be moving
forward confidently into the twentieth century, which Canada's
great Prime Minister, Sir Wilfrid Laurier, had declared to be
peculiarly Canada's. What might have appeared to an outsider to
be flaws or restrictions were seen by Blairlogie as advantages.
The roads around it were certainly bad, but they had always
been bad so long as they had been roads, and the people who
used them accepted them as facts of their existence. If the greater
world wished to approach Blairlogie, it could very well do so by
the train which made the sixty-mile journey from Ottawa over a
rough line, much of it cut through the hardest granite of the
Laurentian Shield, a land mass of mythic antiquity. Blairlogie
saw no reason to be easily accessible.

—What's Bred in the Bone, 1985

RENFREW, ONTARIO, where Rupert published and edited the
Renfrew Mercury from 1919 to 1925, was very different from the
southwest Ontario towns where he and Florence had spent the

early years of their marriage. Brantford, Ingersoll and Thamesville were located on rich farmland, were easy to reach by road and were relatively homogeneous socially, having been settled primarily by English immigrants. Renfrew, sixty miles northwest of Ottawa, lay on thin soil that barely covered the rocky Precambrian shield; in 1919 it was accessible only by rail, and, small though it was, it exhibited deep social divisions based on ethnicity, language and religion.

The town had begun a century earlier as the centre of a farming and lumbering region in the Ottawa River valley, but when hydroelectric power came along, milling and manufacturing became its chief source of income: flour, woollen textiles, iceboxes, sashes and doors. By the time the Davieses arrived, Renfrew had achieved a population of 5,000 and, since its incorporation in 1895, had made enough material progress—waterworks, sewers, paved streets, hydroelectric power, a public library—for one of its native sons to conclude in 1923 that, "Altogether, Renfrew at its century-old point is generally conceded by experienced travellers to be one of the best-looking, most efficiently equipped towns of 5,000 people to be found in any part of Canada."

But Davies, coming to Renfrew in 1919 as a child of five, didn't see it that way. Neither he nor his parents found the town an easy place to form attachments. His brothers were pleased to exchange village life for that of a substantial town and generally enjoyed their years there. For Davies, however, its primary aspect was its "bleak, malignant ignorance." For him the inhabitants of Renfrew were "troglodytes"—"a bitter, evil, ingrown, ignorant pack of ruffians." His voice becomes harsh as he exclaims: "Lord, what a hole of a place that was!" His fictional Blairlogie in *What's Bred in the Bone*, which mirrors all this most keenly, is far from doing Renfrew justice. But Davies, an unusually perceptive child, was buffeted by his experience of the town's underside, and his negative reactions were reinforced by his parents' own feelings of rejection. The Renfrew that flourishes in Davies' imagination is what he perceived as a precocious, lonely, often unhappy boy.

Davies' Renfrew is, in its own way, just as highly coloured and idiosyncratic as his Thamesville had been. He remembers huge horse-drawn drays shaking the ground as they brought lumber into town from the woods; the governess cart with matched bay ponies and top-hatted coachman Billy Lepine, carrying Thomas A. Low's wife about the town; horse-drawn funerals on the way to the cemetery, the hearse bearing a cross for a Catholic or an urn for a Protestant; the droshky-like long-distance winter cabs—horse-drawn, coachman on a box outside at the front and enclosed body painted black below and green or red above. He remembers the local billiard parlour where his brother Fred hung out when he skipped school. It was called "The Better 'Ole" in homage to Bruce Bairnsfather's famous First World War cartoon (where the old soldier says to the quivering recruit sharing the shell hole with him under bombardment, "Well, if you knows of a better 'ole, go to it"). The Gospel Tabernacle, which occupied a store, had a garish poster of the seven-headed Beast of the Apocalypse in the window. At Donahue's blacksmith shop, men would idle the time away jawing, chewing wads of tobacco, hawking spit, and boys would entice unsuspecting victims into licking a frozen runner on one of the upside-down cutters awaiting repair outside.

Davies remembers the ancients Orange and Aaron Wright, who themselves could remember the days when the Indians occupied the land. Aaron possessed a beard that, in Davies' recollection, hung to his knees. His mind's eye also sees Canon Quartermaine, a local Anglican cleric, in full clerical garb, including the flat hat with rosette in front and, in inclement weather, an Inverness cape. Davies knew that local gossip said that Quartermaine had not kept the various funds in his care (church, Children's Aid, his own) rigidly separate, and he had heard of Quartermaine's horror when his activities were investigated. He also knew of at least five families who kept a retarded child in the attic. A schoolfriend once pointed maliciously at the light shining from the top floor of Davies' own house, accusing him of "a lunatic relative, a hideous freak, or some other shameful secret." And Davies had heard tales about E. H. Stevenson, a local undertaker and embalmer. Stevenson was said to have left the corpse of a man who froze to death on a table while doing other work, when suddenly its legs thawed, shifted and catapulted it to the floor. His shrieks were a great source of amusement to the town. When a religious girl died at the age of sixteen (Davies could never quite view her as "a budding saint because she was enormously fat"), Stevenson, who had the job of preparing her corpse, apparently let it be known that "she had eaten a huge supper the night that she died and he had to use double the amount of embalming fluid to get her hard enough for the final orgies [last rites]."

Although Florence and Rupert had easily woven their lives into the fabric of three southwestern Ontario farming centres, they found it much more difficult to penetrate Renfrew's complex, deeply stratified society. In their experience, Renfrew was not a town that accepted newcomers easily. And indeed others have testified that when the Davieses moved there in May of 1919, Renfrew was a very closed community. They were not alone in being rebuffed. Outsiders typically remained outsiders; locals would begin to accept them only after they had lived in Renfrew for twenty years. Newcomers coped by socializing with each other.

The problem was compounded by the widening gap between Rupert and Florence. His sense of betrayal at the revelation of her age had become a significant wedge between them. And her shy, reserved temperament made life more difficult for her. Residents remember her as "very withdrawn," "high hat," "over-shadowed by her resplendent husband" or "self-sufficient." And the bouts of bronchitis and asthma that kept her in bed for weeks at a time isolated her. Davies remembers that when Rupert would suggest entertaining, she was most likely to respond nega-tively and, if pressed, would rush off and throw up. Occasional theatrical expeditions with other Renfrewites to the Russell Theatre in Ottawa seem to have produced no warm friendships either. Only St. Andrew's Presbyterian Church appears to have given her a strong contact with the community. There she and Rupert met Percival Kirby, the church's organist. He too was an "outsider," an Aberdonian, whose profession gave him no place in the town's social hierarchy, and he quickly became a good friend of the family.

Even at the church, Florence made few friends until, toward

the end of their stay, the issue of Church Union arose. Rupert was initially in favour of the move to link Presbyterians with Congregationalists and Methodists in a new United Church, but he so disliked the unionist party's aggressiveness that he and Florence joined the opposing group and, for a time, attended church less frequently. When the issue came to a vote in January 1925, the Non-Concurring Presbyterians lost both their church and their minister. But this drew the band of them together. According to Arthur, his parents began to attend services more regularly, and his mother at last began to get to know and like native Renfrewites among the dispossessed Presbyterians. Where she had once thought Colonel Irving's wife (daughter of the wealthy Barnet family) "stuck up," that lady was now "the salt of the earth." It was probably about then that Florence became president of the Ladies Aid of St. Andrew's Presbyterian Church.

Rupert had a somewhat easier time of it. He quickly became active in the Board of Trade, and as editor of the *Mercury* he joined the local Rotary Club when it was established in 1922. As a theatre enthusiast he became an honorary official of the Dramatic and Operatic Society formed in 1923. A keen Temperance supporter, he became president of the South Renfrew Temperance Association during his last year or so in town. And he and Arthur, both good singers, soon joined the church choir. He also served briefly as the superintendent of the Sunday school. Like his father and grandfather, he was a lifelong Liberal, and he soon made friends with Thomas A. Low, one of the town's leading businessmen, another "outsider" who had not come to Renfrew until he was eighteen. Rupert campaigned for Low in the December 1921 federal election, though, according to one Renfrewite (a political rival according to Davies), his opinion carried little weight: he "lacked the common touch." Be that as it may, Low won the election by a comfortable margin. Arthur recalls that Rupert had a splendid time making forays into the hinterland by long-distance cab, keeping audiences of twenty to twenty-five amused in a succession of rural school-houses until his candidate arrived. Davies too remembers his father's politicking but was more struck by the condition of the hotels his father was obliged to use: "The beds so dirty that the traveller was obliged to wear everything but his boots; the pillow so filthy that it had to be covered with a spare shirt; no water to wash in, as it was assumed that those so effeminate as to wish to wash their faces would do so at the barber's; no chamber-pots, as 'the fellas generally just steps outside'; the food an indigestible mass of fried pork...."

With a staff of about fifteen, the *Mercury* and its associated job printing plant constituted a considerably larger operation than the *Thamesville Herald*. No longer a one-man band, Rupert could now focus his energies on editing and publishing, and in the estimation of the previous editor and publisher, W. E. Smallfield, he succeeded: "In the regularity of its editorial expressions, in the quantity of district correspondence and in the number of special features introduced, there has been improvement which has warranted the increase which has come in both circulation and advertising patronage...." Rupert soon bought out his only competitor, the *Renfrew Journal*, and in one triumphant week in September 1923 he cleared off the resultant debt. This was "Old Home Week," the town's celebration of the hundredth anniversary of the arrival of its first settler. Rupert rose to the occasion with a special commemorative thirty-six-page edition instead of the usual eight or ten pages, and he printed the official programs, the posters and small bills as well. The entire staff worked overtime. Rupert got by on catnaps for the week, and the whole family pitched in. Davies remembers himself and his mother bringing great containers of coffee and mountains of sandwiches every evening at eleven or twelve. That week was exceptional, but there is no question that Rupert worked very hard in Renfrew. Davies remembers him often taking to his bed for the weekend, having his meals brought to him, refusing to answer the telephone and working his way through a briefcase full of reading.

By the time he sold it in 1925, the business had doubled, and he had won the town's respect for "bringing the *Mercury* along." But all his efforts had not integrated him into the community. Many thought him pompous and suspected that he "felt himself a cut above people." His habitual costume—walking stick or cane, spats, stiff collars with turned-down corners and bow-ties, hat tipped just so—made the boys on the street regard him as a stuffed shirt. He was still an outsider in Renfrew.

Rupert's three houses epitomized his climb up Renfrew's social ladder. Davies once described the town as "a three-layer cake— the Scotch, the French, and the Poles," and in a passage in *What's Bred in the Bone* that draws directly on his recollections of Renfrew he elaborated on this a little: "The best of the town's money and business was firmly in the hands of the Scots, as was right and proper. Below the Scots, in a ranking that was decreed by money, came a larger population of Canadians of French descent, some of whom were substantial merchants. At the bottom of the financial and social heap were the Poles, a body of labourers and small farmers from which the upper ranks drew their domestic servants." (As a broad generalization this is true enough, but there were many more Irish in Renfrew than French Canadians, and you could have found Scots in all the layers of the cake.)

When they arrived in May 1919, the Davieses were dismayed to find that the house W. E. Smallfield had arranged for them at 166 Cross Street (now 198 Cross Avenue) was in the Polish section of the town. The house itself, which had two storeys and a finished attic, was pleasant enough—plain, newly built of red brick and possessed of indoor plumbing. The Davieses soon planted trees, dug a garden and established a lawn on the raw land surrounding the house. But the ashpit on the next lot remained a problem. Whenever carts dumped their loads, a powdery dust would cloud up and gradually settle over the garden, and Rupert and Florence came to detest it.

In other places where they had lived, it was the custom for people new in town to hold a reception and to announce it in the social column of the local paper. So Florence inserted a notice in the "Personal and Travel" column of the *Mercury* of November 21, 1919:

> Mrs. W. R. Davies of 166 Cross Street will be "at home" on Wednesday, Nov. 26th, and afterwards on the first and third Wednesdays of each month.

She expected only a few neighbours and prepared accordingly, and was stunned when a much larger number arrived. The Renfrewites had assumed that Florence's "at home" was an "open house." When the teacups ran out early in the proceedings, Mrs. Low sent Billy Lepine for a hamper of cups and saucers, and other ladies rushed off to get extra china. The resulting mix-up could have laid the basis for a firm bond between Florence and the neighbourly ladies of Renfrew, but instead, in her defensiveness, she was resentful, suspecting that people came "to see what was in the house and finger the stuff and make remarks."

The girl who "came in by the day" seems to have been an additional annoyance in Cross Street. She was dwarfish and grunted noisily in the kitchen as she ate. She had joined the Salvation Army and was buying her uniform article by article, making Florence's "life a burden about whether she should wear the bonnet or the chapeau." As Bella-Mae Elphinstone she plays a role, larger than she did in life, in *What's Bred in the Bone*.

In the fall of that first year, Davies, now six, began to attend kindergarten in the old wing of Renfrew's Central School (which also housed the teachers' training college), a couple of short blocks away at the end of Cross Street closest to the centre of town. He could not read yet—no effort had been made to teach him—but he had been looking forward to school, because he thought he would know how to read as soon as he got there. What a disappointment at the end of his first day when he "took a volume of the encyclopedia from the shelf, opened it and waited for it to tell me something!" Worse, he found that reading would not be taught until the following year. He remembers little of school that year and was probably home ill much of the time. He had a debilitating six-week bout of whooping cough, which was treated with twice-weekly painful injections in the back just above the kidneys, and a set of respiratory ailments (flu, wheezes, coughs, bronchitis) that have become lifelong annoyances. As always when he was ill, his mother read aloud to him, kept his spirits up and was generally "the most kind and tender of nurses."

The following year (1920-21) he progressed through Junior and Senior Primer under Miss Allie Clements and Junior and Senior First under Miss Mabel Stewart. Miss Clements, whom

Davies recalls as having "lemon-coloured hair" but who says herself that it was "a good blazing red," was impressed by Florence's pride in her son and by how companionable she was with him, talking to him as if he were another adult. She remembers that Davies had "a lot of information that nobody else his age had" and that he was a joy to the many student teachers who passed through the classroom, since "You could always be sure of an answer from Robertson. And he always looked so interested...." It was while Miss Clements was his teacher that he made his first stage appearance in Renfrew, as one of thirteen "froggies." In a green suit and cap, he hopped and croaked and sang a ditty about "Mr. Bullfrog Grave and Stern." A few weeks later he recited "If Santa Claus Lived In A Shoe?" during a Christmas concert.

In Miss Clements' class, he discovered that reading and writing went together, and that writing was the more onerous by a considerable margin. He was taught what he later came to regard as the "cheap and nasty hand" devised by Joseph Carstairs, still taught in North American schools. In an article on the history of handwriting that he wrote in 1956, he recalls its miseries in detail: "'Feet flat on the floor! Sit up; don't slump! Arms FREE! Now class—OVALS! One-two; one-two...' And after a few tight ovals had been described by the steel pens filled with water, inkpowder, fluff and hairs, they would begin to shoot uncontrollably up and down, as the tension of small muscles increased."

Learning to read meant laboriously learning to recognize the words in the *Ontario Primer*'s first story, "The Little Red Hen," which were printed in the script he was being taught to write. In the accompanying pictures he noticed that "the Little Red Hen was larger than the cat, the dog and the pig with whom she shared the farmyard," but as a child he had no idea why this should be so. Much later, he concluded that "the Little Red Hen was morally bigger than the cat, the dog and the pig, so she was drawn larger, just as saints in ikons are drawn larger than pagans or people of mere ordinary virtue."

He often walked home from school at noon with a frail little boy by the name of Mousie Stevens. Mousie, as he learned later, was illegitimate, and his mother worked as a cleaning woman. One day he asked Mousie what he was going to have for lunch

PRIMER

The Little Red Hen
found some wheat!
She called the cat
She called the dog
She called the pig

and was given pause, even as a child of six, by the reply: "I don't know because every day at noon the sun comes down and it gives my mother what we have to eat." Not long after this, Mousie died. Davies was frequently sent for milk to the house of a Polish family by the name of Narlock, at the end of the street where the town stopped and fields began. This was a different culture shock: their main floor, where the shrivelled, immensely ancient grandfather resided, seemed to be all kitchen, and the cows were sheltered right outside it. In winter the Narlocks would heap manure up to the windowsills to keep the house warm.

Some of his encounters were entirely in the imagination. The house on Cross Street had a finished attic, and there he met his second witch, "a little, bumpy, nut-cracker woman with glowing eyes and a terrifying look of malignance," crouching on the other side of the door in one of the closets under the eaves. Afraid to attract the attention of the spectre, he froze, until his mother's call from below released him. On another occasion he awoke, terrified, to see a witch squatting on the foot of the bed. For a long time the witches he had met in fairy-tales and stories appeared in waking dreams and haunted his nights, chasing him to tear out his "liver and lights" or threatening to bake him in a pie. Years later, when his youngest daughter Rosamond was

afraid that a witch might descend the attic steps into her bedroom in the night, Davies knew exactly how to deal with her terror: together they placed her school Bible on the third step, just
inside the door, to trap the witch in the attic.

These were not his earliest visitations. In Thamesville he had
had a recurrent vision just as he slipped into sleep "of God, and I
could see his private parts." He was tormented (as he had been
when he glimpsed his grandmother without her clothes), certain
that "this was the most awful and evil thing that could possibly
be." Yet he could not rid his mind of it. In Renfrew, a balancing
vision came to him, of such force that he was unable to speak
about it, even to his wife, until he was over fifty. He remembers
that he was outside walking along Cross Street when suddenly he
stopped, looked up in the sky and saw Christ floating upward
and looking down at him. He was wearing his blue robe and
white gown, his arms were outstretched and he was surrounded
by a great mandala of light, "and right in the middle of him was
a globe of the world, circular, going around and around and
around." The transfiguration was no doubt familiar from Sunday
school, but the globe at the centre of the figure was new and
strange to him. He did not encounter it again until 1964, in
Toledo, Spain: "In the Orphanage a 15th century painting that
brought me up short: Christ as World Ruler, with a representation of the globe inside his body—just as I used to see it in a
recurrent vision before I went to sleep, when seven or eight.
Have never seen anything remotely resembling it at any time."
Later still he learned that what he had seen was "a vision of the
Unus Mundus, the One World, the Totality and interdepen-
dence of all things." Readers of *The Manticore* will recognize this
as one of the dreams David Staunton recovers from his childhood at his analyst's request.

It was also during the first two Renfrew years that Davies began
to lay his theatrical experiences up in long-term memory. From
this time on he has been able to recall what he saw on the stage
in sufficient detail to use it in his discussions of the history and
development of theatre. An example is *In Sunny France*, which
Davies saw in February of the year when he was six. It was the
first of many amateur performances he was to see between 1920

and 1925, including *The Royal Chef, H.M.S. Pinafore, The Arrival of Kitty, Officer 666* and *Charley's Aunt.* It is likely to have been an eminently forgettable evening, but his memory has preserved it whole.

In Renfrew, as in Thamesville, there was only one theatre, the O'Brien Opera House, named after its owner, Senator M. J. O'Brien, a leading local industrialist. It had two sets—an interior one of "oak & red silk panels" and an exterior one "with a rushing stream which stopped abruptly in the middle of the stage." Even then Davies knew how the performance was staged, and the newspaper bears out his account. As with *The Royal Chef* two years later, an impresario (in this case the well-known Wilson MacDonald, who also directed, played the piano and sang) arrived in town with a railway car filled with scenery and costumes and set about producing a musical comedy. Every local talent he could lay his hands on, however trifling, was included.

Here's what Davies could recall in 1979 about *In Sunny France* and *The Royal Chef:*

> These musical comedies were not tightly crafted, if I may borrow an expression popular in the modern theatre. They could be enlarged to include anything anybody in town could do, which included whistling and playing the musical saw. There was always a "Prologue in Fairyland" in which virtually every female child under thirteen appeared, dancing, sometimes rather morosely, to the music dispensed by the talented director at the piano. There was always a number called "The Foxtrot of the Hours," or the "Two Step of the Flowers," or something of that kind, in which every female schoolteacher under fifty had a brief solo, as an Hour or a Flower. The costumes were gorgeous but decent.
>
> The highlight of the evening was when the talented director himself appeared on stage and sang a song filled with references to local notabilities. These were not pungent lampoons. I recall one which ran:
>
> I taxi'd round to Mrs. Airth's
> To have a little frolic;

I ate some cake the dear girl made
And nearly died of colic.

On January 25, 1921, and again on December 11, 1924, he had a chance to see quite a different kind of performance. *Uncle Tom's Cabin* was his first nineteenth-century melodrama. "Tom-plays" appeared every year on stages across North America from the 1850s until the end of the 1920s. Seeing one was a rich experience, even in the third-rate versions that reached Renfrew. The players, an unkempt lot with remnants of the make-up from the previous evening's performance still visible, would drum up business during the day with a parade, led off by a black band big enough to make a great noise, followed by a barouche in which the managers rode and bowed to the crowd, then a dray bearing Aunt Chloe, Uncle Tom and a cabin about the size of a dog-house. Then came the vicious-looking bloodhounds (mastiffs in Davies' experience); and finally Little Eva, in another barouche, throwing leaflets out from side to side. Davies must not have been the only one to demur at a Little Eva who was pushing forty. Yet the show enthralled the audiences at the matinees Davies attended, loggers, agricultural workers, wives and children alike. Davies included, they were thrilled by Eliza's escape across the ice of the Ohio River, carrying her infant son and pursued by roaring bloodhounds. They were roused to laughter by Topsy's shenanigans. A pin could have dropped at the death of Eva, as the slaves sang "Nearer My God to Thee," and when Uncle Tom fell under the whip of Simon Legree. But they were not allowed to wallow in pathos. Moving briskly, the play jerked them from tears to hilarity or exultation and back again.

Davies feels lucky to have seen this play when he "was still innocent, before the coming of that critical spirit that robs us of so much pleasure." He is glad to have seen it too with an audience "just barely literate if literate at all" and as uncritical as he. But even in this time of innocence he was not wholly swept away, and he felt gleefully superior to a much-hated bully who was. When a huckster came on stage at intermission selling pictures of the leading actress as Little Eva St. Clair for twenty-five cents, Davies himself resisted, feeling no desire for a picture of an old woman pretending to be a child. "But Murray Dagg, who had been crying bitterly during the play because he was so affected by Little Eva, unbelted a quarter for a picture of this wretch." Davies remembers feeling a surge of power and thinking: "That fellow is a cream puff. He can punch the socks off me but he's a cream puff."

He also took note of the tricks of stagecraft. Far from diminishing his pleasure, his inside knowledge thrilled him and contributed to his fascination. He was aware of the boxes planted at strategic intervals on which Eliza crossed the Ohio, of the three-foot-wide strips of gauze that created the heaving waves, of the wire that raised Little Eva to heaven, of the dummy rolled into her bed, and of the thick padding Uncle Tom donned just before Legree lashed him to death. His mother told him about a version of the play she had seen as a child, which led him to realize that plays could be staged in different ways. Hers had had "two Lawyer Markses and two Topsies: the point of that was when Marks was thrown out of a door on the left side of the stage, his identical twin immediately rushed in from a door on the right side, and felled his assailant from behind, with an umbrella. When Topsy fell through a trapdoor apparently into the cellar, her double immediately slid down the bannisters onto the stage, as if from upstairs."

As soon as Rupert could afford to do so, part way through their second year in Renfrew, he moved his family to 137 Raglan North, a house with a big garden on the town's long main street. The family referred to it as "the Handsome Campbell house" after its owner, although, according to Arthur, "neither the house nor Mr. Campbell were handsome." But it was larger than either the Thamesville or the Cross Street houses, better situated than the latter and, in Davies' view, a house of "very considerable charm." The neighbourhood was more typical of Renfrew than Cross Street in that people came from a variety of backgrounds and represented the full social scale.

Soon after they moved in, they acquired excellent household help. Victoria Campbell (who is recognizable as Victoria Cameron in *What's Bred in the Bone*) became their live-in cook-general. She was in her late twenties and had the energy and household skills that Florence Davies lacked. She was not only a fine cook but a veritable whirlwind who cleaned the windows, waxed the floors, did the washing and tidied the house. Of Scots descent, she was very religious, and tidy if unfashionable in appearance, with her hair parted in the middle and pulled back in a bun. She was a paragon, and she knew her worth. When Florence was ill, Victoria Campbell got into terrific wrangles with any nurse who attempted to patronize her. She immediately became an important figure in Davies' life. She told him all sorts of things in the kitchen while preparing the cookies, pies, cakes and roasts. Samuel Marchbanks recalled one of them: "Many years ago I knew a cook whose father and brothers were bakers, and she told me that they always kneaded their dough with their feet, prancing rhythmically in the large wooden mixing tub, with their trousers' legs rolled up." And it was she who told Davies all he was allowed to discover about the problem play *The Unwanted Child*, which children were not permitted to see. Having attended the "Ladies Only" matinee on March 25, 1924, she let him into

the secret by declaring: "Bobby, it was about a girl who Went The Limit."

In September 1921, Davies and several other children were uprooted from Central School and transferred to the North Ward school (officially called Victoria School, and the original of Carlyle Rural in *What's Bred in the Bone*). The move to the Handsome Campbell house had taken Davies into a new school district, and for him, "It was like the expulsion of the Acadians."

Getting to the new school was a trial for a start. He had the choice of the short route (roughly half an hour) by way of the foot-bridge over the briskly flowing Bonnechère River or the considerably longer route over the main bridge. He chose the hundred-yard-long foot-bridge, which at that time was a rough affair suspended on cables, with boards underfoot and fence wire angling up at the sides to provide handholds and to prevent pedestrians from tumbling off. In winter, when the wind roared down the river gorge, it would swing the bridge and lift the spume into the air, icing the boards and the wire and terrorizing the timid.

The school was populated largely by the children of Scots farmers. Davies, at eight, already looked different from most of his schoolmates, a spindly child dressed in neat jackets rather than the more usual sweaters and much-mended hand-me-downs. Totally unathletic, never a participant in after-school sports, he attracted the bullies, and recess became a hated, ongoing battle. He remembers fighting back with his tongue and with his fists, and winning about half the time, but he is well aware that he looked like an awful sissy, and indeed that is the way some contemporaries at the North Ward school remember him.

He was shocked by the common practices of his classmates. Each spring he watched in horrified fascination as boys stuck straws into the cloacae of frogs from nearby ponds and competed to see who could inflate his frog the most, unaffected by its frantic writhings. From time to time they would take a razor blade to the testicles or ears of a cat while the animal yowled. It is little wonder that Davies thinks that many of the denizens of the North Ward school represented a debased form of humanity.

It took a special breed of teacher to keep these brutes in order, but Miss Belle Eady, an "old maid school marm," had what it took. Davies' first year at the North Ward school, 1921-22, was her last. She was short, fat, spectacled and wore black dresses with small white flowers on them. She taught the older children in the second-floor classroom, while a second teacher oversaw the younger children in the room below. Davies, who was just beginning Junior Second (and would complete Senior Second that year too), was assigned to the dragon's lair, and since he had personally little or nothing to fear from her, he undoubtedly trembled with pleasure to watch as she humbled his adversaries.

Miss Eady often administered the strap in full view of all the children in the room. John G. McNab (whose father, the school inspector, admired Miss Eady) remembers that his brother Murray once got "two lickings in one day from Belle Eady." Davies recalls that when a smart-alec whipped his hand away after two or three whacks so that the strap came down on her own knee, she "went to work with that strap and hit him around the face and head and all over the place until he was truly sick of the strap." According to another Renfrewite, she was capable of letting "a war whoop out of her [that would] scare you out of your skin." Davies remembers the way she would light into "some cringing lout," flaying him with her tongue: "The trouble with you…is that you're just stupid. You're stupid clear through from the soles of your feet to the crown of your head. And I'm not surprised because I taught your father and I taught all your uncles and they were just as stupid as you are."

Davies, the son of an ardent Liberal and Welshman, classed Miss Eady as a bigoted Tory and an overly enthusiastic Scot. She was full of romantic tales of The McNab, the chief who had come out with his clansmen in 1825 to settle land in nearby McNab township. Davies was her student during the election in which his father supported the Liberal, Thomas Low, which brought their opposed political convictions to a full boil. So powerful an impression did Belle Eady make on Davies that he later remembered her as teaching him for three years, instead of slightly less than one.

Renfrew's school nurse, Miss Elizabeth Orford (whom Davies later caricatured in his Marchbanks columns as Miss Toxaemia

Dogsbody, Reg.N.) worked hard to institute a program in the schools to provide undernourished children with free milk. It was a good idea, but its execution at the North Ward school left much to be desired. The milkman (whose brother-in-law was on the school board, according to Davies) would leave day-old milk in a covered pail at the school door, where it would stand warming in the sun until recess. Miss Eady would then pour it into glasses brought from home for the purpose, glasses that gradually became encrusted and filthy as the weeks limped by, since the school had no water to wash them in. Davies, numbered among the needy because he was underweight, eventually became so disgusted by the souring milk and the dirt that he threw up. After what must have seemed like an eternity, his parents managed to extricate him from the toils of the milk program.

The foul reek of the school's basement privies nauseated him so much that he couldn't bring himself to use them. (Nor, one guesses, did he use the outhouse he discovered on the dilapidated farm of one of his schoolmates, which was equipped not with toilet paper or newspaper but with an indescribably filthy old undervest.) As a result, being kept in after school was a real test of his endurance. He probably developed here the amazing powers of retention for which Samuel Marchbanks gave thanks a quarter century later: "A summer cottage can be a lovesome thing, God wot! but not unless it has proper plumbing. I am no lover of those old and picturesque privies which have assumed the gravity-defying obliquity of the Leaning Tower of Pisa. Employing a special form of Yoga I transcend the physical side of my nature and avoid them utterly." At the North Ward school, even the children stank. Davies claims that many of them were "sewn into their underwear in the autumn and unsewn in the spring," with the result that, in a schoolroom overheated by a hot wood stove, "they became foul and smelly beyond mere bad smell." In 1954, during his one return to Renfrew, Davies toured the old school just before it fell to the wreckers. Renfrew legend has it that Allan Gay (then the supervising principal) and his wife accompanied him on this descent into the past and that as they reached the end of the tour Davies sniffed and said, "Same old smell—shit and piss."

Not surprisingly, Davies rejected the standards of the schoolyard and upheld his parents'. His brothers, as grade school boys,
had been mortified when their father drew attention to himself
by singing solos in church, by carrying a bamboo cane on
Sundays or by using a baton to direct the massed Thamesville
church choirs when no one in the village had ever seen a baton.
But Davies, when faced with derision at his father's dress or
when boys wrote "fuck" on one of the Eton collars he wore to
Sunday school, was indignant at the "bloody-minded riff-raff"
and their derisive opinions. To have felt otherwise would have
been to ally himself with people whose language, behaviour and
general demeanour appalled him.

So he became noticeably solitary. A contemporary remembers
seeing him playing croquet, alone, in the yard of their second
Renfrew house, making no effort to find companionship. His
parents were aware that he was miserable, but they could not
grasp what made him so. As a result, they resorted to their
favourite nostrum and dosed him both on Friday night and
Saturday morning to ensure a thorough purgation of his bowels.
And no doubt they had recourse to Dr. Tyrrell's Domestic
Internal Bath. But these measures did not improve matters. It
wasn't until 1923, when Davies was merely promoted instead of
achieving the usual "honours," that his father finally concluded
correctly that the school was the source of the problem. By
threatening to send his son to the Catholic school, he got Davies
out of the North Ward and back to Central School in time for
Senior Third with Miss Eva Millar in 1923-24 and Junior
Fourth with Mrs. Easton in 1924-25.

Davies' disgust at the North Ward school's filthy privies and
fetid atmosphere heightened the effect upon him of his family's
obsession with cleansing and purgation of the bowels.
Defecation, and everything associated with it, acquired the kind
of unacknowledgeable significance for him that most people of
his generation reserved for sex. What is surprising is that in the
following decades he was able, through his reading of psychology
and his self-analysis, not only to acknowledge this energy but to
incorporate it into the discussable. His struggle to understand
himself encouraged him to discuss the subject, even to twit his

fellow Canadians for their own refusal to talk about it. The Marchbanks columns and Davies' private letters and diaries contain a plethora of references to purgation, costiveness, losing control, flatulence, farting, excretion, plumbing and so on. Years later, he channelled this energy into his writing in episodes like Hector Mackilwraith's humiliating experience with borborygmy in *Tempest-Tost* and David Staunton's with his bowels turning to water in *The Manticore*, but it was not until *The Rebel Angels* that he took the subject and explored its implications fully.

It was from the North Ward schoolyard that his dislike of the Common Man stems as well. Davies feels that the Common Man is the Common Boy writ large. He mistrusts those "who stand four-square on their simplicity and native virtue." Given real power, they would become worse tyrants than Ivan the Terrible or Hitler, "because their tyranny is rooted not only in ignorance but in a kind of native, unredeemed awfulness." Consider this passage from 1945:

> Hullabaloo today about the results of the British General Election, which is interpreted in some circles as a mighty triumph for the Common Man. I suppose it is, for it has turned out of office Winston Churchill, who certainly ranked high among the Uncommon Men of our times. I confess that I find the modern enthusiasm for the Common Man rather hard to follow. I know a lot of Common Men myself, and as works of God they are admittedly wonderful; their hearts beat, their digestions turn pie and beef into blood and bone, and they defy gravity by walking upright instead of going on all fours; these are marvels in themselves, but I have not found that they imply any genius for government or any wisdom which is not given to Uncommon Men.... In fact, I suspect that the talk about the Common Man is popular cant; in order to get anywhere or be anything a man must still possess some qualities above the ordinary. But talk about the Common Man gives the yahoo element in the population a mighty conceit of itself, which may or may not be a good thing for democracy which, by the way, was

the result of some uncommon thinking by some very uncommon men.

On the other hand, the North Ward school was not wholly a descent into Stygian darkness. For one thing, it had its own brand of theatre—old-fashioned playlets, called dialogues, that were designed to point a moral. Davies watched one in which a town boy debated with a country boy as to who had the better life. Another "was laid in a human stomach. Various characters appeared there, of which some were quarrelsome and harmful like Piece of Pie and Slice of Cake, and others were of a noble and uplifting nature like Fresh Vegetables and Wholewheat Bread. The hero and heroine were handsome young Mr. Apple and Miss Glass of Milk." This last may well have been one of the dialogues performed in a concert that included "The Model Child," "The King of Foods," "Mother Goose Health Play," "Merry Microbes," "Our Friend Milk" and "Six Year Molars." Davies participated in several of these earnest pieces, learning his lines easily and enjoying himself mightily. He played Dr. Ipecac in one dialogue about a school that had an epidemic of pink-eye, and a newspaper editor in another called "'Press' Prize Christmas Poems."

Such dialogues were often part of school concerts, which required an astonishing amount of preparation. Miss Eady's concerts were so well put together that other teachers often came to see them. The Health Concert the North Ward school presented on April 10, 1922, was typical of her efforts. Read its program and raise before your mind's eye the ghost of an Ontario school-room in the third decade of this century—the blackboards deco-rated with chalk drawings of chicks and bunnies, the children alert and well-drilled, the presence of officials and parents giving a sense of occasion and Canon Quartermaine in full Anglican rig, making Davies cringe as he brought proceedings to a close, "humorously" announcing: "Now children, I have a great treat for you. We're going to have ice-cream and we're going to have it right now! And now, I will point to me, and you all point to yourselves, and say 'I,' and then we all 'scream,' and so we have 'I scream'!" It cannot have pleased Davies that the proceeds raised by this affair went to "the fund which Miss Orford, the school nurse, is raising with which to purchase milk for the undernourished school children." Note the many Scots names.

Flag Salute.

Chairman's Remarks—Mr. J. McN. Austin.

Chorus—"Upon the Heights of Queenston"—The School.

"Who Killed the Winter"—Sterling Stewart, Hobson Perry, Jeannie Beall, Jean Christo, Katharine McCabe, Dugald Jamieson, Dalton Bertram, Lillian McIntyre.

Health Dialogue, "The House That Tom Built"—George Loken, Frank Church, Pansy Barr, Mack Scott, Jack Austin, Willard Jamieson, Ted Vickers, Fred Stewart, Robertson Davies.

Chorus, "The March Wind"—The School.

Recitations, "How I Fooled my Teacher"—Marion Jamieson; "The Vulture"—Myrtle Church; "Marion's Ironing"—Grace Ross.

Motion Chorus, "The New Moon"—Borden Wilson, Thelma Corbett, Anna Mick, Gilbert Simpson, Mary Flower, Harry Perry, Chrissie Eady, Irene Crow, Beryl Christo, Marion Jamieson, Dorothy McGregor.

Dialogue, "Hiring Help"—Murray Barr, Carl Eady.

Solo, "My Dear Soul"—Miss Call.

Reading, "A Bear Story"—Miss McLaughlan.

Dialogue, "Mrs. Brown's Visitors"—Gladys Morphy, Muriel Bengry, Doris Crowe, Elsa Stewart.

Chorus, "The Birdies' Complaint"—The School.

Recitations, "Little Lamps"—Geo. Butt; "The Candy Shop"—Kenneth Toner.

Reading, "Selection from Drummond"—Miss McLaughlan.

Health Dialogue, "The Germ Drive"—Keith McGregor, Fred Amey, Kenneth Christo, Ida Barr, Eva Morrison, Margaret Thomson.

Motion Chorus, "Jack-in-the-Pulpit"—Floella Simpson, Lois Stewart, Dora Roberts, Harriett Beall, Esther

Cornett, Mary McManus, Marguerite Peever, Myrtle
Church.
"The Birds' Ball"—The School.
Valedictory—Muriel Hollingworth.
God Save the King.
Congratulatory Addresses—Canon Quartermaine and W.
R. Davies.

Davies enjoyed learning, no matter what school he was in.
John G. McNab, who sat across the aisle from him in Junior
Third at the North Ward school, has a clear recollection of
Davies' comment on the whitewashing episode in *The
Adventures of Tom Sawyer*. Miss Milliken had asked for the meaning of: "Tom gave up the brush with reluctance in his face but
alacrity in his heart." Davies volunteered "that Tom Sawyer was
pretending that he didn't want to let the other fellow paint the
fence, but he would have been happy to throw the brush at
him." This answer so impressed McNab that he began to view
Davies as "very artistic" and "a very erudite person," though he is
sure that he did not know the word "erudite" at the time. Miss
Eva Millar often asked her students in Senior Third at Central
School to write brief essays. For her, Davies "wrote the most
delightful things, just delightful, and some of them she could
quote." She considered him her most outstanding student and
often talked warmly about the experience of having had him in
her class. During Junior Fourth at Central School he must have
been doing his best, so enchanted was he with his teacher. Arthur
remembers that the family meals were eaten that year to the endless refrain of "Mrs. Easton says." What Mrs. Easton said "was
coming right down from the mountain top."

The readers then in use in grade schools throughout Ontario
were full of selections from British, American and Canadian
poetry and prose. They were very much to Davies' liking, and
they stocked his mind with phrases, lines and verses that he
never forgot. Each reader contained selections that soared a little,
or, in a few cases, far beyond the grasp of the students who struggled with them, but Davies apparently liked the pieces that were
"tough chewing" or that remained "splendidly mysterious." As a

child he willingly memorized and tried to crack hard nuts like F. W. Bourdillon's "Love" (*Second Book*), Joseph Addison's "The Vision of Mirzah" (*Fourth Book*), William Cullen Bryant's "To a Water Fowl" (*Fourth Book*) and Ben Jonson's Pindaric Ode, which begins "It is not growing like a tree" (*Fourth Reader*). As an adult, he approves of such "educational time bombs," which may lie in the mind for years before exploding into meaning, or whose splendid language lasts for a lifetime.

Looking back, he feels that although the commonplace, the trashy, the narrowly moral and the passingly fashionable found their way into the readers, a high standard of taste and a fine ideal stood behind the bulk of the selections. He thinks that Ontario educators were trying to set forth "a coherent body of literary knowledge in which everybody could share," and is pleased to reflect that although English writers were given more space than American and American more than Canadian, Canadian writers appeared shoulder to shoulder with Sir Walter Scott, Dickens, R. L. Stevenson, Longfellow, Lowell and Whittier. Nonetheless, it is noticeable that he mentions no Canadian writer by name and quotes from no Canadian author when he discusses the readers. (Canada was represented primarily by Charles G. D. Roberts, Archibald Lampman, Wilfred Campbell, John Richardson and Egerton Ryerson.)

The one subject that Davies could never fathom was arithmetic. He spent interminable hours after class at both Central and North Ward schools as teacher after teacher tried to make him understand its simplest principles. It is hard to recapture the waste of time and spirit these hours represent because Davies does not talk about them much, but year after year his ineptitude was a humiliation and a source of frustration.

Home did much to compensate him for the miseries of arithmetic. There, Davies read voraciously. What he read supplied information, broadened his horizons, stimulated his emotions, raised questions, even held him in thrall, but it did not, in his opinion, influence him as profoundly as the reading he did much later. This seems to be true (with the notable exception of Victor Hugo's *Notre Dame de Paris*). Nonetheless, Davies, who has the urge not just to experience his life but to possess it, often recalls, revisits and reassesses books he read as a child. What did he read? All sorts of things, many of them written in the nineteenth century: Jessie Fothergill's *The First Violin* (1896), George Wilbur Peck's *Bad Boy and His Pa* (1883), Johann Rudolf Wyss' *The Swiss Family Robinson* (1812-13), Evelyn Everett-Green's *Sir Aylmer's Heir* (1890), William Kingston's *Snowshoes and Canoes* (a book of Canadian adventures), Thomas Hardy's *Tess of the d'Urbervilles* (1891), Daniel Defoe's *Robinson Crusoe*, a children's version of Jonathan Swift's *Gulliver's Travels*, Louisa May Alcott's *Little Women* (1868-69) and *Little Men* (1871), Andrew Lang's collections of fairy-tales, William Harrison Ainsworth's *Rookwood* (1834), R. M. Ballantyne's *The Coral Island* (1857), Mary Shelley's *Frankenstein* (1818), Marshall Saunders' *Beautiful Joe* (1894), Frances Eliza Hodgson Burnett's *Little Lord Fauntleroy* (1886). Dent's *Everyman's Encyclopedia*, looking frustratedly for information on sex and with the intention of becoming a polymath. (He abandoned this ambition as soon as he perceived that science, mathematics and pure reason were beyond his capacities.) O. S. Fowler's *Science of Life*, an old-fashioned book on sex, which he found hidden away in a trunk in the attic. The Henty books that his brothers had had before him, and *The Victor Book of the Opera*, which was in the family library. *Cole's Fun Doctor*, a two-volume, nineteenth-century, Australian book of jokes, put by his bedside to cheer him when he was ill. Dickens' novels in abridged versions for children and, in order "to get the full glory" of his brother Arthur's performance as Buzfuz in *Bardell vs. Pickwick* at the December 1921 commencement exercises at the collegiate, all of *Pickwick Papers* when he was eight. The funny papers. *Striving to Help*, a Sunday school prize won by one of his parents. Goethe's *Faust* when he was ten or eleven, because his parents had seen Gounod's *Faust* at the Russell Theatre in Ottawa. (He found it heavy going and was staggered to find God speaking in the Prologue, for his Presbyterian soul could not conceive how anyone could write down the words of God.) The pages of advertisements at the back of boys' books. He yearned to get his hands on *The Boy's Book of Magic*, Louis Hoffmann's *Modern Magic* and *Later Magic* and Robert-Houdin's *The Secrets of Stage Conjuring* and

Confidences d'un prestidigitateur but only acquired and read them years later when they began to turn up in rare book catalogues.

He revelled in the many magazines his parents took: *Scribner's,* the *Atlantic Monthly,* the *Saturday Evening Post* from the United States; the *Strand, Pearson's Magazine,* the *Sketch,* and *Punch* (for its pictures) from England; *Saturday Night* and *Maclean's* from Canada. They introduced him to some of the best short-story writers of the day—P. G. Wodehouse, Conan Doyle, W. W. Jacobs, Rudyard Kipling and Somerset Maugham. He recalls devouring Maugham's "supposedly cynical tales of adultery with a powerful appetite, because, although I was not sure what adultery was, I knew it was wicked." In similar spirit he took tremendous pleasure in an article by a bishop entitled "Is Nudity Salacious?" Apparently, "The bishop thought it need not be, if encountered in the proper spirit, but he gave a lot of enlightening examples of conditions under which it might be, in his word, 'inflammatory.'" The magazine *Rod and Gun* repelled him.

The *Youth's Companion,* which came from Boston, taken especially for him, and the big red annual volumes of *Chums,* which came from England in time for Christmas each year, did not fully capture him. He admired the American boys in the *Youth's Companion* but felt a certain distance from their uncritical patriotic adulation of figures like George Washington. He was fascinated by the English boarding school boys in *Chums,* but he felt he had little in common with their splendid adventures together, the pranks they played on their schoolmasters and the concept of upholding their school's honour on the playing field, since he had no close friends, was taught by women and disliked sports. As in the case of his parents' stories about their North American and Welsh forbears, these fictional characters represented distant worlds.

His mother taught him something about reading aloud, which he took to heart and which was reinforced by several school-teachers of her generation. It was a system she had been taught as a child: Pause for a count of one at a comma, of two at a semi-colon and of three at a colon or period. Let the voice rise when a sentence ends with a question or an exclamation mark, and pause at the end of a paragraph. When drawing to the end of a piece of reading, slow the pace a little, and always read clearly. It is well to remember Florence's advice when reading Davies' books, for Davies, who as a boy and a youth recited stories to himself in bed at night and who still runs his sentences past his mental ear before committing them to paper, thinks of his books as aural experiences. His punctuation is a set of signals for reading aloud. Usually when he wants a reaction to what he is writing, he does not hand over his manuscript: he reads it aloud.

Davies wrote his first piece of journalism in this period at his father's request. Many decades later, without the benefit of access to the *Mercury*'s files, he produced the following details about it: he wrote it when he was about ten or eleven; it was a report of a lecture given by the Reverend Mr. Radley of the Methodist Church, called "A Visit to Shakespeare's Birthplace"; Mr. Radley had palsy, so it was an agonizing business whenever he had to turn a page; his father did not criticize what he wrote, but did go over it "and made it right to go in the paper"; and he was paid twenty-five cents for doing it (big money to a boy who got no allowance). He attached so little importance to the object itself (perhaps because writing was taken casually in his family, where everyone wrote for the paper at one time or another) that he did not even read the piece when it appeared and it did not occur to him to clip and keep it.

In fact, he actually wrote the report at the age of nine, for it appeared on the front page of the *Mercury*, February 16, 1923, thus:

MR. RADLEY LECTURES ON SHAKESPEARE

To Interested Audience in the Methodist Church— Numerous Illustrations Shown.

A very enjoyable lecture was given by Rev. Mr. Radley, in the Methodist Church on Friday evening last on "William Shakespeare and His Country." The lecture was illustrated with lantern views, the lantern being operated by Mr. M. H. Winter. The first part of the address was on the beautiful Shakespearean country. Mr. Radley said that Charles

Kingsley in "Westward Ho!" and Blackmore in "Lorna Doone," taught us to love Devonshire; Dickens gives us a glimpse of country life in rural England, and also takes us along quiet stage roads. Shakespeare also gives us glimpses of some of the most beautiful portions of rural England.

Pictures were shown of Shakespeare's home, Anne Hathaway's cottage, the field where John of Gaunt fell, and many other historic spots. A very interesting description of Stratford-on-Avon was given by the lecturer. The evening was a very enjoyable and instructive one, and many of those present expressed their appreciation of Mr. Radley's address.

During the evening Mrs. M. H. Winter sang "Husheen" very acceptably. At the conclusion of the lecture the audience was invited to the platform to see a number of other views which Mr. Radley had gathered when visiting in the Old Land, including one of a round church, at Mr. Radley's boyhood home.

Another piece of writing that Davies did outside school has not survived. He knew that the coarse Mutt and Jeff shows he had been forbidden to see at the O'Brien Opera House were about comic-strip characters, and he wrote a three-page play of his own, based on his favourite comic, "Our Boarding House." As Davies describes it, Gene Ahern's cartoon was "about people in a boarding house, owned by Major Hoople and his wife, who talked, and talked and talked, in large balloons that almost filled the space in the single panel." Writing it gave him great satisfaction, but he showed it to no one because he did it when he ought to have been working on homework. Looking back, Davies credits this early exercise with teaching him that plays are largely "an exposition of character through dialogue."

Music continued to introduce him to powerful emotions and uncommon personalities. During a visit to the Canadian National Exhibition in Toronto, he fell under the spell of Signor Creatore and his concert band, succumbing without a murmur to Creatore's romantic appearance ("his hair fell to his shoulders in glistening black ringlets"), his unabashed gusto ("his manner

of eating could only be described as vivacious gormandizing")
and his "richly emotional music" (Rossini, Von Suppé, Auber,
Verdi). He revelled in the showmanship the bandmaster brought
to the "Miserere" from *Il Trovatore*:

> Before it was played there would be a short pause while the
> principal cornet player left the bandstand and removed
> himself to a considerable distance, in the darkness (for this
> was inescapably a piece for the evening concert). The
> dreary howling of the monks was heard, and the plaint of
> Leonora, and then, magically,
>
> > Ah, I have sighed to rest me,
> > Deep in the quiet grave—
>
> It was the principal cornet, personating the imprisoned
> Manrico, far away in the darkness. It would have drawn
> tears from a brazen image. When it was over, Signor
> Creatore was forced to bow again and again.

Even more powerful was a rough version of Verdi's *Rigoletto*
that Davies encountered in a Chautauqua tent in the summer of
1921 or 1922. He was already familiar with the opera excerpts in
the family's record collection, and he had images of some of the
characters and singers in his mind from the record sleeves and
from *The Victor Book of the Opera*. He "knew that opera meant a
play in which people sang, and that it was imbued with an inef-
fable magnificence," but as yet he had had no direct experience
of it. The Chautauqua version was certainly a dieter's introduction to opera's feast, since it began with a confusing plot summary, had an upright piano for accompaniment and was sung by
three men and three women with only mediocre voices. When
their turns came, one or more of the six "hurled themselves out
of their chairs toward the front of the stage, and roared defiance
to the world. They gestured violently; they sobbed...." But to
Davies, it was all glorious: "I did not understand the story, but
my heart beat in time with the music, and it seemed to me that I
grew a foot in the two hours I passed in the Chautauqua tent

that night. This was emotion on a scale undreamed of. This was a reality surpassing anything that had come my way before. This was a distilled essence of life; this was the way people behaved when they took off the masks which all adults seemed to me to wear; this was noble. A veil had been rent between the greatness of mankind and myself, and I knew that I would never be the same again." And indeed he had gained much. This early apprehension of a richer, more splendid life under the everyday veil had far-reaching consequences for Davies. It fostered in him an intense interest in the means of experiencing it, not only in the theatre but, later, through dreams and the exploration of the unconscious.

Davies began piano lessons at the age of eight under Percival Kirby, the Presbyterian church organist. He would sit

> on the piano stool, toiling through pieces called *Violet, Rose,* and *Mayflower* while [Kirby] was sunk deep in a dilapidated wicker armchair, with his feet on top of the upright piano—yes, he was an exceedingly tall man—waving one hand gracefully to give me the time. At intervals there would be alarming sounds from the remainder of the house—shouts and inexplicable thuds, and weeping; sometimes a female arm would appear through a crack in the door, beckoning my teacher peremptorily out of the room. He was a man, I soon discovered, who was not blessed with tranquillity in his domestic arrangements. This seemed to me to be extremely romantic. It was in his house that I first saw china thrown in anger; one day as I was approaching the climax of *Jonquil,* the door burst open and a child rushed in, with a dinner-plate following close behind it. The child ducked, my teacher ducked, and I ducked, as the plate smashed against the wall. Then the thrower of the plate appeared, and everybody laughed hysterically, and there were some embraces, and then we all had pieces of cake to steady our nerves. This was *La Vie de Bohème* as we lived it in rural Ontario, and all things considered it was life-enhancing and educational.

Kirby, who lived in the house next to the church, and who often came across in his carpet slippers to play the organ, was the first of a number of church organists Davies got to know over the years. Together they grew into the character of Humphrey Cobbler, the eccentric organist in the Salterton novels.

Although he still had no close friends, toward the end of his stay in Renfrew Davies joined other boys in attending the Saturday afternoon movies. They cost ten cents, which was money he had to ask for, although it was forthcoming when he needed it. He saw the Mack Sennett comedies and films starring Charlie Chaplin, Tom Mix, Fatty Arbuckle or the Keystone Kops, and drank in the current serial episode (one starred Reginald Denny as the good-guy pugilist who always beat the crook in the weighted gloves). He remembers seeing the Gish sisters in *Orphans of the Storm* and *The White Sister*, Richard Barthelmess in a number of movies including *Tol'able David, Sonny, The Bright Shawl* and *Way Down East*, as well as films of *Lorna Doone, The Hunchback of Notre Dame* and Robin Hood. From time to time he saw bilingual silent films, the captions in English on one side and French on the other. The accompanist, a chain-smoker who played with great rapidity, would leap, when religious feeling was called for, to a little harmonium. Sometimes Davies brought some of the other boys home to serve as actors or audience for impromptu plays, many of them inspired by the movies.

What really fired his imagination was the time he finally got to "do" the midway at the Canadian National Exhibition in Toronto. He had been to Spark's circus, which came to Renfrew most summers, and was enormously impressed on his first visit by a barker "talking about how you would see the lion consume fifteen pounds of raw, bloody meat." Every autumn he had attended the big agricultural fair at the local fairgrounds, but he had not been allowed to see the monsters and horrors in the side-shows. He got to the CNE while he lived in Renfrew, on Press Day when his father had special privileges. One year his brother Arthur indulgently accompanied him the full length of the midway—the House of Mirth, racing monkeys, bathing beauties and all—and he finally got to see the freak show. He had a good stare at the dwarfs, giants, hermaphrodites, living skeletons and the like, hoping "that they might impart some great revelation to me, some insight which would help me to a clearer understanding of the world about me." One of the things he noticed was that little people—midgets or dwarfs—"were always getting the knife in first. They looked for the shortest man in the crowd and said, 'Hello, Shorty.' And they'd got him first, you see, and everybody laughed at him before they laughed at them but there was a terrible defensiveness about it."

The summer of 1924 brought a major event, which suddenly expanded Davies' world. Rupert, who was president of the Canadian Weekly Newspapers Association, had attended the second Imperial Press Conference (for editors of daily papers) in Ottawa in 1920. As a result of his interest, membership in the Empire Press Union was extended to editors of weekly papers the following year, and he immediately decided to mount a trip to acquaint the Canadians with leading editors in Britain and to give them a chance to hear "some of the Empire's great statesmen discuss Imperial questions." So many of them had been involved in the First World War in one way or another that the trip soon expanded beyond the "Motherland" to Belgium and France.

It was no easy matter to organize a tour for a hundred and seventy-one people, comprised of over a hundred editors, plus wives, and a few children, to Belgium, France, England, Scotland and Ireland, especially when the tour included presentations, receptions, dinners and garden parties to meet dignitaries like King Albert of Belgium, Marshal Foch and President Doumergue of France, King George and Queen Mary and assorted burgomasters, Lord Mayors and councillors in every centre along the way. But Rupert loved every phase of the adventure, from his ground-laying journeys in 1921 and 1923 through the trip itself.

Davies, towed along in the wake of the hundred and seventy when they sailed on the C.P.R. steamship *Melita* from Montreal in June until they arrived back at Quebec City on the *Montlaurier* seven weeks later, was so awash with the multiplicity of impressions that flooded in upon him that he took years to absorb them fully. Now he had seen where the Great War was fought, seen actual places where the characters in his books lived and walked where his father had grown up. He saw for himself that life, as the British and Europeans conceived it, was lived very differently than it was in Renfrew.

One of his deepest impressions came from the two-day tour of the battlefields in Belgium and France. In every city and town they had visited, there had been a great laying of wreaths at the Tomb of the Unknown Soldier. And as they visited the sites where Canadians had fought, they saw what remained of the trenches. One of those sites was Ypres, where, in *Fifth Business*, Davies has Dunstan Ramsay surprise a German machine-gun nest and collect a fragment of shrapnel in his left leg.

In Antwerp, Davies, the son of Temperance parents, had his first glass of beer, "so bitter but, to the parched throat, so refreshing." Later, in Paris, at a buffet luncheon, he discovered some oddly shaped glasses with bubbly stuff in them that he took to be a superior sort of lemonade. He consumed a good number. During the afternoon he felt unusually cheerful, but that evening, at a performance of *La Bohème* at the Opera Comique, he felt so ill that after the first act his parents hustled him back to the hotel, where he threw up at the top of the stairs. The bearded French doctor they summoned quickly diagnosed inebriation, and Rupert and Florence were so relieved that, instead of being angry, they thought it was hilarious. They commemorated his fall from grace with a parcel on the Christmas tree that year in which lay a Temperance tract called *The Shadow of the Bottle*. (It should be added that seeing wine and beer consumed in a civilized manner on the trip had the effect of gradually liberalizing their attitude toward alcohol. In later years, Rupert would take a drink fairly regularly, Florence used a little brandy for her asthma and wine began to be served at dinner on special occasions.)

Davies was also exposed, on the continent and in London, to grotesques—cripples crawling along on carts, their twisted legs dragging behind, their hands gnarled and their fingernails like talons; creatures with elephantiasis; young people with no teeth; individuals holding lupus cushions to hideously swollen, cancerous faces; human beings who were little, shifty, trembly, ill-fed and poverty-stricken. He had read in Dickens of such beings, but now they were on the streets in front of him.

The other end of the social scale was equally instructive. In 1924, Edwardian elegance had not wholly faded from London; suddenly Davies could see his father's sartorial elegance against a backdrop that suited it. He observed that gentlemen still wore top hats and morning dress as a matter of course in the afternoon. Men went to see their bankers in top hats. George V's trousers were creased at the sides, as his father Edward VII's had been. Every manservant at the Cecil Hotel where the Davies stayed had three uniforms—"a sleeve-waistcoat, stiff collar and black tie for the morning, a livery with trousers and a dress coat and white tie for the afternoon, and for the evening knee-breeches, a full eighteenth century livery and powdered hair." All this confirmed him in rejecting the standards of Renfrew, where, when Colonel Lennox Irving once appeared in formal attire, his brother-in-law Harry Barnet had come along and said, "Hello, Lennox. You're all dressed up!" and struck a match on the front of his starched shirt.

Toward the end of the trip, Davies and his parents broke away from the main group to visit his great-uncle Dr. Robert Robertson and his wife on the Isle of Wight and to go to Wales. Robertson, a general practitioner in Ventnor and a specialist in tuberculosis, had generously donated his services to the local sanitarium free of charge for fifty years. In St. Catherine's, his great-uncle's house, high on a cliff above the sea with gardens stretching between the house and the precipice, Davies encountered a kind of domestic luxury altogether new to him. A housemaid would appear in his bedroom in the morning to close the window and bring him a cup of tea and a biscuit! And in Wales he finally saw for himself the landscape, places and people that filled his father's memory. Soon after, they rejoined the main party and embarked on the voyage home. He was as dreadfully seasick westbound as he had been eastbound. Seasickness continued to plague him through the 1930s, then bothered him no more.

Davies acquired and read a book on this trip that influenced him deeply. He had been so awed by the Cathedral of Notre Dame in Paris that his mother bought him an English translation of Victor Hugo's *Notre Dame de Paris*, often translated as *The Hunchback of Notre Dame*. Looking back in 1967 when he purchased a new translation, Davies acknowledged to himself that this had been one of his "truly formative books," which by then he had read three times.

As a boy he had been drawn in by the melodramatic plot and its vividly drawn characters. He was particularly struck by the episode in which the poet and playwright Pierre Gringoire is swept along by a group of fake grotesques, who discard their sores and crutches and proceed to an evening of revelry in the Court of Miracles, where "they hung the poet up with bells all over him and said that if any woman would marry him they would let him go, but if he rang the bells, they'd kill him." Just before Gringoire encounters the grotesques there is another image that seems to have sunk deeply into Davies' consciousness. He has been following Esmeralda through the night streets of Paris, and by the flickering light of an oil-soaked wick at the feet of a street-corner statue of the Holy Virgin, he sees her attacked. Quasimodo then knocks him out, and he returns to his senses on the paving in front of the statue. Compare *Fifth Business*, where Dunstan Ramsay has a battlefield glimpse of a statue of the Virgin by the light of a dropping flare just before he loses consciousness. In the chapters that follow, Gringoire is propelled from hope to despair and back, again and again, in a series of surprises of a kind that Davies springs, rather more sparingly, in his own books. And several of the novel's figures—the hermitess Gudule in her cell, the beauteous Gypsy girl Esmeralda, the learned alchemist and lustful priest Claude Frollo, the hunchback dwarf Quasimodo—grasped Davies' imagination so strongly that years later he introduced similar characters into his novels *Fifth Business* and *The Rebel Angels*.

Home from his adventure and in a school he liked, Davies found that Renfrew was beginning to grow on him. He and his family had moved into a third house, one of the substantial residences at the south end of Raglan Street (now number 494). Its surroundings were pleasant: there was an established garden; it looked across the street and a broad stretch of Smith's Creek to the fairgrounds; to the rear there was a large barn and behind it a ravine, good settings for the plays he put on with other boys. It had a name—"Kildonan"—like the Barnets' nearby "Coleraine Hall," and wood had been used lavishly in the interior, particularly in the panelled library with its octagonally patterned, hardwood floor, probably because John Mackay, the man for whom the house had been built, was the son of a man with large lumber interests.

Davies became more venturesome. In particular, he pursued an interest in magic. The boys' magazines he read were full of magic and ventriloquism, and he sent away ten cents for a gadget advertised in the *Youth's Companion* that promised to turn anyone into a ventriloquist once it was inserted in the mouth. When he got no reply, he told his father about it, and Rupert shot off a stiff note to the magazine, bringing an apology from the *Companion* and the gadget from the advertiser. But, "of course, like all these things, it didn't work very well." In Arthur's recollection, Davies' sleight-of-hand didn't go any better. One night as the family was sitting on the verandah, Davies "came and said he could make an egg disappear and reappear. So he was dressed in a little jersey and a pair of long khaki pants and he stuffed the egg into a little pocket. He put the egg in this pocket. Then, of course, the culmination of the trick was to make the egg reappear. So there was more squirming around and finally he broke the egg in his pocket! End of trick."

The famed Blackstone came to town on February 24, 1925, and bodied forth the marvels Davies had read about. His advertisement in the *Mercury* on February 20, with its whiff of evil and promise of exotica, was designed to ensure brisk ticket sales. And among the marvels on his posters was an intriguing pixie, "from whose mouth, in a balloon, came the words: 'Lord, what fools these mortals be.'" (Compare Puck in *Tempest-Tost* above the Snak Shak's food counter, where the balloon now says: "Lord, what foods these morsels be.")

Rupert, too, was finally settling into Renfrew. Having achieved one of the town's best addresses, he thought he "was fixed for life," as he wrote in *Far-Off Fields*. It is possible that Rupert's financial success, Florence's warming toward her fellow

Continuing Presbyterians and Davies' tentative socializing might in time have ameliorated their harsh view of the town. But they moved away in the summer of 1925.

Two events toward the end of his stay cast dark shadows over Davies' recollection of Renfrew. One was the two- or three-day visit to Central School of Arthur Wellesley Beall, the Ontario Department of Education's itinerant lecturer on eugenics and personal hygiene.

Davies' curiosity about sex had been aroused in Thamesville when, prompted by his brothers' warnings to keep away, he had discovered a drawing "of a woman with enormously exaggerated breasts and private parts" on the inside of the door of the boxcar in which the family had packed their household effects for transportation to Renfrew. In the North Ward schoolyard he, who had never heard his brothers or his father tell a dirty joke or use a dirty word, had been surrounded by the ripest sexual innuendo. He was sickened and repelled when the boys hinted that such and such a girl was pregnant, or that a woman had had an abortion and stuffed the resultant mess down the privy. But he did not dare to raise these subjects at home. Although he was deeply convinced that what he was hearing was irreligious and evil, he was quite unable to put what he heard from his mind. His trip to Europe had stimulated him further. In Belgium, there were plenty of statues "of women with breasts like kettledrums, & nipples like champagne corks, & something mysterious between the thighs whch sculptors indicated only by a lump. I was in a fever of curiosity, but of course with no one to satisfy it. For in spite of the obscenity of the children I knew—ignorant without being innocent, & vile without imagination—I knew nothing whatever of sex except as a dark world which constantly impended, all the more terrifying for being utterly unknown."

By the time Beall came to address the senior students in Davies' public school, he was in his sixties. He had been in the Department of Education's employ since the turn of the century, and would continue to tour the province's public and high schools until well into the 1930s. His book, *The Living Temple*, provides the basic script for the performance Davies witnessed. Addressing both boys and girls in Lessons 1 to 7 (which were covered in the first day or two), Beall inched his way toward the reproductive organs, masturbation and sex with such mincing delicacy that his hearers must have been thoroughly bewildered. He recurrently exhorted them to be "A.1," be clean, love Canada, and treat their living temples, their bodies, with reverence. This meant refraining from smoking, drinking, telling smutty stories, swearing, looking at dirty postcards, singing dirty songs or touching or kissing another girl or boy. Beall divided the world into two camps—"The Devil's Dump" and "God's Honor Roll." To stay on the right side of the line, the children were to refer to the triangle-motto (Beall drew it on the blackboard):

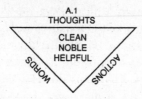

At the eighth lesson, Beall dismissed the girls (who, as Davies recalls it, were then instructed by a nurse). Now he got down to business. Throughout, he had presented mothers as objects of veneration. Now he pushed each boy to acknowledge that his own mother had put her life on the line for him: "For on the day that you were born your mother went down into the Valley of the Shadow of Death so that you might live. Hands, now please, to the top storey and repeat: 'On the day that I was born my mother went down into the Valley of the Shadow of Death, so that I might live.'"

From the beginning he had urged the children to see their bodies as living temples. Now he drew a parallel between the temple in Jerusalem and the living temple of the body, suggesting that the most holy place was the genital organs, and that each man, as his own high priest, might go in unto the holy place only once a year and only when wearing clean white garments. (What he can have meant by this is not clear.) According to Beall (and in the following summary I emulate his use of capital letters), the Most Sacred Place in the male body was the LIFE GLANDS, whose LIFE FLUID had three functions, two of them to feed the muscles and the nervous system. It was important to keep the Life Glands clean and leave them alone. If a boy habitually allowed the Life Fluid to bleed away (as a boy might allow his life blood to flow away by cutting the vessels of the wrist with a jack-knife), then he would certainly go out of his mind and have to be committed to a hospital for the insane. Beall told a story of a boy who suffered just that fate: "When they took him to the hospital he was crazy. But he got worse and worse. He couldn't keep his hands off the MALE PART of his body—a half dozen times a day he was playing with it, and bleeding away the precious LIFE FLUID, until one day the doctors came along and cut off the two LIFE GLANDS, just to keep the miserable dregs of a miserable existence from all being frittered away." Now he introduced the boys to the word penis, cautioned them darkly against letting any other boy touch it and observed that the more it was used the weaker it became. In conclusion, he declared that "*The Third Function* of the LIFE FLUID is FATHERHOOD—after marriage—and 'ONLY' after marriage," for, he argued, while the boys would all agree that it was dreadful to kill a baby, it was even more dreadful to bring "a new baby into the world, unless that baby has an A.1 father and an A.1 mother, to give it an A.1 start."

Davies remembers Beall as a squat toad with lower eyelids that drooped red like a hound's and a white moustache that straggled over an unpleasantly wet mouth. The lectures were more horrific in the flesh than on the page, for in the heat of presentation Beall actually exposed his own penis. He also made points omitted from *The Living Temple*. In particular, he linked sexual purity to the vigour of the British Empire, associating sexual indiscretions with bringing the Empire to its knees and delivering it over to the horrible Hun. Beall can be found, as Dr. G. Courtney Upper, in *What's Bred in the Bone.*

Davies found the harangue as revolting as the North Ward schoolyard. And he was still frustrated, since his grasp of the facts of sex was still confused and he had no courage to discuss the subject with his parents. Beall's mawkish, fake-religious assault on his sensibilities was the more troubling because it seemed to have the approval of the school. He was tremendously relieved later to discover that his father despised Beall and had tried to dissuade the school board from inviting him.

Beall's views on motherhood were, on the other hand, shared by his parents, certainly by Florence. In *World of Wonders*, Magnus Eisengrim recalls the attitude that was a daily reality in the Davies household: "Those were the sunset days of the great legend of motherhood. When your mother bore you, she went down in her anguish to the very gates of Death, in order that you might have life. Nothing that you could do subsequently would work off your birth-debt to her. No degree of obedience, no unfailing love, could put the account straight. Your guilt toward her was a burden you carried all your life." When Davies was impudent to his mother or "sauced" her, she became a rampaging virago, going so far as to lash him with a pony whip that his brothers had bought at the fall fair in Thamesville. Tears on both sides then brought a general retreat. The matter was only resolved when he physically abased himself before her, the symbol of the sentimental altar of motherhood. He apologized, there were more tears, and finally she forgave him. Here is a comparable scene in *Fifth Business*:

> My father and Willie came home, and there was no supper. Naturally he sided with her, and Willie was very officious and knowing about how intolerable I had become of late, and how thrashing was too good for me. Finally it was settled that my mother would come downstairs if I would beg pardon. This I had to do on my knees, repeating a formula improvised by my father, which included a pledge that I would always love my mother, to whom I owed the great gift of life, and that I begged her—and secondarily God—to forgive me, knowing full well that I was unworthy of such clemency.

The offending Davies was required to bow lower than this: he had to kiss Florence's shoe. He hated the grovelling, but even more he despised paying lip service to a sentimental notion of motherhood that had little to do with his actual relationship with his mother.

Here was another of the unacknowledgable tensions that burdened Davies for years. Like his brothers, and for that matter most boys of his day and class, he was expected not only to feel grateful to his mother for "the great gift of life" but also to his father for support, guidance and counsel of his unworthy self. He was exhorted time and again to "Honour thy father and thy mother that thy days may be long upon the land which the Lord thy God giveth thee" (Exodus 20:12). He did feel gratitude and proffer honour, but he felt them to be onerous tributes, rather than gifts.

The other event that shadows Davies' memory of Renfrew concerns Francis Xavier Boucher. An achondroplasic dwarf— "heavy-headed, short-legged [with an] ugly mask of a face always grinning like a dog with a tongue hanging out"—Boucher was a conspicuous figure in the town. During the latter part of 1923 and through much of 1924 there was a modest advertisement in the *Mercury's* "Classified Business Directory" that ran

F. X. Boucher
Up-to-the-minute
Clothes Pressing, Cleaning and
Repairing
Phone 316   Dominion House Block
Our Slogan—Courtesy & Service

He was making a success of his business: on February 13 and 20, 1925, he ran a much bigger ad announcing that he had moved into larger premises due to the pressure of business. Then, suddenly, he (and the ad) disappeared. It was a mystery, until Davies found out what had happened from Rupert. For years members of one of the local lodges had concluded their induction rites by persecuting "Bushy." Full of booze, they would shanghai him from his shop, make him strip and give him a bath at the lodge. Then, according to Davies, "they would chase him around the room with wet towels slapping them at him while he had to run, and, 'you know, Bushy was a great little guy—he always went along with the gag—he had as much fun as anybody—it was just an absolute hoot.'" But this time Boucher hanged himself in the back of the shop. Davies gave this story dramatic vigour in *What's Bred in the Bone*, where F. X. Boucher appears as François Xavier Bouchard.

Davies' immensely detailed and extensive memories of Renfrew continue to contain tremendous energy. He loathes the place at the same time as he treasures the storehouse of highly coloured images and stories that he amassed during his six years there. He made use of only a fraction of what he remembers in the creation of the fictional Blairlogie. When at Christmas 1986 I gave him *The Story of Renfrew*, a collection of reminiscences and articles by present-day residents of the town, he replied with a fascinated exuberance:

...what a compilation! How revealing of the way in which Renfrew wishes to think of itself! How devoid of any illuminative, characteristic detail, or anything that might suggest a dark thread in the tartan! And it is, as you say, a rather sloppy job, and the confusion of F. X. Boucher with Mr. Pausé is only one of the errors. The Pausés—pronounced locally Posy—were a dwarf brother and sister, who had independent means, and always dressed very fashionably; Mr Pausé always carried a tiny walking-stick, and when he walked down Raglan Street with his little sister on his arm children sometimes jeered at them; and then Mr. Pausé gallantly rushed at them with his cane raised and would have thrashed them except that they were more agile than he. Both Pausés, alas, were frail little hunchbacks and could not have stood up to the morlachian toughs who attended Renfrew's schools. But the picture is Bushy to the life, and captures his observant look.... Another picture in the book which electrified me was that, on 231, of Little Lura Troke. She was the heartbreaker of the ten-to-twelve years old set, a dark beauty with an aquiline nose (very rare in childhood and promising a hook in maturity) & corkscrew curls of a rich, dark chocolate colour. And there she stands, right down to her elegant kid gaiters. Well do I recall that a friend of mine, another boy in the Presbyterian Sunday School, fell under her thrall, and dared not speak his love. But on Sundays after we had had our dose of *The Shorter Catechism*, I used to walk with him up and down Lura's street, casually, as though there by chance, in the hope that the Fair Enslaver might appear and cast him a glance. But no. Ah, Lura, did you know what devastation you wrought among the youth of Renfrew? I rather think you did.... So many memories were aroused by the book. There is a piece by Sam Shields, which does not reveal him as a lord of language; I went through school with Sam, who was always head of his class because he was "smart" and could do Mental Arithmetic and could read more and faster than any of us.... I was interested that Sam recalled the DiColas, our one Italian family; the girls were not beauties, but they were not bad, and Mrs. DiCola polished them up and rouged them and, in the minatory local phrase, "put them on show" and they all got Italian husbands from elsewhere.... it is a very selective book. Even Colonel Lennox Irving, the local butt, is spoken of with respect, nor is it hinted that Miss Edith Airth, a greatly loved schoolteacher, was the bastard of Old Carswell, who used to sneer at her publicly—not when she was present, but in barbershops and other forums of opinion.... What a lot of pleasure you have given me, and you have made me think again about Renfrew. Was I wrong? Were my parents wrong? There can be no final decision in such matters. But I saw what I saw, and heard what I heard and when my thoughts turn to Renfrew the sun is never shining in the vision. A child's impressions? Of course, but I think some consideration has to be given to the nature of the child. I was a *very* observant child and my intuitions were acute.

P.S. The book contains two pictures of Len Wright, who with his family, were our only blacks.... Oh, the day when their daughter Eunice, who was my age, snatched a *boy's* bicycle and declared she could ride it, and did so until she fell foul of the crossbar and gave a piercing shriek. Consternation! Eunice carried into the school—it was recess—and laid on a desk. Dr. Burwell sent for. Grave faces on the lady teachers. Had Eunice—O, the *frisson* of it!—been deflowered by the bicycle? History is silent on the subject.... And the Froatses, much gloated over in the book, but nobody says that two of them were albinos, and wore dark specs to school. They made tombstones.... Nor is it hinted that Tom Low went bust before he died and is thought to have taken his own life. Certainly my Father reported that he was all swelled up and horribly discoloured in his coffin.... Oh, the opportunities missed by the editors of that book!

Chapter 4

KINGSTON AND UPPER CANADA
COLLEGE: 1925-32

As they are approached over the water Quebec is noble,
Montreal mighty, and Toronto strenuously aspiring, but
Kingston has an air of venerable civilization which warms the
heart; domes and spires, and the moral yet kindly outlines of its
houses of refuge and correction give it a distinction of which any
city might be proud.
                    —Samuel Marchbanks, "Canada's River of Romance,"
                                                    21 November 1942

It has long been fashionable for writers of autobiography to
abuse their boarding-schools, at which they declare they were
unhappy, misunderstood, bored and ill-taught.... Only fools
expect to be happy all the time. Only people of primitive
perceptions think that youth is a time of unalloyed enjoyment.
Occasionally I meet people who assure me that their schooldays
were the happiest time of their lives, and I pity them; I wonder
what they have been doing with the years that have passed since
they left school forever.
                            —"A Chapter of Autobiography," 1979-80

IN THE SUMMER of 1925, the family moved to Kingston, at the eastern end of Lake Ontario, where Rupert had taken over the loss-making *Daily British Whig*. The move was suggested to him by J. E. Atkinson of the *Toronto Daily Star*, and he responded to the opportunity only reluctantly, since he had no desire to uproot himself yet again or to take on a daily paper. It was running at a loss when he bought it on July 1, but within a year he managed to put it in the black, and he eliminated his only significant competition as expeditiously. His friend Harry B. Muir was persuaded to buy the *Kingston Daily Standard*, and on December 1, 1926, they amalgamated the two papers as the *Kingston Whig-Standard*, Muir to manage the business side and Rupert the editorial and news. Almost immediately the paper prospered, permitting Rupert to make (as he said with considerable understatement) "investments in many other companies which were very profitable." By 1928, when he sent his youngest son to a private school, he was well on his way to becoming a wealthy man. Having invested wisely, he was unaffected by the stock market crash in 1929, and by 1932 he could afford to buy and maintain a large country house in Wales as a summer home.

To Davies' twelve-year-old mind, the contrast Kingston offered to Renfrew was auspicious. This city of 22,000 had presence, and, viewed from the lake, its mature trees and the disposition of its domes and spires formed a skyline of considerable charm. Its many public institutions were distinctively housed, and the blue-grey stone of the early buildings of the "Limestone City" imparted an impressive coherence to the whole. Kingston was Davies' home until he left for Oxford in 1935. His play *Fortune, My Foe* and the linked Salterton novels, *Tempest-Tost, Leaven of Malice* and *A Mixture of Frailties*, draw their settings and many of their characters from the city and its inhabitants as he knew them then.

Whereas Renfrew had been barely a generation away from the rough and tumble of pioneering life, Kingston was a long-settled city. The French had built Fort Cataraqui on the site in 1673, and after the British captured and renamed it Fort Frontenac in 1758, it remained a military centre. Many United Empire Loyalists settled nearby when they were displaced by the

American War of Independence, with the result that a district capital was established there in 1784 and called King's Town, for George III. Fort Henry and four Martello towers were added in the first half of the nineteenth century. By 1835, Kingston seemed the logical place to build the first of several penitentiaries, and, after Confederation, the infant Canadian Army established the Royal Military College there for officer training. In the 1920s, the military buildings lent weight to Kingston's skyline, as they do today.

As Upper Canada's leading centre for the trans-shipment of goods during the early decades of the nineteenth century, Kingston quickly developed into its largest town and an administrative centre of justice, education, religion and government. The first court-house was built in 1796. In 1841 "Queen's College at Kingston," later Queen's University, was founded. Both the Roman Catholic and Anglican Churches established cathedrals there, the one in 1848 and the other in 1862. Most importantly, in 1840, Lord Sydenham, the governor general of British North America, selected Kingston to be the capital of the Province of Canada, the union of Upper and Lower Canada.

By 1842 construction had begun on an imposing limestone parliament building of classical design, and some four hundred stone houses were built. Quite suddenly, however, in 1843, the decision was reversed. Sydenham's successors moved the capital to Montreal (and subsequently to Quebec City, Toronto, Quebec City again and finally Ottawa). Having been in the right place for more than fifty years, by mid-century Kingston was in the wrong one. The commercial focus of Upper Canada had shifted to Toronto. Kingston grew very slowly through the second half of the nineteenth century, so the core of the city continued to be dominated architecturally by the early limestone buildings. To Davies, the failure of the city's reach for political eminence provided it, as he told a BBC-TV audience in 1983, with "the melancholy of romance." Since the flood of immigration to Canada early in the twentieth century largely passed Kingston by, its people and institutions still reflected their British extraction with considerable faithfulness through the 1920s and '30s.

Well before his university days, Davies had become thoroughly aware of Kingston's Loyalist roots, its military history and its association with Canada's founding fathers. Had he not had pointed out to him on the grounds of Alwington House the very tree (looking suspiciously young) on which Lord Sydenham had fatally struck his head when thrown from his horse in 1841? Had he not seen the fusty offices on Wellington Street where Sir John A. Macdonald, Canada's first prime minister, had commenced his legal practice in 1835? A favourite local legend concerned Archdeacon George Okill Stuart and his ruinous mania for building. Stuart had built "Summerhill," a dwelling so large that it housed the whole of Queen's College from 1854-58, and he had embarked on another house that remained unfinished when he died, one Davies and his contemporaries knew as "Archdeacon's Folly." (Stuart prefigures Prebendary Bedlam in *Tempest-Tost*, who built "four houses of real beauty" in Salterton, including Old Bedlam on the university grounds and St. Agnes' where the Websters live.)

Rupert's first house in Kingston was at 138 Albert Street. But the house that became Davies' real delight was their next home, which bore the name "Calderwood." Like Sir John A.'s "Bellevue House," it had been built in the style of a Tuscan villa a little before 1850. Douglas V. LePan has written a poem called "Tuscan Villa" that evokes it strongly for Davies. However, when it first caught Rupert's eye, little remained to link it with Bellevue or its Italian precursors. It had become the property of the Canadian government, which used it as a married officers' residence during World War I and as a rest home for soldiers after the war. In the early 1920s it had been seriously damaged by fire, and the extensive grounds and gardens had been allowed to run wild. This provided Rupert and Florence with the opportunity to exercise their own taste, and no sooner had Rupert leased it than they plunged happily into rebuilding and refurbishing. Davies, who had now been uprooted for the fifth time, began to recognize that decorating and renovation were among his parents' shared pleasures. When completed late in 1928, the low servants' wing with its bedrooms and basement kitchen had been entirely reorganized and rebuilt, and the main section of the house had been made exceedingly comfortable. Rupert equipped Calderwood with a billiard table, although Fred, the veteran of "The Better 'Ole," was the only member of the family who knew how to play. They had the exterior painted yellow with green trim.

Rupert hired a Welsh gardener to tend Calderwood's several acres and lay out extensive gardens. The lawns, apart from an area set apart for croquet, were to be inviolate, off limits to adults and children alike. (One marvellous day, as his granddaughter Miranda recalled, Rupert broke his own rules, piled all the grandchildren into his grey convertible and drove over the lawns in mad figures of eight. The children were so excited—and incredulous—they gasped: "Aaaaah, we're on the GRASS!") At first Florence worked on the gardens herself, and even when confined to a wheelchair she took a keen interest in them, whacking the weeds with her stick and keeping the gardener on his mettle.

In the summers, during the years when he was at Upper Canada College and Queen's University, Davies became an unpaid gardener's helper. This experience loses nothing in Samuel Marchbanks' "Diary": "Gardening is an undemocratic pursuit: Somebody crawls through the flowerbeds, weeding and grovelling like the beasts that perish; somebody else strolls in the cool of the evening, smelling the flowers. There is the garden-lord and the garden-serf. When we are all socialists gardens will vanish from the earth." He became intimately acquainted with the gardener's shed as well, which, fantasticated as a conservatory, became the setting for some of the action in *Tempest-Tost*.

To Davies' great delight, Calderwood housed three ghosts. Two—an old man who had shot his wife and a billiards player who had died of heart failure—refused to materialize during the Davieses' tenure. But the third, one Dr. H. A. Betts, who had reputedly drowned his daughter Augusta in the bath, showed up twice. The doctor appeared to guests of the Davieses, descending the stairs in evening dress, but not to the Davieses themselves. The family lived in that house until Florence died in the late 1940s. It was demolished in 1969, to make room for an addition to the Penitentiary Staff College at 443 Union Street. Only two outbuildings—the gardener's shed and the coach house—survive.

Davies found plenty of old-world drama in the Kingston of the 1920s and '30s. The Penitentiary still hanged criminals. The lash was still employed. The father of a boy he knew, a guard at the Penitentiary who administered floggings with a broad, perforated strap, might, as it seemed to him, have been a character out of Dickens. And on the evenings when his parents dined with the warden and were served by the criminals, *Great Expectations* felt quite real to him.

The streets of Kingston were as vividly costumed, to Davies' eye, as the Cecil Hotel in London had been in 1924. You might see "a groom in the full dress uniform of the Princess Patricia's Regiment or of the Royal Canadian Horse Artillery, standing out-side a door with two horses, his own and that of an officer. And if you hung around you would see an officer marvellously gotten up in that green uniform with silver froggings and so on and so forth...come down the steps and hop on a horse and away they'd drive, the groom riding half a horse's length behind the officer." He remembers the cadets from the Royal Military College chang-ing their plumage with the season—scarlet tunics topped by white helmets with gold spikes in summer, little capes plus pill-box hats in autumn, grey fur and blue greatcoats in winter. The two cathedrals hinted at the streets of Canterbury and the Vatican. The Anglican clerics paraded in rosetted black hats and gaiters; the Roman Catholic priests' black hats were seemingly cast of iron. From time to time a gaudy cardinal or papal nuncio would visit. Davies recalls that on these occasions the aged Roman Catholic archbishop, "who had, in the Irish phrase, 'sur-vived his wits,'" had to be carried through the streets, mitre and all, by two hefty young priests. Some Queen's professors affected pince-nez, and all wore academic gowns on the campus—unlike the undergraduates, who wore shirts and ties, sweaters and slacks or suits. On fine days, too, begowned lawyers could be watched, chatting on the court-house's neoclassical portico.

All this institutional costumery had its perfect counterpoint in the Gypsies who appeared every summer on the streets of Kingston. Davies claims that the most beautiful girl he ever saw was sitting on the tilt of a caravan outside Anderson's store. And he admired the hags, too, and their way with words: "A gypsy who could address an Ontario housewife with legs like gateposts and a face like a meataxe as 'pretty lady' while attempting to sell her a ten cent comb for a dollar was an artist, and I have a weakness for artists."

For Kingston, and for Salterton in *Tempest-Tost* as well, the premier social event of the year was the Royal Military College June Ball. Davies never managed to attend, but his parents went every year. (By 1934 he had become so experienced in theatrical make-up that he "touched up" his father's moustache for the occasion and "painted" his mother as well.) He was hugely amused to discover that some of the older ladies wore the same dresses year after year (a custom he saluted in *Tempest-Tost*).

"At Homes" survived in Kingston until the Second World War. At Bishop's Court, the Anglican clergy entertained many Kingstonians at tea on Sunday afternoons, and private citizens like Miss Mowat, the niece of an early premier of Ontario, kept an afternoon once or twice a month when they were "at home" to their friends.

Kingston's mellowness and its cast of costumed characters deeply satisfied Davies, but it was music and drama that were its greatest gift to him. Kingston was just large enough to attract and hold performers and road companies for a day or two as they travelled between Toronto and Montreal. They played the Grand Theatre downtown or Grant Hall at the university. Yet the city was just far enough from Montreal, Ottawa and Toronto to have to create and sustain a separate cultural life. The Kingston Art and Music Club organized exhibitions of painting and evenings of chamber music, some with imported notables. Its Drama Group mounted frequent evenings of plays and readings. Faculty and students of the university presented concerts, plays and lectures, many of which were open to the general public. Choral performances were often of a high standard, typified by those of the fine choir of the Anglican cathedral.

Rupert was not so absorbed by the *Whig* that he did not take advantage of these opportunities with his family. He often took Davies to public lectures, and the whole family were frequent attenders of concerts. An *a capella* performance of sixteenth-century music by the English Singers in November 1927 held them spellbound and spurred Rupert to buy their recordings of motets, madrigals, ballads and folk songs by Gibbons, Morley, Weelkes, Byrd and Dowland, as well as modern work by Vaughan Williams, Percy Grainger and Peter Warlock. The family played the discs so often that only the ghost of music past remains on them now in Davies' collection. They were equally struck by a concert by tenor Edward Johnson in 1927 or '28. Johnson sang "Sunrise and You," the sentimental drawing-room ballad he had made peculiarly his own. Although the music was undistinguished, "Edward Johnson did what great artists can do, and used the ordinary little song as the foundation on which he raised a creation of romantic regret, and the fleeting nature of youth and love, which was entirely his own." (In *A Mixture of Frailties*, Monica Gall does something similar with the neglected song "Water Parted" when "She performed that feat, given to gifted singers, of making the song seem better than it was, of bringing to it a personal significance which was not inherent in it.")

Rupert joined the Drama Group of the Art and Music Club. He and Florence continued to be passionate play-goers and with Davies saw good touring companies doing musical comedies like *Rose Marie* and *No, No, Nanette*. Each year they saw the Dumbells, a famous troupe of entertainers that had been formed from the Canadian Army's Third Division in 1917. Rupert, on his frequent business trips to Toronto, would occasionally take Davies and Florence along for a theatre evening, and there were several family trips to New York where they saw the Marx Brothers in *The Cocoanuts* and *Animal Crackers* and Marilyn Miller in Jerome Kern's *Sunny*.

Davies experienced one performance with particular pleasure. Early in 1927 he had been tilting his head oddly and keeping his right eye almost closed, and a family friend suggested checking his eyesight. It turned out that glasses were needed. When he finally got them, black-rimmed and sturdy, Rupert cheered him up with a trip to Toronto for the D'Oyly Carte *Mikado*. Even the jaded critics raved over Ricketts' costumes for the production, with their "appearance of pure Japanese fabric exquisitely designed," splendid gold embroidery and authentic curled pigtail bag on the top of the Mikado's head. Davies, finally able to see the costumes and the setting clearly, found the subtleties of colour and texture so beautiful as to be almost painful.

This was a time when Rupert, full of enthusiasm and ambition at forty-six, was thrusting his energies outward, constantly expanding his world. He was very attractive to women, who gravitated toward him on social occasions, and it is clear from his accounts of his travels that he enjoyed the attentions of the bright and talented ones among them. Florence, now fifty-five and frequently ill, was jealous of his easy social conquests and suspicious of their extent, although Davies remembers his father as being "absolutely rigid" in his refusal to respond to the "blandishments" of the women, who "were all over him." Florence for her part no longer had the energy or the will to make new friends, although she liked Kingston and had settled easily into St. Andrew's Presbyterian Church. When necessary or when pressed, she could put forth an effort, and she did so with charitable work during the Depression. Occasionally she entertained, rather stiffly, at a tea party for fifty or sixty people on a Sunday afternoon, with a musical trio in attendance. But her interest had by now essentially narrowed to her immediate family, and Rupert had to entertain his political friends alone.

Florence's growing isolation made her increasingly dependent for stimulation and affection on the company of Rupert and her sons, and more and more resentful of anything that took them outside her sphere. But Rupert would not be limited by her, and the older boys, grown up, were living their own lives by now. (Although she particularly hated anyone to leave the house on Christmas Day, Fred, her eldest and her favourite, handsome and charming, made little of going out to see his friends.) So she focused her possessive attentions on Davies. He, just entering his teens, was not in a position to flout her wishes as easily as Fred, but he was just at the age where it was important to establish a degree of independence. He experienced the ensuing struggle as a battle for control of his life, and it embittered his feelings toward his mother for years. He loved his mother and fully accepted his filial obligations, but he fought against her unwanted domination with a subtle campaign of resistance. In his chosen territory—words—even the articulate Florence was no match for her son. He would slyly present her with unpalatable bits of the Presbyterian dogma he was learning in Sunday school, "because I knew in her heart she didn't take much stock in it either, but she thought I should." Or he would say things in ways that lay outside her ken. Years later he felt a shock of recognition at the scene in Peter de Vries' novel *Comfort Me with Apples* in which "a young man was sharply rebuked by his father for making jokes your mother can't understand." He understood the strategy well: "Oh, I know about that. It was a kind of disloyalty." It came as a relief to him to learn from his father "that she was afraid of me. And I thought, good, *good*, that's the way it must be. Because if she wasn't afraid of me, she would have eaten me."

Fred and Arthur, who had both worked for their father at the *Mercury* during the family's last year or so in Renfrew, now began to work for him at the *Whig*. Fred managed the job printing plant, until that operation was eliminated with the amalgamation of the papers. After working for a while in the advertising department, he left and took a succession of jobs. Arthur became a reporter and, when the two papers merged, city editor. Both of them lived at home, Fred sporadically as he moved from job to job and Arthur steadily. This arrangement continued until the two married, Fred in 1932 to Muriel Porter (and again in 1937 to Kathryn Stanfield, sister of Robert Stanfield, long-time Conservative premier of Nova Scotia and later leader of the national Progressive Conservative Party), Arthur in 1934 to Dorothy Eleanor Porter (and again in 1969 to Jean Rowe).

For Davies, younger than his brothers by eleven and ten years respectively, they were practically old enough to be parent figures, and unfortunately they had little sympathy with either his interests or his opinions. Shortly before the move to Kingston, for example, Davies asked Arthur one Sunday why he had to go to Sunday school, which he despised. Arthur replied "in an immensely superior way, 'So that the elders can get a little peace while you're out of the house.'" Both Arthur and Fred were of a much more conventional cast of mind than he, and his idiosyncrasies irritated them. He remembers that when he began to see the makings of an actor in himself and to speak openly about his ambition, Arthur said irritably, "I wish you wouldn't tell people that when you finish the university you're going to go on the stage. It's embarrassing." Davies felt little respect for their judgments on him. When he failed his examinations and they were quick to reprove him, he resented it, knowing that neither of them had shone at school.

In spite of their differences, Davies and Arthur appear to have managed to coexist without excessive acrimony. Not so Davies and Fred. Arguments between them were a daily occurrence. The two grated on each other continually and never managed, as long as Fred lived, to put their relationship on a happy footing. Although Fred was Florence's favourite, he often found himself in Rupert's bad books for overspending his income, sometimes to the extent that his creditors hounded Rupert, and it seems likely that he took out part of his frustration on his younger brother. At one point, Davies, in the midst of his adolescent growth spurt, had begun to slouch, as teenagers do. Fred, intensely irked, claimed that his brother was turning into an eccentric "mollycoddle" and urged him to work out at the YMCA. This suggestion was unwelcome on several grounds. It involved exercise—which Davies hated—and although it was unmentionable to his parents, he believed the local branch to be, as he said later, "an absolute hive of homosexuality." What he liked to do after school was to walk down to the *Whig* office to snip reviews, articles on actors and theatrical pictures from the Montreal, Ottawa and Toronto papers for his scrapbook, and return home with his father at suppertime. The dinner-table sniping between the disgruntled Fred and the resentful Davies gradually diminished, but it never entirely lapsed.

Rupert eventually asked one of the physical education specialists at Queen's to suggest some remedial exercises for the slouch, and with his help Davies improved his posture. A factor that may have contributed to his problem was aching arches. For a time he wore rigid aluminum arch supports prescribed by a specialist in Toronto, but they reduced him to a painful hobble, so he quietly stopped wearing them. The problem vanished on its own when his feet had grown enough to support his new height comfortably.

(A slight congenital malformation of the inner ear, which still causes dizziness from time to time and which did not come to light until he was in his sixties, probably contributed to Davies' lack of skill at sports and prevented him from learning to ride a bicycle or drive a car.)

Although Davies attended Sunday school at St. Andrew's Presbyterian Church, certain of its doctrines repelled him; they did not square with his own conception of God. As he remembers it, Jesus was presented as a "big softie who loved everybody and forgave everybody." Davies hated "the pictures of that bearded lady in a nightie being wonderful to everybody." Hymns like "Tell me the stories of Jesus" with its lines

> Words full of kindness,
>   Deeds full of grace,
> All in the lovelight,
>   Of Jesus' face

almost made him "throw up." For his part he continued to believe that God was "terrific" (causing great terror, violently impressive, of tremendous intensity), a Deity to be both admired and feared. The notion that "God is not mocked: for whatsoever a man soweth, that shall he also reap" (Galatians 6:7) struck home to him then and still does today. Davies could not accept the notion that Christ had died to atone for our sins, because he could neither believe that God would demand such a sacrifice of His son nor that He would permit people to escape the consequences of their actions. Despite his reservations, he persisted with the 107 questions of *The Shorter Catechism*, a process begun in Renfrew, until he had mastered them sufficiently to be given a Bible and take communion with the congregation.

Every year Davies found new ways to bring theatre into his daily life. He made himself a stage about two feet high by three feet wide, with a proscenium arch, and his mother supplied it with curtains, weighted at the bottom so that they would fall properly. Unfortunately, when he tried to make puppets for it, he found he had no skill for that kind of work. His co-ordination was poor and he simply could not translate the instructions he found in books into reality.

Nothing of a theatrical nature happened in Senior Fourth at Victoria School under Miss Scammel (1925-26) but a classmate at Kingston Collegiate Institute (KCI) the following year remembers Davies dressing and speaking in a dramatic manner: "when Robertson arrived at High School with a long flowing artist's tie, we all thought he was a bit of a 'weirdo' or whatever word we had in those days, to use for anyone who was 'a bit different.'" The classmate remembers that his contemporaries sniggered at the ties and at an old-fashioned frock coat that Davies wore in the winter, and considered his way of speaking theatrical. Davies himself, however, points out that his parents were sticklers for proper dress and would never have countenanced such bohemianism. He says that ties were usual at the Collegiate and that his were his brothers' discarded four-in-hands. His coat, too, was ordinary.

When Davies' class presented the trial scene from *The Merchant of Venice* to the school assembly on a Friday afternoon, he was given the role of Shylock, his first chance at Shakespeare. To get it right he studied William Winter's three-volume *Shakespeare on the Stage* and questioned Rupert about Henry Irving's performance in the role. He performed it so convincingly that Jack Telgmann (as Antonio) was almost afraid to open his shirt! Overnight, the sniggers died away. The class performed the scene once more at a special public entertainment and again at a concert organized by the city's central council of Home and School Clubs.

In 1927 Canada was celebrating its Diamond Jubilee year, sixty years after Confederation. English-speaking Canada was still in its own mind very much a Dominion under the British Crown, and Kingston was perhaps particularly mindful of the strength of its ties to the past. Like numberless towns and cities across the land, it marked the year with pageants and celebrations. Davies played central roles in two of them. The first, presented at St. Andrew's Presbyterian Church, featured a solemn procession of guardian spirits, goddesses of fame, fathers of Confederation

(Davies played Sir George-Étienne Cartier), a herald, personifi-
cations of the provinces, pioneers and the like. The second,
sponsored by the city and performed by schoolchildren, was the
centrepiece of a long program made up of patriotic songs,
hymns, a maypole dance, a flag drill, a physical culture exhibition and the presentation of Diamond Jubilee medals. "The
Romance of Canada" bears comparison to the spectacle conceived by Davies and Tyrone Guthrie forty years later for
Canada's centennial in 1967, and two excerpts from the program
capture the tone of the pageant:

> I. Entrance—"Britannia" attended by her "daughters,"
> India, South Africa, Australia, New Zealand,
> Newfoundland and the Irish Free State.

> VI. Entrance—The Fathers of Confederation [this time
> Davies was Sir John A. Macdonald], who exactly sixty
> years ago framed the British North America Act of July
> 1st, 1867, the present Constitution of our fair Dominion.

Davies claims that he didn't take it very seriously. He "liked the
chance to clown around and show myself off," and in his view
the parents and schoolteachers must have been amused by "kids
dressed up absurdly and spouting quotations from the greats."
Nonetheless, despite the comic-strip character of the occasion, he
was as impressed as anyone with the importance of these symbols
and traditions. It was in 1927, too, that Florence gave him an
article on the emblems and coats of arms of Canada, the earliest
surviving record of his lifelong interest in heraldry.

Even summer camp provided an opportunity for drama.
Davies went to Camp Ahmek in Algonquin Park when he was
about thirteen. He liked the boys he met there, found the food
excellent and thought the place well run. Of course, the camp's
basic interests—canoeing and swimming—were skills he was
never good at. He hated the early morning plunges into cold
water and couldn't find any enthusiasm for the camp's "phoney
Indianry," which required the boys to address the director, Taylor
Statten, as "Chief" and to imagine themselves in Council Rings

during the big Saturday night campfires. But he was largely free to do what he wanted, and Ahmek seemed to understand his kind of boy surprisingly well. While he was there, Augustus Bridle, the drama critic for the *Toronto Daily Star*, was brought from Toronto to direct a pageant of the Jesuit martyrs Fathers Brébeuf and Lalemant. Bridle was an abysmal director. He couldn't articulate his ideas effectively, and his notion of a directorial "coup" was to simulate the Indians' cutting out of Father Lalemant's tongue by secreting a piece of raw beef from the camp kitchen until the last moment, when it was removed and flung into the fire.

At the end of his second year at KCI (May 1928), Davies became involved in a very ambitious dramatic venture. The school's newly formed Dramatic Society staged Sheridan's *School for Scandal*, with Davies as Sir Peter Teazle. This long play is a risky choice for inexperienced actors and directors because it requires excellent diction and a feeling for the eighteenth century, and the action must flow briskly. The *Whig*'s reviewer managed to scrape together six paragraphs of praise before letting the cat out of the bag: "A few suggestions which possibly would improve the production this evening are, first and foremost that every character should speak more slowly and more distinctly"; otherwise "the audience gets only a very imperfect impression of the plot." The assistant to Miss Mabel Edwards, the teacher who had organized the Dramatic Society and directed the play, was J. Elliott Butterworth, a recent arrival from Ireland. "A very queer little man, a very crooked little Irishman, all soft, silky and insinuating," he had set up shop in town as a "Teacher of Piano, Singing and Elocution." He had his eye on Davies as a potential student, but met firm resistance: "to talk like Butterworth would be to mark yourself a kind of an idiot. When he was reciting Satan's address to the sun out of *Paradise Lost* it was enough to make you blush out of embarrassment." The silky Butterworth was the inspiration for Bevill Higgin in *Leaven of Malice*.

From now on Davies was always writing. He entered all the contests—for best junior short story, best poem in the school, best essay on Confederation, best essay about Canada's progress since Confederation. He placed second in the story and the poem, first in his class in the Confederation essay, and won a twenty-five-dollar award from the IODE for tying for third place in the Lower School (grades 9 and 10) with his piece on Canada's progress. The three poems that survive from this period reveal Davies, at fourteen, in command of a broad vocabulary. He was characteristically playful in his shifts of perspective, and the subjects he chose will be recognized by readers of his novels. "Peculiar" deals with the dreadful jokes teachers tell. "The Bedeviled Curate" concerns a young cleric who meets the Devil. The best of the lot, the six-stanza "The Hero Worshipper," bears quotation. It tells of a general who so admired Napoleon that he aped his hero's interests and appearance, until,

> One day there came a subaltern
> And, smilingly, he raised the question,
> "You know that 'Nap' was taciturn
> Because he had the indigestion.
>   You model on him, I've heard tell,
>   Perhaps YOU colic have, as well?"
>
> The General thought, then he replied,
> "I copy Bony, and all that,
> To outwardly be he I've tried,
> But indigestion, NO, that's flat,
>   I, even for Napoleon's sake,
>   Decline to suffer tummy ache!"

The piece of writing he enjoyed most at KCI was his dramatization of the scenes from Dickens' *Great Expectations* in which Pip meets the sinister lawyer, Mr. Jaggers, and later dines with him. The scenes mount to a dramatic climax when Jaggers exposes the powerful, branded wrists of his serving woman and hints that she is a murderess. Davies handled it so well that it was used as the basis for a Friday afternoon school assembly.

Davies failed Latin in his second year at KCI, under a teacher who failed to enliven Caesar's reports from the battlefield. Mathematics was still impenetrable, although he did enjoy his

assignment at the public library to find out about the lives of figures like Pythagoras, Thales and Archimedes, and he did pass the
examination. So Rupert and Florence decided that he should try
for a scholarship to Upper Canada College in Toronto. This was
the most prestigious of Canada's private residential boys' schools.
It had a century of tradition, a good academic reputation, and
many of its students came from socially prominent families.
Davies himself knew nothing about the school, but he studied
hard for the entrance examinations and was downcast when he
did not win the scholarship. His parents were now affluent
enough to pay the fees, and his spirits rebounded when they
decided to send him anyway. Davies' fictional Colborne College
(Sir John Colborne, first Baron Seaton and lieutenant-governor
of Upper Canada, helped found UCC) in *Fifth Business*, *The
Manticore* and *What's Bred in the Bone* owes much to his experience of UCC, and to his recollections of the men who taught
him there.

There are reports that Davies (now fifteen) presented an even
more arresting appearance on his first day at UCC than he had
at KCI. According to one journalist: "He arrived at that elegant
seat of learning attired in a wing collar with a four-in-hand tie
and similar accessories down to somewhat Elizabethan shoes
with buckles. A young boy in such affected dress has two choices:
he can submit to ridicule and beatings or he can attempt to carry
it off. Robertson chose the latter course. 'How he did it I have no
idea,' recalls a classmate. 'His arrogance rather paralyzed everyone. He stared us all down.'" And a friend tells a similar tale
about Davies' appearance that day. He remembers that he came
wearing "spats and a sort of grand stock at the neck," clothes that
earned him the title "Viscount Willingdon" (then governor general) from the school's "cruder fellows." This friend is convinced
that Davies set out to attract attention. Davies recollects this first
day quite differently. He says that he wore pretty much what
everyone else did (suit, shirt, tie) and that his shoes were a fairly
ordinary sort fastened by a strap. His old-fashioned, hard,
detachable and turned-down collar *was* peculiar, but the school's
clothes list had specified that kind for Sunday use, and once he
found out that nobody else wore them, he jettisoned the lot.

Be this as it may, his long apprenticeship in self-defence and self-definition in the schoolyards of Renfrew and Kingston had taught him how to meet derision, and he found those lessons valuable once again. He not only didn't mind being different, he delighted in the performance he could give. While he was at UCC, Davies created a persona that dazzled his fellows—a matter not of costume but of manner. One of those who admired his performance described the general effect he created: "…he made it very clear that he was incomparably superior to any of the rest of us in so many ways, you know, but not arrogantly—charmingly." He projected superiority with such assurance that many saw him as "wonderful," "marvellous," "brilliant." He played into this by inventing a splendid name for himself—William Ruthven Vanderlip Devereux Robertson Davies—and hoodwinked his contemporaries to the point that one of them checked *Who's Who* before talking with me, to see whether his full appellation had been made public. (He took the extra names from Florence's side of the family). Those who were unsympathetic, on the other hand, saw him as arrogant, haughty, intimidating and deliberately odd.

Davies was fortunate to be at UCC while W. L. Grant was its headmaster. Grant was a man of breadth and originality who set a high standard for masters and boys alike. UCC under his guidance was a place where an unconventional boy like Davies could find a niche. However, as an administrator, he could be capricious, and it was this side of him that Davies encountered first. A day or two after he arrived, Grant informed him that he had actually won the scholarship he had sat for but that it had been given instead to a needy boy, the son of a clergyman's widow. Davies was shocked and resentful, not about the money, but about the loss of recognition. Evidence of intelligence was important at UCC. For the first time he realized that wealth could be a bar to honours.

He then received worse news: his intelligence test results had placed him in the most junior form in the school. In mathematics this was no surprise, but the mark in English stunned him. He had thought to demonstrate his prowess by giving a whole new meaning to "One fine————, Little Red ———— was

walking through a deep, dark ————, carrying a ———— of
———— to her ————," but his originality was unappreci-
ated by the master who graded it. As a result his score was so low,
he was told, that had he "entered the Army as a private" he
"could never hope to be promoted to Corporal." After this, it
hardly surprised him to find that his roommate was the clergyman's son who had been awarded his scholarship. This boy,
unused to eating a heavy evening meal, awakened Davies regularly by sleep-walking and throwing up in the washbasin in the
middle of the night.

Parts of the school program were unappealing to Davies, given
his physical ineptitude—team sports (made much of at UCC)
and drilling with the cadet rifle squad. In addition he disliked
and disapproved of the fagging system, whereby he, like other
new boys, was assigned for a year to a senior and expected to do
menial tasks for him. Also, he valued his privacy greatly, and
there was very little of it at UCC. Breakfast (8:00-8:20) was followed by physical drill (8:30-8:50). After a quick change into
school clothes, there were prayers, a Bible reading, a harangue
from the headmaster and a hymn (9:00-9:20). Classes (9:30-
12:30), mail, lunch, a brief free period in which no one was
allowed to return to his room, classes (1:30-3:30), sports and
punishment drills, finally ended with an hour of free time. But
then came dinner (6:30-7:15), study (7:30-9:00), prayers, a further study period and finally bed (10:30). Rooms, each with a
washstand, basin and jug for hot water taken from a tap along
the hall, were shared by two or three boys. The baths and toilets
(in doorless cubicles) were communal, so cleanliness too had to
be achieved in public.

Happily it turned out that there were ways around most of the
problems. He soon got himself moved to a different room. And
as a hopeless wrecker of the marching cadence of his cadet platoon, he was promoted to corporal in charge of the medically
unfit, whose major duty was handing out, collecting and storing
the rifles. Once he discovered that music could be substituted in
the sports time slot, he started piano lessons. This was triply
ingenious, since it not only excused him from sport but gave him
a patch of solitude in the middle of the day for practising—and

he could read while doing his scales. He was also quickly advanced to a form appropriate to his abilities, though several masters continued for a time to think him incompetent.

Although his confident self-advertisement impressed the other boys, his private assessment of himself was considerably harsher. He did well enough in history, for instance, but his reading oppressed him: there was so much he didn't know! He was still no good at Latin, which meant that he could not take Greek. He began to grasp that French and German were keys to whole civilized societies, but his courses provided practically no opportunity to move beyond the languages to their literatures. In all these areas his newfound inadequacies stirred up in him a lifelong thirst for learning.

Mathematics, however, was by now almost a lost cause, and here UCC failed him. Despite special tutoring at Regiopolis College in Kingston in the summers, any lingering hopes were dashed by his last two years at UCC in the classroom of Lorne M. McKenzie. McKenzie, a sarcastic Presbyterian Scot, was the sort of mathematics teacher that the good students found stimulating, but the tension they enjoyed in his classes was excruciating stress for the others. McKenzie believed in work for its own sake, and he had little patience with those he thought to be laggards. The likes of Davies filled his eyes with blood and flushed his face peony-red. He shouted, jeered, mocked and stormed. He wrote derisive comments on tests and assignments and would assign scores well below zero if the student used the wrong method as well as giving an incorrect answer. With his shock of black hair and the bluish jaw of a man who has to shave twice daily, McKenzie became an apparition for Davies, who later used him as the core of the character Hector Mackilwraith in *Tempest-Tost.*

In Davies' final year, McKenzie regularly demanded that he report with the little third-form boys (whom Davies otherwise, as prefect, had in charge). When Davies struggled at the blackboard, he would prompt one of them to correct him: "Here is this boy and he is supposed to be a clever boy, but he can't do these trivial problems. So you show him how it's done." Finally one day he called Davies a liar. They asked Grant to adjudicate, and he, convinced that Davies was beyond help (having already

sat the junior matriculation examinations in algebra and geome-
try two or three times, always with a mark of zero) decided to
excuse him from further math classes. All three were grimly
aware, however, that this decision would make entrance to an
Ontario university impossible.

Money was another source of continuing anxiety. Most of the
boys had a set allowance from their parents, but Davies was on a
different system, which probably resulted from Rupert's unhappy
experiences with Fred. There was no money to spend just as he
pleased. When he applied to his father and explained what it was
to be used for, in due course a reasonably generous sum would
arrive. But from time to time he would find himself without
resources. "You go through trembling agonies at that age because
you want to be able to do the things that other people do and
you cannot bring yourself to say that you cannot afford it."

These inadequacies sapped Davies' self-confidence and raised
the cost of sustaining his jaunty public pose. Sometimes he
wasn't up to the task and gave way to one illness or another, usually a variation on the family bronchial and chest ailments, once
rising to chicken pox. By now he had started smoking—occasional pipes and cigarettes at UCC; cigars came some years
later—and this wouldn't have helped. He was in the infirmary
often enough that Grant noted it in a letter to Rupert Davies on
December 11, 1930. His contemporaries assumed that his avoid-
ance of exercise was a factor. One of them commented that his
face seemed so pasty that, had one poked it, the indentation
would have remained for quite a while.

Davies wanted to acquire many skills, and he was prepared to
work hard and long to do so. While at home one Easter, he
opened Edward Johnston's *Writing and Illuminating and
Lettering* in the Kingston Public Library and felt his heart leap at
the beauty of Johnston's italic hand. He "was at once seized with
a strong desire to be able to make pages of writing as beautiful as
those in the book." He laboured through the vacation, making
little headway in overcoming the style he had been taught in
Renfrew. But he had found his ideal, and with the help of the
copy of Johnston's book he later purchased at Oxford, over the

decades he gradually managed to approximate his mentor's italic
hand.

W. Robertson Davies 1926

His good acquaintance, stern and staid
May lend him Wisdom's arms. 1930

and I shall be watching for you eagerly next
Friday. If you arrive in Kingston around 1. p. m.
1933

Joul: (the Gentle man in him outraged) So that's what you want, is it?
Physical adventure! Ann Blare, the glamorous courtesan! 1937

I am returning the page proofs to you under
1947   separate cover. I have made Hengist

I supported Macdonald in his contention
that he should have the final word 1954

July 4: THURS: rather a scramble
getting away from the coll. & I 1963

January 20: the COC prod. of Die Fleder
1987   maus. We went expecting

Robertson Davies 1994

By now, eyeing the possibility of an acting career in England, he had begun to practise to eliminate his Ontario accent. Owen Classey, UCC's modern languages master, had rigged a number of record players with headphones so that students could improve their accents in French, German or Spanish. Since the great actor Johnston Forbes-Robertson was acknowledged to be a master of elocution, Davies apprenticed himself to four of his recordings. With the assistance of Classey and a dictaphone, by the time he left UCC he was rolling his "r"s and had acquired a slight Scottish accent.

He was already skilled in repartee when he arrived at UCC; he had absorbed it from his parents' table talk and sharpened it in the hurly-burly of the playground at the North Ward school. In Kingston he had spoken "like an actor," a phrase that suggests broad gestures and extravagant speech. But he continued at UCC to practise and strengthen his vocabulary and diction. Years later, speaking to high school students, he asked: "Do you talk to yourself? Do you ever, as you walk along the street, or ride in a bus, make speeches to yourself? You should, you know. That is the way to practise the use of words. Talk to yourself, and listen carefully to what you are saying. Then correct it." And many years after that, he told a university audience that rhetoric is to be practised "in the head, going carefully over each sentence, rejecting an adjective or an adverb utterly, or perhaps changing it for a better one; polishing up the jokes until they sparkle and rubbing the ironies until they gleam wickedly, forming your thoughts, indeed, into prose." A model Davies may well have had in mind was Aldous Huxley's *Antic Hay*. One summer while he was home from UCC he was bowled over by this novel about a young English schoolmaster who throws over his job, invents inflatable trouser padding for the comfort of bony posteriors and finds a new confidence with the ladies by assuming a splendid false beard. He was fascinated by Huxley's capacity to make a comic construct of life. The book's bright, irreverent, fresh turn of phrase delighted him, as did its easy scholarship and amusing characters.

His labours as an apprentice to the art of conversation were sometimes obvious. A friend who spent a lot of time with him through this period remembers his audible colons and semi-colons: "His words came out as if they had been really planned and polished for a half an hour the night before for tomorrow's conversations." He may not yet have followed the advice he later gave the high school students: "Cut out the hot air and the nonsense; rigorously exclude anything that you do not believe to be true; do not attempt to deceive yourself with fancy tricks of expression." It is also likely that his conversation was gaudy with quotation, since he memorized easily, and may not yet have assessed the dangers he acknowledged years later when he observed: "To be apt in quotation is a splendid and dangerous gift. Splendid, because it ornaments a man's speech with other men's jewels; dangerous, for the same reason. A man who quotes too easily risks the loss of any capacity he may have had for personal expression; he has only to dip into the filing cabinet of his memory and—presto!—the witty, or impressive, or brilliantly compressed essence of what somebody else had thought is his to utter."

Novice or not, at UCC he was enjoyed as a conversationalist. Talking with him was fun. His friends recall the tremendous pleasure of long, rambling debates. His talk was pointed, and from time to time it would convulse his companions into gales of uncontrollable laughter. The Renfrew word-slinger was not entirely transformed into the genial companion, however. Those who did not know him well or whom he disliked could find themselves made to look foolish when they made the mistake of disagreeing with him. He was quick to sense vulnerability. Though he usually enjoyed downing an opponent, he has always regretted one of his successes. In his first year, the head prefect of Wedd's (his house) had given Davies a dressing down in front of several other prefects for failing to perform his duties as a fag properly. When this boy bragged that he had the power to make life "pretty awful" for him, Davies responded:

> "Well, no, you can't make life pretty awful for me. You can punish me, you can do things to me, but you cannot make life really awful for me."
>
> He said, "Why not?"

And I said, "Because you haven't got it in you. I look at
you and I see somebody with a weak face and I know that
whatever you may do, you really haven't any power." And
do you know, he turned an awful colour and his friends
sniggered and he sort of chewed at the air a little. And I
thought, "I have speared that poor dolt," and I was sorry
afterwards, but I had to do it. I mean I wasn't going to take
that from him.

One friend felt that Davies sometimes changed his colour from
one day to the next. He had the uneasy feeling "that he was
always acting." Which Davies would surface: the kind and generous soul, the reformer, the railer and scoffer, or the advocate of
old-fashioned attitudes? Generally he was a small-"c" conservative (politically usually Liberal) but in some respects he was ready
to flout the establishment. Davies was devouring George Bernard
Shaw's plays and prefaces at the time, underlining as he went.
Shaw was disapproved of in many quarters, and it was provocative to read him, as he did, in church. One of his friends was forbidden by his father ever to ask Davies to the house again.

The pieces Davies contributed to the *College Times* in his last
three years preserve several of his poses. In "Modern
Advertisement" he reacts against the blaring and obstreperous
wooing of the public, arguing that advertising must "tone itself
down or become played out." In another, titled "I," he works his
way toward the declaration, "It is our egotism which makes life
worth living."

In two other contributions, Davies attempted a pose of astonishing difficulty. Taking Alexander Pope's pastorals and John
Gay's town eclogues as his models, he emulated those eighteenth-
century poets and succeeded remarkably well. His heroic couplets catch the rhythm, tone and feel of the earlier works without
copying individual phrases or lines. Here is a passage drawn from
the third section of "Scholasticum," which describes a typical
UCC day:

For school masters, in fairness be it told
Must pander to young fools instead of old,

Yet old fools too, they must perforce assuage
For Parents plague the poor, distracted sage;
"Is Willy well?" "How long is Nolly's bed?"
"Is Dick a favorite?" "When is Percy fed?"
While boys, like hogs, spurn each scholastic pearl
Which in their path the febrile ushers hurl.
O Masters, men born free, but self-enslaved
Upon your mossy tombs this verse be graved;
"Restrain thy tears, whoe'er shall tread this sod
Here lives a man who tried to be a god;
God-like, but human he employed his years
Trying to make silk bags from porcine ears."

His work was sufficiently accomplished to move B. K. Sandwell, UCC Old Boy and one-time editor of the *College Times*, by now editor of the Toronto weekly newspaper *Saturday Night*, to write Davies a complimentary letter. The second of these long poems, which took as its subject the main social event of the UCC year, the annual ball of the rifle battalion, is equally impressive. Both were good enough to win the school literary competition in 1931 and 1932 and its prize of $25 worth of books at Britnell's Book Shop. Davies is now rather ashamed of these efforts, because in his eagerness to be able to buy books without having to justify his choices to Rupert, he wrote in a manner carefully calculated to impress the school's judges.

If sparkling talk and interesting poses had been Davies' only claim to fame, it is unlikely that he would ever have convinced his schoolmates of his brilliance and superiority. But he won the school's extempore speaking contest three years running as well, with smoothly flowing, well-organized, funny speeches on "Modern Painting," "Choosing a Career" and "Ritual." And his writing moved him up the ranks of the *Times* until in his final year he became editor, a position in the gift of the headmaster. As editor he was to some degree influenced by his father, a keen typographer. He eliminated the ornamental headings created by earlier generations of UCC boys, put into use the new type selected the year before and reduced the number of pictures for the sake of economy. He also (and here his own prejudices came into play) cut the length of games reports, abbreviated comment on the Sunday evening addresses and eliminated the joke page. None of this pleased the conservative among the students and masters. Nor did a number of his editorials. The one in which he declared that most of the school's yells were outdated and silly, for example, wounded the feelings of Sergeant-Major Carpenter, the school's drill sergeant, gym master and enthusiastic yeller. Nonetheless, it was clear that during his editorship the *Times* was well run.

What really won the admiration of boys and masters alike, however, was the flair he displayed in the school's Gilbert and Sullivan operettas. These were a new venture, probably inspired by the D'Oyly Carte's immensely successful visits to Toronto in January and April 1927 and in October 1928. Although Gilbert and Sullivan were *à la mode*, staging an operetta at a boys' school was a risky business. Sydney Hermant remembered the other boys jeering as the singers involved in the *Pirates of Penzance* (he among them) went in and out of the prayer hall for noon-hour rehearsals. He was teased for his participation and was greatly relieved that he hadn't the burden of one of the female roles. He was also aware that the majority of the masters did not approve of the exercise, and that W. L. Grant was allowing it on sufferance. But Richard Tattersall, then in his fourth year as UCC's music director, knew what he had to work with, and he felt that the time was ripe for a musical venture of this sort. He was determined to make a good fist of training his unruly, unsophisticated group of schoolboys, and they sensed his determination. He seemed to some a *Punch* caricature of an artist, wild in dress and manner.

In Hermant's view, Davies must have appeared to Tattersall "like a lifeboat to a drowning man." He cast him in the patter song role, which requires a baritone, a good sense of rhythm, good pitch, but not necessarily a splendid voice. With the help of Ramsay Duff (music) and F. J. Mallett (acting and stage movement), Tattersall brought the operetta off splendidly on April 29–30, 1929. The boys playing girls' parts did surprisingly well. Davies' performance was singled out for special comment. The Toronto *Evening Telegram* critic, for example, noted that

"W. R. Davies' Major-General Stanley was remarkable. Every word of his quick-fire catalogue song was made delightfully. Surely one of the 'liberal' professions will claim this young man." The jeers faded, and for a time a Gilbert and Sullivan operetta became an annual, much anticipated event at the school.

H.M.S. Pinafore (with Davies as Sir Joseph Porter, K.C.B.) and *The Mikado* (with Davies as Ko-Ko, the Lord High Executioner) followed in the next two years, each one greeted as an improvement on the previous year's offering in reviews that pointed to Davies' performance as exceptional. By the time *Iolanthe* came along (with Davies playing the Lord Chancellor), the critics were full in their praise. Edward W. Wodson of the *Evening Telegram* observed:

> The work of the entire company was so good that you might leave the story at that. It was "Iolanthe" with a touch of beauty in every line and a smile in every cadence. But the principals excelled, too. W. R. Davies as the Lord Chancellor was as good as the best Toronto has seen for many a day. Not an accent of Gilbert's lines ever missed its mark as this talented young Chancellor sang or declaimed them. Every word was winged with a directness that delighted. The "nightmare" song showed you how volubility could be made eloquent and how rhythm could link nonsense with wisdom when she cared. "Said I to Myself, Said I," was better than Henry Lytton's own. And he danced like any corybantic shepherd of the Inns of Court and put a touch of real dignity in his moment of dramatic surprise.

Davies' contemporaries recall his performances in superlatives. One declared that he played his roles "gorgeously...virtually in D'Oyly Carte standard." Another remembered thinking him "magnificent and so did almost everybody.... he was head and shoulders over everybody else as far as performance went." He delighted them by sending up some of the masters, including Grant himself, in Ko-Ko's "Little List" and its counterparts. Few were aware that he was (and is) a nervous performer. A friend, confessing his own shakiness and apprehension one evening before one of these performances and envying Davies' composure, was startled when Davies told him: "I feel as one about to lose his lunch." "Well, what about supper?" asked the friend. "I didn't have any supper," replied Davies, tense, but, as his friend noted, "still articulate."

Davies also managed excellently as Malvolio in *Twelfth Night* (1930) and Captain Bluntschli in *Arms and the Man* (1931). Frank Rostance, one of Toronto's best amateur actors, told the headmaster that Davies' Malvolio struck him as "superior to that given by the Stratford Players last year." A newspaper critic felt he played the role of Bluntschli, the Chocolate Cream Soldier, "with a nicely placed derisive quality and an ease of manner."

Davies later drew on his observation of these productions when he came to write his Oxford B. Litt. thesis on *Shakespeare's Boy Actors.* Boys could play female roles convincingly, he found. But other kinds of sexual questions were raised as well. During *Twelfth Night* he found himself attracted for a week to a lad playing one of the female roles. Guilty and disturbed, he told no one, including the other boy, and the feelings abated. The experience seems to have been the only one of its kind for him, but it made it easier for him to understand the same-sex attractions that a few of his friends were going through at the time. (He wasn't aware of much overt homosexuality at UCC: one boy was expelled for being caught in bed with another, and he sensed that some of the seniors' oppression of the little boys originated in this kind of feeling, but that was all.) Critics attending the performances commented on one boy's delightful femininity and another's "saucy independence."

Davies found other uses for his acting skills as well. He acted as adviser to one of four competing casts in Lord Dunsany's *The Golden Doom* (1930), and produced *The Monkey's Paw* (1931) with a cast of junior boys. He also won the school's annual reading contest in 1930 with a passage from *Henry VIII* and came second in 1931 with Browning's "My Last Duchess." (In 1932, although his reading was commended, he missed a prize because Browning's "The Bishop Orders His Tomb at St. Praxed's Church" was deemed a poor choice.)

Although Davies was often oppressed by his inadequacies, he was cheered by his contact with several of the masters at UCC. The headmaster, W. L. Grant, was unusually supportive, valuing as he did Davies' independence of mind. Grant's daughter Alison noted of Davies that "He was quite brilliant, and my father thought, of course, that this was wonderful, just marvellous."

Grant inspired UCC by word and by example. He impressed on the boys that "much has been given to you and much will be demanded of you." He would speak briefly at morning prayers, and at greater length during the Sunday evening services. He was a dramatic speaker, and he could grab an audience. Davies vividly remembers the Sunday evening when Grant suddenly shouted, paraphrasing one of Luther's letters to Melancthon, "Live in the large! Dare greatly, and if you must sin—sin nobly!" (Davies gave the phrase to John Scott Ripon in *A Mixture of Frailties* many years later.) He taught some of his best lessons by example—that a well-trained mind can be playful, that entertaining takes care and skill, that a good marriage can be "a long, long, wonderful talk, full of points scored, jokes craftily prepared and suddenly exploded, and a sort of companionship attainable by no other means."

In one extempore speaking contest, Davies tactlessly contrasted the inexpert portraits of school worthies on the Prayer Hall walls with what painters of genius might have achieved. He won the contest, but Grant took him aside afterward and cautioned him about life's realities. Several of the school's governors were in the audience and had not been amused. He must, as the Headmaster warns Francis Cornish in *What's Bred in the Bone*, "be careful with words like 'hack,'" since "the world's full of hacks." He must learn to keep his "claws in." (Interestingly enough, Francis Cornish doesn't win the prize—a worthy plodder carries it off, and Francis is given an under-the-table recognition of his talents by the Headmaster and told to keep quiet about it—which recalls the episode of the entrance scholarship.)

Davies treasures a moment when he was walking, one fine spring day, on the cinder track in front of Grant's house. "The Headmaster seemed to rise out of the ground at my side. 'Walk with me,' he said, 'and I'll tell you all about the Oscar Wilde scandal.' Therewith he proceeded to do so, in a richness of detail and with a use of words that I thought only boys knew, that left me stupefied but elated. He thought I was old enough and sensible enough to know about such purple sin, and—because his historical training and gift of rhetoric made it possible—he made it known to me as the Victorians had experienced it. The tiny sprout of my historical sense received a manuring that day which has enabled it to grow into a sturdy tree."

It was Grant who appointed him editor of the school paper; it was certainly Grant who made him a prefect (there were five for each of the school's four houses, usually selected from the school's top students and athletes). It was Grant who had him appointed to the Board of Stewards, the group of senior prefects and captains of various sports who advised the principal and had a number of administrative duties.

Two other masters, both teachers of English, were also important to Davies. H. P. Blunt, broadly educated and humorous, made literature entertaining and enriching. Mr. Wright challenged and stretched him. As Davies had polished off the senior matriculation examination in English at the end of his second year at UCC, when he was sixteen, Wright set him work well beyond the usual range of the curriculum. He suggested he read Robert Browning's long, difficult poem *The Ring and the Book*. At this point Davies had already seen *Caponsacchi*, a play loosely based on the poem, and had been "absolutely knocked endways" by it. He bought the Everyman edition at Britnell's Book Shop, on the way to hear Healey Willan playing Bach at St. Paul's Anglican Church, and, arriving half an hour early, started reading. By the time Willan began to play, he was fully in Browning's grip. *The Ring and the Book* is Browning at his most ample and most psychologically penetrating; Willan was an accomplished, subtle interpreter of Bach. The combination transported Davies into "another world."

Browning taught him a good deal. Davies, making his way through the poem's multiple versions of the events of a murder and trial by people of vastly different personalities and perspectives, was brought forcibly to comprehend how character and circumstance distort experience. He could see, for example, how

Caponsacchi, the Canon who rescues Pompilia from her irate husband, inadvertently causing her to be accused of adultery, projects upon her (in psychological terms) much that springs from his expectations about her, rather than from the woman herself. Davies also saw the effects a writer can create by shifting perspective from one character to another. He would return to this poem again and again.

Davies respected all his masters. If he often found himself bored in class by a subject or by the way it was taught, he still found them an interesting study as individuals. They were anything but an ordinary group. One was a good teacher when sober, but a walking warning of the dangers of drink; another doubted and was miserable because he could not quite bring himself to convert to Catholicism; a third had sailed the oceans and was reputed to have survived shipwreck and cannibalism. On Prize Day, when they wore their medals and ribbons, it was evident that many had served in the First World War, and many had been heroic. But it was clear, too, to all the boys, that the war had drained them physically and psychologically. Mr. Potter, for example, had a silver plate in his head, and no one laughed when he climbed the heating pipes in class and clung there, like a great bird in his gown at the top of the room. Davies was mindful of these men when he created Dunstan Ramsay in *Fifth Business*.

Outside regular class hours, Richard Tattersall, the Scottish music master, played a pre-eminent role in Davies' musical education. Initially (following after Kingston piano teacher Harold Packer, who had distinguished himself by playing tone poems which were musical portraits of his fiancée), Tattersall gave him piano lessons, but he soon recognized that Davies lacked the facility to become an accomplished pianist. Davies evidently had special sensitivity to music, however, so Tattersall encouraged him to concentrate on gaining a broad musical knowledge, with an eye to becoming a critic. Tattersall, the guiding spirit of the UCC Music Club, encouraged the boys to attend concerts and recitals all over the city and would often run over the scores with them in advance. He talked about music until Davies was starry-eyed. A man of pronounced preferences, he was devoted to Bach and the other great Germans, scornful of the likes of Offenbach.

Tattersall's musical passions vivified for Davies the human chain that links us to the great figures of the past. One day he declared that the title of Chopin's *Revolutionary Étude* was misleading. He would show Davies how "the Master" meant it to be played. How did he know this?—because he had been taught by his master in Germany, and his master had been a student of Leschetizky's, and Leschetizky's master was Chopin himself. He played the study, as Davies has "never heard it played since, and it was absolutely like heaven and earth opening."

In *World of Wonders* he made use of one of Tattersall's tales to establish the way the immensely rich and powerful Jeremias Naegeli lived in his Swiss castle, Sorgenfrei. Years before, Tattersall had responded to a Glasgow newspaper advertisement—"Organist wanted for employment in a private house. Must be a gentleman"—and found that his employer was to be the millionaire industrialist Andrew Carnegie. The organist's duties at Skebo Castle, Carnegie's great country house nearby, were specific but not onerous. He was to play Bach chorales while Carnegie ate his breakfast, and after a free day, he and Carnegie's many male secretaries would be responsible for taking any unaccompanied ladies in to dinner (the reason a gentleman was wanted). After dinner he was to hold himself ready as soloist or accompanist, whichever was required.

Davies, unlike Bernard Shaw, has never made his living as a music critic, but Tattersall's training gave him a firm base of musical knowledge and whetted his appetite for more in the years after he left UCC. He bought Percy Scholes' *Oxford Companion to Music* as a Christmas present for himself in 1938, immediately read it right through, and has consulted it at least once a week since. When he could afford it, he bought Grove's *Dictionary of Music and Musicians* (then in nine volumes), and he refers to it often as well. Though he almost never performs for an audience, he still plays the piano almost every day, and he often sight-reads his way through operas, church music, choral music and oratorios in order to get a grip on their musical construction. When listening to music on "the gramophone" (never "the record player" or "the stereo") he continues to be enough of a student to like to follow the score. Music, and his knowledge of musical technique, have found their way into his writing in many ways. He has used symphonic devices in his novels—for instance, the "disappointed climax," in which, as he once explained, "You lead people right up to some extraordinary expectation, then cut it off. And they're much better pleased than if you went on and boomed and crashed and groaned your way all through it. You leave it to them to complete what has to be said, or heard." On the whole, "the concentration necessary to listen to music attentively, *as music*, is also effective in banishing triviality and falsity of thought and emotion, and thereby releases anything that has been forming in the writer's mind which has its origin in the creative depths of his nature....sometimes the artist in one form is quickened, is impelled to create, by serious experience of the other. And thus it is with me."

It was not all that easy to hob-nob with young women at a residential private school. Girls remained for Davies objects of curiosity, idealistic romanticism, supercharged eroticism. (His character David Staunton in *The Manticore* had erotic dreams throughout this period about women he couldn't recognize, and sometimes about frightful hags who ravished him.) Davies fell mistily head over heels in love with one girl or another from a distance, but he had little contact with the species and very little notion of how to go about putting them at their ease, or how to be easy himself in their company. Even at Kingston Collegiate, he had not found it easy to meet girls. They entered school through a different door, sat on the other side of the room and were addressed as "Miss So-And-So." Often enough he did not even know their first names. Of course, at UCC girls were present only on special occasions. And the prudery of the day was also a high barrier to knowledge: the school doctor's two sex lectures were so opaque that no one was the slightest bit wiser for them. (The doctor was clear on one point, however: self-abuse marked the face. He could easily pick out the guilty in the group before him. At this one of the lads fainted dead away.)

Davies' sex education was better advanced by Powys Mathers' translation of *Mademoiselle de Maupin*, which he read by flashlight after lights-out. In it he found, as he said many years later, "the descriptions of sexual encounters exquisitely managed, being at once intense and delicate in their atmosphere," and encountered lovers who were "sophisticated adventurers" while being "neither coarse nor yet cripplingly innocent." But of course this was little help in the daily life of UCC, where it seemed the order of the day to be mooning after remote, unattainable figures. The worst fight during Davies' time at UCC occurred when one boy insulted film actress Loretta Young. Another promptly punched him and they went to the floor, too riled to remember that disagreements should be reported to the sergeant-major and settled under the rules of fair play in the gymnasium.

He went stag to one school dance and tried his luck, but his method of coping with girls—talking a lot—tended to scare them into silence, and he feared that they viewed him as something of a clown. In his final year, at the suggestion of his housemaster, he invited Alison Grant, the headmaster's daughter, to the Rifle Company Dance. He was eighteen, she was sixteen, and it was not a relaxed occasion. He sent a note of invitation; she replied with a note of acceptance. He arrived in black tie; she wore a dress of "stiff stuff that rustled a lot" and felt "rather scared of his wit and intelligence." When the moment the two non-dancers had been dreading finally arrived, Davies remembers saying: "I suppose you dance very well?" Fortunately she had the courage to admit that she didn't dance at all, which freed him to declare: "Well, neither do I. Let's see how it goes." Once they had discovered that dancing was not for them, they sat, talked, ate, visited and generally had a "high old time."

UCC provided him for the first time with good friends of his own age. Although he had initially, like any new boy, felt like an outsider, it didn't take long to find those with similar interests. It is fair to say that there was a "UCC set," to which he did not belong—the sons of Tories, many of them related through family ties, well known to each other since birth. Nonetheless, through the operettas, the school paper and the music, drama and current affairs clubs, he rapidly built friendships with many boys who shared his love of music and theatre and who were reading as widely as he. For the first time he had a chance to get to know and like a number of Jews, among them Sydney Hermant, Robert Eisman and Arthur Gelber. He spent time with Edward Wade Devlin (whose play *Rose Latulippe* was performed in the Dominion Drama Festival in 1933 and 1934) and Arnold Smith (who became a distinguished diplomat and the first secretary-general of the Commonwealth in 1965). Years later, Davies noted that "hardly a day passes" that he does not see somebody whom he had known at UCC.

One of the close friends he made was Charles (Charlie) Cadogan Campbell, the son of the head of the French department at Queen's University. Charlie, whom he had met first in Kingston, was already set on becoming an Anglican clergyman. It was Charlie who introduced him to Huxley's *Antic Hay*. Then there was Gordon Haggarty Robertson (like Davies, crazy about the theatre and headed for an acting career), Archie Macdonald (interested in folk dancing and in playing and making recorders), Donald Ryerson (musically able and mathematically gifted) and John Pearson (mechanically clever and a voracious reader of philosophy). The latter four constituted themselves, with Davies, into a little band of individualists. They got together in one or another of their homes (all but Davies lived in Toronto) or in Murray's Sandwich Shop, on Yonge Street between St. Clair and Delisle, just a short walk from the school. Some of their schoolmates were jealous of their closeness and of their philosophic talk (exaggerating its seriousness); others, who considered them eccentric, referred to them as "those shits." In response the five called themselves the Sterquilinium (or dungheap), the name probably suggested by Pearson, who had a keen interest in Latin. In letters Davies later referred to them as "the Brown Brotherhood," "the Brownies," "the Sterqs."

Two of the boys, like Davies, were obliged to wrestle with their mothers for their freedom. Gordon Robertson's sweet, well-bred, possessive mother "just couldn't bear for Gordon to be in the hospital, even though he had TB." John Pearson's mother, too, by Davies' and others' accounts, was a difficult, controlling woman, in fact a real shrew. One observer who knew Mrs. Pearson thinks that Mrs. Bridgetower in the Salterton trilogy was modelled on her. Mrs. Pearson had sparse, greying, dark hair wound carefully around the bald spot at the top of her head, and she made snide remarks. Her son, like Solly Bridgetower, had his room on the third floor of their large house. In retrospect, Davies seems to have had a disproportionate number of acquaintances whose mothers "were eating their sons right down to the cob."

May 1932 brought Davies' time at UCC to a close. Two years later he told a friend that he remembered singing "Praise my soul the King of heaven" at the last chapel service "in a voice charged with emotion" and climbing into the taxi that would carry him to the train station "with the air of one going to a scaffold."

He remained in regular contact with the "Sterqs" for several years. Then Donald Ryerson and Archie Macdonald's paths diverged from his, Gordon Robertson died of tuberculosis in 1936, and John Pearson kept in touch only sporadically until he committed suicide in 1958.

Davies had made the most of such opportunities as the school afforded in music, drama and writing, but his academic performance was another matter. Unlike most of his friends he had not accumulated enough credits to enter an Ontario university. To be admitted even to the extended four-year Pass or five-year Honours B.A. programs (and he very much wanted to go), it was necessary to pass twelve junior matriculation papers. Continuing to senior matriculation involved five subjects, two papers each, and permitted one to cut a year from either university program. Davies' examination results are summarized laconically in the school's ledger: "Jr. Matric, Ont. (9 papers), Hon. Matric, Ont. 31/32 4 papers."

He appeared to have reached an educational impasse. For well over thirty years he revisited this in his dreams: he would arrive for the matriculation examinations unprepared, or would find that he could not understand a word of the question paper, or be forced to leave the Mastership of Massey College because he had never matriculated in maths. There were a thousand variations on this theme.

If his formal academic attainments at UCC were disappointing, he managed nonetheless to acquire a remarkably extensive grounding in another discipline. In class, he had found himself thinking: "...there's got to be something better than this!"—and he found it in Toronto's theatres. Mathematics humbled his spirit, but the splendours to which the stage could rise exalted it. His love of drama and his curiosity about its history were virtually inexhaustible, and so it is no exaggeration to say that his real education in this period was outside UCC's curriculum. In this he was assisted by his parents. With their financial support he supped his fill before the cumulative impact of the Depression, radio, the talkies and time wiped out much of what had survived from the theatre of the nineteenth century. The veterans of the Victorian and Edwardian theatre still visited Toronto's stages and, like his parents' and Tattersall's stories, their performances extended his vision backward in time.

He kept a partial record of his theatre-going in his first diary, starting in January 1928, the year he went up to school, and ending in March 1931. It was a chance encounter with the great English actor-manager Sir John Martin-Harvey, preserver of Sir Henry Irving's Victorian repertoire and acting style, that galvanized him into making it: Martin-Harvey had presented *Scaramouche* and *The Cigarette Maker's Romance* at Kingston's Grand Theatre on January 13 and 14, 1928, and Davies was deeply impressed. The next morning, a Sunday, as he was out in front of the house on Albert Street, a remarkable figure in a fur coat and cap appeared, looking just like his father's picture of Irving in *The Bells*, and, in a distinguished accent, asked how to get to a house in the neighbourhood. Davies gave him directions and then rushed inside to get this brush with his theatrical hero on paper.

Here are his jottings about his theatre-going during his first year at UCC (as transcribed into his "Theatre Notes" in May 1964, with punctuation, abbreviations, occasional misspellings and errors and later glosses intact):

> 1928: Sept 10: wth. WRD to Royal Alex to see George Robey: song as an Egyptian Mummy; 'a farce in his face' like Doggett. Oct 1: *When Crummles Played* impressed by incidental music: Folair & Miss Bravassa sing 'The Expiring Frog' from *Pickwick* as the entertainment at Mrs.

Millwood's: sat next a man who had seen Irving in *Robespierre.*

1929: Jan 7: saw *Interference* at the Empire (stock co.: much taken with Frances Dade, a pretty actress who soon went to Hollywood. Jan 26: *Faust* at R.A.: good touring co. wth. distinguished settings by N. Bel Geddes. Feb 2: *M.N.D.*, touring co. from Hart House directed by Dora Mavor Moore; played dully in dark green curtains; Elaine Wodson was Puck. Feb 8.: Maurice Colborne Co. in *John Bull's Other Island* at R.A.: Barry Jones as Peter Keegan. Feb. 22: Archibald Flower visits U.C.C. to talk abt. Memorial Theatre & we are asked to contribute: most of us give $1—a week's allowance. Mar. 1.: I am cast as the Major-General in *Pirates of Penzance.* Mar. 2. to *Merchant of Venice*, Stfd. co.: a v. bad understudy played Shylock for Geo. Hayes. Mar. 6. Stfd. co. in *The Shrew.* Mar. 8. Stfd. co in *Hamlet*: Geo. Hayes—a bad Polonius, Kenneth Wicksteed: Hayes used imaginary portraits instead of the two lockets. —Also saw *Merry Wives* twice: Roy Byford Falstaff & Hayes, Dr. Caius.= *Pirates* postponed because of suicide of Wm. McHugh, vice-principal: the buzz was that he had lost heavily in the stock market, presumably on margin. *Pirates* performed April 19 & 20.

These notes suggest the surprising breadth of Davies' theatrical interest at fifteen. Part of the "1928: Sept. 10" entry about the British music hall comedian George Robey is a good example. According to the Toronto critic Hector Charlesworth, Robey was so funny "when he was brought on as a mummy in the Egyptian skit 'Rameses' that he reduced his audience to weakness." Much of his impact must have depended on his facial expression. Davies' observation that Robey had "a farce in his face" is a phrase drawn from *Roscius Anglicanus* (1708) in which John Downes says of Doggett (an actor who died in 1721): "he's very aspectabund, wearing a farce on his face, his thoughts deliberately framing his utterance congruous to his looks." With regard to the man who had seen Irving in *Robespierre*, Davies claimed in 1947 that he had made notes of fifty conversations with people who had seen Irving act.

The *John Bull's Other Island* entry dates Davies' first exposure to Shaw. He promptly began to spend his pocket money on Shaw's plays. Davies' March 8 observation—that George Hayes when playing Hamlet saw imaginary portraits in the air instead of consulting the two traditional lockets with their pictures of Claudius and Hamlet Senior—reveals his acquaintance with William Winter's *Shakespeare on the Stage*, which he had read earlier in Kingston.

In these and later notes Davies usually named the theatre as well as the play. He attended the Royal Alexandra on King Street most often, the theatre to which Magnus Eisengrim brings his Soirée of Illusions in *Fifth Business* and *The Manticore*. Davies had known it from many excursions with his parents, as he did the Princess at the corner of King and University Avenue, both of them touring houses, decorated in old-fashioned plush and gilt. The very fabric of these houses—like that of the other two Victorian/Edwardian theatres, the Victoria and the Empire, both of which presented weekly repertory—evoked an earlier day. Davies also frequented a very new playhouse, of a very different kind, Hart House Theatre at the University of Toronto, and was interested in the differences between the old and the new. The older downtown theatres came fully equipped with wings, raking pieces and often a different ceiling for each change of scene; in the experimental university theatre, curtains and mood lighting largely substituted for scenery.

During the three years before UCC and his four years at the school, when he went to a Saturday matinée with friends almost every week, he tasted virtually every flavour of theatrical fare that Toronto could offer—one-man and one-woman shows, music hall, mime, revues, experimental plays, pantomime, musicals, farce, classics, operetta, opera, contemporary plays. And on weekend visits to his mother's sisters in Brantford he saw the vaudeville acts that he later drew upon when describing the dreadful winter circuit in *World of Wonders*.

It was evident to Davies that Canadian plays were rarely produced, although the Hart House Players presented a Canadian play evening once a year. It was evident, too, that Toronto's

Canadian actors were either amateurs who made their living outside the theatre or members of weekly repertory companies, surviving from week to week. Obviously, he would have to go elsewhere if he wanted a serious acting career.

Sufficient exposure gave Davies insight into individual actors' skills and companies' styles. He knew which actors the D'Oyly Carte would cast in which roles, and he recognized and enjoyed that company's peculiar handling of the chorus as "a single character, multiplied by thirty." He became familiar with the strengths of the principal actors of the English Stratford-upon-Avon company and appreciated how its brisk ensemble acting and understanding of the poetry set it apart from the star-dominated companies. He had special information in the case of the Hart House Players, who were at the forefront of the Little Theatre movement and mounted productions of Ibsen, O'Casey, Maeterlinck, Yeats and Shaw. Several members of this company (most of whom aspired to become full-time professionals) were masters at UCC.

Davies knew just as much about the critics. Montreal had one regular drama critic and Toronto had four, and even before arriving at UCC he had regularly clipped their reviews. In Montreal there was Morgan Powell, deeply learned in the theatre and (unusually) bilingual. In Toronto, there was Dr. Lawrence Mason of the *Globe*, who reported but never judged or criticized the plays he saw. Edward W. Wodson of the *Evening Telegram*, who wrote under the curious pseudonym "Yenmita," loved everything. Augustus Bridle of the *Toronto Daily Star* raved incomprehensibly, and Hector Charlesworth of the weekly paper *Saturday Night* concentrated on the actors, their performances and their careers.

Of course Davies was not unusual in being a theatre buff, but he was unusual in being able to cultivate and indulge his enthusiasm while still so young. He could do so because his parents willingly financed his theatre-going. So sympathetic were they that Davies felt questions would have been asked had he *not* presented a theatre bill at regular intervals. He was also lucky because he was exposed to the last examples of a repertoire and a school of acting that would almost immediately vanish. He saw

James T. Powers, Otis Skinner, Mrs. Minnie Madern Fiske, Miss Henrietta Crosman and Seymour Hicks in the buildings that were created in their heyday, and he read the reviews in which Hector Charlesworth placed them in the context of forty years of theatre-going.

His intense contacts with these survivals from the Victorian theatre give Davies' theatrical memory extraordinary reach. But his curiosity about the theatrical past had even more to feed on. From time to time he could see "fossil theatre" and gain an even better insight into what had enchanted the Victorians, including his parents. William C. Gillette, "dry of voice and hawk-like of profile," came out of retirement briefly at seventy-five to take the leading role in the play, *Sherlock Holmes*, a part he had played a generation before. The D'Oyly Carte performed Gilbert and Sullivan's operettas just as Gilbert himself had ordained, and Davies even got firsthand experience of what that meant when UCC hired members of the company to help train the boys, first in *The Mikado* and then in *Iolanthe*. Mr. Jackson was a tenor, and Mr. Stewart was the company's stage director for many years. Stewart in particular made the boys feel that their efforts were being measured by Gilbert himself. He had worked with people who had worked with Gilbert; he used prompt books of the operettas with Gilbert's notations transcribed into them (Davies still has copies); and he would say: "Boys, you must pronounce every word with the uttermost clarity; I daren't think what Mr. Gilbert would say if he heard you dropping a syllable." Occasionally, when they had done a creditable job with one of the operetta's elaborate dances, "Well, children, I think Mr. Gilbert would have been pleased with that."

Sir John Martin-Harvey, the preserver of the romantic acting style of Henry Irving, was no longer attracting huge audiences when Davies saw him. Davies was conscious of his parents' enthusiasm for Irving, and he found that Martin-Harvey put him in touch with a past he had already discovered to some degree himself. He saw him first in April 1926 in a melodrama called *The Corsican Brothers*, playing both brothers. Davies loved the doubling of roles, the dashing sword-play and the easy elegance of Martin-Harvey's bits of "business," like the moment in the first act when one of the brothers, "without appearing to give the matter any attention, rolls himself a cigarette with one hand, and lights it with a flint and steel." He was entirely convinced by the actor's ability to evoke the mystic link between the two brothers. To him, at twelve, it was as if the high, distant, chivalric world of the novels of Sir Walter Scott had suddenly come gloriously alive. When in 1929 he saw Martin-Harvey playing Sydney Carton in *The Only Way*, a melodrama based on Dickens' *A Tale of Two Cities*, he was as moved as he had been as a child watching *Uncle Tom's Cabin*. On the other hand, he was puzzled that Martin-Harvey would frequently cast his wife, Nina da Silva, a fine comedian, as a young, beautiful heroine, since she was overweight, ageing and ugly. Davies pondered this at length over the years and drew on his mature conclusions in creating Milady Tresize in *World of Wonders*.

In Kingston, Davies noticed that performances by Martin-Harvey's and other English touring companies drew an audience very different from the American companies'. It was an audience, older and fewer each year, whose hearts' allegiance was in the Old Country and who got their dress suits and bunny coats out of mothballs to show their respect for English theatre. In Toronto a broader audience attended, but even there the shift in taste away from the Victorian repertoire and acting style had reduced its size substantially by the time Davies saw *The King's Messenger* in 1932. However, those present could not have been more enthusiastic. After the first act, there were three curtain calls, after the second, four, and after the third, nine calls and a curtain speech, which Martin-Harvey began all too revealingly: "We have played to larger audiences but never to one more appreciative and attentive."

When Davies looked for reference books on the theatre and its Victorian past, there was not much to be found. The few compilations that existed, like *Who's Who in the Theatre*, were not easily accessible, so he began to create his own. At home and at UCC, he gathered articles and pictures on acting, stagecraft, theatrical make-up, the lives of theatre figures and actors in their famous roles, from English magazines including the *Strand*, the *Sketch*, the *Tatler*, the *Sphere*, the *Windsor Magazine* and the *London*

Magazine. He pasted them, together with the cuttings he'd gathered at the *Whig*, reviews of productions in which he appeared himself and some clippings on literary subjects, into scrapbooks. But it was not enough. By the time he left UCC in 1932 Davies was ready to become a collector. Almost all the necessary conditions were in place. He had a broad subject (drama), a particular period (the nineteenth century), and one actor (Martin-Harvey) that fascinated him. He could get his hands on very little of what he wanted. The acting repertoire of the nineteenth century, for example, seemed to have disappeared from booksellers' lists and was unavailable in Canadian libraries.

After his last year at UCC came to its discouraging end, Rupert took him off to Britain for the summer. Looking back in *Far-Off Fields*, Rupert explained: "I felt I could now afford to visit Britain each year if I wanted to, and I thought I should like to have a place to settle where I could control my own meals and my own fires. I had found it a bit chilly many times when staying here and there." But this said nothing of his longing for the lovely Welsh countryside where he had spent his boyhood; nothing of the life he could have there—riding, walking, reading, visiting and entertaining; nothing of his desire for a bolt-hole from his marriage. Fronfraith Hall, Abermule, 179 pleasant acres with a large house ten miles from Welshpool, struck Rupert and his youngest son as just what was wanted, and that summer Rupert bought it. This was to be *his* place. "I cabled Robertson's mother on his suggestion, and she came over"—not "my wife" but "Robertson's mother." Florence did come, and she returned the next summer (1933) to share in the furnishing of the house. But after that, except in 1936, Rupert made the voyage without her.

Having established himself in Wales, Rupert gave his son the opportunity to gorge himself on theatre of a quality hitherto outside his range, and to make a start at acquiring the theatrical books he yearned to own. Summer 1932 was the first season of the new Memorial Theatre at Stratford-upon-Avon, and Davies saw seven Shakespearean plays in a row, acutely aware of the greater physical resources available to the company when it was not touring. He inspected the building with the eye of one who had contributed a dollar to its construction and extracted technical information from the stage manager.

Then came the Malvern Festival. This was its fifth summer, and the Festival was attempting the feat of conveying the history of English drama in a single week by presenting, in chronological order, plays chosen from every century from the sixteenth to the twentieth. The plays were performed in the evening, and during the day there were lectures on English drama by Frederic Boas, Bonamy Dobrée, Allardyce Nicoll and Lascelles Abercrombie, all eminent scholars. Not surprisingly, Davies found it marvellous. At his first Ben Jonson play, *The Alchemist*, he was eager to see how Cedric Hardwicke, amply represented in his scrapbooks, would play Abel Drugger. He knew that the great eighteenth-century actor David Garrick had been so brilliant in the role of that dull character that he had repeated it every year from 1747 until 1776. Hardwicke began to show him what could be done with the part as soon as he stepped on to speak the prologue: "...he faced the audience with a look of such trusting simplicity and innocence—a look which was an invitation to every dishonest person present to step forward and strip him naked—that he was irresistible."

Although Davies' passion for theatrical information was well-nigh infinite, performance was his touchstone. On Friday morning Dobrée's lecture convinced him that Dion Boucicault's *London Assurance* had an impossible plot, mechanical wit and slight characterization, but on Friday evening the performance he saw was delightful. Davies usually read each play in preparation for the evening's presentation, but he recognized that reading was an unreliable guide to dramatic effectiveness. Dull on the page could still prove amusing on stage; structural elegance only sensed in the reading could be electric in performance; plays apparently unappealing to modern tastes could become palatable if served up by fine actors. A bonus to the Festival was the opportunity to observe the likes of Dean Inge and George Bernard Shaw in the large public gardens behind the theatre.

In London he saw a fine revival of John Galsworthy's *Loyalties* and caught the young John Gielgud in Ronald Mackenzie's *Musical Chairs*. (At Malvern he had also glimpsed Ralph

Richardson, likewise at the beginning of his career, playing Captain Face in *The Alchemist.*) He saw, among a handful of less memorable contemporary pieces, the much-touted musical version of *Twelfth Night*, in which both costumes and stage sets were in black-and-white. (Viola was played by the beautiful Margaretta Scott. Five years later, when she appeared in *Traitor's Gate*, Davies himself had one of the supporting roles.) As at Stratford and Malvern, he gathered his impressions into a good, thoroughly readable article for the *Whig*. In the daytime he bought copies of nineteenth-century social drama, costume plays, farce and melodrama that he found in the barrows in front of the bookshops on Charing Cross and Tottenham Court Roads, or in Samuel French's catalogue. There was so little call for these at French's that they had to be dug out of storerooms. His acquisitions were for the most part dull enough reading, but this just further whetted his curiosity about these once-popular entertainments.

By the end of the summer of 1932, Davies had accumulated a knowledge of theatre that was more broadly based and more thoroughly assimilated than that of most university graduates in English literature.

Chapter 5

QUEEN'S: 1932-35

"I suppose Mrs. Forrester cast her because of her looks. Well, I for one have never thought much of them: she looks a regular Dolly Varden, in my view." Just what Mrs. Bridgetower meant by this condemnation was not clear. But Solly knew it of old, as a phrase used by his mother to describe any girl to whom she thought he might be attracted.

—*Tempest-Tost*, 1951

It was because of his daughter Griselda that he had agreed to lend his garden to the Salterton Little Theatre for an outdoor production or, as Mrs. Roscoe Forrester preferred to call it, "a pastoral". The particular pastoral which had been chosen was *The Tempest*, and Griselda, who had just been released from boarding-school, was named as a possible person to play Ariel. It had been Mrs. Forrester's intention from the beginning that the play should be done at St. Agnes'....

—*Tempest-Tost*, 1951

MANY PARENTS ARE less understanding with sons who fail their examinations than was Rupert. Not only did he offer Davies a diverting trip abroad, but he took up his son's cause as well. On

June 17, 1932, in a *Whig-Standard* editorial headed "Universities, Examinations, and Mathematics," he sympathized with "protests against the inclusion of mathematics in the compulsory examinations necessary for an arts course," arguing that "Mathematics may be a brain developer but it is of very little use in practical life, and it does not seem fair that it should act as a barrier to students, who are clever in other subjects, entering the university." In private he gave Davies some practical advice: "There are always people who are good at mathematics and who for that reason are disposed to be honest, whom you can hire to do it for you. *You* don't have to bother with it!"

However, the return to Kingston brought Davies thumping to earth. He was excluded from university and did not know what to do next. Although he wanted eventually to become a professional actor, neither he nor his parents seem to have considered a theatrical training, either in the United States or in England. Suddenly, however, the university's door opened. W. E. McNeill, Queen's vice-principal and treasurer, suggested to Rupert that Davies should attend as a special student, which meant that he could go to classes, do the assignments and write examinations, but not take a degree. Davies doesn't know how his plight came to McNeill's attention (given Rupert's local prominence and the frustration animating his June editorial it is possible to guess), but he was immensely grateful to get the chance.

The university where Davies spent the next three years was then one of Canada's four major post-secondary institutions. In academic reputation it stood third, after the internationally recognized University of Toronto and McGill University and ahead of the University of Western Ontario. It had a long history of solid teaching in arts and science, in the applied sciences and in medicine. Many national figures had been educated there. Queen's was modelled on the Scottish universities, having originally been founded by the Presbyterian Church of Canada in association with the Church of Scotland as a college to train young men for the ministry. Although the ties to the Presbyterians were broken in 1912, Queen's continued to emphasize its Scottish origins, and often carried all before it on the sports fields with its supporters chanting the Gaelic battle-cry "Cha Gheill."

From the beginning, Davies was a highly unconventional member of the Queen's community. Having decided not to submit to the usual freshman hazing, he simply absented himself from it, and never wore the Scotch cap imposed on first-year students. No one ever thought of him as a freshman. He looked and acted older than his classmates, and because he was feeling defensive about his status he added another layer to the persona he had constructed at UCC. Freed from the rigid dress code of UCC, he now also expressed himself in his choice of clothing. He is remembered as projecting superiority, discouraging familiarity and affecting dress both relatively formal and flamboyant—a black fedora, a tweed jacket with leather patches at the elbows, a cane for the long walks to and from Calderwood and either huge, colourful bow-ties or long, splendidly flowing four-in-hands. One girl so admired his two "perfectly gorgeous" purple ties that he was moved to give them to her. Now arrived at his full six-foot height, and gaining in girth, he looked not unlike G. K. Chesterton. Asked later about his choice of clothes, he commented that it put him in the company of other aspiring actors, like Arthur Sutherland, Lorne Greene and Gerald Chernoff, who dressed with flair, and that it was not *that* unusual; after all, hats were the order of the day, and many students wore three-piece suits. More, he observed: "why embrace mediocrity when you have so much of it in yourself and are trying to get rid of it already?" He aspired to be a citizen of a larger world. He wanted to set himself apart from those of more limited outlook. "I didn't want to be like those other people. I thought so poorly of their ideas and their outlook on things and their awful simplicity. They never seemed to see even what was in front of their noses."

Davies, as a special student in Honours English, had greater freedom to pick and choose his courses than the other students. He took no first-year courses during his three years, no reading courses and (unfortunately as it turned out later) no Latin. But he took the English courses prescribed for the second-, third- and fourth-year English Language and Literature students, and instead of the usual five courses in a minor and six in other subjects, he took one pass English, three history and the equivalent of three courses in "Mental and Moral Philosophy," which included philosophy and psychology. His formal work-load was roughly a third lighter than that of the regular honours students, leaving him considerable time for other pursuits.

One of the subjects he wanted to explore was psychology, and under Professor George Humphrey, an "absolutely splendid" teacher who later became Professor of Psychology at Oxford, he took several courses, in which he was introduced to Freud for the first time. At Humphrey's suggestion he read Havelock Ellis' four-volume *Studies in the Psychology of Sex* (1897-1910), which was at that time sequestered on the reserve shelves and had to be approached through the office of the head librarian, Dr. Ernest Cockburn Kyte. Over twenty years later, he placed Ellis' great work with Burton's *Anatomy of Melancholy* (a book he also read at Queen's) "at the top of any list of books in English which are at the same time notable works of science and admirable as literature." It opened his understanding to the width of the behaviour range that constitutes normal sexual activity.

He both liked and respected the four professors in the English department, who gave him a thorough grounding in the canon of English literature. At least one of them became the source for a character in a play and a novel. George Herbert Clarke, who taught him both "Shakespeare" and "The Victorian and Georgian Periods," was a "full-packed and meaty lecturer." He was also, as Davies said years later, "entrapped in a grotesque, retrospective love-affair with every one of Shakespeare's heroines."

The department's other full professor, James Alexander Roy, was a Scot who fled to the heather every summer, returning to his Canadian exile only on the first day of term. He taught Davies "English Literature from 1780 to 1832" and "The Classical Age." Like all teachers, he imparted more than he knew, and Davies warmed to him. In a lecture on the Romantic poets, Roy once observed sorrowfully, "You have to recognize that most people are mutts," and incapable of experiencing anything but the bluntest emotions. His own emotions were strong, if impulsive. He once bragged to Rupert (and thus Davies heard) that he never had any difficulty in finding bed partners, as there were always ———— and ———— (a member of the faculty and the daughter of a professor). Gossip reported that his first marriage had ended at the church door. Davies recalls that a choral speaking group, performing a new poem by Roy,

> Would I were back in the Highlands
> In the desolate lonely places...

was disconcerted by a burst of laughter from the audience; it was widely known that he was in jail at the time on a charge of drunk driving. Years later, in *Fortune, My Foe*, Davies used him as the model for Professor Idris Rowlands, and Roy recognized and enjoyed the portrait. Later still, in *Murther and Walking Spirits*, Davies evoked Roy again in the character James Alexander King.

One of the department's two associate professors, Henry Alexander, who taught the single-semester courses on Old English (Davies failed) and Middle English, inspired Davies to a teasing column in the *Queen's University Journal*, where he extolled the virtues of Anglo-Saxon literature and claimed: "I am seriously considering the organization of a Society for the Resuscitation of Anglo-Saxon Language and Customs. I am awarding a handsome prize (a stone hatchet gaily decorated with tufts of human hair) and a banquet of seal's blubber and reindeer cheese to the scop who will compose the best thirty thousand lines (or 'fragment,' as all Anglo-Saxon poetry is 'fragmentary') with the title '*Alexanderdammerung.*'"

Wilhelmina Gordon, the department's other associate professor, taught him Spenser and Milton. She demonstrated convincingly that a test of a person's command of good English speech is to be able to read Milton acceptably: "...it is a question of cultivation showing itself through whatever kind of speech it is and a sense of rhythm and composition which is absolutely vital." Davies considered her an excellent teacher and was tolerant of the occasional moments when she "couldn't refrain from lighting into the Catholic Church...even referring to Catholics as Dogans which is inexcusable, but as a daughter of a Presbyterian parson, she had strong feelings." A woman of distinguished appearance, then in her late forties, she wore skirts of the

Gordon tartan and would embellish her evening dress with a scarf of the same pattern. He remembers her as having a strong sensual nature, probably because she unexpectedly kissed him once.

Davies tutored in Professor Gordon's courses and occasionally in Professor Clarke's during his last two years at Queen's, having earned the job with two As in the English courses he took in his first year. As tutor, however, he had to mark "forty-eight loathesome essays every fortnight." Marking kept him at his desk night after night, and interviews, as he wrote in a letter at the time, meant "sitting in a horrible room with sixteen corners and a slanting roof under the eaves of the Arts Bldg. and receiving students hour after hour, and explaining to them that there is no such word as 'termendulously' or that a sentence without a verb is frowned on in literary circles." Twenty years later, writing *Leaven of Malice*, he faced Solly Bridgetower with the similar task of marking fifty-two essays by First Year Science men on "The Canterbury Pilgrims and their Modern Counterparts." However, although Davies groaned and grouched, he was glad of the job because it gave him privileges and money ($75 a term) to spend as he chose.

Davies says that he did not do much writing at Queen's. Partly, he said later, he was repelled by the spectacle the other student writers presented. At the meetings of the Queen's English Club the ghastly poetry and fiction were as appalling as the presumptuous efforts at criticism. One student was so obsessed by writing that he withdrew from classes to compete for a substantial cash prize offered by the *Atlantic Monthly* for the best new novel, modelled the hero on himself and became so involved with his Junoesque heroine that he bought an extra seat for her at the movies and sought her opinion on the films. He was certain he would win, so much so that he nearly committed suicide when the prize went to someone else. This was hilarious enough, but disturbing in its way, and when Davies finally chose to write professionally he was careful to impose cool discipline on himself, wary of the wayward energies of the imagination.

Davies did write "odds and ends of things as it became necessary." He kept a diary, primarily, he says, about rehearsals of plays, and in August 1933 he told a friend that he was "writing a sonnet sequence (a hell of a job)." He wrote for particular situations—a Gothic horror story in the manner of E. T. A. Hoffmann and Edgar Allan Poe to amuse people at a party, the twenty-two columns called "The Bookshelf" for the *Queen's University Journal* and some theatrical pieces.

Davies now considers his efforts in "The Bookshelf" "impudent, know-it-all student stuff." True enough, two of the columns do suggest an insufferable side to his pose of superiority (one of them advising incoming students to acquire culture by becoming "intimately acquainted with ten really good books" and another informing them how to read), but most of the columns anticipate his mature attitudes and opinions, describing books he valued, most of them concerned with Wales, the theatre or music. Some of them, like George Borrow's *Wild Wales* or *Ellen Terry and Bernard Shaw: A Correspondence*, he has continued to read and treasure. At least three—Cecil Gray's *Peter Warlock*, Sir John Martin-Harvey's *The Book of Martin Harvey*, and Sacheverell Sitwell's *Liszt* (especially the chapters about Paganini)—became source books for his fiction. His published reminiscences of his reading in this period mention none of these: the emphasis is on his enthusiasm for nineteenth-century drama, the fiction of John Cowper Powys, the fine careful prose of Havelock Ellis and his preference for Sinclair Lewis and H. L. Mencken over Ernest Hemingway, Thomas Wolfe and F. Scott Fitzgerald.

Theatre-going was not what it had been at UCC. Road companies had almost stopped visiting cities as small as Kingston by 1932. But he tumbled into all sorts of amateur enterprises, and they provided all the exasperations, exhilarations and hilarity that mark the designs of ill-equipped enthusiasts on art. The first seems to have been a production of the Coventry Nativity Play shortly after Christmas of 1932, which he and his friend Charlie Campbell co-directed. The actors were children from the Sunday schools in the parish of St. George's Anglican Cathedral, and the production was warmly received. Early in 1933 he acted in three presentations by the Kingston Drama Group. In February he played an antiquarian in love in John Hastings Turner's slight

but entertaining *The Lilies of the Field* and then the wife's lover
in John Masefield's *The Locked Chest*. In April he directed several
episodes of John Galsworthy's *Escape* as well as acting the parson,
and Rupert, also a member of the Group, turned in a creditable
performance as a farmer.

The Locked Chest stands in Davies' mind as a truly terrible play.
It concerns a Viking woman married to a miserable farmer, and
for part of the action Davies, playing the lover, was concealed in
a chest. The chest was large, but he was hot and sweaty when he
finally emerged at the end of the play. In their pursuit of authenticity the Group went so far as to secure a tub of cows' horns,
boil them up in Daisy Miller's kitchen, extract the sludge and
sew the horns onto their helmets. "And the stench of this stuff
was awful, and, of course, it clung to the costumes, and we all
smelled like a glue factory." Terrible or not, the production was
chosen as one of the Group's contributions to the first Dominion
Drama Festival. (The DDF, the brainchild of Lord Bessborough,
Canada's governor general at the time, became and remained for
almost four decades a great national amateur competition, filling
the vacuum between the touring companies' collapse and the rise
of indigenous professional theatre in the 1960s. Rupert was a
member of the original committee and a local organizer for some
years.) As a result, the play came under the eye of the regional
adjudicator, E. G. Sterndale-Bennett. It was no surprise to
Davies when Sterndale-Bennett said that he "felt the monotony
of voice and gesture more in this play than in any other at this
festival."

Escape presented a difficulty for the Group that Davies considers typical of the period. The young man who is the play's central figure is walking in a park at night when he is accosted by a
young prostitute; a policeman accuses the girl of soliciting and
insults the young man. The latter punches the policeman, inadvertently kills him, is arrested and ends up in Dartmoor. "But
the thing is, in a place like Kingston, who do you get to play the
part of the prostitute? And there was grave difficulty. No local
actress would touch it, so, finally, Mrs. Miller, with enormous
self-sacrifice, played it herself. But on the program it appeared as
'A. N. Other' played it, you see? And, of course, everybody knew

Daisy. You couldn't miss her at a thousand paces! But there it was, you see. A kind of frightful delicacy that went on in those days, which is utterly gone, thank heaven."

In March 1933 Davies handled the stage direction for a university production of Bach's *Peasant Cantata* (with his brother Arthur a tenor in the chorus), and in May he produced Clara L. Burnham and George F. Root's operetta of *Snow White and the Seven Dwarfs* for the Kingston Girl Guides. Although the muses had apparently boycotted both the libretto and the music, Davies cheerfully informed his friend Donald Ryerson: "The production, I need not tell you, is inspired, artistic and novel."

The Sterqs, with whom Davies kept in touch in letters and visits, remained his only close male friends. But he was now meeting girls and taking them out. Having no sisters, fresh from an all-male private school, uneasy in his relationship with a possessive mother, he had nothing to give him a balanced view of women, with the result that romantic fantasies took quick root. The first girl he fell for was Clare, the daughter of Daisy Miller. Clare, who had a part in *Escape*, had chestnut hair and rosy cheeks, and her ladylike demeanour and speech added to her appeal.

His feelings for her are threaded through his letters to Donald Ryerson from the summer of 1933. He and Ryerson had decided to create an operetta for the Girl Guides to be performed the following February, Davies to write the lyrics and continuity and Ryerson to arrange the music. On August 6 Davies wrote that he had accomplished little because "Clare has gone to Quebec for a month, and previous to that time I had many important things to tell her and subsequent to it I could only write Russian lyrics for the opera, sheer Chekhov. A recent development has raised me to the highest pinnacle of elation and I shall now work with a rush." The following day he sent Ryerson a list of the characters he planned—a King, a Queen, a Princess, a disguised Prince, Pompey (a black child, slave to the Princess), the evil Prince Ivan, his base accomplice Sforzando, a sneaky Sorceress and three separate choruses.

On August 13 he sent Ryerson the words of Act I, begging him to "Forgive my erratic method of working but I spend these days in alternate fits of exaltation & deep depression according to whether I have a letter from Clare or not, and anything I am doing suffers a corresponding change." Through the balance of August and during September all appeared to be going smoothly. Davies completed most of Acts II and III, and chose the tunes that Ryerson was to arrange from *Folksongs of All Nations* and *Songs of England.* But then on October 5 he wrote: "Two weeks ago Clare went to England to go to a finishing school and she will be away for a year. I feel completely lost, much, much worse than I thought I should. We had several long talks before she left, and she has become engaged to the Lieutenant I told you of. She tried to let me down gently, but it was an awful shock and I feel really quite different, and rather glum. It is a good thing for me that she is a kind-hearted girl and considered my feelings much more than she need have, or I think I should have done something very foolish."

Fortunately, the fall term had already begun and he had much to keep him occupied. Ryerson, in Toronto, was similarly busy, and work on the operetta soon fell into abeyance. Even while working full-tilt on the operetta in August, Davies was designing settings for the Drama Group's fall pantomime, *Alice in Wonderland,* and with the arrival of autumn he and his brother Arthur as well were swept into preparations. With Mrs. Therese Fuller and Mrs. Dorothea Goodfellow, he prepared an acting version of *Alice's Adventures in Wonderland* and *Through the Looking-Glass.* Arthur made and painted the papier mâché masks. Davies took on two roles—the King of Hearts and the Gryphon—which required him to show up at many of the rehearsals, and very quickly, Colonel Stewart's daughter Elizabeth, who played Alice (and looked the part) caught his interest. By the time *Alice* delighted its audiences on December 8 and 9, Davies was taking her out and enjoying her friendship mightily.

Actually, he carried more than one fair damsel in his imagination when he walked the streets of Kingston between eleven and twelve at night. At that time he was steeping himself in folk songs and old ballads, full of doubles and phantom lovers. He had become interested in the Russian writers and in the *lieder* of

Schubert and Schumann, the lyrics of Heinrich Heine, the poetry of Goethe. As he walked, he mused about those who had walked these streets decades before, thinking thoughts like his. He would pause before a house "which had the beauty of having been built well and having been lived in and having been loved by a lot of people," or the home of a girl who had captivated him, and through his mind would flow Heine's "Der Doppelgänger" in Schubert's setting and James Campbell McInnes' voice:

> Still is the Night, the streets never waken,
>   Here dwelt my Sweetheart in days of yore;
> Long since hath she the town forsaken,
>   Though the house still stands where it stood before.
>
> There stands too a man, aloft stark-staring,
>   And wrings his hands, a woebegone wretch;
> I shudder, seeing his face despairing—
>   The moonlight shows me my own pale fetch.
>
> Thou white-faced fellow, my phantom double,
>   Why apest thou my love's despair,
> That many a night wrung my heart with trouble
>   In that same spot, in the years that were?

Davies' performance in *Alice* brought him to the attention of a Mrs. Sweezey, who lived in Montreal but who was attending Queen's that year to read philosophy. She invited him to produce *The Importance of Being Earnest* for a New Year's party at her country house some five miles outside Kingston. He accepted, and found himself in a household ridden with tension. At this week-long house-party, rumour floated free about the difficulties in the marital life of his host and hostess. Mrs. Sweezey was a woman of many aspects. She collected young men. A couple of months after his first encounter, Davies wrote that "she had been reading Wilder's *Woman of Andros* and saw herself as a Great Hetaera, bringing out the genius in young lovers like the Marschallin in *Der Rosenkavalier*. There was just enough colour in this pose to give it life." She also played the faithful, much-tried wife, and as an evangelistic Anglican was "apt to rhapsodize about Jesus being a Great Poet, rather than a prophet." More interesting to Davies, she was the rival of her daughters Margaret and Eleanor. She warned Davies particularly against Eleanor, the younger, claiming her to be cruel and inconstant (this of a girl just turned eighteen).

Life at Mrs. Sweezey's was not dull. During the week of the party her husband's brother knocked Davies down in the course of a row (he responded quickly and effectively). There were fits of gaiety and bouts of tears. And he found himself "utterly infatuated" with Eleanor. He was himself so amusing (in Eleanor's recollection) that he couldn't open his mouth without provoking gusts of laughter. When *The Importance of Being Earnest* was finally staged, Davies (Dr. Chasuble) and Eleanor (Miss Prism) had time to chat as they waited on the back stairs for their entrances. After she had returned to Montreal, and they exchanged letters, she says she "began to fall for him."

Home from the house-party in January 1934, he immediately began to rehearse in Marjorie Pickthall's poetic drama *The Woodcarver's Wife*, which he now considers a "bejesus awful play." It was the Drama Group's Dominion Drama Festival entry for that year. Its plot, as set forth by the *Whig*, concerns a French-Canadian "wood-carver who used his wife as a model for a carving of the Virgin Mary he was creating. He complained that his wife had not suffered enough to comprehend the facial expression of sorrow which he wished to portray in his carving of Mary holding the dead Christ in her arms. He arranges that his wife's lover should be killed before her eyes. Overcome by grief, she unconsciously adopts the expression of sorrow for which the artist has been striving. He calmly proceeds with his carving." Davies played the wood-carver. Unpromising though this sounds, Davies so threw himself into his part that, as he told Ryerson in a letter on February 14, "At the recent Drama Festival here I did a piece of acting which was, I know, the best thing I have ever done. It was technically very faulty but I grasped the part thoroughly and was commended by the adjudicator for my 'perfect sincerity.' I am not boasting nor am I posing as a soul tried by suffering, but I am convinced that I was able to act because I had, just once, felt very deeply [in loving Clare]. A few more shocks and I suppose I will be battered enough to call myself an actor."

In the same letter to Ryerson, he suggested that they tackle their operetta for the Girl Guides again that summer, and he confided his indecision between his fondness for Elizabeth Stewart (the girl who played Alice) and his infatuation with Eleanor. The latter was to visit the following weekend. Davies wondered: "will the sight of Eleanor banish Elizabeth from my mind? or will Eleanor upon a second sight fade beside the very fresh, airy and virginal Elizabeth?... My whole trouble is that I become infatuated with a girl in five minutes and then am unhappy about her for a week." Elizabeth later provided the point of departure for young Fredegonde Webster in *Tempest-Tost*. His mother did not make these passing attractions any easier to cope with; she appears to have had an uncanny ability to discover where his affections lay and to deride and demean the girls who attracted him. Always possessive, she clamped down on him when he stayed out late.

Davies' fancy turned itself more and more firmly to Eleanor, whom he described to Ryerson as "one of the loveliest girls I have ever seen," but ironically, he had already made the first of a number of moves that were fatal to a long-term relationship with her. He had succumbed to the impulse to send comic valentines to her, her sister Margaret and her mother. Gross parodies of the sort of old-fashioned Victorian valentine that was overloaded with lace, tinsel, ribbon and heart-felt sentiment, they were printed on cheap paper, garishly coloured and included a caricature and an abusive verse for good measure. Davies couldn't resist them; indeed, they still have appeal for him. He regretted their demise in the *Peterborough Examiner* on three separate occasions in 1941, 1946 and 1951. A verse he quoted in 1951 is typical:

> You think you're a Dandy
> And all hearts do please
> But in actual fact
> You're a big hunk of cheese.

The valentine he chose for Mrs. Sweezey twitted her for trying to be one of the students while still demanding the respect due her seniority. It ended with the phrase "your halo is bent." The one to Margaret mocked her hypochondriacal tendencies. Eleanor no longer remembers hers. Unfortunately, the recipients did not appreciate his joke. Mrs. Sweezey (who in Davies' view possessed little sense of humour) ignored her card. Margaret found her own amusing, but she never forgave the insult to her mother—and never let Eleanor forget it.

As Eleanor came to know Davies better that spring during several long visits when she stayed at the country house outside Kingston, she was more and more drawn to him. But at the same time she was increasingly bewildered by his satiric streak, which often vented itself in barbed comments on her mother and sister and in ridicule of the books her father chose to read, books that she felt to be unexceptionable.

Davies was involved in one more theatrical enterprise before the end of term, co-directing (with Wilhelmina Gordon) the Faculty Players in *Everyman* early in March 1934. Shortly afterward, he returned to UCC to attend that year's Gilbert and Sullivan operetta with the Sterqs, taking with him (as he told Ryerson in a letter arranging details of his visit) his "most thrilling waistcoat and stock for the event." Late in May, Ryerson came to visit, and the two laboured some more over the operetta, which then dropped from view.

That spring he witnessed a scene that was to be replayed annually, almost always to the same conclusion. It began with Rupert announcing his intention of going to Wales, wondering whether Florence were well enough to accompany him. She, disliking travel and finding her bronchial and asthmatic problems exacerbated by the damp of Wales, temporized, and eventually she admitted that she didn't want to go that year.

Then he said: "Well, I don't want to go and leave you."
She: "Oh, no, no. You'd better go if you've made your plans, if you really don't want to stay here."
He: "Well, I think I'd better go. I've got to look after the

place, you know. There are all kinds of things that have to be done and I just can't leave it standing there."

When he left for Britain in June, Rupert took Davies with him. As in 1932, he devoted much of his time to theatre-going, this time at Ludlow, Stratford-upon-Avon, Malvern and London, and as on the earlier trip he wrote up his impressions for the *Whig*. He had begun to experience the pulse and tug of his father's beloved Wales, and the life at Fronfraith leaps from the pages of his letters to Eleanor:

Last week Plaish Hall, an old Tudor mansion in Shropshire, was sold up, and Dad and I went to the sale, three days in a row, forty-five miles there and back. A fine sight: big marquee with a refreshment tent attached, and porters who carried all the things around the audience, to be seen. A lunch-break of half an hour. Very odd group assembled— the country English and Welsh—and they bought curious things; I am not one to speak for I bought a zebra skin rug because it was so cheap, and Dad bought a sewing machine that won't go. It is a madness. But at least we didn't buy any stuffed peacocks or cracked chamber-pots, or po-boxes described as antique log boxes. Many dealers there, a devious lot buying for re-sale, sometimes on the spot.

Did I tell you about our errant cow? The farmers around here won't sell us milk; need it all. So Dad bought a nice little gun-metal coloured cow from Norman Lloyd. But she was used to a big herd and lonesome with us. On Tuesday she took off and for an hour and a half we chased her up hill and down; I was on the lawn in my slippers when the cow dashed past, pursued by Dad and Joe Peate, the groom; I joined the hunt but the cow rushed into the woods, down the hill, and then, gorblimey, right up it again to the very top—about three-quarters of a mile of steep scrambling. At this juncture we were joined by two gardeners, Sam and Bill Haycock, and they tried to win the cow with love, calling it endearing names in Welsh and

English—it was a Border cow, and presumably bilingual. We finally chivvied it down the mountain to the driveway, where it pranced up and down for a time, and then took off again down a ravine and got mired in a bog, and we feared it would breathe its last and £20 would be shot to hell, but it got out on its own, seemingly refreshed. The Haycocks kept saying 'Coom coom, there's a pretty maid, there's a good little wench,' until we got her into one gate of the stable-yard, and I was set to guard the other. She made two or three very creditable attempts to jump the five-foot brick wall; Joe said, 'If her jumps that, begod I'll put her in the Grand National!' Then came the job of milking her, though Dad suggested she be allowed to burst as a punishment. But Sam and Joe held her head, Bill tried to milk her, and Dad very gingerly held her tail, which she used as a club. No milk. Bill kept saying over and over, 'Indeed to goodness, sir, 'er elders be full but the wench won't give down, that's where it is!' By this time the milk apparatus on the cow was swollen to the size of a small blimp. We drove over to Norman Lloyd, who laughed like a hyaena, who came and took her away and presumably milked her, for I heard no bang as of a bursting cow.

Found out the other day that our neighbour, Mrs. Buckley-Jones, was formerly Mrs. Heseltine, mother of Philip Heseltine, or Peter Warlock, the composer of some marvellously beautiful songs. Killed himself a couple of years ago, quite young.

On Saturday we visited a family called Bebb, who live in a splendid Tudor farmhouse called Y Cwm. Charming people and wonderful food, but farmer Bebb had ill-fitting false teeth, and I don't mean just slightly ill-fitting. He sucked perpetually, making noises like suds in a drain; he had, in his youth, taken part in a tithe-war, when some very rough things happened. Indeed, rumour has it that policemen's testicles were nipped off and later eaten, but these things are hard to prove. The farmer was a realist;

took us to his room and said 'Perhaps you'd like to wash, and if so, the jerry is under the bed'. Told us also, over tea, about having his teeth out. A travelling dentist did it in the kitchen. 'When he was done there was blood to your ankles', then the new teeth were installed, ready-made. Total cost, five pounds.

This afternoon we went to visit the famous printing office of Gregynog, generally admitted to be one of the finest in Britain; the hobby of the sisters of Lord Davies of Llandinam, Misses Gwen and Daisy. Under the care of a really glorious woman, Mrs. Dora Herbert-Jones. They also have a concert-hall attached to the house, filled with splendid Monets, but with a fine El Greco on a screen in front of the organ; the people on the estate provide singers for a choir of forty; now where but in Wales would you find that?... Mrs. H-J is a noted interpreter of Welsh folk-song, and has a wonderful private collection, acquired in workhouses, almshouses and among old folk everywhere. She sang for us, and it was quite marvellous to hear the old songs in the old language. Has two delightful children, Elsbeth and Huw. The girl plays the 'cello, is about fifteen, and delightful.

This past weekend we entertained my Father's Aunt, Miss Margaret Robertson—Auntie Maggie—who is 80, and weighs about 65 pounds and eats her weight at every meal. An old sweetie, very cultivated; one of the first women to get a degree from the University of Wales and never forgets it. She is deaf, but likes me to play the piano for her, which I have to do at the top of my voice, so to speak. A true Robertson; gets up at seven, takes a cold bath, and has a two-mile walk before breakfast.

Yesterday (Aug. 31) we went to see the Welsh National Theatre at Plas Newydd in Llangollen. Wonderful old house (once lived in by the famous Ladies of Ll, who were very nice Lesbians when it wasn't polite to say so). Met the director, Evelyn Bowen (first wife of Robert Speaight). An oddity, quite handsome with v. black hair and v. light eyes but the damnedest makeup you ever saw…but is v. brainy and really very nice. We saw a play done in the ruins of Valle Crucis Abbey.

By the time Davies returned to Kingston he was refreshed and ready for anything. In his last year at Queen's (1934-35), he took over the book review column in the *Queen's University Journal*, carried on with his tutoring and, despite his anomalous status, presided over the English Club. But his great achievement came in two amateur theatre productions that are still remembered in Kingston.

Soon after the term began, Arthur Sutherland, who had been on the executive of the Drama Group with him the previous year, approached him. Sutherland was now president of the Queen's Dramatic Guild, the student dramatic society. The Guild had been pulling in large audiences and building up its bank balance with popular comedies like J. B. Priestley's *Dangerous Corner*, but it was criticized by members of the faculty for not doing serious work. Sutherland wanted Davies to help retrieve its reputation. A classic was obviously the thing, and money would be no object. Davies rose to the challenge with alacrity. They quickly settled on *Oedipus, King of Thebes*, hitherto performed in Canada only by Sir John Martin-Harvey's travelling English company. Davies, who has never liked Yeats' austere translation of Sophocles' great tragedy, plumped for Gilbert Murray's, as appropriately "above a mortal mouth" with its ringing, soaring verse. The production was to be grand, nay, grandiose.

Since there was no financial constraint vis-à-vis costumes and staging, he assembled a cast of forty-four. The principals were carefully rehearsed and he kept the pace brisk. A bright thought was to persuade the girlfriends of the key players on the Queen's football team to appear "practically stark naked" as Jocasta's nymphs and attendants, ensuring that the audience would be large (if unfamiliar with the verse). Donald Ryerson was engaged to write original tunes, which were to be played on one of Archie Macdonald's recorders as background.

Wilhelmina Gordon had emphasized to him "that the Greeks did not exploit physical misery," that "the dénouement takes place off stage and the audience is just aware of it," that the blinding of Oedipus is "usually just indicated by a black tape tied over his eyes." But Davies arranged for blood by the bucket. Every night when Gerald Chernoff as Oedipus came on after blinding himself, there was gore (strawberry jam and cochineal stuff) streaming down his face and onto his gown. A couple of girls would scream horribly, and their unspeakable terror would stampede the chorus off the stage, up the aisle and into the lobby, shrieking and dropping their sandals as they went. Finally Chernoff, the "blood" still dripping, would make his exit, led groping through the audience by a small child (borrowed from Tiresias' landlady). These ploys had the desired effect.

The production attracted record audiences. According to Davies, "you couldn't get standing-room or even clinging-to-the-ceiling room whenever we played." The *Journal* reviewer declared that the Guild "outdid themselves." "The startling suddenness of Oedipus' entry, after he had blinded himself, was the highlight of the performance and Chernoff's acting from that point to his final exit left nothing to be desired." Eleanor, who was by now a student at Queen's, was in the audience, and she was impressed with Davies' capacity to transform the Gerald Chernoff she knew off stage into the magnificent Oedipus she saw on it.

The fall term was fully occupied by *Oedipus*. A series of lesser theatrical projects consumed the winter months—a truncated *Oedipus* for the DDF regional festival (honourable mention); Bach's *Peasant Cantata* with the Glee Club, the Faculty Players and a group of dancers; the lead in *Everyman* with the Faculty Players; parts in a Pirandello vehicle and in a comic sketch for the Queen's annual revue, called *The Campus Frolics*.

Davies saw a great deal of Eleanor, often joining the group assembled at her family's house for Sunday tea, going for drives (with her at the wheel), for walks, to dinner and to concerts. From time to time she would come for a meal at the Davieses', and he persuaded her to play Good Deeds in *Everyman*. When she sometimes failed to show up for a dinner date or for some event for which he had bought tickets, claiming that she just couldn't allow herself to be tied down, he was irked but not put off. She went to dances with other people, but he discouraged too much of that by seeing other girls and getting a mutual friend to tell her about it.

Come spring, Davies submerged himself in a second major production, which braided together many strands from his experiences of the previous three years. The Drama Group wanted to do a Shakespearean play *al fresco*, using Calderwood's garden. Rupert's passion for plays temporarily overcame his obsession with his lawns, so they got their wish. *A Midsummer Night's Dream* was chosen, with Davies to direct.

He was thoroughly familiar with the play by now, having seen it in 1929 (with Elaine Wodson as the Puck with fetching legs), in 1932 and 1934 at Stratford-upon-Avon in Elizabethan dress and again in 1934 in London. In the Stratford and London versions Puck had been played by men (the one a goblin, the other a faun), "a relief," Davies had declared in the *Whig*, "from the traditional Puck in a Robin Hood costume, usually played by a girl." Not surprisingly, his Puck too was male. The London production in Regent's Park had shown him how useful clumps of bushes could be for concealing such things as wireless and lighting equipment, and convinced him of the value of an orchestra playing Mendelssohn's music. It had also provided splendid opportunities for processions and dances. All of these elements would be incorporated in Davies' production.

Every theatrical group Davies had worked with made a contribution. The actors were drawn from the three major amateur associations: the Kingston Drama Group, the Faculty Players and the Queen's Dramatic Guild. Daisy Miller (who co-produced with Miss Margherite Mullin) held some of the rehearsals at her home, and the cast included Rupert Davies (Egeus), Professor G. H. Clarke (Bottom), Eleanor (Hermia) and Davies himself as Lysander. Even the Girl Guides were called in to usher and help direct traffic with the Boy Scouts.

Directing this production was far from easy. Early in the proceedings, as he contemplated teaching "Clarkey the first principles of acting" and guiding all the professors through the comic scenes, Davies groaned. "They are so stupid, and one has to be so tactful with them." In the end they all did well enough, though some for the wrong reasons. Professor Clarke as Bottom provided considerable amusement "in a kind of solemn way, because his short-sighted determination to get everything right was really very funny."

Old, half-blind Miss Mabel Gildersleeve presented another difficulty. She had belonged to the Drama Group for decades and regarded herself as an expert on make-up. Fortunately, since she had done the make-up for *Alice in Wonderland*, Davies knew what to expect and had arranged to have Charlie Gates take charge of that responsibility. Unfortunately, she couldn't be stopped. Before each performance she materialized with her dry rouge and box of crayons and, peering through a great magnifying glass, proceeded to dab about on faces with ghastly results. The adults only needed a little time to make repairs, but many of the thirty or so children playing the fairies went on looking grotesque. Davies hoped that the audience would assume "it was some kind of advanced view."

In the end, according to the *Whig*, the large audience was "thrilled." "Lavish, spectacular and sincere the performance was an unqualified success, artistically and financially." There were rough patches—processions that took so long the orchestra had to cover the gaps, a few anachronisms, like a box of matches and a Hudson Bay rug, exits so speedy they belonged on a racetrack—but none of them interfered substantially with what was clearly a triumph. It was a thoroughly satisfying conclusion to his years at Queen's.

The performance and the term complete, he ground to a halt. He spent a week or so "lying about with every nerve twitching, eating bland foods and feeling my pulse every now and then." He had Ryerson come for a visit, continued to see a great deal of Eleanor and brooded over what to do with himself. Although he had completed many of the requirements for an Honours B.A., and had performed exceptionally well in a number of his courses, there would be no document from the university attesting to it. And of course there was also nothing official to say that he had acquired a great deal of practical stage experience.

Once again a door opened unexpectedly. That spring, when

someone from Queen's (probably Professor Roy) suggested to Rupert that Davies apply to Oxford, he sent off applications to Balliol with recommendations from Wilhelmina Gordon, A. E. Prince (his history professor) and W. Hamilton Fyfe (principal of Queen's and Quince in *A Midsummer Night's Dream*). Balliol was one of the larger Oxford colleges, known for its high academic standards and for welcoming students from other countries. An advanced degree from Oxford would allow Davies to become a professor of drama if he failed to carve out a niche for himself as an actor. But there was no reply, and he assumed that Oxford was not for him. Well into August, however, a cable arrived from Rupert, saying that he had been to Oxford to see the tutor for admissions at Balliol. It was all right. He would be admitted. (Later Davies found out that his initial application had been mislaid.)

The prospect of leaving Canada forced Davies to consider his relationship with Eleanor. He loved her, and he desperately wanted assurance that he would not lose her by going off to Oxford. So he proposed. But she had just finished her first year at university and, only nineteen, she was far from ready to commit herself to him—or anyone else for that matter. She was attracted to him, enjoyed his marvellous sense of humour, liked going out with him, but his satiric streak made her uneasy, and her sister was set against him. She sensed that they differed on fundamental matters, and she feared that his strong personality would swamp hers. She did not love him, and said so. But she also assured him that she did not love anyone else and that his chances were good. Should her feelings toward him deepen, she would tell him so immediately.

Davies, unable to stand the uncertainty, pressed her for an answer. He assured her that saying "yes" would not mean an official engagement. Finally she capitulated. But she looked so miserable that he promptly released her from her promise. It was no comfort to the enamoured Davies that in the midst of such a scene, part of himself was registering and judging every nuance of his own behaviour and storing away what it perceived for future use.

He left for Oxford on anything but an emotional even keel.

Chapter 6

OXFORD: 1935-38

The meeting was to take place in ffrench-Pritchard's rooms, and full evening dress was demanded. The company arrived smiling, as men may well smile when they are assured of good food, good drink and good company. They were not many in number, but they clearly thought themselves great in spirit.

—"A Forest of Feathers," 1942

DR. VON HALLER: ...You told her you loved her?
MYSELF: On New Year's Day. I said I would love her always, and I meant it. She said she couldn't be sure about loving me; she would not say it unless she was sure she meant it, and forever. But she would not withhold it, if ever she were sure, and meanwhile the greatest kindness I could show was not to press her.
DR. VON HALLER: And did you?
MYSELF: Yes, quite often. She was always gentle and always said the same thing.

—*The Manticore*, 1972

1935-36

DAVIES AND MID-1930S Oxford hit it off beautifully. Entering this society of dons and students that valued individual prowess

161

of almost any stripe, Davies, an unabashed Welsh-Canadian, was ready to bowl it over. In these years he seized life by the scruff, became a central figure in the Oxford University Dramatic Society, loved (disastrously) and, surrounded by good friends, began to acquire an adult understanding of himself and his past.

As to costume, his performance was by now much larger than life. His hats, broad-brimmed and high-crowned in black or fawn, were rolled up on one side, down on the other. His jackets were of Welsh tweed, in blue or heather. With dinner dress, he wore an old-fashioned stock of black barathea or claret velvet, a large ring, a monocle or pince-nez on a black ribbon, and he carried a stick. (Despite many reports to the contrary, he did not wear a full-length cape or cloak, either then or later. This is so even though he ordered "a cape in a splendid peat-coloured tweed" at Hall's in Oxford thirty years later, observing to himself: "For all my life people have declared I wear a cape: now I shall do so in truth." What he ordered in 1965 was an Inverness cape—a standard coat, with a cape to the elbow. But he was, and is, easy to envision in the full-length version.) The letters he wrote affected the long "s" and his envelopes were sealed with a lump of red wax. Three or four years his junior, the Oxford undergraduates were, as one of Davies' contemporaries at Balliol observed, "amazed, sometimes a bit impressed, and partly amused" at the drama of his self-presentation. They also admired his seeming possession of a breadth and objectivity of outlook that they themselves lacked. A young Celt in imperial Rome, Davies was determined to demonstrate his independence and his worth, and Oxford settled back to enjoy the show.

The class distinctions of the Old World had begun to make themselves felt as soon as he boarded the *Empress of Britain* in Montreal. It was a floating social layer-cake. Lord Bessborough, returning to England after his stint as governor general, and Cardinal Villeneuve of Quebec, bound for Rome, were both in first class. Since Bessborough had the ship's one private dining room, the Cardinal had to make do with a screened-off portion of the main dining area. Nonetheless, the less important of his attending clerics, assigned to second class, kept trying to impress Davies, who was also in second class. They would observe:

"Well, last night I was up in first class, and I was asked to dinner with Zeminence. You know that's a pretty considerable distinction to have dinner with Zeminence. And Zeminence said...." Davies, seated for meals at a table with two teenaged girls, was doing a little impressing himself: he posed as the Cardinal's Protestant secretary.

In third class were some French-Canadian Franciscans on a pilgrimage to Rome. Davies described them in a letter to Eleanor Sweezey as "rabble," "undersized and somewhat dotty in appearance, but [they] laugh a lot, as the Saint himself was reputed to do. But at what?" Also in third class were several other Oxford-bound Canadians, among them Douglas V. LePan. Since Davies was in second, LePan did not meet him until they stood at the ship's rail looking toward Cherbourg or perhaps Le Havre. For LePan, there is something "a little emblematic about that because Rob has usually been, economically certainly, and perhaps socially as well, a class above me."

Davies arrived in Oxford at midday, "sun shining through mist, making magic of the city," and put up briefly at the Mitre. His rooms at Balliol were soon assigned—No. 8. Staircase XXII at the end of the Garden Quad, off a small courtyard, reached through an arched passage. (The rooms vanished in a 1967-68 renovation.) There was a modest sitting room with a mirrored fireplace, two easy chairs, a chesterfield, a desk and a capacious bookcase. The stone floor was garishly carpeted. Davies installed two huge chests of books in the bookcase, hired a small piano and hung two reproductions, Dürer's *Madonna with Many Beasts* and his "great favourite," Bronzino's *Allegory of Time*, which depicts Venus and her son Cupid in incestuous embrace, surrounded by allegorical figures. The Bronzino had captured his attention in the National Gallery in the summer of 1932 or 1934. Although it had been "improved" by the addition of a wisp of drapery over Venus' lap and a frond of foliage over Cupid's rump, and although it was obscured by dirt (which concealed the pair's thrusting tongues), the painting fascinated him. He was drawn too by the face of one of the allegorical figures, which resembled Eleanor Sweezey's: he discounted its lion's paws and sting-tipped serpent's tail.

Like every undergraduate before him, Davies had to get along without central heating. The sitting room was warmed by a soft coal fire (and the scent of burning bitumen still raises Oxford to his mind). But since the days of the Founder—John de Balliol's wife Dervorguilla—late in the thirteenth century, there had been "no form of heating whatever" in the tiny bedroom. Nor was there running water—just a jug and basin, a slop-pail and a "jerry." Each morning his scout, or manservant, would deliver water, cold for washing, lukewarm for shaving. The lavatories, also unheated, were in a brick shed some distance away. They were nicknamed "Lady Perriam," in memory of the woman who had given Balliol funds to erect a building on the land—"A poor requital for her generosity," reflected Davies in 1961. The baths were in the basement, presided over by Cornell, a cheerful man with one arm, who hurried his charges along. Since the baths were arranged in pairs, "the next man is likely to slop over into your tub; the Hon. Lyulph Stanley, who is an extrovert, sings Gilbert and Sullivan in the tub, and slops fearfully." By January, Davies had retreated from the chill, dirt and communality of the baths; he heated water on the fire to sponge himself down in the privacy of his rooms.

Oxford, of course, had been at the costume and ceremony game much longer than Davies. At the freshmen's dinner, black tie was required, and formal admission to the college and university a day or two later demanded a dark suit, white shirt, dark tie, gown and cap. Each student was made to sign his name in Latin, first in the college register at Balliol and then in the university register in the Clarendon building. (Davies' given name, William, converted without too much difficulty to Wilhelmus.) Latin too was the language in which the vice-chancellor charged the freshmen to keep the Statutes, which, *inter alia*, laid down that one must not shoot arrows in the Broad, nor (more to the point) be out of college after 9:00 p.m. ungowned, and never later than midnight.

All the special college events called for dressing up. At the annual Gaudy on November 25, which was the feast day of Balliol's patron Saint Catherine, everyone appeared in "full fig." The Indian students were especially colourful, and Davies, conspicuous in his stock, inspired cries of "Pickwick!" They toasted the college in large silver goblets of mulled claret, ate a good dinner and made merry till one o'clock in the morning. Official university business, too, was transacted with panoply and pomp. Little academic processions—the vice-chancellor in full academicals, preceded by three mace-bearers, for example—were often to be met on the streets. University and college clubs met in white or black tie; the little dining societies ate in sartorial splendour; and it was a rare week that did not include a formal occasion of one sort or another.

It took no time at all for Davies to disobey the Statutes. On the evening of the fifth of November, Guy Fawkes Day, he accompanied Elliott Emmanuel, a fellow Balliol undergraduate, to a performance of Marlowe's *Dr. Faustus* by the Munich Marionettes. On their way back to college they found themselves in the midst of a fight between students and townies, Davies "enjoying it, holding my specs with one hand and punching likely subjects with the other." Just as the students had begun to lift a car by its back wheels, Davies was nabbed by a buller (a university functionary in a blue suit and hard hat) and conducted to a proctor, "velvet bands on his gown, snowy lawn tabs under his white tie, bland as a custard, soother than the creamy curd":

> "Are you a member of the University, sir?"
> As I was wearing a gown and a Balliol scarf, this was simply *pro-forma*, but not to be outdone in politeness I replied "I am, sir."
> He took out a little book and a pencil and (fine touch) one of the bullers lit a match for him to see by, and he continued: "I must ask you for your name, initials and college, sir."
> "W. R. Davies, of Balliol, sir," sez I.
> "Thank you, Mr. Davies. Will you return to your college now? Good evening."

When he and Emmanuel presented themselves to the proctor at 9:30 a.m. several days later, they got "a severe warning about brawling" but no fine.

Davies' chief tutor at Balliol was the Reverend M. Roy Ridley. "Not a good tutor, but a great influence," according to Kenneth Garlick (later Keeper of Western Art at the Ashmolean Museum). Ridley, tall, slim, elegant and gracious, delighted in his resemblance to two figures of literary fame. Garlick recalls that he would stroll in front of the bronze of Dante above his mantel, casually aligning his profile with that of the poet. And he was compared by some to Lord Peter Wimsey, Dorothy L. Sayers' high-amateur detective, but when asked if he were Wimsey's original, he replied, "No, because Lord Peter, with his pleasing vacuity of countenance, was created long before I had the pleasure of meeting Miss Sayers. But perhaps a coincidence of age and college, and even the intermittent use of an eyeglass, are foundations enough for a legend." He encouraged the association by keeping Sayers' novels on display and, once, did a little amateur detecting himself. When Pat Moss, a Canadian student at Balliol, was burnt to death in a haystack during the early hours of May 15, 1936, Ridley sleuthed around the scene, magnifying glass in hand, until he was warned off by the police. By coincidence, Davies himself was drawn into this incident. Henry Davis, a good friend of Moss', had seen Moss at dinner and coffee. Giles Robertson, a distant cousin, saw him at ten. Davies, too, had said goodnight to him on the Broad outside Trinity. Reports of these encounters confused Davis, Robertson and Davies, and so, for a time, it was thought that Davies knew Moss better than he did. He was interviewed by Scotland Yard. Later, Davies came to believe that Moss had been murdered after a high-stakes card game, by one of a group of drug-takers and gamblers. But no one was brought to trial.

Ridley advised Davies to read for an undergraduate degree in Pass Moderations. This meant he would have to prepare for examinations in Anglo-Saxon, Latin, the history of Greek drama, and English drama and criticism, an unattractive mixture of challenge and boredom to Davies, who had failed Anglo-Saxon at Queen's, done no Latin since UCC and had covered much of the ground in the other two subjects already. However, he plugged through the required Anglo-Saxon texts under John N. Bryson, his lesser tutor at Balliol, and swotted up his Latin under

Sutton, a "crammer." He attended J. R. R. Tolkien's lectures on the Anglo-Saxon period (inaudible) and Miss Keith's on the Greek drama (good but solemn). Much better were the tutorials with Ridley on Elizabethan and Jacobean drama and criticism. Ridley was editing the New Temple Shakespeare at the time (Davies had used his *A Midsummer Night's Dream* at Calderwood), and he co-opted Davies in his first year to assist him on the remaining volumes. Ridley shared Davies' passion for live drama and, as a director of the Oxford Playhouse and a member of the committee of the Oxford University Dramatic Society, would often entertain actresses and actors in his rooms. No matter how early the tutorial—and Davies' were at 9:00 a.m.—it was accompanied by a "Roy Ridley Special," a glass of sherry mixed with a generous dollop of gin (a drink Davies still pours on occasion for himself and offers to friends). Ridley poured these all day for himself as well as his students, and went on to burgundy with his dinner at high table and port afterward, without betraying the slightest sign of intoxication.

A. D. Lindsay, Balliol's master, was not an important influence on Davies. He was a member of the Labour Party, a fervent Quaker and one who strongly believed in the importance of discussion in democracies. He held an open house once a week where students were encouraged to talk about anything and everything, and took particular interest in those—like Edward Heath—who were reading Philosophy, Politics and Economics in preparation for public life. In Davies' experience, he had precious little time for those in the arts and sciences. Neither Lindsay's socialism nor his passionate commitment to political debate struck answering chords in Davies; they bypassed each other's enthusiasms. But he did appreciate the blunt forthrightness with which the master and other teachers at Oxford assessed his work.

Balliol's denizens included Mr. Tylor, a blind legal don, a man of fierce independence who made his way around the college unaided, having long since memorized the number of steps to and from everything. Tylor, who played chess by mail, was regarded as a legal genius. Davies was struck by his behaviour at meals and at college functions, and, as he wrote to Eleanor

Sweezey, took note of him in Lady Perriam "shaking the vinegar off his pickle." When Davies based Pargetter in *The Manticore* on him years later, Tylor's sister wrote to compliment the portrait.

A tide of undergraduates flowed through Davies' rooms. Early in the first term, Lionel Massey (the son of Vincent Massey, then Canada's high commissioner to London), hypersensitive to protocol, would bound in to communicate a discovery "about whether one is supposed to walk on the grass, or spit at the Dean, or whatever." Clifford Macfie, who had neighbouring rooms, came to play flute and piano duets and to borrow books on psychology. A Mr. Ning, who looked fifteen but proved to be a prefect of the Hong Kong police force and the father of many children, came for help when he got stuck reading English. Charles, Lord Shelbourne, came to smoke Davies' cigarettes and chat about the theatre. From time to time, too, one girl or another would come for tea and talk. Livia de Gidro-Frank, a Hungarian countess and a "very bouncy girl" who tried every chair in the place before settling on the floor, loved disputation. Conversation with her became "a species of spirited fight." For Douglas LePan, who came over from Merton to talk about literature, Davies played and sang Elizabethan airs by Dowland, Attey and Hume. Kenneth Garlick remembers Davies declaiming from the lectern on his desk, once from Isaiah. Horace W. Davenport, an American Rhodes scholar at Balliol and a student of physiology who shared Davies' love of the theatre, provided an appreciative audience for impromptu demonstrations of the great actors of the past in the role of Hamlet. "Unfortunately," wrote Davenport to his mother, "they require space, and he is often interrupted by knocking over furniture."

Undergraduates often sought Davies' advice. Because he was older than they, and because of his interest in psychology (Ellis' *Studies in the Psychology of Sex* was prominent in his bookcase), he found himself consulted on many issues. Should family wishes be defied in choosing a career? How should one deal with a homosexual attraction to a youth of sixteen? And what should be done "when you kiss a girl and she says 'Oh, now you've spoiled everything!'" or "when a girl you have been rushing for six weeks invites Another to her college dance?" Of course, he learned a good deal himself from these interchanges.

One story that particularly fascinated Davies was that of the Catholic student James Pope-Hennessy, who was sorting out his sexual orientation. He was the scion of a distinguished family: his grandfather was reputedly the original of Trollope's Phineas Finn; his father had been the British representative to the Vatican and military attaché to Washington; his mother was Una Pope-Hennessy, the biographer; and his brother John was so sensitive to art that he functioned as a kind of touchstone of a painting's authenticity—confronted with a genuine Fra Angelico, he fainted. (Davies claims that this story is true and it may be so; John, later Sir John, did become an internationally respected authority on painting and sculpture.) But what riveted Davies was James' sex life—his involvement with one of the "college homos," his passion for a girl and subsequent recoil, his love for one tough or another. How, he wondered, could someone of James' refinement and sensitivity be drawn to a boor who couldn't string two words together? He asked, and the reply, "Oh yes, but you notice how his hair grows at the back, how it hangs on his neck," sent shafts of light into territory he had previously encountered only in books. When someone referred to Davies as "the Havelock Ellis of Balliol," he mused: "I wish I were. But the fact is that I am extremely curious, and will listen, and this nosiness consumes a lot of time."

Outside Davies' rooms, Oxford and the countryside beckoned, and he often went exploring on foot with friends. Parties were frequent. Vincent Massey hosted a tea for the Canadians at Oxford, as did Lady Tweedsmuir at her manor outside the city. Old Reverend Nathaniel Micklem, friend of G. H. Clarke of Queen's, had Davies to dine at Mansfield College. During eights week he drank beer, ate strawberries and cheered on Balliol's boats from the upper deck of the college barge, the furthest concession to sport he felt inclined to make. Uninterested in politics, he did accept an invitation to dine at the Oxford Union that first autumn, and in his final year he gave one of the leading "paper" (prepared) speeches, affirming that the arts do have a place in the university. Wearing the required white tie and tails, he carried the day. Davies was not even mildly drawn to the university's communist cells, though, like everyone else, he was solicited to join.

While at the Union he had a good look at the murky Pre-Raphaelite murals of Malory's *Morte Darthur* in the library. His interest in them had been heightened by a caricature of Max Beerbohm's depicting Benjamin Jowett, the acerbic master of Balliol, confronting Dante Gabriel Rossetti as he worked on *Sir Lancelot's Vision of the Sanc Grael*: "And what were they going to do with the Grail when they found it, Mr. Rossetti?" The mural later figured in *What's Bred in the Bone*.

One thing Davies *was* interested in was music. He went frequently to evensong in one or another college chapel and regularly to Balliol's fine bi-weekly Sunday concerts. Edward Heath was organ scholar at Balliol, and from 1936 to 1938 Davies sang with the Choral Society Heath organized (the men were drawn from Balliol with one or two from Trinity, the women from Somerville and Lady Margaret Hall). Once a term they contributed one of the Sunday evening concerts, giving the thousandth of the series on November 27, 1937. Later, writing as Samuel Marchbanks, Davies recalled an item in its repertoire: "Once, when I was a mere youth, I belonged to a choral society which rendered an echo-song by Orlando di Lasso, dating from the 16th century, and which consisted wholly of one part of the choir shouting Italian equivalents of Phooey and Boob at each other, with an occasional Ha Ha thrown in to give an air of gaiety."

When there was something special to be heard, like the Oxford Bach Choir singing the *St. Matthew Passion* on Sunday, February 27, 1938, Davies went along with a friend or two. Here is Davenport describing the day to his mother: "We had to get up in the morning in order to hear half of it before lunch and after lunch we went back to hear the rest of it. It is of course very fine music, but it was rather badly treated by the amateurs. Rob who knows it very well raged and stormed for hours about the way that the performers thought they were conferring a favor on a great work of art by singing it badly. He had the score with him and at every bad place he would groan or cast his eyes towards

heaven." In Davies' recollection, Davenport's own contribution
to the day was to remark in a penetrating voice as the women of
the choir—unmarried dons and professors' wives—filed in: "Ah,
there they come, the great army of the unenjoyed!" As readers of
A Mixture of Frailties will have realized, Davies made use of what
he learned at this performance in creating the background for
Monica Gall's humbling encounter with the *Passion.*

The Balliol English Club was Davies' chief college club, and he
was elected to it practically upon arrival. Its discussions were
larky, ebullient, attitudinous, in fact just typically undergraduate.
Prior to the meeting of Sunday, May 17, 1936, Davies and several of his friends carefully organized a practical joke. Horace
Davenport had spent the day preparing a paper on Modern
American Poetry, expressing it as far as possible in American
slang. He invited John J. Espey (another American Rhodes
scholar) over from Merton, while Davies invited Douglas LePan.
After dinner the four, together with William L. (Willie) Sachse
(another Balliol American), clustered in Davies' rooms to lay a
trap for the native know-it-alls of insufferable pretension.

When the club assembled, Davies served everyone "mint julep
to drink to stimulate the American atmosphere, which it certainly did." Davenport's paper, slangily provocative, created
"somewhat of a sensation." Then the hoaxers expounded upon
the New England poet Elias Cabot (of the Cabots that talk only
to God) who had studied at Harvard and lived on a cranberry
farm in Connecticut. Although his work was still unfamiliar to
the general public, the well-informed knew that it fell into three
periods—the "yes," the "no," and the "ahh." After the early
Rooted Green and *Naddars and Pads,* he had most recently published *Welded Brick.* The hoaxers knew people who had studied
with him and so they were able to recount a few personal reminiscences, and Espey read several of his own poems as Cabot's.
Enticed by all this dangling bait, the fishes rose to the surface.
How could they not, when, as Davies himself observed, "...it is
against all rules for an Oxford man to admit that anyone else
knows something he doesn't know..."? Two of them had read
reviews of *Welded Brick* in the *Saturday Review;* another made an
extended (but necessarily vague) comparison with Emily

Dickinson; and James Pope-Hennessy thought he remembered his parents meeting Cabot in Washington when his father was British military attaché there. As Davies said in a letter, "Cabot was a huge success and we who had begotten him lingered after the meeting to toast him in a good 1924 rye."

In the spring of 1936 Davies was elected to the Leonardo Society, Balliol's oldest club (he still wears its plum tie with rampant gold Balliol lions), and occasionally he was asked to meetings of clubs at other colleges. Unfortunately he struck no answering chord either at Balliol or at Pembroke's Johnson Society with papers on his beloved, but unfashionable, Victorian theatre. His audiences were unbudgeably convinced that it was terrible stuff.

Davies went often with his friends to the New Theatre, the city's only commercial house, and to the Oxford Playhouse. But the theatre that mattered most to Davies in Oxford was created by the Oxford University Dramatic Society. In November he was invited to join the OUDS, and it became his chief university (not college) club. The club mounted two major productions every year, one indoors in either the Playhouse or the New Theatre in February and the other outdoors in one of the college gardens in June. Rehearsals lasted for three or four weeks, and performances spanned one (usually six evenings and two matinées). The OUDS being a club for men only, the members took the male roles, but professional actresses were brought in to act the key women's parts. Dons' wives and students from the women's colleges were allowed to play the lesser female roles. Professionals were also brought in to direct, create the sets and design the costumes, an arrangement that opened a channel of communication with the London stage, which was invaluable to the theatrically ambitious. Davies involved himself in all six major productions in his three years at Oxford.

In February 1936, the OUDS performed *Richard II*. Helen Highet (later famous as Helen McInnes, writer of mysteries like *The Venetian Affair*, *The Salzburg Connection* and *Ride a Pale Horse*) was the Duchess of York. Florence Kahn, the American actress, married to Max Beerbohm, played the Duchess of Gloucester. Though only in her late fifties, she seemed over seventy to Davies, who wrote to Eleanor Sweezey that she was "A positive old dear but acted in the manner of an earlier day; she told me that no less a person than Augustin Daly had told her the secret in Shakespeare was to have a gesture for every line— and so she did, slowly and unforgettably." She asked for a screen in her dressing room, "Because you see, Mr. Davies, my husband Mr. Beerbohm will be calling for me, and I must have a screen to dress behind!" Because of her, Davies met Beerbohm himself— "that fabled figure, very elegant and the pineapple of polite- ness"—and at the supper after the final performance heard his informal and characteristically witty speech in response to the toast to "The Guests."

Vivien Leigh played Queen Anne. She was breaking up with her first husband, Leigh Holman, at the time, and he haunted the corridor outside her room with their small daughter. Wrote Davies: "Miss L. swears at them both with a foulness of mouth that would be shocking anyway, but is terrible from such a face, and when addressed to a child! I think she has a screw loose. In spite of her beauty she sometimes has a really terrible stinking breath, which is sometimes a sign of disorder that is beyond the merely physical. Oons, what a fury! as somebody says in some old play I can't at the moment put a name to." Davies is inclined to read considerable significance into personal odours. When a man he knew later at *Saturday Night* in Toronto was arrested for spying during the Second World War, he felt that the man's cor- ruption had made itself known in his "frightful breath" and the personal odour that recalled "a privy."

John Gielgud, then in his early thirties, directed the produc- tion, and Glen Byam Shaw assisted. Davies already knew Gielgud's quality as an actor and a director—he had seen him as a sensitive, consumptive Joseph in *Musical Chairs* in 1932 and a lyrical Romeo in his own magical production of *Romeo and Juliet*, with Glen Byam Shaw playing Benvolio, that January. And as stage manager he got an intimate view of Gielgud's direc- tion, since it was his job to "'sit on the book,' i.e. make notes of every move and effect the director wants in the large prompt- copy, which eventually becomes the Bible of the production." There was nothing of the flighty, irresponsible, romantic artist about Gielgud: he was businesslike, used everyone's time well and was courteous in curbing the students' rambling discussions. Thoroughly prepared, he knew what he was after, and he would experiment with moves and groupings until he achieved it. Never bookish, he was nonetheless sure-footed on questions of period, rank and class. Watching him was humbling. He kept doing marvellous things, and everyone would exclaim "How does he do it?" Davies, who knew how he did it, reflected that the greater puzzle was how he *thought* of it. Reviewers placed Gielgud's *Richard II* among the best efforts of the OUDS. The Society was impressed with Davies, too, and promptly elected him to the management committee. "This is considered meteoric!" he observed gleefully. More important, John Gielgud complimented him. In the 1940s and 1950s, when he was angling for a London production of his plays, Davies sent them to Gielgud.

In March he stage-managed the OUDS annual "smoker," which was reputed to be "the most obscene show in England." Although it probably did not achieve this distinction, the students were able to douse their inhibitions very satisfactorily just the same during its offerings of "Salacious Sketches," "Sexy Songs" and "Wanton Words." After the third and final performance, there was a bacchanalia at which glasses were thrown and Lord ———— "had a habit, whenever he was put in a chair of saying 'My God, I'm peeing,' as indeed he was." The "homos" were "in a great state, and one silly kid was sold under my nose…for thirty shillings—a great joke, but the infant was anxious to fulfil his part of the bargain." Finally people began "to be sick indiscriminately" and Davies left. It struck him nonetheless that "there is a very good side to such an affair. At Queen's there was never very much recognition of a common humanity between faculty and students, and certainly not of the dark or Dionysian side of that humanity. But here it is, and a very good thing, too. Dons can be dirty and dons can be silly, as when the Dean, A. B. Rodger, sings *The Hole in the Elephant's Bottom* at parties; but dons can also be learned and dons can be authoritative because they have lived lives with many dimensions, and we all know it. The silliness is often very endearing."

In June the OUDS performed *As You Like It* in Magdalen Grove, with Davies stage-managing again. Horace Davenport handled the lighting, and, fresh from the success of the Elias Cabot hoax, he and Davies devised another. They made a presentation to the Sir Richard Steele Society at Merton College on a new German lighting device called the Boehmann Frame, which caused light to bend around objects and thus eliminated ugly stage shadows. Again they gulled the English. Not only was the tale swallowed whole, but when the Mertonians inspected the lighting in Magdalen Grove they commended Davenport and Davies on the miraculous absence of shadow, apparently oblivious to the very real shadows produced by the spots and floods concealed in the trees.

This *As You Like It* was probably overly ambitious in its use of animals—a horse, several goats, a dog or two and Magdalen's herd of deer. The kid insisted on climbing a tree to nibble the wires. The billy-goat, lecherously pursuing the nanny, kept Audrey and Touchstone (on-stage) and Davies (off) busy trying to outmanoeuvre him. When a newspaper photographer asked Nova Pilbeam (then sixteen, playing Rosalind) to hold the goats' leashes for a picture, the billy promptly mounted the nanny, to the young actress' dismay. As for the horse, the plan was for Orlando to launch into the play's opening speech—"As I remember, Adam, it was upon this fashion..."—at which the wicked brother Oliver, alerted by the wave of a handkerchief, would spur the horse from the distant trees and arrive just in time to deliver his lines. All went well until dress rehearsal, when the horse struck an electric cable with its iron shoe, gave a dreadful roar and fell dead to the ground. Davies watched amazed as someone piously covered the horse's head, leaving its erect penis and expiring ejaculation fully exposed to the public view.

Lastly, there was Val Rogers (Jaques), who insisted on eating a symbolic grape at each of the Seven Ages of Man and throwing away the stem at the climactic "Sans teeth, sans eyes, sans taste, sans everything." Thea Holme, the director, vetoed the idea firmly, but he slipped it past her on opening night anyway, and almost choked himself in doing so. Nonetheless, the production went off reasonably well: it attracted capacity audiences and the critics were kind. But, wrote Horace Davenport to his mother on June 19: "Back stage is a better show than in front. Davies who is a superb stage manager and I wear our dinner jackets during the shows, just part of the OUDS tradition of elegance." Fifteen years later, some of the sillier aspects of the production got into *Tempest-Tost.*

As far as most observers could tell, and even to a friend as close as Davenport, Davies' first year at Oxford had been a great success. Yet within a matter of days of his display of elegance, probably before the end of the play's run, he was diagnosed as suffering from "a severe nervous breakdown and also a bad heart condition" and was sent off to Fronfraith without sitting his examinations. His private year had had a very different complexion from the one he had seemed to his friends to be living. Despite his appearance of nonchalance, he had become increasingly upset, couldn't concentrate on his courses, and finally he fell apart. Davies, the sympathetic attendant to the woes of Balliol's lovelorn, was himself in great need of understanding and good counsel. Having fallen for Eleanor Sweezey, he had projected on her an amorous fantasy, and it had taken him over.

From the time of the New Year's party at the beginning of 1934 when he had begun to pursue her, Eleanor had been much less committed to the relationship than he. Once at Oxford, he had fallen prey to the anxieties of insecurity. Head over heels in love with a girl who would not commit herself to him, he became more and more depressed by his situation as the year went on. It was a deeply humiliating position. Indeed, when he read Maugham's *Of Human Bondage* that year he recognized a parallel to his own anguished servitude in Philip Carey's mortifying surrender to love for the waitress Mildred Rogers. Much later he found it again in the agonized letters of Thomas Otway, the Restoration dramatist, to Elizabeth Barry.

But he could not extricate himself from the role of adoring, abject admirer in the letters he wrote to her every day. He who had been "Davies" to his friends at UCC, "Robertson" or "Rob" at Queen's and "Rob" at Oxford, signed himself "Bob" to her, a childhood nickname she liked (and he did not). When he tried to express his love, his prose sagged and whined. Humility did not sit easily on him, and occasionally he would rear up to demand that she love him, to point out one of her faults, to urge her to bow to his wishes. But he was so terrified of losing her that apologies, explanations and declarations of love followed hard on the heels of these assertions. As month followed month with no hint that his love was returned, his mood darkened and his health suffered. By November he was fatigued and irritable. (At the time his eyesight had deteriorated, which didn't help. He needed and bought new glasses.) When he went home for the six-week Christmas break, as he did again in 1936 and 1937 (the nine-day winter North Atlantic crossings a misery of sea-sickness), he got no further urging his suit in person. In February, he was sufficiently prostrate at the feet of his beloved to send her a Victorian sentimental valentine, one that had been carefully preserved in a lady's scrapbook for almost a hundred years until he saw it in a pleasant old shop and thought it just right for her.

Within days of sending the valentine, things went further awry. He discovered that Ridley had "put me to work on Tacitus, when it should have been Pliny! Quelle misericorde! But hard on me, as I must start all over again; he thought I was to do the same work as another man he supervises, named Garlick; apparently he gave Garlick my work!" He had to prepare afresh about half of the set translation for the Latin examination, which, like his other three examinations, fell at the end of March as Hilary term drew to a close. "And this got on my nerves frightfully and I was very, very depressed." (Kenneth Garlick has no recollection of Ridley confusing him with Davies.)

By March, Davies had another particular reason to be depressed. He had urged Eleanor to visit him in Wales for six weeks in the summer, and, when she demurred, made the tactical error of pressing her hard, countering her excuses. At this she decided to end their relationship. Undoubtedly, her decision was the right one, because their personalities and interests were ill-assorted. She, who later became a medical illustrator, drew meticulously; he loved whimsicality and doodles. She majored in mathematics; he found it incomprehensible. She loved to dance, although by her own account she was "about as musical as a bull frog"; he was no dancer, but responded powerfully to music. And, while she did not suffer from stage fright and could perform easily, she did not share his passion for the theatre.

Letters and cables volleyed back and forth. Davies, labouring on his Latin and Anglo-Saxon, began to suffer eyestrain, and a cold that he was suffering got so bad that it took Ridley's attention. He shipped Davies off to his own physician, Dr. Raymond Greene (brother of the novelist). Dr. Greene prescribed an inhalant and medication to control his cough.

Greene diverted him with a tale about Reverend Father Alphonsus Joseph-Mary Augustus Montague Summers, a figure who came to intrigue Davies so much that he would write about him and collect his books for the rest of his life. Summers, a rotund scholar of many enthusiasms—occult phenomena, Restoration drama, liturgy, late Latin literature—had cut an eccentric figure in Oxford shortly before Davies' time, trudging along in his soutane, buckle shoes, round spectacles and a large shovel hat, carrying a huge umbrella like Sairey Gamp in *Martin Chuzzlewit*. He was always accompanied by a thin, pimple-faced, pallid young man dressed from head to foot in black, or by a rangy, ugly black dog. The young man and the dog were never seen together, and it was suspected that the dog was Summers' familiar. Greene told Davies of being summoned once when Summers was ill and finding him "in a great big bed like a catafalque with a huge crucifix on top of it, holy pictures all around the room, and it was like a rich abbot's cell in a monastery." Summers was gloating over an illustration in a huge and rare volume of medical oddities, picturing "some woman who had an extraordinary malformation of her privy parts," and he asked Greene: "Could there really be one like that?" Davies, still as fascinated by the grotesque as when he had stared at the midway freaks at the Canadian National Exhibition, loved the notion of a living curiosity relishing a printed one. He became a collector of such books himself when he could afford them.

Unfortunately, Greene's efforts on Davies' behalf could not solve his very real problems, and he failed his end-of-term examinations.

At this juncture, J. Max Patrick intervened. Patrick was a red-haired Canadian from St. Catharines, Ontario, president of the Balliol English Club and interested, like Davies, in psychology.

There had been some thought of Davies producing Milton's
Samson Agonistes for the Balliol Players with Patrick in the lead
because (as he says himself), "I'm 6 feet 4 and then was a rowing
hearty bulging with fine muscles—born for the part as it were."
Accordingly he spent two weeks at Fronfraith with Davies that
April between Hilary and Trinity terms. They soon gave *Samson*
up as impracticable, but, conscious that Davies was "depressed in
soul," Patrick persuaded him to unburden himself. On returning
to Balliol, Patrick wrote a long letter to Eleanor Sweezey, in
which he brought both youthful self-importance and considerable penetration to bear on his assessment of Davies' state of
mind and character:

> As for you, I do not know you, and Rob has told me prac-
> tically nothing about you. The roses bloom where you
> walk as far as he is concerned; you are heaven and he is a
> worm unworthy and the like. Under the dramatic veneer,
> as you know, he means it with terrible force....
>   Rob is really a very gentle, exceedingly generous, most
> sympathetic, loving, timid, affectionate, deeply emotional,
> and deeply sentimental person. But he was brought up in a
> family, who, in exterior at least, are constantly ironical,
> sour, biting, cynical. He naturally fell into this way of exte-
> riorizing himself. Moreover, being exceedingly sensitive, he
> was constantly being hurt; his excess of emotions was
> laughed at; he found them hard to control; as a child he
> was a persecuted "sissy"; an unfortunate complex as regards
> mathematics brought him constant humiliation. As a
> result he became in his manners and behaviour suspicious,
> cynical, destructive, and exhibitionistic. The suspicion,
> cynicism, and destructiveness were defence mechanisms
> against the intolerant cruel world which kept hitting him.
> The exhibitionism canalized him off to the theatre, and
> has been put to good use. It is noteworthy that he adopted
> a ready-made defence—the cynicism of his family. In a
> sense this was fortunate—for the real Davies is still there,
> if anything in increased force because it has been so pent
> up and repressed. Give him a chance to be generous, and

he overflows; ask him about it, and the defence mechanism pops up, and he gives the impression that he was generous only in a mechanical way, and then rips apart the bad points of the characters he has been dealing with.

The actual fact—I found it hard to accept at first, but I am convinced that it is true—is that he is so conscious, though in an inexpressible way, of people's good qualities, that he takes them for granted. He was not aware until I told him, that people took his destructive portraits seriously: he did not know that the vividness with which he debunked a thing so influenced his hearer that all the life and beauty went from it. It is that feature, I think, which repelled you as it has repelled me—the ease with which he could sour and embitter one's attitude towards people and things. But to him, to the real him, these descriptions have no particular force: they are merely his way of thumbing his nose at the objectionable side of the world. By so doing, he actually eliminates the nasty side for himself, and has only the good part left. It is his mental method of evacuation....

At the same time, I well realize that the real Rob has bad points as well—it is supersensitive; when aroused it is liable to extreme excitement, anger, and even violence, it is often lazy, and, in spite of wide sympathy and real generosity it is a bit self-centred.

But it has a capacity of genuine greatness about it—with all its storms and superficies, there is a something there which must be given a chance to develop. The danger of your affair is that it may sour and embitter him permanently. Even though it has ended, it can be made a sweet and cherished memory, working in the other direction. *If he can be convinced that you really understand and respect him, that you appreciate the fine qualities of the real Rob, and that you will have a real friendship with him on that basis, this will be accomplished.*

Patrick urged Eleanor to write to Davies to "say with sincerity that you love him as a friend, that you have confidence in him, and that you respect him—with perhaps a word or two to encourage him in his career...." She appears to have done so and she continued to write as a friend. Patrick felt that he had himself alerted Davies to "what a false hard impression he makes on the world," with the result that Davies was making some effort to "change his exterior." Certainly, from this time onward, Davies seems deliberately to have curbed his tongue.

However, he was in the grip of something more powerful and more destructive than could be put right by a few letters and modest reform of his persona. He managed to put up a good front for most of Trinity term, but he was actually sinking into a depression, which manifested itself in constant fatigue, irritability and fits of dizziness that caused several bad falls. In June, when he told Dr. Greene about his misery over losing the girl he loved, Greene counselled him wisely about psychosomatic illness. He also told him that he must take care because he had a "dicky heart" and packed him off to his parents in Wales. The local doctor there found nothing wrong with his heart, which allayed some, but only some, of their concern. And no wonder. His spirits were so low that even his handwriting was affected. Normally he wrote as if on ruled paper, but on June 25, shortly after reaching Fronfraith, the lines in a letter he wrote trailed morosely downward to the right.

1936-37

Davies' friends rallied to him. Douglas LePan visited, and John Espey sent a letter in the form of a poem. Horace Davenport forwarded a Shakespearean dialogue, which inspired Davies to reply with a long poem of his own headed "Penillion for Davenport the American from Ap Robert the Bard, known as the Snipe of the Severn." Rupert urged him not to see this breakdown as final, telling him about the similar collapse he himself had suffered in New York, and had recovered from, at about the same age.

On August 5, Davenport came to Fronfraith and was startled to find it a luxurious country house, not a rough mountain cabin. For the first time in almost a year he experienced the pleasures of hot and cold running water and an extravagance of bathrooms. Rupert was "in residence," and the house was fully staffed. (When Davies was there between terms in his father's absence, life was much simpler: one woman coped with the cleaning and the meals.) Davenport immediately wrote his Oxford tailor to make up and send grey flannels. He described Fronfraith's setting to his mother: "I can't describe the beauty of the place. The house is high on a hill, and from the terrace can be seen miles of rolling hills. The slopes are wooded and in the valleys are little rivers. The scene is peaceful and green and well arranged, quite different from the snug untidiness of the English countryside." When he had met Davies' parents in Oxford that June he had found them to be "pleasant and kindly people …who just say what they think," not the "first-class hammer throwers" of whom he had been warned. But his first night at Fronfraith found him in a battle with Rupert over the upcoming 1936 U.S. presidential election (Alfred M. Landon versus Roosevelt), which lasted until everyone went to bed:

> I continued to explain to him that I didn't have any set political views, but he insisted on thinking me a Socialist. He is an absolutely perfect example of the employing class. He is doubtless very good and public spirited, but he is completely incapable of seeing any other point of view. All labor men are wicked agitators and all people out of work are lazy bums. He kept telling me that when I got older I would have a wife and family to support and I would get ahead in the world and then I would see things as he does. He is the archetype of a man not naturally logical or sceptical, corrupted by success. Otherwise he is perfectly decent, and I shall try to avoid discussions of politics.

On August 18, George Humphrey, Davies' psychology professor at Queen's, came to visit with his wife and daughter. Concerned about Davies' continuing gloom, Rupert and Florence asked his advice. He alleviated Davies' dark mood a little by suggesting that a marriage to Eleanor would have been unwise and recommended that he see Dr. Robert D. Gillespie, Physician for Psychological Medicine at Guy's Hospital in London, one of Britain's foremost psychiatrists.

Davies was, of course, interested in psychiatry, and was immediately receptive. He quickly came to admire Dr. Gillespie's elegance and distinction. (Like other top-ranked London physicians
of the day, Gillespie wore morning dress and top hat on his hospital days.) They had one or two introductory visits, ten days of
intensive treatment in late September and regular Saturday
morning sessions in the fall and winter (after which Davies usually went to a play). This self-searching was probably what
prompted him in 1937 to begin to record his inner life and
thoughts about family matters in the chunky, octavo diary with
marbled board covers and black, tanned leather back that he still
uses from time to time. Davies found it "a thrilling experience to
be thoroughly probed by someone who has no axes to grind, and
can tell you about yourself without affection and without ran-
cour." Although he told his Oxford friends little about the treatment, he made no effort to conceal that he was seeing a
psychiatrist. Some of them worried about the impression it
would make on his potential employers in the future.

In a letter he wrote at the time, Davies explained, with youthful exaggeration, that he was "undergoing that very rigorous
process known as psychoanalysis," but it would be more accurate
to say that he underwent a series of counselling sessions. Neither
a Jungian nor a Freudian, Gillespie was a problem-solver, and he
sorted Davies out with expedition. It did not take him long to
recognize that the love affair that had precipitated the breakdown
was only part of what ailed his patient. Davies' frustration with
the work he was doing at Oxford had made a contribution.
Finding that he had already done the equivalent of an undergraduate degree and was ready for advanced work, Gillespie got
in touch with Ridley. The latter, no doubt feeling some chagrin
at his part in the previous year's fiasco, reoriented Davies' study
program toward a B. Litt. (a research degree). By mid-November
Ridley had proposed a congenial thesis topic, arranged for Nevill
Coghill of Exeter College to supervise it and suggested lectures
on practical matters, like thesis preparation, the use of a research
library, Elizabethan handwriting and the principles of editing,
this last with R. W. Chapman. Formal permission for Davies to
try for a B. Litt. came two or three weeks later. (That year and

the next, Davies also attended lectures by Edmund Chambers, C. S. Lewis, Holmes Dudden, Brett Smith and Nevill Coghill, none of them an outstanding speaker but all, to Davies, cork-full of wonderful information.) With challenging, sympathetic work to do, Davies shook off his lethargy and applied himself effectively.

As Gillespie explored Davies' childhood and youth with him, it became evident that his upbringing had contributed to his internal conflicts. Gillespie encouraged him to speak of the things he had repressed or only partly sensed. They talked about the concern his parents must have felt before he was born, remembering the frailty of Arthur and the death of the stillborn child, and they concluded that he had been an unintended, probably not much wanted baby. They looked at what it had meant to him to have been so much younger than his brothers and to have been the child of parents whose attitudes were old-fashioned, almost Victorian. With Gillespie's help, Davies came to recognize how oppressive he had found his parents' oft-reiterated demands for gratitude toward his mother for the gift of life and toward his father for financial support and guidance. After Gillespie and he considered the scenes in which he knelt to ask pardon of his mother and the later episodes of adolescent resistance, the doctor finally observed: "You know it's perfectly obvious what's wrong with you. You have been disastrously badly brought up." Davies felt: "Whew! I don't have to be grateful any more." Freed of the burden of demanded gratitude, he could be more honest with himself about the negative feelings he harboured, particularly toward his mother. In turn, gradually over the years he came to value the positive elements in their relationship and to penetrate through his youthful projections to the person she really was.

In sorting out Davies' amorous frustrations, Gillespie was concerned that the obsessiveness of the affair might have masked an underlying homosexual inclination, but (to Davies' relief) he quickly rejected that possibility. He examined Davies' theatrical ambitions, too, to see whether his expectations there were as unrealistic as they had been in love—was he perhaps eager to reform the stage?—and was satisfied when Davies told him he just wanted to join one of the admired London companies and work along the lines it had already established. When Davies admitted that he wasn't sure that there would be a place for him in the theatre, Gillespie's reply struck him as genuinely wise: "Well, of course, it is just a fact that we attract what we are, and if that is for you, that is what will happen to you." Finally, Gillespie brought him to see that his love for Eleanor had been a projection of his own needs. He came to realize that he hadn't really known her. Although the reciprocity he yearned for did not exist, it was not her fault.

That admission helped him to put his depression down. But it took a long time after the sessions with Gillespie ended to integrate what he had learned about himself fully into his understanding. His relationship with Eleanor, which taught him much that he would use later in his work, now made him wary of succumbing to infatuation, for he knew the delusive power of romantic attraction at first hand. Henceforward he determined to keep his feelings carefully bounded, and to choose his marriage partner on different grounds than enchantment. The writer's art, he came to think, must consist in distillation and alchemy. It must be the very opposite of a venting of raw, uncontrolled emotion. In time, as he found fresh ways to come at what had happened to him, he tugged on different strands of the experience in creating characters and situations for his plays and novels.

For decades he shrank from recalling the emotional tailspin of his first Oxford year. On one level, he had no desire to revisit his young, foolish, pathetic self. But he recoiled too from the dark feelings he had experienced in the depths of his obsession. Here his extraordinary powers of recall were a liability, for they opened the possibility that the remembered despair might grip him again. When, in the late 1960s, Eleanor returned most of the letters he had written to her, he could not bring himself to reread them. Several years later, in August 1972 as he prepared to write *World of Wonders*, he thought they might be of use, presumably in creating the background for Roland Ingestree, but again he shied away. He did not reread them in fact until 1983, while writing *What's Bred in the Bone*. Then he thoroughly exorcised his ghosts, and, for the first time since 1940, went to visit Eleanor Sweezey.

Like many who harrow their souls under the probing of a psychiatrist, Davies experienced a surge of energy and a lightening of his mood. By November he reported: "I can say with full conviction that I am happier now than I have ever been in my life. I seem to have a much better grip on everything. My work has improved to the point where my tutor is really delighted, and I get through it with an ease which I never knew before."

This is likely to have been the year when he bought a number of volumes by Freud, including the five-volume *Collected Papers*, *The Interpretation of Dreams*, *Introductory Lectures on Psychoanalysis*, *Wit and Its Relation to the Unconscious* and *Beyond the Pleasure Principle*. He was certainly making a study of psychology the following summer (1937), looking for himself on every page, finding no simple answers. The more he read, the more complicated it seemed. For a time he tried noting down his dreams to see what could be made of them in Freudian terms, but he was very conscious all the while of how easy it would be to delude himself.

He also read at least two books, *The Book of the It* and *Exploring the Unconscious*, by Georg Groddeck, whom he still regards as one of this century's great diagnosticians. Groddeck was a psychoanalyst who believed that body and mind are both expressions of "It," a force that comes into being at the moment of conception. He was convinced that patients must be understood holistically, and he regularly used psychoanalysis to treat organic disease. At his clinic in Baden-Baden, the patient would rest for several days, eat lightly, be soothed by warm baths and be thoroughly purged; then, before asking questions, the doctor would let "It" speak to him through the body's sounds, textures and smells. These books made a deep impression on Davies, who introduced phrases and ideas from them throughout his writing. Many of these were probably reinforced by their appearance in other contexts, but it is worth noting that Groddeck was convinced that death is always voluntary, an idea Davies has used several times. In *The Book of the It*, Groddeck makes some play with Terence's "*Humani nil a me alienum puto*" ("I count nothing human indifferent to me"), the tag that Davies placed on the masthead of the *Peterborough Examiner* in 1951. In the same book, he calls the nine months in the womb a paradise, a notion Davies used in *World of Wonders*.

In one part of *The Book of the It*, Groddeck writes persuasively, in more detail than can be related here, about the hatred that he believes to be unconsciously entwined with women's love for children. In extreme cases this might move a woman to avoid having children at all, by remaining celibate and single, by refusing sex with her husband or by succumbing to a disease that would preclude intercourse. It might make her body inhospitable to conception or bring on a miscarriage. It might manifest itself in the nausea and vomiting of early pregnancy and was always an aspect of the birth process, the casting of the child from her body. In another section Groddeck speaks powerfully of the lasting hatred a child may conceive toward its mother if it is not breast-fed and experiences unassuaged hunger. Davies may here have found important and helpful insights in his efforts to come to terms with his own and his mother's feelings. They are similar in character to the travel diary entry made years later on August 1, 1966: "But I have sometimes wondered if my fearful & life-denying mother hated me in the womb & marked me for life? She cd. have done it: a v. strong character, devoted to negative ends. Dutiful as a mother, but not loving. Sometimes I think this early struggle is the key to my character, both its strength & weakness, & its sudden descents into despair." Davies' struggle with his mother cast a long shadow forward. His attempts to understand her and her meaning for him, and to achieve a fairer view of her than that of the hungry child or resentful adolescent, has produced several of his characters and energized several books.

As the work with Gillespie drew to a close, Davies made the decision to break with the Presbyterian Church. This was a move that had been in the making a long time. He disliked Presbyterian Sunday school in Renfrew and Kingston but had yielded to family pressure to go. Later he had attended St. Andrew's in Kingston, but the more he learned about Presbyterianism the less comfortable he felt with it. As a teenager, he resented the doctrine of predestination: it seemed to him unfair that though you might have been damned before the foundation of the world, you still had to behave like one of the elect on the chance that you were predestined for everlasting life. He disliked the didacticism of the Presbyterian church services and the dull cadence of their discursive prayers. Then he had been exposed to the formal beauty of the Anglican *Book of Common Prayer* at UCC (where excellent classes in scripture had given him a good general introduction to the Bible and some aspects of theology). By the time he reached Queen's, his friends were aware that he was interested in Anglicanism and that he attended high Anglican services during occasional visits to Toronto. At Oxford, finding the English strain of Presbyterianism repugnantly harsh, he became a regular at Balliol's Anglican chapel services. Almost immediately the college chaplain, Canon Pym, a man of bright intelligence, took an interest in him. With his help, Davies came to recognize that the splendid surroundings of the Anglican service and its ritual and poetry were important to his worship.

At five o'clock on Monday, March 1, 1937, not coincidentally the feast day of St. David, patron saint of Wales, he was confirmed in Christ Church Cathedral by the Bishop of Oxford. This was, of course, a declaration of independence from his parents, but it was a modest one. There was ample precedent for his choice on both sides of the family. His mother's relatives, the Langses, were Anglicans, and his father's mother had been an Anglican before she married.

During this second year at Oxford, Davies rented pleasant, large quarters on the top floor of Canterbury House, a four-storey building by the gate of Christ Church College in King Edward Street. The ground-floor suite was occupied by Basil Sabouroff, a Bulgarian of Davies' acquaintance, who entertained his friends to lunch on Wednesdays. A careful host, he habitually tried out the menus himself on the previous day. Such hospitality was not unique. Oxford was full of little dining clubs. Davies, Horace Davenport, Willie Sachse and John Espey had themselves founded The Long Christmas Dinner Society, named after Thornton Wilder's play, that fall, and it met in its members' rooms until June 1938 (it is still listed as one of Davies' clubs in

Canadian Who's Who). They entertained each other, and occasionally guests, with as many flourishes of dress, cuisine and occasion as they could comfortably muster. Meals were inexpensive and relatively easy to manage, since those who lived in college could make arrangements with the college kitchens and those in digs with their landladies.

On St. David's Day, following Davies' confirmation, the Society dined gaily in his rooms. Davies had festooned the premises with leeks. Horace Davenport had had his scout polish the handle of his new stick, so that, as he wrote his mother, "What with my black hat and chesterfield and white kid gloves I was sufficiently elegant. Willy wore his top hat at the request of Davies who wants to impress his landlord. LePan and Espey were also there. We had an excellent soup combining the flavors of asparagus and indian corn followed by Davies' weakness, vol-au-vent, with fried potatoes and onions. The sweet was a very good trifle, though I never could understand why such a dish is called a trifle. The sparkling Burgundy sparkled throughout." Their high spirits were further assisted by a large bowl of Cardinal Punch, "a delectable beverage involving two bottles of claret, several lemons, and a quantity of spice...served hot."

Davies often wrote light verse for parties on the river or other occasions, carefully incorporating the names of everyone present. On this evening he may well have read a poem, as he did later that year on the Eve of All Hallows (after Willie Sachse had gone down from Oxford) when he presented the assembled with "An Apostrophe to *Time*":

> Cherish this evening, all-destroying Time,
> Nor blot the page wherein this feast's recorded,
> Spin out the hours to years;
> Let the slow-bleeding sandglass set no curst confine,
> Let not the stinting minutes banish unregarded
> Our laughter and our tears.
>
> Trumpeting Fame, lackey to shadows, hold thy peace;
> Here *Davenport*, stranger to chymic glory,
> *Espey*, unread, and *Davies*, unacclaimed,

Are met together in a dirty den
To drown our woes at ease
In cups unnamed and high-resounding story;
Let the faint wraith of recollected *Sachse*
Sit in the midst and banish all our fears;
Here is true greatness found, and here
Renaissance England is herself again.

Before the evening was over, Willie Sachse was playing Davies'
piano under the impression that it was an organ, and none of the
others felt it worth correcting him. Davies recalls that they were
all "very frail" the next day. Davenport remembers that it was the
last time he was really drunk. He was unable to work for three
days afterward. Years later, Davies looked back on occasions like
this and commented to himself in his travel diary: "What asses
we were & how happy!"

The February 1937 OUDS production of *Macbeth*, stage-
managed again by Davies, was a major trial for him. Hugh
Hunt, subsequently well-regarded as a theatre director, was then
only twenty-five or twenty-six. He changed his mind incessantly,
designing the set three times with the result that it could not be
assembled until the day before the opening, and even then didn't
fit together properly. He failed to arrange for special effects until
the last moment. The tricks themselves—"ghosts, magic, fire,
lightning, horses' hoofs, bells, visions, boiling cauldrons and
God knows what not"—were legion. His lighting strained the
eyes of the audience and created hazards for the actors, uneasily
groping their way onstage. Lady Macbeth (a fine performance by
all accounts) created her own difficulties. Margaret Rawlings, a
well-known actress whose work Davies had admired while at
UCC, was of an imperious disposition, her tone was acerbic, and
her companion, the beauteous Toska von Bissing, flirted with
the men of the OUDS. Miss Rawlings herself would cosy up to
Davies before the curtain every night, hoping to improve the
lighting for her scenes. By consensus the production was judged
lacklustre, but Davies' own part in it brought him credit. When
it was over he served notice. He would not stage-manage again;
with a thesis to write, he could afford neither the emotional

energy nor the time for the job.

It is hardly surprising that the committee raised the ante in their reply. Loath to lose his organizational and theatrical skills, they made him junior treasurer and asked him to act in their next production. To their surprise, and the dismay of some among them, Davies in accepting brought North American energy and attitudes to bear on the Society's affairs. He had the dining room redecorated, overhauled the menu and fired the antiquated waiters. He also set about to recover £1,700 in back dues, writing scores of notes informing delinquents that he would put matters in the hands of The Foreign and Colonial Debt Recovery Association within the month if they did not pay up. By autumn the debt had plunged to £700.

May brought the Coronation of George VI. This was a theatrical extravaganza in itself, the final scene, as it were, in a medieval play. After George V's death in January 1936, Davies had watched the recorder and the vice-chancellor of the university, in the presence of the mayor, mace-bearers and assorted bewigged grandees, proclaim the accession of Edward VIII. Trumpets blew, bells pealed, flags rose from half-staff and the crowd shouted "God Save The King!" During the university's week of official mourning, he and the other students, save a few malcontents, had worn black ties. After the unwanted drama of Edward's abdication, preparations sped forward for the coronation of his brother Albert as George VI. To Davies' delight, Rupert, who as president of the Canadian Press Association was entitled to a seat in Westminster Abbey, transferred the place to him.

Appropriate costume in Davies' case meant morning clothes, spats, ascot and gloves (and an opal tie-pin he borrowed from Davenport). When it proved impossible to get lodgings in London, he was put to the further expense of a car and chauffeur to drive him to the Abbey and back. He dressed and breakfasted at 2:30 a.m. on the great day and, because of the crowds, did not get back to Oxford until 11:45 p.m., having neither eaten nor drunk all day. He also managed not to have used the Abbey's improvised facilities, but he did note that they were labelled "Peers and Peeresses, and Ladies and Gentlemen, so there would be no unseemly mingling of the waters of Empire."

High in the triforium of the north transept, seated with the world's press, most of them in full academic dress, he could spy a multitude of details invisible to those below. He had a clear view of the orchestra and choir assembled on the rood screen, attentive to the baton of conductor Sir Walford Davies, in his Oxford Mus. Doc. gown, all white brocade and pink sleeves. He could watch Lord Berners, the composer, in the midst of the peers, peeresses and members of Parliament directly below, following the music in his own score. The peeresses' coronets "were fulfilling a double purpose, for they had them filled with sandwiches with which they refreshed themselves when opportunity offered." He drank in the impressive pageantry, and he appreciated the emphasis on the religious character of the occasion. As he wrote in his report for the *Whig-Standard,* "I would not have missed it for worlds, and am now a Monarchist for life." (He is still a monarchist, valuing the Crown as a tradition and symbol of permanency that stands above temporary governments.)

The OUDS June production that year was *Twelfth Night.* Davies as Malvolio was in a role he already knew well from UCC. John Gardner, then Organ Scholar of Exeter College, directed the music. The three professional actresses (Phyllis Konstam, Rachel Kempson and Alexis France) handled their roles well; Molly McArthur designed exquisite costumes; and Esmé Church directed imaginatively. At the opening performance, everything conspired to create an enchanted interlude that laid down magical memories for the young and gave one reviewer a glimpse of Arcadia: "The O.U.D.S. production of 'Twelfth Night' in the beautiful setting of the Fellows' Garden of Exeter College is a delightful summer evening diversion. A starlit sky, shimmering leaves, darting swifts and a lazy fountain make Illyria very real." An extra performance at Downham, Surrey, drew an audience of three thousand. It was a triumph for Davies, for both Oxford and London reviewers singled out his performance for special comment. Half a century later Rachel Kempson would recall that he played Malvolio "with brilliance."

The assessment that mattered most to Davies was that of Tyrone Guthrie, whose productions at the Old Vic were attracting attention in London, and who had come at the invitation of his colleague Esmé Church. As Guthrie explained in 1948 in a draft of an introduction to Davies' first collection of plays, he was "rather impressed with his performance. It had gravity and wit—a combination all too rare." Guthrie "was even more impressed with his conversation at supper later the same evening. One could tell in a moment that he was a Boy from the Dominions—a Pioneer—bred of the Wide Open Spaces: fat and scant of breath, like Hamlet, he wore very thick glasses which dangled affectedly from a very thick ribbon; his voice, like that of Miss Annie Laurie, was low and sweet, with an accent impeccably metropolitan; his turn of phrase courtly, spruce, picked, elegant, urbane; his turn of mind original, sophisticated and merry. His personality had a kick like a mule; one suspected too a mule's obstinacy."

1937-38

Davies' theatre calendar was as full in his last year at Oxford as it had been during his final year at Queen's. Many opportunities opened up as a result of the warm critical reception for his Malvolio. All year, tempting possibilities came by, any of which might boost him into the London theatre. The OUDS immediately offered him the part of Lear for the following February, but he turned it down as beyond his capabilities.

Alan Hay, a student who had inherited a fortune at twenty-one, invited him to join the OUDS group he was taking to the Arts Theatre in London during July and August to present a season of three or four plays. Hay would manage the productions himself and follow the usual OUDS practice of bringing in a professional director and one or two actresses for each one. Hay was a Roman Catholic and had decided to begin with G. K. Chesterton's very Catholic play, *Magic.* This was an offer within Davies' capacity and he was soon in London playing the role of the conjuror, under the direction of Glen Byam Shaw. However, the production was not a strong one. The notices of its two-week run in July were good rather than transported (Davies drew respectable but brief comment), and its audiences were dispiritingly cold. Realizing that they were simply not good enough, the company called a halt during rehearsals of a second play (a

Norwegian drama by Helge Krog), though not before Alan Hay took a bath financially.

This fiasco led to a rebuff of another sort. Urged on by Olga Edwards, a young actress who had had a part in *Magic*, Davies wrote a play while he was in Wales that August and September. This seems to have been his second such attempt, for in a letter in August mentioning that "a young actress" wanted him "to write a play for her," he went on: "I have already tried that for another actress, but she rejected it, saying bitterly that England would only accept 'that sort of thing' from Norwegians or Russians." The current play was strongly influenced by Terence Rattigan's West End success *French Without Tears*, which Olga Edwards admired. Both are variations on a house-party—Rattigan's is set in a villa on the west coast of France where several young men have come to live and learn French, Davies' in a country house on the Shropshire side of the Welsh border where two Rhodes scholars studying at Oxford have been invited for Christmas. In both plays, three young men fall in love with the same young woman: two are obvious about it, and the third is a sardonic individual, secret and reluctant in his love. As the plays end, the woman pursues the man who does not want to yield to love.

Rattigan's play is an airy confection eminently suited to the skills of the young Rex Harrison, Trevor Howard, Jessica Tandy and Kay Hammond, who acted in its first production. Davies' play, more ambitious and less successful, was rather heavy-handed in its exploration of the motivations of the young people, in part because it became a vehicle for re-examining his relationship with Eleanor Sweezey now that Gillespie had helped him reach a clearer understanding of it. The young poet, about to depart for India, tries to extract a promise of marriage from the heroine in a scene that clarifies and expands on the one in which Davies, about to depart for Oxford, had proposed and been refused. The sardonic young man brings the heroine to heel, handling himself in a manner that Davies no doubt wished he had managed in real life. This character protects the heroine and, as her confidant, is wise and full of good advice. When he finally admits that he loves her, but has no intention of doing anything about it, *she* decides to pursue *him*.

Davies called his play "Three Gypsies" after the ballad that begins "There were three gypsies a-came to my door." It tells of a fine lady who leaves her "new-wedded lord," her "silk-finished gown" and her "goose-feather bed" for a life "in a cold, open field/Along with the wraggle-taggle gypsies, O!" In Wales, Gypsies with elaborately decorated caravans were often to be seen, each one (in Davies' recollection) with a beautiful young Gypsy woman nursing her baby on the tilt and an old hag sitting on the back, with a man and several mangy dogs walking along beside. The link between the ballad and the play appears to lie in the heroine's rejection of a wealthy marriage for a lover who may lead her a merry chase. Davies sent the play off to Esmé Church and others, and in return (as Horace Davenport reported to his mother) "got a pretty good number of razzberries from several theatrical women in London for the excellent reason that the chief female character is not entirely a sweet and wholesome lady."

Back in Oxford in September, and settled into comfortable lodgings on the second floor of Longwall House opposite Magdalen Grove, he plunged again into theatrical endeavours, with Oxford seemingly hanging on his every move. He had made a sufficient impression during his first year that comments on his dress, appearance, conversation and even his colds appeared from time to time in the student publications the *Isis* and the *Cherwell* from the autumn of 1936 onwards. In the first term of his final year he was profiled as an "Isis Idol"—the ultimate undergraduate accolade. The magazine ran lightly down the roll of his theatrical achievements, from "his first appearance on any stage at the age of four as an Israelite child in an opera called 'Queen Esther'" to his OUDS Malvolio the previous June. The opening paragraph and one sentence from the conclusion sketch the Davies that Oxford contemporaries recall:

Unless someone pretty desperate comes along, Robertson-Davies looks like being the last of the real undergraduate 'figures' in Oxford; not that there are no others who might qualify for such a title, but alas, none are backed by any of that culture or brilliance which make such figures worth noticing. Any day you may see the form of Robertson-Davies, almost Chestertonian in its greatness, proceeding with stately gait up the Broad, with a genial nod and a smile to chance acquaintances, and a deep but dignified bow for the more favoured few. If you are fortunate, this important-looking figure will halt to exchange a joke with you, and when he laughs, he will shake all over and the roar will reverberate from the Broad to the High. Dignity, however, will remain…. Yes 'presence,' that's the word that sums him up best of all, I think.

The song lyrics he wrote for Alan Hay's contribution to the OUDS annual one-act-play night that November were "neat" according to the *Isis* reviewer. With much anxious effort, he directed the Merton Dramatic Society in a good performance of Auden and Isherwood's play *The Ascent of F6* a week later. But he was so exasperated at the experience that he wrote an article for *Light and Dark*, attacking amateur actors, and Oxford amateurs in particular, for their refusal to work on technique and their failure to bring passion, intellect and imagination to their roles. Leslie French (Puck in the 1934 Regent's Park *A Midsummer Night's Dream* and director of the upcoming OUDS production of *Much Ado About Nothing* in February 1938) rushed to the defence of amateurs, and the OUDS especially, in a lively letter published in the *Isis*. In an amusing reply, Davies maintained his ground and complimented the OUDS (and by implication French) on its recent acting. The two letters may in fact have been a promotion for *Much Ado*, in which Davies played Dogberry. Reviewing the production for the *Isis*, Nevill Coghill declared his portrayal "the best and most polished performance I can remember in any O.U.D.S. production since Robert Speaight played Peer Gynt. It was a masterpiece of controlled buffoonery."

Davies had been thinking of attending the Old Vic's drama school after Oxford. Now he was suddenly presented with a new option. French was convinced the Victorian poet Swinburne was a homosexual and wanted Davies to write him a play centring on the pathos of Swinburne's rejection by a girl who didn't like him because he was short and odd-looking. French would find backing and play the lead. Davies was bucked up by this evidence of confidence in his powers and, riding a wave of enthusiasm, decided to write *ten* plays, persuading himself that playwriting could become habitual with practice. He was leery, nonetheless, of pouring too much into this particular play, given his experience with the last two efforts. He was right. French liked the outline but never gave him the go-ahead to finish it. Instead he had another suggestion for him—playing roles like Polonius with a company touring four Shakespearian plays that summer. But that too fell through.

At Fronfraith in April 1938, Davies simmered with further ideas for plays, his mind full of folklore, Gypsies and Wales. He bought and read (as a change of pace from Penguin paperbacks and ghost stories) *Zadkiel's Dream Book*—actually two books bound as one, *The Universal Dream Book* by Zadkiel and *The Popular Fortune Teller* by Sibly The Great Astrologer—and found it brimming with curious lore of charms, incantations, lucky days, dreams, nativities, fortunes (by tea leaves or coffee grounds) and much more. He was drawn to experiment with a play based on Isaac Craigfryn Hughes' romance *The Maid of Cefn Ydfa*, a kind of compendium of Welsh folk tales, at least in part because it concerns a popular young woman whose love for a bard results in disaster. Davies soon realized that he was not the person to do this justice, but he still wanted to set a drama in the beautiful Welsh border country around Fronfraith and Welshpool where his ancestors had lived for generations. Before the vacation was over, he had written two brief outlines and had made a start on the play that eventually became *A Jig for the Gypsy*.

His last appearance on an Oxford stage was as Christopher Sly in the OUDS' *Taming of the Shrew* in June 1938. As the character for whom the play is ostensibly performed, Sly has to look attentive and amused, and not to distract the audience unduly. Davies, amply supplied with drink, kept his Sly within bounds.

All these activities demanded bursts of energy; few of them required great concentration. The same might be said of the various examinations he sat that year, all of which he passed after taking the precaution of paying a shilling to touch the lucky

baby in the arms of the Gypsy woman who appeared in Oxford
at such strategic moments. His thesis, on the other hand,
required sustained attention from the moment Ridley proposed
the topic in November 1936 until early May 1938, when he submitted it to the English Board. Davies claims that he never did
any work during term at all, and one might be inclined to accept
this, given all the things that had occupied him in Oxford, were
it not that his own and Horace Davenport's letters regularly
mention his efforts on the thesis. Possibly he means that he did
not do the actual writing (as opposed to the reading and
research) during term. He did that during his 1938 Easter vacation in Wales.

The line of investigation proposed by Ridley—whether the
female parts in Shakespeare's plays had been conditioned by the
fact that they had to be played by boys—could not have been
more suited to Davies. It set him to work on a playwright whom
he had idolized from his earliest childhood. It meant looking at
the plays from both an actor's and a writer's perspective, and he
could do both. It required him to consider the needs of a stage
populated entirely by the male sex, and he had acted on such a
one at UCC. He needed to know something of boys' capacities
as actors, and also about Elizabethan music and voice training.
Not only did Davies have considerable experience of watching
his contemporaries on-stage at UCC and in professional productions such as *Peter Pan*, but he had loved the vocal music of
Shakespeare's period since he had first heard Cuthbert Kelly's
English Singers in 1927, and when Kelly performed at Balliol he
had consulted him about the training and repertoire of
Elizabethan choirboys. The thesis that emerged was lively and
singularly unacademic in style.

Once he had completed and submitted it, Davies began to
worry. Much was riding on its success. There were no diplomas
to attest to his academic capacities—no junior or senior matriculation, no Queen's B.A., no Oxford B.A. If his thesis passed
muster, he would finally have a piece of parchment to certify success in this last and most challenging tussle with the educators.
At first he worried because his thesis could only suggest what boy
actors' training must have been, not prove what it was. He feared

this might bring immediate rejection. Several weeks later, he heard that the thesis was going forward to examination, but he was in anguish about his examiners. Sir Edmund Chambers and Percy Simpson were the leading authorities on Elizabethan the-atre and the work of Ben Jonson, and Simpson was reputed to be a crabbed pedant. He was sufficiently uneasy to shave off his beard. On the morning of the big day (Thursday, June 9) he threw up three times, got himself "all dolled up like a plush horse" and proceeded timorously to the Examination School at the appointed hour, 2:30 p.m., prepared for a two-hour grilling.

As it turned out, his anxiety was unfounded. The examiners immediately made it clear that they liked his work, mentioned one or two errors of fact that needed correction, and then Chambers, settling back in his chair, reminisced about seeing Ellen Terry play Imogen when he was a young man. In a quarter of an hour the two had sent him on his way, and Davies rushed over to Horace Davenport's. Finding him out, he left a note:

Dear Horace:
    A 15 minute viva: no questions—only comments, all favourable. They advise me to publish & both said they greatly enjoyed reading it! They wished me well in my career!
    I die, I faint, I fail!

                                                                            Rob

He didn't descend to earth for two days. He cabled the good news to his parents and sent his mother a coloured print of an Oxford scholar in his robes to commemorate the event. That night he rehearsed Sly in *The Taming of the Shrew* and went to a college ball. The next day he went out on the river with friends, in the evening there was another rehearsal of the *Shrew* followed by another college ball, and after *that* a drive with Michael Benthall (fellow member of the OUDS and later director of the Old Vic), during which they drowsed off and woke up in a ditch.

On June 23 he took his B. Litt., in the same group as Horace Davenport, and was pleased to find that Oxford's leave-taking was just as rooted in tradition as its welcome. As he knelt to receive his degree, the vice-chancellor thumped the side of his head with a heavy Bible in a practice perpetuated at Oxford since the Reformation, a reminder that he "must never be neglectful of God's revealed word." Of all the many academic honours he has since received, only one has topped it in his own mind—the honorary D. Litt. Oxford conferred on him in June of 1991.

Chapter 7

THE OLD VIC: 1938-40

"I think the world of you, Maria. So let's stop this foolishness and talk to the point. Will you marry me?"

"Why should I marry you?"

"That would take a long time to answer, but I'll give you the best reason: because I think we have become very good friends, and could go on to be splendid friends, and would be very likely to be wonderful friends forever."

"Friends?"

"What's wrong with being friends?"

"When people talk about marriage, they generally use stronger words than that."

"Do they? I don't know. I've never asked anyone to marry me before."

"You mean you've never been in love?"

"Certainly I've been in love. More times than I can count. I've had two or three affairs with girls I loved. But I knew very well that they weren't friends."

"You put friendship above love?"

—*The Rebel Angels*, 1981

As HE LEFT Oxford, Davies' ambitions were confidently focused on a theatrical career. The stage was a world of order and fine conceptions, and he believed that it could offer him, too, the ennobling potential that seemed to transfigure the lives of his theatrical icons. But his immediate need was simply for financial independence. His father was generous enough, but Davies still had no access to money that he could spend without explanation. At Oxford, money matters had been somewhat easier than before, since he was allowed to draw on Rupert's London bank account at need. But there were still rasping accountings required, whether for his Oxford expenses or for what he spent on the antiques Rupert directed him to pick up at one sale or another, and for what was needed to live at Fronfraith between terms. Rupert, perusing his bank-book, would say:

"Forty-five pounds! What did you spend forty-five pounds on?"

"Well, I spent it on the occasional table you said that you wanted."

"Forty-five pounds! It seems an awful lot. You've been living very high."

This sort of thing undoubtedly affected Davies' choices in many ways. A good example was book collecting. Influenced by Rupert, he had developed an appreciation for fine papers, well-designed type and imaginative book design. He was attracted by the lovingly produced volumes from the Gregynog Press, and browsing in Blackwell's and Rota's he quickly became interested in first, rare and unusual editions. If it had just been a matter of scrimping on living expenses to buy them, his collecting could well have taken this line. But any major expenditure invited Rupert's inquiry. In any case, his particular interests in the nineteenth century, and in the odd and the eccentric, would have sent him to the barrows as well as to Blackwell's. So it was from the inexpensive, unfashionable and out-of-date that he began to build and form his collection. He bought, for instance, the early joke book *Nugae Venales, or a Complaisant Companion, Being new Jests, Domestic and foreign Bulls, Rhodomontados, Pleasant Novels,*

Lyes and Improbabilities (1686), a prized acquisition whose resources he has tapped many times since. He also began to collect first editions of the Sitwells and now possesses them all, except a few by the prolific Sacheverell. He was, of course, unsympathetic to the popular prejudice against wealth and the aristocracy, which predisposed him in the Sitwells' favour through the years when they were relatively neglected. And he admired the grace, erudition and application they brought to their writing. Since their books sold only moderately well, he could pick up their first editions for a song on the remainder tables.

In the same period he discovered the delights of leafing through playbills, the precursors of the modern theatre program. Typographically old-fashioned and surprisingly long, they invited him to play detective, tracing actors from one role to the next. The playbills were inexpensive, so he bought some, and it was for the same reason that he was able to acquire his first two nineteenth-century theatrical tinsel pictures (depictions of costumed actors embellished with bits of coloured tinsel). He coveted, but couldn't buy, the big collections of eighteenth- and nineteenth-century plays like *Bell's British Theatre* and Elizabeth Inchbald's *The British Theatre*, although they sold for modest sums like twelve or eighteen pounds a set, and later he counted himself lucky to get them for many times that amount. Over the years he has bought all the books he yearned to acquire while at Oxford.

Evidently, he needed a job. When Horace Davenport's friend Mrs. Eloise Hirt proposed to use his thesis as the basis of a program for the BBC called "The Stage's Jewels," he worked up a talk about the boy actors of the Elizabethan theatre, selected some illustrative scenes from the plays and co-directed the program with her. But although he hoped for an opening at the BBC, it did not materialize. He also took steps to get his thesis published. Ridley gave him a recommendation to J. M. Dent and Sons, and after some revisions, in January or early February of 1939, W. Robertson Davies' *Shakespeare's Boy Actors* appeared under their imprint. Just a few hundred copies were sold, but the *Times Literary Supplement* reviewed it, commending Davies for "the most useful and comprehensive survey of the subject" and singling out his chapters on the comedies and on the training of boy actors as particularly valuable—no mean achievement for a first book. Sadly, the war intervened at just this moment, bringing with it a paper shortage, and the unsold copies were pulped. As Marchbanks has it, "It appeared between the Anschluss and the outbreak of war and these trivial distractions ruined it."

Davies wrote some sketches and lyrics too, among them one on Neville Chamberlain's return from Munich, a "Paean to the P.M.," and submitted them to Norman Marshall at the Gate Theatre—but nothing came of it. Fortunately, Alan Hay had decided to take another flier on a Catholic play. This time it was Morna Stuart's dramatization of Sir Thomas More's last years, *Traitor's Gate*. Hay chose Leslie French to direct, and French hired a number of excellent actors. He invited Davies to play the Duke of Norfolk. The company went on tour, perhaps in late September, certainly by October 1938, then settled in at the Duke of York's in London on November 17. Before the London opening, however, Charles Carson took over for Davies, who was deemed to have insufficient weight and experience. He stayed on at a reduced wage, as assistant stage manager and player of off-stage music. Though the reviews were better than those of *Magic*, there was no clamour for seats, and the run ended on January 14, but not before it cost Hay and the play's backers a great deal of money.

Davies and Hay had taken a flat together (in Leith Mansions on Grantully Road, overlooking the Paddington Recreation Ground in Maida Vale) with another OUDS friend, Philip John Stead. Stead, a dry and witty Yorkshireman, was scraping a living as a cinema critic for the *New English Weekly*, writing features and occasional drama criticism for the *Times* and acting as story editor for Paramount Pictures. In their sanguine moments they dreamt that an announcement might appear one day outside the Drury Lane Theatre:

ALAN HAY presents **ROBERTSON DAVIES** in *King Lear*.
"This play will run.
Great performance by Davies"—STEAD.

But when *Traitor's Gate* closed, Hay was in a bad way. The other two carried the rent, made sketchy breakfasts, cooked sausages for late supper and shared the date pasties and other goodies that Stead's mother forwarded every week. Stead and Davies ate out as well, but Davies suspected that Hay had to survive on what came his way at the flat. The unpleasant situation gave him new insight into the hazards of theatre finance.

Stead and Davies found each other highly congenial. The tales Stead collected from the prostitutes and low-life characters at the local, "The Hero of Maida" (named after the Duke of Wellington), and his stories of his eccentric Great-uncle Bingham still lodge in Davies' memory. Among the notes for *The Lyre of Orpheus* is this one: "P. J. Stead's Uncle Bingham, Rabelaisian old ruffian—peeping into a young bride's hall closet—'No dead bairns in there!'" They loved to quote at each other from the Elizabethan and Jacobean dramas. Davies, knowing that Stead was enamoured of their next-door neighbour, would greet him with "Have you had Ford's wife yet?" (referring to *The Merry Wives of Windsor*), and Stead could make no effective riposte, since Davies was so close-mouthed about his own affairs that his friend never knew he was seeing women at all. They did make a point of handing their rent money, together, to their aged land-lady, whose rooms were crammed with curiosities from her hus-band's years in India, in order to hear her croak, with a suggestive leer, "Would you like to see my green monkey?"

On one of their long rambles through London they came upon an escapologist, struggling to free himself from his chains near Henry Irving's statue behind the National Portrait Gallery. (Davies put the incident to excellent use years later in *World of Wonders*.) On another occasion they happened upon a *Punch and Judy* show, and Davies, who had seen *Punch* only once before as a boy of twelve in Toronto, happily settled in to watch, adding his shilling to the hat as it passed. But Stead muttered darkly and lit into the puppeteer after the show for departing from tradition, astounding both him and Davies with his unex-pected knowledge. Eventually Stead wrote a book on the subject, *Mr. Punch* (1950), which Davies reviewed. Davies himself intro-duced Punch briefly into *Fortune, My Foe* in 1948, and certainly

Stead's book influenced Davies' handling of Punch's major role in his play *A Masque of Mr Punch* in 1962.

Good news now arrived from the blue. Tyrone Guthrie wrote, inviting him to join the Old Vic Company. This was the opportunity Davies had been hoping for, and he accepted promptly.

The theatre itself could hardly have been more romantic. Opened in 1818 as The Royal Coburg (Prince Leopold of Saxe-Coburg was its patron), it had started off staging sensational melodramas. Renamed The Royal Victoria in 1833 in honour of the young princess, it had been successively a "penny gaff," a music hall, a Temperance amusement hall and finally a venue for light opera and some serious acting. When Lilian Baylis took it over in 1912, she changed the focus to Shakespeare and mounted the entire Shakespearean canon between 1914 and 1922, something no one had ever attempted before her. When Davies arrived in December 1938, it was still Victorian in appearance: the nineteenth-century flies were intact, the auditorium was still charming, if shabby, in fawn and gold, and Rudolphe Cabanel's ornamented roof could still remind play-goers of the theatrical grandeur of another day.

Davies found a familiar production in rehearsal. It was a revival of the imaginatively Victorian *Midsummer Night's Dream* that he had seen when the Old Vic had first presented it at Christmas 1937, which took the building and its atmosphere (and Mendelssohn's music) as a starting point for its costumes, sets and manner. Davies, of course, already knew both play and music well from his own Kingston production in May 1935.

Ben Webster, then in his seventies, played old Egeus, while Davies was cast as Snout. During the long stretches when both were off stage, Webster would invite Davies to his dressing room and while away the hours with theatre stories. He had played Cecil Graham in the first production of *Lady Windermere's Fan* in 1892 and remembered Wilde well from rehearsals. In 1896, with his new wife May Whitty, he had accompanied Sir Henry Irving on his fifth, or perhaps sixth, tour of America. A spry old actor by the name of Henry Howe, an eighty-four-year-old whom everyone called "Evergreen," had fallen ill in Cincinnati, and Webster and Whitty had visited him in hospital every day until the company moved on to Chicago. They were amply repaid for their kindness by Howe's stories of an even earlier day in the theatre, vivid evocations of the shade of William Charles Macready, with whom he had appeared in the first production of *The Lady of Lyons* in 1838, and, equally gripping, the scene when as a boy wanting to go on the stage he had approached the great Edmund Kean in his garden at Richmond to ask advice.

"Why, cocky, you're a Quaker!" cried Kean in amazement.

But Howe said that, in spite of his upbringing, he was determined to act in Shakespeare.

"Well, cully, can you *starve*?" growled Kean, turning upon the boy with a look which pierced his very soul.

Davies, with his passion for nineteenth-century theatre, was transported. It was such a hall of mirrors he inhabited! Here he was in a grand old Victorian theatre, in a fine Victorian production of a classic play, listening to an old actor who had performed with his father's idol Henry Irving and who could show him, through all the mirrors, the way back to Macready and Kean. What more could life offer?

Overseeing, directing, animating every aspect of *A Midsummer Night's Dream*, Tyrone Guthrie was a fountain of invention. He possessed a brilliant theatrical imagination, and since he delighted in the classical repertoire he poured tremendous energy into keeping that repertoire accessible and fresh for his audiences. At thirty-eight he was already well known for effective ensemble productions, as a skilled manager of crowd scenes and as a deviser of artful stage business. Tall and commanding at six feet, five inches, he was more (and perhaps less) than human. A born leader, truly charismatic, he was clearly in touch with the forces of the unconscious, and indeed in their grip. This seemed to Davies to be the source both of Guthrie's genius and of his disasters, for he was less well endowed with the controlling faculty of judgment. Generally a pleasant and courteous man, he brooked no nonsense from his actors, and his tongue, guided by his powerful intuitions, could cut like the whip of Simon Legree.

He could be a thoughtless, even cruel tormentor, pillorying old Ben Webster for lapses of memory. In time Davies came to recognize that Guthrie's penchant for anticlimax, the zany and the savage, as well as his unease with the softer emotions, were signal shortcomings.

Davies got to see more of Guthrie than most other junior members of the company because his position combined the roles of actor, student, dramaturge and teacher. He was given modest speaking parts and, like the students in the Old Vic's drama school, understudied larger roles and attended performances and rehearsals whenever he was free of other duties. The apprenticeship was enough in itself to keep him fully occupied. The company was always performing one play and rehearsing the next. That winter and spring, Davies played Stingo in *She Stoops to Conquer*, understudied Mr. Hardcastle, and was so bowled over by the script that he learned the whole play by heart. In *An Enemy of the People* he had a tiny part in a crowd scene and understudied Dr. Stockmann. In *The Taming of the Shrew*, Guthrie gave him four minor roles: a zany, Curtis, the Pedant and the Widow (and at a couple of matinées he went on as Christopher Sly, his understudy role). Davies made a tall and conspicuous figure, at his six very solid feet, and by the time he appeared in his third change of costume, the audience had recognized him and began to laugh. When he returned as the Widow they guffawed—just as Guthrie had anticipated. But the Widow was Guthrie's private joke, too, for it amused him to see Davies, who had thought long and hard about men and boys in Shakespearean female roles, trying to put his ideas into practice.

Davies also did dramaturgical work for Guthrie, cutting the texts, smoothing the transitions and digging up whatever historical material might be needed, as it was for the *commedia dell'arte Taming of the Shrew*. In addition, he taught in the drama school. Here is how a Swedish student described him and his lectures in a letter to her mother in January 1939:

> Every Friday we hear extremely interesting lectures by one
> of the actors. By the way, a wonderfully nice man, whom I
> have been going out with now and then. He speaks about

Tradition in the Theatre. Started with Greece and Rome, then the Middle Ages. First in Italy and then in Spain. Next Friday will be about the Renaissance in France. He is a funny man. They say he was a huge success at Oxford. He is unbelievably learned and funny and correct; glasses, a bit round shouldered with butterfly instead of tie, with a broad-brimmed light-coloured hat. Do you recognize the type, mother? He is the first human being I have been going out with, who calls me Miss Rydbeck and not Birgitta.

Davies took lessons once a week from Bertie Scott, a brilliant voice and singing teacher whom Tyrone Guthrie had brought from Belfast. His expertise was of the physical kind, a skill of the sort that (like acting or musical performance) is handed down from one generation of practitioners to the next. He often referred to his own teachers—the Welsh baritone David ffrang-con-Davies and Irish bass Harry Plunket Greene—quoting Greene's assertion that "all a singer needed was two teeth and a sigh." He was quotable himself: he could "spit y'up a cupful o'phlegm any morning in the week." He earnestly advised his students to "breathe the muhd," to assume their characters so deeply that their very breathing would reflect the effects of emotion, age and class. A little stumpy man, a chain-smoker of Craven A's, in appearance Bertie perfectly personified the stage Irishman of the English music hall. He was bald and fifty-seven, and his roving eye was well known to his wife, who told Tyrone Guthrie, "He can't resist a good pupil," and kept an eye on him over the transom. Indeed Bertie Scott was irresistible, and Davies let him flower spectacularly as Murtagh Molloy in *A Mixture of Frailties*.

Working at the Old Vic meant long hours and appalling conditions, gulping ghastly food on the run. But it was exactly what Davies wanted. He found it exhilarating, and he was not too busy to enjoy a new romance. Birgitta Rydbeck, the nineteen-year-old Swedish drama student who described his lectures to her mother, was blonde, beautiful, always elegantly dressed. He still remembers her arriving at the theatre for a performance of *A Midsummer Night's Dream* one wintry night. In her fur coat, hood and muff touched with snow, her face flushed from the cold, she appeared to him as a snow princess—and not only to him. Catching a glimpse of her, one of the leading actors exclaimed, "My God, I think that's the most beautiful thing I've ever seen in my life!"

Birgitta was not just marvellous to look at, she was fun to be with, and in the early months of 1939 Davies often took her out to the theatre and for a snack afterward, willingly putting up with her tendency to order the most expensive items on the menu. She was quite oblivious to the fact that he was struggling to survive on a meagre Old Vic salary. When she was ill in March he sent her a bucket of daffodils with a brief funny letter and later a copy of *Shakespeare's Boy Actors* with the note: "This is not a book which I could possibly recommend as reading for one who is ill—However, the cover is a very pretty colour, and you may find the book useful for holding doors open, throwing at cats, and other similar purposes. WRD." By April (and probably earlier) he was light-heartedly in love and enjoying the sensation, at least in part because she represented romance rather than reality. How could he propose marriage to a girl so obviously accustomed to wealth when he was earning so little? Aware that he was "in love" with her, Birgitta noted in her diary that "we have made an agreement that both of us will behave as if he were not."

Birgitta's diary and letters in 1939 reveal that she too very much enjoyed their dates. She thought him "*wonderful*," appreciated his help with her work and noted that he was "unbelievably entertaining, intelligent and perfect in every way." On the other hand, in appearance he was far from her "fairy-prince." She knew she was not in love, and she was a bit uncomfortable about the amount of time they spent together, in part because of the other students' attitude toward the relationship. As a Swede, she was already different from the others, and she won herself no popularity by spending time with one of the teachers. When he urged her to work harder on her faulty English, she began to think of him as "a sort of symbol for all my five elder brothers at home." Reflecting in maturity on the person she knew in 1939, she said:

> I think Rob was very vain—about his looks. He used to talk about his feet—proudly—about his high arched insteps. Which made me giggle. That hurt him. He wore his hair longer than anyone else. He had thick glasses. He was rather on the fat side. He liked to move his body with grace. Was quite particular about his clothes. I think he was very shy. People who seem—and are—extremely self-confident, very often have one side to their personality which is filled with shyness. Perhaps because they want to find themselves perfect in every way. And nobody is.
>
> I think Rob had a very high opinion about himself. About his brains, his learning. About girls, sex and so on I think he was very shy. But how am I to tell? I was quite strictly brought up and shockingly innocent and immature. I fell in love about every three weeks in different persons. Most of them were of course ignorant about the fact.

Davies did not spend all his leisure on Birgitta. He also saw a good deal of Brenda Newbold, who had come from Australia in 1936 at nineteen to attend the drama school. She had done such a fine job "holding the book" and prompting for Guthrie's *Henry V* (with Laurence Olivier in the lead) that the stage manager had asked her to stay on as his assistant in 1937. When her boss went on tour in the early months of 1939, she became the Old Vic's first woman stage manager. Her duties included compiling information for programs, co-ordinating times and places for costume fittings, finding props, letting everyone know about shifts in rehearsal time, organizing changes of scene, having the actors called as they were needed on stage, recording all the details of the production, doing anything the director wanted and generally ensuring that everything ran smoothly in performance. She also acted small roles.

Brenda had been introduced to Davies in Oxford when she went up to see the OUDS *Shrew*, and he arrived at the Old Vic just when she was about to take over as stage manager. She was young for this responsibility, and (she recalls) unnecessarily "formal" and "pushy" with the actors and backstage people. When Davies once failed to materialize for a rehearsal she gave him a scolding, then learned that he hadn't been told about it. She was so officious in ascertaining whether to spell Davies' name with or without a hyphen that another actor commented: "It's tuppence to speak to Brenda!" But her initial stiffness passed quickly. When Guthrie directed her to raise the curtain for *A Midsummer Night's Dream* at a particular point in the overture, she knew she wouldn't be sufficiently musical to recognize it and approached Davies, whom she had overheard discussing music knowledgeably with Guthrie. He was happy to help out, and before every performance he would come to her corner and count the forty-eight bars for her.

They quickly became good friends. Her charm, zip and style appealed to him, and she had three additional qualities that were rare in women of his experience—punctuality, sensitivity to his pocketbook and a ready sense of humour. She never left him languishing on the street-corner wondering whether she would turn up. She insisted on footing the bill every other time that they went out together, well knowing the limits of an Old Vic starting salary. And, wonder of wonders, not only did she tell good jokes, she was alert and responsive to his own sallies. Davies never felt with her that tossing out a joke was like "throwing a stone into a pool of tar...a kind of gradual subsidence but no resonance at all." Nor was she overawed by him. If she saw things differently than he, she said so. He was struck by something she said not long after they met, and asked: "Oh, where did you read that?" She hooted with laughter and declared: "You don't believe *anything* unless you've read it!" Like him, she had had an earlier disastrous love affair, and the common experience created a bond between them. Although she was evidently competent and practical, she aroused his protective instincts nonetheless. When she proposed that he should take a "lonely" student to the Vic-Wells Ball in March, it being well known to everyone but Brenda that the girl in question virtually sold her services for money, he was convinced that she knew nothing about people and needed someone to watch out for her. (The

William Robertson, Davies' great-grandfather, for whom he was named.

Elizabeth Marchbank Robertson, William's wife and the source of Samuel Marchbanks' surname.

Samuel Davies, Davies' great-grandfather, from whom Samuel Marchbanks got his given name.

Marv Ann Evans the Angel, Samuel Davies' second wife.

E.G. Whitehead

Jemima Robertson, Davies' great-aunt.

J.H. Anderson

Walter and Jessie Davies, Davies' grandparents, in 1888. Rupert and Percy at the back, Elsie in the middle, Robertson on his father's knee, Mary on her mother's.

Dixon

Rupert Davies, Davies' father, as a young man in about 1900.

Swithin King

Florence McKay, Davies' mother, in 1898.

The house in Thamesville where Davies was born.

Davies at the age of one.

The *Thamesville Herald* office. Rupert Davies at the platen press at the back, Fred at the stone in the middle, Arthur reading a paper at the front.

Frederick William Lyonde and His Sons

Fred, Florence, Arthur, Robertson, and Rupert Davies in 1926, in Kingston.

Davies (centre) as the Rt. Hon. Sir Joseph Porter, K.C.B. with the other principals in the UCC production of *H.M.S. Pinafore* in 1930.

Davies, aged eighteen, in 1932.

Eleanor Sweezey at eighteen, in 1934, soon after she met Davies.

Van Dyck Studios

Fronfraith Hall.

ROBERTSON
DAVIES
(STAGE
MANAGER)

Davies as stage manager of the OUDS *Macbeth* in February 1937.

Davies, at twenty-two, stage-managing the OUDS production
of *Richard II* in February 1936.

Davies as the *Isis* Idol for November 17, 1937.

Davies in 1938 or 1939.

Davies as Dogberry in the OUDS production
of *Much Ado About Nothing*, February 1938.

Brenda and Robertson Davies, after their marriage
at Chelsea Old Church, February 2, 1940.

Brenda, Rosamond, Jennifer, and Miranda Davies in 1947.

Christian Lund, National Film Board

Detail of final tableau of the Coventry Nativity Play. Mary (Elizabeth Mitchell) is before the altar with the child in her arms. At her right is the Angel Gabriel (Clifford Trollope) and at her left Joseph, the Carpenter (Arthur Green).

costume ball was a fascination in itself: he could watch people like the cripple who came as Nijinsky in *L'après-midi d'un faun* exposing their innermost desires through their choice of disguise. The ball showed up years later in one of the scenes of *A Mixture of Frailties*.)

Like Davies, Brenda had decided young that she wanted a life in the theatre, and for much the same reason. There had been difficult and painful passages in her childhood, and the theatre seemed to promise a finer, more splendid world. At twelve in Melbourne, she'd seen a play performed by students of Clyde, Australia's leading girls' boarding school, and become "passionately keen to act." She attended Clyde for four years (1931-35), and, like Davies at UCC, played leading roles in the school theatricals. For a year after she left school she acted with Little Theatre groups, as Davies had at Queen's, and then spent a brief time with the professional Gregan McMahon Players. Her mother, who had always wished that she herself had had a chance to act, was sympathetic to a theatrical career, so in 1936 arrangements were made for her to make the eight-week voyage to London to audition with Lilian Baylis for a place at the Old Vic's drama school.

While Davies was exploring London's theatrical resources from his Oxford base, Brenda engaged herself in the same pursuit. This was a remarkable period in the London theatre, when you could watch actors like Laurence Olivier, John Gielgud, Ralph Richardson, Michael Redgrave, Athene Seyler, Peggy Ashcroft, Edith Evans, Margaret Rutherford, Alec Guinness and Vivien Leigh. When he and Brenda got together, they found it as interesting to explore the reasons why plays missed the mark as to celebrate the productions where everything trembled into a balance that took their breath away. In that winter and spring of 1938-39, after going to the theatre together (frequently the Sadler's Wells ballet, where they could get complimentary tickets), they often enjoyed their post-mortems as much as the performances themselves.

Their relationship was not at all confined to the theatre. After a long day they both welcomed exercise and fresh air, and Davies soon began to walk Brenda home. She lived in a flat at 40 Tite

Street with her mother and sister, who had come out from Australia that September. (Davies would lodge Giles Revelstoke in this flat in *A Mixture of Frailties*.) Although they usually arrived late, Mrs. Newbold would often invite Davies in for delectable food, and he would compliment her on "the only drinkable coffee in London." There, in addition to the hospitable and witty Mrs. Newbold, he got to know Brenda's sister Maisie and Maisie's fiancé, the Australian painter Peter Purves-Smith. Soon he was included in Sunday picnic jaunts in Pete's car.

Once acquainted, he and Pete set out together to amuse the girls. Pete would draw caricatures of Davies, and Davies would respond in derisive verse. In one pastel, Pete sketched Davies on a wooden chair, in a blue shirt, three-button jacket, flowing purple tie and handkerchief. It was a study in circles—heavy black goggle specs, globe-like head capped by dark hair, arms curving around an ample body to folded hands. Davies replied with "Admonitory Lines to Pete":

> You, Peter, with an artisan's rascality,
> Paint what you see, and call your daub Reality.
>   Shunning the artist's noble task of seeing,
>   Stripped of its outer guise, the Essential Being.
> The hang of my hair, the myopic twist of my head,
> The Quietist fold of the hands and the curves of my Torso
> Tentatively scribbed in inferior green and red
> Are tolerably what I seem, or a little bit more so;
>   But this Baroque exterior conceals
>   More than mere trumpery Talent ever reveals;
> Pencil can never capture and control
> The Perpendicularities of my Gothick Soul.

This sort of thing delighted Brenda, who had suffered through the miseries of dyslexia in her early years at school, and for whom writing and spelling were never easy.

When the Old Vic recessed at the beginning of May 1939, Davies had made no decisions in any area of his life. He enjoyed the company of Brenda, but he liked taking Birgitta out too. In May and June, Brenda was away in France with her family, and

he wrote to keep her up to date on his activities. Between May
and August, when Birgitta was home in Sweden, he wrote her too,
letters that she describes as "very personal" and "revealing." Years
later she reread them and decided not to throw them out, because
they were "so beautifully written and they touched my heart."

During this period he had slowly come to realize that acting
was not his *métier*. At a party, the critic Lionel Hale demanded:
"What the hell are you doing on the stage? You ought to be writing, and if you don't get off the stage I am going to put you off,
and I can do it." Davies was hardly encouraged by Guthrie's
observation: "Oh, I don't think you're as bad as Lionel suggests.
If you keep on you might develop quite a nice little career playing grotesques." But Hale's pronouncement was not as crushing
as it might have been, since Davies had by now shifted his long-
term ambition from acting in plays to writing them. Guthrie
suggested, however, that he might have a future in directing, and
with that in mind gave him a contract to come back for the
1939-40 season to act, teach, do dramaturgical work and start
learning to direct.

In May and June he returned to Canada to visit his family. His
father, now president of the Canadian Press, was preparing to
visit the European correspondents of the Associated Press to
strengthen the CP's sources of information in the coming conflict. In Kingston, Davies gathered fresh material for his theatre
history lectures and began to lay the groundwork for a tour of
Canada by the Old Vic Company that Guthrie wanted to promote. Once back in England, Davies wrote to Vincent Massey,
still Canada's high commissioner, on July 2:

> For some months past I have been wondering what sort
> of National Service I should offer myself for in the event of
> war. A close study of the Government Handbook on the
> subject has not been very helpful, and in any case, as a
> Canadian I should prefer to do something which would be
> of help to Canada if the need should arise.
>
> At present I am working as an actor at the Old Vic, and
> as a teacher in the Dramatic School there, and also in pro-
> paganda and lecturing work connected with that theatre.

This keeps me busy every week-day from 10:30 a.m. to 11.30 p.m. and often on Sundays, so that I really cannot find a minute for any other sort of training or work; in the case of war, however, I should like to be quite clear about what I am to do, as seriously defective eyesight closes the usual sorts of military service to me. As you know, my training has been entirely academic and literary, and I thought that this sort of skill might allow me to make myself useful in some capacity.

I am sorry to trouble you in this matter, but as I am resi-dent in England and yet not English there seems to be no place where I fit in. If you can give me any advice in this matter I should be deeply grateful as at the moment I do not know quite what I should do. If you should want to get in touch with me a letter to the Old Vic, Waterloo Road, S.E.1 will always reach me. I am

Yours most sincerely
Robertson Davies

Massey, who knew Davies' father politically and was acquainted with Davies himself as a contemporary of his sons Lionel and Hart at UCC and at Balliol, replied that he would get in touch if the need arose.

Davies therefore settled into furnished premises (soon named "Hell Hall") at 19 Ovington Mews, Knightsbridge, not too far from Tite Street, which he occupied off and on for the next seven months. With the rest of the troupe, he got on with prepa-rations for the Buxton Festival in Derbyshire. For four weeks, beginning August 28, they were to play *Romeo and Juliet* (Davies as Old Montague), Norman Ginsbury's *Viceroy Sarah* (Davies understudying Prince George of Denmark), Shaw's *The Devil's Disciple* (Davies as Uncle William and understudy for Anthony Anderson) and Goldsmith's *The Good-Natur'd Man* (Davies as Mr. Honeywood's footman). For the Goldsmith play, he created a forty-two-line prologue in heroic couplets, using images and ideas that might have occurred to the eighteenth-century play-wright. In performance, the prologue was presented without ref-erence to Davies' authorship, and no one questioned it.

While the company was still rehearsing in London, Davies, Brenda and Maisie spent a weekend at Fronfraith visiting places and people. The Welsh singer Dora Herbert-Jones, learning of Maisie's interest in art, showed them the extraordinary collection of Monets that Davies had himself first seen in 1934 (it subsequently went to the National Gallery). In the same period, he went to a fête on Hampstead Heath with Birgitta and another girl, where an astute fortune-teller told him that he would soon be married, but not to either of his companions of that day.

War's imminence now forced decisions on them all. The company had hardly reached Buxton when Birgitta's parents summoned her home. Two other students hastily married so that the girl, a German, would have British citizenship. Only three of the four plays had opened when Chamberlain announced on September 3 that the country was at war. The actress Sonia Dresdel promptly threw her arms around Davies, saying, "Tell me it isn't true, Rob. Tell me it isn't true. There isn't going to be a war, is there?" as if he could somehow change the course of history. Planes passing over that night—British, it was later learned—fuelled fears of disaster and bombings. On Monday, September 4, theatres, music-halls, cinemas and places of entertainment were closed throughout the country because of "the danger involved in the assembly of large numbers of persons in places where it is not feasible to provide adequate protection against the effects of bombs." The students and junior members of the company, Davies among them, were set to filling sandbags and heaping them around Buxton Hospital—part of a curious effort to make public buildings "less vulnerable in air attack"— and the Actors' Equity Association compiled an emergency register of its members, listing whatever non-acting skills they possessed.

By this time Davies had been sufficiently exposed to the theatrical realities to have abandoned rosy visions. He now knew about the agonizing gaps between jobs, the boredom of bit-actors in long-run successes, the struggle to educate children or support aged parents on intermittent pay. And in this new crisis, he discovered that the clown Frederick Bennett had once held a key position in a bank, matinée idol Stewart Granger had been a doctor, someone else was a trained nurse. Evidently the theatre was a siren that had lured many to a life of insecurity. Respecting the sacrifice that so many theatre people had made, he began to question his own ability and fitness for it.

The company's already slim salaries were now cut to the bone, with the result that those at the lower end of the scale could no longer afford both a bedroom and a sitting room. Marie Ney, one of the leads, offered her own sitting room as a place where some of the juniors could eat their meals, and Davies and Brenda (with Maisie, who had been sent to them by Mrs. Newbold to escape the anticipated bombings) were among those she took under her wing. Unfortunately, the Good Samaritan was also a good vegetarian, and Davies, not of her persuasion, observed of the boiled potato:

> when you put some salt and pepper on it, you've done everything you can do for that potato. And by the time you'd eaten two of them you were wondering if really the Germans shouldn't come and end all this right away.... Another member of the group who was living under Miss Ney's benign direction was Max Adrian, who was an extremely fine actor, and a great comic. He used to tease her.... "Now, Marie dear, are you perfectly sure that you haven't got a nice little steak waiting for you in your bedroom when we finish these awful potatoes. I can't stand this any more, Dear. I'm going to go out and get a piece of meat...." She kept assuring him what valuable salts lay in the potato. The rest of us who couldn't afford to go out like Max and have decent meals took to buying big blocks of chocolate and little half bottles of brandy and consuming them in our bedrooms. And you know, that is an awful diet....

On the fourth or fifth of September the future looked black and hopeless. Davies and Brenda went for a walk in Buxton's Municipal Gardens. The war probably meant that they would have to return to Canada and Australia before they were ready. Davies was still exploring his theatrical options, and Brenda knew that she, too, would need more experience if she were to fulfil her dream of founding a theatre in Australia. She was beginning to suspect that she would never get that experience, since only men could become stage directors in England. But going home to Australia without credentials represented failure. As they talked, the two of them found that they had become more than just good friends. It became clear that for both of them, separation was an unacceptable prospect. Before they left the Gardens that day, they had decided to become engaged.

For Brenda, of course, marriage and a life in Canada meant a major uprooting. There would be virtually no professional theatre opportunities there. But she believed it would give her a richer, more interesting life than the alternative that lay before her. Davies, for his part, felt that they were on solid ground in committing themselves to a lifelong partnership: they knew each other well and were not blinded by romance. He was mindful of his earlier experience in coming to the view that friendship was a necessary basis for marriage. It seems unlikely that Arthur Cornish's proposal to Maria Theotoky in *The Rebel Angels*, which stands at the head of this chapter, duplicates the one in the gardens in Buxton, but it certainly expresses Davies' enduring convictions about love, marriage and friendship. Like Arthur, he believes that "…marriage with anyone whom I do not think the most splendid friend I've ever had doesn't interest me. Love and sex are very fine but they won't last. Friendship—the kind of friendship I am talking about—is charity and loving-kindness more than it's sex and it lasts as long as life. What's more, it grows, and sex dwindles: has to." Decades later, when Davies wrote in his travel diary on May 30, 1984—"B. gets me in order & on my way like the dear & loving *friend* she is"—he was paying his life's companion the greatest of compliments.

As luck would have it, Rupert was in Wales at that moment. He had made the crossing from Calais to Dover on August 31, having finished his tour of Associated Press correspondents on the Continent. Since he was unable to get passage to Canada for three weeks, he had settled in at Fronfraith. It was not easy for Davies and Brenda to find even a day to visit him, since the theatre in Buxton reopened (like the other provincial theatres) on

September 9. But finally they left after a performance a few days later and made their way through the black-out to Wales. Brenda drove Pete's car with the headlights off, and Davies clambered out to read the signposts, both of them half expecting bombs to fall at any moment. Little more than an introduction was accomplished by the initial encounter with Rupert, however. He had strong reservations about Australians. He had also hoped that his son might make a brilliant marriage, possibly to a daughter of one of the local gentry, and he greeted Brenda, later his favourite daughter-in-law, with reserve.

The engagement ring Davies bought for Brenda was a Tassie. Eighteenth-century jeweller James Tassie had, by a technique now lost, invented a special glass that could be tinted to resemble various gems, with which he created both intaglios and cameos, many of them replicas of ancient and famous stones. Like Giles Revelstoke's Tassie ring in *A Mixture of Frailties*, Brenda's was an intaglio. Its fine workmanship pleased them both. Already interested in the history of costume, Brenda found her curiosity aroused by the ring, and gradually, over the years, she has become a knowledgeable collector, particularly of intaglios and cameos. As an Australian, she has a special affection for opals.

Brenda brought into the relationship with Davies her own and her family's stories. Although they did not strike as deeply into his imagination as his own, they nonetheless had the psychological power that often accompanies tales of people bound to each other for good or ill, and they were important to Brenda. Later he went to see the places where she and her family had lived and was as curious as she when some new bit of information about her people came to light. Her ancestral tales have had their own impact on his life and writing.

Her family story begins with her Scottish great-great-grandfather, Peter Peterson. From the tombstone of Peterson's first wife in the graveyard at Walls in the Shetland Islands, Brenda and Davies learned that he had been the minister of a Congregational church, which, when they visited it, proved to be very plain and humble. In the mid-1800s Peter Peterson's five sons left the manse and travelled to the corners of the earth. One, who reached Bombay, became a professor of Sanskrit. Another, William Peterson, Brenda's great-grandfather, sought his fortune on the Australian goldfields, fetching up at Forest Creek in Victoria in 1852. Brenda's grandmother on her deathbed claimed that William was the illegitimate son of the laird. Presumably that was why William had called his house in Australia "Melbe," after Melby House, the laird's home. But Davies found himself sceptical of "this ancient scandal, so long dead & so late & so dimly heard." He was inclined to accept the opinion of Brenda's Aunt Elsa that the tale was "just sheer invention to provide a little class to the family which otherwise had none." Leaving the islands after a visit in 1963, he reflected "how glad one is that one's stock was from clean, decent, wind-swept places, & not from the slums of Naples or Cracow. The strong strains which unite in our children are country strains, with the physique—& alas the Calvinist strenuosity—that such an inheritance brings."

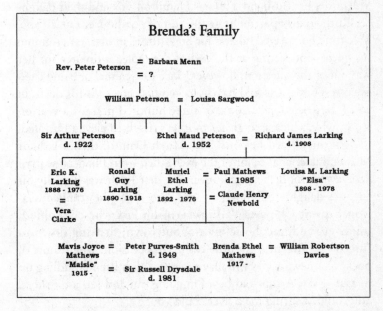

Brenda's Family

Rev. Peter Peterson = Barbara Menn
= ?

William Peterson = Louisa Sargwood

Sir Arthur Peterson
d. 1922

Ethel Maud Peterson = Richard James Larking
d. 1952   d. 1908

Eric K. Larking 1888 - 1976 = Vera Clarke

Ronald Guy Larking 1890 - 1918

Muriel Ethel Larking 1892 - 1976 = Paul Mathews d. 1985 = Claude Henry Newbold

Louisa M. Larking "Elsa" 1898 - 1978

Mavis Joyce Mathews "Maisie" 1915 - = Peter Purves-Smith d. 1949 = Sir Russell Drysdale d. 1981

Brenda Ethel Mathews 1917 - = William Robertson Davies

In Australia, William, who reputedly slept with a Bible and a Shakespeare under his pillow, found gold, but his partner made off with it. Fortunately, he realized that supplying food to the mining camps was a surer thing than prospecting, and he founded the concern that eventually became Messrs Wm. Peterson and Co. in Melbourne. When he had prospered sufficiently in the import and export trade, he built "Melbe" on Balaclava Road, East St. Kilda, Melbourne. William also came to be part owner of the Dillalah station in Warrego district, Queensland, and of two other huge tracts of grazing land in New South Wales, on one of which the great silver mine at Broken Hill was found after it had passed out of his hands. He married Louisa Sargood, whose brother owned "Rippon Lea," the great Victorian house now preserved with its gardens as a showplace and park in Melbourne.

William's son Arthur, Brenda's great-uncle, became a judge of the High Court in England and was knighted. Often, when in London, Davies and Brenda stroll past the house at 39 Cheyne Walk where Sir Arthur lived in the early 1900s. Occupying the lower floors himself as a bachelor, he supported his mistress Valentine, her husband Thomas Hamilton Fox and their daughter Ruth in an apartment at the top of the house. For a time, Valentine Fox played hostess for Sir Arthur's parties, entertaining his guests and sitting at the end of the table. A divorce for her was out of the question, however, since the scandal of being cited as co-respondent would have wrecked his career. At his death in 1922, he settled an income of three hundred pounds a year on Ruth, which increased at her mother's death to eleven hundred. (The money freed her husband, Hugh Dalton, then a Labour M.P. and later chancellor of the exchequer, from financial worry.) To Davies' mind the implication was that Ruth was actually Sir Arthur's daughter. He loves to speculate about the strained relationships at Cheyne Walk, imagining Fox, the cuckolded, impoverished, alcoholic man-about-town, drifting down to "touch" Sir Arthur for a little cash. On occasion, when short of pocket money, Davies will play the scene with Brenda, sidling up to ask: "I say, Arthur old boy, I'm going out and I'm a bit short. You couldn't spring me a fiver could you?"

William's daughter Ethel Maud married Richard Larking, a junior in his firm. Larking was a German-educated Englishman who added to the family fortunes so handsomely that, after his death in 1908, his widow, his four children and his grandchildren were able to live in considerable style for some seventy years. Larking was the great figure in the life of his third child, Muriel Ethel, Brenda's mother, although he died when she was only sixteen. For her he created "Sun Pictures," a book of hand-written poems, decorated with little water-colour drawings. An enthusiastic amateur photographer, he took many pictures of his "Mimi" in which she looks every inch a rich man's pampered daughter. In one photograph he appears himself with camera and tripod, wearing knickerbockers and a fore-and-aft cap. (The book and photographs came into Brenda's possession at her mother's death in 1978, just in time to inspire one side of the portrait of the Senator in *What's Bred in the Bone*. The name of his house, "St. Kilda," recalls the address of "Melbe".)

Ethel Maud thought of herself as belonging to Australia's upper crust. It was inconceivable to her that her children or her grand-children should be educated anywhere but the private schools where they would meet the right people. She was a pillar of the Anglican Church who occupied herself by making calls in her carriage and, when at home, by making fine lace. If Muriel wanted to do something useful with her life like nursing: "No daughter of mine will ever...." If Brenda wanted to act: "No granddaughter of mine will ever...." After Larking died she took the children to Europe. Eric took engineering in Manchester, Ronald studied at Cambridge and Muriel spent a year in each of France and Germany, learning the languages and a little Cordon Bleu cooking.

Just before the First World War, Muriel married Paul Mathews, a friend of Ronald's at Cambridge who had taken a first-class degree in mathematics. With Tolstoy, he believed in getting back to the land and decided that apple orcharding in the depths of Tasmania was the life for him and Muriel. He established his unskilled, pampered wife in a tiny cottage that had most recently been inhabited by sheep, and there they had two children in quick succession, Maisie on September 1, 1915, and Brenda on January 17, 1917. This was not the life for which Muriel had been prepared, but she stuck it out until 1920 when, her health shaken, she retreated to her mother's great Victorian house "Woorigoleen," in Toorak. A few years later they all moved to the large modern house at 234 Orrong Road in Melbourne, which was Brenda's and Maisie's home for the rest of their childhood and adolescence. It was a house of women—Mrs. Larking, Muriel, Maisie, Brenda and, infrequently, Muriel's younger sister Elsa visiting from England.

Muriel tried to obliterate the memory of her marriage, which officially ended in divorce in 1924. She tore up her photographs of Mathews and cut him out of pictures of them both. Her daughters heard it her way and came to regard their father as a menacing figure. Brenda understood little of her father's side of the story until 1958, when, at Davies' urging, they and one of their children met him and his wife over a hotel lunch in Manchester, England. The visit was a powerful lesson in point of view. The frighteningly shadowy figure of Brenda's childhood produced photographs of his own parents and of himself with his original young family. The man who had placed her mother in the intolerably primitive setting, who had played the piano while she had tried to cope, now appeared to be a passionate man who had needed a "warmth & flow of emotion" that Muriel had been incapable of giving. He spoke kindly of Brenda's mother and grandmother. By this time in his sixties, he was "a tall, heavy man, with a huge head & a mass of bushy iron-grey hair: looks like a musician." He had remarried and become an electrical engineer and a special lecturer to postgraduate students at the University of Manchester. To Davies' mind this was "a psychological adventure to be cherished." It has been a continuing adventure, for Davies and Brenda saw Paul Mathews at intervals after that until his death in 1985 and they have kept in touch with his children.

In 1925, Muriel married again, just as disastrously as before. Claude Henry Newbold had enlisted in the air force at eighteen or nineteen, flew many missions, became shell-shocked, and after the war succumbed to alcoholism. According to Elsa, whom he had been seeing, Muriel set her sights on him just to prove that she still had it in her. She appears to have misjudged her powers, imagining, erroneously, that she could save him from drink. The marriage was difficult for everyone. Maisie and Brenda felt assaulted when their boarding school announced one day that they would henceforth be called Maisie and Brenda Newbold. To confuse matters, their legal surname remained Mathews. Newbold, a drunk and a nuisance, made Brenda's adolescence miserable until she was sixteen, when he and her mother parted. (Davies suspects that marriage to Muriel was no easier for him than it had been for Mathews.) But Brenda coped with him, and the experience stiffened her backbone.

Elsa, Muriel's sister and Brenda's aunt, studied at the Slade School in London, became a painter and settled in St. Ives. In 1936, she arranged to come home to Australia in order to accompany Brenda to London. It was she who made Davies a gift of the cane that had belonged to her brother Ronald. Noting its arrival in his travel diary for December 28, 1969, Davies described it as "Malacca, with ivory head of a monkey; press a button & its tongue sticks out. V. Edwardian, & v. Ronnie." On January 1, 1970, came a second, rueful entry: "Elsa's monkey stick has given up the ghost: has not been excessively or roughly used: just won't do its trick any more: some inner spring broken. So I take it to Smith's in New Oxford St. & they will not touch it—no workmen who understand such work. So to Swayne & Adeney, from whence it came so long ago: same story. They lament the passing of such artificers, but there it is.—" But there it did not remain, for when a cane like this is broken in *World of Wonders*, art improves on life. In the novel, the man who was born Paul Dempster patiently figures out what is wrong and rights it, to the delight of its owner and the little girl who broke it. Brenda's aunt also influenced Davies' writing in another way. His visits to her in St. Ives during the 1960s and '70s gave him the understanding of a painter's view of Cornwall that he used in *What's Bred in the Bone*.

Davies did not visit Australia until 1968. Until then the land where William made his fortune, where Richard Larking indulged his beloved Mimi, where Muriel Mathews cleaned up the sheep droppings, where Brenda had coped with her drunken stepfather and where she was schooled had seemed to him to be "a play of extraordinary interest but with only the vaguest scenery." When he finally took a month and a half to tour the country with her in 1968, they visited Brenda's sister Maisie and her second husband, painter Russell Drysdale, at their beautiful home "Bouddi Farm," and stayed for a time with Brenda's mother at 20 Grange Road, Toorak, Melbourne. So stirred was he by at last seeing for himself the surroundings in which Brenda had led her early life that he found himself dreaming about people who had figured largely in Brenda's childhood. At every step he was conscious that this was "v. much B's occasion as the memories are all hers." But the trip placed a setting for her memories on the stage of his own mind. Now he could "see" Melbourne and the surrounding state of Victoria, for instance, as England with an occasional "palm-tree, or some wild burst of strange & beautiful bloom" and with magpies, kookaburras, and everywhere the "ghostly-grey shapes" of gum-trees "with hair tossed as if by fright." But, compelling though it all was, and glad though he was to have seen it, he went only once. Australia is an alien land, a strange, separate place, one that does not spark his imagination.

When it became clear in September 1939 that the West End theatres would remain dark for some time, Guthrie quickly cobbled together a tour for the Old Vic Company. They played the Opera House in Manchester, the Streatham Hill Theatre in Streatham (*Saint Joan* opened here with Davies playing the Archbishop of Rheims, and *Viceroy Sarah* was dropped), the Prince of Wales Theatre in Birmingham, the Grand in Leeds, the Golders Green Hippodrome and, finally, the Prince of Wales in Cardiff. Because Guthrie and Esmé Church were both called away for long periods, Davies and Brenda carried a good deal of extra responsibility. The pressure drew them together. Brenda displayed a practical kindliness that future friends would find characteristic. She found fruit and vegetables for her friend Basil Coleman to give some variety to his desperately limited vegetarian diet. And she made sure that Davies, whose night vision is poor, got back to his lodgings in the black-out every evening.

Shortly before Christmas, the troupe disbanded in Cardiff. Though many of London's theatres were active again, the Old Vic did not reopen until the following September. With hundreds of actors still out of work, there was little hope of a job for Davies. It was time to return to Canada.

Davies and Brenda immediately began to organize their wedding. The parson of Davies' parish turned out to be a gloomy sort, so they decided to be married in Chelsea Old Church since many actors had been married and buried there. They established residence by depositing a suitcase of their belongings with a friend (Canadian actor Robert Christie) who lived in the parish, arranged for the triple reading of the banns and selected February 2, Candlemas, as the great day. This is the day of the Purification of the Virgin Mary, the day when priests bless the candles to be used in their churches during the coming year.

On Friday, February 2, 1940, a modest group gathered in Chelsea Old Church. On the bride's side were Mrs. Newbold, Maisie and an Australian couple, friends of Mrs. Newbold's who had known her family since the First World War when Mrs. Larking kept open house in London for Australians on leave from the front. On the groom's side was just one person, Elsbeth Herbert-Jones, daughter of Dora Herbert-Jones, the Welsh singer. Michael Benthall, the OUDS friend with whom Davies had fetched up in a ditch in the euphoric days after his B. Litt. oral, was to have been best man, but the army revoked his leave at the last moment.

Tyrone Guthrie had cautioned Brenda against marrying a Welshman, lest he prove untrustworthy and make her unhappy, but had reconciled himself to the event and was to give the bride away. He took the precaution of shaving before he came, as he wrote his mother, lest it be thought that Brenda was "associating with sausage-frying Bohemians." At the church, he wondered why Brenda Newbold was being married under the name Brenda Ethel Mathews, distracting Brenda to explain her legal name to him on the way up the aisle. Davies had chosen the organist's music with care—at the beginning Bach's "Jesu, Joy of Man's Desiring," then the wedding march from Mozart's *Nozze di Figaro*, for the signing of the register the minuet in Handel's *Samson* and finally the "Trumpet Tune" often attributed to Purcell but actually by Jeremiah Clarke. In a letter to her mother, Elsbeth Herbert-Jones described the wedding as "very fine" to her Welsh mind since "everybody spoke so well." The Australian friends had a small reception at their apartment for everyone afterwards.

The honeymoon began innocuously enough. As always, it took a while to get to Fronfraith—a train to Manchester, a second to Shrewsbury, a third to Welshpool and a little local to Abermule. From there, Sam Haycock drove them in the pony-trap the half-mile or so up the steep hill to Fronfraith through the snow of the harshest winter for years. The house had been more or less readied by Sam's eighteen-year-old daughter, Daisy, who was to look after them. She met them at the door with an oil lamp, because Fronfraith had no electricity, and wished them well. In return, Brenda gave her a piece of wedding cake and told her that if she put it under her pillow she would dream of her future husband.

The honeymooners settled in, finding life in the big house rather more arduous than they had realized. It had never been this cold when Davies was "baching it" in April, certainly not in the summers. That February the pipes had frozen, so water had to be lugged in pails to the bathrooms and heated on the large oil stove in the bedroom for washing. But they were young and energetic and used to theatrical digs, so they took these as minor inconveniences. Daisy seemed to be having a little trouble coping, but they assumed that her difficulties were caused by the large, unhandy house. During the days, they went for long walks through the snowy landscape to see the places and people Davies knew so well, including Mrs. Buckley-Jones, who lived on a neighbouring hill four miles away. And they took the pony-trap and went to see Dora Herbert-Jones.

On their return to Fronfraith one day after lunch and tea with Mrs. Buckley-Jones, they discovered that Sam Haycock had summoned the doctor from Newtown. Daisy had to go to the hospital immediately. So the doctor, Davies and Sam Haycock carried her down the sweeping three-storey staircase in Fronfraith's central hall and out to the doctor's car, while Brenda stood at the bottom to light their way with an oil lamp. Fantastic shadows played along the wall and a nauseating, rotten-potato stench rose from the sick girl, but the doctor would not tell them what had happened, and when they and Sam Haycock took the pony-trap to the hospital a couple of days later, none of them was allowed to see Daisy. Davies finally got it out of the doctor (who had been loath to speak in Brenda's presence lest he offend her sensibilities) that Daisy had blood-poisoning from a botched abortion. Within days, Daisy died.

After a telephone consultation with Rupert they decided to hold the funeral from Fronfraith. On the day of the service Sam Haycock, his sons Tom and Bill and a couple of other men carried the coffin down the long hill and up another to the Llanmerewig Church. The grief of the Haycock men, all of them strong farm labourers, was terrifying; they wept and wept throughout the service. In the cemetery outside, the grave had been dug down to the clay, and water had oozed into it. As the coffin splashed into the water, Bill's wife gave a terrible shriek. When the graveside ceremony was over, the parson's wife, who was very conscious that the Davieses were the "quality" present, ignored the distraught family and the other mourners, leapt across the grave, seized Brenda by the hand and said, "Well, Mrs. Davies, you have had a remarkable beginning to your marriage, haven't you? You've seen the joy and you've seen the sorrow."

The wedding was attended by more ill omens than this. The capable woman who replaced Daisy as housekeeper, a Gypsy from the nearby village of Llandyssil, was hit by a car and killed less than a week after they left Wales. Within the year, Davies' sole wedding guest, Elsbeth Herbert-Jones, who as a nursery-school teacher had accompanied a shipload of evacuated children out to Australia, died after the ship in which she was returning to England was torpedoed. And the very church where they were married was destroyed by bombing.

On the first of March 1940, St. David's Day, they sailed with just a few other passengers from Liverpool on a Canadian Pacific liner that zigzagged its way alone across the wintry Atlantic, its lights blacked out, its sole defence a few depth charges. They felt fortunate to be married and together, when so many of their friends and acquaintances were being called up, divided from their loved ones and sent off to war. Every moment seemed precious, for no one knew what might happen. The glowing lights of St. John, New Brunswick, moved them deeply when they arrived out of the blackness; no lights had shone after dark in wartime Britain since the third of September.

Chapter 8

EDITOR AND JOURNALIST: 1940-63

To be an editor was to be a geyser of opinion; every day, without
fail, Old Faithful must shoot up his jet of comment, neither so
provocative as to drive subscribers from his paper, nor yet so
inane as to be utterly contemptible. The editor must not affront
the intelligence of the better sort among his readers, and yet he
must try to say something acceptable to those who really took
the paper for the comics and the daily astrology feature.

—*Leaven of Malice*, 1954

No man's newspaper writings should be saved and produced in
evidence against him.

—Samuel Marchbanks, "Diary of a Complacent Man,"
23 Oct. 1948

SETTING OUT TO earn his living in the spring of 1940, determined to win renown, Davies had made a fortunate choice in the
woman by his side. Where his mother had been caustic and dominating, Brenda was warm and nurturing. Having lived with
hypochondriac parents, he found her optimism about matters of
health both surprising and bracing. For her part, Brenda was
determined to make their marriage work, and she was undeterred

by the isolation and loneliness that his occupation at times created. Although she regretted giving up a career of her own in the
theatre, the transition to the roles of wife and mother didn't
cause her undue stress, probably because those roles called upon
skills she possessed and enjoyed. She treated their household
help—when they had it—with consideration, and as a result the
household ran smoothly. And she sewed and cooked well, which
made life more pleasant, particularly at the beginning. Since he
was never able to drive a car, her love of driving turned out to be
especially useful. In 1945 or 1946 they bought their first car, and
later they owned a series of Jaguars and then BMWs.

Brenda provided Davies with emotional ballast, steadying him
against his highs and lows. It became a great safety valve for him
that he could speak freely in her presence, since he constantly
had to bite his tongue and curb his acerbic pen. He found
Brenda, who enjoyed his verbal extravagances, the best of listen-
ers: responsive, critical and always sympathetic. And her aesthetic
sense, more strongly attuned than his to landscape and architecture, helped him to see and enjoy effects of colour, light and line
that would otherwise have escaped his notice.

He supported her, too, in different, but equally significant,
ways, and was always as determined as she to make their marriage work. From the beginning, he saw her as a partner; he
wanted her free to do the things that interested them both, and
so he encouraged her, as soon as they could afford it, to hire help
with the house and children. He early recognized (and editorialized about) a woman's need for money to spend at her own dis-
cretion. From the outset she managed the budget and made most
of the purchases; he accepted her decisions without quibble. He
was generous with gifts, delighted in her accomplishments, took
pride in her appearance and injected imagination and surprise
into their daily lives, whether in whimsical birthday place-cards
or by dusting an angel for the top of the Christmas tree with silver and gold. He was always able to entertain her—leading the
Canadian actress Amelia Hall, who had once been a guest in
their house, to observe: "I think any man that can make his wife
laugh at breakfast is a marvellous husband."

While Davies cast about for something to do, the two of them lived with Florence and Rupert in Kingston. Fruitlessly, he went to Toronto from time to time to follow up leads at the Canadian Broadcasting Corporation and at the *Globe and Mail*. The war had cast a pall of uncertainty over everyone. At dinner that April or May, Davies heard Mitchell Hepburn, Ontario's Liberal premier, assure his father that, by the middle of June, Hitler would be sitting in Buckingham Palace dictating peace terms.

On the advice of his father's friend Duncan MacArthur (minister of education in Hepburn's government), Davies went to see W. H. Clarke of the educational publishing firm Clarke, Irwin. It turned out that the company could use an introductory text on Shakespeare, and he began to plan one in the evenings. Brenda, for her part, was becoming acquainted with his family and background at first hand. She and Davies went to tea with Eleanor Sweezey and her sister Margaret because Brenda wanted to make a cordial gesture toward the woman who had been so important in his life. The gesture made, the two women never saw each other again.

Beginning on March 18, Davies filled in at the *Whig* most days for the ailing W. Melvin Ashton, his father's editorial assistant. This temporary work familiarized him again with the concerns of a conscientious local newspaper—the local, provincial and national issues. His father seems to have written most of the staple editorials. Davies' own contributions—pieces on literature, drama, opera, psychology and language—broadened the range of the editorial page and lightened its tone.

Although Rupert liked what he was doing, Davies quickly realized that he would be unwise to stay. Working with his father, who was alternately dominating and protective, he would never become his own man. And he found it excruciating to work with his older brother Arthur, who felt free to interfere, question and judge his work. Arthur, general manager of the *Whig* at the time, disapproved of his light-heartedness. It was wartime: the editorial page should reflect the seriousness of the situation. But Davies set out to raise people's spirits with editorials like "That Oxford Twang" (April 8), "Too Many Baths" (April 9) and "The Devil Got Him" (May 25). The final straw was "Merry-Go-Round"

(July 4), a cheery couple of paragraphs about the pleasures of the old-fashioned steam calliope whose wheezy strains had drifted up to the windows of the *Whig* from a little itinerant fair in the marketplace below. Arthur was furious. But the piece attracted favourable comment, and Rupert was pleased.

Brenda had been having problems of her own. Rupert and Florence had welcomed her, but there really was no role for her at Calderwood. Uneasy, difficult and unwell, Florence had little interest in anyone besides her husband and sons, and she turned mealtime conversation almost entirely to the past. Moreover, Brenda had quickly become pregnant and was expecting a baby in December. It was time to get out from under the parental roof.

Although he had nothing to go to, Davies gave up his job and moved them to Toronto. For the moment they were in limbo. They rented a furnished second-floor flat in a Victorian house (since demolished) on Selby Street. Their German landlady, Mrs. Ida Schneider-Bassanesi, was as deep in limbo as they. The RCMP had interned her Italian husband on suspicion of Axis sympathies, and she had had to cope financially by retreating to the attic. The living room and sun-porch in her own flat, now the Davies', were decorated in depressing black, so Brenda bought yards of bright red fabric, made curtains and covered the cushions to cheer it up. Privacy was a rare commodity in Selby Street, for Mrs. Schneider-Bassanesi shared their kitchen and bathroom, and the couple in the apartment below kept an eye on their comings and goings too. Indeed, the wife often arrived unannounced by way of the back stairs. But all these people were generous and kind. The couple below drove Brenda to the hospital for the birth of Miranda on December 24 and between them, with Mrs. Schneider-Bassanesi assisting, almost drove Davies mad with helpfulness while she was away. Davies consulted "Chevreul's pendulum" (a wedding ring hung from a thread or hair over the abdomen of the pregnant woman, which swings to and fro for a boy, in a circle for a girl), and found it to be accurate. Miranda (Prospero's daughter in *The Tempest*) Nichola (the feminine of Nicholas, a favourite saint of Davies) Rhiannon (a mythical Welsh princess) was the first of three daughters.

Davies was called up for military service in 1940, and again a couple of years later, but was turned down both times because of his poor eyesight. Like many other men rejected for the armed forces, he became a regular blood donor. While looking for a job he made enough to get by with a thrice-weekly column for the editorial pages of the *Whig* and the *Peterborough Examiner*. (The *Examiner* was purchased in 1935 by Rupert and his partner, Harry B. Muir; in 1939, after Muir's death, Rupert bought his interest.) The column first appeared on August 1 under the heading "Cap and Bells." It was signed by "Samuel Marchbanks," since Rupert felt it wise to disguise the presence of yet another Davies on his newspapers. The name, like Davies' own, was drawn from both sides of his father's family. One of Rupert's grandfathers, William Robertson, had married Elizabeth Marchbank (sometimes spelled Marjoribanks)—whence Marchbanks. The other name saluted Samuel Davies, he who had married Mary Ann the Angel and become the first Nonconformist mayor of Welshpool.

With only one break, Marchbanks kept his columns up until 1953. In the first he introduced himself as "roving reporter, book reviewer, art, music and drama critic, trained snoop and funny man." He intended to amuse and entertain, but not simply to be funny. This fool or jester would rail "against the World, the Flesh and the Devil." In fact, he rarely jested; by 1941 the heading "Cap and Bells" had gone, replaced by titles reflecting the subjects of the day. Marchbanks also soon extended his range beyond the original program, adding character sketches and articles about special days of the calendar. Both of these were to become frequent topics in Davies' journalism over the next two decades.

Davies wrote the Marchbanks columns in the evenings, often with the column-inch foremost in mind. But it is here that the preoccupations that later characterized his novels made their first appearance—in particular his delight in the exceptional, peculiar and eccentric, and his conviction that the past illuminates the present.

While in Mrs. Schneider-Bassanesi's flat, Davies wrote *Shakespeare for Young Players: A Junior Course*. For his intended audience of grade eight students, he briefly drew on what he had learned in England and concentrated on what he wished he had been told himself as a student, including a description of how to "breathe the muhd" *à la* Bertie Scott. But the heart of the book was his choice of twelve surefire scenes for performance. Three he had seen played by young actors—the murder scene from *Julius Caesar*, in which his brother Arthur had appeared at the Renfrew high school; the trial scene from *The Merchant of Venice*, in which he had himself scored a triumph at the Kingston Collegiate; and the carousing scene in *Twelfth Night* in which, at UCC, Maria, Sir Toby Belch and Sir Andrew Aguecheek had schemed against his Malvolio. The others he chose either for unambiguous, strong emotion or for rough-and-ready comedy. Canadian artist Grant Macdonald (a Kingstonian, theatre-lover and Davies' friend since Christmas of 1935, when they had met on the crossing from England to Canada) supplied evocative line drawings for each scene, the first of a series of collaborations with Davies. *Shakespeare for Young Players* did well, selling, according to Davies' editor at Clarke, Irwin, "in classroom material loads" for more than thirty years.

On October 29, Harold F. Sutton, the literary editor of *Saturday Night*, at that time Canada's leading weekly journal of opinion, accidentally drowned. On the advice of a friend, Davies resolutely squelched his feelings of delicacy and applied immediately for the job. He needed no introduction to the editor. B. K. Sandwell was a UCC Old Boy who had noted Davies' prize-winning poem, "Scholasticum," in the school paper back in 1931 and had written him a complimentary letter. In March 1939 Sandwell had also reviewed *Shakespeare's Boy Actors* warmly, declaring Davies "one of the most brilliant students ever sent by Canada to England." He summoned Davies the day after he submitted his application and hired him on the spot at $42.50 a week. Davies' first review appeared November 16, 1940, and he took over officially as literary editor on November 23.

This became an apprenticeship not so much in journalism, though that was important for him, as in helmsmanship and direction. Sandwell, albeit a Canadian nationalist, was anything but parochial. Under his guidance, from 1932 to 1951, *Saturday*

Night held a central position in Canadian discussion of the arts, business and politics and provided a well-informed, characteristically Canadian perspective on international affairs. Davies described him once as "a liberal humanist"—"a man whose boundless goodwill was controlled by an alert, informed and free intelligence." Sandwell brought astonishingly diverse talents to his convictions at *Saturday Night*. At university he had majored in classics, and before taking on *SN*, he had been successively drama editor of the *Montreal Herald*, editor of the Montreal *Financial Times*, an assistant professor of economics at McGill and head of the English department at Queen's! By the time he hired Davies, he had good people in place in all parts of the paper.

Sandwell set high standards. Despite frail health, he worked long hours, steadily writing or dictating pieces distinguished by an air of civilized argument. He was a convinced libertarian who reigned courteously, appreciatively, judiciously, undogmatically. But, as Davies once commented, he could also "cut a man's head off so neatly and so swiftly that the victim did not realize what had happened until next time he sneezed."

At *Saturday Night* Davies conducted "The Bookshelf," writing some of the reviews himself and assigning others. The page continued to review books (especially Canadian books) on a wide range of subjects, but Davies changed its feel by reducing the length of reviews and by encouraging a lively, crisp style. He also wrote much of "The Passing Show," the page-three column of wisecracks, rhymes and whimsies. At least once a month he was "At the Theatre," and from time to time he hid behind pen-names like Eleanor Rumming, Margery Maunciple and Amyas Pilgarlic. Since Hector Charlesworth (now the paper's music critic) and Sandwell were often ill, he contributed quite a few unsigned music reviews and editorials as well.

In a journal entry for October 1, 1941, Claude Bissell, then starting out as an academic, recorded his impression of Davies as *Saturday Night's* young literary editor. The occasion was a luncheon given by E. J. Pratt, the most distinguished Canadian poet of his generation and a professor in the English department at Victoria College in the University of Toronto. Davies appeared "plump, with horn-rimmed glasses, flowing moustache, English speech" and Bissell had "a feeling that each word has been carefully patted into shape before it emerges." In recalling this encounter with Pratt a quarter of a century later, Davies added further detail. A man of "sweet, genial and kindly nature," Pratt

> was wearing a new hat—such a hat as one would not expect a poet to wear, for it was a stiff, rather aggressively coloured object, perhaps a little too close to a terrible headgear of the day which was called a Whoopee Hat. 'Do you like it?' he asked me, and I liked him so much that I made haste to say that it was indeed a very fine hat. 'This is what I like best,' said he, and removed the hat to show me that, fixed in the ribbon, was a small metal airplane. His delight in that airplane was part of the charm of his open, innocent nature. But it was not what I would have called a poet's hat; I was wearing one of those myself—a large-brimmed, black hat that gave notice to the world that beneath it great thoughts were boiling. But whatever the hat, there could be no doubt as to which of us was the poet.

Davies now settled into the daily rhythm that he would maintain for more than twenty years. Almost every day of the week would see three periods of intense work. Weekday mornings and afternoons, and Saturday mornings, were given to writing for *Saturday Night,* and the evenings usually to his own. Apart from the long shadow cast by the war, life was satisfying. When he had a play, ballet or concert to review in the evening, Brenda would come along. Home, too, was now more pleasant. The second-floor flat had proved too arduous once there were baby paraphernalia to contend with, so in 1941 they moved to a Victorian two-storey working-man's row house on Aylmer Avenue, next door to Vincent Bladen (professor of political economy at the University of Toronto) and along the street from Richard Tattersall (Davies' UCC music teacher). (The house was swept away a decade later during the construction of the Yonge Street subway.)

During this period they made several lifelong friends. Grant Macdonald introduced them to the graphic designer Clair Stewart and his wife Amy, daughter of J. S. McLean, the wealthy philanthropist who had made his money as president of Canada Packers. They discovered Clair to be a painter of exquisite pictures and, though more conservative in his taste than Davies, just as careful and interested in his dress. Davies and Brenda strongly appreciated his wicked, understated, slyly expressed sense of humour. Amy, quiet and unassuming, but more direct as a conversationalist, proved to be a gardener of extraordinary imagination. The four of them continued to see a good deal of each other over the years.

At *Saturday Night* Davies got to know Graham McInnes, the paper's art critic, who later went to the National Film Board in Ottawa and later still entered Canada's foreign service. Graham's family tree was studded with artists: the painter Burne-Jones was his great-grandfather, the novelists Angela Thirkell and Colin McInnes his mother and brother, and his father was the baritone James Campbell McInnes, whose singing of "Der Doppelgänger" had moved Davies so during his years at Queen's. Davies and Graham loved to quote *Babbitt* to each other and make scatological references in their letters. Like Brenda, Graham and his wife Joan had grown up in Australia. When the four got together the conversation was wide-ranging and uninhibited, accompanied by shouts of laughter as Davies and Graham capped each other's stories and jokes. Joan persuaded Brenda to audition for soap operas at the CBC, and she got a couple of bit parts, becoming a regular on "The Story of Dr. Susan" as Dr. Susan's English friend, who blathered on endlessly to her on the telephone.

Christmas at Calderwood in 1941 was not a wholly pleasant occasion. The previous year they had missed the family gathering because of the birth of Miranda, so only now did Brenda find, to her unease, that the senior Davies' obsession with the past extended to the custom of placing Christmas presents under the tree from the dead or long-vanished. One of them, for Rupert's spinster sister Elsie, proclaimed itself to be from the man she had given up in order to keep house for her father. Brenda found this deliberate flick of a raw nerve more than a little disconcerting.

She was also surprised to find that the opening of gifts occurred in the afternoon, *after* Rupert had had his nap—an ordering of events, she would discover later, that was not geared to small children.

That Christmas Day Arthur R. Kennedy, editor of the *Peterborough Examiner*, died. It had been clear for several days that he was gravely ill, and Rupert had had time to consider who should succeed him. The two key men at the *Examiner* were H. L. Garner and G. Wilson Craw. Harold Garner, the general manager, had come from the *Globe and Mail* in 1937. He was a principled, genial man who was able to attract and keep good staff. Wilson Craw, the paper's managing editor as of January 1, 1942, was equally valuable. A Peterborough native, he pre-dated the Davies-Muir regime, and his knowledge of local politicians' activities and community sensitivities was deep. Rupert told both men flatly that he wanted his youngest son to be the paper's editor. His reasons were at least partly dynastic. As he told Garner, "If Robertson is going to be part of this...he should help to build it." On the other hand, Rupert had no intention of jeopardizing the paper by giving his inexperienced son total control. Rather, he planned a period of apprenticeship under Garner and Craw during which Davies' name would not appear on the masthead.

During the Christmas festivities Rupert made his wishes clear to his son. Davies recognized the challenge, the substantial nature of the post and the financial benefit to himself. But he also felt the offer as an imposition. Living in Peterborough had little appeal, and he had no desire to leave Toronto or *Saturday Night*, where he had been building a satisfying life free of his father's domination. But, as usual in their battles of wills, his father won. On March 1, 1942—St. David's Day—Davies took over as editor of the *Examiner*, and his father was careful not to interfere with his editing of the paper.

The year 1942 was not a propitious time for a lover of drama and music to move to Peterborough. In its earlier days, the town had had a succession of entertainment houses, a music-hall, an opera house and finally a grand opera house that could attract touring companies, but none had survived the Depression. After 1935, the only dramatic performances to be seen were church and school fare, and at the outbreak of war even these had stopped. The city had had a Conservatory of Music, and the Kiwanis Club had sponsored a music festival, but both folded during the 1930s. The Madrigal Singers, a fine women's choir, disbanded when its leader moved to Toronto in 1942. Many members of choirs and bands had been called up for military service. Only the Community Concert Association remained, presenting three evenings of music a year. And it was not easy to get to Toronto for an evening's entertainment from this central Ontario city of 25,000. On the roads of the 1940s and '50s the drive could take as much as three hours.

Many of the Peterborough area's early nineteenth-century settlers had been poor Irish Roman Catholics. A few were well-educated (and Anglican)—like Thomas Stewart and his wife Frances, who came from Ireland, or like Thomas and Catharine Parr Traill and J. W. Dunbar and his wife Susanna Moodie, who had emigrated from England. Their memoirs, letters, botanical studies and fiction formed a small literary legacy, in which their descendants in the district took great pride. Peterborough had quickly expanded as a lumbering town, and timber remained its chief source of wealth for more than fifty years. Then, capitalizing on the development of hydroelectricity on the Trent River system, it shifted to manufacturing. Canadian General Electric was the largest employer in the city when Davies arrived. As in Renfrew, the highest institution of learning in Peterborough was the Normal School, which trained grade-school teachers.

At the time the Davieses arrived, the town was stratified into "the Old Families, the Irish Families and the New People," groups that rarely socialized with each other. Newcomers often remained outside "society," even after passing their entire adult lives in the town. In 1942, Peterborough was even more closed in upon itself than usual, because the war had taken many of the men away. Families were self-absorbed. People said, "Oh, you must come to dinner" but never set a date or got in touch. Davies associated this coldness with the "real" Peterborough for years; he continued to feel its chill until he left in 1963. But it is not the only Peterborough he encountered, nor the only one he acknowledges. When he departed, the town was turning itself into the sort of place he would have enjoyed much more, due in part to the foundation of Trent University.

For the first few months, he lived at the Empress Hotel during the week and spent weekends in Toronto with Brenda and the baby. Then in June they moved to 572 Weller Street, a house Rupert had arranged for the *Examiner* to purchase and rent to them. Rupert also backed a bank loan (speedily repaid) to help with their moving and setting-up expenses.

Wilson Craw greeted Davies from the "real" Peterborough on his first day at the *Examiner*: "Well, I suppose you realize you have come to the arse-hole of Ontario Toryism!" Craw was not just talking politics; he was talking of a mind-set that hated change. There were many in Peterborough who had no desire to explore beyond the city limits. There were even more who were deeply suspicious of anything new. Brenda met this attitude during her first afternoon of rolling bandages at the Red Cross, where she overheard two elderly ladies spiritedly discussing their travels. Less was definitely better: the winner triumphed by revealing that she had never been as far away as Toronto. And when Brenda introduced herself to old Mr. Kerr, a lawyer for the Old Families, in the street, he inquired: "And who were you before you were married?"—that is, which of the Old Families did you belong to? Davies himself met this often. Many of the natives were suspicious of people who had too much education: he was told more often than he cares to remember, "You know, if you think too much, it'll send you crazy!" Davies, who had not only taken a research degree but had done so *abroad*, was doubly suspect on that account. The role of education, it was felt, was to provide the rationale for Peterborough's cultural assumptions. It was difficult to believe, he was often told, that "a man of your education" could say whatever he had just said.

Davies and Brenda made the "real" Peterborough uneasy for many reasons. Their accents were unfamiliar; Brenda, not Davies, drove the car; they enclosed their front lawn with a picket fence (everyone knew that fences were only to enclose back yards); and in the summer they often ate out-of-doors, a major oddity in those pre-barbecue days. In public (not in private) Peterborough was dry, but Davies was editorially in favour of liberalizing the liquor laws. He had afternoon tea in a cup and saucer; everyone else in the office had coffee in paper cups. His modest departures from normal business dress attracted attention as well. People took notice of his flowing coat, long Oxford scarf, colourful vests, broad-brimmed hats, and—they hardly knew where to look—his beard. He was young enough to be off fighting in the war, and yet here he was, safe in Peterborough. Unless you got to know him (and sometimes when you did) you suspected him of eccentricity, haughtiness and snobbery.

The beard measured the gulf between Davies and the town. Clark Gable or David Niven might wear natty little moustaches, but Davies, when he first arrived, sported generous moustachios. Had they known that their new editor was also the Samuel Marchbanks of the editorial page columns, the townsfolk might have guessed that a beard was coming, for on April 7, 1942, there appeared in the *Examiner* an editorial headed "What About Beards?" which defended them as "an honourable badge of masculinity through the ages." Later that same year, reviewing a pictorial atlas of 1878, Marchbanks confessed to a "sneaking fondness" for whiskers and argued that "a man without his beard is like a horse with a docked tail—smarter and more efficient, no doubt, but lacking that noble wildness which nature intended." It was actually a three-week bout of flu in late February and early March 1943 that presented Davies with the opportunity to grow the beard he has worn in one form or another ever since. He was well aware that, to the "real" Peterborough mind, beards were associated with the unshaven, rough lumberjacks who used to emerge in spring from the woods to lie about the streets in drunken stupor, but he took a stubborn pleasure in demonstrating the converse. The result was more or less what his father had experienced on the streets of Renfrew: hooligans threw pebbles at him, shouted insults and yelled from their bicycles at his daughter Miranda—"Hey, Davies! Why's your old man wear a beard?" Occasionally, however, he managed to turn the tables: when the *Examiner*'s newsboys were making a ruckus one afternoon in the alley below his office window, he leaned out and boomed down:

"Don't you know that *God* is watching you?"

Most of the opportunities that wartime Peterborough provided for mingling had little appeal for either Davies or Brenda. Faced with a similar situation in Renfrew, Rupert had joined one of the town's dominant churches, sung in its choir and involved himself in the controversy over the formation of the United Church; he had been active in the Board of Trade, Rotary, the Temperance Association and Liberal politics. Davies felt no inclination to do any of these. The church he and the family attended sporadically for a few years from 1944 onward was little St. George's, in the working-class part of town. He did not join a church choir or a men's luncheon club. He was not really much interested in trade or politics. For a few sessions he was persuaded to join a discussion society of Scots working men, but he extricated himself when he realized how little could be achieved by untrained people grappling with problems they knew nothing about. He was not invited to join the Fortnightly Club, a group of professional and business men who met every second Saturday night in the members' homes to hear papers on literature, art, education and topics of national character, but, having a low opinion of the level of its discussions, he would have refused had he been asked. Herb Dobson, his doctor, "rushed" him for the Masonic Order more than once, putting the question without fail in the midst of his rectal examination, but the answer remained no. He did serve on the board of the Victorian Order of Nurses and for many years on the executive of the Community Concert Association. Brenda, no more clubbable than he, didn't involve herself in a church or church group and had no interest in afternoon teas and bridge. Early on, when she did attend a tea, conversation came to an abrupt halt when she casually referred to her "screw" (which she knew only as English slang for salary).

Nonetheless, Davies met the community's leaders, determinedly accepting every invitation to talk to a club, group or organization in town until he had made the full circuit. He spoke on "Some Aspects of the Theatre" to the Women's Art Association and on "How to Read a Newspaper" to the Women's Association of St. Andrew's Church. He was not yet as effective a speaker as he later became, but he was certainly no bore, and, according to a university professor who heard him speak to recruits at the army camp, he was already able to gauge his audience accurately, neither speaking down nor over-simplifying.

Meanwhile, their second daughter, Jennifer (English for Guenevere) Minerva (Roman goddess of wisdom, and a family name on Davies' side) Angharad (Welsh for "the loved one") had arrived on October 16, 1942, and Brenda had hit on a novel method of making child-raising a more stimulating experience. Hearing Dr. William E. Blatz speak early in April 1943 about the nursery school he had established at the Institute for Child Study in Toronto, she decided to organize one in Peterborough, where many women living with their parents or in-laws were coping with children in cramped quarters while their husbands were overseas. With advice from the Institute she hired a trained kindergarten teacher, had a local carpenter fence the front yard and make play equipment, enrolled about a dozen children and arranged for at least one of the mothers to help out each day. St. David's Nursery School flourished from 1943 to 1949, an enterprise well ahead of its time. It closed when Brenda became too busy with theatre commitments to carry it on, to the regret of those who sought stimulating, professional care for their children.

In 1943 and 1944 both Davies and Brenda taught weekly classes at the YWCA. She gave "Talking of the Theatre" alone the first year, and with Davies the second, and he did "How to Look at Pictures" the first year and "Reading for Pleasure" in the second. The second year Corporal Gordon H. Roper, who was stationed at the army camp on the outskirts of town, was "volunteered" to give a course. Roper, who had been an instructor in English at the University of Chicago and was soon to become a professor at the University of Toronto, assumed that he would be invited to give a course on literature. But when the prospective instructors assembled around a table at the "Y," a strange, bearded figure at the other end pompously commandeered the course on literature for himself and assigned him one on political science. A few days later, after the twenty-odd groups had met for the first time, everyone assembled in the gymnasium for a "mixer" of social games. The Davieses and Ropers retreated from this and over drinks discovered a broad community of interest that banished Roper's initial negative impression and produced a warm friendship. Roper loved the wonderful moments when Davies would throw himself back and guffaw. It was through the Ropers that the Davieses met several other congenial spirits— two widely read army doctors and a very English Anglican priest, Reverend E. C. Moore, the rector of modest little St. George's. When all these, except Father Moore, left at the end of the war, the Davieses kept in touch with the Ropers.

William Breyfogle, Jr., and his wife Betty lived just across the road from the Davieses and were pleasant acquaintances until they, too, moved away shortly after the end of the war. Breyfogle had gone to Oxford on a Rhodes scholarship and had studied in Munich, and at this time he was publishing freelance pieces in American magazines. Betty Breyfogle remembers that, like the Davieses, she and her husband found Peterborough a very dull place in the 1940s.

Davies' chief channel of communication with Peterborough was the *Examiner*. He gave himself whole-heartedly to the task of editing the newspaper and quickly settled into an orderly pattern—"Rise at 7.30; breakfast 8; office at 9 and a business morning; lunch break 12 to 2, including half an hour's nap; 2 to 5.30 office again and write for newspaper; 5.30 to 8, home, drink, dinner, talk to children and play the piano; 8 to 11, write on book or whatever it may be; 11 to 12.30 a drink, a snack, and a long talk with my wife; 12.30-? read in bed. I do a six-and-a-half day week and am not fond of vacations." Each "business morning" he proof-read the editorial page that had been set in type overnight, scanned the editorial pages of twenty-five or so Canadian papers and the *New York Times*, answered his mail, wrote fillers, prepared letters to the editor for the printer, allocated books for review, collected his ideas and wrote the lead editorial before walking home to lunch. In the afternoon he did the balance of the editorial writing and, after a few years, reviewed the day's work over tea at 4:00 or 4:30 with his assistant. From the beginning he equipped himself with a well-padded chair and a large desk in a private, book-lined office, and when the building was renovated in 1954, he achieved real quiet by having the office door lined with lead. He was equally focused in the "leisure" hours he gave to columns, reviews and other writing. As a result his output was astounding. He told Graham McInnes in 1947 that he usually wrote 12,000 words a week as Davies and 2,000 as Marchbanks, and thirteen years later he was still producing 12,000 words a week.

Although his father took care not to interfere, Davies' editorial approach nonetheless owed something to Rupert's advice. As he left for Peterborough, for example, his father had said: "Now, remember. If you are the editor of the paper, you have the loudest voice in the community. So be careful how you shout." Rupert had often spoken of the importance of praising people: "You must hand out the bouquets." Nonetheless, it was certainly Davies' own convictions that moulded the paper. He impressed on the *Examiner* staff (as one of his assistants said years later) "that a newspaper was not a scandal sheet that gossiped only about the weaknesses and horrors of the human condition, but that its correspondents should also gossip about the greatness and achievements of humankind." The voice he chose for himself was that of teacher, expert and counsellor.

When he arrived, the editorials occupied the first three columns of the editorial page, but from June 1942, when the page was reduced from seven columns to six, only the first two. The previous editor had written without inspiration on the usual topics: business, politics and the war, but his speciality was folksy pieces with a rural flavour, often in rhyming prose. They make painful reading. This sample from an editorial entitled "Wealth" is characteristic:

> The man who died had shared his wealth, of course kept nothing for himself, three sons and daughters two; of dollars some got quite a lot, perhaps more than they really ought, while others got a few.
>
> 'Twas then the family had a spill, and some one tried to break the will, they found some one to blame; they argued that their father's head, was spinning when he took to bed, he might have been insane.

Davies was, of course, "something completely different." Suddenly the editorials began to range over new subjects—psychiatry, religion, the arts, language, insanity, education, sex (VD, birth control, sex education in the schools, studies of human sexuality), special days of the calendar, centennials, character portraits of exceptional people and, in the 1940s, probably because of Brenda, Australia. He, and later his associate editors too, believed that the *Examiner* should support worthy local initiatives like the preservation of the town's market hall and the establishment of a university. He thought it should speak out sharply when a local crown attorney was drunk in court, when the city's Little Lake was found to be polluted by industrial effluent, when there were problems with the police force. He routinely promoted local cultural events and made a point of addressing Roman Catholic issues from time to time, knowing that fully a quarter of his readers were members of that church. By 1942 Rupert had been appointed to the Senate as a Liberal, and perceptive readers could see that Davies' sympathies too generally lay with that party. But he tried to be even-handed in his political editorials. The stance was typically small "l", but not egalitarian. His tone, like B. K. Sandwell's, was that of well-bred discussion rather than disputatious or crusading.

As was the practice at the *Whig*, Davies concluded the editorial columns with "Notes and Comment," a few brief, mildly funny fillers similar to *Saturday Night*'s "The Passing Show." These were sometimes loosely based on similar pieces from the other papers to which the *Examiner* subscribed. Davies enjoyed rewriting such pieces to give them greater point or local relevance, and he was quite conscious that he was not the only Canadian editor so occupied. As he scanned other editorial pages day after day he saw jokes modified and repeated from one coast to the other. This was wit, not as Oscar Wilde fresh minted it, but as *Nugae Venales*, the old joke book he had bought at Oxford, collected it, and some of the jokes were very hoary indeed. For Davies that was part of their charm.

From the beginning he recognized his lack of expertise—and for that matter, interest—on many subjects central to the region's concerns: agriculture, the economy, Parliament, international affairs, science. By 1945 he had hired an assistant editor to deal with these areas. His first associate, who lasted only a year, was a graduate of the Ontario Agricultural College who wrote knowledgeably about farming and provincial agricultural policy. The second, Thomas J. Allen, came in 1947 and stayed for a decade. A Peterborough native, he willingly did many of the editorials on what he called the "bread and butter stuff, like surfacing roads and garbage collection"; he also took an interest in international affairs. The third, Ralph Hancox, recently from England, succeeded Allen in 1957 when the latter moved to the *Toronto Daily Star*. By 1960 he was carrying the brunt of the editorial duties and himself required an assistant. In 1963, when Davies moved to Toronto, Hancox took over as editor, and he held the post until the end of 1967, when he became magazine editor for the Canadian edition of *Reader's Digest*. Hancox was passionately interested in politics, and he was able to persuade Davies and the board to send him on reportorial excursions to Ottawa, Paris, Washington and New York, all ventures usually far beyond the pocketbook of a paper of the *Examiner*'s means. He also brought a strong interest in science, mechanics and physics to the editorial page.

After September 1942, the third column on the editorial page was reserved for articles "outside the usual editorial scope." Davies made sure that it was always worth a glance. Marchbanks filled it three times a week until November 1942, then twice weekly until 1948, and finally Saturdays only until 1953. Once a week it offered book reviews: initially by Samuel Marchbanks; from 1948 to 1952 by Tom Allen, Hilda Kirkwood and Davies as RD, SM (Samuel Marchbanks), OBC (Our Book Critic) or OB (Our Book); a couple of years later by Arnold Edinborough; and still later by Ralph Hancox. Commentators on the Canadian scene like Bruce Hutchison, Grant Dexter, J. H. Gray, A. J. Thomas, Geoffrey Vivian, Peter Eliot and Lester B. Pearson featured regularly in the third column, and, as time went on, Peterborough writers found a place in it as well. When the *Observer* of London was selling its foreign service through Canada in 1949, Davies seized the opportunity to run columns by Ivor Brown, Julian Huxley, Nora Beloff, Kenneth Harris, Lord Dunsany, Philip Toynbee, Bertrand Russell, Rawle Knox, *et al.*, and persuaded his father to take the service too, making the *Examiner* and the *Whig* its first customers. When the *Globe and Mail* wanted exclusive rights several years later, the *Observer* refused to cut the Davieses off, and so, twice a week until the service was discontinued, some of the finest columnists writing in English appeared in the *Examiner* and the *Whig*.

Of his own third-column contributions, after November 13, 1943, the Saturday slot was the one that kept Davies sane. With the example of Eleanor Roosevelt's "My Day" to inspire him, Samuel Marchbanks here turned diarist. He wrote a paragraph for each day of the week, and gradually developed his crusty old self in doing it. His creator was under the necessity of guarding his tongue carefully in his editorials, but Marchbanks—an outspoken old rascal, a lover of good talk, food and wine, a devotee of the arts and of genius in all its forms—could give the back of his hand to any and all who did not share his enthusiasms. It was through Marchbanks that Davies invited Peterborough citizens to draw closer. He walked the city they knew, mentioned the performances they attended, mocked Toronto with the rest of them and laboured under the burdens of ordinary life. But he did not let them get too close. His readers were never made privy to the playful, ever-shifting parabolas by which Marchbanks' life intersected Davies' own. Fairchild, Marchbanks' brother, drew heavily on Davies' brother Arthur. The immediate family was usually concealed behind phrases like "an Australian lady of my acquaintance" or "a child I know," and the latter usually exposed the eternal child in Marchbanks himself:

> Helped some children build their blocks this evening, and built several temples for their delight: my taste inclines toward the Byzantine. Also built a passable reproduction of Stonehenge and then, to please the children, built a sidewalk leading up to its front door. ("Diary of a Likeable Old Duffer," 18 March 1944—Miranda was three and Jennifer one.)

> A Young Woman whom I know who is just learning to read kindly undertook to read me a story from her schoolbook

today. It was one of those pieces about a king who promises
his daughter's hand to any man who can make her laugh. It
is this sort of promise which makes me wonder about the
psychological make-up of fairy-tale characters.... ("Diary of
a Worried Woodsman," 9 October 1948—Miranda was
almost eight, Jennifer nearly six and Rosamond one.)

Sunday: Awoke to find that it was raining outside, and that
the water closet in March-banks Towers had become
plugged; a child, in a fit of wild merriment, had cast its
shoes into the maw of the monster and made it costive.
Oh, the bitterness of domestic life! Plumbers, like doctors,
should be on call at all times, but they are not, so after
some ineffectual and half-hearted groping I resigned myself
to this stroke of fate....
Monday: Plumber arrives first thing and operates successfully on the patient upstairs; the atmosphere of the household brightens visibly, but the shoes are beyond reclaim.
("Diary of a Gourmet," 6 November 1948.)

Sometimes family events are just off-stage. When their
youngest daughter, Rosamond (a family name among the
Cliffords on Brenda's side, recalling Rosamond Clifford, mistress
of Henry II) Bronwen (Welsh for "the white breast") was born,

Circumstances made it necessary for me to take a walk
through town at half-past five this morning; I had the
streets to myself and was able to look about freely. Was
astonished by the fact that a great number of my fellow
citizens appear to sleep in sealed rooms; if they get any
fresh air, it is certainly not through their windows. I dread
to think what my old school nurse, Miss Toxaemia
Dogsbody, Reg.N., would have said about this; retrospective fear of that old harridan has compelled me to open my
window on nights of bitterest cold, and because of her
admonitions I still brush my teeth up and down, instead
of crosswise which is much more fun. ("Diary of a
Hospital Visitor," 19 April 1947.)

The Dame of Toorak
  Cooked and raked out the cinders
For her elderly Ma,
  Gammer Larking of Flinders;

For her Ma and her daughters
  She worked like a black,
And she smiled through it all,
  Did the Dame of Toorak.

One daughter was pretty,
  Artistic, and lazy;
She was wed to a painter
  And drove him nigh crazy;

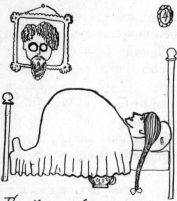

The other, as fair,
Was prolific, alack!
And she called, in her pains,
For the Dame of Toorak.

So the Dame packed her shawl-strap,
  And o'er the salt sea
To chill Canada sailed
  From fair Antipodee;

"I'll wash off the baby,
  And hurry right back,"
To her Ma and her Mais,
  Said the Dame of Toorak.

But when she got there
  And the baby was born
She lingered to slave
  Evening, noon, night and morn;

She mopped up the pee,
  Hung the clouts on the rack,
And threw dung down the drains,
  Did the Dame of Toorak.

Sped the year to its fall,
  'Twas the hour of return;
Though they bawl and create
  An emotional churn—

"It is useless to plead,
  For I've got to go back
To my Mais and my Ma,"
  Said the Dame of Toorak.

So they piped their damp eyes
  And looked merry and hearty;
And they all cut up dog
  At a grand farewell party;

Then she hopped on the 'plane
  In her best toque and sacque
And off into the blue
  Sped the Dame of Toorak.

Davies created "The Dame of Toorak" as a keepsake for his Australian mother-in-law Muriel Ethel Newbold on the occasion of her 1947 visit (when Rosamond was born). Each verse was illustrated on a separate page.

Marchbanks dealt lightly, but tellingly if his readers had known it, with Davies' most worrying illness. All through the summer of 1947 Davies thought he had hay fever because he was short-winded. In September, Dr. Dobson precribed a medicine to clear his respiratory system, which left him feeling drugged and sleepy. He had tests for allergies. Then, a couple of weeks later, X-rays revealed a fibrous mass in his chest. Dobson immediately sent him to Dr. Richards of the Ontario Institute of Radiotherapy at Toronto General Hospital (TGH). The two doctors decided on a three-week course of deep X-rays at TGH that November, and a second course in late May and early June the following year, the maximum possible. Brenda had to pry the diagnosis out of Dobson: Hodgkin's disease (normally fatal). The treatments themselves drained Davies' energy and his spirits. Images of death recurrently rose to his mind. But he clutched his despair to himself and said little to anyone other than Brenda. Even Tom Allen, who had just begun work at the *Examiner* and who had to cover for Davies while he was in Toronto, was told practically nothing.

Countering his gloom was Brenda's certainty that he was not going to die and his own grim conviction that, with four dependants, he could not afford to. In Toronto, Clair and Amy Stewart invited him to stay with them during the treatments. Gradually, he returned to health and the threat of death faded, although Dobson insisted on a complete physical examination every six months in case of a recurrence. To this day it is not clear whether Davies actually had Hodgkin's disease; he is inclined to suspect mononucleosis. In some ways the experience was Davies' war, his confrontation with the death that men of his generation faced in Europe. It brought him to terms with the fragility of his own hold on life. Early in the episode he tended simply to soldier on, determined to get things done no matter how he was feeling; when it appeared that he was to live after all, his relief was expressed in new exuberance and a new direction in his writing.

Marchbanks records much of this—breathlessness, hay fever, medication, lethargy, allergy tests, X-rays, ghastly treatments in Toronto and the aftermath—but he so fantasticates it that many readers undoubtedly thought it was just another of his many exaggerated minor ailments. Here's part of the column about his second stint at TGH:

Monday: Today I finished the series of treatments which have occupied my time during the past month. "You've been a good patient, Mr. Marchbanks", said the nurse as I climbed off the gridiron; "we've put 124,000,000 veloci-pedes through you and you haven't batted an eyelash". (She may have said something else, but I think it was veloci-pedes; these measurements of electricity are very confus-ing.) I said nothing. When one is praised by nurses it is best not to be too enthusiastic. They may like you so much that they insist on further treatments. I silently cursed the Atomic Frier, into which I have been slid like a roasting fowl for a month, and escaped to the cubby-hole where my clothes had been left....

Wednesday: Set out for my place of business today and met two men. "Hello, I never expected to see you again", said one of them. "Nope, heard you were a goner", said the other. "Ridiculous", said I haughtily. "Well, you can't blame us", said the first man; "it was all over town that when you came back it would be in a box". "Pooh, pooh", said I, being unable to think of anything which properly expressed my feelings. "What was wrong with you, any-way?", asked the second man, screwing up his eyes as though he thought that he could produce X-ray vision in himself by that means, and look right into my inside. "Well, if you wish to know", said I with dignity, "I had a slight case of cradle-cap, and I have been taking treatment for it". They went their way muttering discontentedly.... Reached my office and was greeted there with great friend-liness, but during the morning a man stuck his head in at the door and said, "Well, well, wonders will never cease. I heard you were on your last legs". Threw a heavy paper-weight at him, but he ducked.

Thursday: One of my temperance friends called on me today. "Do you think it is going to be permanent?" he asked, in the voice which doctors use when enquiring after one's elimination. "Will what be permanent?" I countered.

"The Gold Cure", he whispered. "I have not been taking the Gold Cure", I said, coldly. "That's what they all say", he replied; "but I heard from someone who knows a man who knows an intimate friend of yours that you had a nasty scare with pink elephants—teeny-weeny pink elephants about the size of cocktail sausages—which you saw crawling all over your counterpane. And this man said that they took you to Toronto in a straightjacket, and drained your crank-case, and.... ("Diary of a Half-Dead Man," 19 June 1948.)

Davies filled the fourth and fifth columns of the editorial page with one or two syndicated cartoons (local cartoonists proved to be expensive and not good enough) and an editorial or two reprinted from another Canadian paper, or possibly the *New York Times, New York Herald Tribune*, the *Observer* or the *Spectator*. This was another place where his own and his assistants' deficiencies could be remedied. The last column was given over to a retrospective feature put together by Wilson Craw, a daily Bible reading bought from a syndicate and letters to the editor. Davies was totally opposed to giving the "Bible Message" a place anywhere in the paper, let alone on *his* page. He saw it as sanctimonious and was convinced that Bible readers required no guidance from the *Examiner*. But he was unable to stand up to Craw. Whenever he would propose to excise it, Craw would rage on God's behalf until Davies gave way. Craw had the numbers on his side, too: when the readers were polled in 1951, sixty letters arrived to support it. It took Davies until 1956 to finally and deviously dispose of it: in this, the *Examiner*'s hundredth year of publication, he successfully argued that Craw's own retrospective feature should get more space.

From 1944 to 1950, Davies contributed one more item to the editorial page, a weekly quotation under the masthead, often drawn from Bartlett's *Familiar Quotations, The Oxford Dictionary of Quotations* or H. L. Mencken's *A New Dictionary of Quotations*. Many lifelong favourites appeared here, giving pithy expression to basic tenets of Davies' outlook on life. "Use three physicians still: first, Dr. Quiet, next Dr. Merryman, then Dr. Diet," for example, ran on December 15-21, 1945, and Bernard Shaw's "My method is to take the utmost trouble to find the right thing to say, and then to say it with the utmost levity" on October 7-13, 1944. Emerson's "A foolish consistency is the hobgoblin of little minds, adored by little statesmen and philosophers and divines," which is still ready to his tongue when he is caught in an inconsistency, appeared October 21-27, 1944. In 1950, however, his friend Clair Stewart created a new heading for the *Examiner*, using a modern Roman typeface, and on July 14, Davies changed the quotation for the last time. The new heading incorporated Terence's "*Humani nihil a me alienum puto*," the quotation he had encountered in Groddeck's *The Book of the It*. He translated it for readers of the *Examiner* as "I am interested in everything human."

Davies selected and edited items for the Saturday op-ed page as well. This came to be the place for reporters, photographers, local writers and historians to contribute special material. And it was here that "Dolly Gray" flourished briefly in 1957 and 1958. Ralph Hancox and Davies couldn't resist the temptation to parody the syndicated advice columns. They decided that Hancox would write to Dolly and Davies would compose the replies. A picture of one of Edward VII's mistresses represented Dolly herself at the head of the column. Hancox's letters were slightly bizarre, and Davies' replies, although based on the too-familiar, expanded into unexpected territory. The first exchange set the tone:

DEAR DOLLY GRAY

I am twenty-two years of age, with mid-brown colouring, 5'3" in height and with 26 bust, 32 waist and 36 hips. I have never had a date though my girl friends tell me I am quite attractive, and I wish I knew what was wrong. I have most of Junior Matric and can dance, but who am I going to dance with? What should I do?

WONDERING

Dolly Gray replies: Poor perplexed lassie, your problem is all too common! But have you checked yourself lately dear, for those simple things which nevertheless make all the difference between popularity and, well — wondering? Are you dainty from top to toe? Sometimes, all unknowing, we may offend with unpleasant breath. (This may be tested by breathing for a short time into a paper bag.) Perhaps you might pay a call on your family doctor, and ask him if you need a tonic. For a figure like yours, stress petite charm, a dress of simple Princess line gives the svelte silhouette, and in your case generous frills and ruching between throat and waistline would be wise. Don't despair, dear. It is always darkest before the dawn and Mr. Right may be nearer than you think!

It wasn't until it became clear that a number of readers were taking it quite seriously that they regretfully brought the skylarking to a close.

Davies wrote the arts reviews—initially just of the three or four Community Concerts and a couple of exhibitions of amateur art, but after the war also of amateur concerts and play performances, the summer stock season, and the occasional touring ballet or drama—a task he later split with his assistant. Some of the visiting professionals were undoubtedly startled to find their work assessed knowledgeably in the local paper. Jan Rubes, the singer and actor, remembers with amusement being ticked off by Davies for his preamble to Mussorgsky's "Song of the Flea": "We must smile, however, at Mr. Rubes' statement that this song was written in protest against the influence of Rasputin at the Russian court: Mussorgsky died in 1881, and Rasputin was born in 1871; at the age of ten his influence at court was probably negligible. It is very well to patronize an audience with little stories, but it is a mistake to assume that they cannot count." When writing about amateur efforts, Davies' objective was to encourage the arts, and he wasted little time on judgment, although his estimate was usually clear enough. Instead he would draw on his knowledge of music and theatre to spark his readers' interest, provide context, open perspectives. The art itself was taken seriously, no matter

how feebly the particular dauber or performer might labour in its
service, and at the same time he took great care not to undercut
anyone's self-worth. He kept his exasperation ("Well, it's for
charity, ain't it, so it can't be bad") for Brenda's or his associate
editor's ears.

The staff at the *Examiner*, initially suspicious that the owner's
son would prove incompetent, or lazy, or arrogant, soon saw that
he was a gifted writer who worked hard and sensibly consulted
Wilson Craw before writing about local matters. Rupert Davies
had already set the paper on a good business footing; now his son
gave the editorial page a compelling and adventurous style that
brought the paper the recognition of its peers. The other ninety-
five or so daily papers in Canada began to quote the *Examiner*
with greater and greater frequency. In 1937, shortly after Rupert
Davies and Harry Muir acquired the paper, the *Examiner* was
thirty-seventh on the list of Canada's most quoted dailies. By
1945, Davies had moved it up to twelfth, in 1952 to seventh,
and by 1959 it had ranked fifth many times. The staff took pride
in working for a paper that attracted that kind of attention.

Besides winning their respect, Davies managed to gain their
affection. In the words of Margaret Rodney McCauley, the
paper's accountant, he had "a nice manner with him," spoke
pleasantly to the men as he passed through the printing plant,
made himself approachable. Christopher Gledhill recalled walking ten feet tall when Davies commended him on his use of the
word "etiolated" in one of his "Peter Piper" columns. For young
reporters passing through the *Examiner* for a couple of years'
training under Wilson Craw, Davies was a father figure, and he
used his position to try to inspire in them his own love of the
English language and its proper use. As long as they had done
their research carefully and quoted accurately, they could count
on his support when there was pressure from the community. To
Tom Allen, educated at Queen's and Oxford, Davies quickly
became a friend; for Ralph Hancox, who had left school at sixteen and was largely self-educated, he was a powerful mentor.

Although the *Examiner* staff warmed to Davies quite rapidly, the
reaction of the community as a whole was much more difficult

to gauge. At the beginning, he often felt he was working in a vacuum, so slight was the feedback. Even then there was the occasional vigorous reaction, however. On October 3, 1942, he wrote
that birth control should be used to bring Canada's population
to a desirable level and keep it there. Hardly an instant had
passed before Monsignor O'Sullivan, the acting Roman Catholic
bishop, stormed into his office.

> [He] planked himself, about six foot six of black angry
> Irishman, in my chair and said: "I hope you realize that
> I'm the Ordinary of the Diocese."
>
> And I thought he was an ordinary indeed, the big,
> potato-eating clod, and we had a real row and he said that
> this advocacy of birth control had to be withdrawn imme-
> diately or he would take steps. So, as I did occasionally
> when I needed advice, I called my father and said: "What
> do we do?"
>
> He said: "Carry the fire into the enemy's camp."
>
> So I wrote another editorial saying that birth control is
> the biggest thing since the discovery of granola, that every-
> body ought to have it and possibly it should be available in
> slot machines and, you know, this kind of business. And
> the old Monsignor was furious and he sent out a letter as
> from the Bishop of the Diocese to every Catholic church
> in the area, saying that all loyal and devout Catholics
> would drop their subscriptions to the *Peterborough
> Examiner* immediately.

The paper lost only five subscriptions, and those were recovered
within two weeks. Brenda's Roman Catholic cleaning woman,
Mrs. Menogue, and her friends, considered that the Monsignor
was overreaching his authority and ignored the proscription.

A later confrontation was more serious. Between 1954 and
1956 the *Examiner* repeatedly criticized the local police force,
and matters came to a head when the paper opposed the
appointments of chief and deputy chief. County Judge John de
Navarre Kennedy, a member of the Police Commission, invited
Davies to his home on December 23, 1956, to ask that the paper

change its stand. Davies refused and instead wrote an editorial exposing Kennedy's attempt to influence his editorial policy. The following July there was a twelve-day investigation into the police department (with Davies among the witnesses) which resulted in reforms and the resignations of the deputy chief and two members of the Police Commission, including Judge Kennedy. Kennedy, who had not expected to find his private conversation made public, became a bitter enemy. Davies, who had previously supported him editorially as a capable judge, bore the rift with equanimity, since he privately disliked the man. He resented Kennedy's habit of patronizing him as "the old hand to the young beginner," when the man had only published three mysteries and an account of one aspect of Canada's contribution to the Second World War. Davies himself had by this time published a dozen books, including plays, novels, *belles-lettres* and criticism.

All editorialists hope that their readers will respond to their efforts. Davies and his associate editors were discouraged, however, especially in the early years, by the quality of the letters that came their way. Most of them were dully disputatious or of the poison-pen variety. Davies resolutely refused to publish unsigned letters, although he permitted a pseudonym if the writer privately identified himself. Until well into the 1950s, only one or two printable letters arrived each day. Not unusually, these reflected the views of the "real" Peterborough—on the editor's nauseating articles on the Kinsey Report; on his appalling opinion that children should be told to drink moderately when they grow up; on his anti-Christian interest in CBC talks by Brock Chisholm, Bertrand Russell and Anna Freud; on his communism (he opposed McCarthy and McCarthyism) and so on.

While Davies was in Toronto for his first series of X-ray treatments in 1947, Tom Allen announced a poetry contest in celebration of Princess Elizabeth's marriage to Prince Philip. On his return, Davies opined that Allen had gotten himself into it and he could get himself out: they were bound to receive "some awful junk." Indeed they did. As it flowed in, Allen began to realize what a witches' brew he had conjured up, the concoction of a rhymery of would-be poets, "chewing their nails and pencils in a farm kitchen," probably for the first time since grade eight. Allen went so far in desperation as to write a few poems himself, but the town's librarian, old Mr. Delafosse, a published poet, in the end bailed him out with some respectable quatrains. These won first prize, and Davies, who had helpfully contributed a series of eighteenth-century heroic couplets over the *nom de plume* of Joseph Harris, was "runner-up." Davies also wrote an eight-line bawdy verse on the view from the keyhole as Philip mounted the marital bed and had it set in print at the *Examiner* for Allen's private amusement, but alas, no copy survives.

Davies or Allen or Hancox would occasionally "prime the pump" by writing pseudonymous letters, usually opposing one of their own editorials. Allen returned from vacation once to catch Davies so engaged. An editorial that had urged Peterborough to turn its sewage into fertilizer had attracted a number of surprisingly good responses. But Allen recognized Davies' style in them, and in any case the time lag between the editorial and the letters was too brief. When he confronted the culprit, Davies owned up. Allen proved more elusive himself when he wrote a letter signed "Mother of Three" protesting the inconvenience of power blackouts at mealtimes. Moved by her plight, Davies deputed Allen to write in favour of rebates in such cases and never did guess the imposture. Fortunately, there were interesting, well-reasoned letters from time to time, and when they did arrive, especially in the early years, Davies paid attention. In January 1943, for example, John Londerville, a Queen's University student, took issue with an editorial that had urged the universities to focus on the liberal arts and admit only the gifted. Davies responded editorially, arranged to meet Londerville and, on November 9, 1943, had him contribute a "third column" on the "Early History of Peterborough Schools." As the years passed, the number of good letters increased. By 1963, when Davies left Ralph Hancox in charge, there was a healthy flow of responsible, thoughtful letters: according to Davies, who is not strong on figures, sometimes twenty or twenty-five a day; in another place he mentions "almost 1,500 such letters a year."

Samuel Marchbanks attracted many delighted readers, but readers who were outraged at the views in Davies' editorials were

repelled by Marchbanks as well. And many were discomfited by
his references to nose-grease, bad breath, spit, tripes, pipe-dottle,
ear-wax, sweat and defecation, as in—

> "What colour would you say this was?" said a woman I
> know today, holding out a piece of light brown material
> toward me. "Isabella-coloured", I replied, after a moment's
> consideration. She demanded an explanation. "Well",
> I said, "though I don't expect you will believe it, there
> was once an archduchess called Isabella who was very
> much provoked about the siege of Ostend which (as you
> very likely do not know) lasted from 1601 to 1604;
> her annoyance was so great that she vowed that she would
> not change her underlinen... until the siege was raised;
> the siege lasted nearly four years and the garment, when
> removed, was an interesting shade between beige and
> taupe, which has since borne the name of the arch-
> duchess".

Be that as it may, the column became required reading, not
only in Peterborough but in Kingston as well, where Davies'
brother Arthur found it advisable to read it before going out to
parties on Saturday nights since people would be talking about
it. Ultimately, and ironically, this helped to kill the column:
Davies could feel his fellow citizens looking over his shoulder,
and finally he could not be free and spontaneous any more.

The newspaper flourished. In 1941, just before Davies came,
the population of Peterborough was 25,350 and the paper's circulation 8,981 (35 percent). By 1951 the figures were 38,272 and
15,484 (40 percent); by 1961, 47,185 and 22,423 (47 percent).

By 1946 Davies had clearly made a success of the paper in his
father's eyes: his name appeared on the masthead as editor for the
first time on June 3. This symbol was correlated with a key
financial decision. The *Examiner* had prospered, but until now
its increasing worth had been masked by heavy wartime taxes.
Recognizing that its book value would rise rapidly once the tax
rate fell, Rupert decided to take this opportunity to pass on the

ownership to his sons, thus minimizing their cost of acquisition. Arthur, who had worked at the *Whig* since 1925, got 50 percent (not the 51 he wanted), Davies got 30, and Fred, who had made a mess of the opportunities Rupert had given him, 20. They all paid for their shares out of the next few years' profits. Arthur became president and Davies vice-president of the Peterborough Examiner Company Limited. As had been the case when Rupert Davies owned the paper, there was no interference with editorial policy. In 1953 there was further evidence of Rupert's approbation when he proposed that Davies assume the editorship of the *Whig*. According to Davies, this suggestion came to naught since Arthur, as general manager, firmly vetoed the idea. (When the post went to Arnold Edinborough on July 1, 1954, Davies made himself available daily, by telephone, during the initial months of adjustment.)

In the 1950s, Davies' work with the *Examiner* moved at least two owners of other journals to try to acquire his talents. After Jack Kent Cooke bought Consolidated Press in 1952, he approached Davies to edit *Saturday Night*. Davies, who had known Cooke for years through his father, was not even mildly tempted by the thought of working directly under a man who, though lively and genial, was also capricious and interfering. A second offer came from Roy Thomson, later Lord Thomson of Fleet. (Thomson was likewise someone he knew through his father. Rupert had gone into partnership with Thomson in the radio stations in Peterborough and Kingston in 1942, and in the 1950s the pair expanded into television in both cities as well.) Thomson dangled the editorship of the Edinburgh *Scotsman* before him, probably in 1955 when the incumbent retired. Davies turned this down too. It appeared that one of Thomson's motives in choosing him was the curious notion that the name Robertson would appeal to the Scots. But Davies couldn't imagine that Thomson would give him the freedom he needed. It was just as well that he didn't take the job, since Rupert had "an absolutely furious fit" at the mere thought that he might desert the family.

Davies had made no effort to market the Marchbanks column to other newspapers, but others approached him—the *Ottawa*

Citizen in 1946 and several western newspapers later on. When he first considered gathering some of the columns into a book, he approached Macmillan, thinking that firm the most likely to be interested. But Macmillan was in an interregnum between Hugh Eayrs and John Gray, and the spiritualist Ellen Elliott, who sat in the editor's chair, did not recognize what Davies had to offer. Clarke, Irwin was more receptive to the idea when it was presented in July 1946. The company made its money primarily from educational books but wanted the cachet that trade publishing could bring and was willing to print worthwhile poetry, plays, novels and essays at a loss. As it turned out, Davies' books usually made back their costs and a little more, and they proved to have the added advantage of attracting other writers into the fold. Davies respected W. H. Clarke's acumen and vision, and he enjoyed working with the firm's editor, R. W. W. Robertson, whose ancestral Robertsons, like his own, hailed from Dumfries. However, his contracts with Clarke, Irwin became oppressive in time, and some of the differences that sundered him from the firm in 1958 were there from the beginning.

The Diary of Samuel Marchbanks moved through a year's worth of columns, from "Sunday & New Year's Day" to the last "Saturday" fifty-two weeks later. Nothing was used from 1944, the apprentice year, but by 1945, the Marchbanksian paragraphs could walk, march, dance and twirl to tunes of Davies' devising, always with a certain rhetorical decorum and in a slightly old-fashioned vocabulary. So he drew on his work from 1945 and 1946, selecting the best from January, then February, and so on, eliminating local references as he went. He wrote a few new pieces and did a little rearranging. Because the column had been written once a week, the rhythm of the year was already built in, but his publishers announced each season with a special page, numbered the weeks with roman numerals and encouraged him to break the monotonous repetition of the days of the week with references to saints' days and other special occasions. The Marchbanks in this collection is home-centred: he does not go out in the world, it comes to him by way of the newspapers, the radio and the mail.

When Davies forwarded the manuscript on March 7, 1947, R.

W. W. Robertson was so delighted that he took it home and read it aloud to his wife, Eleanor, as he did with later books. Like Davies later manuscripts, it was beautifully typed and required virtually no editing. But Robertson made a few modest excisions—of the dedication and the four mock verse quotations for the verso of the pages marking the seasons—and this got him into hot water with his author. He acted as he did, he said looking back, because paper was in short supply in the years immediately after the war; eliminating the dedication saved a page in every book. But that was not what he said in his letter to Davies:

(a) They [dedication and mock quotations] add nothing to the book.

(b) They are not in the spirit of the book. The book, you will remember, is tragic, mystic and sublime—but not funny! These are very very funny!

(c) (And this is the most important) We are all devotees of the DIARY here. We hope that it is going to have a great success and we feel that it is going to give our fellow Canadians a much needed lesson in the art of not taking ourselves too seriously but we don't want to do anything to destroy that lesson by going one inch too far.

Missing Robertson's irony, Davies reacted angrily:

I disagree completely with yr letter of 19 September. I have been writing & publishing this DIARY for 4 years, & in that time I have put everything under the sun into it, including a great deal of verse of the type of these mock quotations. The public thinks them funny, and that is what counts. The *Diary* is a grab-bag: some like one thing in it, & some another. It has no homogeneity & no plan. When you talk about "the spirit of the book" you talk of something which, so far as I am concerned, does not exist. In writing the *Diary* I have been guided by one principle & one only—"*Anything for a laugh*". If the dedication & half-title quotes make a few readers laugh, that is all to the good.

Perhaps you mistake my motive in writing the *Diary*. It is not, as you suggest "to give our fellow Canadians a much-needed lesson in the art of not taking ourselves too seriously": it is, simply, to say my say as I please: there is nothing educative or highbrow about it. If I may say so, I think that you take the *Diary* too seriously when you say that it is not meant to be funny; it was never meant to be anything else.—In short, I should like the half titles used, though you may can the dedication if you don't like it. And I think that the Autumn quote—

> *Crows doze, choughs cough, shrews snooze etc*

should be attributed to Hardy, rather than Crabbe.

When the *Diary* appeared in the fall, the dedication and the quotations were gone, but the conflict between Davies' sensibility and Clarke, Irwin's continued to simmer.

The second Marchbanks volume was quite a different sort of book. Davies once told his friend Gordon Roper that the major influence on the columns between January 1947 and May 1949, from which he drew *The Table Talk of Samuel Marchbanks*, was Logan Pearsall Smith. That careful stylist, who wrote several modest volumes of tasteful reflections and, after a final polishing, gathered them into *All Trivia*, may indeed have affected Davies' style—one could learn much from Smith about *le mot juste*, pacing and rhetorical control—but not in any obvious way. Davies already knew much about the nice management of parallelism, inversion, exaggeration, climax and anticlimax, and his exuberant earthiness and turn of thought were certainly foreign to Smith. A more important influence on the columns of these years was the change in Davies' own life. The war was over, Canada's cultural life had revived, and Marchbanks was sallying forth to participate.

When Davies and his publisher began to consider a second volume in May 1948, Robertson suggested that he make it an old-fashioned day book or commonplace book. But the new, gregarious Marchbanks was already something of a conversationalist, and once Davies actually settled to the task in the first four months of 1949, he thought that a collection of table talk would do him better justice. He chose the best bits from the columns of 1947 and 1948 and presented them as observations uttered during a seven-course formal dinner. The manuscript was forwarded to Robertson on May 12. The latter suggested the removal of a number of paragraphs that repeated *Diary* material and, at the same time, requested the addition of new material to make the book longer. On May 30, Davies forwarded fifty-six additional selections taken from the first five months of 1949.

Robertson—conscious that Clarke and his wife Irene (head of the trade book division) were "very good church-going people" who wanted to publish "clean books"—cut out the paragraph that began: "Worked on my garden this afternoon, scattering fifty pounds of a fertilizer called Milorganite, which is made from the excrement of the citizens of Milwaukee; in spite of my considerable experience as a book-reviewer, I do not suppose that such a quantity of American ordure has passed through my hands in a single day before." The offended Davies wrote him a sharp note declaring that he did not like censorship; indeed, he said, the annoyed publisher of the *Whig* (i.e. Rupert, who, like Davies at the *Examiner*, ran the column on his editorial page) had barely been persuaded not to sue. As it turned out, neither Clarke nor his wife was offended by the passage; indeed Clarke had to comfort his shaken editor with the observation that Davies was probably just joking! Robertson wrote a letter of apology.

That fall *The Table Talk of Samuel Marchbanks* was presented to the public (like the *Diary* before it) with decorations and jacket by Clair Stewart. Both books were welcomed warmly by reviewers across Canada, with only one or two exceptions. The *Diary* sold about 6,000 copies in the first year or so after publication, and the *Table Talk* probably did as well.

From September 1949 to December 1950, the Marchbanks column took an entirely new form. Davies was feeling his oats now that his brush with death had passed and it appeared that he had a life to live after all. Impressed with Smollett's use of the epistolary form in his novel *Humphrey Clinker*, he decided to turn Marchbanks into a correspondent. New characters appear, and events begin to take place. Marchbanks travels abroad, Dick Dandiprat puts a skunk in his car, Osceola Thunderbelly wants to get out of jail (or into it). Many characters are as one-dimensional as their names (Haubergon Hydra, Doctor Raymond Cataplasm, the legal firm of Mouseman, Mouseman and Forcemeat), but they live up to them outrageously. Marchbanks now administers the reply direct when severely provoked, but otherwise comports himself with his accustomed whimsy and well-read urbanity.

Davies sent the first three columns of "The Marchbanks Correspondence" to W. H. Clarke in the fall of 1949. Robertson thought it a lively new departure, and once it became clear that the *Table Talk* could sell as well as the *Diary*, Clarke wrote on April 3, 1950, to say that a third Marchbanks volume would be a good idea. But when "The Correspondence of Samuel Marchbanks" arrived early in 1952, the underlying difference between Davies' and the firm's tastes became a serious stumbling-block. This Marchbanks was "the crusty old curmudgeon, the ribald Rabelais, laying about him in all directions," but Clarke, Irwin preferred "the real Marchbanks," whose mind, rich from a lifetime of reading, expanded easily around the universals of human experience. The firm found the ribaldry excessive, thought the running stories weak, disliked the flat characters and

Davies' suggested title page for
"The Secretary of Samuel Marchbanks"

found earlier themes repeated. In short, it was no go.

A year elapsed. Then, early in 1953, a discussion developed about a different kind of volume—an "Almanack" or perhaps a "Secretary," whose contents, Davies wrote, "would be divided into Drawers and Pigeon Holes, Secret Hiding Places, and Spillings (these last being fished up from behind the Drawers)." Contracts were drawn up and signed on March 21, the title "Marchbanks' Almanack" won the day on March 28, and Davies began to forward his twelve-part manuscript, a piece at a time, most of it in May, with the last two parts sent on June 15. In fact, it paid little more than lip-service to the notion of an almanack. Although each section was dedicated to a particular sign of the zodiac and began with a paragraph-long, tongue-in-cheek horoscope, what followed was an odd *mélange*—letters from "The Correspondence of Samuel Marchbanks," selections from Marchbanks' 1951-53 diaries, and even, in several sections, a playlet. Clarke, Irwin's reader liked much of it, but the letters' "low" humour continued to be a stumbling-block. The volume seemed repetitious and incoherent. Chatto and Windus, the English publisher with whom Clarke, Irwin had placed *Table Talk*, had similar concerns. The publisher's letter to Davies has not been preserved, but he reacted to it on June 23 by forwarding substantial almanack-like additions for each section—an "Enchantment," "Health Hints," and three "Apophthegms of Wizard Marchbanks," plus a few odd bits. This made no difference. On August 13, 1953, R. W. W. Robertson telephoned to decline the collection "on the ground it was not up to standard." Disgruntled and shaken, Davies left the rejected manuscript in his drawer for more than a decade.

Late in 1952, Jack Kent Cooke tempted Davies with "a really high price" (probably somewhat less than the $70 per column he was to command in 1958) to become *Saturday Night*'s literary editor. He accepted, and held the post from January 10, 1953, until March 28, 1959. But, as he had foreseen when Cooke had approached him earlier, the association was not a comfortable one. In December 1954 he withdrew from the editorial board in order to dissociate himself from the magazine's political stance, but Cooke still irritated him. He would phone at half past twelve on a Saturday night to say: "We're having an argument here in my house. Is *War and Peace* really the greatest novel that's ever written or is it not? Now, I want a *yes* or a *no.*"

Patronizing and infuriating as he might be, Cooke had a sense of humour. Davies had argued in a lead "Books" article that the sexual impotence of Thomas Carlyle was probably at the root of his obsession with force. On his next visit to Toronto, Cooke surprised him:

> "You know, I'm supposed to fire you."
> And I said, "Why?"
> And he said, "Well, Max Beaverbrook has been on the trans-Atlantic telephone to me saying that I've got to fire you because no Scotsman was ever impotent and Max would not allow it to be said [that he was] in a Canadian paper."

And Cooke "rolled around and beat the desk and shrieked with laughter."

As literary editor of *Saturday Night* (then a weekly magazine), Davies handed most of the brief reviews to others—R.M.T. (Ruth Martin Thompson), M.A.H. (Margaret Heideman), F.A.R. (Fern Rahmel) and occasionally T.J.A. (Tom Allen), B.E.N. (Brenda), S.Y. (Scott Young), all of whom lived in the Peterborough area. Occasionally he wrote one himself over the initials S.M. (Samuel Marchbanks), but he saved most of his attention for his lead articles, which, at 1,200 words, had sufficient length for a measured expression of his thoughts. Addressing himself to the intelligent generalist reader, he wrote with assurance and generosity, confident of his grasp of the traditions that underlay contemporary writing in Britain, the United States and Canada, and certain of what was central and what peripheral among current books. There was little that fell outside his range in those six years. Novels, short stories and plays; collections of letters, diaries, biographies, autobiographies and criticism; reference books and compendia; books on psychiatry and psychology, art and architecture, sex and love, costume and fashion, cookery and etiquette, folklore, humour and crime—all received space. The publication of special editions allowed him to talk about the value of finely produced books and about the classics.

The books he chose for review were distinguished, in Bernard Berenson's phrase, by their "life-enhancing" qualities: enthusiasm, zest, enjoyment, craftsmanship, the capacity to tell a story grippingly and entertainingly. If they stimulated the spirit, broadened its range of sympathy or provided food for the intellect, Davies would undertake to reveal the nature of the delight they held in store. Abundance, grandeur, sweep, imagination, inspiration, power, genius—these were the qualities that made for greatness in his eyes. If one or more of these were present, then the "flaws" the critics pounced on mattered little. As for the critics themselves, he displayed a writer's prickliness when dealing with their works, unless he felt himself in the presence of genius or special gifts. Critics who were themselves writers he treated with sympathy: such hybrid beings were capable of memorable prose, familiar with the anguish of creation and quick to discern fakery. The academics, on the other hand, were discounted unless their prose was sound and their judgments tempered with humility.

In these articles Davies was at the top of his bent as a reviewer. They caught the attention of Alfred Knopf, the most literary of the major American publishers, admired for the quality of his list and the design of his books. On March 31, 1958, Knopf proposed to Davies a collection of pieces under his imprint. The initial exchange of letters makes it clear that both men were thinking of something more than a gathering of already-published material. What Knopf and his editors were hoping for was an idiosyncratic, opinionated, controversial survey of the contemporary literary scene. The *Saturday Night* columns explored the main currents of western literature, and if Davies had stayed on that course Knopf might have got exactly the book he wanted. But Davies considered his options during the summer of 1958, and as he drafted his first chapter and prepared an outline for the balance of the book between September 18 and October 15 he decided to explore a number of literary meanders and bayous instead. He explained to Knopf: "The theme of the book is that as everybody has now been taught to read it is interesting to see what they actually do read, and that there are whole classes of books which are very popular and which never receive critical attention. I want to give them some of this commodity, though I do not think that they will like it."

Four subjects of the popular, but uncriticized, books that Davies chose to examine were self-help, sex and love, humour, and pornography. Because universal literacy had become a social objective in the Victorian period he grounded his discussion of this popular literature in nineteenth-century examples, before proceeding to those of this century. He exposed the dross in most such books and discussed how to recognize what little gold there was in them. His two remaining subjects—Victorian best-sellers and Victorian plays—were passions of his own. He presented them as rich, complex forms of escape literature replete with strange literary conventions, notions of character, taboos, laws and social assumptions. He saw them, too, as giving access to a past that provides a sometimes lurid perspective on our own age. Davies is an effective apologist for such forgotten books, many of them plucked from his own shelves. A fair number of them have made appearances in his novels and plays.

He devoted his opening and closing sections to the art of reading. To get the full measure of a book, he urged readers to give it an aural dimension, trying the cadences of sentences and lines on the inner ear and imagining the characters as if they were speaking with the voices of appropriate actors. Plays, he suggested, should be given a mental performance in the course of a single evening. The reader should not let the critics choose his books for him: he should make his own choices, and having done so, give them his full mental and emotional attention. Davies hoped the exercise would help to create a large group of literate general readers in North America. Unfortunately, these sections are weak and unpersuasive. Divorced from the books that inspired them, they reveal what Davies himself would be the first to admit: his strength does not lie in abstract thinking or in the systematic exposition of ideas.

As he started to work in the fall of 1958, Davies tentatively titled the volume "*AT LARGE AND WITH ORNATURE*," since he was feeling "more and more like John Leland, Henry VIIIth's antiquary, who said that in his catalogue of the manuscripts in the monasteries he 'desired to be somewhat at large, and have ornature.'" But Knopf cautioned against a title that conveyed so little. The manuscript Davies carried to New York in December 1959 was entitled *A Voice from the Attic*, which probably seemed just as unsatisfactory. It refers to "Cold Colloquy," the fifth section of Patrick Anderson's "Poem on Canada," in which Canada says:

> Yes, I am one and none, pin and pine, snow and slow,
> America's attic, an empty room,
> a something possible, a chance, a dance
> that is not danced. A cold kingdom.

Knopf received the book warmly, despite his disappointment in its theme. He had wanted a book on contemporary writers that would set the critics on their ears; what he got instead was a book on literature's byways by a virtual unknown. He knew it was unlikely to sell well (and in its Knopf edition it did not). He and his editors insisted on cuts of about 3,500 words from the sections on Victorian best-sellers and plays, cuts that now seem regrettable, since the book is read these days primarily as background to Davies' novels and plays and for what it reveals about Davies himself.

In 1955 *Saturday Night* shifted to bi-weekly publication, and in 1958 Davies sensed that the magazine was going rapidly downhill. Quick to take advantage of the situation, B. H. Honderich, publisher of the *Toronto Daily Star*, telephoned on September 17 to invite him to write a book column for the *Star* syndicate. By the end of the month Davies had resigned from *Saturday Night*, effective at the end of the year, and had begun negotiations with the *Star* about a column to run Saturdays, commencing January 1959. However, when Arnold Edinborough was appointed editor of *Saturday Night* on November 8, Davies agreed to stay on, workaholic as he was, although he was already editing the *Examiner* during the day, working on *A Voice from the Attic* in the evening and anticipating fresh demands from a theatre project.

He wrote at the time: "It seems obvious that I could undertake the *Star* work and then throw it off if it became burdensome, but that is not the way my character works, and I am particularly anxious not to neglect anything of greater importance in order to do it. The real trouble is that after I have argued myself out of doing the *Star* job, a voice within me says 'But it would probably be very good fun,' and so frivolous am I that all my life I have tended to do things for fun rather than because common sense supported them. And so immoral is life that this frivolous course of action has never given me any great pain." A deal was struck with the *Star* for $125 a column. At the insistence of the *Star*, he dropped the *Saturday Night* job in March.

What the *Star* wanted, as its assistant managing editor, W. B. Spears, explained in October 1958, was "a chatty, not too cerebral, general interest column about books and those who write them, written for ordinary people and not for specialists." Topicality was not essential, but liveliness and occasional controversy would be welcome. Length—eight hundred words. In reply, Davies envisioned "using the greatest possible freedom of treatment in writing it, making it sometimes a book review, sometimes a consideration of an author, living or dead, sometimes funny, sometimes satiric, and most often a mixture of all these." He wanted the column to be distinctively Canadian, and he intended to review those British books that were available in Canada but not south of the border. The heading he chose—"A Writer's Diary"—indicated that the shift from the balanced, mainstream position of the *Saturday Night* columns to the idiosyncratic, personal one of *A Voice from the Attic* was to be repeated in the move from *Saturday Night* to the *Star*.

Davies took seriously the title of his column. For four weeks, beginning with March 28, 1959, and on a few subsequent occasions (May 30, July 25, August 15, September 5, 1959), he framed the column as a diary, similar to the Marchbanks diary in form and tone, but focusing on writers and writing and unambiguously referring to his own experience. In this vein he wrote about visiting his publisher, and about such other authorly occupations as collecting books, compiling scrapbooks, making notes, gathering quotations. Once he cast the column as a playlet composed entirely of proverbs. The reviews pursued his usual interests—established and current fiction, books on clothes, psychology, music, words, handwriting, smells, plumbing and collecting.

During the first three months, he appended a bit of Canadiana to each column. To remedy Canada's lack of "a mythic history from which we can draw refreshment, marvels and grotesquerie," he quoted sententiously from eminent public figures and others. But his real purpose was mischief: "What I wanted to do was to see how long it would be before somebody questioned these quotations, because I have an unflattering theory about Canadians that they will accept almost anything that is told to them with a sufficient degree of solemnity." His brother Arthur no doubt twigged on February 7, 1959, when the quotation was "the best quatrain of a Canadian poetaster, Miss Patience Minchell." Miss Minchell was the "witch" who had lived next door to the Davieses in Thamesville. And Raleigh Parkin wrote to ask for the source of the quotation attributed to his father, Sir George, before the end of the month. Of course, Davies did supply authentic Canadian flavour from time to time when he addressed Canadian literary issues and reviewed Canadian books.

The syndicate quickly sold the column to nine Canadian papers in addition to the *Star* itself—the *Montreal Star*, the Ottawa *Journal*, the *Kingston Whig-Standard*, the *Peterborough Examiner*, the *Winnipeg Tribune*, the Regina *Leader-Post*, the *Calgary Herald*, the Vancouver *Province* and the *Victoria Daily Times*—as well as to the Philadelphia *Evening and Sunday Bulletin*. By 1961 the *Providence Journal* was also running it. Reader feedback was instant, copious and positive. The managing editor of the *Montreal Star* was so pleased that he wrote to say that his paper would gladly pay more. But when the syndicate expressed its dissatisfaction with sales in the summer of 1961, Davies decided to bow out. He had begun to stale and was miffed by the cuts Nathan Cohen (the *Star*'s new entertainment editor) had been making in his column. He expressed his frustrations freely to Arnold Edinborough: "It pays handsomely, but it is whoredom. You are one of the few people I know who would understand this. To write about Corvo and Logan Pearsall Smith for housewives in Sioux Lookout is all right for a while, but in the end it makes one a Tinpot Pontiff—the peer of T. Cholmondeley Frink in *Babbitt*, if you happen to recall him. The *Star* can take their money and ingest it anally, if I make myself clear."

His last "A Writer's Diary" appeared on June 16, 1962, and although the *Star* pressed him for a number of years to resume it, he refused. He had, he says, taken note of Cyril Connolly's opinion that anyone who persists in reviewing books, week after week, once he has reached the age of fifty is a hack, and in 1962, Davies was just a year from the deadline. (He always adds that Connolly failed to heed his own warning and went on reviewing books until the week he died.) And so his career as a book reviewer and columnist ended just a year before he left the editorship of the *Examiner*.

At the beginning of January 1963, Ralph Hancox replaced Davies on the masthead of the *Examiner*. Davies continued to do some writing for the paper until he moved to Toronto in June. Thereafter, he kept in touch by telephone and made occasional contributions to the editorial page, primarily reviews of the Stratford Festival and holiday pieces from abroad. He found satisfaction in turning out one of these 1,350 word articles in a morning, for it confirmed that the craft he had practised so long had not deserted him.

Davies' last major link with journalism was severed on March 31, 1968, when the *Examiner* was sold to the Thomson chain. The decision was relatively sudden. Davies, his brother Arthur and Fred's widow Kathryn had continued to plan for the long term, and between 1965 and 1967 they had invested $1.5 million in an addition to the building, a new press room and a specially designed press. But Arthur wanted to put his financial affairs in order before retirement, and he knew that if he owned 50 percent of the *Examiner* at his death, the taxes on the estate would be sufficient to cause a forced sale. Arthur was uneasy, too, about keeping the family's assets so committed to the *Examiner* now that none of them was actively involved in its day-to-day management.

So they invited tenders from five large Canadian newspaper organizations. Formal offers came from Thomson, Southam and Free Press Publications, the winning Thomson bid being substantially the highest at $3.1 million. Thomson agreed to maintain existing benefit plans and staff.

Arthur was pleased since, like Davies, he knew Roy Thomson and his son Ken well through his father's long association with them in broadcasting. In his experience, "Their word was as good as their bond any time." But Davies had mixed feelings. The financial outcome was satisfying, for it largely freed him from worries about money, but he hated the fact that he, and not Arthur, had to call the staff together to tell them the news. There was some spite in him as well. His regret at committing the paper to Thomson, who he knew would reduce it to a money-mill, was much diminished by an incident that had happened shortly before he left Peterborough. The printers' union had threatened the *Examiner* with a strike because their international wanted to establish a precedent-setting settlement before negotiating with a paper in the United States. Davies, no advocate of the "common man" and no supporter of unions, remembered that Harold Garner, the paper's general manager, had assisted these men with loans, and he saw their threat as a lapse of loyalty, evidence of malignance, lack of principle and loss of memory— evidence, in short, of the spirit of the North Ward schoolyard in Renfrew. Thus, although the sale of the *Examiner* to the Thomsons cast him in the role of Mrs. St. Clare in *Uncle Tom's Cabin* selling the slaves to Simon Legree, part of him "didn't give a damn." But he did care deeply about the paper that was so much the product of his imagination and standards, and, paternalistically, about the people who had served it and his family long and well. With that part of his mind, he hoped that the Thomsons meant what they said when they promised to maintain the paper's high standards.

Chapter 9

PLAYWRIGHT AND DIRECTOR: 1940-50

———— • ————

...I think that it is wrong to call pieces which are written for the theatre in Canada "plays", for that word suggests lightness, fantasy and ease of accomplishment. Canada will only respect her theatre when plays are called "works". Canada has a high regard for anything that involves toil. Therefore I think that in future I shall describe all my plays as "works", and if they ever reach the apotheosis of print I shall take care to call them "The Complete Works of Marchbanks". Let triflers talk of plays; Canada wants to be given the works.

      —Samuel Marchbanks, "Diary of Picklemas,"
               18 September 1948

T HERE IS DOUBLE irony in Marchbanks' rueful reflection. When Davies did collect and publish his dramatic "works" he called them *Eros at Breakfast and Other Plays, Four Favourite Plays* and *Hunting Stuart and Other Plays*. But despite their air of "lightness, fantasy and ease of accomplishment," they were the product of self-discipline, hard work and regular habits, the old Presbyterian virtues, reinforced in his case by UCC, Queen's,

Oxford, the Old Vic, *Saturday Night* and the *Peterborough Examiner*. His daughters were all conscious of growing up in a household where work was being accomplished. Most evenings after they went to bed, and for part of most weekends as well, their father would write at his small desk in the living room of the Weller Street house. Later, in the Park Street house, he spent similarly long hours in his study where he had greater privacy.

Of course, one person's "work" is another's consuming interest. Even in his leisure hours, Davies was constantly engaging himself in one activity or another, restless to accomplish something new. Over the years he has filled scrapbooks on many subjects. One, for instance, which he began in the early 1940s, contains "Clippings Relating to Oddities, Absurdities, Curiosa, Crime and Suicide, and Strange Manifestations of the Holy Ghost." Others concern murder, romance, advertisements, theatre, clocks, musicians and political cartoons. Jennifer came to believe that life is for working; since there is so much to be done, you should not waste the time you have. Rosamond, seeing her father's long hours bearing fruit in novels published, plays directed and staged and books reviewed, was convinced that she, too, could have a productive career.

None of the girls resented the hours Davies poured into his writing. He had always spent time that way, and he had plenty of energy left over for them. He and Brenda took them along to concerts and plays, organized expeditions to museums and movies, drove out into the country for frequent walks and picnics. In his playful moods with them he sometimes surprised adults who knew his more formal public self. Once, as a neighbour watched, he became a shambling bear, with the aid of a fur coat, "woofing" and "grrring" to the girls' excited squeals and shrieks. Amelia Hall, getting off the bus in 1950 for a visit, heard the following exchange:

> Rosamond (aged three): "When are you leaving, Miss Hall?"
> Davies: "Now that's not the thing you ask a guest or she might take umbrage and leave at once."
> Rosamond: "What's umbrage?"

Davies: "It's a very large dark umbrella that people get underneath when they're annoyed."

Having to account for every penny spent, one of the bugbears of Davies' adolescence, was not a problem for his daughters. They were free to dispose of their modest regular allowances (and later their clothing money) as they chose.

Sunday afternoon and evening were (particularly when Miranda and Jennifer were young) a time for tea around the fireside, accompanied by stories, read with great drama by one parent or the other. Jennifer's friends were fascinated by her parents, who actually encouraged children to form their own opinions and listened to what they had to say. Davies admits, however, that his banter was not always a success. One little girl who had timorously contributed to the conversation at dinner was collapsed into silence by his reply: "That, dear girl, was a terribly subversive statement!"

Although it was Brenda who ensured that the girls learned to ride their bicycles, skate and swim, and she who dealt with the practicalities of child-rearing, it was primarily Davies who brought music into their lives. He was an opera enthusiast, a regular listener to the Saturday afternoon radio broadcasts from the Metropolitan Opera and, from 1950 on, an attender of the performances of the Toronto-based group that eventually became the Canadian Opera Company. His musical tastes were tremendously catholic, embracing folk song, Elizabethan choral music, hymns, carols, a wide range of symphonic and chamber music, eighteenth-century catches, oratorio, band music, Gilbert and Sullivan, the incidental accompaniments to plays and Victorian drawing-room ballads; he stopped short only at twelve-tone music, jazz, the products of Tin Pan Alley and all sentimental, semi-religious ditties. When the girls were tiny, he played "duets" with them at the piano, encouraging them to play the most dramatic and demanding note, like "Pop" in "Pop Goes the Weasel." And when they began to study the piano, he reviewed the question of lessons annually: if they wanted to go on, they would have to make a commitment to practise. Miranda did persist, and by her teens her duets with him had advanced to the

level of Mendelssohn's "Fingal's Cave." Davies sang nursery songs
with the girls too, and when they were older, the family developed a repertoire in three- or four-part harmony—second
soprano, alto, baritone and sometimes tenor, "growled" by
Miranda. Driving expeditions were enlivened with rounds and
canons, including the eighteenth-century

> Twine gentle evergreen, to form a shade
> Around the tomb where Sophocles is laid.

So the girls came to love classical music, with an exuberance that
most children and adolescents reserve for popular songs. They
delivered Purcell's "I Attempt from Love's Sickness to Fly in
Vain" with such gusto to Jamie Cunningham (the theatre director) when he was thirteen, in 1953, that he has never forgotten
it. As teenagers, all three sang in the school choir, and Miranda,
for a time, essayed a career as a singer.

Davies' frequent poses, his delight in role-playing, challenged
the girls' perceptiveness. People who didn't know him well were
often taken in, confusing an attitude with opinion; years earlier
at UCC, one of his friends had watched his procession of guises
and decided that he was always acting. Miranda felt that she
always had to read between the lines "to know where his centre"
was, something "pretty tricky for little children." Her experience
was of "a very mercurial sort of father, not a solid father who
gives one a protective, strong environment, but of one who is
entertaining and enticing and fascinating and alluring and glamorous and utterly adorable." Brenda, on the other hand, was the
needed strong centre. Miranda always knew exactly where *she*
stood; while Davies might be playful and tease her with his irony,
the family's values were never in any doubt.

The standards and interests of the Davies household were, of
course, in many respects strikingly different from those of the
community around them. The girls found themselves living in
two different worlds. But whereas Davies as a child in Renfrew
had demonstratively rejected the community's standards, his
daughters did not. The gap was not nearly as emotionally
freighted for them as it had been for him. They responded to the

divergence according to their temperaments: Miranda strove to be accepted as one of the gang, privately believing her parents' standards to be superior; Jennifer acted one way outside and another at home, confident that her parents would recognize the necessity of this duplicity; Rosamond was critical of the way the family fenced itself off. Nonetheless, all three girls felt comfortable in Peterborough, and when they were sent at grade eight to Bishop Strachan School, a private Anglican girls' boarding school in Toronto known for the excellence of its academic and music program, each of them considered it an emotional deprivation. Miranda and Jennifer now accept their parents' decision as the right one, but Rosamond was miserable at Bishop Strachan and finished high school at another Toronto private school, Thornton Hall.

When Davies and Brenda arrived in Canada in 1940, the theatre world they had known in London seemed heart-achingly distant. Wartime Toronto was visited by touring productions from England and the States, but it hadn't a single local professional company. Peterborough had only movies and the radio. The sense of deprivation was immense as they stared back over the thousands of empty miles toward London's hothouse of directors, designers, actors and audiences.

Faced with such a tremendous loss, Davies acted with characteristic energy. He reached back to the London theatre world—by writing plays for it. His "eventual aim and hope," he told W. H. Clarke in 1944, was "to be a playwright," and he made it his goal (though he did not say this publicly until 1947) to succeed in London's West End. Between 1943 and 1960 he wrote twenty-six scripts—ten radio playlets, eight one-act plays and eight full-length pieces—all of them theatrically inventive. His characters are extraordinarily diverse, firmly drawn, vigorous and memorable. The dialogue is literate, often witty, sometimes sharp, and it flows easily. As a result, his plays were very successful—when he addressed a concern that his audience could share. The plays that tackled Canada's cultural philistinism—especially *Overlaid*, *Fortune*, *My Foe* and *At My Heart's Core*—struck such a powerful answering chord that they were widely and frequently performed, and by the 1950s Davies had come to be generally regarded as the country's foremost dramatist. Ironically, the awakening of theatre arts that he helped to foster in Canada ensured that these plays would soon come to seem dated. But they will undoubtedly be revived from time to time, precisely because they are vigorous, interesting depictions of a particular moment in the evolution of the Canadian psyche.

On the other hand, Davies got into trouble with his audience more than once by taking a light-hearted attitude to subjects that were felt at the time to be above such treatment. And when he tackled subjects primarily of private interest to himself, he was much less successful, because in these cases his chief failing as a dramatist—discursiveness at the expense of dramatic tension—became excessively costly. Two of his full-length plays have never been produced, and several have been performed only once or twice.

Davies learned a great deal in the course of this tremendous outpouring of energy. The process of creating the plays led him to discover subjects and characters in himself that spoke very powerfully to him. By the time he came to write his novels, he had come to understand himself much better. As with all his serious work, writing the plays involved him in a kind of ongoing self-analysis, a process that had fascinated him ever since his introduction to psychology at Queen's, and particularly so after his sessions with Dr. Gillespie in London.

From the beginning, Davies saw writing as a matter of recording communications from the unconscious. In a light-hearted 1948 talk, he described the process, basing his account on "a certain amount of practice and a few vague intuitions." When an idea occurred to him that seemed "to demand embalming" he would immediately jot it down, lest it vanish, in a notebook he always carried for the purpose (and still does). Then the idea would seem "to acquire a life of its own," presenting itself in dramatic form, growing and sometimes transforming itself utterly, until it settled into a final shape. Only then, when it had become "an aching tooth which has to be pulled," would he commit the play to paper. He has described the process of writing his plays and novels in similar terms ever since. When an interviewer asked, soon after the publication of *Fifth Business*, how he went about developing a character, he replied: "You don't. The character arises in your imagination and then you go ahead. I know this sounds terribly pompous and grandiose, but you don't really do it; it's something that happens and you write it down. You can't sit down and say, 'Now, I think I'll think up a funny Jesuit,' and do it, because you'll get a mass of eccentricities; you won't get a live person. But if one arises in your mind, and he's got all his oddities and you see him hopping around and doing things, then you just write down about it. This is what imagination is. It's not invention, you're more passive than that. You listen to your ideas; you don't tell them what to do." And in 1989, after describing the writing of *Fifth Business*, he concluded: "It is this sort of explanation, I know, which persuades some critics that an author is indeed an *idiot savant*, who does not know what he is doing. But that is a misunderstanding of the creative process. The author may not know consciously every detail of his story when he begins it, but his Unconscious knows, and it is from the Unconscious that he works."

Davies has had much material to integrate and resolve. His father's stories of Wales were a part of his family inheritance; his mother's tales of Ontario pioneer life were another. His battles for dominance with his mother, his striving to satisfy his father, his contests in the Renfrew schoolyard, his struggles to come to terms with his romantic sensibilities, his memories of the camaraderie of the Oxford and London years—all these provided his unconscious with a massive hoard on which to draw. From the beginning, his unconscious also presented him with figures and stories of a mythic nature, which he didn't satisfactorily understand until he had read and absorbed Carl Gustav Jung's works in the 1950s and '60s. As he delved and wrote, he felt an almost-religious sense that "by gaining knowledge of oneself and indirectly of other people you gain some apprehension of some aspects of God." He believed then, as, indeed, he does now, that one's best creative work is an offering to God.

Davies reached out to the theatre not only by writing but by directing and acting, with Brenda, primarily in Peterborough. Between 1943 and 1960, the two of them were involved in thirty-seven productions, and Brenda directed or performed without him in sixteen more. In so doing they made a substantial contribution to Peterborough's community life, which is gratefully acknowledged and warmly remembered today by many who worked and acted with them.

The experience was invaluable to Davies, not just as a way of keeping the magic of the theatre alive for himself, but as training in the arts of persuasion and communication. In the role of playwright, searching for his voice, he didn't always interest others in his vision. As a director, one who often had to work with inexperienced amateurs, he was a good deal more successful. Few in the Canada of the 1940s had his breadth of theatrical exposure, fewer still his intensity of interest in technique. He drew on his observations at the Old Vic and on his own considerable roleplaying experience, with the result that he was frequently able to transmit his conceptions effectively to his actors, making his perspective theirs. Almost always the performance reached out and drew the audience into the magic circle as well. There were failures, generally when he hadn't sufficiently considered the preconceptions and expectations of his audiences, but these were few, and he learned from them how to hone the persuasive narrative voice that later was crucial to his success as a novelist. Together, he and Brenda, in the thick of the ferment from which a professional theatrical fraternity was beginning to emerge, made a tremendous contribution to the post-war revival of the theatre arts in Canada.

Davies' transmutation of self-discovery into art actually began not with plays but with fiction. In 1940 he wrote "Mr. Paganini Complies," a cautionary little tale that presents the first of the mythic characters that emerged from his unconscious. A popular song of the moment, "Mr. Paganini," written by Sam Coslow, had caught his ear:

O Mister Paganini, please play your rhapsody,
And if you cannot play it, go on and sing it;
And if you can't sing it, you'll have to swing it—

Davies derides such cheapenings of the masters and reacted by writing a story in which the virtuoso violinist responds to the slangy invitation. Appearing in a dance-hall, Paganini displays demonic powers greater than any Coslow could have conceived, stripping off the dancers' façades, exposing their deep insecurities, forcing them to exhaustion in a fandango and ultimately causing one to commit suicide. The dancers and their chaperones, unable to face the forces unleashed within them, repress their memories *en masse*. (Years later Davies endowed his magician Magnus Eisengrim with a hint of the same demonic force.)

In "A Forest of Feathers," a novel begun on November 15, 1942, the leading character is an Oxford student. Drunk for the first time, and prodded into introspection by a new acquaintance, the young hero is "set on the path to self-knowledge" when he finds "a measure of truth in the cup…a reflection of what lies deep within himself." He sees that he wants to spend his life in the theatre rather than in the family business—and the very next day he is invited to join the OUDS. But Davies abandons his theme of self-discovery to take a nostalgic detour through Oxford, as his hero walks the streets, visits Blackwell's, attends a performance at the Playhouse and spends an evening with the Long Christmas Dinner Society. Virtually all the characters have real-life originals. The central figure is modelled on Michael Benthall, Davies' friend from the OUDS. Horace Davenport becomes Homer Fenwick, and Davies himself shows up as Llewellyn ffrench-Pritchard (or Taffy for short), a student whose research project is an edition of the seventeenth-century jest-book *Nugae Venales*. At the middle of the seventy-third manuscript page, Davies called a halt: the novel was turning out to be "silly." Rereading it in 1988, he judged it "too autobiographical" and "too Oxford-enchanted," and he was right: the loving evocation of Oxford dissipated all the dramatic tension in his *roman à clef*.

The first of Davies' serious plays, still a prentice piece, was written hesitantly and with much revision between mid-1943 and April 1944. At different times he called it both "The King Who Could Not Dream" and "King and Caliph." Once again it is an exercise in self-exploration. The King in question is the glum Æthelred the Unready, ruler of Wessex from 976 to 1016, during whose reign many Christians made pilgrimages to Jerusalem expecting the second coming of Christ, only to be killed or sold into slavery. In Act I Davies makes effective use of historical detail in establishing Æthelred, the key figures in his court and the harsh conditions in his restive, Viking-plagued kingdom. As the act ends, the King grants his Queen, Emma, her heart's desire, permitting her to go to Jerusalem, but as the second act opens we find her a slave at Caliph Montasir's cosmopolitan court in Samarquand. She falls in love with the Caliph, in whom she finds the qualities she had hoped to find in Æthelred. (Davies intended one actor to play both men, to make the point that they were of the same clay, although differently moulded by circumstance.) In the third act Emma returns to Wessex, intending later to rejoin Montasir. But word arrives that the latter has been overthrown and killed, and that the Vikings are about to attack Wessex. At this Æthelred decides to retreat with his Queen and his Fool to Normandy, saying "…we must go upon a journey, to friends and safety, to find, perhaps, the greatest mystery of all—ourselves." There the play ends.

Although Davies had chosen the subject with an eye to the London stage, the play's implicit comment on contemporary life was a good deal more relevant to his own situation than to a London audience's concerns. Sidelined in dour Peterborough (Wessex), yearning for the theatrical life of civilized London (he paints a Samarquand filled with magical entertainment, feasting, amusing talk and dancing girls, a place where a great alchemist thinks he has discovered the elixir of eternal youth), Davies saw himself in both Æthelred and Montasir. Unfortunately for the play, he did not manage to make his theatrical Samarquand a believable counterpoise to Wessex, nor is his Caliph a serious alternative to Æthelred.

In the spring of 1944 Davies decided to try his hand at writing for radio. He persuaded the Victorian Order of Nurses and the Victory Loan Campaign to let him publicize their activities in fifteen-minute slots on CHEX, the local station that his father and Roy Thomson had started in 1942. In the four scripts for the VON he indulged his love of Victoriana, reminding the Order of its roots. One script depicted the fatal ailments that had dispatched so many of Peterborough's Irish pioneers; another contrasted the nursing methods of Dickens' drunken Sairey Gamp with those of Florence Nightingale; a third recreated the battle for anaesthetics in childbirth; and the last one looked at the differences between Victorian and modern child care. They were larky, lively little pieces, but they did not always carry their audience with them: when Little Eva's illness was whimsically diagnosed as "strabismus of the Novachord" the nurses attending in the studio whispered in puzzlement.

His six Victory Loan playlets (three in spring 1944 and three more in spring 1945) were similarly light-hearted. As with the VON dramas, none of the scripts survive, so the description of one in the *Examiner* for May 10, 1944, will have to do duty for all. The other five were studio productions, but this was part of a full evening of entertainment in the Collegiate auditorium—a *very* full evening: the Royal Canadian Army Medical Corps band from Camp Borden played a dozen numbers, a pianist two more, a soprano sang three songs and two choirs from local schools sang six! There were also two duets and, of course, a long speech by a Victory Bond salesman. Mid-evening, Davies' "The Temptation of Anthony Blinker" was performed and broadcast. In this adaptation of *Everyman*, a good spirit urges Anthony to buy Victory Bonds and an evil spirit counters her efforts. Davies, playing the evil spirit, "put everyone in the mood with a spine-chilling laugh." Alas, although the players understood what Davies was up to, the levity missed its mark: the Victory Loan was not felt to be a joking matter in Peterborough. When he and Brenda finished producing the last of the playlets they decided glumly that "you could die in Peterborough of unrequited jollity."

By September 1944, when Davies brought W. H. Clarke up to date on his activities in a letter, his opinions about Canadians' attitudes to the arts had begun to find a central place in his writing. At the time he was working on "a one-act piece on a Canadian theme—a little comedy about Frontenac and Bishop Laval who, you may recall, had a tiff about a production of Molière's *Tartuffe* at Quebec." Probably completed by February 1, 1945, this play was called *Hope Deferred*, referring to Proverbs

13:12, "Hope deferred maketh the heart sick: but when the desire cometh, it is a tree of life."

Hope Deferred is set in New France (now Quebec) in 1693. Two bishops, the zealous Saint-Vallier and the saintly Laval, challenge Count Frontenac, the governor. In their view, a pending performance of Molière's *Tartuffe* poses a threat to the piety of the simple folk in their care. Frontenac and his protégée, Chimène, a Huron Indian who has just returned from Paris where she has been trained as an actress, are just as convinced that artistic expression is central to a life of civilized complexity and subtlety. When the bishops succeed in banning the performance not only of *Tartuffe* but of all other dramas, Chimène regretfully decides to return to Paris, where she can employ her skills. She and Frontenac can only hope that Canada will, some day, come to value the arts more highly. This is a strong little play whose four characters speak persuasively from their deepest convictions, and its relevance to the plight of drama in Canada is clear. Davies' depiction of Frontenac, whose desire to mount plays is frustrated, and of Chimène, who has no outlet in Canada for her training, is only too self-referential.

Between July 23 and September 30, 1945, Davies wrote the three-act play *Benoni*, later retitled *A Jig for the Gypsy*. Originally conceived in 1937 at Fronfraith, it grew out of Rupert's stories of Welshpool and the election of 1880, when Montgomeryshire returned its first Liberal member in a century. The character of Richard Roberts, a local Liberal Party worker, is based on Davies' grandfather. But unlike the family tales, which centre on the sufferings of local Liberals at the hands of the Conservatives and on their electoral triumph, the play is focused on a Gypsy, Benoni Richards, a near-legendary figure who, like the alchemist Avicenna in "The King Who Could Not Dream," has special psychological insight and possesses arcane lore. When she is persuaded to read the Liberal candidate's teacup, the general truths she perceives are seized upon by his supporters to sway votes. The powerful local Conservatives then retaliate by having her evicted from her home, but by the end of the play she has managed to regain both a home and a livelihood. In the secondary plot, a young girl falls in love with a prig, blinded to his character by Ruskin's eloquent idealism—the first of a series of characters to reflect Davies' insight that his reading of German romantic poetry had unbalanced his immature sensibilities and made him prey to ill-founded romantic feeling.

A Jig for the Gypsy richly evokes Victorian Wales, and it possesses a notably strong central character in Benoni. Davies' portraits of Jack the Skinner, Pugh the Photograph, and Conjuror Jones are equally vivid. But the play needed cutting and reorganization to make it move along more briskly. Its relevance to a contemporary audience is also far from clear.

Davies completed *Overlaid,* his most frequently performed play, in a first draft titled "Intermission Time," by Christmas 1945. The action is set in a farm kitchen in Smith township not far from Peterborough, where Pop, a seventy-year-old farmer, is listening to the first half of the Saturday afternoon Metropolitan Opera radio broadcast. Ethel, Pop's religious, respectable daughter, has no time for opera, and while the radio is turned down during the intermission he irritably tries to explain to her that food for the soul is as important as food for the body. Then the insurance agent arrives to announce that his policy has matured. Pop, the self-proclaimed "bohemian set of Smith township," gleefully tells them how he plans to use the $1,200 windfall:

> I'd go to New York and spend it—that's what…. I'd get some stylish clothes, and I'd go into one o' these restrunts, and I'd order vittles you never heard of—better'n the burnt truck Ethel calls food—and I'd get a bottle o' wine—cost a dollar, maybe two—and drink it all, and then I'd mosey along to the Metropolitan Opera House and I'd buy me a seat right down beside the trap-drummer, and there I'd sit an' listen, and holler and hoot and raise hell whenever I liked the music, an' throw bookies to the gals, an' wink at the chorus, and when it was over I'd go to one o' these here night-clubs an' eat some more, an' drink whisky, and watch the gals that take off their clothes—every last dud, kinda slow an' devilish till they're bare-naked—an' maybe I'd give one of 'em fifty bucks for her brazeer—

As this draft ends, Pop is bent on turning his dream into reality.

When Davies read "Intermission Time" aloud to Tyrone Guthrie at Christmas, Guthrie suggested that the play would be stronger if it gave Ethel her say, too. Davies took his advice, but first he injected snatches from the radio commentary during the opera intermission to reinforce Pop's position on the vitality and beauty of art. Then, when Ethel has her turn, she proves to want

> A headstone. A granite one.... We ought to have a proper family plot, with a chain fence round it, and a headstone with the family name on it. A headstone! Oh, a big family headstone! We could get that plot surrounding mother, right on the crest of the hill, and it'd be seen from every place in the cemetery. A headstone! Not a broken pillar, or a draped urn, or anything flashy and cheap, but a great big block of granite—the gray, not the red—smooth-finished on the faces, but rough on the sides and top, and the name on the base, cut deep! Dignified! Quiet! But the best quality—the finest in the cemetery. I want it! I want it! Then Mother and I, and Lover and Jim and you could all be there together at last—

Pop cannot withstand her. He signs the insurance cheque over to her. His own convictions are "overlaid," a conclusion truer to Davies' sense of contemporary reality than the initial draft had been.

Overlaid is powerful and compelling. The two visions of "life properly lived" are contrasted effectively in the attitudes of the central characters. Davies manages to make Pop's and Ethel's revelations wholly credible. Ethel and the insurance salesman, mouthpieces for convictions that Davies knew were widespread in the society around him, are absolutely in character.

The unhappy endings of *Hope Deferred* and *Overlaid* in part reflect Davies' frustrations at the *Examiner*. Every day as he scanned the editorial page, the Bible Message would stare back at him from column six, the triumph of Wilson Craw's morality over his own aesthetic principles. Every year, too, Craw would want the *Examiner* to review the latest annual compendium of sermons that his minister had published at his own expense, and every year Davies would reply that it was improper to review vanity press books. But in 1944, not long before *Hope Deferred* took shape, Craw had prevailed. Davies gave way in an extra Marchbanks column that appeared in the *Examiner* but not in the *Whig*. So there was probably more than a little of his own rueful chagrin in Frontenac as he acquiesces to the bishops: "These good men exert a dreadful pressure…they are so sure that they are right that they bend us to their will when our hearts and minds tell us that they are wrong." And at the end of *Overlaid*, when Pop gives his daughter the insurance money, he says: "There's a special kind o' power that comes from the belief that you're right. Whether you really are right or not doesn't matter: it's the belief that counts."

In fall 1946 Davies wrote *Eros at Breakfast: A Psychosomatic Interlude.* This is a sophisticated one-act comedy that takes place in the solar plexus of young Mr. P.S. (Psyche and Soma), who falls in love while eating breakfast. The characters appear in uniforms appropriate to the parts of the body they represent: Aristophontes, from the Intelligence, wears a dress collar, white bow tie and academic gown; Parmeno, from the Heart, "*a hussar's uniform, with a pelisse, sabretache and every possible redundancy of military grandeur*"; Crito, of the Solar Plexus, "*an indoor, or palace uniform.*" The fantasy is anchored by references to Mr. P.S.'s outer world—the cereal he eats, the dance he attended, his marks at university, a poem he has written, cultural conditions in Canada and so on.

This depiction of an inner world is a generally light-hearted construction of the *terra incognita* that Davies was struggling to know. But a few lines suggest that he was beginning to focus on difficult points in his relationship with his mother:

> ARISTOPHONTES, *sententiously, as though repeating something he has said for years*: Mr. P.S.'s mother is a Good, Kind Woman. She would do anything in the world for him. Remember how ill she was when she bore him. She is completely wrapped up in him—
> CRITO, *languidly*: I wish she were dead.

A deftly executed whimsy that has received many productions, *Eros at Breakfast* is full of flashes of insight and remains judiciously within its artificial bounds.

King Phoenix, written between October 1946 and February 1947, was once again conceived for the London stage. Reading Geoffrey of Monmouth's *Histories of the Kings of Britain*, Davies had come across King Cole, the "merry old soul," and became intrigued with the idea of a king whose reputation rests on his jollity. The play that gradually took shape in his mind is set in a legendary Celtic Britain several hundred years before the Roman conquest. The immensely long-lived King Cole, his daughter Helena, the Shepherd Lug and the brewer Boon Brigid inhabit a seemingly permanent pastoral golden age. But the giant Gogmagog, surviving as a ghost from an even earlier era, serves to remind the King that time passes, and inevitably brings change. The malevolent Archdruid Cadno and the Phoenician trader Idomeneus indeed prefigure a diminished, human-scale future when, if Cadno has his way, "science" will subjugate nature. The monarch's greatness of spirit contrasts with the meanness of the Archdruid, who tries without success to kill King Cole. When the King does meet his death at the play's close, it is in a manner of his own choosing: with his face painted like the sun, merrily drunk on Boon Brigid's beer, he dances along the top of the Druids' great new stone circle at the vernal equinox and deliberately falls to his death as the first ray of the morning sun strikes the sacrificial stone. Like the vegetation gods of primitive myth, he dies to rejuvenate his era, and his spirit lives on in his daughter Helena, who dons his gown, a beard and a wig, reddens her face and, in the image of her father, presents herself to the people as their new monarch.

Once again, as in *Overlaid* and *Hope Deferred*, Davies contrasts a generous openness to life's rich potential with the narrowing impulses that bring death to the soul. His characters are vivid and memorable, and the Golden Age is richly realized. But quasi-historical plays that build on myth are expected to have contemporary political application. This play, written like "The King Who Could Not Dream" essentially out of his own frustrations, didn't strike the right chord with his contacts in the London theatre.

Getting any hearing at all for the early plays was not easy. There was almost no indigenous theatre in Canada during the late war years, and although the London stage was presenting new works by the likes of Terence Rattigan, Peter Ustinov, J. B. Priestley and Emlyn Williams, Davies was too far away to take its measure. He did have one professional connection in Tyrone Guthrie, who encouraged him from the first. On reading "The King Who Could Not Dream," Guthrie recommended that it be sent to John Gielgud. The latter, however, tactfully claimed that Æthelred's reputation as "The Unready" was an insurmountable obstacle for an actor looking for a star vehicle. Guthrie then suggested that Davies approach Dame Sybil Thorndike about producing *A Jig for the Gypsy*, but this too led nowhere. In February 1947, when Gielgud was passing through Toronto with his production of *The Importance of Being Earnest*, Davies gave him the script of *King Phoenix*, but on Gielgud's return to Toronto with *Love for Love* in July, he received another no, albeit kindly and at length, over lunch. Gielgud could not afford a failure, he said; a mythic era was difficult to stage convincingly; he feared that people would identify King Cole with Churchill and the Archdruid with Attlee. Guthrie saw this play too, but with no result.

In 1945 Davies sent W. H. Clarke the plays he had written during the previous eighteen months. They were returned. He sent *Overlaid*, and later other one-act plays, to Andrew Allan at the CBC for the radio "Stage" series (this aired from 1944 to 1956, presenting classics of drama and new works by Canadian writers)—again to no avail. Then he discovered the Ottawa Drama League Workshop's competition for Canadian one-act plays. Early in 1946 he submitted *Overlaid* under the pseudonym Cymro (Welshman), and in May he was jubilant to find that he had beaten out forty-six other contenders for the $100 first prize. The judge of the competition, Charles B. Rittenhouse, producer for the Montreal Shakespearean Society, deemed *Overlaid* "one of the finest plays ever written in Canada" and declared it "A hilarious folk-comedy that could stand comparison with the best of E. P. Conkle." This sounded extremely promising—until Davies consulted French's catalogue, where he discovered Conkle to be "a concocter of gummy fantasies"!

The prize did create new possibilities, although not all of them bore fruit. The Drama League always produced the three best plays from its contest, and so *Overlaid* was given a workshop performance in Ottawa on October 27, 1946. Dora Mavor Moore was at that time planning the first season of her New Play Society (which would perform many new Canadian plays); when the prize was announced, she wrote to ask for a script, but she did nothing with *Hope Deferred* for fourteen long months, and Davies got his manuscript back only after he wrote her a letter that she found "distasteful." Neither approached the other again. When Davies decided to enter a play in the 1947 competition, he made sure to do so with a sophisticated piece that would defi-nitely not invite comparison with E. P. Conkle. Using the pseu-donym Phelim (for Phelim Brady, the Bard of Armagh), he sent them *Eros at Breakfast*.

With the end of the war, the Davieses were able to establish contact with the professional theatre once more. Over Christmas 1945, Tyrone and Judith Guthrie came to visit from New York, where Guthrie was directing his wife's adaptation of Andreyev's *He Who Gets Slapped* for the Theatre Guild. They stood as god-parents to Miranda and Jennifer at their christening in St. George's Anglican Church. There was invigorating talk about Davies' plays, about the London and New York theatre and, on Christmas night with the Davies clan at Calderwood, about the-atre in Canada. Guthrie, who had produced a series of radio dra-mas on Canadian history in Montreal in 1931 and who thereafter viewed Canada as a land of theatrical potential, expanded on "the possibility of bringing the Old Vic Company to Canada to play in a travelling tent theatre."

In 1946 the Davieses went to New York to see the visiting Old Vic company perform Sophocles' *Oedipus Rex* and Sheridan's *The Critic* (as a double bill), both parts of Shakespeare's *King Henry IV* and Chekhov's *Uncle Vanya*. After their six dry years it was like "water in a thirsty land." *Uncle Vanya* struck Davies par-ticularly, reminding him "so poignantly of much of life in our own Dominion, where blighted hopes, frustration and waste of spirit are more common than we usually acknowledge." Davies viewed Chekhov, like Ibsen, as a spokesman for Canadians. Later he was to call Ibsen Canada's greatest playwright.

By 1946 Canadian amateur theatre had begun to revive. Davies threw himself vigorously into the first opportunity that presented itself, and it laid down images in his mind that would have a strong impact on *Fifth Business* years later. Father Moore, the priest of little St. George's Anglican Church, wanted to inspire his congregation with a greater sense of reverence, and the two of them hit on the idea of producing the Coventry Nativity Play that Christmas.

When Davies had produced the piece in 1932 with Charlie Campbell, he had used the text of the Everyman's Library edition. This time, wanting a tighter, more graceful, clearer script, he made his own adaptation. Like the original, his version presents the prophecy of Isaiah, the Annunciation, Joseph's reproaches to his "unfaithful" wife, the journey to Bethlehem, the shepherds in the fields, their visit to the Christ child, the arrival of the three kings, Herod's rage and the slaughter of the innocents. But he added a final tableau showing Mary enthroned with the Holy Child in her arms, and a brief epilogue based on several lines from John Bale's *God's Promises*.

By August he had sketched the settings and the seventeen characters in nine-by-twelve-inch water-colours to guide the parishioner making the costumes. The action was to be set in medieval, not biblical times: Isaiah was to be costumed as a bishop, Herod's messenger as a jester, his soldiers as knights, and Herod himself would carry an orb and sceptre. Only the archangel Gabriel—"an apparition in a wine-red cloak and emerald green turban, with hawk-like features," according to the *Examiner*—would be out of time.

Davies and Brenda helped to make the props and costumes. They turned the worn upholstery fabric from their chesterfield inside out to serve as Isaiah's cope, and Davies painted a dove on the back to represent the Holy Ghost. Old curtains from the *Examiner* offices were dyed green, red and yellow by the ladies of the church. Miranda, going on six and enchanted by it all, remembers her parents making Isaiah's mitre and the crowns for Herod and the Three Kings out of stiff stereotype moulds from the *Examiner*. They painted the surfaces dark, scrubbed them lightly with almost-dry gold radiator paint to give them a richly worked appearance and then stuck on some of her glass marbles with red sealing wax to serve as jewels. With a little work, gourds from the vine on the side of the garage, impaled on sticks, became sceptres.

In the last week of September, Brenda and Davies cast the play, and St. George's blue-collar congregation produced a carpenter to play Joseph, a blacksmith for Gabriel and a butcher, a brick-layer and a shipper to portray the three kings. John Hooper, St. George's gifted young organist, decided with Davies to retain two of the four songs from the old play—"In Excelsis Deo" and the "Coventry Carol"—and to intersperse selections from *The Oxford Book of Carols* throughout. He put together a small *a cappella* choir, consisting of himself, his wife, Davies, Tom Allen and two others, and practised them in four-part harmony.

In performance, the parishioners of St. George's, like the guildsmen of Coventry centuries earlier, were marvellously effective. The play was offered "as a service to God" on four evenings in December, and in the packed, candlelit, little white church everyone present genuinely felt afresh the wonder and mystery of the birth of Christ. As the players, the singers and Father Moore moved down the aisle at the play's end, singing "O Come All Ye Faithful," John Londerville wanted "to step out and go with them." For a musical child like Miranda, it was sheer magic.

The play was repeated in 1947 and again in 1948. By 1947 the choir had swelled to fourteen, and the National Film Board sent Christian Lund to take photographs of the production. By 1948 the choir had established an independent existence as the Coventry Singers. Davies sang with the group for several years and often suggested music for it, like Peter Warlock's choral works or Vaughan Williams' arrangements of folk songs. To encourage the Singers, the *Examiner* (which often supported local musicians this way) sponsored a series of pre-Christmas broadcasts each year on CHEX radio, and later on television. The Singers are still performing.

Midway through the play's 1948 run, while his mind was still filled with its powerful images of motherhood—Mary as the

Virgin of the Annunciation, Mary berated by Joseph as a strumpet and whore, Mary the loving mother in Bethlehem, Mary enthroned with the child Jesus in her arms—Davies' own mother died, ending a decade of semi-invalidism. He arrived at Calderwood as soon as he could and found her body laid out in the drawing room, with an expression so grim that it looked as though (in her own words) she "could have chewed nails."

Davies' mother has haunted his dreams throughout his adult years. Typically she appears to him as Medusa and turns him to stone. This night was the most terrifying of her manifestations, for after he fell asleep in the room that had been his as a schoolboy and college student, her ghost appeared above the bed, "utter ferocity and anger on her face," her hair floating around her head "like something out of Blake," her presence so vivid as to be almost palpable. He leapt up, and tried to dispel the vision by sitting up for a time and drinking a glass of water. Then he returned to bed and fell asleep, but the apparition came to him again. "And I thought, if this happens three times, I will die. So I sat up all the rest of the night." Describing the visitation on another occasion, he conveyed the ghost's malevolence even more forcefully, saying it "tried to kill me."

Of the ghost of Hamlet's father, Davies once observed: "The ghost is not terrorizing, it is *awesome*, because you know that something very frightful is happening in Hamlet's life—something that makes him see the ghost of his father. Which means that a very deeply held fantasy and conviction of his is projected into the outer world so that he actually sees the figure of his father and hears his voice. But what his father says is rather what Hamlet expects to hear, or what he fears may be true.... Ghosts and apparitions arise from unconscious psychological disturbances." In these terms, the apparition of his mother was a projection of his own unconscious sense of guilt at winning his independence from her, especially during his adolescence, now recalled so forcefully by the room and the bed he had occupied during those years. That night he was convinced that the fury of the ghost reflected the fact that she was dead and he alive, that he had eluded her clutches at last. But Davies has since had several other ideas about these psychological disturbances and their emanations. He has seen the ghostly visits as representations not of his real mother but of the "ogre of the nursery" who is so important in one Freudian theory about writing. And he has also linked them to his chronic asthma. In *Archetypal Medicine* (1983) Alfred J. Ziegler describes how mothers of asthmatic children confusingly alternate between smothering tenderness and resentment of their offspring, and he vividly evokes the hag-ridden nightmares that asthmatics consequently experience. When he read the book, Davies "immediately recognized the evil spirit which haunted me on the night of my mother's death."

After the service in Kingston, the family took Florence's body to Brantford for a second service and interment in Mount Hope Cemetery. At the funeral parlour, Ross Beckett, its director, took Davies in to see his mother. She looked "all right, as all right as people do when they're in their coffins." But when Beckett confided, "You know, in her last illness your mother had lost a good deal here [at the bosom], so I put in some padding because I thought it would give her a more ladylike appearance," Davies thought, "Well, Beckett, if my mother knows about *that*, you're for it!"

Florence left everything to Rupert, requesting that her jewellery be given to her daughters-in-law as a memorial. She made no bequests to her sons because, like many women of the time, she considered that her possessions belonged to her husband.

The revival of the Dominion Drama Festival in spring 1947 signalled the end of Canada's theatrical winter. Davies supported the DDF in many ways, serving as a governor from 1948 to 1958 and as a member of its executive committee from 1950 to 1953. Samuel Marchbanks reviewed the annual playoff each year, and Davies often acted as adjudicator, speaker, panelist or workshop conductor.

It was in 1947 that the Ottawa Drama League entered *Overlaid* in the Eastern Ontario Drama Festival (a preliminary, regional round of the national competition), giving Davies his first chance to see one of his plays staged. And when, in May 1947, he won the ODL's playwriting competition a second time with *Eros at Breakfast*, there was a network of Little Theatres to pay heed to Charles Rittenhouse when he deemed it "an original, satiric fantasy," proof, together with *Overlaid*, that "drama is at last coming of age in Canada."

It was also in May that Colonel Robert J. Bolton, president of the Peterborough Teachers' Council, approached Davies for help in a new dramatic venture. In Bolton's view, the city's school-teachers should make a contribution to the community that would dispel the rigid, sober image the community associated with them. He recommended forming a choir or presenting a play. The teachers agreed, and although none of them had much experience in the theatre they had decided to "try something in the drama line."

Davies, who understood their frustrations very well, leapt at the opportunity for Brenda and himself to create some theatre in Peterborough, and in effect to play Pygmalion to the teachers' Galatea. They arranged live-in help (first Sylvia Pedak, and a year or so later her mother, both recent migrants from Estonia) to free up Brenda's time. Nor did they falter when the mistaken diagnosis of Hodgkin's disease took Davies to Toronto for X-ray treatments in November: Brenda just carried on with rehearsals in his absence.

It was quickly decided that the group would present an evening of drama (repeated once or twice) in January or February each year and would work toward entering a production in the Dominion Drama Festival in a year or two. It was agreed too that non-teachers could be recruited to strengthen the group. So emerged the Peterborough Little Theatre. The Davieses sought out plays with large cast lists in order to spread the burden and share the interest of acting as widely as possible, and since amateurs need nine or ten weeks of rehearsal time, they looked for plays whose language and ideas would sustain the cast's interest. If costume dramas could be found, then so much the better: dressing-up was a great aid to the untrained actor's imagination. That first year they chose to present an evening of one-act plays—Shaw's witty *The Dark Lady of the Sonnets*, in which Shakespeare lobbies Elizabeth I for a publicly supported national theatre; Davies' own *Overlaid* (at a teacher's suggestion); and finally Anatole France's wise and hilarious farce *The Man Who*

Married a Dumb Wife, based on Rabelais' anecdote of a medieval French judge who foolishly imagines that his happiness would be complete if his pretty new wife could speak.

At one end of the attic of the Central School the teachers constructed a rough rehearsal stage, and Davies, who did most of the directing (Brenda usually played leads after the first year), set to work. He was kindly and patient with the inexperienced actors and managed gradually to pull coherent performances out of them. He strove for clarity, tried to expose the plays' allegros, andantes and climaxes, and sought to keep the stage "picture" interesting and balanced. For actors who did not speak well, he invented action to make them appear to possess weight and character. He was particularly good at showing his actors how to move on stage—how to use a sword, what to do with gloves, how to flourish a hat. In other parts of the school, after consulting with him, art teachers produced designs and models for sets and costumes, and the home economics and shop teachers executed them. Davies and Brenda passed on hints about things like how to transform old fedoras into medieval hats. Brenda made her own and Davies' costumes. They held a workshop on make-up at their house, with Miranda agog on the fringes of the group.

Their enthusiasm was infectious. Swept into the adventure, the teachers gradually began to ask questions and try out their own ideas. Volunteers for even the mundane assignments were easy to find. And morale rose sharply when Davies threw the resources of the *Examiner* behind the enterprise: there were news pieces during the weeks of preparation and a staff photographer took eight-by-ten inch glossy photographs of the building of sets, rehearsals and scenes. Tom Allen (and sometimes in subsequent years Herbert Whittaker or Arnold Edinborough) reviewed the opening performance.

On January 20, 1948, Galatea was ready for her unveiling. As Prologue, Fern Rahmel stepped forth in cap and gown and, in Davies' rhyming couplets, explained to the audience that, although teachers were thought to be dry and academic—sweeping aside the gown to reveal the evening dress beneath—"*Tonight we are not teachers, we are actors!*" She urged, as the *Examiner* reported, "the acceptance of the theatre as a civic necessity and pleasure."

The evening was a revelation. The productions had a polish and coherence that set them apart from other local amateur drama that had sprung to life in the churches and schools of Peterborough. The sets, designed by Earla McVannel and Gertrude Cox, were unconventional and imaginative. The teachers handled themselves competently, even splendidly. The outdoor scenes of *The Man Who Married a Dumb Wife*, played broadly with a great deal of mime against the musical background of Respighi's "The Birds," were alive with street people and vendors crying their wares. As Fruit Hawker, Musa Cox threw "oranges, the biggest ones I've ever seen, into the audience." The surgeon, doctor and apothecary who were to restore the wife's speech carried a full line of ghastly saws, catheters and squirts, and Davies (listed in the program as Samuel Marchbanks) "came on playing great huge pipes," cavorting across the stage in "a dancing bear sort of performance." Brenda (listed as Seraphina Marchbanks) was, according to the *Examiner*, "pertly vulgar" as a Street Dancer.

The following month, February 1948, the Ottawa Drama League won the Fulford Shield for best one-act production at the Eastern Ontario Drama Festival with *Eros at Breakfast*, and in March, the Montreal Repertory Theatre presented a program comprised of *Overlaid*, *Hope Deferred* and *Eros at Breakfast*, receiving warm reviews. In May, *Eros at Breakfast*, as the only Canadian play in the final festival, automatically collected the Sir Barry Jackson Challenge Trophy for best production of a Canadian play. More significantly, Davies beat out eight others for the $100 prize awarded to the best-written Canadian play in the regional festivals. Samuel Marchbanks, not to be outdone, handed out some laurels of his own in his column, including "The Marchbanks Scold's Bridle for the Most Tactless Remark: Awarded to a lady from the West who approached the only Canadian playwright to have a play in the Festival immediately after its performance with the query: 'Well, and when are you going to write a novel?'"

With Davies making himself felt as a coming Canadian playwright, Samuel French published an acting edition of *Overlaid* that year (1948), and in the next few years virtually every Little Theatre in Canada performed it. In a striking demonstration of its popularity, four of the twelve competitors in the Central Ontario Drama League's first All-Canadian One-Act Play Festival in 1953 chose to present *Overlaid*! The organizers opened each of the festival's four evenings with a different production of the play.

In May 1948, Clarke, Irwin decided to put together a collection of Davies' plays for publication. Called *Eros at Breakfast and Other Plays*, it was to include *Hope Deferred*, *Overlaid* and *Eros at Breakfast*, as well as several others written in 1947 and 1948. Davies himself eliminated one candidate after Brenda told him that its effect on her was "like chewing mothballs." Titled "The Man Who Had No Personality," it was written when he thought he might die of Hodgkin's disease. Centred on the trial run of a machine, invented by two physicists at a national radio corporation, which picks up the voice of God, it questions many things that Davies ordinarily holds dear—ambition, personality and the possession of a strong ego. Another possibility, "Coping with Babylon: A Theatrical Trifle," was scrapped because Clarke, Irwin saw the subtitle as altogether too apt. A third candidate, Davies' adaptation of the Coventry Nativity Play, was rejected on the grounds that it was different in kind from the others.

That left *At the Gates of the Righteous*, whose title is drawn from Proverbs 14:9: "The evil bow before the good, and the wicked at the gates of the righteous." A slight play written for adolescents, it views life through a jaundiced eye, probably because Davies wrote it while he was feeling ill. Set in 1860 (a period in Canada Davies knew through his mother's stories), it is about the seventeen-year-old son of a Presbyterian minister who, with a friend, runs away from home in hot-headed disillusionment with his parents and society. He seeks out a gang of highway bandits, believing them to be latter-day Robin Hoods, but finds their attitudes conventional, even sentimental. In the end the bandits tie the teenagers up and move on, intending to become a church organist, an evangelist and a phrenologist, the better to rip off the public.

Also to be included was the taut, effective one-act play *The Voice of the People*. Completed that June, it aired a pet vexation. Many newspapers in the early decades of the century published letters to the editor under the heading "The Voice of the People." But that heading (a partial translation of Alcuin's "*Vox populi, vox dei*"—"The voice of the people is the voice of God") had never appeared in the *Whig* or the *Examiner*. In Rupert's view, letters to the editor were neither the voice of God nor the voice of the people: "They're the voice of half of a dozen idiots that get into the paper." Davies, who had received his own portion of badly conceived, ungrammatical, anonymous, abusive letters full of etceteras, takes aim in the play at the ill-founded prejudices of barber Shorty Morton, who reads and comments on the evening paper to his family and follows up with a letter to the editor. Shorty and his family are contrasted with Sam North, the electrician who is fixing their stove. Inspired by Thamesville's Sam West and Peterborough's Roy Powell, Sam has much good sense and injects it, in brief and pointed observations, into the discussion.

In the summer of 1948, Davies completed *Fortune, My Foe*, his first full-length play set in Canada. Once again he lashed out at Canada's cultural aridity, amplifying a swelling sense across the country that things must change. Displaced persons had been arriving in Canada in huge numbers during the early post-war years, and at the same time gifted young people in the arts and in academe, despairing of their future in Canada, were emigrating, especially to the United States. This time, however, Davies' play struck a newly optimistic note. It argued that Canadians could create their own culture, a message that spoke powerfully to the new generation. The Canadian actor David Gardner, then a student at the University of Toronto, considered it an important nationalistic polemic, and Donald Davis, likewise a young Canadian actor at the university, was challenged by its argument that "Canada was a garden that was worth tilling." When Clarke, Irwin published *Fortune, My Foe* in October 1949, the reviewers celebrated it as a rare appearance of a full-length Canadian play. By 1967, it had logged more than a hundred productions.

The action opens in a speakeasy on the Cataraqui River over-looking Kingston. Canada's indifference to its academics has embittered Professor Idris Rowlands and has driven his young colleague Nicholas Hayward to undertake a research project, purely (and cynically) to win a lucrative university position in the United States. (Davies resuscitates here the project he had invented for Taffy ffrench-Pritchard in "Forest of Feathers," that is, preparing a modern edition of the seventeenth-century jest-book *Nugae Venales*.) Franz Szabo, a marionette master recently "displaced" from Europe, enters with his puppet, Mr. Punch. Szabo has served a sixteen-year apprenticeship to his art and has perfected the skills honed by generations of practitioners before him. He commands the marionette repertoire, and during the play he patiently and deftly makes a little stage and marionettes to go with it that would have turned the schoolboy Davies green with envy. After he performs the windmill scene from *Don Quixote*, two educationists, his potential employers, attack the great classic's many "deficiencies." Their moralizing, which symbolized for Davies a painful ignorance on the part of many Canadians of the depth and richness of their European artistic heritage, provokes Szabo and the inebriated Rowlands to an impassioned defence of Art. The old professor sends them packing, these people who "have a simple belief in their own power to do good," in a move that contrasts positively with the conclusions of *Hope Deferred* and *Overlaid*. Szabo declares that, even in Canada, the vision and tenacity of the artist will carry him through to success. And, in a frequently quoted speech that reveals Davies himself coming to a difficult recognition, Nicholas Hayward tells Szabo:

> If you can stay in Canada, I can, too. Everybody says Canada is a hard country to govern, but nobody mentions that for some people it is also a hard country to live in. Still, if we all run away it will never be any better. So let the geniuses of easy virtue go southward; I know what they feel too well to blame them. But for some of us there is no choice; let Canada do what she will with us, we must stay.

It was in 1948 that summer stock groups began to spring up across Canada, among them Arthur Sutherland's International Players in Kingston. Sutherland had known Davies at Queen's, and finding that he had written two acts of a play set in Kingston, he pushed Davies to finish *Fortune, My Foe* quickly. Sutherland scheduled it as the final offering of the summer. Davies directed, Grant Macdonald created the sets, and Sutherland produced and played Edward Weir, a character based on Robert D. Owen, the managing editor of the *Whig*. Macdonald, a native of the city, understood precisely what Davies intended by his opening stage directions: "... *across the Cataraqui River the Kingston skyline may be seen in an autumn haze. Let no scenepainter carelessly represent this by the usual huddle of flat roofs and false fronts which might serve as the skyline of most small Canadian cities: two cathedrals, a domed City Hall, the towers of limestone churches and a mass of river-shipping in the harbour make this one of the most picturesque prospects in Canada, and in this light, one of the loveliest.*"

Edward Weir was not the only character with an original in Kingston. Idris Rowlands was based on James A. Roy, Davies' professor at Queen's and the author of the recently published *The Scot and Canada* and *The Heart Is Highland*, both poignant expressions of the yearnings of first-generation Canadian immigrants for their lost homelands and the cultural traditions they had left behind. Buckety Murphy was inspired by an old reprobate who drank shoe polish, prying an occasional dollar out of Rupert Davies with inventive tales about the cry he had emitted at his birth. Chilly Jim, the proprietor of the speakeasy, recalled Dollar Bill, a bootlegger who had run a blind pig in an old seaplane hangar on the Cataraqui River. Inevitably, Davies and Macdonald knew much more about these characters than was spelled out in the stage directions, and the details they supplied were recognized and appreciated by the local audience.

The company was no more perfect in its lines than any other weekly rep, but this *Fortune, My Foe* had special qualities. The actor who was to play Idris Rowlands had a fine voice, so Davies adapted the old Elizabethan song "Fortune My Foe" to give him a chance to sing—and found the title for his play in doing so.

Brenda served as stage manager and gave the production a professional finish. William Needles, later a stalwart of the Stratford Festival company, turned in a first-class Szabo. With only five days for rehearsal, Davies achieved an effect he always strove for as a director, "an everchanging succession of beautiful and significant stage pictures." The production played to full houses for two weeks, a record run for Kingston, and the play quickly became "the much talked of *Fortune, My Foe*."

The Kingston production had hardly ended before the CBC presented a fine radio interpretation of *Overlaid* on September 19 in its "Open Air Theatre." But on October 17 the CBC's "Stage" series gave *Fortune, My Foe* a clumsy production from which, as R. W. W. Robertson observed, "any grace and any humour were ruthlessly excised." Davies' displeasure was increased when he discovered that Lister Sinclair had earned $500 for adapting it while he, the playwright, had received only $300.

In December, the Peterborough Little Theatre, with only three short plays to its credit, began rehearsals for *The Taming of the Shrew*. The play-within-a-play convention suited them very well, because elaborate sets were beyond their budget and they could pretend to be a very tatty travelling company improvising with very few properties in a big room in a lord's house. And Davies had researched all the necessary *commedia dell'arte* details for Guthrie in 1939. Nevertheless, the leap the teachers were asked to make was breath-taking. This production would be performed not only in Peterborough but at the Dominion Drama Festival, and no other group had attempted a full-length Shakespearean play in the history of the festival. John Londerville remembers saying "Sure" when Davies asked him to play Petruchio, and then nearly dying when he discovered what he had agreed to. But the twenty-seven actors (Davies made a brief appearance, *à la* Hitchcock, as the tailor) brought extraordinary will and discipline to the task.

Brenda played Katherina. As always when she and Davies worked together, they had so thoroughly discussed and debated the play that he "understood what she didn't need to be told, and she understood what I didn't need to say, so that directing her was simple." Nine-year-old Miranda, watching her practise, especially relished Katherina's declaration: "I will be angry!" As in her later roles, Brenda turned in a good solid performance, striking and strong, full of warmth and grace, funny (when required) without being clownish. Her habitual briskness and her trained Australian voice were a combination that a couple of years later struck a fellow performer as bracing, "like clear cold water." She herself assesses her talent coolly, by Old Vic standards, and feels that her upbringing, which stressed proper behaviour and control of feeling, inhibited her from doing anything truly exceptional on stage.

Peterborough audiences loved the production, from the acrobatic zanies who changed the scenery to the incidental piano music by Purcell and Warlock. But not until the teachers played the Eastern Ontario Regional Drama Festival in Brockville on February 19, 1949, did they sense how exceptional it was. The adjudicator, Robert Speaight, was so caught up by it that he "just threw away his pencil." When they finished, he came out of the audience on the run to declare that he had witnessed "a brilliant production from first to last…. a brilliant essay in Elizabethan stagecraft…. a light-hearted lark, animated by the spirit of the Italian *commedia dell'arte*." At the festival's close, since the other outstanding entry was the Ottawa Drama League's polished, near-professionally acted *Fortune, My Foe*, Speaight had to choose between Davies the playwright and Davies the producer. The playwright won. *Fortune, My Foe* took best play (and a place at the finals), best full-length play and best actor. Although "well-drilled and disciplined," the Peterborough actors were judged to be "standing not on their own feet, but, so to speak, on the feet of their director." But Brenda's "quicksilver" Katherina won her best actress. Later, Speaight recommended that *The Taming of the Shrew* also be invited to the DDF finals in Toronto.

All this created a stir, which Grant Macdonald described for Davies on February 23:

Dear Rob,
    Congratulations!
    I find this response to your work the most heartening indication that there may yet be a Canadian theatre. That

you should happen to be a Canadian is a circumstance of great fortune for the country and I cherish the hope that there will be a theatre here in which it will please you to enjoy at least part of your career. It seems to me inevitable that your plays will be done in London once they become aware of them over there....

I got back, Monday, from a two-week visit to Toronto. Socially, I have rarely had such a fling. I was not at one party where you were not one of the topics of conversation, and only once did I start it. I put one woman into quite a dither of excitement by telling her there was going to be another Samuel Marchbanks.... I met Robert Gill, director of drama at Hart House, who had just that day read *Fortune, My Foe*. I admired his complete acceptance of it, when I consider the reactions of some producers we know. He would love to do it but fears the students could not do it justice.... My friend, Nancy Pyper, heard you talk in Toronto last month and was much stirred. She knows the difficulties of doing anything about theatre in Canada as perhaps few others do, and felt utterly sympathetic towards your views....

After the week of the DDF finals in late April, it was clear to all that Davies had become a major force in Canadian drama. Clarke, Irwin had published *Eros at Breakfast and Other Plays* (Grant Macdonald designed the jacket) on April 22 in order to get complimentary copies into the hands of everyone who mattered in the DDF before the playoff began (thus setting the stage for *Eros* to become Davies' second-most-produced play, and for *The Voice of the People* to become a staple with amateur groups across Canada). The Introduction by Tyrone Guthrie offered some penetrating observations about Davies' grapple with his parents and with Canadian mores.

On the afternoon of April 28, Davies took part in a panel discussion about the writing of plays in Canada. That evening, after the Ottawa Drama League's performance of *Fortune, My Foe*, there were cries of "Author," and he took a bow. Then it was announced that the DDF had been invited to send a one-act play to the Edinburgh Festival in September, and that it had elected to send the ODL with Davies' *Eros at Breakfast*. On the evening of April 30, the Peterborough Little Theatre performed *The Taming of the Shrew* in Toronto's Royal Alexandra Theatre. Although the production got lost on the large stage and the intimidated teachers were not at their best, Davies and Brenda were a high success. *Saturday Night's* B. K. Sandwell longed to see Brenda "in a more poetic and less rompish comedy." In the audience, David Gardner was electrified by Davies' balletic, flowing tailor. The production won Davies the award for best director. *Fortune, My Foe* took best Canadian play in the finals (over one competitor), and Davies took home the $100 prize as author of the best of the ten Canadian plays in the regional festivals. Tom Allen recalled that as he, John Hooper and Davies walked toward the Royal York Hotel, Davies euphorically chanted: "It's so easy! It's so easy!" Allen interpreted this to mean that it was so easy "to get into the swing, to be somebody, to get close to the high and the mighty, even though he was based in Peterborough." It was so easy "to make waves."

On May 10, *Saturday Night* published Grant Macdonald's drawings of Brenda as Katherina and of Davies as the tailor, a gratifying coda to a week of triumph. That May, too, in an article he wrote for *Mayfair*, Davies inadvertently offered some insight into his casting of Brenda as Katherina—the woman who rebels against the hierarchy of the traditional marriage but ends by acquiescing entirely to it. In "Advice to a Bride," Davies opined that "your husband, whether you like it or not, is your Lord and Master. If he is a decent fellow he will not insist on this too much, but it is part of your job to bear it in mind. By making yourself subservient to him you will find a freedom and happiness you will never get by demanding 'equal rights,' and, paradoxically, you will have more influence with him than you could achieve in any other way." A wife's job is to create "a good home (which really means a pleasant atmosphere)." This is a far more traditional expression of the role of a wife in marriage than either of the Davieses now maintains, but it apparently expressed Davies' own view, and probably that of Brenda, too, at the time.

Back in Peterborough, something new and exciting had already come up. On meeting Davies at the opening of the Kitchener-Waterloo Little Theatre's production of *Fortune, My Foe* the previous December, Michael Sadlier, a young Irish-born Canadian actor who had been looking for a base for a summer stock company in eastern Canada, had been persuaded to consider Peterborough. The combination of a city newly interested in plays, a 410-seat, air-conditioned auditorium at Queen Mary School, a large tourist base in the surrounding lake country and guaranteed support from the area's newspaper editor had settled his choice. Sadlier's Peterborough Summer Theatre presented a season of ten or more plays each year from 1949 to 1957, and, together with the Straw Hat Players, through to 1961.

The first season opened in June with *Fortune, My Foe* directed by Davies (Brenda playing Ursula Simmonds). Before the season had run its course of eleven weeks and eleven plays, Davies had directed two more productions—*Blithe Spirit*, with Brenda as Madame Arcati, and *The Importance of Being Earnest*, with Brenda as Lady Bracknell. In addition, Brenda played Beatrice Lacey in *Rebecca*. Over the next four years, while Sadlier guided the enterprise personally, Davies directed five more productions and Brenda acted in those and in three others. In this period Davies also had some impact on the selection of plays. It was he who added Wilde's *The Importance of Being Earnest*, Shaw's *Arms and the Man* and *Pygmalion*, and two Victorian melodramas, *East Lynne* and *Ten Nights in a Barroom*, to the usual list of West End and Broadway successes. Of course, the *Examiner* supported each production with news pieces, editorials and reviews (many written by Davies). The family went to every play, good, bad or indifferent. Jennifer was taught the responsibility of a theatre audience at these performances. "I learned to clap, because there were often about three of us, and us laughing and clapping and carrying on because Daddy felt it strongly as a responsibility to encourage them." She almost burst with pride when her parents were involved as director and actress, and she loved the excitement of this different world, although she has never herself aspired to a life in the theatre. Miranda, too, until she was sent to summer camp, lived and breathed summer theatre. She went to the rehearsals and got to know all the actors' names. As she watched her mother, she aspired to become an actress herself.

The Summer Theatre brought the Davieses together with many actors then active in radio and summer stock, a number of whom—Robert Christie, William Needles, Betty Leighton, Kate Reid, Barbara Hamilton—were soon to become prominent in Canadian theatre. Some became friends, and all were grateful for the family's generous hospitality. Brenda often organized a pleasant Sunday picnic as a diversion before dress rehearsals. And when Needles (a friend since the Kingston *Fortune, My Foe*) took to his bed with a slight nervous breakdown before the summer of 1952, Davies' telephone call got him up, packed and to their house in Peterborough, where he was cossetted through rehearsals with rum-laced egg-nog every night. When Robert Gill (the influential director of the Hart House Theatre in the years after the Second World War) stipulated that he would direct and act in summer 1953 only if he could stay in a private home rather than a rooming house, the Davieses took him in.

Neither Brenda nor Davies saw the Summer Theatre as a means to a new theatrical career. It was invigoration they wanted—a chance to escape the stifling proprieties of Peterborough. When six-year-old Jennifer escaped one afternoon from the back garden to tear naked down the street with her father in hot pursuit, and the Summer Theatre people happened upon the scene in their battered truck, did they worry about the propriety of nudity on a public street? Did they help to catch the speeding child? No. To the Davieses' delight, they cheered and egged Jennifer on. Although the under-rehearsed, under-funded theatre gave far from ideal performances, the Davieses prized it anyway. Seeing a "good-natured piece" in another summer theatre years later, Davies noted in his theatre diary: "But the *spirit* of the prod. was excellent; one was invited to enjoy it and one did & all the crudities & ineptitudes faded in the general effect. We were reminded of our own days with the Pb<u>ro</u> Summer Theatre, where goodwill covered so many defects."

In September 1949, Davies and Brenda visited Britain for the first time since they had left it for Canada in 1940. They wanted to be at the Edinburgh Festival for the Ottawa Drama League's *Eros at Breakfast,* which they hoped might provide the opportunity at last to break into the London theatre. Marchbanks memorialized the trip in letters later selectively collected in *Marchbanks' Almanack,* and under his own name Davies sent reports on the Festival to the *Globe and Mail* as well. His reports, which enthuse about the positive response of Scottish audiences to his play, the ODL's polished acting and Grant Macdonald's beautiful set, are alive with optimism and hopefulness. But in his heart of hearts he must have realized that this venture would not win the attention of the influential London producers. Certainly Philip Hope-Wallace, the *Manchester Guardian's* respected critic, who judged the production excellent and the play a "slight but highly diverting little one-acter," knew this. In *his* report to the *Globe and Mail,* Hope-Wallace said flatly that the Canadian participation in the Festival was undeservedly a failure because it had attracted neither the audience nor the critical attention it clearly deserved.

In Edinburgh, the Davieses saw Tyrone Guthrie and were impressed by his command of the open stage in two Festival productions. (It was three years later that Guthrie commissioned Tanya Moiseiwitsch to design a splendid thrust stage for Canada's Stratford Festival.) They visited Rupert in Wales, now at Brookland Hall, which had the comforts of central heating and electricity that Fronfraith had lacked. There they also saw the Welsh folksinger Dora Herbert-Jones and enjoyed the sight of Gypsy caravans on the road. In London, Brenda and Davies paid homage at the statue of Henry Irving behind the National Portrait Gallery, where street entertainers and escapologists still plied their trade, and they caught up with John Stead, who was preparing to write his book *Mr. Punch.* At the Old Vic their friends had long since vanished, with the exception of one competent woman who had not been promoted from her pre-war post. For Brenda, this was convincing evidence that as a woman she would have had no hope of rising to the directorial level. Davies for his part had long since concluded that he would never have achieved the first rank either as an actor or as a director. They had chosen rightly in 1940.

On February 16-18, 1950, the Peterborough Little Theatre made some unintended waves with an evening of one-act plays: John Heywood's *The Play of the Weather* (co-directed by Brenda and Davies), Davies' own *The Voice of the People* (directed by Fern Rahmel) and O'Casey's *The Tinker's Wedding* (directed by Davies, with Brenda playing Sarah Casey). The O'Casey play, which portrays an ugly, greedy, old priest and a couple that elects to live in sin, roused indignation among some of the city's Irish Roman Catholics, a number of whom surged to their feet and swept out, including, to Davies' huge amusement, the local crown attorney and his mistress. Letters of outrage descended upon the *Examiner*, many of them taking offence at Davies' program note, which had unwarily stated that the choice of play was "not unmindful of Peterborough's rich Irish heritage" in "the city's centenary year." There were in addition rebukes from the pulpit. Although Davies' *Hope Deferred* had dealt with religious opposition to freedom of dramatic expression, neither he nor the teachers had anticipated the strength of this reaction. Nor was this his only experience of it. The *United Church Observer* accused him of making cruel fun of a drunkard and a bum in *Fortune, My Foe*'s Buckety Murphy. And a Peterborough district Baptist minister attacked *Overlaid* for making fun of "good people" in its portrayal of Ethel.

At My Heart's Core, the full-length play which, with *Overlaid*, seems most likely to become a Canadian theatre classic, was written between January 17 and April 7, 1950. Michael Sadlier had asked Davies to write a play to mark the hundredth year since Peterborough's incorporation, and he decided to write about three of the area's exceptional pioneers: the botanist Catharine Parr Traill; her sister, author Susanna Moodie; and the letter-writer Frances Stewart. Several other characters have historical antecedents: Frances' husband Thomas Stewart is, of course, one. Edmund Cantwell is based on a couple of sentences about a "Mr. Cantwell" in Frances Stewart's *Our Forest Home*. A minor character, Phelim Brady, recalls a local Irish pioneer who had put his deceased wife's body up on the roof for the winter, and (as his name suggests) the Bard of Armagh. Davies' approach in the play was dictated to a large degree by his mother's tales of the cultural deprivations suffered by the early settlers, a topic still relevant in his view to contemporary Canada.

In the background of the action is the unsuccessful December 1837 Rebellion led by William Lyon Mackenzie against the governing Family Compact of Upper Canada, and Lord Durham's subsequent *Report* to the British, which prompted the establishment of responsible government in the colony. While the loyalist men of the settlement are away fighting Mackenzie and his insurgents, Mrs. Stewart, Mrs. Traill and Mrs. Moodie are needled into rebellion themselves by the diabolic Edmund Cantwell, who plants the maggot of discontent in their breasts, voicing what each has long felt "at her heart's core."

Thomas Stewart now arrives home. The uprising has fizzled out, but he is convinced that political reform is needed. In the first of many mock trials in Davies' writing, he sets out to ascertain what has been going on in his absence. He taxes Cantwell with his provocations, but the latter, undismayed, accuses him and the ladies of being "a tight, snug, unapproachable little society." After Cantwell leaves, Stewart plays Lord Durham and cuts through the problems he has found. Mr. Moodie is to have a government post, which will give Mrs. Moodie financial security and time to write. And he satisfies his wife that she has made the right choice in him.

Like *Fortune My Foe*, *At My Heart's Core* spoke positively to contemporary Canadians. Culturally impoverished Canada might be, but the challenge of staying to make things better was, in Davies' view, worth accepting.

That year the Summer Theatre played in two cities. *At My Heart's Core* had its "world premiere" in Niagara Falls' Summer Theatre on August 22 and another, "official premiere" in Peterborough on August 28, where descendants and relatives of the play's three central women were sprinkled through the auditorium. Davies directed and Brenda played Mrs. Stewart, the role he had written for her. Both audiences were enthusiastic.

Like *Fortune, My Foe* before it, *At My Heart's Core* attracted immediate attention from theatre groups. Several had plans to stage it (among them the Canadian Repertory Theatre in Ottawa which invited Brenda to play Mrs. Stewart again) even before the play appeared in print in November 1950. This time the reviewers referred to Davies in phrases like "Canada's best-known contemporary playwright," "Canada's leading playwright," "Canada's foremost playwright of the day," "rapidly becoming Canada's leading playwright." By the early months of 1952, *At My Heart's Core* had been performed more than fifty times. Like *Fortune, My Foe*, it was televised by the CBC in 1953 and continued to be performed across Canada through the balance of the 1950s and into the '60s.

Unquestionably, by 1950 Davies had achieved a dominant role in Canadian theatre. His plays had challenged the country's self-conceptions and encouraged the cultural aspirations of a new post-war generation. He had brightened his corner as well: under his leadership, Peterborough had more and better amateur theatre than ever before, and it had acquired a professional summer season. And as a director he had made his mark in every forum available to him—local amateur theatre, the DDF competitions and summer stock. His plays were being performed by amateur and professional groups across the country and had a growing readership. But despite it all, he was a profoundly dissatisfied man.

In the first place, he didn't want to be judged by local standards only. Although there had been a tremendous upwelling of dramatic activity after the war, much remained to be accomplished before the country would be capable of supporting anything like the splendour of London's theatre. Just how much was the burden of Davies' submission to the Royal Commission on National Development in the Arts, Letters and Sciences (known as the Massey Commission). Davies was approached in April 1950 to prepare a memorandum on the state of theatre in Canada, and he had almost finished it before he went to the DDF finals in Calgary, early in May. On his return he revised it completely in the light of a long discussion with Michel Saint-Denis, co-director of the drama school at the Old Vic and adjudicator of that year's finals. In Davies' memorandum, Lovewit and Trueman, two characters from a 1699 pamphlet about the English theatre, discuss Canada's shortcomings: audiences were unfamiliar with the English dramatic classics; teachers taught plays they had never seen performed; there were few real theatres; professional actors could find no stage work in winter…the limitations of amateurs…the state of criticism…the needs of playwrights…and on and on. They argue that a country like Canada could and should possess a living theatrical tradition. Its classics should be the common possession of a civilized people; its actors should inherit skills honed down the ages; its critics should be able to recognize and celebrate great performances and theatrical events; its playwrights should be able to learn by watching their plays rehearsed and performed. Possibly, travelling companies, led by gifted directors and business managers and performing a broad repertoire, including the classics, might be a place to begin. But they should be encouraged to spring up of themselves and to succeed on their commercial merits. Government should assist by establishing a training centre for the theatre arts and helping to lighten the expenses of travelling companies and playwrights, but Davies opposed the notion of a state-supported National Theatre.

Another source of frustration for Davies was his lack of success in placing his plays abroad. Nothing had come of the Edinburgh Festival venture. Kitty Black, the leading reader of plays for H. M. Tennent, the London producing company, wrote bluntly, in a letter that Davies has quoted often, "You must realise that no one, but no one, has any interest in Canada." When he had sent plays directly to eminent actors and producers he knew (*At My Heart's Core*, for example, went to both Gielgud and Olivier), they would let them gather dust for months or years without reading, returning or even acknowledging them. Employing an agent had produced little better result. By 1950, he was using Stephen Aske's literary agency to hawk his wares to London producers, and by 1953 he had switched to Graham McInnes' agent, John Johnson at E. P. S. Lewin & Partners. But the net result of his and their efforts was just one BBC Welsh Region production of *Benoni* on August 6, 1952 (rebroadcast twice) and an amateur production in Ealing, by an experimental group called the Questors, of *A Jig for the Gypsy* in September 1954. Clearly what he was writing did not speak effectively to the needs of English producers. Davies must have inwardly acknowledged this, for since *King Phoenix* in 1947 he had written no plays "on spec" for the London stage. Nor would he do so in the future.

Davies was further aggravated by the treatment his plays received in the hands of bad amateurs: it was almost beyond bearing. After a production of *Fortune, My Foe*, for example, in which a character unfamiliar to him spoke lines of "stupefying vulgarity and foolishness," he was told by the director: "Oh, you know that newspaper man you put in? Well, it wasn't a very good characterization; he wasn't stupid enough for a newspaper man. So I re-wrote it...." Davies knew that he would be judged by this man's meddling, yet the state of theatre in Canada was such that he felt he must bite his tongue and be polite. Also, when he had offered the Ottawa Drama League *At My Heart's Core* free of royalty, in appreciation of the group's influential early productions of his plays, its committee of amateurs turned the play down (which he could accept), and then went further, telling him that the play was badly written, unactable and probably a money-loser. Then, at a London (Ontario) Little Theatre performance of *At My Heart's Core* in May 1951, he overheard one member of the local committee remarking to another, chuckling, "Well, here we go for another of these rotten Canadian plays we do out of duty." The production they gave his play was so sentimental and perfunctory that he felt it had been mauled. Yet he also felt he had to pretend to be grateful that it had been performed at all.

He found it exceedingly painful when an adjudicator lit into an untried play on the basis of an amateur performance. (He would have found it no less painful, no doubt, to have a play faulted after it had been given a fine professional production, but then, presumably, he would have felt that the play had had a fair chance.) When, for example, the North Toronto Theatre Guild gave *King Phoenix* its première production in March 1950, Herbert Whittaker directed the play imaginatively, but the cast was less than ideal. Yet, on the basis of this performance, the Toronto critics criticized the play sharply, and when the group entered it in a regional drama festival soon afterward, the play drew patronizing comments from the adjudicator. According to R. W. W. Robertson in a report written that autumn: "Its reception...cut him to the quick and the harsh criticism of the play by the regional adjudicator rubbed salt in a wound which has not healed to this day." Likewise, when the Peterborough Little Theatre entered Davies' own production of *King Phoenix* in the 1953 Eastern Ontario Drama Festival, the adjudicator drew peals of laughter at Davies' expense. "Moments of memorable brilliance were spoiled by passages of memorable banality," he said. The plot resembled "the libretto for a 19th-century opera to which the music had never been supplied." When it was still judged the best Canadian play in the Festival (over one contender), a visibly distressed Davies left one of the teachers to accept the trophy. Afterwards, many took smug pleasure in his humiliation.

Davies put his feelings on paper in a seven-page comic dialogue titled "Playwright's Plight" (later part of the 1953 "Marchbanks' Almanack" manuscript). Mrs. Henbane, president of a woefully amateur drama club, meets Apollo Fishorn, wildly impractical Canadian playwright. Her group (five hundred paid-up members, twelve active) intends to perform his historical fantasy about Napoleon's desire to "ruin" Laura Secord. They are tired of doing the old Broadway and London successes that every Little Theatre offers; now it is time for "something that nobody can possibly call commercial." Although Mrs. Henbane has held the script for eighteen months, she hasn't read it, preferring to select the play on the strength of Fishorn's name, which "stands for the finest in Canadian drama—such as that is." With the benefit of her two years' experience as president, she proposes to help him "shape it for the stage" and when he protests, she informs him that "it'll be rewritten, or it won't be done." The play calls for thirty-seven characters (only one of them a woman) and a crowd, but Mrs. Henbane can cast it from "eight women and a rather undecided boy." Fishorn envisages sixteen changes of scene, including a grand panorama and a vision, but when they rewrite, she says, "it will all take place in Laura's cottage, and we'll do that with some old gray curtains." Finally, "goaded beyond endurance he draws a small bow and arrow from an inner pocket and shoots her dead."

If he ruled out writing for London and for Canadian amateurs, that left the Canadian professional theatre. As he said in a letter at the time, "They adopt a thoroughly business-like attitude toward the play, their artistic standards are high and what particularly pleases me as a playwright is that they allow me to know my own business and do not itch to re-write and tinker with my plays." But in 1950, he had already achieved as much as such groups could then offer—namely, summer stock productions that would run for a week. Nonetheless he was hopeful, given the startling advances since the war, that it would not be too many years before there would be a Canadian professional theatre of high standard that would offer him more scope. When that happened, he thought, he would write for it. In the short term, however, he decided to try his hand at a novel, and so he turned to the writing of *Tempest-Tost*.

Chapter 10

THE SALTERTON TRILOGY: 1950-58

He has written full-length plays, continues to work at them, and hopes that they will be produced in England. If, by the age of 40, he has not achieved this aim, he says he will turn to novels.
    —Graham McInnes, *Saturday Night*, 26 April 1947

By the development and integration of personality Dr. Jung does not mean rampant egotism or "personality" as salesmen or show-people use the word; he means self-knowledge, particularly of those parts of the mind which we usually seek to ignore, and those parts of the personality which seek their gratification in aggressive and hostile attitudes and actions towards others. Such self-knowledge is a curb on egotism, not an encouragement to it.
    —Robertson Davies, *Saturday Night*, 24 May 1958

BY THE LATE 1940s the Davieses had begun to find friends and genial acquaintances in Peterborough. The Little Theatre introduced them to a large number of the city's teachers, a number of whom, like Fern Rahmel, became friends. They met the head of the Grove School in nearby Lakefield (some of the staff were involved in the Nativity Play in 1947 and 1948) and from then on were invited annually to the school's New Year's fancy dress ball. Once Davies went as a Gypsy, another time as a rajah, and most notably as a Puritan, bearing a banner that read "Circumcise therefore the foreskin of your heart, and be no more stiffnecked" (Deuteronomy 10:16).

In the early 1950s they formed warm friendships with psychiatrist Tom Currier and his wife Sheila, writer Scott Young and his wife Rassy and insurance agent Ross Thompson and his wife Ruth. Ruth Thompson, Scott Young and Brenda all reviewed for Davies at *Saturday Night*. Ross Thompson acted and Sheila Currier acted and then served as production manager in the plays Brenda directed for the local St. John's Players. The four couples saw a lot of each other socially, but the occasion remembered best by all is the annual Boxing Day family party at the Davieses' Park Street house. The children started things off at about 4:30 with an entertainment. In 1953, for example, this took the shape of a puppet performance by Miranda, Jennifer, Rosamond and the Thompsons' sons of "The Tragedy of Dr. Faustus." The script was a four-page adaptation by Davies for the three glove puppets the children happened to own at the time: their bearded king, wearing a cap, became Dr. Faustus, their devil became the fiend Mephistopheles and their kitten the philosopher's cat Vitzliputzli (a minor demon in the old German play that Goethe had used as a springboard for his *Faust*). Helen of Troy was personated, according to Davies' note in the margin of the script, by a doll, "stark naked." There were some good sound effects—the off-stage voices of an angel and a demon, a blinding light, a scream and a clock striking twelve.

After the entertainment came supper, charades and a rousing game of "Homicidal Maniac." This was hide-and-seek with a difference. Everyone drew lots, the black spot designating the Maniac. The lights went off and everyone hid. The Maniac then sought out and "choked" his (or her) victims, who each gave a frightful shriek and fell to the ground. The object was to produce the maximum number of shrieks before someone tapped the Maniac and identified him. The moonlit Park Street house, with its back stairs, attic stairs, full-length mirrors and many closets, was an ideal setting for the game, and it filled with screams and giggles as the eighteen of them skulked about.

On occasion the Davieses joined the Youngs, Tom Allen (from the *Examiner*) and the Edinboroughs (if they happened to be visiting from Kingston) to go tobogganing. As they careered downhill, Davies' and Edinborough's beards would fill up with snow and their chins become frost-bitten; afterward the adults would warm up with hot buttered rum at the Youngs' in Omemee.

By the mid-1950s the Davieses were part of an enjoyable social circle whom they saw for drinks, parties and dinners. At one party where spirits ran high and a séance was attempted, a number of the revellers managed to levitate Davies in his chair, only to lose their concentration and drop him sprawling to the floor!

Robert B. Porter, who came to town in 1956 to be chief librarian, became a friend, as did his wife Valerie, in 1958 or 1959. When Porter advertised in the *Examiner* for an assistant, Davies addressed a pseudo-application to "Bwana" Porter, couched it in extravagant African English, signed it from someone who purported to be "the fruit of Porter's loins" and had it mailed from Nigeria. He tried a more elaborate hoax in 1961 when the local Historical Society was gathering material for a museum. Porter was on the executive, and Davies sent him a little album containing photographs of Peterborough residents, circa 1867, which he had found in a Toronto shop. In the covering note he drew attention to a leaf of an old letter tucked into the album and asked Porter to decide whether it should go to the Society. The album itself is in the museum today, but the letter fragment didn't quite make the grade. It certainly looked authentic enough. Written in a nineteenth-century hand, on laid paper, it began mid-sentence with a reference to the making of sugar and "maple sass" and ended in the midst of some homely particulars of pioneering life. But the long middle section revealed a scandal: Mrs. Frances Stewart had been found *in flagrante* with the young curate Clementi in the vestry of St. John's Church! Porter was agonized. Mrs. Stewart was a local icon, the almost-saintly wife of the man who had organized the settlement of the area. The Reverend Vincent Clementi was a respected pioneer of local education and a descendant of the composer Muzio Clementi.

Porter could imagine the reaction in Peterborough if the letter were made public. But then he realized that each horrific sentence was just too deliciously phrased, just too atrocious. So, writing Davies a letter of thanks, he took the hoax letter to the next meeting of the Society's executive and watched gleefully as they were deceived in their turn. One member even declared that the letter would have to be suppressed. Porter found out later from Ralph Hancox that Davies had taken the paper from an old book, stained it with coffee and tobacco juice and cooked it a little in an oven to age it.

Contrary to his 1947 statement to *Saturday Night*, Davies did not wait until his fortieth birthday before starting his first novel. He began *Tempest-Tost* on September 18, 1950, shortly after he turned thirty-seven, and it took the form it did because he was discouraged by his experience as a playwright. He had originally conceived *Tempest-Tost* as a play, and so had written his usual notes about the plot and characters and prepared two outlines. Then, picnicking on a hillside with Brenda and the children in June 1950, he thought: "To hell with it. You write a play and then you have an awful time getting it quite badly done by incapable people. I think I'll try it as a novel, and see how it goes as a novel." If he did that, he would not have to depend on others to display his characters to advantage. He could direct, set the scene, light the action and costume the cast himself. And all the powers of persuasion he had been developing as he worked with amateur theatrical groups, trying to bring them to understand and share his vision, could be exercised directly on his readers instead. His manuscript, instead of being subjected to the indifference and carelessness of theatre people, would receive the attention of publishers who, in his experience, would respond courteously and promptly.

The play became a novel with startling economy of effort. He was able to use practically everything he had in hand, filling out the larger fictional form with things that were at the top of his mind at the time. The conception in his first note for the play made it into the novel virtually unchanged:

A Shakespeare play is to be performed by some amateurs, out-of-doors, in a large garden owned by a Senator? The background of the play is rehearsal and performance.

The mainplot: a member of the cast is a highschool teacher, a bachelor whose life has been a success by his standards; he is now 40-45. He becomes infatuated with a girl in the play who is 18-20, just out of a private school and eager to try her attractions. She pays no attention to him, except for a word or two & a general flirtatiousness. As the production goes on his jealousy and torment grow until he finds her kissing a young man. He then tries to kill himself, but his suicide is ineffective and is hushed up, though some people know about it.

As readers of the novel will realize, the bachelor schoolteacher is Hector Mackilwraith and the girl is Griselda Webster, daughter of the wealthy man who owns the garden. With some adjustment of detail, the three scenes of the projected play—the first in the gardener's shed, the second during the second-to-last dress rehearsal and the third in the midst of a performance—provided the novel with its beginning, middle and end. All ten of the original characters of the play survived into the novel, and Griselda's thirteen-year-old sister, the precocious Fredegonde, who with her champagne cider was to have framed the drama, makes an appearance in the scenes that open and close the novel as well.

Amateur acting groups were very much on Davies' mind at the time. In his recent submission to the Massey Commission he had argued that in the theatre amateurs are distinguishable from professionals in two ways. They cannot give the theatre the time and energy it needs, and (less excusably) they tend to indulge the pernicious notion that the talented among them should exercise their gifts on-stage with restraint, in order to avoid exposing the weaknesses of the rest of the cast. Professionals, on the other hand, give themselves wholly to the theatre and recognize (however painfully) that talent is and must be ruthless in its demands. Having decided to explore this territory, Davies, smarting from his unhappy experiences with amateur productions, might easily have produced biting satire. He was certainly capable of it. But satire is not a comfortable genre for him. He recoils from pessimists. At Oxford he had been dismayed to learn that others cringed from the force of observations he tossed off quite casually, and since then he had deliberately guarded his tongue. So while in *Tempest-Tost* one can often see a glint of the bright épée of the satirist, Davies kept its point well sheathed.

In Davies' outline, the action was to have taken place in a very specific spot, namely the garden of Calderwood, his father's house in Kingston, and the amateur production enacted there was to have owed something to his 1935 production of *A Midsummer Night's Dream*. But the richly imagined milieu of *Tempest-Tost* went well beyond that. In fact, the decision to turn his knowledge of Kingston to account in creating the novel's town of Salterton was quite fortuitous. Late in April, *Maclean's* magazine had asked him for an article about the city, which he had forwarded at the end of June. But when Pierre Berton, as Article Editor, returned it, asking for a radical rewrite, Davies decided not to recast it. The novel was taking shape in his mind, and he decided to draw on this material to make the city itself a subject, second in importance only to the amateur production in which his characters were involved. So the first chapter cannibalizes the first eight pages of the *Maclean's* article to introduce the fictional city of Salterton, a community that takes much satisfaction in its past glories (including the moment when it almost became Canada's capital). It is proud in setting its own rules and in possessing such marks of distinction as a Roman Catholic *and* an Anglican cathedral, a fine court-house, Waverley University, a large and forbidding prison and many beautiful homes of local limestone. Davies then gave the Websters' home, St. Agnes', a history that combines those of Summerhill, Archdeacon's Folly and Calderwood itself. And a few pages later he pillaged his recollections of Calderwood's grounds and Alwington's to construct the garden where the Little Theatre is preparing to produce *The Tempest*, his favourite play.

As he moved further into the novel, Davies' memories of Kingston came more fully to bear. He follows his characters into their homes and out to various events; he portrays their evening meals, their entertainments and their falling in love; and as he does, we see the social gradations of Kingston/Salterton through his amused and privileged eyes. When Valentine Rich needs to settle the affairs of her recently deceased grandfather, Dr. Savage, the offer of his library to interested clergymen memorializes an event well remembered in Kingston and creates the opportunity for one of the book's great set-pieces. In 1930, Dr. Bruce Taylor, clergyman and retiring principal of Queen's University, had placed a small notice in the *Whig* to say that "members of the Kingston clergy who wished to come and see if there were any volumes they would like in his extensive theological collection were bidden to do so on a particular day." Davies' account of what ensued makes the most of its comic potential, beginning with the modest notice in the newspaper and rising to frenzy:

> By half-past eleven two hundred and thirty-six clergy-men had passed through the library, some of them three and four times, and the shelves were bare. Dr. Savage's bequest had been somewhat liberally interpreted, for an inkwell, a pen tray, two letter files, two paperweights, a small bust of Homer, a packet of blotters and an air-cush-ion which had been in the swivel chair were gone, as well. The widest interpretation had been placed on the word "library" in the advertisement, for some of the visitors had invaded the upstairs regions and made off with two or three hundred detective novels which had been in the old scholar's bedroom. Even a heap of magazines in the cellar-way had been removed.
>
> "I don't think there is a scrap of printed matter left in the house," said young Mr. Maybee.

But Salterton is not simply a portrait of remembered Kingston. The play production does obviously draw on Davies' 1935 *A Midsummer Night's Dream*. Laura Pottinger, the ancient make-up lady, is a comic expansion of Mabel Gildersleeve; Griselda Webster is like Eleanor Sweezey in having access to a car and dri-ving when she goes out on dates; Solomon Bridgetower, the director's assistant, owes much to Davies. But this production also recalls the OUDS' 1936 garden production of *As You Like It*

—in its sensible, pleasant professional woman director, in the horse that steps on a live wire during the rehearsal and in Professor Vambrace's "business" with the seven grapes. And once Davies had thrust Hector Mackilwraith into the middle of the play production and imported the Snarey trio from Thamesville to interfere with its music, his construction had gone well beyond what he remembered of Kingston. Salterton is not a photograph but a comic composite lit by imagination.

The creation of Hector Mackilwraith, like the invention of Salterton, represents an important step in Davies' creative development. Mackilwraith is his first serious study of an emotionally impoverished man in the midst of a mid-life crisis. When Davies first laid his plans in June 1950, he intended to exact full comic vengeance on his hated UCC mathematics teacher, Lorne McKenzie, in the course of "a light and amusing story." And he did endow Mackilwraith with McKenzie's physical appearance, his methodical approach to life and his narrowly conceived, punitive teaching techniques. But toward the end of the second chapter, the character began to assert himself in an unanticipated way. As Davies explored the upbringing that had turned Mackilwraith into such a narrow human being, it soon turned out that the character's background was rife with the humiliations that Davies had himself suffered at the North Ward school in Renfrew. When Davies got to the passage where Mackilwraith, as a boy, refuses to be browbeaten into entering the ministry, he realized that "Hector was rather more of a handful than I thought he might be."

From then on, ridiculous though Mackilwraith often is, the reader is made to feel sympathy for him. Burdened very young with heavy responsibilities, he never has the leisure to pursue an interest or develop a capacity other than those that lead directly to a good teaching job and paycheque. When, at forty, his starved spirit pushes him to try acting, Shakespeare's poetry works powerfully on his uneducated sensibilities, and he promptly falls in love, in a courtly, idealistic way, with young Griselda Webster, the first girl who smiles at him. In trying to attract her attention he becomes painfully aware of his age and of the limitations of his approach to life. So completely is he disconcerted that he ceases to take pleasure in his job, goes off his food, loses sleep. In the end, mistakenly convinced that Griselda has given herself physically to another man, he "atones" for her sin by making an inept attempt at suicide, a gesture both funny and sad. But it purges his overwrought emotions and it brings him a little of the feminine warmth he has yearned for: Valentine Rich comforts him and, as the book ends, Griselda (whom he has worshipped from afar) speaks to him as a friend and kisses him goodnight. (The book's readers, however, are left to decide whether this catharsis will result in a genuine growth in his personality. Not until *Fifth Business* and *The Manticore*, after Davies had reached his late fifties and absorbed the thinking of C. G. Jung, was he ready to pursue characters like Mackilwraith through their mid-life crises to the painful realignments that would allow them to meet the challenges of the second half of life successfully.)

Davies completed the novel that he had originally subtitled "The Life, Pathetic Love, Tragical Death and Joyous Resurrection of Hector Mackilwraith, B. A." expeditiously. The new form seems to have given him only one serious technical concern, which he addressed to R. W. W. Robertson in November. Was the 120,000 words he projected too short? too long?

It may seem curious to you that I should make an enquiry of you at this time when the novel is still in the process of being written. It is very often said that a story must find its own length and that the number of words contained in it should be sufficient to tell its story adequately and no more. However, I seem to function rather like Anthony Trollope than like the artistic gentlemen who talk in the terms which I have mentioned above, and if I am told that a piece of work should be a certain length, I adjust my inner machine accordingly and it appears at that length. I suppose this is because I am basically a low journalist and not an artist.

Robertson didn't help much. He did recommend a minimum of 80,000 words but "hesitated" to fix an extent.

The first draft of *Tempest-Tost*, like those of the earlier plays and later novels, is remarkably free of revision. His play drafts from the 1940s, handwritten with a fountain pen, look almost like fair copies, so rare is the crossing-out of a word or sentence. But they were not: Davies made his decisions about structure, sentence and word in his head, then confidently wrote from inner, clear dictation. Revision, which came at the end, was simply a matter of adjusting words and phrases and adding stage directions. The novel (and his subsequent work as well) was written with similar assurance, but with an important difference. Anticipating that he would find it too tiring to handwrite a substantial book, Davies switched to a typewriter for *Tempest-Tost* and used one for almost all his writing thereafter. The change required little adjustment, since he was used to working at a typewriter at the *Examiner*. With this first novel he also established a procedure that served him for most of his later writing: on completing his first draft, he revised it by hand, had a typist prepare a fresh copy, revised *that* by hand, and then had this polished version newly typed for submission to his publisher. The eight sections of the final copy of *Tempest-Tost* were delivered to Clarke, Irwin at intervals between May 15 and 22, 1951, just eight months after the writing had begun.

With the manuscript off his hands, Davies experienced periods of dizziness, probably the result of the congenital malformation of his inner ear. He told Robertson: "I hardly dare mention this to the people who have been convinced that I have been dizzy for many years, but it is a nasty thing, and control of it involves a great deal of pill-taking." But he ploughed right on, doing the necessary proof-reading, directing an early summer production of *At My Heart's Core* (Brenda playing Mrs. Stewart) at Brae Manor in Quebec, and assisting with the move, on July 12, to the pleasant 1850 house at 361 Park Street North that he and Brenda had bought in May.

Late in July, revisions were called for. Clarke, Irwin had noted itself uneasy about several aspects of the book, and Irene Clarke had instantly taken exception to one incident in particular. As written, the episode of the horse's death included the sentence: "At the instant of shock, his penis had extended to its uttermost."

In Irene Clarke's opinion this was "unworthy" of Davies. It wasn't his "best self speaking," he must "take out the horse's penis"! Davies managed to argue her around, but then Chatto and Windus, who were to publish the book in England, objected to this and other passages as well. In Davies' opinion, their discomfiture with the horse and with Mackilwraith's attempted suicide was a misjudgment. They had "mistaken my book for a *funny* book to be read by old ladies at Torquay on winter afternoons. It is a *comic* book, and one of the comic things about life is the way in which the lovable and venerable may, in a moment, in the twinkling of an eye, become hideous, grotesque and even hateful." But he grumblingly allowed himself to be persuaded by Cecil Day-Lewis, then senior reader for Chatto and Windus (and an established poet), to replace the sentence about the horse's electrocution and to cut out two chunks of Mackilwraith's background, one describing the family diet and the other recounting an ill-advised attempt by Mackilwrath's mother to sell his father's theological books. All three excised passages are characteristic and well deserve reinstatement.

Davies met the challenge of the new genre with astonishing skill, modulating from quoted speech and thought, to reportage of both, and on to summary, as if he were an old hand with narrative techniques. We hear the hum of the characters' thoughts as we watch them in action. The tone is consistently warmed by the narrator's comic and humane vision. But the pacing is less secure. The action begins slowly, the play production and the side glances at Salterton interfere with each other, and the story is derailed too long by the flashback to Hector Mackilwraith's early years.

When *Tempest-Tost* was published that October, in a charming jacket by Grant Macdonald, most Canadian critics welcomed it as new evidence of Davies' broad talents. They admired his ability to create character and telling situations and enjoyed his "wit, humour and cogent observation" (to quote L. F. C. of the *Hamilton Spectator*). Such weaknesses as they discerned (primarily the implausibility of Mackilwraith's suicide and the book's lack of plot) were brushed over as of little importance. William Arthur Deacon in the *Globe and Mail* was one of the few hostile assessors, and potentially the most damaging. But his estimate of the novel as "no more than a casual fragment of impressionistic reporting" without "solid core" or "serious purpose" didn't prevent strong sales (about 5,000 hardcover copies in Canada, a figure matched by the two later Salterton novels as well). When Rinehart published it the following July, the American reviewers liked it too, although their notices were briefer. Chatto and Windus' British edition in the same month attracted even less attention.

Davies had made his revisions to *Tempest-Tost* in Wales. The previous year Rupert had sold his second Welsh country house, Brookland Hall, and purchased massive Leighton Hall, which stands across a valley from Powis Castle, its rival in size and grandeur. Having retired from business in January 1951, he was free to indulge himself, and on March 1 he did so, accepting the ceremonial and honorary post of High Sheriff of Montgomeryshire. Created by Henry VIII, this position required Rupert, to his delight, to wear a traditional cocked hat, lace collar, sword, dark-blue velvet breeches and buckle shoes to open the County Assize Court and (as things fell out) to proclaim the accession of Elizabeth II. Under-sheriffs and heralds accompanied him on these occasions, their banners displaying his coat of arms.

Eager to share the pleasures of all this with his family, Rupert invited his sons to spend the summer with him and his new wife, Margaret Esther McAdoo. A Calgarian, she was the same age as Davies and, like Rupert, she was a descendant of an old Welsh family. Leighton Hall was a huge, Victorian extravaganza built in 1851, surrounded by formal terraces and gardens. Its first owners, Liverpool banker John Naylor and his wife, had outdone themselves in the three-storeyed great hall. Under the oak-timbered roof, the stained-glass windows of the clerestory depicted the arms of the tribes of Wales. A bronze and ormolu clock, whose works occupied the tower, indicated the seconds, hours, days, months, seasons, signs of the zodiac, the time at Leighton Hall, the time at Greenwich and the phases of the moon. Huge paintings of *Napoleon Crossing the Alps* and *The Temptation of*

Christ hung on the end walls. Portraits of the Naylors, larger than life, flanked the main doors. Their initials were carved everywhere. An immense Austrian sideboard from the Great Exhibition of 1851—a veritable altar to gluttony, carved with a profusion of allegorical figures, life-sized hounds, fruits, flowers, meats and game—dominated the south wall. (It makes an appearance, along with the clock, in Liesl Naegeli's amazing Swiss castle in *The Manticore*. When Rupert later had the sideboard dismantled, he distributed some of its lesser parts to his family, and Davies' portion—two cornucopias and young Autumn—lent splendour to his own Thanksgiving board for many years.) Rupert's own portrait later joined the Naylors', and was described thus by Davies after his father's death in 1967:

> *My Father* by Cleeve Horne. As big as the Naylors, & over the fireplace. He is in Court dress, as High Sheriff, & seems to have been taken by surprise in some handsome house. Excellent legs, & the right knee a little bent as though he might do a bow, or a minuet, at once. *Chapeau bras* & white gloves in his right hand; the left rests on the hilt of his sword. The only American thing about him, his horn-rimmed spectacles. Expression quizzical; only someone who knew him wd. recognize this as a sign of self-consciousness. He looks amusing, & amused.

Rupert went to great pains as host. He would ask his grandchildren, "Would you like to hear some fairy music?" and at his pull of the concealed lever in the great hall the thirty-seven fine bells of the clock would chime out in a sacred or national air. With the exception of Rosamond, who was often left out because she was at least five years younger than the rest, they all had a splendid time, riding the ponies and exploring. Davies himself had fun as the turbanned and bearded substitute for the fortune-teller at the local church fête. He knew his game, as Marchbanks later divulged:

> (1) everybody is worried about a boy, a girl or a child, according to age;

(2) everybody is short of money, regardless of income, and likes to be told that they will find money worries decreasing as they grow older, which is likely to prove true;

(3) a stroke of good fortune is likely to come to everybody within three months, and may confidently be predicted;

(4) nobody believes utterly in fortune-tellers, and very few people utterly disbelieve in them.

But the visit was not wholly pleasurable for the adults. Leighton Hall was not yet the appealing, comfortable home Rupert would later make it in his many summers there. Rationing was still in effect in Britain, and renovations were barely complete. His new wife had not yet settled into her role. And Rupert had been foolish in inviting the two sons who had never gotten along well—Fred and Robertson—to visit together. The tensions that had exploded between them years before in Kingston had never been resolved.

Although Fred could be charming when he chose, the disastrous course set by Florence's indulgence and Rupert's rigidity had produced in him a self-centred, outspoken, often unpleasant person, who, when angry, could be uncontrolled and terrifying. All his life he was an embarrassment to his family. An observer in Renfrew remembers him making insulting remarks about the food at a dinner at Thomas A. Low's cottage, when it was his own lateness that had spoiled the meal. An able mechanic, he had been an asset in Rupert's printing business, but he understood nothing of managing people nor of controlling expenditures, and when Rupert, in 1932, gave him the Kincardine *Review-Reporter*, a prosperous weekly newspaper, he ran it into the ground. (It was absorbed by the *Kincardine News* in 1937.) His life had then trailed away into "managing" his wife's money, serving as his father's gofer, working at jobs that went nowhere and running through astonishing sums of money borrowed from his mother and Arthur.

When it occurred to Fred that Davies' writing was probably lucrative, he repeatedly angled for a share in the profits by supplying plots and experiences for him to turn to account. Davies kept putting him off, but inevitably there was unease and awkwardness.

Fred could also be amazingly insensitive with children. Once, knife in hand, he threatened to cut off Jennifer's thumb because she had persisted in sucking it longer than usual. All through the visit at Leighton Hall, there were heated words, as Davies reacted to Fred's insulting behaviour, particularly as directed toward Brenda. Matters were exacerbated further by the fact that he found Fred's wife Kathryn intensely disagreeable. This was the last prolonged period the brothers spent in each other's company. On March 7, 1954, according to a report in the *Examiner*, Frederic Rupert McKay Davies was killed near Nassau in the Bahamas "when his car went out of control and hit a tree."

By March 1952, Davies was contemplating a new Salterton novel, or perhaps two. In May he talked of completing this next novel (which would "have as its centre the newspaper of the city") by the following spring, and on November 28 the first two sections were in R. W. W. Robertson's hands. At this point, he intended to call the novel "A Barber's Chair." This is a reference to a favourite quotation of his from *All's Well that Ends Well*, which was also to have supplied the titles for the book's six sections: "The Barber's Chair," "That Fits All Buttocks," "The Pin Buttock," "The Quatch Buttock," "The Brawn Buttock" and "Or Any Buttock."

Work on the novel was halted in 1953 when he took on *Saturday Night*'s book page, reshaped "The Correspondence of Samuel Marchbanks" into "Marchbanks' Almanack" and made a substantial contribution to a book commemorating the first year of the Stratford Festival, all this in addition to directing for the Little Theatre and two summer stock companies! His overtaxed system rebelled by succumbing to *lichen planis*, itchy red spots whose initial visitation persisted for a year and a half. It still flares up whenever he pushes himself too hard. The recurrences of this "fretting scall, or tetter," this "shirt of Nessus" make him, he says, feel like a leper. It kept (and keeps) him from wearing a wrist-watch. But he resumed work on the novel (wisely dropping "the whole buttock device"), and finally got it finished in the spring of 1954. The first part, now slightly revised, reached Robertson March 23 and the sixth and last a month later.

What kept Davies on track through all the distractions was a
theme that had been shaping itself in his imagination for a long
time: what if a small city newspaper slipped up and printed a
notice that proved to be a hoax? It could easily happen. At the
Examiner during one amazing week in 1946, a prankster had
unsuccessfully submitted an item which implied that two people
were married (they were not), and a second had succeeded in
placing a birth announcement on behalf of a newly married couple. By the time he wrote the first of his "Notes for Novel in
Progress" in his "Works in Progress" notebook in spring or summer 1952, the core idea was clear and much of the book's life
was present in embryo:

> *Theme*: a false engagement notice is inserted in the
> *Salterton True Briton* and the book tells of the annoyance
> this causes and the changes it brings about in the lives of
> several people directly & indirectly affected. ∞ The notice
> inserted by a man who is aggrieved against the editor &
> the two parties whose engagement is announced: an E. B.
> party, a singing & elocution teacher refused privileges of
> university library by Pearl Vambrace? slighted by Solly
> Bridgetower who will not let him read Shakes. or advertise
> his talents in his classes? Editor has refused him puffs. Feels
> himself excluded by Salterton snobbery. Notice inserted on
> Hallowe'en? His landlord & landlady, George and Kitten?
> Name: Bevill Higgin & insists that 's' be left off. ∞ Does
> *Time* visit Salterton to investigate the scandal? ∞ Involved
> are Humphrey Cobbler & some friends who are found by
> the Dean dancing in St. Nicholas' cathedral on
> Hallowe'en.

Sketches for the novel's main characters followed, then outlines
for the first three sections and, more roughly, for much of the
fourth and a little of the fifth. As was to be his practice in writing
novels, Davies did not plan the final section, in order to leave the
story free to draw its own conclusion.

Where *Tempest-Tost* reflects Davies' youthful delight in
Kingston's history and architecture, and especially its amateur

theatre, *Leaven of Malice* celebrates the civilizing influences he had come to appreciate as a young man: the newspaper, the Anglican Cathedral, the university. He had an insider's knowledge of each of them. He knew a little about St. George's Cathedral from the time when he had co-directed the Coventry Nativity Play there with his friend Charlie Campbell in 1932, and more from what Charlie, who had intended to become an Anglican priest, had told him. He was familiar with the university from his years as an undergraduate and tutor there. The newspaper, of course, he knew best of all. The book would be a comedy of manners, but in taking a comic, sometimes farcical look at the daily struggle of the talented and principled against the smug, the self-satisfied and the narrow-minded, Davies never diminishes the complexity of the war being fought. The two young people who fall in love and begin to seek independence from their parents are inhibited not so much by the tyranny of their elders as by the love and duty they feel toward them. And even the most principled of his characters is infected, however briefly, by the spitefulness abroad in the community.

The story begins with the hoax announcement in the "Engagements" column of the Salterton *Evening Bellman* on October 31:

Professor and Mrs Walter Vambrace are pleased to announce the engagement of their daughter, Pearl Veronica, to Solomon Bridgetower, Esq., son of Mrs Bridgetower and the late Professor Solomon Bridgetower of this city. Marriage to take place in St Nicholas' Cathedral at eleven o'clock a.m., November 31st.

It then follows Gloster Ridley, the *Bellman*'s editor, through the events of November 1. Walking to work in the morning, Ridley wonders whether he will be given an honorary degree by Waverley University and mentally begins to compose a lecture that he is to give at the university that fall. At the office, he reads his mail, edits the letters to the editor, is interrupted by old Mr. Swithin Shillito, scans the editorial pages of other papers, concocts "Notes and Comment," allocates books for review, has his ear bent by the reporter Henry Rumball on the subject of the epic novel he is writing, consults his managing editor Edward Weir and writes a leader on the St. Lawrence Seaway. All this follows the pattern of Davies' mornings at the *Examiner*. The subjects, though not the manner, of Shillito's editorials "Whither the Toothpick" and "A Vanishing Amenity [the walking-stick]" recall or anticipate Davies' own "The Vanished Button Hook," "A Place for the Toothpick" and "The Solid Gold Toothpick." The novel that Henry Rumball labours at is the epitome of all the hopeless novels that preoccupied one reporter or another at the *Examiner*. In 1952 both the *Whig* and the *Examiner* had run editorials on the subject of the St. Lawrence Seaway. Edward Weir is based on Robert D. Owen, the *Whig*'s managing editor, and Swithin Shillito draws on certain antiquated hangers-on whom Davies had noticed at the Kingston paper as an adolescent.

The repercussions of the spiteful notice begin to spread through Salterton. Dean Jevon Knapp is affronted that the Vambraces had not contacted him before announcing a wedding in his Cathedral; Professor Vambrace is insulted that the notice links his family and that of his arch-enemy. The fusty Tory lawyer Matthew Snelgrove (whose original is Peterborough's Mr. Kerr) encourages the Professor to sue the newspaper for libel; and Pearl Veronica Vambrace and Solly Bridgetower, the innocent pair, who had seen nothing of each other since they had participated in the Little Theatre production of *The Tempest* four years before, find themselves not only linked in the minds of Saltertonians but literally tied together in a silly game at a party. Davies kneads this light dough very skilfully, pulling us into the lives of the Dean and his eccentric organist Humphrey Cobbler, Ridley, Pearl and Solly, and bringing us to feel concern for their welfare when the things they care about and have worked hard to establish are threatened.

But the leaven of malice is countered by a leaven of goodness. Solly Bridgetower, suffering the *longueurs* Davies himself experienced as a tutor at Queen's when marking undergraduate essays, hates teaching and takes no joy in academic research. Fortunately for him, Humphrey Cobbler counsels him and helps him to find and accept his calling as a writer. Gloster Ridley, bedevilled by unreasonable feelings of guilt over his wife's incurable insanity, so much so that he has concealed her existence and has yearned for honours to shore up his self-esteem, luckily has a good friend in Mrs. Fielding, who helps him to come to terms with himself. Although the newspaper faces the prospect of a damaging libel suit, Ridley and those who work for him fortunately believe in the value of good investigative journalism, and reporter Henry Rumball finally discovers the hoaxer to be one Bevill Higgin, an elocution teacher who had wanted to spite Solly, Pearl and Ridley for minor and imagined slights. (Higgin is based on J. Elliot Butterworth, the "Teacher of Piano, Singing, and Elocution" who had assisted in the 1928 Kingston Collegiate Institute production of *The School for Scandal*. Butterworth had unscrupulously persuaded the couple with whom he boarded, and in whose front room he taught, that they possessed musical talent, and had managed to part them from much of their savings. When he gulled them into performing a concert, the young Davies was equally appalled by their ignorance and his opportunism.) The book ends happily and romantically, since those who wish to provide the community with a principled newspaper, fine music, cultivated and wise preaching (and possibly a good novel) emerge victorious, and a new, legitimate engagement notice is scheduled to appear in the newspaper.

Reading a draft of the first third of the book in December 1952, R. W. W. Robertson had noted perceptively: "I think Mr. Davies is riding his invention with a snaffle in an effort to keep out extraneous matter. Time and again I thought that he was off on some alluring bypath, as for example the earnest reporter and his great Canadian novel, *The Plain that Broke the Plow*, but just as I began to inquire if this side-trip was necessary, it became evident of itself that it was...." Over the next year and a half Davies fulfilled this early promise, producing in *Leaven of Malice* the most balanced of the three Salterton novels. He had managed to bring all the elements that were slightly out of kilter in *Tempest-Tost* under control. The plot is tidily woven up and the structure neatly contains the action. The three characters (Gloster Ridley, Solomon Bridgetower and Pearl Vambrace) who achieve a degree of self-knowledge do so with the aid of mentors and confidants who keep the focus squarely on the key issues. And the title *Leaven of Malice* is entirely apt. (Davies did not give it to the book until January 1954, but the phrase, which comes from *The Book of Common Prayer*, was in his mind from the beginning. He had included it in his preliminary notes for Bevill Higgin.)

As the sections reached Clarke, Irwin in March and April 1954, R. W. W. Robertson responded with appreciative notes. Once again, however, Clarke's wife Irene sought changes. This time she wanted a romantic ending, with a satisfying love scene between Solly Bridgetower and Pearl Vambrace. Early in May, Davies made two half-hearted attempts (one double-spaced page each) at "putting another 1/2 lb. of sugar in the cake," but neither suited. He did not forget her ill-judged interference.

On the advice of Leonard Woolf, Chatto and Windus immediately agreed to publish *Leaven of Malice* in Britain, but Rinehart declined the manuscript in the United States, as it had earlier declined *The Table Talk of Samuel Marchbanks*. Davies had been feeling for some time that he ought to be more professional about the business side of authorship. It seemed likely that an experienced agent would serve his interests better in the United States than his Canadian publishers had done, and might perhaps also bring a useful perspective to the standard contracts he signed in Canada. So he accepted Scott Young's offer in June 1954 to introduce him by letter to Willis Kingsley Wing, Young's own New York agent. By July, Davies and Wing had come to an agreement. (In 1965 Wing became president of Collins-Knowlton-Wing, a subsidiary of Curtis Brown Limited of New York, and continued to do Davies' work until 1968. After Wing retired, Davies stayed on, as he did later when Collins-Knowlton-Wing was absorbed into Curtis Brown in 1976 with Perry Knowlton as president.)

When Davies informed W. H. Clarke that he had placed his affairs in Wing's hands, the firm was alarmed by the financial implications. It earned fees for placing Davies' books in Britain and the United States, and sometimes also by printing the books for the other markets. In the short run, its position was impregnable, however, since the contract for *Leaven of Malice* empowered it to function as Davies' agent outside Canada. But when both Knopf and Harcourt Brace refused the book, Clarke, Irwin itself engaged Wing to act on its behalf in the American market. Wing placed *Leaven of Malice* with Scribner's, the first publisher he approached.

The novel, in a jacket by Clair Stewart, appeared in September 1954 to Canadian reviews that relished its gallery of distinctive characters, the comic situations, the wit and well-honed style. Comparisons with Stephen Leacock were frequent. (Aptly enough, when *Leaven of Malice* won the Leacock Medal for Humour for 1954, Davies was introduced at the awarding ceremony as "the man of many faucets," a reference that Leacock would undoubtedly have been delighted to include in his lecture "We Have With Us To-Night.")

Although the reviewers saw little point in dwelling on weaknesses, it probably exasperated Davies to have them say, even in passing:

> Its plot may be slight…. (the *London Free Press*)
> …it is scarcely a plot…. (the *Hamilton Spectator*)
> The plot is slight enough…. (the *Cornwall Standard-Freeholder*)
> There is little or no plot…. (the *Kingston Whig-Standard*)

Annoyed by similar complaints about *Tempest-Tost*, he had told a correspondent: "I cannot say that I think very much about plot myself, for the lives of most people appear to me to be plotless. However, I am always happy to oblige my critics and I am hoping to cram in enough plot into the next book to fulfill their needs for a long time; I shall then be able to write my subsequent books without any plot at all." In similar vein he had told his editor that *Leaven of Malice* "would have a Wilkie Collins plot, a thick, rich, dark-brown, stewy sort of a plot."

When *Leaven of Malice* appeared in Britain in February and in the United States in July 1955, the critics in both countries paid serious attention. It struck them as wise in its knowledge of human nature. They compared Davies' work to that of Trollope, Joyce Cary, Evelyn Waugh, J. B. Priestley and Sinclair Lewis. In

England the book attracted substantial reviews from Nigel Nicolson and Elizabeth Bowen, and in America from the major New York papers. The *New York Times Book Review* recommended it for seven weeks. American hardcover sales rose to about 7,000, the best achieved by any of the Salterton novels on first publication.

Through much of 1955 Davies' left leg had been giving him concern. There were prolonged periods of numbness, and often when he got to his feet at the end of a concert or play, it would give way. He could stick a pin into it at such times with no sensation of pain. After fretting and worrying for a while, Davies consulted Dr. Dobson, who couldn't find the source of the trouble and said, "but I think we should open up your back and see if you have a slipped disc." Davies remembered the result of Dobson's diagnosis of Hodgkin's disease in 1947, however, and declined. Soon after this, in November 1955, he met a woman who spoke enthusiastically about the Alexander Technique, and he followed up the introduction she gave him to her teacher in New York.

Shaw and Aldous Huxley had awakened Davies' interest in F. M. Alexander and his Technique much earlier. In *London Music in 1888-89* (1937), Shaw had written briefly of Alexander's "far reaching science of the apparently involuntary movements we call reflexes" and of his "technique of correction and selfcontrol which forms a substantial addition to our very slender resources in personal education." In *Ends and Means* (1938), Huxley had claimed that Alexander's method of physical re-education increased mental and moral self-awareness and self-control at the same time as it relieved physical strains. Davies had sent for Alexander's *The Universal Constant in Living* in 1941, but from its murky, pretentious prose he had been able to gather only that Alexander believed physical ills to result from misusing the body, not from organic weakness or infection.

In January 1956 Davies and Brenda went to New York for a week of lessons with Lulie Westfeldt. A short, slight woman, then sixty years old, she was living proof of the efficacy of Alexander's teaching. Weakened by polio at the age of seven, she had lived in a wheelchair for years as the result of the deterioration caused by a so-called "corrective" operation (which immobilized her right ankle) when she was thirteen. Yet Alexander had got her walking again during her first six months of lessons in 1929-30, and by the end of his first Training Course for Teachers, which began in 1931 and lasted four years, she moved gracefully, even buoyantly.

What Lulie Westfeldt had learned from Alexander and passed on to the Davieses was a particular alignment of the head, neck and back that Alexander believed to result in the most efficient use of the whole body, an alignment apparently assumed instinctively by animals. Standing, sitting, lying down, walking, one should "think" the body into this special relationship, saying inwardly: "The neck free, head forward to go up, back lengthening and widening." She guided their bodies into the appropriate alignment with her hands and helped them to isolate and eliminate the tensions that interfered. Of course, achieving the proper stance at a lesson, with the help of a teacher, was one thing. Putting it into operation in daily life was quite another, for that meant abandoning deeply ingrained, wholly unconscious physical habits. To assist them, Lulie suggested contemplating an action such as walking, or reaching, or writing, but not doing it. Since the mere thought would call the old tensions into play, Davies and Brenda slowly learned to distinguish "right" from "wrong." She then taught them to focus not on the general action with its habitual responses, but on its component elements, with the result that they eventually learned to move in a more economical, relaxed way.

Back in Peterborough, they took turns teaching each other twice a day and consolidated what they had learned. They had absorbed enough that Davies was soon able to stop clenching his leg into the hip socket; its circulation and sensation quickly returned to normal, and on the few occasions when the numbness returned he was able to alleviate this problem, which Lulie Westfeldt had suggested might well have had its root in an undiagnosed brush with polio in childhood. For her part, Brenda learned how to relax the tension of the jaw that had arisen years before when she had struggled with the frustrations of dyslexia at school.

From then until Lulie Westfeldt's death in 1965 they went every six months for a week's lessons, usually to New York, occasionally to Sandgate, her farm in Vermont. Her wisdom and cultivation extended well beyond her teaching, and they came to care deeply about her. Davies considers her to be, like Brenda, one of the women who have taught him the things of real importance in life—"interesting, practical, sensible things." He read and commented on early drafts of her book *F. Matthias Alexander: The Man and His Work* in 1957 and 1958, and he and Brenda each wrote a testimonial in October 1958, which appeared over their initials when the book was published. In 1959 Davies sent her to his agent, Willis Kingsley Wing, but she was unable to find a publisher until 1964.

After her death, it took them several years to find another Alexander teacher. Between 1969 and 1977 they had lessons with Peter Scott when they were in London, in 1979-80 with Richard Ireton when he visited Toronto and in 1980-81 with Jean Robinson in London. In the early 1980s Toronto finally acquired several teachers of the Alexander Technique, and since 1981, Davies has gone once a week (and Brenda bi-weekly) to Kevin McEvenue.

For Davies, the benefits of the Alexander Technique were substantial. In 1958, he reported an increase in his physical well-being. The new way of sitting made long hours at his desk less exhausting; the new way of walking made his favourite (and only) exercise more pleasurable. He felt that his powers of physical and mental endurance had expanded and that the method had given him a new means of self-exploration. Over the succeeding years there were additional gains. The feet that had caused him such difficulty in adolescence lengthened by a half size and became more comfortable. The writer's cramp that plagued him in the early 1970s finally yielded to the Technique. And his relationship with Brenda gained a new dimension as well. Where Davies had had virtually no physical interests and Brenda had many (she skates and plays badminton and tennis), now he had some contact with this side of her world. As they worked together and discussed their progress, their understanding of each other deepened.

Inevitably, the Technique appeared in Davies' writing. In *A Mixture of Frailties*, voice coach Murtagh Molloy enjoins singer Monica Gall: "Feet a little apart. Let your neck go back as far as it will—no, don't move it, *think* it and let it go back itself. Now, *think* your head forward and up *without* losing the idea of your neck going back. Now you're poised." And again: "Ah, your jaw's tense. Get your neck *free*; think it free, and your head forward and up, and your jaw *can't* tense. Come on now, try it again." Or again, in *World of Wonders*, one of the older actors in Sir John Tresize's company gives young Paul Dempster some advice on how to achieve a relaxed control of his body: "It's mostly your back. Got to have a good strong back, and let it do ninety per cent of the work. Forget legs.... The main thing is to trust your back and forget you have a front; don't stick out your chest or your belly; let 'em look after themselves. Trust your back and lead from your back. And just let your head float on top of your neck. You're all made of whipcord and wire. Loosen it up and take it easy. But not slump, mind! Easy."

When suffering from boredom at UCC, Davies had thought desperately: "...there's got to be something better than this." He'd wished that reality were sharper, brighter, more intense emotionally, more splendid. He thought he had found what he sought in a Chautauqua tent at a performance of *Rigoletto* during his tenth summer—this, he was convinced, "was the way people behaved when they took off the masks which all adults seemed to me to wear." As he matured he did satisfy his yearning to some degree in the heightened world of the theatre. But that was a world apart. At bottom he was sure that he was missing something; life must be more vivid than it seemed. As we shall see, it was ultimately C. G. Jung who opened his eyes. But it took a long time for him to perceive this, and his consequent shift in perspective was not complete until he tackled *Fifth Business*. In the 1950s, when he first began to read Jung, he saw him primarily as a possessor of insights that might assist his ongoing voyage of self-discovery.

As a student and young man, Davies had been bowled over by Freud's persuasive eloquence and his brilliant psychological insights. As late as 1960, he was persuaded by Dr. Edmund Bergler's *The Writer and Psychoanalysis* to accept a Freudian theory about why writers write. He gives the gist of Bergler's argument in *A Voice from the Attic*:

> Authors are attempting to solve an inner conflict through the sublimatory medium of writing, says he, and it has been his invariable experience that the conflict is that of a psychic masochist at war with his Mother Image. This alarming image is not his real mother, or his mother as she appears in his Oedipus complex, but is rather "that giant ogre of the nursery, the pre-Oedipal mother." We need not examine this concept in detail, but it is of interest that in Dr. Bergler's opinion this inner tension results in the aggressive and rebellious nature which is common to writers. Nor, it need hardly be said, that aggression and rebellion necessarily manifest themselves in an obvious fashion: they may be confined to a deep level of the writer's work. But they are there. This cast of mind also, in Dr. Bergler's view makes writers what he calls "injustice collectors," people who have a strongly developed sense of grievance, which again need not appear in obvious ways.

There were probably two things that attracted him to this theory. On the one hand, it proposed a positive outcome—namely, writing—for his negative feelings about his mother. And on the other it emphasized that a writer's Mother Image—the pre-Oedipal ogre who threatens to devour or starve or castrate him—has nothing to do with his actual mother, and everything to do with a newborn's very real fears as he first comes to terms with the discomfort of life outside the womb. At the time of reading Bergler's book, Davies was in the midst of striving to view his mother more objectively and with greater fairness, and Bergler's theory contributed to this impulse by simultaneously offering a justification for his dark negativity and by suggesting that it was directed at a nursery phantasm rather than at the woman herself.

However, although Davies, with his immense interest in self-knowledge, had chewed over Freud's theories for years and had made occasional use of them in his criticism, he had never espoused a Freudian outlook, never erected a character on the basis of his theories. The reason for this only slowly became clear to him. When he was a young man he had not recognized how much Freud's temperament and outlook repelled him, but as he approached middle age, he began to feel profound unease and dissatisfaction with the great man. Freud had little to say to patients over the age of forty-five. His deep pessimism had begun to grate on the basically optimistic Davies. Freud's dogmatism, his unwillingness to admit to reservations or uncertainties, troubled him. His view that religion is an illusion was frustrating as well: Davies had once hoped to learn something about religious belief from Freud's investigation of the psyche. And Freud's insistence on the central role of infantile sexuality in all subsequent experience seemed wrong-headed and reductive of life's possibilities. Surely a man elected to become a writer (to take one telling example) "for some better reason than because he was scared of his mother before he developed his Oedipus complex"!

Curious to find out why Freudians so disparaged Carl Gustav Jung, Davies began to read Jung. (Brenda accompanied him, debating and sharing insights with him as they progressed from book to book.) Although the Swiss psychologist's slow-moving, heavy style had nothing of the Viennese's grace, Davies found that his theories, broad reading and turn of mind were deeply satisfying. Unlike Freud, Jung took keen interest in the challenge of the second half of life. He proved to be an optimist, and was willing to change his mind in the light of subsequent experience. To Jung, sex was only one of a number of important elements in life. A Jungian analysis was constructive, setting a patient's problems in the context of his present life and culture, drawing on insights from the world of myth, fairy-tale and legend. Jung had much to say about the creative mind and about religion. His conviction that man's intellectual and psychological capacities evolve very slowly, which minimized the differences between a classical Greek and a contemporary European, was one that Davies found sympathetic.

The shift in Davies' allegiance was not instantaneous. The first

Jung he read was *A Modern Man in Search of a Soul* in 1953, followed by *The Practice of Psychotherapy* in 1954, *Two Essays on Analytical Psychology* in 1955 and *Symbols of Transformation* in 1956. After that he acquired and read the balance of the great Bollingen translation of Jung's works (1953-73) more or less as it was published. He also read broadly about Jung: introductions, biographies, handbooks, letters, interviews. Two secondary sources in particular—P. W. Martin's *Experiment in Depth* (read in 1955) and M. Esther Harding's *Journey into Self* (in 1956)— were early, major sources for a coherent overview of Jung's theories and of Jungian analysis. As late as January 21, 1956, however, Freud still commanded his primary loyalty. In a review of the second volume of Ernest Jones' biography of Freud on that date, Davies exhorted: "Compare what he writes with Jung's cranky, self-justifying account of his break with Freud, and we soon see which is the greater man."

Within months Davies had begun to transfer his allegiance, in a move that appears to have been a deliberate confrontation of the crisis of middle age. On June 16, 1956, he wrote R. W. W. Robertson at Clarke, Irwin: "I very badly need some new ideas and a thorough overhaul of many of my old ones. I could name dozens of cases—and so could you—of authors who have rushed through life outfitted only with the ideas that they picked up between the ages of eighteen and twenty-four, which has not been enough provision for a lifetime. The result is that much of what they write after forty is old stuff which is only redeemed from mediocrity by the fact that their skill in writing has increased. I am extremely anxious to avoid this pitfall if I can and, therefore, I want to take some time to read and even more time in which to do absolutely nothing." The play and the novel he planned that year and the next were much influenced by Jung. When he referred to Jung's influence and theories in *Saturday Night* later in 1956 and in 1957, there was a new note of respect. Many of the drawings (including one of the cross with a serpent trailing around it) that he hung as decorations in the house for Christmas 1957 were based on illustrations in one of Jung's books. By May 24, 1958, he had moved far enough to suggest that "as a therapeutic method his form of depth-psychology seems to be both safer and more lastingly effective than Freud's."

Jung's respect for the psychological insights embedded in medieval astrology probably prepared the ground for Davies' decision to consult a New York astrologer, Hugh McCraig. Brenda's old friend Jackie Kornfeld had insisted that, as a writer, he ought to see this extraordinary man, so he visited him on December 8, 1958, in his dark little room at 15 West 44th Street. McCraig cast his horoscope on the basis of data Davies had forwarded beforehand, and told him (according to his diary):

> I am not as needful of people as many. I live much in my mind, & my health is bound up with my mental health; avoid drs.' drastic remedies & trust my intuitions abt. myself. Am highly intuitive & shd. trust it: will be increasingly concerned with metaphysics. Am entering an important stage of my life whch will mount for many yrs. My writing is especially successful when it relates past to present. The collaboration with T[yrone]. G[uthrie]. will be difficult but if I treat him with kid gloves his jealousy of me may be blunted. (Do not believe this of T. G.) The Casanova play will be a marked success. I am on an upward pathway. Will retain health and semblance of youth & be increasingly wth. young people. Will live into my eighties, wth gd. health. Brenda is an 'old Soul' & in many respects my teacher: respect her intuition....

There was enough astute perception (and, as it turned out, accurate prediction) here to win Davies' respect for the powers of this strongly intuitive practitioner of the ancient science of astrology.

He also consulted M. Esther Harding, a New York Jungian analyst, on May 8, 1959. Reading her *Journey into Self*, a view of *Pilgrim's Progress* in Jungian terms, had so intrigued him that he considered entering analysis with her. But she discouraged him. His plan of taking a long weekend once a month (or possibly a fortnight every six weeks) would not work: analysis had to be continuous. Besides, he had no "gross symptoms," and he had plenty to keep his feet on the ground—a wife, children, a demanding job. From his single encounter with Harding he carried away an indelible impression of a woman with a hearty, easy laugh, and one "splendidly at home in her life; frank, charming, wise, and without being in any way beautiful or young, certainly one of the most fascinating women I have ever encountered." She became one of the sources for Dr. Johanna von Haller in *The Manticore*.

The message that family friends received in the Davieses' 1961 Christmas card was in effect an announcement that the transfer of his allegiance from Freud to Jung was complete, although it took years more for Davies to assimilate Jung's ideas fully:

Was it Frazer who froze Old Christmas,
With frost from the Golden Bough?
   Was his mirth destroyed
   By Sigmund Freud—
Say, where is Old Christmas now?

From the deep Unconscious grottoes
Where the Jungians take their stand,
   Archetypical, unreformed,
   Old Christmas rules the land;
Wafting crypto joy
   To each girl and boy
With lavish, numinous hand!

When Davies read Jung's autobiography, *Memories, Dreams, Reflections* (1961), it became clear why his views were so sympathetic. Jung's upbringing, outlook and experiences were surprisingly similar to his own. Freud was a Jew who had grown up in the city of Vienna, but Jung and Davies had both grown up close to the countryside, comfortable with fields, farm animals and rural people. Their Protestant childhoods had produced similar ethical frameworks. Like Davies, Jung had found mathematics incomprehensible and had hated gymnastics. He had read and been struck by Goethe's *Faust* at an early age. His mother, too,

had had a frightening, witchlike quality. Indeed, Davies sensed
that in writing about his mother Jung was slightly pulling his
punches, as he himself had (and would) in writing about his own
mother. Jung's boyhood waking dream of God dropping an
enormous turd on the cathedral in Basel from his throne high in
the sky put Davies in mind of his own horrifying childhood
vision of God's private parts. Jung had recognized as he began to
investigate his own psyche that "It was most essential for me to
have a normal life in the real world as a counterpoise to that
strange inner world," and Davies too felt that his career and family provided him an anchor against the currents of his imagination. Like Davies, Jung thought of his successive books as
recording stages in his inner development.

Not until *A Mixture of Frailties* did the impact of Jung's thinking
on Davies begin to make itself felt in his work. The result is a
book of mixed impulse, which reaches out to encompass much
more of life than the earlier books. Parts of it are set in the
comic, dispassionate mode of *Tempest-Tost* and *Leaven of Malice*,
but much of it follows the career of the central character from
the viewpoint of a committed, sympathetic observer. Whereas in
the earlier books Davies' own standards are implicit, here he uses
persuasive mentors to articulate and argue them. And the world
of the novel has expanded from a self-satisfied, isolated, small
Canadian city to all of European civilization.

The book opens with Mrs. Bridgetower's funeral and the ensuing tea, where characters from the two earlier novels are reintro-
duced. With the reading of the will it is clear that although Mrs.
Bridgetower has died physically, her domineering spirit lives on.
According to the will's provisions, her son Solly, her friend Laura
Pottinger and St. Nicholas' Cathedral are all to receive bequests,
but only if Solly and his wife Veronica (the Pearl Vambrace of
the earlier novels) produce a male heir and christen him
Solomon Hansen Bridgetower. Until that time, the income from
the estate is to be used to give a young Salterton woman a train-
ing abroad in the arts. Solly, Laura Pottinger and Dean Jevon
Knapp (with the interfering assistance of lawyer Matthew
Snelgrove) are saddled with the task of its administration.

The novel's lesser (and sometimes frustratingly sketchy) story concerns Solly Bridgetower and his struggle to carry out his mother's wishes and to get free of her control. He learns to manipulate the other executors into locating a suitable candidate and supporting her training. But his mother's dead hand rests heavily on his personal life. In accordance with her will, he and Veronica live in her huge house (but without her wealth to manage it with) and strive to produce the obligatory heir. At the stillbirth of their first child they come close to despair. But in the end the required child is produced, and Mrs. Bridgetower's domination is broken.

The major story of the novel concerns Monica Gall, the young soprano who receives the scholarship. The dead hand she must shake off in order to transform herself into a great artist is nothing less than her whole upbringing. Her father, a maintenance man at the Salterton Glue Works, where she is a clerk, holds no brief for ambition; he makes her feel that any attempt to rise in the world is a criticism of him. Her musical taste has been set by an aunt who likes pretty "drawing room music" and believes that great artists are simple, fine lovers of all that is sweet in life. Because her mother is a keen adherent of the Thirteenth Apostle Tabernacle, Monica sings with its Heart and Hope Gospel Quartet, from a repertoire including "Eden Must Have Been Like Granny's Garden" and "Ten Baby Fingers and Ten Baby Toes, That Was My Mother's Rosary."

When Monica gets to London, everything changes—her horizons are broadened entirely. The great conductor Benedict Domdaniel manages her training, arranging for her to study with voice coach Murtagh Molloy and composer Giles Revelstoke. He also sets her to learn several languages, arranges for her to spend a Christmas in Wales at a country house and ensures that she is advised about clothes, manners and general culture by a sophisticated, wise American woman living in Paris. Monica falls in love with Revelstoke and becomes his mistress. He writes songs especially for her voice, and she becomes the chief interpreter of his work. When it transpires that her training is not costly enough to consume the income from Mrs. Bridgetower's estate, she underwrites the first production of Revelstoke's opera *The*

Golden Asse in Venice. Every aspect of her training moves Monica further from her family's values, a gulf that is made more apparent when she comes home to be with her dying mother. When, finally, she returns to Salterton to consider her options after Revelstoke has committed suicide, it is clear that her family's attitudes no longer have any relevance for her, and the reader is led to expect that she will marry Domdaniel and pursue her singing career.

From the beginning, Davies had intuitions that this novel would be a more serious matter for him than *Tempest-Tost* and *Leaven of Malice*. On February 8, 1955, for example, he wrote Gordon Roper: "I do not go very deep because, as yet, I dare not; but I shall do so. In my next novel, now a-brewing, I want to get into my bathysphere and go as deep as I can; it is about a girl who is trying to rise above a sordid home background."

He completed the plan for the novel by June 5, 1956, outlined the three opening Salterton sections in his "Works in Progress" notebook that September and wrote them between September 30 and January 15, 1957. In spite of his intention to dive deep, he cast these sections in the comic mode of the earlier books. But then his pace slowed. He had to begin the time-consuming business of breaking in a new assistant editor of the *Examiner*, Ralph Hancox, at the beginning of February, and the material of his novel was beginning to insist that it be given different treatment. In his notebook he listed thirty-six elements that might become part of his singer's training and experience (he rejected many of them), then planned (and probably wrote) the fourth and fifth sections. Then he made more notes and set down the outlines for the next three sections. As he wrote, he kept saying to himself: "Oh, come on, you know this isn't the way you're supposed to write!" But where he had been very much the detached observer of his characters and action in *Leaven of Malice*, he felt warmly sympathetic toward this heroine and keenly involved in her unfolding story, and his narrative tone reflects this shift in attitude.

In mid-June he was working full-out again, with the story "expanding in a way which I had not expected." By July 19

(Hancox carried the editorial page at the *Examiner* alone that summer), he had the novel three-quarters written. He wrote to Horace Davenport: "It is harder to write than anything I have yet attempted, & on a larger scale. It gives me the jim-jams, for in it I am not relying on my talents as a funny-man to get me by. I am—so help me—trying to be a serious novelist. Of course there are some larky bits in it, & some of the grotesquerie which is inseparable from my view of life, but basically it is serious." October saw him wrestling again, now with the ninth and last section (notes preceded, interrupted and followed the outline in his notebook). He wrote to the Guthries: "...I have run into a very bad patch with my writing, and stuff keeps coming out which is pure *Peg's Paper* or even *The Happy Mag*. To my horror sentences frame themselves like this—'Judge of our heroine's amazement when she opened the door, only to discover that Truman Thoroughgood, deemed by her to be in Rome, stood on the threshold, his finely moulded lips parted in a shy, sweet smile'." Nonetheless, he had copies to his agent by the promised deadline at the beginning of December.

The plunge in the bathysphere had brought him face to face with his mother. In the years since her death Davies had been mulling over everything he knew about her—her background, upbringing, marriage—and he had been considering his experience as her son, all in an effort to understand her better and to see her through adult eyes. To some degree this reassessment appears to have been driven by the guilt he felt at having judged her so harshly and having entertained such negative feelings toward her. He found that Jung's ideas opened hitherto-neglected avenues of exploration. But although, as always, the act of writing clarified his perceptions and produced self-knowledge, all the various things that were in his mind about his mother and her background are still not fully explored, or drawn into relation one to the other, or dramatized in this novel as he could do it years later in *Murther and Walking Spirits*. In *A Mixture of Frailties*, and in his mind, they retained an unresolved emotional power.

Davies had already, in his first two novels, explored some of the negative aspects of his relationship with his mother through Mrs.

Bridgetower's treatment of her son Solly. In *Tempest-Tost*, for example, he had given this tyrannical semi-invalid his own mother's uncanny ability to sense his youthful romantic inclinations and blight them with an ironic phrase. But *A Mixture of Frailties* brought a more comprehensive, ultimately fiercer confrontation.

In the details Davies ascribes to Ma Gall and the Gall family, but touches on only lightly, it is clear that many aspects of Florence's family and personal history were in his mind. Ma Gall shares Florence Davies' pioneer ancestry. Her old Ontario Loyalist expressions—"there; let 'em eat till they're pukin' sick," "slopdolly housekeeping," "she's got a butt-end on her like a bumble-bee" and "independent as a hog on ice"—were a part of Florence's inheritance from her pioneering forbears (although Ma's illiteracy and rough speech are very much her own). Her morphia-induced delusions of being in a bawdy-house in the nights before her death are similar to the delirious deathbed ramblings of Lavina McKay, Davies' maternal grandmother. Aunt Ellen Gall, the milliner whose fiancé had died before they could marry and who plays the piano well, combines attributes of Florence's sisters Cynthia and Martha. Jessie Fothergill's *The First Violin*, which this aunt owns and which Davies uses to establish the sentimental musical taste of an earlier day, was a book of Florence's that he had read when he was a boy in Renfrew. Ma Gall's marital travails reflect some of Florence's own: she is considerably older than her husband; Grandpa Gall had opposed the marriage on that ground and also because her family were odd; her family did not want her to marry anyone; young Alfred Gall, like the young Rupert, was bent on marriage and would not listen. Alfred Gall buys Monica large stocks of necessaries like toothpaste, convinced, as Florence was when Davies left for Oxford, that such things were not available in England. And Ma's letters to Monica, written every Sunday afternoon, flatly recording the small details of life and describing the Sunday menu at length, recall the letters Davies received from his mother at UCC and abroad.

One of Davies' deepest resentments of his mother surfaces in a detail in the novel. Giles Revelstoke's mother is a pretty, frivolous woman who does not know one note from another, and has no notion that her son is a composer of genius. The height of her ambition for him is that he should give up his bohemian life in London, marry a local girl and settle down to a country life in Wales. She and her second husband, Griffith Hopkin-Griffiths, do not attend the memorial concert for Revelstoke, and they never see a performance of his most important work, *The Golden Asse*: "When it was on in London Griff was seedy and we simply didn't feel up to the journey at that time. And then when it was done in Venice, we had already been to Baden, where we've gone for years—really I don't think I could face the winter without it—and what with the extra expense, and the time it was done, and everything, we simply didn't make it." Such behaviour was characteristic not only of the real woman upon whom Mrs. Griffith Hopkin-Griffiths was based (Mrs. Buckley-Jones) but also of his own mother. To his knowledge, Florence never read his books, although *Shakespeare's Boy Actors*, *Shakespeare for Young Players* and *The Diary of Samuel Marchbanks* had all appeared before she died at the end of 1948. When he directed *Fortune, My Foe* for Sutherland's International Players in Kingston in the summer of 1948, he wanted to make the special arrangements that would make it possible for her to attend, but she wouldn't go. And she never asked him about the production or how it was received. Like Revelstoke's mother, she didn't acknowledge her son's special gifts and powers.

Other parts of the novel reveal Davies digging deeply into his vexed relationship with his mother. Mrs. Bridgetower dies shortly before Christmas, when Florence had died and when Davies himself had had the terrifying visitation from her ghost. Until now he had kept his distance from that experience, as he had from his seemingly inexplicable childhood vision of Christ. But Jung, who described many such psychic emanations and valued them as communications from the unconscious, freed Davies to recall and consider such happenings and to conceive of characters having similar experiences. At one point his narrator observes: "If it were still the fashion to see ghosts (and it may be asked if such revelations are not a matter of fashion, or, if a more pretentious phrase is demanded, of intellectual climate) Veronica

Bridgetower would very often have seen the ghost of her mother-in-law, Louisa Hansen Bridgetower."

Living in her dead mother-in-law's house, unable to change a thing, Veronica feels the pressure from Mrs. Bridgetower, imbuing Solly's love-making with desperation, rendering him impotent for a time, increasingly dominating his personality. She comes to believe that the dead woman may even have strangled their long-awaited son with its own navel-cord, and she begins to fear a second pregnancy. Later, eight months pregnant, Veronica is awakened in the night by what she takes to be a rattling storm window in her mother-in-law's bedroom, and goes to investigate. She screams and is found on the floor, in labour, thoroughly terrorized. A short time later, the long-desired male child is born in Mrs. Bridgetower's bed, an outcome that moves Humphrey Cobbler to pronounce: "And serve Ma Bridgetower damn well right.... She got the first child, but Veronica was too many for her this time. Now Molly, nobody's going to convince me that Veronica didn't have some kind of wrestle with that old woman in the middle of the night, so shut up! That's love. That's devotion, and I call your attention to it...." But this "happy ending" does not deal fully with the energies released by the compelling ghostly passages. It is difficult to imagine the frightened, floored, labouring Veronica as victorious over her mother-in-law. And her despairing sense that Solly has become more and more like his mother is ignored in the general rejoicing over the birth of the child. Davies was not yet fully in control of his material; in later books, he was to manage it better.

Ma's surprising deathbed assertion that she herself possesses "quite an imagination" springs from Davies' own determination to be fair to his mother. Ma continues: "That's where you're like me, Monny. Always remember that. You got that from me." Then Monica accepts her declaration and expands on it:

> For in Ma, when she told tall stories, when she rasped her family with rough, sardonic jokes, when she rebelled against the circumstances of her life in coarse abuse, and when she cut through the fog of nonsense with the beam of her insight, was an artist—a spoiled artist, one who had

never made anything, who was unaware of the nature or genesis of her own discontent, but who nevertheless possessed the artist's temperament; in her that temperament, misunderstood, denied and gone sour, had become a poison which had turned against the very sources of life itself. Nevertheless, she was like Ma, and she must not go astray as Ma—not wholly through her own fault—had gone. In these songs she would sing of the spirit which might have been her mother's if circumstances had been otherwise. Alice had not hesitated to say that she had killed their mother by giving in to her wilfulness. Well, it was not true; what was best in her mother should live on, and find expression, in her.

However, the opening sections of the book, which establish Ma Gall's character, contain little evidence of the tall stories, the rough jokes, the coarse abuse or the insight. What this passage actually concerns is Davies' relationship with Florence. Davies had come to believe that his mother had possessed great, but thwarted, imaginative qualities, and to feel that he had inherited his imaginative reach from her. The bite she gave to conversation and family stories with her fresh, sharp tongue did play a part in nurturing his own imagination. But his supposition is largely rooted in his conviction that she was a writer *manqué*, her powers turned in on themselves by her lack of opportunity. It is true that his mother had reported local happenings for the *Thamesville Herald*. She had contributed competent stories and verses to the Davies family's annual "Yuletide Magazine." And after her death Rupert had discovered that she had done a fair amount of writing in secret. But there was no hint of exceptional talent in any of it. Davies' tribute to his mother's imagination, by way of Ma Gall, is likely to have been an attempt at filial compensation for the many negative feelings he had entertained toward her from adolescence onwards.

One aspect of Ma Gall that has nothing whatever to do with Florence is the manner of her death. On July 19, 1957, Davies appealed to his old friend and physiologist, Horace Davenport:

I need a disease. Specifically, I am at work on a novel in which the heroine's mother must die. She is a woman of vulgar nature, about 50-55, who has been a lifelong heavy eater, & in particular an eater of sweet things—jams, pastries, conserves & all the sugary stuff. What could she die of that is legitimate, yet has a touch of style to it? Science is so meddlesome nowadays that there are not too many good diseases left to fiction. I see by the *Encyclopaedia* that gormandizers may become *lardaceous*, but this is not fatal. Diabetes is no longer a killer. Is fatty degeneration still a possibility? And can it be combined with a nice, monstrous dropsy? I should be *so* much obliged for a good, authentic medical horror which a greedy woman could die of.

Davenport returned five typed pages headed "Plausible Deaths for a 50-55 year old Woman who Overeats," which focused primarily on Acute Pancreatitis and Acute Cholecystitis, but canvassed other possibilities and dealt with all of Davies' queries and speculations. Not surprisingly, given Ma's last name, Davies chose Acute Cholecystitis (interference with the emptying of the gall bladder by a stone or malfunctioning cystic duct). He then appealed for (and received) more medical details, and on August 17 reported: "I have killed her, discreetly, with *cholecystitis*, not harping on detail, which I always think a bore in novels. But I like to have the background right."

Davies' plunge in his bathysphere also resulted in the articulation of deeply held convictions about the nurturing of an artist, drawing heavily on the details of his own life in England and Wales, when he (like his heroine) was being educated and having his horizons broadened. His characters live in places he knew (for example, he gave Revelstoke the Tite Street flat where Brenda had lived with her mother and sister). A few people he had known became minor characters. Monica Gall sings a minor role in the *St. Matthew Passion* in the Sheldonian Theatre, where he had himself heard the Oxford Bach Choir perform this work in 1938. And she goes to the Vic-Wells Ball, as he had in 1939.

Monica Gall's three main teachers all had their beginnings in real people. The most directly rooted in actuality is Murtagh Molloy: he is a portrait of a man Davies knew well, Bertie Scott, his voice coach of the Old Vic years. Benedict Domdaniel depends rather more on extrapolation and invention. He is a freehand drawing of the great conductor Sir Adrian Boult. Davies had met Boult, and had had a chance to observe him— tall, bald-headed, splendidly moustached, a fine figure of a man—when he conducted at the Gregynog Festival in Wales. Davies also knew quite a lot, through Dora Herbert-Jones (a great friend of Boult's), about matters like the strenuous exercise program that lay behind Boult's impressive physique and the strap that he wore at night to train his moustache.

Giles Revelstoke's original was Philip Heseltine. Although Davies had never met Heseltine, his depiction was based to a considerable degree on special knowledge. Cuthbert Kelly's English Singers had introduced him, in Kingston in 1927, to some of the delicate songs Heseltine had written under the pen-name of Peter Warlock, and in the intervening years he had become familiar with many more. Davies associated Heseltine's music with Christmas (hence Revelstoke's Christmas visit to Wales) because of his many settings of carols. In the summer just before he began writing *A Mixture of Frailties*, Davies ordered the music for a large number of the Warlock songs (seeking out editions in the original keys) and by October had acquired twenty-five. Although Giles Revelstoke's compositions set different lyrics than Warlock's, they preserve the musical qualities Davies had discerned in the composer—brilliant instrumental writing with occasional muddled passages, high tessitura, sensitivity to the poetry and the rhythms of English, frequent variations in time signature, an "other-worldliness."

Besides being familiar with Heseltine's music, Davies knew his mother and stepfather, the Buckley-Joneses (accurately depicted as the Hopkin-Griffithses). Their house, whose spacious bathroom became the scene of Monica Gall's first sexual experience, was only four or five miles from Fronfraith. In frequent visits to it between 1932 and 1940, Davies had seen musical manuscripts in Heseltine's hand, played his piano and pianola and talked of him with his mother, stepfather and son Nigel. Reading Cecil Gray's *Peter Warlock: A Memoir of Philip Heseltine* (which he had reviewed for the *Queen's University Journal* in 1935), Davies had taken note of Heseltine's influential music master at Eton, his resentment of Beecham's masterful conducting and his own aspiration to conduct opera, his editorship of the *Sackbut*, his violent controversy with Ernest Newman, his certainty that he was always in the right, his cats and mistresses and menagerie of hangers-on, his feuds and vendettas, his flat at 12A Tite Street and the manner of his suicide. He based much of Revelstoke on these sources. But the facts that inspired him certainly didn't bind him: the portrait is highly interpretative.

The novel's treatment of art and artistic expression was an articulation of Davies' long-developing convictions, drawn into new coherence by his reading of Jung. For Davies, as for Jung, art is "self"-centred. At the beginning, Monica is torn between loyalty to her parents, who dislike ambition, and her dream of becoming a great artist. Presented with an opportunity to realize the dream, she seizes it, auditioning and paying the stiff fee required to get the opinion of a great musician on her potential. But if she is to get anywhere as an artist, as her first mentor, Sir Benedict Domdaniel forces her to admit, she must acknowledge the claims of her talent. She must want to sing, not for some vague altruistic notion of bringing refinement to others, but for herself. (It is relevant here that when Davies was writing the last section of the novel, he declared that it "will be the best thing I have written. I have felt it more deeply than anything else, and if it is a failure, do you know what I shall do—I shall just sit right down and write another and better one, that's what I'll do. It is my fate to write, whether I do very well at it or not, and more and more I do not care what people think of my stuff.")

Domdaniel argues that there are two kinds of singers. Romantics use music as a vehicle for their sexuality, forming a personal magnetism between themselves and their hearers, whereas bards intend their music to be a distillation of life's beauty and delight. Monica thinks she has bardic potential, and time proves her right. But the achievement requires long, hard struggle. She must uncover her full vocal resources and learn to control them. She must study to present herself effectively on stage and off, and she has to learn to speak several languages well, her own included. In submitting to voice coach Murtagh Molloy, Monica is placing herself at the end of a long chain of practitioners. Molloy teaches her what he learned from ffrangcon-Davies and Harry Plunket Greene, just as they had taught him what they had absorbed from their own teachers, and so on back into the past, just as Davies studying piano at UCC under Richard Tattersall had found himself at the end of a chain of masters and students reaching back to Chopin himself or, as an apprentice at the Old Vic listening to old Ben Webster, he was given a glimpse of William Charles Macready and Edmund Kean. In yielding to her teachers, Monica masters the resources that lie within herself.

If her music is to distil life, she must expand her emotional range. Her teachers set her to see (as Davies had set himself to learn) what other artists had distilled from it on the stage, in painting, in the literature of song. But her own experience is her chief resource. She must learn to grasp the essence of each feeling, to recapture it and to use it in performance in such a way as to evoke it in others. The capacity to do that, as Giles Revelstoke tells her, is the product of self-knowledge: "Poetry and music can speak directly to depths of experience in us which we possess without being conscious of them, in language which we understand only imperfectly. But there must be some of us who understand better than others, and who give the best of ourselves to that understanding. If you are to be one of them, you must be ready to make a painful exploration of yourself."

Monica's self-exploration, which has much in common with Davies' own, is curiously passive. Like his, Monica's discoveries about herself come not from deliberate, directed thought, but from being quiet enough to hear below the surface of her mind. It is a process of recognizing, of becoming conscious of things. We are told "…she was a little surprised to discern that what she had really been thinking about, and longing for, was immortality…" or again "…she felt, stronger than ever before, the mixture of elation and dread which she was learning to recognize as part of her professional life, part of her fate." What gives her a clue to what she thinks deep down is the music she hears at the back of her mind all the time, music which is not particularly original but which is not anyone else's either. Here Davies created a parallel rather than a direct equivalent to his own experience. He too has been haunted by music since childhood, but what runs in his mind is other people's melodies—trashy ballads heard in his youth, show tunes, Elgar's *Enigma Variations* and the like. At Queen's, George Humphrey had suggested that such music is a clue to the unconscious, and so, far more self-analytic than his heroine, Davies often tries to discover why a particular tune has thrust itself into his mind, sometimes successfully, but more often not.

Monica hears her mother and Giles Revelstoke in her own inner ear, as Davies daily hears Rupert and Florence giving their opinions of his doings in their familiar idioms. She wonders: "Is it perhaps my substitute for thinking—orders and hints and even jokes from deep down, through the voice and personality of someone I've loved—yes, and feared?"

As Monica wanders in Paris from the museum of the Opéra to the Panthéon and on to St. Étienne du Mont, it comes to her that reason, judgment and logic are not easy or productive methods of problem-solving for her, while feeling is. Davies had reached the same conclusion about himself. At UCC, his teacher H. P. Blunt had introduced him to Plato's four ways of encountering the world and of interpreting the experiences it presents: thinking (the use of logic), feeling (making accurate, coherent value-judgments), sensation (perceiving phenomena through the senses) and intuition (sensing the intangibles in a situation). When Blunt set the schoolboys to assess their strengths and weaknesses in these terms, Davies' ineptitude with mathematics had made him depressingly aware that thinking was not one of his strengths, nor likely to become one. His powers of sensation, too, had seemed to him to be weak. Now, following Jung, he had come to view the four functions as pairs: thinking and feeling as means of making judgments; sensation and intuition as kinds of perception. In Jung's experience, most people were strong in one function, and moderately so in a second from the other pair. Davies concluded that in his own case feeling was dominant and intuition a close second. (This did not mean that he could not present a case in logical terms, only that he would do so to persuade others, after he had reached his decision by other means.) But his powerful intuition, tremendously important to him as a novelist, could be exhausting. Brenda says that "...he is very aware, terribly aware, too aware of what other people think and even the ambience given out by them. He suffers from this terribly...that's why he's shy and withdrawn, because actually the effect on him of people is so strong and he can remember everything about them and, you know, what they're like and he knows what they feel. He knows what's going on behind the blank, the brick wall, and you pay a high price for that."

As Monica Gall embarks for England to begin her training, she hopes to be transformed from a clerk at the Salterton Glue Works into an internationally known diva. Through good teachers, unremitting labour and self-examination, she *is* changed and (after the conclusion of the book) she does become a famous singer. When she returns to Canada on the occasion of her mother's final illness and death, everything sets her apart from the environment in which she had been raised—her speech, clothes, demeanour. Her recital displays her hard-won interpretive range and the special qualities of her now fully trained voice. The metamorphosis she has undergone exemplifies the kind of growth and change Davies believes everyone who meets the challenge of life must make. It is a realization of the truth at the heart of Apuleius' *The Golden Ass*, the classical story that Revelstoke turns into an opera, which treats of "the metamorphosis of life itself, in which man moves from confident inexperience through the bitterness of experience, toward the rueful wisdom of self-knowledge." *The Golden Ass* is clearly one of the great legends which, according to Dean Knapp in his closing sermon, "We dismiss...at our peril, for they are the riddling voices by means of which great truths buried deep in the spirit of man offer themselves to the world." In Jungian terms, these "great truths buried deep in the spirit of man" are the archetypes.

Davies' first title for the novel was "Water Parted." He took it from the song by Thomas Augustine Arne that Monica sings at her recital in Salterton:

Water parted from the sea
  May increase the river's tide—,
To the bubbling fount may flee,
  Or thro' fertile valleys glide.

Tho' in search of lost repose
  Thro' the land 'tis free to roam,
Still it murmurs as it flows
  Panting for its native home.

To Monica it speaks of a longing for spiritual fulfilment, of a yearning, ultimately, "toward all the vast, inexplicable, irrational treasury from which her life drew whatever meaning and worth it possessed." However, Brenda thought "Water Parted" ill-advised as a title: it did not grab the attention, its meaning was not immediately apparent, "water" sounded feeble. But *A Mixture of Frailties*, which comes from the *Miscellanies* of Sir George Savile, seventeenth-century marquess of Halifax, suffers from similar deficiencies. Of all the titles Davies chose for his novels, it is the least felicitous.

The book precipitated the break with Clarke, Irwin that had been brewing for some time. When Wing submitted the manuscript to the publisher on December 6, 1957, the firm refused to accept him as Davies' agent. It insisted that the option clause in the contract for *Leaven of Malice* included world rights for this subsequent novel. Without world rights, Clarke, Irwin argued, it could not arrange joint production for the United States, Britain and Canada, which is what made it possible to produce a handsome book and keep losses to a manageable level. (A summary of the accounts for Davies' books sent to Wing showed losses on each one, a much gloomier picture than the one R. W. W. Robertson remembered when interviewed.)

This was difficult for Davies to contend with, given his long association with the firm. Nonetheless, he politely sent R. W. W. Robertson a copy of the letter he had written to W. H. Clarke in July 1954 explaining his reasons for putting his affairs in the hands of an outside agent. And Wing pointed out to Clarke,

Irwin that the option clause in question did not convey world rights. It said merely that "The Author agrees to allow the Publishers a thirty-day option on his next following book-length work on terms to be arranged, which option period shall begin on the day the complete manuscript is received by the Publishers." The trade understood "terms to be arranged" to mean that the territories to be granted, the rate of royalty to be paid, the advance and subsidiary rights all had to be negotiated.

On April 3, 1958, unable to get the terms it wanted, Clarke, Irwin regretfully declined the manuscript and accepted the loss of its most popular trade author. A factor in its decision was the reaction of one of its readers, who thought that there was "too much ribaldry in the book" and concluded: "I think Mr. Davies has wasted his talents and intelligence, to some extent, on a book that is not altogether worthy of him."

Davies, for his part, was relieved. W. H. Clarke's death in 1955 had elevated Clarke's wife Irene to the presidency of the firm, and he associated with her all the elements in it that had irked him over the years—its Temperance and Methodist attitudes, its opposition to smoking, its love affair with sugar. He had never been comfortable at its book launches, always "teas" at which the centrepiece was a sweet cake crudely reproducing the delicate jacket designs in icing. Davies and Grant Macdonald shared a private indignation at being asked to slice the cake and eat a piece of it at the climactic moment, thus symbolically destroying the book. However, his relations with Clarke, Irwin did not end in 1958. The contracts he had signed between 1942 and 1955 kept his early plays and novels under its control for many long and, for Davies, exasperating years.

Having gotten wind that Davies might be in the market for a new Canadian publisher, John Gray of Macmillan contacted him in January 1958 and reached agreement with Wing about Canadian publication of *A Mixture of Frailties* in April. Chatto and Windus, who preferred Davies' earlier comic style, disliked the new novel and rejected it; in the end, Weidenfeld and Nicolson published it in England. Scribner's welcomed it warmly in the United States. Its copy-editor produced one of Davies' favourite publishing stories when she wrote:

You refer in *A Mixture of Frailties* to a Mr. Henry Purcell, the composer. Will you give us his name and present address so that we can check if it is all right to quote the words that you use in the book?

Davies sent a copy of the correspondence to Scribner's with a note:

My Dear Charles,
    If I could give you the present address of Mr. Henry Purcell, I'd be the happiest man in the world!

When the book appeared in Canada and the United States in August and in Britain in November, the reactions of newspaper reviewers were much more mixed than for *Leaven of Malice*. Many liked some things and disliked others. They contradicted one another: some thought the characters were two-dimensional and unbelievable, others thought them richly realized; some relished the comic opening and disliked the rest of the book, others the opposite. Monica's affair with Giles Revelstoke aroused disapproval in some quarters. Many sensed an archetypal pattern behind her story and compared her to Cinderella or Galatea (but none saw the parallel to *The Golden Ass*). American reviewers were most frequently capable of enjoying the novel as a whole, possibly because they viewed the Canadian and the British parts of the book from an equal distance. They and a few Canadian reviewers recognized *A Mixture of Frailties* as a work larger in scope and richer in conception than its two precursors, leading them to expect good things from Davies' pen in the future. On reading the thoughtful notice in the Montreal *Gazette*, Davies was moved to write: "I think & hope that at last I may be getting my rightful place in Canadian letters, as the most *serious* writer they have & more truly of the country than the 'sincere' boys— whose sincerity is perhaps more accurately described as naiveté."

Chapter 11

PLAYWRIGHT AND DIRECTOR: 1950-60

The pattern of work was surprisingly regular. Domdaniel would find fault with a passage, and suggest how it might be re-cast: Revelstoke, after argument, would re-write the passage in his own way: Domdaniel, having first said that the new version would do splendidly, was likely to find in a few hours that it was—well, not quite right, and suggest further revision, usually along the lines he had originally proposed. Revelstoke would again re-write, producing something manifestly inferior to what he had done before. Domdaniel would then suggest that the earlier revision be used—with a few changes which he could easily make himself, to spare Giles trouble. But Giles did not want to be spared trouble; he wanted the music as he had written it in the beginning.

—*A Mixture of Frailties*, 1958

DAVIES AND BRENDA continued to apply great energy to local amateur and professional theatre right through 1960. They directed and acted for the Peterborough Summer Theatre until 1953, sometimes as many as three productions a season. From

1951 to 1954 they did a production each summer at the Brae Manor Theatre in Knowlton, Quebec. In 1955, Davies directed *Ten Nights in a Barroom* for the Straw Hat Players in Port Carling and Gravenhurst, with Brenda as the drunkard's wife, and Brenda directed *Visit to a Small Planet* for them in the 1959 season mounted in conjunction with the Peterborough Summer Theatre.

Davies directed the Peterborough Little Theatre's major winter production each year until 1953—in 1951 it was *Twelfth Night* (with Brenda as Olivia and himself as a priest), in 1952 *The Merry Wives of Windsor* (Brenda as Mistress Page, Miranda as Robin Page, Jennifer as Robin, himself as Pistol), in 1953 *King Phoenix* (Brenda as Boon Brigit, himself as a servant). Most years the group competed in the Eastern Ontario Drama Festival, and did well. Finally, in December 1953, he reprised the Coventry Nativity Play, co-directing with Brenda. The Little Theatre, fully fledged by now, carried on successfully without him: in 1955, for the first time, it took the top award at the Eastern Ontario Drama Festival with John Londerville's production of André Obey's *Noah*.

When Davies stopped directing plays in Peterborough, Brenda ended her local acting as well. But she continued to direct, and between 1955 and 1960 she was involved in productions for the Little Theatre, the skating club, the Cobourg Opera and Dramatic Guild and the Eastern Ontario Drama League's workshop. The group with which she worked most intensively was the St. John's Players, whose members had approached her and proposed to pay her a modest fee if she would take them on. She directed good repertory-standard presentations for them in April or May each year from 1957 to 1960. Whatever the production might be, Davies was involved. They had vigorous discussions about interpretation, direction and staging, and during the productions he would sometimes lend a hand backstage, painting screens, applying make-up, making wigs and props, dressing the cast and injecting a little whimsy. His best effort in this respect was probably the impressive-looking armorial crest for the curtain of *Trelawny of the "Wells,"* with the motto:

CANNI
BORO
URUM
BRELLA.

Recalling the scene that had greeted him when he first arrived in Peterborough in 1957, Ralph Hancox exclaimed: "Some of the plays that were put on in Peterborough were first class! You know I get so impatient with people who talk about Canada and Ontario being a cultural wasteland, and about imported American culture...because, in fact, in Peterborough, people could have seen five or six plays by Oscar Wilde, a couple or three Shakespearean plays, Pinero...." He did not realize that this was anything but typical of small-city Canada or that it had sprung into being in response to the stimulus provided by two people.

What the Davieses had begun survived and flourished. In the 1960s Peterborough's amateur groups came together to form the Peterborough Theatre Guild. The Guild bought one of the city's churches and converted it into an intimate 200-seat theatre, and began to mount a season of plays every year.

Despite his 1950 decision to put off playwriting, Davies had hardly completed *Tempest-Tost* before he was writing another play, and for amateurs at that. In fall 1951, Alan Stephen, headmaster of Upper Canada College's Preparatory School, inquired if Davies might provide a play to mark the Prep's Jubilee Year. Delighted to be asked to create something for his old school, Davies immediately agreed. In early October he came up to view the gym, which was to be the theatre, in November he forwarded a title and cast list, and on January 2, 1952, he followed with the completed script of the one-acter, *A Masque of Aesop.*

Of the five plays he wrote during the 1950s, this is the only one that has been widely performed (it was given in many schools across Canada over the years) and it is the most likely to stay in the repertoire. In creating it, Davies made use of what he had learned from performing in "dialogues" as a boy in Renfrew—that children like thumping morals. He also made sure that the play exercised just those skills that his Oxford thesis had taught him boys can master—"good declamation and a broad, direct acting style."

The action can be summarized briefly. A crowd of angry citizens in Delphi is bent on drowning Aesop for his "objectionable" views, but the god Apollo insists on a fair trial for the fabulist. At the trial, three of Aesop's fables are wittily dramatized: "The Belly and the Members," "The Town Mouse and the Country Mouse" and "The Cock and the Pearl." Apollo, impressed with the wisdom demonstrated by the plays, reproves the citizenry for their self-centred blindness. But because Aesop has behaved in an arrogant manner, Apollo decrees a punishment: his writing will be read chiefly by children, and few will remember it when they become adults.

The play was performed at UCC on May 2 and 3, 1952 (and again in 1954, 1961, 1965 and 1991). It gave Davies great pleasure to have W. L. Grant's widow, Maude, write to say, "This was not only generous but imaginative and to me it adds a dignity & quality to the school that only the fruits of the mind & spirit can give. I cannot help thinking of my husband's delight in this...." It was likewise gratifying to hear that his mentor B. K. Sandwell had told the headmaster, "I don't know whether you realize, Stephen, that that play will be being played in a hundred years' time."

Clarke, Irwin brought out ordinary and educational editions of *A Masque of Aesop* in 1952 and 1955, illustrated by Grant Macdonald, and Davies contributed both his performance fees and his royalties as a gift to the school. By 1954, $250 had accumulated, and when he was consulted on what should be done with it he suggested, "what about spending a reasonable sum of the money for as long as it lasts on a really large and splendid cake to be eaten by the Dramatic Society after they have given a performance? There is nothing that makes people so hungry as acting and I would rather think of the boys having something to eat than looking at a picture of me or watching one of their companions, who happens to have a particularly brassy nature, getting a copy of Macaulay's *Essays* on prize day." The school elected to use the $50-$100 that rolled in annually for the next decade on a supper each year for the thirty members of the dramatic club.

In June 1952, Stratford, Ontario, announced its intention to hold an annual Shakespearean festival. Davies immediately wrote an editorial urging Peterborough to host a summer festival itself. The idea was not a new one; observers like Herbert Whittaker were certain that the many summer theatres that had sprung up would soon lead to a permanent theatre or festival, probably in Kingston, where Sutherland's International Players were active, or in Peterborough, because Davies was there. But within weeks, Stratford had spiked potential contenders' guns by hiring Tyrone Guthrie, who let it be known that he saw the venture as a means of increasing Canada's artistic prestige, not as a money-maker. Since this was just the sort of development Davies had been hoping for (and Peterborough hadn't responded to his editorial urgings), he decided to give Stratford his unqualified support.

In December it looked as if Brenda might be able to make a professional contribution to the Festival when Guthrie asked her to stage-manage. She was sufficiently tempted to travel to Stratford to discuss the job with him, but when it became clear that she would have to leave her family for three or four months of the year she turned the offer down. Davies' own involvement began in the early months of 1953 when, at Guthrie's urging, he was asked to advise the Festival's board of governors. At the end of May he was invited to become a full member of the board (he stepped down in 1971), and he began to travel to Stratford regularly (usually by train) for its quarterly meetings. He often found himself bridging a gap between the board and the artistic director, particularly at the meetings in which the program for the coming season was presented, because, unlike most of the others, he could speak of, and to, the director as an equal. His familiarity with theatre and with the Shakespearean canon carried a great deal of weight with the board. It was partly at his encouragement that the Festival was broadened to include non-Shakespearean classics and experimental productions.

Clarke, Irwin published three books to commemorate the Festival's first years—*Renown at Stratford* (1953), *Twice Have the*

Trumpets Sounded (1954) and *Thrice the Brinded Cat Hath Mew'd* (1955). In the first two, which were illustrated by Grant Macdonald's portraits of the actors in costume, Davies shared the writing with Tyrone Guthrie. In the third, Tanya Moiseiwitsch's costume sketches were used to illustrate pieces by Davies, Guthrie, Moiseiwitsch and conductor Boyd Neel. Davies' task was to memorialize the magical, landmark productions of those first years, and he succeeded amazingly well. While his reading of Freud is evident in his description of the emotional power and central relationships in the plays (as it is also in many of the book reviews he wrote in the 1940s and early '50s), these pieces gain their particular force from his familiarity with theatrical history. He could allude with equal ease to the stage conditions of Shakespeare's day, to the work of the great British actor-managers—David Garrick, Henry Irving, Herbert Beerbohm Tree and John Martin-Harvey—and to many of the most notable twentieth-century productions. And having seen at least nine of Guthrie's earlier productions and himself been involved in seven more, he was unique in his ability to put the great director's work at Stratford into perspective. The series ended after W. H. Clarke, its guiding spirit, died in the summer of 1955.

In 1953 Davies wrote the first of his influential reviews of the Festival, which appeared in the magazine *Saturday Night* each summer until 1958. The best of his reviews, which set the productions against the long sweep of theatre history, convey all the delight of an enthusiast who is reliving a savoured experience. Together with his *Examiner* reviews from 1960 to 1967, the *Saturday Night* pieces represent an important part of the chronicle of Stratford's progress from season to season.

His enthusiasm was, indeed, so evident that one wonders whether Davies the reviewer bent the truth in his passionate desire to see the Festival succeed. The frank letters he wrote to Tyrone Guthrie each season about the productions have unfortunately disappeared, but the private notes he kept on his theatregoing in the 1960s often reveal a harsher judgment. For instance, of Peter Donat, who played Troilus in the 1963 *Troilus and Cressida*, the notes say: "A good production by Michael Langham, but perhaps not enough emphasis on Troilus' disillusion, which may have had something to do with Peter Donat, who is not really a romantic actor—just a handsome man. He thinks a man in love shows it by clumsy tumbling about and being tongue-tied. He fumbled and left out some of his great Act 1.i speech 'O Pandarus, I tell thee, Pandarus, etc.' He was often out in his lines, & missed 'heel the high lavolt,' a favourite phrase of mine. He was coltish, rather than a young prince." In his review Davies softened this to, "As Troilus, Peter Donat suffered not only from first-night nerves which made him mangle a few speeches, but from lack of that nobility which is expected of a son of Priam."

At intervals Davies has also written half a dozen articles for the Festival's souvenir programs, given five papers at the Stratford seminars and three public lectures, and contributed to *The Stratford Scene 1958-1968*. And he has written many occasional articles and editorials that have helped to publicize the Festival.

In the summer of 1954, after he had completed the writing of *Leaven of Malice*, Stratford presented him with a stimulating dramaturgical project. Guthrie raised the possibility during July of staging something that would be both Canadian and classical for the 1955 season. When Davies responded by suggesting a Canadian version of Ben Jonson's *Bartholomew Fayre*, Guthrie, immediately enthused, invited him on the spot to make a suitable adaptation. (Jonson is Davies' favourite English dramatist after Shakespeare.) The board confirmed the proposal in a letter on August 9, and so Davies found himself with the challenge of making Jonson's great, sprawling portrayal of London's stall-keepers, thieves, fools, schemers, ballad-singers, pimps, gulls and hypocrites accessible to modern audiences, with the luxury of knowing he would get a thoroughly professional production.

Guthrie wanted cuts and clarifications of the text, plus newly written scenes in place of some of Jonson's. Davies set to work in the early months of 1955 (it was clear by the previous October that production would have to be delayed until 1956) to transform *Bartholomew Fayre* into a Canadian "Bartholomew Fair." Working with a text of the play taped page by page onto large sheets of paper, he shifted the setting from 1614 London to

1956 Stratford, modified the vocabulary, cut a lot, added a bit and rewrote several pages near the end. The resulting typescript was still voluminous, and when Guthrie saw it on April 10 he wanted more excisions and more new scenes. By now it appeared that the adaptation would not be performed until 1957, since Guthrie would not be directing at the Festival in 1956.

From this point on, unfortunately, things went badly awry. In the fall of 1955 Michael Langham succeeded Guthrie as the Festival's artistic director, and Davies, sensing that Langham was not himself interested in staging the adaptation, wrote Peter Bennett, Stratford's managing director, on November 9, offering to free the Festival from any financial obligation to him if he did no further work. If he completed a final draft, however, he would expect to be paid. Bennett did not reply, but Davies saw Langham on January 4, 1956, and got the go-ahead from him. Over the next four months, he reduced the length of the play by half, made the language more accessible, substituted a French-Canadian folk-singer called Rossignol for Jonson's Nightingale and replaced Jonson's puppet show with a beauty pageant.

In June 1956, his agent sent the script to the Festival. Langham read it and told Davies on August 8 that he hoped to include it in the program for 1957, and failing that, that it would be done within two or three years. But when Davies read the minutes of the October 25 meeting of the executive committee, he found that Langham did not expect to produce the play in the foreseeable future. Bennett then belatedly wrote to accept Davies' offer of the previous autumn. Davies understandably felt betrayed. He thought then (and believes still) that the Festival had decided not even to pay him for his work. After considerable hesitation, he decided to insist on payment, which finally resulted in a cheque for $500 for a three-year option (never exercised) on stage rights.

The correspondence reveals that Bennett knew neither that Langham had encouraged Davies nor that the play had been completed and submitted. Once he discovered what had happened, there was no question of not paying Davies. But how much? Stratford had no experience in dealing with living playwrights. Although Davies and his agent had long before settled between themselves on the modest fee of $500 (which he intended to donate to the building fund) plus a share in profits when the play was produced, the agent had not communicated these details to Stratford in the draft agreement he had forwarded in June 1955 (to which Stratford had never responded) nor in later letters. As soon as Davies mentioned the $500 figure to Bennett in a letter on March 1, 1957, contracts were sent and payment was forthcoming.

No one comes out of this story well. Not Guthrie, who set Davies to work, then deserted him (by November he had had the adaptation for "some months" without offering an opinion). Not Langham, who encouraged Davies, then decided that he was not the right director for the adaptation, but failed to tell him of his change of heart. Not Stratford, whose right hand seemed not to know what its left was doing. Not even Davies, who should have insisted on a contract right at the beginning.

I have seen no record of Guthrie's reaction to the script, but it evidently didn't enthuse him. Failing his participation, the play's chance at performance was poor: its new character and scene make it impossible for Stratford or any other theatre to offer it simply as an update to a classic play, and the joshing local and contemporary references are often strained and heavy-handed. "Bartholomew Fair" has never been produced, although several directors have asked to see it.

In the fall and winter of 1955-56, Davies undertook (unpaid and without a credit in the 1956 program) a dramaturgical job for Michael Langham, creating several brief scenes to fill out the story of the Host of the Garter and the German visitors in *The Merry Wives of Windsor*. Davies titled them

The 'Lost' Scenes from
THE MERRY WIVES OF WINDSOR
restored from the 1599 Duodecimo
and edited with notes by the
Dark Horse of the Sonnets.

The 123 new lines blended so well with Shakespeare's that the opening-night critics did not even notice their presence. The actors, but not the audience, had the benefit of Davies' humorous scholarly notes, which explained unfamiliar words and references, pointed out parallels in contemporary texts and provided sources. (In 1975 "The 'Lost' Scenes" were used again, in the production of *Merry Wives* at London's Mermaid Theatre.

Davies and Brenda have been faithful patrons of the Festival. When the permanent theatre was built in 1957 they offered to endow seats in the names of Lilian Baylis (Brenda's mentor, famed for mounting the entire Shakespearean canon at the Old Vic), Sir Edmund Chambers (Davies' thesis examiner at Oxford and an eminent Shakespearean scholar) and Sir Henry Irving (Rupert Davies' favourite actor, revered in Canada for his Shakespearean performances). Since Irving had been spoken for already, they made up the three with Sir John Martin-Harvey, who was also famous in Shakespearean roles, and whose performances had so enchanted Davies as a boy. (The seats, including Irving's, are located on either side of aisle six at B27-29 and B30.) The *Examiner* and the *Whig* made substantial corporate contributions to the Festival. Davies and Brenda were made Permanent Members in 1979 in recognition of their continuing generosity.

For some of the insiders, Davies' sense of humour was one of his main contributions to the Festival. In the early days, when no one knew whether the tremendous artistic and financial gamble they were all taking would succeed, he jokingly recommended that the Festival should announce that it possessed a hitherto-unknown Shakespearean play brought to the new world by the Pilgrim fathers—and he offered to fake the manuscript himself. His reaction to the design for the permanent theatre that replaced the tent in 1957 was a grumble: "Well, all we're doing is putting a cheese safe over the stage!" And a couple of years later, he suggested in a letter to Tanya Moiseiwitsch that the new theatre should have its own ghost. He recommended Iris Warren (then still alive) for the position. In 1962, when the witches' cauldron scene was cut from *Macbeth*, "doubtless because of the difficulty of securing the properties necessary to its apt performance," he wrote to Moiseiwitch again. In the identity of Leonard Greymalkin, representative of "FRIAR BACON &

FRIAR BUNGAY: Necromantic Suppliers and Supernatural Warehousemen (Founded 1594)," the firm "who had the honour of victualling this extremely effective scene for Mr. Shakespeare himself in 1606," he submitted quotations on nineteen items. The first was "Toad, that under cold stone / Days and nights has thirty-one / Sweltered venom sleeping got…" for which he had:

> IMMEDIATELY AVAILABLE in unlimited quantity from our own gardens. True *Bufo vulgaris* as supplied to Mr. Shakespeare. $3. per doz.

For the nineteenth ("Cool it with a baboon's blood"), he offered:

> True baboon, per carafe (approx. 1 litre) of superior bouquet and body, $15. Canadian native baboon, bottled by Bright's Winery (screw-top returnable bottle) $3.

While Davies was working on adapting *Bartholomew Fayre* for Stratford, he had also begun to write for the young Crest Theatre in Toronto. Having made a success of their summer stock company, the Straw Hat Players, Donald and Murray Davis had decided to try producing plays in a permanent theatre during the winter season. The brothers knew Davies' dramas well. Donald had directed *Overlaid* and acted in *Fortune, My Foe* while a student at the University of Toronto, and the Straw Hats had performed *Overlaid*, *Fortune, My Foe* and *At My Heart's Core*. After their first short season in the early months of 1954, they asked Davies for a new play to lead off their second season that September. He offered them *A Jig for the Gypsy*, a particularly appropriate choice, since they are of Welsh and Gypsy descent. Herbert Whittaker came in to direct, Donald Davis played Jack the Skinner, his sister Barbara Chilcott played Benoni, and the play pulled good houses in its two-week run. Clarke, Irwin published the play that fall, following the text of Whittaker's script with its cuts and additional stage directions. But it has been revived only once, at Theatre Lennoxville in the summer of 1973. (The Davises were again involved. This time Donald Davis directed, and Barbara Chilcott played the role she had created nineteen years before.)

This success set the Davises to dreaming ambitiously of playing roles especially written for them. Why should not Davies write for the Crest as Shakespeare had written for the Globe, O'Casey for the Abbey and Chekhov for the Moscow Arts Theatre? No one, complained Donald Davis, was writing romantic plays full of panache and style. Their desires complemented Davies' own, so he agreed to write a romantic play with their particular characteristics in mind. He did not mention to them that he already had in hand a detailed scenario for such a play, prepared two years earlier.

Davies had long been fascinated by the pretenders to the English throne—and by their supporters. At Oxford he had noted, but not joined, the White Rose Society (whose aim was to "restore" Prince Rupert of Bavaria to the English throne), and he was intrigued that many Scots (including Canadians of Scottish descent) adulated the dissolute Bonnie Prince Charlie, who, after all, had scorned the Scots people and preferred to speak French instead of English. Evidently there was something to the royal jelly—what gave it its power? Davies wove it all up into a play, *Hunting Stuart*.

He began the actual writing (under the working title of "The Last Chevalier: A Comedy") on February 1, 1955, kept at it while he was taking his initial run at adapting *Bartholomew Fayre* and completed it that August in Port Carling and Gravenhurst while directing *Ten Nights in a Barroom* for the Davises' Straw Hat Players. The first act introduces Henry Benedict Stuart, a minor and self-effacing Ottawa civil servant, and his social-climbing wife Lilian. She prides herself on her taste and on her Scots forbears, contemptuous of her husband's "foreign" background. (Davies also devotes quite a few pages to the doings of Stuart's low-brow aunt.) Then two scientists, a biologist and an ethnopsychologist, arrive, and it soon transpires that they believe that Henry is a direct descendant of the royal Stuart house. They are specialists in heredity, and they want him to serve as a guinea pig to test their theories. To convince the sceptical, they produce an anaesthetic powder that releases "ancestral memory," and, wonder of wonders, it evokes in the henpecked Henry all the opinions and charming arrogance of that famous wencher and drinker, Bonnie Prince Charlie! But this isn't good enough for Lilian, and she demands more proof. It isn't long in coming. Henry, who has found new resources in himself under the influence of the powder, demonstrates the Royal Touch by curing his aunt's arthritic hand. As the play ends, it is not clear whether Henry will make a bid for the throne or offer himself to science.

Directed by Robert Gill, *Hunting Stuart* opened for a two-week run on November 22, 1955, to good reviews from all the Toronto critics, except Nathan Cohen, who called it "laborious," "illiterate," "fatuous" and attacked it for its "barnyard" view of sex. Davies had introduced a phrenologist halfway through the play whose hands wander suggestively from a girl's skull to her neck and shoulders, although no further; and at one point Henry, thinking himself the lascivious Pretender, carries the woman scientist off-stage to the bedroom—without accomplishing anything. The Crest received letters and telephone calls expressing "shocked revulsion" at these indecencies. But so many more Torontonians telephoned and wrote to purchase tickets that the second week saw the biggest gross of the Crest's short history. (Surprisingly, John Johnson, Davies' London agent also found the script offensive, so Davies transferred his affairs there to Messrs. A. P. Watt.)

A good notice in *Variety* caused a flurry of interest in New York, but this gradually dribbled away. By the fall of 1956, only the producer Richard Charlton was still evincing strong interest. Between December and the following February, at the behest of Charlton's director, Norman Lloyd, Davies shortened the early part of the first act, rewrote a good part of the third and strengthened the conclusion. In this version Henry arranges to fly to Scotland to present himself as pretender to the throne. But in the end Charlton let his option lapse.

It is likely that the ebbing of interest resulted from the play's failure to pursue its animating idea seriously enough. Davies believes that a person's character is in a very real sense dependent on the cumulative experience of his ancestors, and the play makes this point; but he spends so much time evoking figures from the past and their amusing doings, and in making one excursion and another, that the underlying theme loses itself. The pattern of *Hunting Stuart* is not unlike that of the early play "The King Who Could Not Dream," which also introduces a royal hero in a bleak situation and transforms him; in both cases the transformation, while fascinating to watch, feels insubstantial, like a magician's sleight-of-hand. The play has been revived by professionals only once, at Festival Lennoxville in summer 1975. Thirty-five years later, Davies returned to the idea that a man can learn much about himself from the lives of his ancestors in *Murther and Walking Spirits*.

For all that, in 1954 and 1955 the Davises were delighted. Davies' plays pulled good audiences. They asked for a new play for the 1956-57 season, and he began to hope that he had finally established a continuing creative partnership with a theatre where he could fine-tune his scripts as they went through their first production. Even before he began to gather his thoughts about the new play, however, he and Brenda did something that he later saw as "an absolutely ill-fated thing." On April 28, 1956, they gave a small dinner party at the University Club in Toronto for J. B. Priestley, the prolific English novelist, playwright and essayist, who was in Toronto on a lecture tour. (Davies and Priestley were acquainted slightly. After reading *Tempest-Tost*, Priestley had invited Davies to visit the next time he was in England, and Davies had done so.) The guests bidden to meet him—Donald and Murray Davis, their sister Barbara Chilcott, her husband, the actor Max Helpmann, Herbert Whittaker and Helena Ignatieff—were all passionately interested in theatre, with the result that there was good talk throughout the meal. Sitting opposite the three Davises, Priestley was fascinated by the family likeness and mused to himself: "'What an entrance these three could make!'" Unable to call to mind a play that would bring three such siblings together, within two days he had decided to write one himself.

Thus, all unbeknownst to Davies, another, far more prestigious playwright was also preparing a play for the single new-play slot in the next Crest season. Davies himself, mindful that Donald Davis had said "I wish you'd write me a big romantic part before my hair goes!" had settled upon Casanova as his central figure—

who could be more romantic than this legendary adventurer in love? And who more interesting to explore than this eighteenth-century Venetian, who in his time had been a priest, a soldier, a spy, a violinist, a gambler, a crook, a librarian and a writer of engrossing memoirs? Davies had been fascinated by him ever since his university days. By now deeply involved in exploring Carl Gustav Jung's psychological theories, he had also decided that the play would be "Jungian." That May, June and July he gathered his thoughts, and by August 25 he had virtually completed a detailed scenario in his "Works in Progress" notebook. Then, as he was about to begin the writing early in September, he got wind of the competition. When he checked on September 13, he found that the Davises had indeed changed their plans: they had decided to do Priestley's play that winter and to delay his own until the following autumn.

Priestley's *The Glass Cage* did excellent business during its run at the Crest in March 1957 (Davies attended on the fifteenth to take a sharp look at the drama that "cut the throat of my Casanova play"). It then went to London and on tour, where it fared badly. The Davises returned to find the Crest in the usual end-of-season financial crisis. So, that August, Davies provided them with a lightly revised copy of his scenario to use as part of an application to the Canada Council for funding, and in February 1958, with production scheduled for the autumn and *A Mixture of Frailties* off his desk, he got down to writing the play he was now calling "Phantasmata." When he forwarded it to the Davises in May, they "rejected" it on the grounds that it was not "Box Office." After discussions, Davies revised the third act. Michael Langham was then interested in directing it, and on July 16 Davies expected it to be performed that fall by a cast that would include the three Davises, Frances Hyland and Powys Thomas. But Langham accepted a commitment elsewhere, Murray Davis took a sabbatical in 1958-59, and Donald Davis took one himself the following year, and then moved to New York for ten years. Davies' hopes of a working relationship with a professional theatre thus fell apart.

The play was published in 1972 under the title *General Confession* (a phrase from the preface to Casanova's *Memoirs*) together with *King Phoenix* and *Hunting Stuart* (as revised for Richard Charlton) in *Hunting Stuart and Other Plays*. Although Kathleen Griffin (who read plays for Sir Laurence Olivier) saw it in 1961, the CBC in 1963, Leon Major in 1968, Jean Gascon in 1969, Paxton Whitehead at the Shaw Festival in 1972 and Michael Schonberg at the Stratford Festival in 1982, it has never been performed.

Despite this, *General Confession* is of special importance in Davies' development. Not only is it his favourite among his plays, it contains the first deliberate exposition of the Jungian ideas that had by now begun to influence his views profoundly.

Whereas "The King Who Could Not Dream" and *Hunting Stuart* had done too little with their theme of self-discovery, the Casanova play can be said to attempt too much. Davies confronts his hero with manifestations of the Jungian archetypes that rule him and takes him far toward understanding them (and himself). But these were unfamiliar ideas for an audience to grasp without some preparation. In addition, the play's very graphic depictions of sexual intercourse and physical humiliation go far beyond the titillations of *Hunting Stuart*. The latter had been good box office in the Toronto of 1955, but this was something else again.

As the play opens we are in a moonlit antechamber of the great library of the castle of Dux, the residence of Count Waldstein, in 1797. An officer in Napoleon's army and the Count's twenty-year-old daughter Amalie have slipped away from a ball. The officer fails to seduce Amalie and is about to stamp off when Casanova, now in his old age and librarian to the Count, reveals his presence in the shadows. He offers his evaluation of the lovers' handling of their roles in the previous scene. Talk turns to the memoirs he is writing: Amalie is curious about his life and about the supernatural powers he claims. To amuse her, he mutters a spell or two, and, to his surprise as well as theirs, out of one bookcase steps the spirit of Voltaire (to whom he talks), from a second issues that of Cagliostro (with whom he fights), and from a third, that of his Ideal Beloved (whom he woos).

In the second act, Casanova and the spirits act out three occasions on which he had fallen in love—first as a youth, then as a young man at the height of his powers, and finally as a mature man of forty-five (Davies modified three episodes from the *Memoirs* to suit his purposes). In each scene, the Voltaire figure plays Casanova's wise counsellor or adviser, the Ideal Beloved personates the woman to whom Casanova is attracted, and Cagliostro represents the individual who ensures that Casanova's objectives come to naught. By the end of the act, Casanova has recognized that Voltaire personifies his own wisdom, that The Ideal Beloved is his inner ideal of womanhood and that Cagliostro is a mysterious force within himself that has jinxed his every striving.

In the third act, having reluctantly acknowledged that such creatures exist within himself and in others, Casanova wonders why they have made their appearance at this time. Is it to judge him? To drive him mad? Or to make him admit guilt? At Amalie's urging he submits to a mock trial. Amalie is to be the judge (though it is clear that he ought to assume this role himself), Cagliostro counsel for the prosecution, The Ideal Beloved counsel for the defence, Voltaire the clerk of the court. Casanova pleads guilty to six of the deadly sins—Pride, Envy, Anger, Gluttony, Avarice and Sloth—but not, surprisingly, to Lechery! He protests that he had always genuinely loved: every time, he thought he had found his Ideal. But he finally admits guilt on this count, too, and with this act, in which he takes responsibility for his whole self, he breaks Cagliostro's hold over him and is restored to vigour. The spirits disappear into their cabinets, Amalie and her officer depart for the ball; dawn breaks; and a serving girl brings Casanova's breakfast. As the play ends, he arranges an afternoon assignation with her.

Now, it is Jung's view that there is a level of the mind which has been shared by all human beings from time immemorial, which he calls the "collective unconscious." This level is populated by "archetypes," which are not innate ideas but rather "typical forms of behaviour which, once they become conscious, naturally present themselves as ideas and images." It is they which are responsible for the similarity of characters, stories and ideas in fairy-tales, myths and dreams around the world. Their presence is normally felt as "numinous," other-worldly, even spiritual. Jung believes that the archetypes play a large part in our lives, appear in our dreams and influence our perceptions of situations and people. Only an exceptional few of us consciously recognize and come to terms with them, but it is essential to do so if we are to achieve real self-knowledge. Jung has given names to the chief among them.

In the play, Davies portrays the confrontation between Casanova's ego and his ruling archetypes—his "Wise Old Man," his "anima" and his "shadow"—with great vividness. In the first act the ego engages them all unknowing (Casanova defers to Voltaire, finds himself attracted to The Ideal Beloved, is repelled by Cagliostro). The three "love" scenes in the second act demonstrate the ego's projection of the archetypes onto others. Attracted to a succession of different women, Casanova is blind to their actual characters and imposes on each of them his own ideal of womanhood. The compulsive intensity of projection is demonstrated in the third episode, in which Casanova is besotted with an eighteen-year-old trollop for a fortnight. He persists in believing that she loves him despite the warnings of his friends, despite the extortionate demands of her "Auntie," despite her disdain and her demands for money. Only when he catches her in the act of intercourse with her servant and is thrown to his hands and knees, ridden,

Wood-engraving from *Endymion* (*Half-tone reproduction, reduced*)

The Anima

Engraving glued inside the front cover of Davies' "Works in Progress" notebook, labelled (by Davies) "The Anima."

flogged and humiliated by her and her lover, is he finally brought, reluctantly, to see her clearly. In like manner he is repelled by a succession of different men, projecting on them one or another of the attributes that he has repressed in himself. If Casanova, Cagliostro and The Ideal Beloved were played by actors who (like the Davises) share a resemblance, the point that they are all parts of Casanova himself would be reinforced.

At the end of the trial in the third act, after Casanova has reached the second stage of self-recognition, Voltaire, The Ideal Beloved and Cagliostro step back into their respective bookcases. This is a visual representation of the withdrawal of projection as the unconscious and conscious levels of the mind begin to achieve their integration. But Casanova still has much to recognize in himself. As the play ends, he is still seeing the world through at least one of the archetypes, for the servant girl with whom Casanova makes his assignation is played by The Ideal Beloved.

For anyone familiar with the theories of Jung, the play is a fascinating depiction of his insights and concepts. But it demands a great deal—probably too much—of anyone without this prior knowledge. Thirteen years later, when Davies came to write *The Manticore*, he managed things differently and introduced a Jungian analyst to explain the archetypes to his character David Staunton and the reader.

For Davies himself, the theory of the archetypes was deeply satisfying. It gave him a satisfactory explanation for the appeal that certain kinds of character and story had for him. Looking back, he could see that the diabolic violinist in "Mr. Paganini Complies" and Edmund Cantwell in *At My Heart's Core* were shadows—the figures who body forth with a whiff of brimstone what we repress in ourselves. In "The King Who Could Not Dream," the alchemist Avicenna had been an instance of the Wise Old Man of great experience and knowledge, speculative, penetrating intelligence and apparently magical capabilities. In Benoni in *A Jig for the Gypsy*, he had created an example of the Wise Old Woman, earth-mother and witch. And in *King Phoenix* he had been drawn to the archetypal pattern that has found recurrent expression in the vegetation myths, that of the death by which life is renewed. Jung's work confirmed and extended his already strong intuitive understanding of the archetypes. And to find that a man of Jung's broad learning and stature took the "collective unconscious" seriously encouraged him to trust his own intuitions and to make greater—and more effective—use of the archetypes in his writing.

In July 1955, the American publication of Davies' second novel, *Leaven of Malice*, stimulated immediate interest in the dramatic rights on the part of New York producers. It also set in motion a complex train of events that resulted in the most grinding of Davies' dramatic failures. Davies was well aware that New York was a reputed graveyard for foreign plays, even those that were signal successes at home, yet he could not help but hope that his own chance at the big time had come at last. To ensure that it did not slip through his fingers, he went to extraordinary lengths. Where ordinarily he would gather his ideas, prepare a scenario and write a draft that would then require only slight revision, on this occasion he conceived plays based on *Leaven of Malice* five separate times, and he tinkered endlessly with the script that finally went into production. Used to working in the solitude of the study, and as a rule free from qualms about the sufficiency of his own creativity, this time he twisted and turned his conceptions endlessly in an ultimately unsuccessful effort to suit the ideas of others. In the end, inevitably, he recoiled; but it is a measure of his hunger for a major theatrical success that his reaction was so long in coming.

He began by presenting "A Plan for Dramatizing 'Leaven of Malice'" (prepared February 8-April 4, 1956) to Broadway producer Joseph M. Hyman, who held an option on dramatic rights from 1956 to 1958. But his scheme did not win Hyman's approval. Manuel Donald Herbert, a producer with the Theatre Guild (which interested itself in producing new, foreign and little-known plays), took up the option late in 1958, but he too rejected the "Plan" as it stood, proposing that Davies collaborate with Tyrone Guthrie. So Davies prepared a new outline, wrote a two-act script called "Leaven of Malice" in spring 1959 and flew to Ireland to work with the flamboyant director for three weeks in July at his home, "Annagh-ma-Kerrig."

Guthrie at home was the emperor of a very large and down-at-heels ménage. Davies noted in his travel diary that Miss Bunty Worby, previously companion and nurse to Guthrie's mother, lived with the Guthries and took her meals with them. The manager of the farm, the couple who managed the house, Guthrie's old paralysed nurse and her daughters lived under the same roof but dined separately. The large greystone country house in County Monaghan accommodated nineteen visitors that month, a few for a meal only, most for a few days to a week. Evenings were often passed in reading aloud or singing. Guthrie read the last chapter of his autobiography, *A Life in the Theatre*, some monologue character pieces he was preparing for the BBC and his libretto for a Nativity opera. Davies read his play *General Confession* and an episode from *Leaven of Malice*. Together they read parts of *A Mixture of Frailties* and, toward the end of Davies' visit, their new script. Christopher Scaife, a professor of English literature at the University of Lebanon, contributed some of his poems, and Joe Hone, Guthrie's nephew, read a passage from a film scenario he was writing about a hideous Galician dwarf. The composer Marc Blitzstein, who had arrived to consult about his operetta of *Juno and the Paycock*, accompanied Scaife and Guthrie as they sang—Scaife with great sensitivity, Guthrie bombastically and at great speed—and Davies played the piano for Guthrie's Irish songs.

Everyone deferred to the great man at Annagh-ma-Kerrig. Davies even contributed to his coffers by pulling groundsel from among the strawberries and picking raspberries to be sold in the village. He and other guests were also pressed into service to proof-read the 144 galleys of *A Life in the Theatre*, and when he insisted that Guthrie pay tribute in it to his mentor James B. Fagan, Guthrie told him to fix it himself. He did so, in a paragraph at the end of the Oxford chapter.

The Guthries pinched their pennies. Cigarette butts and butter floated in the dishwater. The linens were rarely changed. Meals consisted of greasy meat, potatoes and starchy puddings. More disconcerting yet was the emotional atmosphere, since Guthrie bullied his worshipping wife about her smoking and drinking in a "lunatic keeper's fashion." After tea one day, Guthrie, nude, his vast paunch a dismaying sight, came into the bathroom to talk while Davies took his bath, a liberty that led the latter to suspect Guthrie of being attracted to him physically. And Davies' unease was not alleviated when his host announced that he would use the bathwater next—to conserve hot water! This incident and a number of others eventually moved Davies to see Guthrie as a repressed homosexual.

In the midst of all this Davies reshaped his play, writing optimistic comments to his diary: "Things begin to move, as T. is getting notions for physical production & these spark off my mind for scenes & dialogue. This is what I had hoped for: & when he is working in this way he is very inspiring & it is all practical, for he knows to perfection what can be done & how." But in truth, he felt it slipping away from him. He rarely took pleasure in the writing, and slept poorly, because at heart he mistrusted Guthrie's judgment. There were days when he had no ideas, days when he fell ill, days when nothing went right. In the draft he had brought with him, the editor Gloster Ridley receives his honorary degree from Waverley University, and as he speaks to the Convocation the plot emerges in a series of flashbacks. Guthrie convinced Davies to reduce Ridley from narrator to an ordinary character, to eliminate a verse chorus and to add a number of silly telephone calls and a sequence of dreams. As a result, the comic, wise, literate overview that had contributed greatly to the success of the novel was lost. The changes coarsened the play, eliminated much of its whimsy and narrowed its focus. Shorn of Ridley's connecting commentary, the action became confusing. The play never recovered, because Davies was unable to substitute a coherent new vision for the old one. The subsequent changes—and they were endless—just got him deeper into the jungle. Typed afresh, the script was now "Malice Domestic: A Comedy adapted from the novel *Leaven of Malice* by Robertson Davies."

In March 1960 Guthrie began to cast the play. In May, responding to Guthrie and producer Donald Herbert, Davies made another round of cuts and revisions, reinstated the verse chorus and added a fresh telephone scene. The resulting script was called "Tyrone Guthrie's production of *Leaven of Malice:* A Comedy adapted from the novel by Robertson Davies." Finally, after the Theatre Guild had its own go at the title in early July, some copies were retitled "Tyrone Guthrie's production of *Love and Libel:* a comedy adapted from the novel by Robertson Davies."

On October 8, when the play went into rehearsal in Toronto, Davies was full of resourcefulness, enthusiasm and eager expectation. A play of his was at last being produced by one of the world's greatest directors. The cast of sixteen principals included many of the Canadians who had made the Stratford Festival a signal success. There were sufficient resources to give it a large-scale production, capable of competing in the big time: that season the New York stage presented plays by Lillian Hellman, Jean Anouilh, Sean O'Casey, Brendan Behan, Tennessee Williams and Paddy Chayefsky. So he coped cheerfully with the daily revisions he was asked to make.

On October 25, over tea and rum, Guthrie declared himself to be Davies' "father in the theatre." Some years later, he made the claim again, even more sweepingly: "You know, we all have fathers in art. I guess J. B. Fagan was my father in art. And I'm your father in art." And Davies admitted the truth of this to himself in respect of the theatre. Guthrie's force-field had certainly been as powerful an influence upon him as Rupert's, albeit in a narrower sphere, and in both cases Davies had found it necessary to establish a careful distance. He acknowledged a debt to Guthrie's advice and support and to his perceptive criticism of his plays. But now he was making his mark as a novelist, and here he would acknowledge no such relationship. It irked him when Guthrie assumed that he had the right to criticize his novels, since he knew that Guthrie was temperamentally incapable of the discipline and dedication required to be a writer himself. He sensed that Guthrie was jealous of his success in that field and of his escape from his influence. So even in the midst of preparing *Love and Libel,* Davies qualified Guthrie's claim; come what may, the theatre was no longer his central focus—or his forte.

The demands for changes continued remorselessly after the opening at the Royal Alexandra in Toronto (mixed notices), on the road tour through the Cass Theatre in Detroit (cold audiences) and the Wilbur Theatre in Boston (full houses), and right up to the opening at the Martin Beck Theatre in New York on December 7 (notices heavily qualified). Through all this, Davies' diary took a positive view of Guthrie's handling of the play, and in public ("A Writer's Diary," October 22 and November 19) he spoke cheerfully about the process of rewriting to please a director and actors. This in spite of the fact that in October he was asked to shift the two-act format to three; in November, to change it back to two, then to three again. He was pushed to tinker with the dream sequence and the finale again and again, to write new scenes and make cuts—of the verse chorus, the telephone calls and, eventually, the dream sequence itself.

Dennis King, the ageing American matinée idol who played the eccentric organist Humphrey Cobbler and saw himself as the star of the show, made things worse. He insisted on entrance speeches, sure-fire jokes and soliloquies. When he did not get what he wanted, he sulked, wept and threatened. When he did get what he wanted, he had trouble with his lines, refused to rehearse and, on occasion, froze on-stage. And Guthrie, nauseated and headachy from bad teeth and still suffering the effects of the heart attack he had had early in the year, let King dominate him. He would approve rewrites, then, under pressure from King, ask for further changes. Inspired by King's example, other actors also pressured Davies. Donald Herbert and his partner, Philip Langner, asked for major revisions on three occasions as well. Under these stresses the play was turned into a tricky, punchy comedy, full of gimmicks and slapdash theatricality. The stage business overwhelmed the script.

On November 29, in spite of Brenda's bracing presence on the tour, the weary Davies "Was desperately depressed for the first time since all this began: for 20 years I have been a writer & never before have I been in a milieu where every consideration came before literary considerations, & the opinion of anybody—the humblest actor, money-counter or baggage man—weighed equally or heavier than that of the author." Finally, on the day before the play opened in New York, he was informed by Herbert and Langner that all the money raised for the play had been spent. If it got anything less than rave notices, it would close at the end of the week. However, it could survive two additional weeks if $20,000 could be raised. Would he contribute $10,000? On the advice of Brenda and Willis Kingsley Wing, he did not, and the play closed that Saturday after five performances.

Amelia Hall recalled that Guthrie dismissed the failure "the way you might dismiss a tray of cookies that you'd left in the oven too long." He told Jack Merigold, his stage manager, "Well, Jack, we didn't make that one. On to the next one!" But Guthrie could afford to take that view: he was in the final stretch of a long, busy, brilliant theatrical career. For Davies, on the other hand, the failure was devastating. Without an established reputation, he feared that he would never be given another chance at the New York or the London stage. But he didn't give up, and characteristically, he remembered to post a note for the cast which one of them preserved:

My dear friends—
  It is too bad that our venture should be so soon over, but—never explain, never apologize. It has been a great pleasure to work with you all, & I hope that I may do so again—soon, and under more favourable stars. Brenda & I wish you all the happiness & success you so plainly deserve.

The Theatre Guild still wanted to mount a London production, so fresh transcripts of the fully worked-out Guthrie production were prepared and the cover labelled, "Love and Libel: Adapted from the Novel Leaven of Malice." But in April, Guthrie, who was fully aware that the Guild would not proceed with anyone else, refused to direct it. He then wrote to Davies that "*of course*" he'd have done it "If it had meant that you & your wife and Little Ones would otherwise have starved...." Obviously, Davies' burning thirst for a major theatrical success weighed little with him.

Chapter 12

MASTER OF MASSEY COLLEGE: 1961-81

...our Guest Nights were ceremonies, and I made it my special care to ensure that they were ceremonies in the best sense; that is to say, that people took part in them because they were irresistible, rather than merely inevitable.... On Guest Nights it was my job to see that things went well, guests properly looked after, and the food and wine as good as the College could manage. They cost us something, these Guest Nights, but they perpetuated a tradition modern universities sometimes appear to have forgotten, the old tradition of scholarly hospitality.

—*The Rebel Angels*, 1981

WHEN *LOVE AND LIBEL* failed in New York in December 1960, Davies was forty-seven. He had made his mark in Canada in a number of ways. He was respected for his fine editorial page in the *Peterborough Examiner*. Through his amusing Marchbanks columns, his authoritative reviews in *Saturday Night* and his more personal "A Writer's Diary" column for the *Star* syndicate he had attracted a wide readership for his opinion about the arts. His Marchbanks books were much loved across Canada, and the

Salterton books had likewise found a receptive audience. But had
Davies written no more than this he would have been remembered only as a minor figure in Canadian literature, and, in spite
of the modest success of *Leaven of Malice* in the United States,
not at all elsewhere. And now his plays, which had been performed widely in Canadian amateur and summer stock theatres
in the late 1940s and early '50s, had met with rejection from two
important new professional theatres in Canada and had failed to
make the grade in New York. At this last great blow to his hopes
of becoming a major dramatist, Davies felt a stunned, deep
despair.

But, of course, Davies did not sink, never to rise again. When
disaster struck in New York, he had already entered upon the
reading and thinking that would make his later work so strikingly different from his early writing. Indeed, by 1960 he had
already made his first set of notes for *Fifth Business*, the first volume of the trilogy that would earn him an international reputation. And suddenly his despond was cut short by an astonishing
offer, one that would delay the writing of those novels until
1968-74.

The offer came from Vincent Massey, who had just completed
his term as Canada's first native-born governor general. Massey
was the grandson of Hart Almerrin Massey, the nineteenth-century Canadian entrepreneur who had made the Massey-Harris
Company the leading manufacturer of farm machinery in the
British Empire. Educated at St. Andrew's College and the
University of Toronto and later at Balliol, Vincent had spent
much of his life in Canada's public service, notably as high commissioner in London (1935-46) before his appointment as governor general in 1952. He was a gifted amateur actor, a
discerning collector of paintings, a lover of music and an influential patron of the arts all his adult life. His grandfather had
been a noted philanthropist (Massey Hall, which he built and
donated to the city in 1894, was Toronto's major concert hall
until 1982) and Vincent Massey, in his turn, could not have
been more intense in his devotion to the public good. But the
generality of Canadians thought of him only as a spare, rather
ascetic man with a long, narrow, dour face, who delighted in

English aristocratic society and could be counted upon to be fastidiously correct. His obsession with protocol was legendary; many chuckled at the story of the two Englishmen of impeccable credentials who were discussing the new Canadian high commissioner and agreed that he had excellent qualities—"But," as one of them plaintively added, "damn it all, the fellow always makes one feel like a bloody savage."

Massey had early taken charge of the administration of his grandfather's large estate, persuading his fellow trustees to use the funds to establish the Massey Foundation, which went on to support numerous philanthropies. It was through his vision that the Foundation gave Hart House to the University of Toronto in 1919. He conceived Hart House as a male student recreational centre in the broadest sense, where men could meet, debate, listen to good music, exercise, attend plays and generally round out their education (women were not accepted as members until 1972). Much later, in 1951, the royal commission he headed was influential in recommending substantial federal government funding for universities and in promoting the establishment of the Canada Council to provide funding for the arts.

Massey, who served as chancellor of the University of Toronto from 1947 to 1953, had come to feel strongly that graduate students needed more from the university than they were getting. Well-taught they might be, but these young men, (and they *were* mostly men at the time), potentially the leaders of Canadian society, were not in his view being adequately prepared for their future responsibilities. The civilizing influences of the Oxford and Cambridge colleges were very much in his mind. If men of special promise were provided with fitting accommodation, then, rubbing shoulders with each other and with senior scholars, being exposed to music and the arts and from time to time meeting established men of affairs, they would acquire a broader grasp of society and their obligations to it. At his persuasion the Massey Foundation announced, late in 1959, its intention to give the university Canada's first residential college for graduate students (apart from schools of divinity). Massey College was to be allied with the university but administered independently by a corporation comprised of its Master and senior Fellows. After consulting the other trustees of the Foundation and the president of the university, Claude Bissell, Massey summoned Davies to Batterwood, his home near Port Hope, on New Year's Eve 1960, and offered him the Mastership. The position included a professorial appointment and teaching assignments in the graduate school.

It might have been expected that such a post would be offered to a member of the faculty. But Massey was familiar with Oxford, where it was not unusual for the head of a college to come from outside the university (in 1948 he had himself been offered the mastership of Balliol, his old college), and he strongly valued the cross-fertilization that came about when persons of accomplishment in diverse fields were brought together in congenial surroundings. He wanted a man who could stimulate the students to see beyond their course work and their research, who could involve them in the arts, who could introduce them to the world of affairs and public policy, who could help, in short, to broaden their eventual contribution to society. Massey felt that Davies was the ideal man for the job: the author of widely read novels and lively plays, editor of a literate, highly respected newspaper, a man as sensitive as Massey himself to English-speaking Canada's British roots. More than that, Davies had a sense of occasion and dress, he spoke well, and he possessed a research degree from Oxford.

All this Massey knew from more than thirty years of observing his man. He had encountered him first as Rupert Davies' son, a contemporary of his own sons Lionel and Hart at UCC and at Balliol. In 1949 he had seen Davies' much-lauded *Taming of the Shrew* at the Royal Alexandra Theatre. Himself a skilled writer of light verse, Massey had been delighted by the lively dialogue Davies submitted to the Massey Commission, and he had appreciated Davies' warm support of his (abortive) effort to establish a National Festival of the Arts in the mid-1950s. When the Foundation's gift of Massey College to the university was announced, Davies the editorialist had been quick to praise it. (Nor did Massey fail to appreciate a Davies editorial on a different subject. He had told Davies of his deep frustration at the Queen's inability to honour him, as she wished, by making him a

Knight of the Garter because of the Canadian Parliament's 1919 decision that no further titles should be awarded to Canadians. Davies had then written an editorial urging the government to make an exception when the monarch wished to honour a native-born governor general.) And, by the by, Massey had enjoyed *Love and Libel*: he told his diary it was "good fun, v. well staged by Tyrone Guthrie but needed a lot of tidying up."

Davies didn't give his answer immediately, but he knew that it would be yes. As early as his Oxford days, he had considered a university teaching career. Initially, he had thought of it as something he might fall back on if he did not succeed as an actor, director or playwright. And from Peterborough, the attractions of university life in Toronto seemed great. He envied the fact that his friends in academe enjoyed the company of their intellectual peers.

Davies had made the most of his opportunities to bring himself to the academics' attention. If it was at all feasible, when his plays were performed by faculty and student groups he made sure to see a performance and make contact with the director and players. On the occasions of his first two honorary degrees (from the University of Alberta in 1957 and McMaster University in 1959), he prepared provocative, insightful addresses. In March 1950, Claude Bissell, who was then dean of residence at University College in the University of Toronto, had invited him to speak to the UC graduating class and was delighted at the wit and elegance of his remarks. In 1956, Bissell (by then president of Carleton University in Ottawa) heard Davies talk about Stephen Leacock on CBC Radio and asked him to speak on Leacock in a new lecture series on Canadian writers and statesmen in 1957. Davies was the only non-academic in the series, but he proved the most impressive lecturer. Gordon Roper (by now teaching in the English department of U of T's Trinity College) had persuaded the College's Literary Society to invite Davies, in 1952, to speak in support of the resolution "That the present environment of Canada is conducive to a distinctive culture." Roper later arranged for Davies to be appointed visiting professor in the Trinity English department, "enriching" four undergraduate drama courses (two in the fall and two the following spring) by giving a commentary in one class hour each week. This brought him to Toronto for two days a week in the academic year 1960-61.

For Davies, then, the Mastership represented a prominent and potentially influential place in a milieu that attracted him. And like Massey, he saw in the college the chance to foster something more valuable in the students than a particular body of knowledge. However, where Massey wanted to encourage in the students a commitment to the public good, Davies had in mind a different kind of growth, namely "that solitary growth, that continuing search for what is enduring in the Self, from which all the great loves, all the high adventures, and all the noble rewards of life have their beginning." This was the search that had engaged him for much of his adult life and that underlay his best work. Davies was further strongly influenced by the prospect of having more time for his writing. Nor was he deterred by considering that some academics would resent his sudden leap to the top of the hierarchy. Of course he realized that many of them would not accept his brand of scholarship as the "real thing," but he was used to seeing himself as an outsider.

Nonetheless, he consulted Brenda before giving his answer. As he expected, she shared his sense that this was an opening they should accept. She knew how desperately he needed a change from provincial journalism. The children's departures to boarding school had increased her own eagerness for a change that would give them a chance to be something other than, in her own words, "the old folks in the country town." To a degree she had already turned her back on Peterborough, having given up directing plays at the beginning of the 1960-61 academic year in order to accompany Davies on the road with *Love and Libel* and to drive him to and from his classes at Trinity. She had hoped that something might come of one or the other, and now that it had, she was ready to make the move.

Davies asked his father's advice as well, and was startled when Rupert replied out of the old-world values that had been ground into him when he was a boy in Welshpool: "Oh, you must do that! You mustn't let that go by! It will raise you right above trade!"

Before accepting the Mastership, however, Davies wanted assurance that the college would be financially independent of the university, which, like all Canadian universities, was state-supported and not heavily endowed. Massey had assumed that, once established, the college could be run on revenue from student fees alone, but Davies knew this would not be possible (in the event, fees covered only about a third of the costs). The university had agreed to discharge any deficits arising from the college's operations and to maintain the buildings as if they were its own, but it demanded and got the right to inspect the books. Davies felt that this arrangement would result in either penny-pinching or the gradual loss of control. However, on February 1, 1961, according to Massey's diary, Massey and his financial adviser Wilmot H. Broughall of National Trust "were able to relieve his worries about the independence of Massey Coll. which must be assured by monies from the Foundation paid to the Corporation operating the College and it now looks as if the way was clear to the acceptance of the appointment of R.D. as Master." In reality, however, the "worries" were not so much relieved as temporarily held in abeyance. Davies had wanted a permanent endowment, whose income would cover the shortfall between fees and costs; instead, the Massey Foundation pledged to cover any deficits itself, but only for the college's first five years.

Davies' appointment was announced in the press on February 24.

The Early Years

Davies accepted the Mastership of an enterprise that had been taking shape for some time under the guidance of the six trustees of the Massey Foundation, many of whom he already knew. He had met Vincent Massey on numerous occasions and knew that they shared many interests. Over the next few years he found that it was often not easy to work amicably with this powerful, sometimes insensitive man, but he quickly discovered that the way to cope with Massey was not to tackle him head-on or to try to badger him, approaches that led inevitably to defeat, but rather to appeal to the genial person behind the stern, impressive, often pompous façade. Massey could not resist Davies' witty thrusts and his flights of imagination, and he loved his jokes—the rawer or dirtier the better. Managed thus, he could often be persuaded to see Davies' point of view. He and Davies often had wonderful evenings together, for Massey was well informed about politics and art, and he had an easy flow of talk, a nice dramatic sense and a capacity for mimicry. He became a valuable mentor, who taught Davies much about dealing with managements, governing bodies and trust companies. In the course of the stressful years during which he and Davies fought to make their shared vision of the college a reality, Davies came to regard him as a third father, after Rupert and Tyrone Guthrie.

Of the other trustees, two had been acquaintances since UCC. Davies was fond of Massey's elder son Lionel, whom he regarded as one of the kindest, sweetest-natured men he had ever known, albeit one who had spent his life in Vincent's shadow. Lionel had served as his father's secretary while the latter was governor general, and was at this time Director of Administration at the Royal Ontario Museum. He was an easy man to work with and gave his time generously to the college. Vincent Massey's younger son, Hart, a prominent architect based in Ottawa, disliked Davies. A very short man, he was in Davies' view embittered by that fact and resentful of those who had the good fortune to be tall. Nor did he share his father's feeling for British traditions. This animosity and difference of perspective produced sharp disagreements as the college took shape.

Davies had not previously met Vincent Massey's brother Raymond, although he knew his work as an actor. (Raymond was well known to millions from his title role in the play and film *Abe Lincoln in Illinois*; later he was similarly identified with his role as the wise Dr. Gillespie in the television series "Dr. Kildare.") Since Raymond lived in Beverly Hills, he attended only the most important meetings of the trustees, but when present, he and his brother provided drama and tension; both men tended to act out their feelings. Raymond's son Geoffrey, a Vancouver architect, was also a trustee, and though more active than his father, he was similarly constrained by distance from

Davies in 1948, when he was editor of the *Peterborough Examiner*.

Christian Lund, National Film Board

Davies as the Blind Beggar and Brenda as the Street Dancer in the Peterborough Little Theatre production of *The Man Who Married a Dumb Wife*, January 1948.

Helen Staples and Donald Munro as Ethel and Pop in the Peterborough Little
Theatre production of *Overlaid*, January 1948.

Grant Macdonald's "Setting for Robertson Davies' *Fortune, My Foe*" in 1948.

Robertson and Brenda Davies with members of the original cast of *Fortune, My Foe*, on Grant Macdonald's set. William Needles (Szabo) is leaning on the bar, Drew Thompson (Hayward) and Glenn Burns (Rowlands) are seated.

Gilbert A. Milne

Brenda as Katherina and Davies as the tailor in the Peterborough Little Theatre production of *The Taming of the Shrew*, as sketched by Grant Macdonald.

Cleeve Horne's portrait of Rupert Davies as High Sheriff of Montgomeryshire.

Robertson, Rosamond, Miranda, and Jennifer Davies in front
of the Weller Street house, Peterborough, winter 1950-51.

Leighton Hall.

LIBERTY

APRIL 1954   10 CENTS

The Double Life
of
Robertson Davies

By Samuel Marchbanks

Walter Curtin RCA

Davies as Samuel Marchbanks on the cover of *Liberty* for April 1954.

McKague

Brenda Davies as she appeared on the cover of *Saturday Night*
for August 28, 1954.

Tyrone Guthrie (far left) rehearsing the cast of *Love and Libel* in 1960.

Ceremonial procession leaving Hart House on the way to lay the corner stone of Massey College May 25, 1962. Dr. F.C.A. Jeanneret (Chancellor of the University), Davies (Master of Massey College) and Dr. Claude Bissell (President of the University) leading off.

The Massey College quadrangle in September 1963. Davies' office (on the ground floor to the left of the bell tower) overlooked the pools.

Jack Marshall Ltd.

Davies and Vincent Massey in the Common Room at Massey College,
September 1963.

Brenda being thanked for directing *Noye's Fludde* in 1974.

Jennifer Surridge

The little Madonna.

Jennifer, Robertson, Rosamond and Miranda Davies in 1993.

Robertson and Brenda Davies at Windhover in 1988.

Davies in his study at Windhover.

participating as fully as Lionel, Hart and Vincent. Wilmot H. Broughall, the last of the six trustees, was the officer of National Trust who looked after the affairs of both Vincent Massey and the Foundation. He has been described as "an astute and cultivated man of affairs, whose sombre appearance masked a rich and allusive wit." He was a regular attender, and Davies was to find him a powerful ally.

Davies soon learned that the trustees had split four to two over the question of design. Vincent, Raymond, Lionel and Broughall had favoured a traditional building, while the two architects, Hart and Geoffrey, argued for a modern one. After considerable wrangling, four Canadian architects, none of them "traditional," had been invited to submit proposals. Vincent, Lionel, Hart and Raymond were all Balliol men, and their fond memories of Oxford were evident in the memorandum issued to the competitors: the building was to have "dignity, grace, beauty and warmth," it should look inward onto a quadrangle, and the resident Fellows' rooms were to be arranged in "houses," each with its own staircase. After the submissions were received, heated discussions resumed—so hot, indeed, that the ordinarily reticent Vincent described them to his diary as "the 'Blood Bath.'" In the end, the trustees selected the outstanding Vancouver architect Ronald Thom, and he had then completed a second, substantially modified, series of plans.

When Davies saw these plans in 1961, he was delighted with Thom's strong, modern interpretation of the Oxford architectural tradition. In a speech to the Ontario Association of Architects the previous year he had asked the architects "to bring a whisper of magnificence, a shade of light-heartedness and a savour of drama into the settings of our daily lives," and he felt that Thom had done just that. (A couple of years later he wrote a little *jeu d'esprit*, "Mimesis at Massey," composed entirely of stage directions, in which the quad from dawn to midnight, and simultaneously from spring to Christmas, provides an ever-changing dramatic setting for the daily and yearly round of events at the College.)

Nonetheless he was relieved that construction was not to begin immediately, since he wanted some changes made, including the provision of more office space for himself, the college secretary and the bursar. Thom gave Davies' office, very satisfyingly, a view of the pools in the quad, and thus partially fulfilled the 1958 prediction by New York astrologer Hugh McCraig that "I shd. live SW of my birthplace & preferably on a hill with a view of water. Will in time move from where I live now & have already begun to meet the more interesting and influential people who will influence my life and thought. Will in later life be v. much a sage and teacher." A speaker's desk was added to the plans for the hall. But Davies, intent on integrating the college firmly into the life of the university, wanted more substantial modifications as well. He wanted to admit married men as non-resident junior Fellows in addition to the college's basic complement of bachelor residents, and in order to provide them with study carrels, space had to be hollowed out under the quad. He wanted to provide a suitable place for the university to carry out the graduate students' oral examinations, and Thom responded by designing a round, domed room, with eighteen desks around the perimeter for the examiners and one in the middle for the examinee. Davies also wanted a small reference library, to ensure that students could work effectively in college, and he wanted room for special rare book collections that would encourage scholarly research on the premises. Thom found space for both in the basement. On the other hand, had it been left to Davies there would have been no chapel. He pointed out that there were five within a quarter of a mile, and no budget for a chaplain. But Raymond Massey, mindful that the Foundation derived its money from his devoutly Methodist grandfather, insisted on one. A chapel was included.

In 1961 Davies and Vincent Massey both refreshed their recollections of Balliol, Davies in May while on holiday abroad, and Massey in June after giving Oxford's Romanes lecture. And Davies, whose travels took him primarily to Portugal, made a point of visiting the country's oldest university, at Coimbra. There he toured the library, the chapel and the examination room, and noted that the last was "splendidly dignified & the same general plan as I devised for Massey Coll."

Also in 1961, the college corporation had its first two meetings, and Davies began, and probably completed, the task of finding quotations to express the goals and spirit of the new college. He named the bell, high in its tower above the quadrangle, after St. Catherine, patron saint of scholars and of Balliol, and he chose a medieval inscription for it, to general approval:

> *VIVOS VOCO: MORTUOS PLANGO:*
> *EXCITO LENTOS: PACO CRUENTOS*
> (I summon the living: I mourn the dead:
> I rouse the sluggards: I calm the turbulent.)

Agreement on the motto for the college crest came less easily. Davies' first choice was the rule which guided the free, well-bred and thus (according to Rabelais) instinctively virtuous inhabitants of the Abbey of Thélème, namely, "*Fay ce que vouldra*" or "Do what you will," expressed much earlier by St. Augustine, Rabelais' source, as "*Dilige, et quod vis fac.*" Originally Davies translated this as "Cherish that which is noble, and you may do as you please"; years later he rephrased it as "Love God, and you may do as you please." But this suggestion had little appeal for the Masseys. They thought the students would take it as an invitation to slack off and wanted instead something that would inspire commitment to public service, along the lines of their own "*Dum Terar Prosum*"—"While I live I burn [to serve]." The factions finally compromised on the concluding words of Horace's "*Dimidium facti qui coepit habet: sapere aude,*" which Davies construes as "To begin boldly is to achieve half your task; dare to be wise."

Further difficulty arose over the choice of the quotation to be inscribed in the dining hall. Davies first proposed "A merry heart doeth good like a medicine; but a broken spirit drieth the bones" (Proverbs 17:22), but the others deemed this unacceptably frivolous. Other short sayings likewise met rejection. The Masseys wanted a long quotation like the passage from Milton's *Areopagitica* that circled the Great Hall of Hart House. So Davies ingeniously linked two passages from the writings of Santayana that maintained the spirit of his original suggestion and encapsulated much of what he sought to encourage at Massey College:

Happiness is impossible, and even inconceivable, to a
mind without scope and without pause, a mind driven by
craving, pleasure or fear. To be happy, you must be reasonable, or you must be tamed. You must have taken the measure of your powers, tasted the fruits of your passion, and
learned your place in the world and what things in it can
really serve you. To be happy, you must be wise.

To Davies' delight, Vincent Massey hired Allan Fleming, one of
Canada's most gifted graphic artists, to design the script for the
signs and plaques of the college. And when the time came,
Fleming himself painted the quotation in the dining hall.

Construction began in the winter of 1961-62, but the laying of
the corner-stone was delayed until May 25, when Prince Philip
was in Toronto for the Second Commonwealth Study Conference, chaired by Vincent Massey. The ceremony, which took
place on the grounds of the University of Toronto, was an elegant and moving one. Shortly before noon a colourful little procession, in dress uniforms and academic gowns, warmed by the
bright spring sunshine and saluted by the bells of the carillon in
Soldiers' Tower, wended its way north from Hart House, up
Soldiers' Walk and along Hoskin Avenue to Devonshire Place. A
university policeman and two sergeants of the Royal Canadian
Mounted Police led the way, followed by the chancellor of the
university and his mace-bearer, the president of the university,
Davies, the lieutenant governor of Ontario, Prince Philip and
finally Vincent Massey. At the site a sizeable crowd, including
hard-hatted construction workers standing on the still-rising
walls, watched intently. The Master presented the college
Fellows and their wives to Prince Philip. Vincent Massey then
introduced the Prince, who spoke with humour and point as the
corner-stone was lowered into place. Four trumpeters of the
Royal Canadian Corps of Signals blew a fanfare written especially for the occasion, and Davies closed the eleven-minute ceremony with remarks linking the college motto "Have the
courage to be wise" with the phrase "a community of scholars"
from the act of the Ontario Legislature that had brought the college into being.

In the months that followed there were many long, exhausting meetings over furnishings, usually held at Eaton's College Street store. Davies, who strongly believes in the civilizing effect of good design and fine workmanship, was well prepared to devote his attention to these matters, but, as the meetings began to stretch on and time was devoted by the Masseys to items such as the monthly washing of windows (Vincent) or whether the chef could produce "a really first class sole meunière" (Hart), he found himself arguing on the side of practicalities. The Masseys considered equipping the dining hall with sterling silver, but Davies, who thought stainless steel a better choice, persuaded them to compromise on silver plate (so much of this cutlery was stolen in the first year that a decision was made to buy stainless anyway). There was no stopping Vincent from ordering leather sling easy-chairs, because they evoked the image of conversation around a fireplace, but Davies found them uncomfortable and they proved to be hard to maintain. And so it went. The meetings certainly had their moments: once, for example, Vincent took exception to the pagoda-like bedside table Ron Thom had designed for the Fellows' bedrooms:

VINCENT: "That's an absurd looking thing. You should take a lot of wood out of there."
  RON THOM: "Well, you can't take any wood out of it: it's structurally the way it is. How could you take any wood out of it?"
  VINCENT: "Well, I'll show you. Can somebody get me a saw?" And Vincent took off his coat and he sawed about a cord of wood off that thing.

By the fall of 1962, Davies had found a bursar and librarian, who, together with the college secretary, would form the backbone of the college administration. The bursar, in turn, hired the staff he needed to run the college. These included Norbert Iwanski, the master carpenter, who in addition to his normal maintenance duties made special furniture like the speaker's desk and later constructed whole additional rooms, and Norman McCracken, the splendidly moustached, retired sergeant-major who became the college's first porter. In 1963, one by one, they took up their duties. Davies and Brenda moved into the Master's Lodgings on June 10, 1963, selling their beloved Peterborough house after much hesitation to Thomas H. B. Symons, the first president of Trent University. Miranda, Jennifer and Rosamond lived with them there for several years.

Davies himself soon came to be as widely recognized as he had been on the streets of Peterborough, a soft touch for beggars as he took his morning constitutional along College Street and around Queen's Park, eyeing the province's official statuary and doffing his hat ceremoniously, for a time, to a strikingly beautiful woman whose morning route crossed his. As soon as they had settled in, he and Brenda left the college staff to cope with myriad last-minute crises and went to Europe for six weeks. Davies needed a rest and he wanted time for introspection.

On the train to Oxford, where he spent three days on his own, Davies settled to his "task for this part of the journey: an examination of my life & an attempt to clear the decks for the next developments. I have some success, but so intimately does this sort of thing affect me I become rather ill, & arrive at Oxford with a headache & some sensations of a cold." He walked the familiar streets and visited a number of colleges, "seeking not only my past, but my present & my future—indeed myself." St. Anthony's and Nuffield provided him with good practical advice on the administration of a graduate college. Ruminating later he observed: "I am rested & refreshed; I have dredged up some good ideas for the coll. &—more important—have achieved a concept of the coll. & an attitude toward it which are coherent & firm without being inflexible. Could not have done this by brooding on the spot."

What had he concluded? That the new college should embody the centuries of collegiate tradition, and that it should be humane and personal, a genuine community of scholars with something of Oxford's merriness. The Fellows should wear their learning easily, unpretentiously. The college should assist its members to prepare themselves for the life opened to them by their education. It would reflect its founders' wishes, even if they differed from his own. As Master, he set himself the goal of ensuring that Massey College would embody these qualities, and that it would encourage the Fellows to realize their capacities as deeply and broadly as possible.

The college opened that fall, and from the start Davies emphasized the formal elements in the Master's role. He presided on special occasions, hosted social events and made himself available by appointment. But though he was not casually accessible at every meal or in the common room, this did not mean losing touch with what was going on. His staff, particularly Moira Whalon, who had been his secretary at the *Examiner* since 1956 and had accompanied him to Massey to become secretary of the college, ate lunch with the Fellows. Not only did she know the senior Fellows well and each student by name, but she kept her ears open. Davies always knew whose wife had had a baby, who was likely to have a breakdown, who had just published a book.

He gave his carefully chosen senior staff his full support. On hearing that the librarian, Douglas Lochhead, would like a cot for after-lunch naps, Davies wrote that he would be given not merely a cot but a divan (and went on to say that his own father attributed his long life to such naps and that he himself followed his father's example). Lochhead, who spent a decade at Massey, felt that he had never worked with anyone more understanding or more congenial. Bursar Colin Friesen, a bank manager in his previous incarnation, similarly appreciated Davies' warmth and forbearance. The staff that Davies nurtured shared his commitment to the college and, in most cases, remained for his eighteen years as Master and beyond.

Massey's ninety or so graduate students were a diverse lot, and chosen to be so. Excellent grades were a primary criterion in their selection, but the college consciously chose its junior Fellows from both the sciences and the humanities and took care to include a substantial contingent of non-Canadians. The twenty or so senior Fellows were appointed, for renewable five-year terms, primarily from among the university's most effective scholars. A few were appointed from outside the university. The first appointments included John Polanyi (winner of the Nobel prize for chemistry in 1986), C. A. Wright (influential dean of the law school), J. Tuzo Wilson (internationally respected geo-physicist) and Robert D. C. Finch (poet, painter, harpsichordist and respected scholar in the field of seventeenth- and eighteenth-century French poetry). In Davies' last year, the list included Boris Stoicheff (physicist widely known for his innovative use of lasers), Northrop Frye (one of the great literary theorists of the century), J. M. S. Careless (eminent Canadian historian) and Douglas V. LePan (poet, novelist and erstwhile diplomat).

The junior Fellows (like the seniors) were all male. Although co-educational residential colleges were at that time hardly thought of, this turned out to be contentious from the start. Practically on the opening day, a parade of female undergradu-ates picketed the college, bearing placards stating that Massey College was unfair to women. Brenda volunteered to investigate and, on discovering that the pickets were first-year students in the midst of initiation, set to their task by seniors at St. Hilda's, the women's residence at Trinity College up the street, she fed them a huge gingerbread cake and sent them happily on their way. In mid-October, however, there was another, more serious demonstration, this time by women in the graduate school. Davies himself ventured out to meet the pickets as they marched around the quad, and for the first of many times he argued, as Vincent Massey did, that their best recourse was to find a wealthy female graduate to endow a similar college for women.

To pull the community together, the Davieses, at their own expense, entertained all the Fellows. At first they tried inviting them to cocktail parties in groups, but they quickly found that as soon as Davies began to hold forth on any subject, other conver-sations would stop. So then they established the fortnightly fall Tuesday buffet dinners, which have since become an institution. Some of the students found these daunting and stiff, but as the Fellows drank their sherry and moved on through an excellent meal, they did mingle, often despite themselves. There were shy intellectuals with no small talk, foreign students uneasy with western social customs, students who had trouble equipping themselves with a suit, uneasy young women imported by Brenda to help leaven the masculine loaf, science men disdainful of the arts and so on—but the suppers added to the warmth of life in the college. For many students they also served, as they were meant to, as an introduction to the manners and decorum of a formal evening in a privileged private home.

The college made deliberate attempts to bring interesting outsiders within the students' reach. The half-dozen journalists who were awarded Southam Fellowships each year were invited to make Massey College their campus base. The university's writer-in-residence usually resided in the college, and room was frequently found for visiting scholars. Davies encouraged the senior Fellows to take meals in college and make themselves accessible. If an academic symposium could be accommodated, it was welcome, particularly in the early years, and if it could not, there might well be a dinner, a sherry party or a reception for the attendees, with Davies playing host. Until 1974, when women Fellows were admitted, female scholars or visitors with their wives were lodged with the Davieses, which meant that a good deal of Brenda's time was spent playing hostess and chauffeur.

Davies had high hopes for the college's library. From the first day it provided a basic reference service, but he imagined that it would grow, with special collections, to focus on theatre. Raymond Massey had promised to donate his theatre books, and in 1962, Davies, considering a donation of his own, went so far as to muse that the result might be "To have one's name perpetuated in a library—the Pedant's Dream." However, Gordon Roper, a senior Fellow from the beginning, took a special interest in the library himself in the 1960s and persuaded Vincent Massey to concentrate on Canadian literature, then too much neglected by universities and their libraries. Later, Lochhead, who had a special interest in printing and old presses, made the history of print and book-making a second area of concentration.

Davies supported both these initiatives and gave the library many books himself, his first donation being three Kelmscott volumes from Sir Sidney Cockerell's library, with William Morris' original designs bound in and inscribed by Morris, which he bought when abroad in 1963. With Lochhead's help he managed to raise the $100,000 needed to buy the Ruari McLean collection of nineteenth-century illustrated books. The money came from college funds, the McLean and Laidlaw Foundations and the university. (Some of the money raised was Davies' own. He regularly passed over to Friesen the honoraria and fees he received for speeches and articles.) He was instrumental as well in getting some fine hand-presses and cases of old movable type: Rupert Davies donated a great deal of type, the *Whig* a standard press, the Thomson newspapers a press from Morris' Kelmscott workshop and so on. Lochhead used the equipment in his bibliography classes to give students practical acquaintance with period printing techniques, and it also imparted a special character to the college's communications, which he printed on special papers, making liberal use of decorative type.

Davies strongly supported Vincent Massey's *hommage* to Oxford. He approved of gowns and Latin graces at dinner, he felt the appropriateness of "Master," "Bursar," "Porter," "Hall" (and "WC" for that matter). He applied on the college's behalf for a grant of arms (they were awarded in 1965). For him these things symbolized the vibrant scholarly life of medieval times.

But how best to expose the junior Fellows to the seniors and to outstanding individuals in the community at large? It was Davies' idea to establish High Table dinners and a Christmas Gaudy. The High Tables were held irregularly in the first year but then settled into a fortnightly rhythm. Outside guests were always invited, and each junior Fellow was asked to attend once a year. It was laid down that guests were not to be asked for favours, nor were they to be quoted outside college. They would meet at six for sherry, proceed at six-thirty to the dining hall (where the senior Fellows stood the juniors in hall wine) and move at seven-thirty to the small dining room or the upper library for dried fruit and nuts. Port and madeira were passed in decanters, cigars and cigarettes in silver boxes, and snuff in a horn. At eight-thirty, coffee and liqueurs were served, and by nine o'clock the guests were on their way, possibly to have a private visit with one of the senior Fellows in his rooms. Davies would often make a few remarks over the port and madeira, drawing attention to the publication of a book, the receipt of an award, the arrival of a child or some other event of significance. The guests were diverse: poets and cabinet ministers, architects and ballerinas, comedians and business leaders.

Gaudy Night was preceded each year by the Christmas dance. This was the junior Fellows' occasion: they conceived the theme, decorated the hall and presented skits and songs in a half-hour revue before a mid-evening buffet. Brenda helped out with the entertainment in the first two years, and Davies contributed a couple of skits, but they bowed out when the juniors made it clear they wanted to do it on their own.

From the beginning, Gaudy Night was the concentration in one evening's entertainment of the best talent that Davies could marshal. He initially conceived it as a purely internal celebration, but so many Fellows wanted to invite guests that from the second year onward Gaudy Night became an evening for the college to entertain its friends. Each year the program included Christmas choral music by the Massey College Singers, often written especially for the occasion. One or another senior Fellow might write special lyrics for them to sing. Or a Canadian composer—Giles Bryant, Keith Bissell, Louis Applebaum, Harry Somers, Derek Holman—might be invited to write music for the occasion. During the first half of the evening, a senior Fellow might read an original poem or an amusing disquisition, or a specially written ballad-opera or cantata might be performed. Davies knew his resources and managed them astutely. When Robert Finch, a poet of distinction and a frequent contributor, expressed reluctance one year, Davies quickly snared him. "But Robert, this year is a double anniversary! It's Beethoven and Dickens!" Finch couldn't resist the challenge of yoking that unlikely pair in verse. Sometimes Davies' contribution to the first part of the evening was more substantial, as when he suggested to Derek Holman a subject for a cantata ("Homage to John Aubrey," "Mr. Pepys and His Music" or "Homage to Robert Herrick"), then selected passages for Holman's use and wrote graceful introductory and concluding verses.

But Davies' major contribution came in the second half of the program. The Master's ghost story, different every year, quickly became the highlight of the evening. Why a ghost story? Davies indulged the belief that a new building like Massey College (or, about the same time, the Stratford Festival theatre) stood in need of a ghost or two. And he associated ghost stories with

Christmas, when they were told in Rupert's family; he himself had made a personal ritual for years of reading Dickens' *A Christmas Carol*. For Davies, the turn of the year is a time when ghostly things approach. Ghost stories also have academic associations for him. Brenda's father had told him about hearing Montague Rhodes James, the biblical scholar, antiquary and palaeographer, reading several of his own at King's College, Cambridge, and he has special affection for the many ghost stories by the Reverend Father Alphonsus Joseph-Mary Augustus Montague Summers, that eccentric denizen of Oxford. At the same time he enjoyed the challenge of essaying a new form of writing, particularly one that gave him such pleasure.

The ghosts he materialized, later collected in book form as *High Spirits*, are certainly an odd lot. The first of them was Davies' own shade, manifesting itself to the college's ninth Master; the second was that of a graduate student who had failed his Ph.D. oral thirty years earlier and was unable to rest until he passed it in every subject; the fourth visitation was from the ghosts of George V, George VI and William Lyon Mackenzie King; in the eighth, Dickens' spirit consumes a graduate student and tans his skin to make a new leather binding for a Nonesuch edition of his works. The stories are recondite, sly and inventive, often topical, and all of them feature the Master, not in his formal outward pose but as the inner man, intrigued and daunted by the apparitions. Davies put great care into his ghost stories and often started work immediately after one Gaudy to prepare for the next. He took pains to strike the right length, rhythm and sound for reading aloud, and his care was rewarded: Gaudy Night speedily became so popular that care had to be taken to ensure that there were enough chairs in the hall.

Davies and Brenda spent considerable time and thought on the college chapel. Since the Masseys wanted it to be ecumenical, they selected the furnishings with this in mind. Both cross and reredos, for example, were late-seventeenth-century Russian. Vincent Massey had asked Tanya Moiseiwitsch to plan the chapel's colours and textures, and thanks to her, Thom and the Davieses, it became a quiet retreat for reflection. Brenda, who had not been brought up a church-goer, made the altar cloths, did the needlework on many of the kneelers and served as one-woman chancel guild for successive chaplains. Davies coped with finding chaplains for the ecumenical service. They came in five denominations: Roman Catholic, Anglican, Presbyterian, United Church and Baptist. For the first five years or so, services (communion and either vespers or evensong) were held twice a month; later once. Davies and Brenda attended almost every service through the long years when only a couple of students and perhaps a senior Fellow or two comprised the balance of the congregation; by the late 1970s, however, there were often as many as twenty. And over the years, many members of the college chose to solemnize important events in their lives there—weddings, christenings, memorials. The Davieses' own daughters, Jennifer and Rosamond, were married in the chapel.

Davies considered the chapel a symbol of the search for self-knowledge. Not long before he became Master, he told an interviewer, "Life is a sort of lonely pilgrimage...in search of God...I think that the way the pilgrimage is made is by attempting to acquire self knowledge...and that by gaining knowledge of one-self and indirectly of other people, you gain some apprehension of some aspects of God." For the service of dedication on December 6, 1963, the feast day of St. Nicholas, patron of scholars, Davies chose scriptural texts that contrasted worldly wisdom and divine wisdom, underlining the primacy of the latter. The College Prayer, which he adapted from the writing of John Woolman, the eighteenth-century Quaker, and had spelled out on the chapel wall, likewise expresses the primacy of divine wisdom. The reredos he and Brenda selected includes a depiction of the Santa Sophia, the Ultimate Wisdom. Speaking at the last service of his Mastership, Davies quoted St. Paul on "the depths and riches both of the wisdom and knowledge of God" and observed that "It is to this wisdom that our College Prayer refers, when it distinguishes between the wisdom of this world, and the wisdom which illuminates and makes splendid the wisdom of this world."

Music, which turns the thoughts inward and is conducive to contemplation, is for Davies another route to self-knowledge. So he was delighted when, shortly after the college opened, Giles

Bryant, a singer and organist, and Gordon Wry, a singer and choirmaster, appeared in his office to propose a small college choir. (This was not quite so fortuitous as Davies usually makes it sound. His daughter Miranda was a member of the fine choir of Grace Church on-the-Hill with Bryant and Wry, and when she mentioned that her father was the Master of a new college, Wry had immediately declared: "Well, of course, what he needs, if he is starting up a university college, is a choir." She arranged a meeting immediately.) Vincent Massey approved, and Wry and Bryant gathered together an exceptional group of eighteen or twenty singers, which included Miranda for a number of years. They sang at every chapel service, drawing their music chiefly from the Tudor, Restoration and eighteenth-century repertoire. They also sang at Gaudy Night and presented one or two concerts a year.

Davies took a tremendous interest in the Massey College Singers. The choir practised every Sunday evening during term in the "green room" in the basement of the Master's Lodgings, which long held the college's only piano. Davies came to every practice, and afterwards, Brenda would serve a light meal and beer, for many years preparing the food herself.

Davies' interest was thoroughly knowledgeable and his musical taste catholic. He kept challenging the choir by suggesting new music. Perhaps they could sing, with great solemnity, something outrageously sentimental from Lizzie Elgie's book of Victorian sheet music? Or the Canadian comic opera *Leo, the Royal Cadet*? Possibly a complex madrigal by Peter Warlock, written in imitation of the work of Gesualdo (the late-sixteenth- and early-seventeenth-century Italian composer known for his astonishing chromaticism) and set to words from *The Duchess of Malfi*? Or something by Gustav Holst?

When the choir early felt the need of an instrument, the college found money for Jan van Daalen to build a small positive organ. In turn this prompted Bryant to seek out long-neglected music by Restoration composers, some of which he then published as the "Massey College Series of 18th Century Verse Anthems." The college bought a substantial library of music for the choir, including some very expensive Musica Britannica editions, and individual copies of Walford Davies' and Henry G.

Ley's *The Church Anthem Book*, a collection that gave Davies particular pleasure. After a time the college paid Bryant, Wry and some of the soloists modest sums. After Davies stepped down, the Singers stayed together for only two more years. Looking back, Bryant observed: "He's a very clever man in that you don't think you are being patronized. You don't come away with the impression that you have been taken over. You don't feel exploited, but somehow, subtly, you used to leave Massey College feeling you were better."

So Massey College sprang, more or less fully armed, into being in the fall of 1963. High Tables, the Christmas dance and Gaudy, chapel services and concerts all took their place in the year's round of events as if they had been going on for decades (or centuries), reflecting Davies' leadership and his personal style. Other events gradually added themselves to the college calendar—the Master's Sherry Party, a barbecue and a dance on the first weekend of term; the Founder's Gaudy early in October, when senior and junior Fellows all drank from the loving cup Vincent Massey had given the college; the Vincent Massey Gaudy in the spring, when they drank again from his gold cup; the Tuesday dinners given by the Davieses; and many other occasions instigated by the senior Fellows, the juniors and the staff. The senior Fellows felt intense loyalty to the college and its ideals; the junior Fellows generally found it friendly and serviceable. Like the senior Fellows, most of the juniors liked the formality that set Massey College apart from other academic institutions. It pleased them that the Master was a man of distinction, never at a loss for words. They appreciated his capacity to warm a High Table or a sherry party with witty, entertaining, seemingly spontaneous talk.

As the college took its place within the university community, it met the predictable criticisms, and plenty of them. The building was assailed by some for turning its back to the street and for emphasizing brick and stone instead of metal and glass. Many were irked that so much had been spent on so few. There was resentment at what was perceived as snobbery, elitism and pretension. Nationalists took issue with the importation of Oxford customs. Women resented their exclusion. Massey College was a fortress, a jail, "Half Souls," "instant Balliol" and a bastion of male chauvinism.

Although Davies more or less maintained his equilibrium through all of this, he often found himself tense and edgy. Some of his moves were certainly easy targets for the critics—for example, the matter of prescribing topics for talk at dinner. Early in the fall of 1963 some junior Fellows in the common room had asked him what he understood by "good conversation," so he offered to post a quotation every day to be pursued at dinner if they wished. These ("Heav'n has no rage, like love to hatred turn'd, / Nor hell a fury, like a woman scorn'd"— *The Mourning Bride* III.viii) appeared for a short time on the notice-board at the entrance to the dining hall. Although most of the students just ignored them, the *Toronto Daily Star* and the *Varsity* (the student newspaper) picked the story up and a legend was born. Fifteen years later it was still being stated indignantly in academic circles that Davies prescribed the topics of discussion over dinner at Massey College. Then there was his declaration: "I always thought that a gentleman sent his laundry out." At the beginning the college had no laundry facilities, and to draw attention to this deficiency, one John Wells, a junior Fellow, washed his socks in the pool under Davies' window. Washers and dryers were installed forthwith, but not before Davies' facetious comment had entered the college annals.

Much more worrisome than the critics was the college's lack of a solid financial foundation. Vincent Massey had assured Davies when he first offered him the Mastership: "You will never have to worry about money." But money proved to be a perpetual concern. Even during the five-year initial period when the Massey Foundation was to cover operating deficits, he never felt certain about what the Masseys would decide from one meeting to the next, given that several of them did not share his fears about the consequences of university control. An endowment still seemed to him to be the answer. So, soon after the college opened he made his one concerted effort at raising capital, for him a grating and distasteful business. He sent out an appeal, printed by Lochhead on the hand-press, to a large number of foundations. But only refusals came back. Many respondents made it clear that they would never support an institution bearing another philanthropist's name. This convinced him that if there were to be an endowment it would have to come from the Masseys themselves—and that it would have to come before anything happened to Vincent, who was well on in his seventies. Broughall agreed, and with the help of Vincent's friend Mrs. Leigh Gossage they persuaded Vincent to their point of view. But this issue divided the six trustees as sharply as the design of the building had done. Vincent, Lionel and Broughall favoured endowing the college with $1,225,000—all but $300,000 of the foundation's remaining capital—whereas Raymond, Geoffrey and Hart, wishing to be able to fund other projects, opposed it.

Lionel's sudden death from a cerebral hemorrhage in July 1965 increased Davies' anxiety. Broughall was equally concerned, and in a letter dated November 5 he sought to persuade Hart to support the endowment, reminding him "of his family's full commitment to establishing, guiding and shaping the college" and arguing that it was "well within the means of the Foundation to provide financial independence for the College and still have an amount which will be quite adequate for the purposes of a family foundation." Far from winning Hart over, however, the letter's tone and assumptions alienated him, and the battle would have been lost right there had Broughall not sought legal advice. It turned out that Vincent, as the sole surviving trustee of his grandfather's estate (the source of the Foundation's money), was free to act as he pleased. So he unilaterally proceeded to make the much-debated endowment, embittering his relations with the rest of the family in doing so and precipitating threats of suit by the other members of the Foundation against himself, Davies and the college. Apprehensive about the possibility of losing control of this endowment to the university, Vincent and Broughall gave it a legal existence separate from the college when they set it up (calling it the Quadrangle Fund) in January 1966. Davies described the episode to his friend Horace Davenport thus:

Have you ever tried to persuade rich people to unbelt? Of course you have. Then you know what I have been up to.

> At last I think the job is done, and we are fairly secure, but it has demanded an awful lot of persuasion, cajolery, flattery and browbeating, not to speak of God knows how much letter-writing, budget-preparing, and tiresome labouring of one obvious fact—that if you found a college and give it your family name and then starve it to death half the world will think you mad and the other half will think you stupid. During the course of this blood-bath our Bursar got an ulcer, the college solicitor got so he could not keep any food on his stomach, and I got an intensification of my skin rash, combined with ennui and *taedium cordis*. But nothing is achieved without these horrors, and colleges are built on the bones of their servants.

At about this time, Davies convinced the university that it should pay for services rendered, and every year thereafter a lump sum was transferred, covering the cost of heat, light, professors' offices, teaching space, the examination room and so on. At Vincent's death on December 30, 1967, a further lump of capital was added to the endowment, the sum that would have gone to Lionel had he lived. With Friesen's careful management, the interest on the capital in the Quadrangle Fund and the sum from the university (adjusted annually to keep abreast of inflation) just kept the college afloat through Davies' Mastership. Money remained a worry, but apart from unsuccessfully courting one wealthy potential donor for a time, Davies made no further serious efforts to solve the problem. He would say histrionically: "...the Bursar and the Librarian and the Master will stand out at the gate with tin cups if we have to to keep [the wolf from the door]," but he did nothing effective about it.

Lionel's death and Vincent's were both felt as major losses in the college. Both men had taken pleasure in attending the institution's special events and had often spent time in the common room. In making themselves easily accessible, they helped to realize the ideal of the college as a place where academe could meet the outer world. When Vincent told Davies of his wish to bury Lionel in a plain pine box rather than a horrible funeral parlour coffin, Davies arranged for the college carpenter to create it. The choir took special care in choosing music for Lionel's memorial service that fall. Many in the college felt a deep fondness for him and crowded to it. Likewise, when Vincent died, forty junior and senior Fellows attended the service in Port Hope that followed the state funeral in Ottawa, and eight of the juniors served as pallbearers. When the contents of Batterwood House were sold by Sotheby's in October 1969, Davies bought a number of items for the college, among them Vincent's desk and chair and the gold cup that was used thereafter at the Vincent Massey Gaudy.

In the years when Massey College was being founded and established, the Davieses' family life was briefly renewed. The girls were all living at home again and, like Brenda, they found themselves swept into the new venture, Miranda, of course, with the Massey Singers. They helped out at the Tuesday dinners and got involved with a few of the entertainments. But for the most part, they were getting ready to leave home.

Miranda completed an honours degree in English at the University of Toronto's Trinity College in 1963. As an undergraduate she had discovered that C. G. Jung's ideas, which so interested her parents, had a powerful appeal for her, too—so much so that she envisioned training as a therapist and only dropped the idea on reading the daunting curriculum that arrived from Zurich. She then qualified as a teacher and taught English and theatre arts for a year in a high school in Scarborough, a suburb of Toronto. (Davies gave her some assistance with an unruly class when he created a brief Christmas piece called "The Pageant of the Rival Holidays." In addition to ten speaking parts, it featured two armies and a crowd, utilizing the energies of all thirty-one of the students in marching, tumbling, fighting, jousting, dragon-killing, dancing and Christmas singing.) At the end of the school year, Miranda moved into an apartment with a friend and began to pursue a singing career, studying at the Opera School at the University of Toronto from 1966 to 1968, and subsequently in London. But success was elusive, so after a few years she combined singing with teaching for a time, in order to prepare for five years of training in child analysis at the Society of Analytical Psychology in London. After qualification she became a senior child psychotherapist and a professional member of the Society and practised in the Health Service as well as privately. She has published clinical papers, has lectured and taught widely and has co-edited a book on Jungian child psychotherapy.

Jennifer had graduated from Bishop Strachan School in 1961, worked at the *Examiner* for a year while at home in Peterborough and spent a year in Rome. After moving to Massey College, she worked in Toronto as a secretary and administrative assistant, principally at the McLaughlin Planetarium. In 1966 she married Colin Thomas Surridge, a psychologist whom she had met while he was a junior Fellow at the college. After a number of years, his work as an administrator in the field of correctional services took them to Jamaica and then to Ottawa. They moved back to Toronto in the mid-1980s. After her marriage, Jennifer held a series of positions as an administrative assistant, and recently she became the office manager of a small company. A skilled needlewoman, like her mother and maternal great-grandmother, she has often taught handwork in connection with one or another specialty shop.

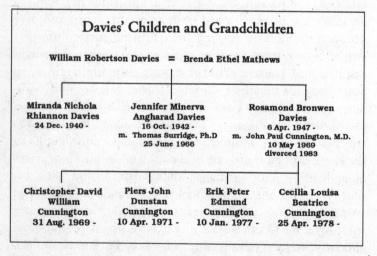

Davies' Children and Grandchildren

William Robertson Davies = Brenda Ethel Mathews

| Miranda Nichola Rhiannon Davies 24 Dec. 1940 - | Jennifer Minerva Angharad Davies 16 Oct. 1942 - m. Thomas Surridge, Ph.D 25 June 1966 | Rosamond Bronwen Davies 6 Apr. 1947 - m. John Paul Cunnington, M.D. 10 May 1969 divorced 1983 |

| Christopher David William Cunnington 31 Aug. 1969 - | Piers John Dunstan Cunnington 10 Apr. 1971 - | Erik Peter Edmund Cunnington 10 Jan. 1977 - | Cecilia Louisa Beatrice Cunnington 25 Apr. 1978 - |

Rosamond went in 1966 to Bishop's University in Lennoxville, Quebec, to do a B.A. in English, and in 1969 she married John Paul William Cunnington. His medical studies took them first to Hamilton, Ontario, then to Philadelphia, where she completed her B.A. at Swarthmore. They then returned to Hamilton, where she took an M.A. in English at McMaster University. They finally settled in Oakville, west of Toronto on Lake Ontario. They have four children—Christopher David William, Piers John Dunstan, Erik Edmund Peter and Cecilia Louisa Beatrice. As she was growing up, Rosamond, influenced by her father's interest in Jung, became conscious of the importance of the inner journey. As an adult she managed the bookshop of the Analytical Psychology Society of Ontario from 1983 to 1985 and edited its publication, *Chiron*, from February 1984 to February 1985. (Davies had helped found this Jungian group in 1970, and he and Brenda were regulars at its monthly meetings for many years.) After her marriage ended in divorce in 1983, she ran a day-care centre for five years, and since 1990 she has co-edited a psychological magazine called the *Mirror*, which views religious faith in Jungian terms.

Teaching and Research

The position Davies was offered as Master included a professorial appointment and teaching assignments in the graduate school. He had made a start at teaching in 1960-61 as visiting professor at Trinity College, and the following year he was made a full professor in the English department at University College. It was felt that he would profit from more experience with undergraduates, so he was given two drama courses to teach at UC, and he continued to do a little teaching at Trinity. At the end of that year (June 1962) he lectured for the university's extension department on the plays to be performed that summer at Stratford, a practice he continued until 1967. He also gave a number of lectures on individual operas for the Opera School. In the fall of 1962, he began regular teaching in the graduate school and continued this until his retirement in 1981.

Although his B. Litt. thesis on *Shakespeare's Boy Actors* was by now twenty-two years in the past, Davies had broad resources to bring to the teaching of drama. In the first place, his practical experience of theatre was considerable. In addition to his student ventures in acting and directing and the Old Vic stint in 1938-

39, he had directed twenty-seven amateur or summer stock productions between 1946 and 1955. By 1960 he had written eight
full-length and seven one-act plays, had adapted two others, had
himself directed productions of five of them and had seen most
of the others staged, often many times. And over the years he
had reviewed plays regularly for *Saturday Night* and the
Examiner.

Moreover, he had been a keen and retentive play-goer from a
very young age. In addition to the theatrical diaries he kept while
he was at UCC and Queen's, in 1957 or 1958, he began
"Theatre Notes," whose purpose he explained in an initial paragraph:

> In this book I want to make a record, as complete as
> memory will allow, of my experiences, chiefly as a *playgoer*,
> but with some references also to what I have done at one
> time and another, as an *actor* & *playwright.* I intend it
> chiefly as a private book, for me & for my children if they
> are interested, but I might at some time use it as a source
> for a book about playgoing. For as long as I can remember,
> playgoing had stood first among all pleasures with me, &
> although to most people it is simply a pastime, I think that
> I have brought qualities to it which raised it above that. I
> have never really been a good actor, (though I have had my
> moments) & it may prove that I was not a good play-
> wright, but I sincerely believe that I have been a good *play-*
> *goer*, & that is something better, perhaps, than having been
> a well-known critic. Critics often do not like the theatre; I
> have never liked anything better.
>
> I shall not make a burden of my book by giving it a plan.
> I shall write as occasion serves, & for pleasure.

He began with a brief summary of his theatre-going experiences in Thamesville, Renfrew and Kingston, then noted the
performances of Marlowe, Jonson and Shakespeare and also of
operas he had seen (lists augmented subsequently in the mar-
gins). A sixty-four-page account of developments in the *Love and
Libel* affair between 1956 and 1961 followed.

At the beginning of 1962, however, he turned "Theatre Notes" into a theatrical diary. In doing so he was mindful that records kept by ordinary play-goers in old-world countries like England had become an important resource in the study of drama. Canada having no such records, he decided to create some for use in his own teaching. During his teaching career he recorded his thoughts on from twenty-nine to as many as seventy-six performances a year—contemporary plays, revivals of the classics, operas, student productions, circuses, puppet-plays. The notes were memory aids, but also memory exercises: here, for example, is what he wrote on January 10, 1963, about a play that had been familiar to him since Kingston, where in 1928 he played Sir Peter Teazle:

> To O'Keefe to John Gielgud's *The School for Scandal*; we both remember his 1938 production as a high spot & I his Joseph Surface as the finest high comedy playing I have ever seen. This was better: gentler, more *easily* elegant & wth. more due attention to the sentimental side of the piece. Also more human: none of T.G.'s [Tyrone Guthrie's] restlessness, & less of J.G.'s frigid elegance. Delightful details: Sir Oliver's costume v. much in the Eastern taste, & old fashioned; Moses not *too* Jewy but given to fur collars & earrings & side curls: the wine bottles *the right shape*; the closet where Sir Peter hides so small that he emerges doubled up; the screen placed so that we can see Lady Teazle's response to the scene. One useful transposition: Act V.i. played before IV.iii, otherwise trivial cuts. Played till 11.20. B. & I so impressed we go again next wk. for a better view.

Davies had, of course, been a collector of theatrical books and memorabilia for many years. He continued to collect at a great rate through the 1960s, and at a reduced pace in the 1970s and '80s. At the heart of this mass of material was a large number of eighteenth- and nineteenth-century plays, a number of which had received his attention in "Making the Best of Second Best" in *A Voice from the Attic*. Some notion of the magnitude of his activity can be gauged from the fact that, by the time he retired, he had in his possession some four thousand melodramas!

Evidently Davies' resources for the teaching of drama were very different from those of most of his academic contemporaries. As a teacher he approached drama primarily as theatre, rather than as literature. While the actual words of dramatic texts were important—at a performance he was always alert to cuts or alterations in the text, and he could quote passages that struck a chord from memory—they were not, for him, the chief thing worthy of discussion. His reading of Jung led him to believe that the theatre communicates *primally*, that it reaches out, like music, not first to the intellect but by gripping the senses and emotions, and that its power is greatest when the characters and situations spring from the archetypes hidden in our unconscious. Without belabouring the point, he nudged his students to recognize these archetypal underpinnings. In his courses on the history of drama he emphasized the nature of the theatre (acting style, stagecraft, scenery, shape of stage, lighting, audience) for which a play was written. He reflected on the ability of great actors to endow plays of no particular literary merit with long and vigorous life on the stage. He noted the frequent failure of dramatic theory to anticipate or account for the success of plays and productions that spoke to new wants in their audiences. He directed the students' attention to once-popular plays whose appeal had faded—what had attracted George Eliot, Thackeray and Trollope to them? When teaching a classic, he would describe its stage history—how the text had been modified to suit the taste of later periods, how it had been differently interpreted, how various stagings had illuminated contrasting aspects of the text. He often brought along a first edition or the playbill of an influential production to assist the students' imagination.

Whether or not they approved of his methods, students did not forget their encounters with Davies. As he saw himself, he was the soul of decorum, never harsh, full of praise for those who earned it, careful to reserve reproof until he could speak to the individual in private. But many students recognized something more formidable in his performance. His appearance was challenging enough for a start. His hair was by now snow-white, but the accustomed moustache and beard remained dark, kept that way with the aid of a dye-pot from the late 1950s until 1981, when, on retirement, he bowed to nature. In the early 1960s, of course, almost all of his colleagues were still clean-shaven. At Trinity that first year, while he was feeling his way, his contributions to "Drama and the Novel," "The Development of English Drama to 1642," "Modern Drama" and "Shakespeare" took the form of lectures, which rather inhibited discussion. One student remembers that "despite the fact that he was periodically fascinating, he had very little capacity of enlivening us. And he had, on the other hand, the capacity, unfortunately, of dumbfounding us. So that when he finally got around to making his observations and saying, 'Well, what do you think?' well, we didn't know what the hell we thought and we were absolutely incapable of expressing it if we did think anything…. Once…in the midst of the utter silence of cowering people, he said, 'God, you're a dumb lot!' And he was right!" By the following year, when he taught "Modern Drama" and a drama survey at University College, he had found his feet. At the end of the survey course, he was given the applause that University College students reserved for professors they enjoyed.

Virtually all his graduate students respected the depth and breadth of his learning and felt the profit from it in the two courses he taught each year between 1962 and 1981, which were variously "The History and Tradition of the Theatre," "English Drama from 1658-1800," "English Drama from 1800 to the Present," "Bernard Shaw and His Contemporaries" and "Nineteenth-Century English Theatre and Drama." One of them remembers and treasures the sudden transformation of a seminar into a sparkling lecture on Boucicault (the nineteenth-century playwright, actor, director and theatre manager), or Gilbert and Sullivan, or "The Edwardian Age." The same student relished Davies' perceptions: "The nineteenth century was bearded and mustachioed. Only actors were clean shaven and stood out because of this. Salvini was an exception with his huge handle-bar moustache" or "To see Lillie Langtry was to have a tiny holiday." To another student, Davies' experience in theatre and journalism anchored his courses in the real world and kept them from floating away into "airy fairy" or "high-falutin" theory. He was struck by Davies' descriptions of the mechanics of the stage of earlier times, by his grasp of the environment in which the theatre operated. The students were impressed not only by Davies' grasp of the facts but, as his readers have been, by the breadth and astuteness of his observation.

On the other hand, the students were markedly of two opinions about the way his courses were run. His idiosyncratic practices inspired anger and unease in some, delight in others. After Massey College opened, he held his two seminars (each for one two-hour session per week) in the "green room" in the basement of his quarters. This was a pleasant place with theatrical prints on panelled walls, books on the shelves, a large central table for the dozen or so students to sit around, a grand piano and an oriental rug on the floor. Here he was both professor and host, a relationship underlined by Brenda's appearance at Christmas and the end of term to accompany the serving of sherry and lunch. Many students were charmed, but some resented the implicit setting of social as well as intellectual standards. At the first meeting of one class, a woman inquired "Are youse Robertson Davies?" and a man flipped the burning tip of his match onto the rug; when they failed to appear for the second class, the other students speculated that they had been asked not to return.

He based grades solely on the students' oral presentations and on their contributions to discussion. The students were to speak from notes, not from prepared texts. In Davies' view, intending teachers should be capable of speaking with authority and in educated English. These rules, very different from those in most graduate courses, generated some tension, especially in those American students who felt themselves at a disadvantage because of their vocabulary and accent. (Erroneously so, according to Davies: it was literacy and grammar that concerned him.) Although the students had no papers to submit, they found themselves preparing just as carefully for their oral presentations. Some felt themselves hard done by when marks were assigned because, with no written work, there was nothing to produce in an appeal to higher authority. However, formal complaints were few. (This might have reflected the lack of written evidence to submit, but on the whole, the students I interviewed felt satisfied that their performance had been assessed justly.)

Davies deliberately maintained a certain distance from his students. Unlike most of his colleagues, he did not keep regular office hours; outside class hours he was available only by appointment. As the students watched him donning his masks—the grand old man of Canadian letters, the Master, the performer, the professor—some of them recognized his need for inner space. But those who took their courage in hand to beard him in his den found him very helpful. If they asked for advice on personal matters, he gave them his full attention, intent on discerning what they *yearned* to do, as opposed to what they thought they *ought* to do. Typically he advised them to follow their hearts. But he never sought this role, fearing the potential dangers of playing the magus, not only for the students but for himself.

In class, it seemed to the students that Davies sometimes played favourites. He was bored easily, especially by those who drew their opinions from critics, and the students soon recognized it as a bad sign when he removed his glasses and began to tap them. Although he usually managed a tactful diversion when a student maundered on, he was occasionally abrupt, even caustic.

Davies' deep convictions on the subject of male-female differences made him an object of suspicion to feminists. In the early years women were excluded from membership of Massey, but it was not only this that excited a sometimes angry reaction. With Jung, Davies is convinced that the principle of Eros dominates women's approach to life, focusing them on feeling and understanding, while the principle of Logos dominates men, focusing them on abstract thought and the making of laws and rules. It seems to him that women are particularly good at psychology: "They're brilliant healers though they're not very often initiators in discovering new techniques." In his view, women care more deeply about the continuance of the race and of culture than men. "They are more pragmatic than men. They are much more domesticated and play safe more than men. Because of their necessity to bear children and bring them up, they place a great deal of emphasis on stability, which men are less inclined to do." (He identifies these qualities in the women most important to him, like Wilhelmina Gordon at Queen's, Dora Herbert-Jones in Wales, the professional women directors he encountered at Oxford, Brenda, his Alexander teacher Lulie Westfeldt, the Jungian analyst Esther Harding.) Men, on the other hand, are more likely to be adventurers and roamers, whose willingness to pursue an abstract line of thought to its logical conclusion has resulted in "wars, constant wrangles, disagreements, economic misery."

Davies feels that universities as they stand are designed to develop men's strengths, and therefore to educate a woman in them is "to try to change her into something which she is not and to belittle and betray what she is." From time to time, however, he would make a comment in class like "Men reason; women intuit," which aggravated the allergies of a generation of women students highly sensitized to patronizing, advantaged males. By all accounts, Davies did not treat the many women in his classes unfairly. They did well or ill according to their merits and experienced no sex bias. A number of women chose him to supervise their dissertations and felt comfortable in asking him for letters of recommendation. It must be noted, however, that in 1973, when he had been teaching graduate students for ten years, Davies was reported as saying that in his experience women were not outstanding students of English literature: "they don't initiate new or venturesome ideas in that realm."

Davies was an encouraging supervisor. As he saw it, it was the student's job to define his subject and to structure his argument, to choose and use the appropriate scholarly texts. It was the supervisor's responsibility to listen, suggest and, when necessary, assist in jumping the administrative hurdles. Davies gave meticulous attention to matters of grammar, style, tone, punctuation and derivation, and encouraged the use of a plain, flexible, graceful, accurate prose, in comments that are often a pleasure to read.

—PLEASE do not use "hopefully" to mean "it is to be hoped." You would not serve junk food at a banquet, and your book must be a banquet. Get your language from Swift, not from Shopsy's.

—"It was a guerilla tactic"; this is guerilla grammar and

needs to be re-cast.

—Not "gold-plated state banquets" but "banquets served on gold plate"—hard food for Midas, I will none of thee!

—*of course* a dead end goes nowhere—trim this.

—The only thing—a trifle, but it is trifles that betray us—is your derivation of "carnival" from *carne vale*, which is dog-Latin, though reasonable Italian. See the big *OED*. Don't change it in the typescript but be ready with an answer if you need one.

At oral examinations Davies loved to watch his fellow examiners (and what he saw informs the comic examination in *The Lyre of Orpheus*). While most examiners were courteous and sensible, a few were quite capable of venting their disputes with a colleague on an innocent student. He prepared his own students well. To calm their nerves he would remind them that their degree was virtually assured; otherwise their thesis would have been halted by the departmental readers. That being the case, they were not to be thrown off stride by what might appear to be hostile questioning: it might well proceed from the examiner's need to show off. Nor should the student allow himself to be baited into giving aggressive or insulting answers to apparently foolish questions. The proper tone was respectful, but not servile. However relaxed the examiners might be, students should maintain a certain formality, out of respect for themselves and for the high degree they sought. At the examination itself, he used the supervisor's traditional opening questions to give his students (as one of them observed) the opportunity "to just spread out your tail like a peacock, and really appear to know the subject."

As Davies had expected, when he arrived at the university many of his academic colleagues were offended by his appointment and snubbed him. The English department was the largest and most influential in the country. It was a time when a doctorate had become a requirement for tenure, and here was Davies, with only a B. Litt., vaulted to a full professorship and a much-coveted appointment to the graduate school. Few had any idea how deep his knowledge of the theatre ran, and his accomplishments as a journalist, dramatist and writer cut little ice at an institution that deemed journalism a trade and practically refused to teach Canadian literature. In 1960, "CanLit" was represented in the U of T's undergraduate curriculum by just one optional course and a single text in "American and Canadian Literature." Even in the graduate program there were only two courses in the subject. Many members of the faculty were quite prepared to think of Davies as a hollow man, a pompous phoney, all form and no content. His performance in three public lectures at Trinity College in January and February 1961 encouraged some who subscribed to this view. Following Oxford practice, he wore his splendid B. Litt. robes instead of the conventional black gown or business suit. Although he delivered his material with flair, some in the audience considered his showmanship a sign of shallowness. And in the course of speaking on "The Curse of Education," "The Curse of Intellect" and "The Curse of Taste," he raised a few hackles in advocating that people should read less, that they should read feelingly rather than critically, and that they should read only what they like. The disfavour of some of his colleagues persisted for a number of years.

Opinion began to shift in 1964 when Nevill Coghill, Davies' former thesis supervisor, lectured at the university. After Davies introduced him, Coghill, widely respected for his dramatic productions, commented that he had seen many Malvolios, but that only two stood out in his memory:

> ...the first of them was that of Professor Davies. It had a deliciously grave dignity, imperiled at every moment by a calculated touch of the absurd, yet somehow maintaining itself in the careful precision of every step and gesture, and the well-timed periods in his speech. I can still hear the note of rapturous awe in his voice and see the glint of his teeth as he said "Jove, I thank thee! I *will* smile!" And smile he did. This was a quarter of a century ago, but for me that smile is as sharp and fresh as yesterday's. The other Malvolio that is etched in my memory as of equal unforgettable distinction came many years later, when I saw Sir Laurence Olivier in the part at Stratford.

From the beginning, however, Davies had the support and respect of key senior figures like Bissell, A. S. P. Woodhouse (the influential head of the English department at University College) and Roper. In 1963 or early 1964, Bissell asked Davies to prepare a report on the initiatives that other Canadian universities were taking in the field of drama. When Toronto proved to be rather behind the times, he asked Davies and Professor Clifford Leech to set up a Centre for the Study of Drama in the graduate school. The two found themselves largely in agreement and quickly planned a course of study to prepare students to become critics, historians and teachers of dramatic literature. They included courses from Classics, English, East Asian Studies, French, German, Italian and Hispanic and Slavic Languages and Literatures to give students a broad exposure to drama. They required a course on the general history of drama and theatre, knowledge of a language other than English, some practical work in the theatre, a thesis or a practical exercise (like directing a play or preparing designs for a production), and the usual general and thesis oral examinations. The Centre assumed control of Hart House Theatre as well, and a nucleus company of four professional actors and a professional director were hired to produce a number of plays each year and expose the students to professional production standards. The Centre came into being in 1966-67, with Davies in a central role. Here, for the first time at the university, he was an insider whose opinions were heeded and whose special knowledge was regarded as a strength.

His colleagues at the Drama Centre—Brian Parker, Clifford Leech, Martin Hunter, Michael Sidnell, Frederick Marker, Lise-Lone Marker, Josef Skvorecký, and Ann Saddlemyer—saw a great deal of him. He would arrive for committee meetings on the stroke of the hour, often with something specific to say, and when the time he had allotted was up he would leave. Belying his poor reputation in some feminist circles, he was a member of the selection committee that appointed Ann Saddlemyer director of the Centre in 1972, making her the first woman director on campus. He was frequently involved in the Centre's thesis examinations, and Saddlemyer recalls his written reports as internal examiner as "always a delight" to read and "always very fair." His examination questions were few, but witty, challenging, often surprising. (On occasion his own plays formed a part of the subject matter.) His colleagues and the theatre professionals who sought his advice came to know that he would give his opinion without pulling his punches. As with the students, he was good at providing the dose of encouragement that made a difference.

Early in 1966, Clifford Leech, one of the editors of the seven-volume *Revels History of Drama in English,* invited him to write the section dealing with playwrights and plays from 1750 to 1880. This being Davies' period, it was a chance to demonstrate his scholarly competence. His contribution, which runs to extraordinary detail on between three and four hundred plays (in 122 pages), unfortunately provides very little in the way of overview, and it is both frustrating and wearisome to read. Fortunately, the index provides ready access to the plums in the pudding, his observations on individual playwrights and plays. Much of what he wrote is astute, including knowledgeable *aperçus* about audiences, and he shows himself surprisingly learned in his discussion of musical accompaniments. Here for the first time he wrote about the dual-role plays that were to figure in *World of Wonders,* and about James Robinson Planché, who was to have some importance in *Lyre of Orpheus.* As usual Davies took care to meet the assigned deadline, in this case July 1968, only then to discover how slowly the wheels of academic publication can turn. For a number of reasons the book did not appear until 1975. By that time it had little effect on his academic reputation.

Non-Academic Writing

During the 1960s, Davies was becoming increasingly concerned about the inaccessibility of his early work. Although he had parted company with Clarke, Irwin in 1958, the firm retained copyright in the ten books it had published, and had neither brought his books out in paperback nor sold the rights to do so to anyone else. The new courses in Canadian literature being offered at Canadian universities typically considered only books that students could obtain cheaply. Davies wished mightily that his early books could appear in McClelland and Stewart's prestigious New Canadian Library paperback reprint series.

M & S was interested in him, too. In 1957 and 1963 the Toronto publishing house had approached him to write the introductions to reprints of Stephen Leacock's *Literary Lapses* and *Moonbeams from the Larger Lunacy*. As Knopf's Canadian distributor, M & S had brought out *A Voice from the Attic* in hardcover in 1960, and in 1961 Davies' Carleton University lecture on Leacock was included in *Masks of Fiction: Canadian Critics on Canadian Prose*. During the next two years, M & S made several overtures to him, proposing to include his work in the New Canadian Library, and in the fall of 1963 Davies and Jack McClelland, the ebullient president of McClelland and Stewart, both wrote to Clarke, Irwin to argue the advantages of putting *Leaven of Malice* into the NCL. This pressure seems to have been the key to Clarke, Irwin's decision to bring out Davies' work in paperback itself—*Leaven of Malice* appeared in 1964, *Tempest-Tost* in 1965, *At My Heart's Core* and *Overlaid* in 1966, *The Diary of Samuel Marchbanks* in 1966, *The Table Talk* in 1967, and *Four Favourite Plays* (*Eros at Breakfast*, *The Voice of the People*, *At the Gates of the Righteous* and *Fortune, My Foe*) in 1968. But Clarke, Irwin's capitulation by no means ended Davies' flirtation with M & S. In January 1965, at the publisher's urging, Davies wrote the little story "Animal U" for a projected series (not, in the end, published by M & S), and in November 1966, while he was working on *Table Talk* to prepare it for republication, he dug the "Almanack" out of his bottom drawer and offered it to Malcolm Ross, general editor of the New Canadian Library and an English department colleague who taught at nearby Trinity College.

Within days, Ross and Jack McClelland had both read the manuscript and were delighted with it. So that Christmas, Davies pulled the book into shape, adding half a dozen new single-paragraph entries (including the quotation at the beginning of chapter one above), and two new letters from Apollo Fishorn, his Canadian playwright. Graduate student Mervyn Noseigh, M.A., now made his appearance for the first time, satirizing a few of the strange growths Davies had recently been discovering in the groves of academe. Finally, Davies drew a set of twelve whimsical zodiacal doodles to open the sections and delivered the revised

typescript on February 21. When the hardcover appeared that fall, followed by the paperback in the spring, the reviewers gave it a warm welcome. Unlike Clarke, Irwin's readers, they enjoyed its "low" humour. Although the *Almanack* repeated points already made in the *Diary* and *Table Talk*, and contained a good deal of incongruous material, this was happily excused in the pleasure of receiving a new body of Marchbanksian reflections.

Unfortunately, the next joint venture between Davies and M & S, a brief book about Stephen Leacock for the NCL Canadian Writers series, chilled their new relationship considerably. When

Davies agreed to write it in 1967, he contemplated the task with little enthusiasm. "The fact of the matter," as he explained to Jack McClelland early in 1968, was that he wanted to be "a Canadian writer, rather than a writer about Canadian writers." Besides, he had said everything he was ready to say about Canada's most famous humourist in his Carleton University speech a decade earlier. Leacock had died too recently for him to write freely: "his fits of melancholy, his heavy drinking, his relations with women, and his brutality to some people who, God knows, invited brutality, are not subjects that can be explored while relatives and close descendants are living. He was a real bag of tricks and to my mind typically Canadian in his failure to understand himself."

But Davies interrupted the writing of *Fifth Business* between January and June of 1969 to produce the Leacock book. Notwithstanding the paucity of new material, it does display a broader understanding of his subject, and it also reveals something of Davies' own development since the Carleton lecture. Once again, he emphasized Leacock's upper-class background, his early poverty, his melancholy and the conflict in his views between Toryism and radicalism. One does sense the physical presence of the Carleton lecture on the desk beside Davies' typewriter, but he had evidently read Leacock's work anew, and this makes itself felt in a new chronological survey of the writer's works between 1906 and 1922 and in his selective commentary on the balance of Leacock's output.

Davies, who had by now been teaching at the University of Toronto for nine years, did have something new to say in discussing Leacock's classroom performances at McGill. "The good professor is himself an example of what learning makes of a man; if he is a dullard, learning must be dull; if he is half-literate, learning is diminished; if he is torpid with boredom and poisoned with scholarly scruple, learning appears as a disease. His job is not to utter ultimate and unchallengeable truth, but to make his students sufficiently interested to take on his subject themselves and confute him if he needs to be confuted. Without becoming a clown of the lecture-hall, a professor must make himself interesting."

In his Carleton lecture, Davies had argued that Leacock had not advanced to novels from his promising beginning with *Sunshine Sketches of a Little Town* simply because the funny short pieces brought in plenty of money, which propped up his self-esteem against the memory of the debilitating poverty of his youth. By 1969, midway through the writing of *Fifth Business*, Davies had come to a different judgment: Leacock had simply not matured as a writer. He had not made the transition from "The godlike view, the assumption by the writer of a power to judge his characters" which he had assumed in *Sunshine Sketches* to "another kind of novel—the kind in which characters are described from the inside, instead of being examined from the outside"—which was the transition Davies was making himself as he left Salterton behind to write the first of the Deptford novels.

When the book appeared in March 1970, Davies wrote M & S a letter which certainly must be one of the most devastating that publisher has received:

> I am sending you with this a marked copy of *Stephen Leacock*. As you will see, the proof-reading has been very much neglected and the general preparation of the book has been so careless that in two places substantial portions of the text have been dropped. Even the material on the back of the cover contains errors. It seems also that the proof-reading has been entrusted to somebody who does not recognize such words as 'acuity' and 'spoliation' and who, on page 43, does not distinguish between £ and $. When the proofs of the book were sent here they were very carefully proof-read and returned with a list of at least 33 typographical errors; my secretary was assured, over the telephone…that the errors we were returning had already been corrected, but clearly this was not so.
>
> I am sending you also some examples of alterations which have been made in the text and I judge that these have been the work of an editor who thinks I do not know how to write. I find this astonishing as I have been a writer for many years and this book is the twentieth that I have had published, and during that time I have had no com-

plaints about my style—on the contrary have sometimes been praised for it. If I were so incompetent a writer as to need the attention you have given me, it would surely have been better not to ask me to write the book in the first place. At present a novel of mine is in process of publication by Macmillans, and when they are doubtful about anything I have written they ask me about it and we clear it up between us; this is the procedure that has been adopted by all the publishers that I have worked with, including Knopf, Chatto and Windus, Scribner's, Secker and Warburg—the sole exception being McClelland and Stewart, who do not seem to value my opinion in these matters.

The Leacock book is such a mess that I am ashamed to speak of it to my friends and could not dream of recommending it to students. It is humiliating to be associated with it. I feel compelled, therefore, to say that I will not sign a contract for *Feast of Stephen* [a Leacock anthology to be edited by Davies], or do any further work on its preparation, until I have a letter from McClelland and Stewart guaranteeing that the whole of the material contained in *Stephen Leacock* will be printed as an introduction, that the text will be what I have written and not what your anonymous editor prefers (even to the matter of punctuation, in which I may be idiosyncratic but certainly not downright silly), and that corrections which I make in the proof will be heeded. I took a great deal of trouble in writing the small book, which you have treated so carelessly, and I should like it to appear in print in a form which does not humiliate me and confuse the reader. When I was approached about writing this book I was assured that the fee was to be small because it was, in a sense, a contribution on my part to Canadian literary studies. I receive the impression from what you have done, however, that you regard these simply as cheap books. I assure you that I am not a cheap author and deeply resent the way in which you have dealt with my work.

McClelland and Stewart immediately fired the careless proof-reader, changed its method of setting books in the series in question and published the corrected text later that year as an introduction to the anthology *Feast of Stephen*. It also republished *Stephen Leacock* (although the title page nowhere acknowledges that it differed in any way from the earlier printing). Davies replied to its letter of apology "...let all be peace between us henceforward." But their relationship did not recover, and his attitude towards the NCL, that had seemed so attractive to him all through the 1960s, changed. In 1971 he told his agent: "I am sorry that McClelland and Stewart are doing the book [*A Voice from the Attic*] in Canada because their New Canadian Library, though quite good, suffers from the disadvantage of always being stocked under Canadiana, a title which unfortunately many readers here pass by without a look." Although M & S continued from time to time to pursue him, he did not give the firm a novel until *Murther and Walking Spirits* in 1991.

In spite of his disappointments with "Bartholomew Fair," *General Confession* and *Love and Libel,* Davies continued to write for the theatre. But it no longer commanded his primary creative energy. He wrote plays only if asked to do so, never, like his novels, because he was driven to write them. And he wrote them in the holes and corners of the time available.

In 1957 Alan Stephen had asked him to write a new play for the UCC Prep, to be performed at Christmas 1958. By June 1958 Davies knew that he would not have time to deal with it that year, but he had given it some thought. Perhaps "it should be called something like *Mr Punch's Masque of Christmas* and be a lively piece about Christmas at schools." The new play refused to come to life in Davies' imagination until, on a visit to England in May 1961, he spied a Victorian, eighteen-inch Punch door-stopper. He had been looking out for one of these for a long time, so he snapped it up, and an expert stripped and repainted it for him that fall in the elaborate traditional costume. In December, he committed himself to completing the long-promised piece and sat down immediately to plan it. By April he was at the writing stage, and copies of *A Masque of Mr Punch* went forward to UCC at the end of May.

In the *Masque*, Mr Punch, who has come to tour Canada, presents a complete *Punch and Judy* show for the media people who have been sent to cover his arrival. But a governor of the Stratford Festival declares that *Punch and Judy* is really a lost Shakespearean tragedy which should be restored from the "dilapidation" it has suffered over the centuries. The "original" version (which wildly parodies relevant bits from *Hamlet*, *Two Gentlemen of Verona*, *Macbeth*, *Richard III* and *Lear*) is then performed. When Punch protests—his public would never stand for a tragic ending!—he is slightingly dismissed. He is told that he has no public, his showman days are over. Mephistopheles then arrives and assures him that he represents the Spirit of Unregenerate Man, an essential element of the human character; sooner or later he'll have to be asked back into the theatre. In the meantime, there'll always be plenty of jobs for him. So the play ends happily, with a song of celebration.

Once again Davies assigned the copyright to the UCC Prep. The first performances of the play (November 29-December 1, 1962) were warmly reviewed, so warmly in fact that Oxford University Press decided to publish it, and the printed version, which appeared in November 1963, brought another round of enthusiastic reviews. Like the earlier *A Masque of Aesop*, *A Masque of Mr Punch* has been widely performed in schools across Canada, including a revival by the UCC Prep itself in 1967.

Canada's centennial year, 1967, was the occasion for two dramatic pieces by Davies. In 1964, the impresario Nicholas Goldschmidt, then chief of the Performing Arts Division of the Centennial Commission, asked him to choose regional collaborators from the Maritimes, Quebec, the Prairie provinces and British Columbia to write a play that could be performed by amateurs across the country. Davies contributed a scene that evokes a 1912 Ontario schoolroom on inspection day. He also wrote a prologue, an epilogue and an introductory scene in which eight characters from the past speak of their experience of Canada, to draw his own and the other four ill-assorted regional scenes into a coherent whole. It didn't really succeed in this, but

Leon Major and Frank Canino, producing and directing, managed a reasonably effective trial production in Lindsay, Ontario, in October 1966. However, the first official performance of *The Centennial Play*, at the Ottawa Little Theatre on January 11, 1967, was a disaster. The director, Peter Boretski, made heavy, ineffective use of film clips and stills, cut the text considerably and, in the words of one critic, turned the play into "a two-hour pageant of scampering naiveté, banality and ineptitude." Davies, well aware of the piece's deficiencies, was frustrated and angry at the hacking the script had taken. He never heard whether any of the sixty groups who had ordered copies before the Ottawa fiasco ever performed the play.

His second contribution to the country's hundredth birthday was the scenario for "The Centennial Spectacle." In 1965, the city of Ottawa had ordered up a massive open-air pageant from Tyrone Guthrie, to be staged on Parliament Hill. Guthrie immediately called Davies to his aid, and during 1966 they worked on it together. They imagined an audience of 6,000-7,500 assembled in huge stands overlooking a playing area of 150 by 50 feet in front of the Peace Tower, to watch a bold depiction of Canada's past and future. As the scenario begins, a huge map of Canada is assembled by appropriate historical figures. Settlers arrive in ships and spread across the land. Britannia and La Belle France, rival matriarchs, establish themselves in Ontario and Quebec, and their followers engage in a spirited tug of war until both are hustled into the hold of a liner and deported. Confederation is achieved, at which the map's separate pieces are lashed into a single gigantic carpet. American investment draws money south over the border. As cities are built the natural beauty of the land is despoiled. Technology comes to the rescue, then ventures too far. But in the end Canadians learn to live in harmony with nature and themselves. "O Canada" is sung, the last of the many songs that accompany and amplify the action.

It was going to be a complex piece of staging, and the preparations were thorough. By the end of 1966, Robert Finch had prepared the French passages that were to alternate with the English, Louis Applebaum had written the music, Marie Day and Murray Laufer had designed the costumes and stage sets. Gratien Gélinas had been asked to do much of the bilingual narration. Nicholas Goldschmidt had been named choral director and a huge cast had been assembled, including the Centennial Choir of the National Capital Area, Les Troubadours de Hull, a seventy-five-member marching bugle band, a one-hundred-piece Concert Band, a choir of one hundred children, members of Ottawa's Little Theatre and of the Orpheus Operatic Society. High school students had been recruited all across Canada for the performances on August 2-12. Guthrie was bubbling with imaginative ideas, and it looked as if he might pull off another of his famous theatrical coups.

Abruptly, and incredibly, the spectacle was cancelled. According to Davies, "Some idiot of an official in the public Works Department—*the Public Works Department*—cancelled it because the construction of the special stage and bleachers was going to interfere with its plans for the Queen's arrival on Parliament Hill." He recalled his helpless anger for John Fraser in the *Globe and Mail* a decade later: "They pay you nothing and then demand impossible things and at the end a minion of the Public Works Department says it's not to be done." Davies resolved never to write for patriotic reasons again.

In the 1970s, the success of the Deptford trilogy produced a brief resurgence of interest in Davies' plays. In 1972, New Press published *Hunting Stuart, King Phoenix* and *General Confession* in *Hunting Stuart and Other Plays.* In July and August 1973 Festival Lennoxville mounted a successful revival of *A Jig for the Gypsy* under Donald Davis' direction and with Barbara Chilcott again playing Benoni. And that fall, the Drama Centre gave *Love and Libel,* newly revised and now titled *Leaven of Malice,* a production at Hart House. For this Davies had done a little fresh writing, adding the character Tessie Forgie, two encounters between Gloster Ridley and his housekeeper Edith Little and a bedroom scene for Dutchy and Norm Yarrow. But for the most part, he constructed the new version from his favourite parts of the five earlier ones: the opening from the script he took to Ireland, the chorus from the initial plan of the play, the dreams from the version worked out in Ireland and later modified and augmented, the telephone scene from the script rehearsed in Toronto and so on. The resulting play (published in *Canadian Drama* in 1981) restored Gloster Ridley to his original importance and brought back the fantasy that Guthrie had banished. Martin Hunter's production of October 11-20, 1973, although slow-paced, did justice to the imaginative moments and drew Urjo Kareda in the *Globe and Mail* to declare that the play "argues persuasively for Davies' astute dramatic discernment. He is our finest conjuror."

On February 14, 1974, the CBC screened a new, one-hour television play called *Brothers in the Black Art* in its series "The Play's the Thing." Written in the early months of 1973, this is very much a memory piece, drawing on facts and incidents that Davies' father had related to him about his early years in the printing trade. It presents three young friends, apprentice and journeyman printers in the early years of the century. They inhabit a rough, drunken world, but these "Brothers in the Black Art" are abstainers who dress fastidiously and pride themselves on their craft. They are romantics, too, who memorize high-flown prose and verse from the books they read and woo their women with song. Jesse chooses to marry a girl who is a real companion to him, while the ambitious Griff marries a woman who helps him on his way and rises to become a newspaper owner, a cabinet minister and senator, leaving his old friends behind. Phil, young and artistic, puts his girl on a pedestal, and when after their marriage he discovers her in bed with another man, he commits suicide horribly by swallowing lye from the print shop. Years later, when Jesse talks with Phil's wife, he realizes that Phil had given his wife only his reverence, reserving his comradeship for his "brothers," Jesse and Griff. Her emotional isolation had led to her promiscuity. The whole story is told by Jesse, now nearing ninety, to a young reporter after Griff's death. The play was published by The Alcuin Society in Vancouver in 1981.

Also in 1974 Davies supplied the off-stage voice of the Great Boyg in the Drama Centre's production of Ibsen's *Peer Gynt,* and Brenda directed *Noye's Fludde,* the fourteenth-century Chester miracle play set to music by Benjamin Britten, for Grace Church on-the-Hill. The three performances on November 27-29 drew capacity audiences and a reviewer was moved to observe: "By concentrating on simplicity, Grace Church has captured a measure of spiritual grandeur."

Commissioned by Leon Major for the St. Lawrence Centre, *Question Time* is Davies' last major play. He wrote the first draft between July 1 and August 27, 1974, and had his revisions completed by the end of January 1975. The play's central figure is Peter Macadam, the prime minister of Canada, a party man, a public man, little more than a mask. As the play opens, the plane in which he is travelling crashes in Canada's far north. Unconscious and in shock, he is brought to an encampment where a shaman and an Eskimo woman care for him, and it becomes clear that his survival will depend on whether he can draw on the resources of his neglected inner man. As the act proceeds, we see him from various perspectives: physically, at the arctic bivouac; inwardly, as he begins to penetrate the arctic wasteland of his unconscious; as a subject of discussion on television news and in the House of Commons; and in the musings and reactions of key people in his life and work.

In the second act, the inward journey continues. Macadam imagines that it is Question Time in the House of Commons, and there he confronts the neglected aspects of himself, personified in the Leader of the Opposition, his wife, a herald and several others. The Leader of the Opposition (played by the same actor) raises key questions that he has been avoiding: Who *is* he? What sort of country is Canada? Why would anyone want to be prime minister? Twice his anima appears to him in the form of an arctic sibyl, La Sorcière des Montagnes de Glace, and their dialogue reveals much about Macadam's state of mind. In the first act he is not ready to listen to her, so she must make her points by selectively echoing his words. By the time the second act is drawing to its close, he has come to know himself sufficiently that he does listen to her; now her words are echoed by him. He has begun to marshal his inner resources, and it becomes evident that he will survive. He returns to consciousness, and a plane arrives to take him to the south.

Macadam's crisis is, of course, an allegory of Canada's own crisis of identity. Here Davies suggests that the country, too, must acknowledge long-ignored aspects of itself, draw them to the surface and explore them, if it is to come to terms with itself.

When the play opened on February 25, 1975, the *Toronto Star*'s Urjo Kareda judged it "a very grand, ambitious, and idiosyncratic disaster," "cool and bossily assertive, instead of sensual and exploratory." This called forth a number of letters and columns in its defence from individual play-goers, and it ran until March 22, pulling 80 percent houses. In fact it was as well attended as the Centre's most popular play of the season. Macmillan of Canada published the play that fall, and it makes compelling reading, but it has never been given another production.

In the summer of 1975, *Leaven of Malice* was revived at the Shaw Festival in Niagara-on-the-Lake, Ontario, and *Hunting Stuart* got a new production at Festival Lennoxville. The first, miscast, under-rehearsed and slow-moving, drew a searing blast from Clive Barnes in the *New York Times*. The second was well cast and directed, moving Davies to observe in his "Theatre Notes" that he had not seen a better production of one of his plays.

In 1976 Brenda played the Countess of Roussillon in Martin Hunter's production of *All's Well that Ends Well*, which played January 22-31 at Hart House. Once she got the role under her belt, Hunter felt she was "quite marvellous...because she has wonderful warmth and wonderful majestic qualities." Writing in his theatre diary, Davies himself thought "Brenda v. good as the Countess—voice, presence & warmth of feeling. Cost her much to act again after a long silence: she worked v. hard, & rehearsed at home every day during the run, & built & built, & was splendid & growing right till the final curtain. I shd. like it enormously if she were asked to act again, for it is really the breath of life to her."

He himself created an opportunity for her to do so in *Pontiac and the Green Man*, which the Drama Centre commissioned for the university's sesquicentennial in 1977. The Centre had earlier considered presenting *Ponteach: Or the Savages of America, A Tragedy* (1766), which is thought to be the earliest play about Canada in the English language. This verse tragedy is exceedingly long and clumsy, however, and Ronald Bryden, then a visiting professor at the Centre, proposed that Davies should write a new play incorporating scenes from *Ponteach* but focusing on its author, Major Robert Rogers of Rogers' Rangers. So that was what Ann Saddlemyer, the Centre's director, asked Davies to do.

Davies set the play in a military barracks in Montreal in 1768, at the close of Rogers' court martial for treason. Davies' Rogers is a free-thinker who despises the bigotry of the English. An admirer of the great chief Ponteach and a sympathizer with the Indians, he is called to account for his presumption. As the court martial proceeds, scenes from *Ponteach* are performed to illustrate Rogers' views on the English and the Indians. (They also permitted Davies to have his say on eighteenth-century acting and playwriting, and to bring Brenda in as Mrs. Belimperia Egerton, manager of the shabby English travelling players who perform them.) At the play's end, Rogers is found Not Guilty. He yearns to join Ponteach in the wilderness, but he is to be confined to barracks until official permission to free him arrives.

Davies wrote his first draft in the summer and fall of 1976, and when Martin Hunter, the director, asked for changes and more changes, he revised and revised again. During this process, unfortunately, the script disintegrated into little more than a succession of scenes, with no clear overall shape. The production itself was seriously weakened by conflicts and differences among the participants—Davies, composer Derek Holman, director Martin Hunter, the student and professional actors, the musicians—so that it is hardly surprising that the critics delivered a gleeful verdict of Guilty on the production, which ran from October 26 to November 5, 1977, in the MacMillan Theatre. When it was all over, Davies observed to Horace Davenport that "The newspapers fell upon it with whips and scorpions.... these public lambastings are hard to bear because, as one grows older, they tend to be from critics whom one regards as Young Squirts, while they regard one as an Old Fogy." No subsequent production has been attempted, nor has the play been published.

The following month Davies made his last gesture of the 1970s toward the theatre. He wrote a prologue for Herbert Whittaker's production of Sheridan's *The Critic*. A graceful tribute to his old friend (and critic), it was warmly received during the play's run from January 9 to 15, 1978, at the Drama Centre's Studio Theatre.

The Later Years

The late 1960s and early 1970s were the years of student counter-culture. Opposition to the Vietnam War was the catalyst for a rupture between the generations that revolutionized student attitudes and for a time put faculties and university administrators severely on the defensive. It was a time when hierarchy was bad; egalitarianism was good. Formality was suspect; spontaneity was natural. Drugs could liberate; privilege was offensive. The students wanted representation on the university's governing council in order to open up the system, and many were prepared to use violence to do it. Even Massey College, despite its founders' vision of community and shared ideals, was not immune.

At Massey College the struggle between students and administration took some time to come to a head. For the first few years the students had seen themselves as part of a working community. They had no interest in forming committees through which to channel their desires to those who ran the college, being content to speak informally to Davies or the bursar as difficulties arose. But by 1966 the students had begun to be curious about the college's statutes. They wanted to see the full list of senior Fellows, read the minutes of meetings of the college corporation and the Quadrangle Fund, inspect the budget and the like. When a junior Fellow was summarily expelled, the students felt that there ought to be some formal means of appeal, and they no longer felt it effective to simply take complaints individually to the Master or the bursar. Davies' formality proved a drawback in this period, because it made him appear cold and uncommunicative. For his part, Davies considered that the governance of the college had been entrusted to him and the senior Fellows by the Masseys, and it was not the business of junior Fellows to question it.

Over the next four years the two sides fenced with each other in an atmosphere of increasing distrust, although some of their confrontations were just good pranks. In the "Great Goldfish Caper" of 1968-69, when the students took the fish from the pools in the quad out past the porter in garbage bags (and wired the bursar to inform him that the fish were on vacation), the administration was not amused and had the drains searched. The fish materialized in Friesen's bathroom a couple of days later. On another occasion, midway through dinner at the last High Table of 1970-71—still, of course, a masculine affair—a junior Fellow rose to announce the entrance of one of Davies' own characters, Miss Gates Ajar Honeypot (she figures in "Dickens Digested," the 1970 Gaudy Night ghost story). A stripper from a local burlesque house, whose degree of nudity depends on the teller of the tale, then entered with a bottle of champagne and a glass, approached the High Table, filled the glass and presented it to Davies. The senior Fellows were embarrassed and uneasy, as the students had hoped. But Davies graciously accepted the glass, toasted the college, bussed her on both cheeks and gave her a little push to send her on her way. Everyone cheered. Despite the levity, the members of the corporation felt increasingly embattled as time went on, and the students continued to feel they were getting nowhere. The administration's modest concessions—dropping the rule that women had to be out of college by 11:30 p.m., for example—did little to appease the junior Fellows, who wanted meaningful democratization of the college's ruling structures and a voice in the use of college funds.

During this period Davies' life was complicated and troubled by Professor W. A. C. H. Dobson. Dobson had been made a senior Fellow at Lionel Massey's suggestion in May 1962, and had initially struck Davies as precisely the sort of person the college needed. He had taken his degrees at Oxford and had lectured there for four years. Head of the Department of East Asian Studies, he was respected for his grammatical study *Late Archaic Chinese* and continued to be a highly productive scholar. His rooms, furnished with tall, chunky Chinese books and *objets d'art*, struck an exotic note. He enjoyed the students and laid himself out to be hospitable to them in regular bi-weekly Friday sherry parties and at his cottage in the summer. And from the fall of 1964 he relieved Davies of the burden of selecting and inviting guests to High Table dinners. All this was to the good. But his self-important airs, his contemptuous behaviour toward Lochhead, Friesen, some junior Fellows and the college staff, and his arrogation of the Master's role at the dessert phase of High Table were less attractive.

Once Dobson separated from his wife in 1967 and began to live in college, he became a mischief-maker whom Davies found it hard, and then impossible, to tolerate. Lending a sympathetic ear to the students' discontents, Dobson would slip them bits of information about the corporation's deliberations. He fuelled their disgruntlement with Friesen, the focus for their complaints about food service and rules, by suggesting that the bursar ought to have a university degree, as was customary at Oxford. To Friesen's embarrassment and relief, Davies faced Dobson down on this one by asking for a vote of confidence in him from the college corporation. It passed on a unanimous show of hands, Dobson's reluctantly included.

Dobson continued to pick away at Davies' authority in a campaign that united lies with innuendo and spiteful gossip. He gave out that he had himself been Vincent Massey's first choice for Master and Davies a poor second. That Davies, who was supposed to have given the place a Canadian stamp, had instead made it a poor imitation of Oxford. That he was guilty of financial mismanagement. That as Master he ought to be a scholar, yet his scholarship rested on a suspect thesis published a quarter of a century before.

Matters came to a head in the "Night of the Green Ghost" (as the students dubbed it) in 1968-69. Davies, wakened by a ruckus in the dining hall (separated only by a wall from his bedroom), threw a green dressing gown over his pyjamas and materialized before an astonished party of High Table revellers—Dobson, a political guest, several Southam Fellows and a number of juniors. Ordering them to cease and desist, he requested the junior Fellows to present themselves in his office in the morning. After dealing with them, he confronted Dobson, and in the ensuing shouting row demanded to know why he was undercutting him with the students. Did he want to be Master? If so, Davies would resign in his favour. Dobson replied: "Oh, no no no no. I'm almost weekly expecting a call from Harvard. I wouldn't want to be bothered with a little tinpot thing like this."

It was clear to Davies that Dobson must go if he was to be secure in his leadership. But the immediate options were limited, because Dobson was popular with the students, and President

Bissell, himself embattled with sit-ins, made it clear to Davies that he did not want an outbreak at Massey College if it could be avoided. Davies therefore decided to bide his time. The opportunity he needed came when Dobson's fellowship came up for renewal in May 1972, and Davies mounted a quiet campaign among the senior Fellows to oust him. As always, their votes were submitted in advance of the corporation meeting, and so, when the renewal was roundly defeated, Davies was able to inform Dobson of the result in a note to save him the humiliation of hearing the result in front of his peers. Fifty junior Fellows (almost all of those still in residence at the time) immediately signed a petition supporting his re-election and presented it to the meeting, but the decision stood.

Davies later took more thorough revenge for the unpleasantness to which he had been subjected: having privately noted a number of curious and discrediting aspects of the man, he incorporated them into the character Urquhart McVarish in *The Rebel Angels* (1981), a portrait recognized by many of Dobson's colleagues. Dobson died in 1982.

The academic year 1972-73 was the most rancorous in the history of the college, but it also laid the basis for future amity. The junior Fellows had persistently asked to see the accounts and the governing statutes of the college, and in November, having finally come into possession of an outdated copy of the latter, they requested the immediate appointment of a visitor, hoping that he might act as an effective conduit for appeals. (The position had in fact been instituted solely to give Vincent Massey a ceremonial role in the college, and it had been quietly dropped when the statutes were amended in 1970.) However, the corporation was happy to comply and named the Honourable Dalton Wells, chief justice of Ontario, to the post. In November and December matters became more acrimonious, and meetings were held that resulted in the students getting representation on the board of directors of the Common Room Club. The tone can be imagined from the final paragraph of the students' report of the December meeting: "Finally, Dr. Davies requested Mr. Vaughan to apologize for having called Miss Whalon [the college secretary] 'a crook.' Mr. Vaughan answered that *he* was deserving of an apology. The Chairman [Davies] observed that it would be a frosty Friday before this happened, and the meeting then adjourned."

After Christmas the students asked for the establishment of an Alumni Association, for representation on college committees and (as they had in 1971) for representation on the corporation. They felt they had reason to do so. Where originally the college had housed seventy junior Fellows, by 1969-70 it had only sixty in residence. The rooms had been used for offices for the Drama Centre and Comparative Literature, quarters for visiting scholars, the writer-in-residence, the occasional Southam Fellow. In Davies' view, it was the senior Fellows who gave the college prestige within the university. Ultimately, he hoped, a way would be found to shift Massey College in the direction of a research college for senior men, while not eliminating the junior Fellows. (In furthering this he made an effort in 1973 to raise money to endow research fellowships for senior scholars; in 1976 he considered housing senior business executives for six-month sabbaticals; and in 1980 he supported giving the Canadian Institute for Advanced Research a base in the college.) The shift did not come to pass (the number of resident junior Fellows remained steady at sixty through the 1970s), but his views were known and naturally made the juniors uneasy.

The 1972-73 year ended with a vote by the corporation to admit women in 1974-75. The junior Fellows had raised the issue informally with Davies at least as early as 1967 and had begun to discuss it in earnest in 1970-71. At a meeting in the fall of 1971, according to the students, Davies produced the following reasons for the exclusion of women: "the Act and the Statutes, the Founder's wishes, the parable of the camel gradually taking over the camel-driver's tent, the ability of eighteen Canadian women wealthier than the Masseys to endow an all-female version of the College, and the fact that the College plumbing system would have to be renovated." Legend claims, probably apocryphally, that he also declared: "Over my dead body will women be admitted into this college." That fall he wrote to the master of Balliol College, who had asked his advice on a similar concern, to say that "If Balliol is prepared to take a lead in educating women as women, I whole-heartedly support the move. If it proposes simply to educate women exactly as it has educated their brothers, I fear that the result will be to spoil a good college for men, without doing anything for women beyond a fashionable gesture toward a mistaken notion of equality."

The following April, the juniors formally petitioned the college corporation to consider women for fellowship on an equal basis with men. In May, the corporation, led by Davies, voted unanimously against it, on the grounds that such a move would violate the trust vested in them under the incorporating act. But when the Masseys received the minutes of the meeting and the letters Davies wrote to each of them soon after, explaining the position the corporation had taken, the three living founders, Raymond, Geoffrey and Hart, wrote back to say that they strongly favoured the admission of women and wished this to be made known. At least in part, their reaction resulted from their experience of an earlier set-to over Hart House. From 1964 onward women had forced their way into Hart House debates, invaded the cafeteria and appealed to the president and the governing council of the university, until finally the president had appointed a committee. This had recommended that women be given the same rights as men at Hart House. Late in 1971 the trustees of the Massey Foundation agreed to change the wording of the deed of gift, and women were given full access to Hart House in January 1972. In view of the Masseys' position, Davies changed course. He began to lobby the other recalcitrants, and in May 1973 he led the corporation in voting to admit women in the fall of 1974. "The Master and Fellows of Massey College Act" was amended the following April, and the first women junior Fellows were admitted on schedule. Davies then championed the election of Ann Saddlemyer, who as director of the Drama Centre was already well known in the college, as the first woman senior Fellow. She was elected in 1975 and in the fullness of time became the college's third Master.

Almost immediately the atmosphere warmed. The student paper, the *Massey College Bull,* had been wont to portray the Master as "the Merlin of Massey" or as "the Manticore" in his

"Manticorium," but in November 1973 it published an interview with him in which he was once again Professor Davies, with valuable and interesting views. Now the junior Fellows began to worry about the awkward realities of sharing their quarters with women. Would it not be best to put them all in one house? The administration, now on the high ground, held firm: no distinctions were to be made; women were to be placed randomly through all five houses.

The arrival of women brought many advantages. There was no longer a need to invite women from outside to bring balance to the Tuesday dinner parties. Manners improved, and bun-throwing at dinner came to an end. Male chauvinism did not disappear entirely, however: even three years later, in the fall of 1977, when the first female junior Fellow to receive her doctorate was congratulated at High Table, one of the senior Fellows quoted Samuel Johnson: "Sir, a woman's preaching is like a dog's walking on his hinder legs. It is not done well; but you are surprised to find it done at all." But the women themselves fitted in as if they had always been there. The tide of student rebellion had made its mark and receded. By 1975-76, the college newsletter noted that "Matters of concern to the Junior Fellows are apt to be scholarly and professional, rather than political. This has brought about a drawing together of the Junior Fellows and the Seniors, and the sense of community has been more marked and more genial than at any time since the first year of our history." Through Davies' final years as Master, the new atmosphere prevailed.

Chapter 13

The Deptford Trilogy: 1958-75

———————•———————

P.m. walk wth. B. & visit the shop of Konrad Welwert at 4
Joseph-Pirchl-strasse; to our surprise he has some polychrome
wood figures & we talk for nearly an hour. He has a gd. St.
Sebastian at $2800 & a charming baroque Madonna, standing
on the globe (encircled by the Serpent) & a crescent moon, at
$3500. We are much taken wth. this latter piece, but we know
nothing of such work, & do not want to pay a foolish price
for it.

     —"A Journey to Austria and the United Kingdom," 1965

MARTIN-HARVEY, SIR JOHN (1863-1944) Actor-Manager.
A very fine collection of about 370 letters, some typed, some
autograph, signed "Jack", to his life-long friend R. N. Green-
Armytage and including about 40 letters from Lady Martin-
Harvey. And other material, typescript, autograph & printed
relating to his career.

     —Offer for sale by Ifan Kyrle Fletcher, Rare Books,
     Prints and Autograph Letters, London, in 1967

WHEN DAVIES, IN 1968, finally got down to his next novel, he
had reached the age of fifty-five. Since the writing of *A Mixture*

of Frailties, his outlook had changed a good deal, and by 1968 he had come to terms with the challenges of his new career as professor and Master of Massey College.

He had sought out new travel experiences as well. From 1961 on he and Brenda began to extend most of their trips beyond Britain to the Continent, although they continued to start or end with London, which had become by now a home away from home. Their London routine had become almost a ritual. They would stay in a hotel (a different one each time until they discovered the Goring in Grosvenor Gardens in 1964) and spend many evenings at the theatre, almost always buying their tickets from the same man at the Army and Navy Stores. They would spend the day browsing, and Davies might buy things like socks, madder handkerchiefs or a silk dressing gown at Liberty's, a light overcoat at Burberrys', a raincoat at Aquascutum, shoes at Poulsen & Skone, a stick of gorse (for lumbago) at Swaine, Adeney's, an umbrella at James Smith and Sons in New Oxford Street (while eyeing the swords concealed in blackthorn sticks and the like) or bound notebooks at Smythson's and Ryman's. From time to time he would find something special: at Ekstein's, for instance, a nineteenth-century ring which, with a new stone, could be engraved with his coat of arms; or at Harvey and Gore a fine fob-seal (circa 1800) of a running fox. His book and theatre collections expanded when there was something appealing at Alec Clunes', Bertram Rota's, Quaritch's, Barry Duncan's, Ifan Kyrle Fletcher's, Travis & Emery's or Bayly's (the last a print shop that he had patronized since 1936). He might see Diana Leavey, who kept tabs on book sales and auctions for him. On every trip they visited the Royal School of Needlework, where Brenda bought wool and had special designs made for her needlepoint. They visited the museums and art galleries regularly, the Victoria and Albert their favourite by a large margin, followed by the National Gallery, the National Portrait Gallery and the Queen's Gallery. On many Sundays they would attend Anglican service, often at the Temple Church. For meals it was frequently the Café Royal, occasionally Martinez, Bentleys, the Savoy Grill, Scott's, Petit Savoyard, Rules or Maxim's. After Davies became a member of the Athenaeum Club in 1964, they ate there, too. He always had his hair cut and washed at Austin Reed.

It was a rare day on which Davies and Brenda did not see a friend or acquaintance in London. At the theatre there might be an actor on the stage whom they knew from the OUDS or the Old Vic. They always looked up opera director Basil Coleman, originally a friend of Brenda's from the Old Vic, now a treasured friend of both. Family might be in town—Brenda's mother, or her sister Maisie and her second husband, the well-known artist (later Sir) Russell Drysdale, visiting from Australia. In the late 1950s and early 1960s, when *A Mixture of Frailties* and *A Voice from the Attic* were being published in England, Davies would also touch base with his London agent (then Michael Horniman at Watt's) and with his publishers, George Weidenfeld and Frederick Warburg.

Expeditions outside London brought more friends to see— Burgon Bickersteth, the retired Warden of Hart House (and J.B. in *What's Bred in the Bone*) in Canterbury, Brenda's father in Manchester, Brenda's aunt Elsa Larking in St. Ives and, almost always, Rupert and his wife Margaret in Wales. Davies and Brenda would drive to Leighton Hall by way of Oxford, where Davies would visit the antiquarian department of Blackwell's, perhaps spend a little time at Balliol, buy an italic pen or get one adjusted at Phillips' in Oriel Street, acquire velvet ties at Hall's or purchase a Balliol tie at Castell's. They might have lunch or sherry at the Mitre. In Wales, Davies and Brenda regularly bought antiques from Andersons' in Welshpool—a set of Regency chairs, Chippendale stools, a pair of early-nineteenth-century card tables. If they didn't go to Tregynon to see Dora Herbert-Jones, Rupert and Margaret would invite her to Leighton Hall for lunch or tea. On Sundays they would attend the service at St. Mary's Church in Welshpool.

By now the ageing Rupert had become difficult to live with. Davies commented in his travel diary: "WRD grows v. old, deaf & tyrannous; civility, never his strong point, is now utterly unknown to him. Shouts down all conversation, puffs & whistles (whistled *tunes* all through the sermon) & is like a large, wilful child: what an egotist!" But Davies, deeply fond of him, was saddened at the end of one of these visits, "for these partings in

Wales cannot be many more, & I have come to associate him with that country more than with my childhood."

Such jaunts as these were as easy and familiar as slipping on an old shoe. But Davies' new travel agenda in the 1960s required more energy. The titles of his travel diaries suggest the new ambitions: in 1961, "Diary of a Journey into Portugal [and England]"; in 1963, "A Diary of a Journey into the Netherlands, Denmark, the Shetland Islands, the Highlands of Scotland, North Wales & England"; in 1964, "A Journey to Spain, Italy, Germany, Belgium and the United Kingdom"; in 1965, "A Journey to Austria and the United Kingdom"; in 1966, "A Journey to the United Kingdom and Austria"; in 1967, "Diary of a Journey to England & Wales & briefly to Paris"; and in 1968, "Diary of a Journey to Australia & Mexico." They usually rented a car for these explorations and Brenda drove. Except for the Shetland Islands and Australia, where it was Brenda's background they wanted to explore, they undertook these new ventures in order to experience at first hand the European origins of their heritage—the convents, palaces, museums, theatres, universities and the rest.

Often it seemed to them that they were travelling in a time machine. In Lisbon, for example, life appeared to move in eighteenth-century rhythms. In the Spanish countryside, they watched threshing floors in use. Time and again Davies was reminded of Act I of Gilbert and Sullivan's *The Gondoliers*, or something like it, and would catch himself, as "one who discerns the truth behind a fiction; for this land of olive groves, cork trees, geranium hedges & charmingly shaped villages, has been known to me only through the *chichi* imagination of stage designers, who make it intolerably weak, smart & cheap." Wherever they went, they sought out theatre. In Copenhagen's Tivoli Gardens, they saw a performance of *Harlequin Kok* at the famous Pantomime Theater, and Davies reflected that he "had never expected to see anything like it...costumes untouched since 1800 at the latest. Delightfully simple-minded. Not really well acted, but the tradition was there, & one could imagine what a Grimaldi might do as Clown. A splendid sorcerer, who came & went by a trap, & suggested what Mozart may have had in mind in *The Magic Flute*. And always the charm of painted sets—so satisfactory. A real time-journey into the past."

During the 1960s and early 1970s Davies continued to work at assimilating the ideas of Carl Gustav Jung. Generally he found that Jung's perceptions extended and tallied with his own, but sometimes they presented quite different ways of looking at things and compelled him to reconsideration. Finding confirmation of his views in an authority of this stature was highly encouraging, and from 1968 on, in speeches and interviews, Davies felt able to speak with new frankness about his deepest convictions instead of masking them with humour or concealing them.

Jung's insights provided him with an overview of the crisis that he and so many other middle-aged men had had to face. In 1968 he spoke of this:

As Jung explains it, in the early part of life—roughly for the first half of it—man's chief aims are personal and social. He must grow up, he must find his work, he must find out what kind of sex life he is going to lead, he must achieve some place in the world and attempt to get security within it, or else decide that security is not important to him. But when he has achieved these ends, or come to some sort of understanding with this part of existence, his attention is turned to matters that are broader in scope, and sometimes disturbing to contemplate. His physical strength is waning rather than growing; he has found out what sex is, and though it may be very important to him it can do little to surprise him; he realizes that some day he is really going to die and that the way he approaches death is of importance to him; he finds that without God (using that name to comprehend all the great and inexplicable things and the redemptive or destructive powers that lie outside human command and understanding) his life lacks a factor that it greatly needs; he finds that, in Jung's phrase, he is not the master of his fate except in a very modest degree and that he is in fact the object of a supraordinate subject. And he seeks wisdom rather than power—though the circumstances of his early life may continue to thrust power into his hands.

Now, the paradox of this change is that it does not make him an old man. What will make him an old man is a frightened clinging to the values of the first half of life. We have all seen these juvenile dotards whose boast is that they are just as young as their sons or their grandsons; they do not realize what a pitiful boast that is…. The values that are proper and all-absorbing during the first half of life will not sustain a man during the second half. If he has the courage and wisdom to advance courageously into the new realm of values and emotions he will age physically, of course, but his intellectual and spiritual growth will continue, and will give satisfaction to himself and to all those associated with him.

Davies had been aware at least since 1956, when he planned the Casanova play, *General Confession,* that the mid-life reorientation required coming to terms with the personal unconscious, particularly with what Jung called the "shadow" and the "anima." The goal was not the Christian ideal of perfection, but rather the integration of the conflicting forces within, the achievement of wholeness, centring one's person not simply in the ego but in the broader "self," which can respond to directives from both the conscious and unconscious levels of the mind. What had been repressed as evil or imperfection must be retrieved, examined, acknowledged and finally developed or brought under conscious control. Likewise the anima (in the case of a woman, the "animus") must be drawn to the surface, examined and integrated into the self. Jung argued that in rare cases this process of integration, extending even deeper into the psyche, could go beyond one's personal unconscious to embrace some of the archetypal contents belonging to the collective unconscious of the race.

From his Oxford days, Davies had known that his serious writing was thoroughly bound up with his pursuit of self-knowledge. He had known that he must pay heed as a writer to what rose spontaneously into his mind from the unconscious, and he had realized that with each new play or novel he achieved greater understanding of himself. Jung helped him to see that in this he was typical of artists, and that an artist is a sort of conduit through which the personal, and more important, the collective unconscious speaks. In a passage from the same 1968 speech, Davies presents self-exploration and writing in an unaccustomedly active manner and reveals that, with Jung, he conceives of the unconscious as having two levels:

> The degree of self-examination that is involved in being a writer, and the stringency of the writer's conscience, which holds you to a path that is often distasteful, necessarily takes you on some strange journeys, not only into the realm of the personal Unconscious, but into the level below that. It is assumed, by many people who have read Freud and Jung, that these descents must always be alarming experiences, because Freud and Jung were so much occupied with people who were very seriously disordered. But the writer is not necessarily disordered, and great rewards await him in this realm, if he approaches it with decent reverence.... That realm of the Unconscious, which is the dwelling-place of so many demons and monsters, is also the home of the Muses, the abode of the angels. The writer, in his traffic with that realm in which dream, and myth, and fairy-tale become mingled with the most ordinary circumstances of life, does not lack for rewards and very great rewards.

It was Jung's view that these "descents" might take the form of dreams, visions or fantasies. That being so, in the late 1950s and through the 1960s, Davies began to pay close attention again to his dreams and his much rarer visions, as he had done after first reading Freud's *The Interpretation of Dreams* at Oxford a quarter-century earlier. He often recorded their contents in his diaries. Many of the dreams seemed impenetrable, but a number, including a waking dream that presented itself in his bedroom at Massey College in the mid-1960s, spoke powerfully to him. In this dream R. W. W. Robertson, his editor at Clarke, Irwin, urged him to write another novel like the Salterton books or, alternatively, a book rooted in their shared Robertson background in Dumfries. The dream also contained a beautifully illuminated vellum manuscript, laid open upon a lectern in the window. A gilded serpent crawled up the lectern and followed the text, its tongue flickering. It said to him, "No, you must write the book you haven't written yet." Davies took this as a warning from his unconscious not to repeat himself, not to attempt pure family history, not to pursue others' ideas in preference to his own.

The novelist, the playwright and the painter weave powerful spells as they give shape to the archetypal stuff rising from the unconscious. And when the reader, the play-goer and the art-lover open themselves to this, the enchantment they experience enriches the spirit. For Davies it is in the playhouse that the conspiracy between artist and audience produces the most powerful magic. As he observed in "Jung and the Theatre," a speech written in 1973: "A fine performance of a great play is one of the most compelling and rewarding experiences our culture provides, and it is also a highly sophisticated version of that experience of which anthropologists have written, where members of the tribe gather together to be told a great dream which is of importance to the tribe." The sharing of the experience is what gives special power to the dream.

By now Davies had come to view certain operas, ballets and classics of the theatre as such great dreams. He had also come to believe that the appeal of much popular entertainment—nineteenth-century melodrama, for example—lay in its ability to evoke the archetypes. Many performers were successful because they communicated with the deepest level of the human psyche—magicians figured as the "Wise Old Man," fortune-tellers as the "Wise Old Woman." Even the side-show hermaphrodite and bearded lady embodied the archetype of wholeness. In a 1968 speech about "Ben Jonson and Alchemy," Davies observed: "Alchemic symbolism...is associated with concepts—perhaps we may call them archetypes—that are common to mankind. Very rarely do we visit a midway or a fair at which a half-man half-woman is not to be seen; that it is a fake is unimportant compared to the fact that people want to see it. I do not think their curiosity is merely prurient; I think they respond to an appeal to the ideal of spiritual unity...."

Davies had always felt that life was more marvellous than it appeared on the surface. He had always suspected that "myth and fairy-tales are nothing less than the distilled truth about what we call 'real life.'" Jung had now supplied him with a theory that substantiated this suspicion and freed him to see life in heightened terms. He could now declare that "we move through a throng of Sleeping Princesses, Belles Dames sans merci, Cinderellas, Wicked Witches, Powerful Wizards, Frog Princes, Lucky Third Sons, Ogres, Dwarves, Sagacious Animal Helpers and Servers, yes and Heroes and Heroines, in a world that is nothing less than an enchanted landscape...."

Davies' reading of Jung also had an impact on his religious beliefs. He had never been conventionally Christian, despite his Presbyterian upbringing and his confirmation in the Anglican Church. From boyhood he had rejected the Christ who loves all and forgives all, whose death atones for the sins of mankind. He felt certain, on the contrary, that a man does, and should, reap what he sows. Early in 1959, in the course of an interview with George Grant, the influential Canadian social philosopher (and the son of W. L. Grant of UCC), he described some of his views, still at that time largely uninfluenced by Jung. He believed in a masculine Creator, indifferent to human life. Shakespeare struck him as being on the right track in *King Lear* with Gloucester's observation: "As flies to wanton boys are we to the gods; They kill us for their sport." He believed in prayer—not as petition for himself or as intercession for others (for he believed that people would and should get what they deserve, and that it was unworthy to protest, whine or beg)—but rather as contemplation. As he saw it, evil and human suffering are the work of the Devil (that is, Original Sin) at work in mortal man. He would not presume to be the judge of others' actions; it was enough for him to decide his own. *The Shorter Catechism*'s "Man's chief end is to glorify God, and to enjoy him forever" was generally a satisfactory statement of the meaning of life. How does one glorify God? By doing one's best work, offering it to Him "as everything must be offered to him whether you think that that is what you are doing or not." He saw life as "a sort of lonely pilgrimage…in search of God," believing characteristically that "the way the pilgrimage is made is by attempting to acquire self knowledge …and that by gaining knowledge of oneself and indirectly of other people, you gain some apprehension of some aspects of God. It must be done alone…in the end, the approach will always be made alone."

He arrived at such conclusions through periodic periods of contemplation. Prodded by anti-religious talk at a dinner party in Paris in 1967, for example, he spent a meditative hour the next day in Notre Dame, recording the outcome in his travel diary:

(a) This world *may* be the result of chance, but does not seem so. For me the strong argument against chance is Art, evinced in such great works of man as Notre Dame.

(b) Man's destiny seems in part determined, in part of his own making & this latter aspect can be influenced by elements in himself whch seem to partner, or call to, or be aspects of, elements of great power outside himself. If he can find a way of linking what he has wth. these greater forces, he is himself greatly enlarged.

(c) These forces do not always seem to work for good, as good is generally understood, & whether a man calls on them for good or ill is a matter of morality. Are these forces of God, then? I cannot believe that God's goodness is comprehensible by man; nor are these forces necessarily all, or partly, of God.

(d) People who profess religion conventionally, or despise & reject it conventionally are much alike in being dead to the spirit. It is hard work to live religiously & laborious to ask for & be granted more than common things.

(e) But it is the only life for me, & rich & glorious in a way the Church never makes real. It is private, not shared. And it does not seem to have much to do wth Christianity as generally understood.

He concluded: "Marvellous morning trying to get this straight in superb surroundings; made me v. happy; I know where I stand."

However, by the time Davies came to write the Deptford novels, these conceptions of God and of evil had been overlaid by his reading of Jung. The latter believed that all religious ideas, all statements made in the scriptures, arise from the archetypes of the collective unconscious. In a lecture Davies gave on the subject of evil in 1976, he explained that Jung saw God as, "at the least, a psychological fact, and at the best as a transcendent authority manifesting itself in man through the activity of the psyche.... For Jung, God was a fact for which evidence existed in the mind of man—which is not to say that God is nothing more than that...." Davies himself believed (as he had earlier and as he does still) in "the existence of a power of good and a power of evil external to man, and working through him as an agency—a God, in fact, infinitely greater than man can conceive, and a Devil vastly more terrible than even the uttermost terrors of human evil."

Jung conceived of God (like the "self") not as perfection but as wholeness, embracing and balancing the great oppositions of good and evil, masculinity and femininity, dark and light. He therefore saw the papal bull of 1950 as an edict of signal importance in its acknowledgement of a female component in what had hitherto been a wholly masculine Christian conception of God. The bull promulgated the Assumption of the Blessed Virgin into Heaven, affirming the union of Mary (as Bride) with the Son and (as Sophia or Wisdom) with the Godhead, and thus gave belated official recognition to Mary's elevated place in worship and belief. Davies, following Jung, was convinced that this move by the Roman Catholic Church "leaves Protestantism with the odium of being nothing but a man's religion, which allows no metaphysical representation of a woman." He came to believe that "the bringing of the feminine principle, feminine values and insights into greater prominence in Christianity will be the greatest revolution in the faith in the last 1,000 years.... The trouble with Christianity is that it's too Hebraically based with its single Father God and its masculine Saviour.... We've got to stop pounding away at the Logos idea (word, reason) and do some serious thinking about the Eros principle; i.e. the principle of love and relationship as women know it...."

Likewise, Davies found himself open to the Jungian suggestion that the Devil is probably encompassed in the being of God, a shift that gave him a vivid way of talking about the necessity of confronting and coming to terms with one's shadow. In 1968, he observed "...we must make friends with the Devil before we can hope to quiet him down. The Devil, who was God's son as much as Christ, must be given his due." And a few years later, in 1974, he said that the Devil seems to him to be "not the commonplace symbol of evil but the symbol of unconsciousness, of unknowing, of acting without knowledge of what you're intending to do. It's from that that I think the great evils spring. The devil is the unexamined side of life; it's unexamined but it's certainly not powerless."

Fifth Business

In 1958 an image began to float insistently to the surface of Davies' mind. It came unbidden, again and again, acquiring more detail and definition with each successive appearance. This is how he first described it, in 1979: "[It was] a winter's night on a village street, which in time I recognized as a street I knew well from childhood.... After a while the scene was peopled by two boys, and one was throwing a snowball, and I knew the snowball had a stone concealed in it." Subsequent accounts added more details. The scene takes place in front of the Davieses' home on Elizabeth Street in Thamesville at about six o'clock on a snowy winter night, one, two or sometimes three days after Christmas. The boys are running along the street and they have been quarrelling. One is hurrying home for supper, the other calling abuse after him. The snowball, spitefully thrown, misses the boy at whom it is aimed and hits a woman in front of whom he dodges. The woman, who is accompanied by a man, is only a casual passer-by, but the snowball hits her head and hurts her so severely that she falls to the ground.

After about two years, the scene had recurred so often to his consciousness that Davies recognized he had to deal with it. Deliberately calling it to mind, he wrote three brief pages of notes, which he dates as "not later than 1960." They may indeed have been written before September 21, 1959, when he told a fan of *Tempest-Tost*: "The next time I write a novel it is going to be about quite a different situation and a very different group of people, though the setting will be chiefly in Canada."

The notes begin: "In a small town a young parson is taking his pregnant wife for an evening walk: a mischievous boy throws a snowball in which there is a rock, hits the woman on the head, hurting her seriously. When the child is born (prematurely?) she loses her reason; after a period of caring for her at home, she is sent to an asylum." The notes continue: the parson's life has been so centred on his wife that without her he loses his grip on himself and his duties. Revenge is to be the theme, revenge on the thrower of the snowball, not by the parson but by his son, whose birth has come prematurely as a result of the incident. Next come speculations about whether the culprit was "a doctor's son & thus a village grandee? & of a different church, provoking denominational feeling? Only two drs. in the village & this makes for another difficulty between them." The notes make brief reference to several possible characters, including the "Editor of village paper & his family." The final note, in a different coloured ink, was almost certainly written later: "Narrator: small-town editor's son, 1st Gt. War veteran & now a master in a private school?—moved to think of it because copy of *Peyton Place* impounded by a zealous assistant?"

Davies was to make use of almost everything in these notes in his new novel, although the story's focus underwent a radical change before he began to write. But the notes make no reference to the boy at whom the snowball was thrown, nor do they draw a connection between the envisioned narrator and that boy.

After several more years had passed, Davies wrote down a new set of ideas for the novel, this time in his "Works in Progress" notebook. They were probably made soon after August 18, 1964, by which time, according to his travel diary, the novel was "pretty clear" in his mind. These notes reveal that a second element that he later saw as crucial to the creation of the novel had by now occurred to him, namely, a reflection on the moral responsibility of children. As a newspaperman he had been aware of many instances of serious crimes committed by children, for which the courts were reluctant to find them culpable. At what point, wondered Davies, does responsibility begin? He had decided that "guilt began with the desire to do evil, though the evil-doer might not fully recognize the lengths to which his evil might reach."

My long-pondered tale of the woman who was robbed of her wits by an act of malignance on the part of a child, & who lives the life of a saint & is requited for it wth. confinement in a madhouse. Setting: Thamesville, as the root. Characters: the Man of Wealth who begins as the Bad Boy; Mrs. Dempster, the saint, wife of a Methodist parson: her son, who becomes a famous conjuror: Andrew Robertson, the chronicler who is the only one to know the whole story.

Possible Scheme of Construction:

1. Section on Man of Wealth: obituary by CP & perhaps a N.Y. paper—self-made, adventurous, endows scholarships & colleges, a great worldly success; an address by his wife to a univ. full of vaunting prose & a dreadful piece of verse by herself (vide Lady Dunn)

2. Section on the Conjuror: the booklet he sells at his performances wth. a fictional life-story & advice to the young

3. The Narrative of Andrew Robertson, who knew the facts & loved Mrs. D. & who makes it possible for the Conjuror to kill the Man of Wealth. A. R. asked to write biog of Man of W. & declines: his narrative the longest section of the bk. & shd. be written first.

the theme of this novel, as it grows in my mind, is Love Denied.

—It cd. be written as an uncompleted memoir of Andrew Robertson, some parts done in full, & others as rough notes, N.Bs, to get in material that wd. be bulky as narrative, but vivid as a note, & capable of throwing light on character of A.R.

—This might be managed as a transcription of a tape

recorded by A. R. after having a stroke, wth readings from diaries, etc.

Not all of this was to find a place in the novel. The division into three sections already hints at the trilogy Davies eventually wrote. (Often, ideas in his preliminary notes that weren't used on one occasion were taken up on another, as with the device of the obituary and the theme of "Love Denied," which found their way into *What's Bred in the Bone*.) He now (still probably in 1964) tried writing a page and a half, but he found that he was still not ready to begin. Four more years passed, and during this interval Brenda discovered the last element that was critical to the novel's creation. At the home of Nicholas Goldschmidt, she heard a theatrical friend quoting what an amusing elderly opera singer had once said about the operatic roles sung in the Europe of her youth: "There were heroes and heroines, she said, and these of course were sopranos and tenors. Then there were villains and temptresses, and naturally these were basses and contraltos. Then, she said dismissively, there was Fifth Business—the sort of roles sung by other singers whose parts were necessary to the plot, but not central to it." The idea and the phrase caught Davies' imagination, and by September 1965 "Fifth Business" had become his working title.

Finally, in 1968, he sat down to make detailed outlines and notes in his "Works in Progress" notebook, and wrote the book that made his reputation. By this time the story was centred not on "the woman who was robbed of her wits" but on the chronicler of the account, Andrew Robertson, renamed Dunstable (and later Dunstan) Ramsay. He was not one of the principals in the scene. He did not put the stone in the snowball and throw it—Percy Boyd Staunton did that. He was not hit by it—Mary Dempster was. He was not born prematurely as a result of it—Paul Dempster was. But if he had not taunted Boy Staunton, and ducked the snowball, the story would not have taken place at all.

Of course Dunstan Ramsay's tale is far from exhausted by his role as fifth business. His life is, in some respects, relatively ordinary—trouble with a domineering mother, rebellious enlistment in the Great War where he is wounded and then nursed back to health by an attractive English girl, decoration for what is seen as an heroic act, a career as a teacher of history at Colborne College, and retirement—but in its imaginative and spiritual dimension it is anything but commonplace. As a boy, Dunstan is fascinated with magic and by the tales in *A Child's Book of Saints* and the *Arabian Nights*. When his seemingly dead brother Willie revives in Mrs. Dempster's presence, he considers it a miracle. Glimpsing a statue of the Virgin as he loses consciousness on the battlefield, he sees Mary Dempster's face upon it and, when he recovers from the six-months' coma, he is convinced that she has healed him. When he learns that the life of the tramp has been transformed by her generosity in Deptford's gravel pit, it is for him a third miracle, and he comes to view her as a saint. Curiosity about the battlefield statue kindles his interest in religion and saints generally, which results in research trips to Europe and Mexico, and in time he becomes a much respected hagiographer, a contributor to the *Analecta Bollandiana* and the author of ten books, including *A Hundred Saints for Travellers*.

Dunstan early perceives that myth is an expression of patterns that recur in history and in individual lives, and later concludes that faith is "a psychological reality" which, when not invited to fasten itself on things unseen, invades and raises "bloody hell with things seen." His penetration into these matters and his growing knowledge of himself permit him to live a more satisfying life (as when he plays the hero or the defeated lover) and to avoid its pitfalls (as when he sees that Boy is unconsciously inviting him to play Gyges to his King Candaules). He recognizes himself as one who must heed "flashes of insight and promptings," one fated to be "a collaborator with Destiny, not one who put a pistol to its head and demanded particular treasures."

But Dunstan still has his blind spots. Although he scorns Boy's obsession with sex, he is just as unbalanced himself in his relations with women. Preoccupied with Mrs. Dempster, he gives little of himself to other women; indeed, he confides little in anyone. He compulsively accepts the entire responsibility for the consequences of the snowball episode and is increasingly dominated by his repressions until, reacting uncontrollably to them at the age of fifty, he is swept off his feet by the primitive beauty of Magnus Eisengrim's young assistant, Faustina, and finds himself pouring out his life story to Eisengrim's partner, the wise but startlingly ugly Liesl Vitzlipützli. When Liesl forces him physically to come to terms with the things he had repressed, he reacts as his namesake St. Dunstan had done to the female devil who tempted him—with a sharp twist of her nose. At the book's climax, Dunstan, as fifth business, finally divulges the secret whose burden he has carried alone—the stone in the snowball—to the two other men whose lives have been affected by it, and his revelation, leading to Boy's death, brings the story of the snowball to a conclusion.

Davies' own life fed into *Fifth Business* in many, many ways, and he was keenly aware of this. A few months before the writing began he told Horace Davenport:

> It is autobiographical, but not as young men do it; it will be rather as Dickens wrote *David Copperfield*—a fictional reworking of some things experienced and much rearranged—a spiritual autobiography in fact, and not a sweating account of the first time I backed a girl into a corner. I choose the word 'spiritual' with intent, for during the past ten years the things of the spirit have become increasingly important to me. Not in a churchy sense—though as Master of this college I have to attend chapel and look serious—but in what I must call a Jungian sense. That may make you laugh, or spit, but through C. G. J's ever-thickening veils of thought and fantasy I discern something that gives great richness to my life, and helps me to behave rather more decently toward other people than my unaided inspiration can achieve. And that is important to me: the world is so full of self-seekers, crooks and sons of bitches that I am very keen to be a decent man—not a Holy Joe, or a do-gooder, but a man who does not gag every time he looks into a mirror.

His memories of Thamesville were central to *Fifth Business* right from the beginning. The snowball scene, the vision that had forced itself upon him, takes place in front of the house where he lived as a child, and several of its elements appear to have originated in the incident in which the Baptist preacher's son had urged him to throw a stone through the window of the Baptist church. Davies' 1960 notes speculate about using certain local characters, and position the narrator as a veteran of the First World War, which dominated the Thamesville he remembered from 1916-19. His recreation of the village is so vivid that the reader observes with Davies just how things looked and felt, and how its residents thought and spoke. Davies' fictional town of Deptford has defined for a generation of readers what it meant at that time and place to be a Canadian.

But memories of Thamesville were a major resource only for the novel's first section and part of the second. Very little in the originating vision, or in the first notes, hints at the material in the balance of the book, apart from the speculation that the narrator was "now a master in a private school." (Although he shares some of Davies' experiences and many of his attitudes, Dunstan Ramsay is no self-portrait. Dunstan is a cranky bachelor, a man who has missed out on the warmth and balance that a good marriage can bring, a dedicated scholar and no artist. Dunstan does draw a little on Mr. Wright, the master at UCC who introduced Davies to Browning's *The Ring and the Book*. Colborne College is itself, of course, based on UCC.)

Dunstan Ramsay, Paul Dempster's first teacher, repeats Davies' own maladroit boyhood attempts in Renfrew at sleight-of-hand and at the village library reads the same books on magic that Davies had himself coveted as a boy (and acquired years later)— Robert-Houdin's *The Secrets of Stage Conjuring* and Hoffmann's two books, *Modern Magic* and *Later Magic*. The notion of involving Paul in "Le grand Cirque forain de St Vite" and its collection of grotesques was probably suggested by the travelling circus Davies saw in Denmark in 1963. Its immensely strong girl acrobat had moved him to speculate about the lives of such people: "what future awaits her? Her present is as clear as that of the dwarves who caper about dressed as chimpanzees—she is an oddity; the dwarves are perhaps to be preferred for they looked intelligent & were v. nice to the children; she looked like a vast, patient animal, & when she thought herself unobserved, trudged & plodded like one." There were earlier inspirations for at least three of the "Cirque's" offerings. A side-show at a small fair to which Davies had taken Miranda and Jennifer in the early 1950s presented an achondroplasic dwarf who danced on broken glass. Louis Chéronnet's *Petit Musée de la Curiosité Photographique*, which Davies has owned since it was published in 1945, includes an illustration of a Heteradelphian, with a grotesque incomplete twin projecting from his body. And the bearded lady was but the latest in a considerable series of them in Davies' writing, stretching as far back as 1941.

Davies' visualization of Mary Dempster as a saint in his notes of 1964 probably owed much to the Roman Catholic iconography he had recently been seeing in Europe. But he had first become curious about saints at nineteen or twenty, having heard them anathematized by the Presbyterians around him as he grew up. At the *Examiner* he devoted several editorials every year to saints, initially the well-known ones like St. David, St. George, St. Andrew, St. Patrick and St. Valentine that even Protestants acknowledged, and over the years many others as well. Whenever there was news of a saint or of a miraculous happening, he would print it. A 1943 editorial, "Saints for Soldiers," makes it clear that he possessed Sabine Baring-Gould's twelve-volume *Lives of the Saints* and that he had come to regard the legends of the saints as invaluable guides to medieval life and custom.

But Davies did not decide to make Dunstan a hagiographer until he and Brenda travelled to Austria in 1965. This jaunt, a family trip that included all three girls and Brenda's mother, was particularly productive for him. They rented a house in Kitzbühel for a month and used it as a base for expeditions to the Salzburg Festival and the surrounding countryside. One day, after admiring the images of St. Florian, St. George and St. Catherine in a small baroque church, Davies mused in his travel diary: "must try to get a gd. bk. by whch to identify saints in London, if one exists; wd. it be a project to write a *Saint-Spotter's Guide*? Or shall I incorporate that in my current novel, of whch I think so much here?" Effectively he did all three: he acquired a handbook of saints (*The Penguin Dictionary of Saints* by Donald Attwater), and his central character is so captivated by them that parts of *Fifth Business* could serve as a reference work.

Dunstan Ramsay's interest in saints very much reflects Davies' own. For *Fifth Business*, Davies drew on the standard sources, such as the *Catholic Encyclopedia, The Oxford Dictionary of the Christian Church* and *The Penguin Dictionary*, but he also went well beyond them, to books like *The Golden Legend* (a medieval manual of ecclesiastical lore), Erich Neumann's *The Origins and History of Consciousness*, Jung's *Man and His Symbols* and Roy Bedichek's *The Sense of Smell* (this last alerted him to the tradition that saints have a delicious odour, which persists after death). He made Dunstan a specialist in Wilgefortis, the female saint who grew a heavy beard, in order to provide the sacred complement to the bearded lady in the "Cirque."

Like so much else in *Fifth Business*, even Dunstan's name is associated with Davies' childhood in Thamesville. It was Rupert who had introduced him to St. Dunstan, reading *The Ingoldsby Legends* to him at bedtime. The tale begins:

> St Dunstan stood in his ivied tower,
> Alembic, crucible, all were there;
> When in came Nick to play him a trick,
> In guise of a damsel passing fair.
> Every one knows   How the story goes:
> He took up the tongs and caught hold of his nose.

On the other hand, the stories of saints that Dunstan Ramsay reads to Paul Dempster came from a book that Davies discovered late. It caught his eye in Bertram Rota's on July 27, 1967, when he noted in his travel diary: "Saw a *Child's Bk of Saints* whch begins wth a Victn. child who assures her papa that she longs for the 2nd Coming & knows Jesus cd. not be crucified again, as Queen Victoria wd. never permit it! I am not sure I can live without this." He couldn't. In August he wrote and ordered it, and he subsequently made effective use of it in the novel.

The 1965 Austrian trip produced more treasure for *Fifth Business*. In Spain the previous year Davies had found himself drawn to the many images of Mary with a crescent moon beneath her feet, a seventeenth- and eighteenth-century interpretation of the Immaculate Conception that was part of the historical veneration of Mary that had ultimately led to the papal bull of 1950. Now, in Kitzbühel, in Konrad Welwert's shop, he and Brenda discovered a polychrome wood figure of "a charming baroque Madonna, standing on the globe (encircled by the Serpent) & a crescent moon." There was a large exhibition of *Schöne Madonnen* in the cathedral in Salzburg at the time, which quickly taught them much about such statuary, and a discussion with a reputable dealer in Salzburg suggested that the price being asked for the little Madonna was the going rate for a fine example. She proved irresistible on a second viewing, and they bought her. Davies carried her in his arms on the airplane to London and later to Canada.

In the course of producing the Coventry Nativity Play at St. George's Church in 1948, Davies had been reminded afresh of the many faces of the Madonna—the innocent virgin of the Annunciation, the woman berated as a strumpet by Joseph, the loving mother of the newborn Christ and finally the Queen of Heaven, enthroned with the child in her arms. Then he had had to rush to Calderwood to confront his domineering mother, a grim-faced corpse and furious ghost. The juxtaposition laid the basis for the sharply dissimilar characters of Mary Dempster and Mrs. Ramsay. Like the Madonna, Mary Dempster is a saint, a harlot, a loving mother and, in the battlefield statue, the Queen of Heaven enthroned with the child Jesus in her arms. To Dunstan she is everything his own mother is not—wise, fearless, trusting, deeply religious, serene and, although a social outcast, a source of comfort and assurance. In contrast, like Florence Davies, Dunstan's own mother, Mrs. Ramsay, is a demon for clean privies, charitable in a practical way, sometimes a shrieking virago, never less than determined to bend him to her will. The scene where Dunstan is forced to abase himself before his mother shows Davies writing with full frankness from his own experiences. Dunstan's confrontations with his mother move him to reflect: "She did not know how much I loved her, and how miserable it made me to defy her, but what was I to do? Deep inside myself I knew that to yield, and promise what she wanted, would be the end of anything that was any good in me; I was not her husband, who could keep his peace in the face of her furious rectitude; I was her son, with a full share of her own Highland temper and granite determination."

Just before Davies began writing *Fifth Business* in 1968, he spent nine days in Mexico City, where, like Dunstan, he viewed several films and stayed at a hotel called the Maria Cristina, whose public room was dominated by "a *Last Supper* at which it appears nobody could touch the lamb, whch lies cold, flayed & repulsive in a dish." He also visited the Shrine of the Virgin of Guadaloupe, not by accident, since he wanted his hero to spend time there too. What he observed became the basis of what Dunstan saw:

> inside the courtyard pilgrims crawl toward the doors on their knees: some have a son or daughter who put a sweater or a scarf under the knees, whipping it from behind the pilgrim to the front, wth. rather comic effect. Many old & ill: many mothers wth. babies in shawls. Inside the church workmen are busy shoring up the edifice, whch tilts alarmingly. Great crowds: whole families carrying candles; we creep up the aisle among them & confront the miraculous cloak on which the Virgin's picture appears; an impressive & handsome picture & the whole church finer & more dignified than I had expected. Saw the bent crucifix, twisted when 'a politician' brought a bomb to the shrine concealed in an offering of flowers; it is thought to be miraculous but a scoffer might say that it was a characteristically inefficient Mexican bomb. The guide had told us the story outside, v. quaintly, of the 'clock' of the peasant, & of the bishop's truly mythical haggle wth. the B.V.M. abt. the Castilian roses. I deeply enjoyed all this, as being fuel for *Fifth Business.*

As Dunstan watches the worshippers, he comes to understand that faith is a psychological reality, an insight that is rooted directly in Davies' reading of Jung.

One of the perceptions deeply woven into the novel is Dunstan's sense that if his life is to be fruitful he must co-operate with fate, allow chance to have its say and heed his intuitions. Again, it was the 1965 Austrian trip that provided Davies with the occasion to work out his thoughts. In Salzburg he had one of the two or three supreme experiences of theatre in his lifetime, soaring performances of both parts of Goethe's *Faust*. He knew the plays well, indeed had prepared by rereading them in translation. The acting and the stagecraft in the old-fashioned, intimate *Kleinen Festspielhaus* gripped him throughout, although he knows only a few words of German.

On the evening when he and Brenda saw the first part, they found themselves stranded. The direct route back to Kitzbühel, which passes briefly through Germany, was closed to them because Davies had forgotten his passport, and Brenda did not want to attempt the unfamiliar, much longer Austrian route in the pouring rain and the dark. Since there were no hotel rooms to be had in Salzburg, they parked under a tree from one until four in the morning, and while Brenda dozed in the back seat, Davies gazed at the "swift-flowing Salzach & the noble night skyline across it" and gave himself over to thought. "*Faust* had put me in the mood for some Jungian speculation: what emerged was a new strength of conviction that the unorthodox ways I have taken in life, & my dependence on intuition, mood & coincidence for guidance—my faith in *me*, as opposed to well-worn paths—is not only the *only* way of life open to me (I have known that for years) but a good, & fruitful & beautiful way & all I have to give to mankind: I have never felt this assurance so strongly & deeply. So when dawn came & we cd. move on, I was greatly strengthened, & I shall always remember this lovely city as a place where I had an important revelation."

Finally, in 1968, with Massey College firmly established and his desk at last cleared of Marchbanks and academic writing, he got down to the novel that had been haunting his imagination for so long. Despite the intensity of the inspiration that animated him, he couldn't escape a feeling of depression. He told Horace Davenport: "I hoped to do so much, and I have done what I could, and it doesn't amount to a very great deal. The joke is that externally I appear to many people to be very successful, because I have an assured air, and talk readily, and look more like a professor than most real professors. (In actual fact, I look like a Stage Professor, although I make no particular effort to do so.) But my desire was to be a writer of some consequence, especially for the stage...." Fortunately, such periods of despondency never undercut his confidence in his creative powers, never dried the flow of invention, certainly never kept him from writing. As an artist he remained confident and optimistic. In the same letter he told his old friend that the genre that now seemed to be most suited to the kind of thing he wanted to say was the novel. "It is here that I repose my hopes. I feel strongly that my best writing is still to come."

As usual, fresh perceptions thrust themselves upon him while he was writing the story. Liesl's question to Dunstan in his hotel room—"Why don't you shake hands with your devil, Ramsay, and change this foolish life of yours?"—owes something to a dream Davies had at the time. In it, the witch who had transfixed him with terror in Renfrew appeared to him again, "and as I dreamed I thought I should once again be frozen by that spell. Not so. I roused myself, and walked toward her, holding out my hands. 'Can't we be friends?' I said. And...the witch became a benevolent figure, took my hand, and was terrifying no longer. I did not need an analyst to tell me what that meant. It meant a measure of self-conquest."

As it turned out, the novel he wrote was an imaginative consolidation of all he had learned over the previous decade. More, it was the work of a man in full command of his creative powers, proceeding intensely and inevitably from beginning to end. No longer did Davies feel the need to distance himself from his characters with comic omniscience as he had in the Salterton trilogy. Now he was willing to risk the more direct expression of his own feeling and thought that was necessary, as it seemed to him, to realize a character from within. He was consistently sure in handling his material, from the scenes rooted in the remembered reality of Thamesville through to those drawn from imagination, like the "Cirque" and the magic show. As he traced the stages by which his hero gains self-knowledge as he moves from the village to the city, from 1917 to 1970, he created a story in which many Canadians recognized their nation's own struggle toward self-recognition and national identity. *Fifth Business* is a wholly compelling book of idiosyncratic vision and can fairly be called one of the important novels of the century.

Davies wrote the first two sections of the novel in the fall of 1968 in time snatched from his work as professor and Master. By December 2, he had written 25,000 words. The following summer, Clair and Amy Stewart loaned him and Brenda "Highfields," the big, airy, barnlike country house near Caledon East, Ontario, that William E. Fleury had designed for them and their many children. Davies completed the balance of the first draft there. He would write at the typewriter in his best hours—9:30-12:30—and after lunch he would rest and do a little physical work. Late in the afternoon he would revise the day's output by hand (for him, typically, this has involved no more than changing an occasional word, or, less often, adding or cutting a sentence), and in the evening he would mull over the material to be dealt with on the following morning. (As a thank-you to the Stewarts, he later had a special Highfields copy of the novel made up, with its title page printed on the Massey College press.)

In the fall of 1969, the typescript proceeded through the usual stages. As she has done for all his subsequent novels, his secretary, Moira Whalon, who had by then been with him for twelve years, raised several pages of queries. As well as copy-editing matters, she would find inconsistencies in the names of characters, illogicalities in the ages assigned to characters from one reference to the next and the like. Her observant eye has rescued Davies from many such errors of detail. The manuscript she produced (which is now in the National Archives of Canada with most of the rest of his papers) has such physical beauty—the typing is impeccable, the typeface large and slightly old-fashioned—that the publisher's editor was deterred from marring it with picayune changes.

Surprisingly, Macmillan of Canada might easily have rejected the novel when it arrived in manuscript that December. One senior editor, who couldn't quite put his finger on why it evoked so little response from him, concluded that "we might well decline if it didn't have the name of Robertson Davies attached to it." But Ramsay Derry, the firm's fiction editor, reacted very differently. Well aware that Davies was by now regarded as *passé*, he feared that this new venture might prove that Davies had been too long away from novels. Instead, about thirty or forty pages into the manuscript, he felt the hairs on the back of his neck literally stand up: he "just knew this was a wonderful book." He wanted to telephone Davies immediately to tell him so, but John Gray, the company's respected president, dissuaded him: more readers should be heard from before a decision was made, and in the meantime they weren't to mislead the author.

Gray himself finally got to it at the end of the month, and found it thoroughly readable but lacking in warmth and immediacy. He thought the letter framework ought to be scrapped, the peculiarly English expressions changed and Mrs. Dempster given more substance. Given Davies' standing and the general quality of the book, however, there was no question in his mind of not publishing, and so, on the last day of the year, Davies received a "telegram from John Gray first thing expressing great satisfaction wth. *5B.*—even as my horoscope in *Vogue* foretold." An uncomfortable couple of months followed during which Scribner's declined the manuscript and both Viking in New York and Macmillan in London considered it. In this interval, in Ramsay Derry's recollection, all three publishers told their author in essence: "Very fine—but, of course, there are a few points…" and none of them said clearly that publication was a certainty.

On March 15, there was a meeting over drinks at the York Club in Toronto between Davies and his Canadian and English publishers, at which Derry remembers Davies asking in exasperation: "What are all these changes you want me to make? Should I change my men to women? Do you want me to put the beginning at the end?" It finally emerged that Alan Maclean, managing director of Macmillan of London (and brother of the famous spy), was concerned about the peculiar title and wanted it to be explained at the beginning of the book. Davies, who had been pre-warned of this concern, immediately fished up from an inner pocket a scrap of paper bearing the required definition—a quotation from Thomas Overskou's *Den Danske Skueplads*. Before they all left the York Club, it was agreed that the book would be published, and that Derry would act as co-ordinating editor.

Davies later rephrased his definition of "fifth business" to the wording that now appears immediately after the title page of the book. He did so, he told Derry in a letter, "in the interest of clarity. My Danish is a bit rusty and I don't think I got it quite right first time." Undoubtedly almost all his readers assumed, as Davies meant them to, that this was another instance of his eccentric learning. His books were well known to contain an astonishing array of obscure facts and references, accurately quoted. A theatre historian who knew that Overskou's multi-volume work was a dull, never-translated account of nineteenth-century productions by Denmark's Royal Theatre might have suspected a rat, but it is hardly surprising that Davies got away with his joke until *Fifth Business* was translated into Norwegian in 1979. The Norwegian publisher, Gyldendal Norsk Forlag, did question the provenance of the quotation, at which Davies immediately and cheerfully admitted that he had invented it and suggested that the firm might "use the story of this mild hoax as publicity for the book."

Years later, Davies would say sweepingly of the Canadian reception of *Fifth Business*: "…in the beginning this story was not warmly received in Canada. But when it gained very warm commendation in the United States and elsewhere, Canada changed its opinion. Many Canadians began to see in the tale of Dunstan Ramsay some relevance to themselves and to their country." Actually, this distorts the facts considerably. Davies' view is probably conditioned by the fact that, soon after the novel's Canadian publication on October 30, 1970, it was given a drubbing in two of Toronto's three major newspapers. Only the *Globe and Mail* took the novel seriously and reviewed it positively. On November 7, however, the *Gazette* in Montreal thought it should take the Governor General's Award for fiction, and enthusiastic reviews had appeared in at least four other major Canadian newspapers before the U.S. publication on November 23. These

Canadian reviewers wrote of Davies as a man of surprisingly diverse accomplishment and saw the novel as an advance over his earlier work.

For most American reviewers, on the other hand, *Fifth Business* was their first exposure to Davies, and for them the novel was a revelation. It fell into none of the usual categories. It was unlike the work of any of the major U.S. novelists of the day. They recognized its craftsmanship, intelligence, perceptiveness and maturity of vision. In reviewing *Fifth Business* in the *New York Times*, Christopher Lehmann-Haupt concluded: "A marvelously enigmatic novel, then, elegantly written and driven by irresistible narrative force. One thinks of 'The Magic Mountain' and 'The French Lieutenant's Woman,' although Mr. Davies hardly needs Thomas Mann and John Fowles to prop him up." In *Book World* (which appears in both the *Washington Post* and the *Chicago Tribune*), L. J. Davies (no relation) declared the novel "a mature, accomplished and altogether remarkable book, one of the best of this or any other season, and it simply cannot be ignored."

In Canada, these astounding U.S. reviews, combined with the positive local reviews and imaginative merchandising by Macmillan (including a book launch at Captain John's Restaurant in Toronto Harbour, virtually on the very spot where Boy Staunton had drowned in his Cadillac convertible), made the novel a sensation. By January 9, 1971, it had risen to first place on the "National Bestsellers" list in the *Toronto Daily Star*, where it held first or second spot until late April and remained on the chart for forty-two weeks. In June, commenting on the book's manifest success, Patrick Scott declared that *Fifth Business* "could only have been written by a Canadian. It is so indigenously Canadian in every respect—and evokes so stunningly the Canadian character and scene—that it stands as a very definition of Canadian content." The hardcover sold 5,000 copies, and 15,000 more through the Book-of-the-Month Club.

It did not, however, take the prestigious Governor General's Award for fiction. That went to Dave Godfrey's *The New Ancestors*. Davies was seen to belong to the generation of Ernest Buckler, Morley Callaghan, Hugh MacLennan, W. O. Mitchell and Sinclair Ross, writers who had made their mark in the 1940s and '50s. Godfrey belonged to the generation of writers who began to publish in the 1960s—the likes of Margaret Atwood, Timothy Findley, Hugh Hood, Robert Kroetsch, Margaret Laurence, and Alice Munro. He represented everything that seemed to be culturally vital and hopeful in Canada. His novel— complex, probing, difficult, committed—seemed to represent an exciting new development in Canadian literature, and it won out over *Fifth Business*, albeit by a close vote.

In the United States, many of the major reviews appeared only after Christmas (in *Saturday Review*, the *Christian Science Monitor*, *Time* and *Newsweek*, for example), so Davies' publisher, Viking, decided to mount a second advertising campaign in February to capitalize on them. As a result, *Fifth Business* made tenth place on the *New York Times* "Best Seller List" on March 28 and April 4 when only 15,000 copies had been shipped, a feat usually accomplished only by books with sales of 40,000 to 50,000. The hardcover sales in the United States were 13,210, plus 10,000 through the Literary Guild. In Britain, where reviews were briefer and more mixed, sales were a disappointing 2,000 or so.

The Manticore

On June 15, 1970, just six months after he submitted the manuscript of *Fifth Business* to his publishers, Davies reported that he was already in the toils of his next novel. "I had meant to keep this on ice for at least a year, but it insists on asserting itself, and notes pile up...." Early the following May, he had the novel planned and had begun writing. On learning that it was linked to *Fifth Business*, Macmillan of Canada urged him to get the manuscript completed before the end of 1971, so that the book could be brought out in the fall of 1972 to capitalize on his earlier success. Davies thought he might just manage this, "but it will be ditch-digger's work and I wish it were possible to arrange a slightly less tight schedule without losing what advantages there may be in publication early in the autumn." He felt much less pressed when his agent managed to arrange a delivery date of April 1, 1972. But he was still going to have to work exceedingly hard in the few months free of teaching and college responsibilities. On a small page tucked into his "Works in Progress" notebook he calculated:

1. Why I Went to Zurich: 50 pp.?
2. David Among Troll Folk: 150
3. A Man's Self-Judgement: 100

June 1-July 17: 37 working days
July 19-Sept. 4: 37 working days
at 5 pp. per day: 370 pp.
or 120 pp. excess
rate may vary from 3 to 5 pp. daily

Fortunately, conditions for writing were ideal. Knowing that he and Brenda had begun to consider where they would live at the end of his Massey College tenure, Clair and Amy Stewart had offered to sell them a hundred-acre parcel of land near their own country house in Caledon East. After seeing Maisie and Russell Drysdale's beautiful house "Bouddi Farm" in Australia in 1968, and after the Highfields summer of 1969, they decided to build a house there, to use first as a weekend and summer retreat and later as their home.

"Windhover," named both for Hopkins' poem and for the hawks in the area, was begun in 1970 and completed in May 1971. The architect was William E. Fleury, who had designed Highfields and had been at UCC with Davies. The house he planned, to their specifications, stands in the middle of the property, with beech woods on either side and a descending sweep of countryside to the east and south. A chunk of stone from Balliol College is built into an outside wall, with the date incised in it. The living areas occupy several levels, flowing into one another up or down a few steps, and provide ample space for large gatherings and comfortable areas for reading, playing the piano or enjoying a drink in front of the fire. Off the dining room is a gazebo-like elevated, screened porch, where there is usually a breeze on the hottest summer day. Davies' completely enclosed, book-lined study is upstairs. The few patches of wall space and the tops of the bookcases hold a number of items of special importance for him, including two that have connections with the book he wrote that summer. Over the window is affixed a piece of oak beam from the Welshpool house in which his father was born. As he explained at the time, it brought to his work-room "something of Wales, and a very strong reminiscence of my father." And above his desk he hung a Karsh photograph of Jung. Many years later he said, "the picture of the great doctor looking wise is a thing which feeds me. I have a sense of touching base."

As usual, Davies not only met but anticipated his writing dead-line for *The Manticore*. He had "a beginning made" on May 5, 1971, was "well into the writing" on May 14 and completed the first section on June 11. By August 28, the first draft was com-plete, and before the end of February 1972 the manuscript was in his agent's hands.

In a description of the subject of the novel, written on June 15, 1970, the emphasis is quite different from that of the final ver-sion. In 1970 the new novel—"not a sequel but associated with F.B."—was to be "about Edward David Staunton, the son of Boy Staunton, whose stepmother, Denyse Hornick, hounds and bedevils him to undertake the task of finding his father's mur-derer. Which he does, but what he finds is something quite differ-ent." By January 13, 1971, when he responded to an appreciative letter from Hugh MacLennan about *Fifth Business*, he had a clearer focus. "I feel impelled to write another novel about the same characters, but from a quite different point of view—that of Edward Staunton, the son of Boy Staunton, who is said to have become a lawyer and a drunk. But I see this man as one of his father's principal victims, but a victim who in the end escapes his father's toils. He adored his father, and wanted to be like him, but for the obvious reason—that sons, in one way or another are impelled to live out the unlived portion of their father's lives, and because Edward is a man of greater sensitivity than Boy—he could not do it.... How does a son face the reality of a dominant and successful father?" In *Fifth Business*, mothers are a brooding presence; the new novel would be haunted by a father.

The story of the "victim who in the end escapes his father's toils" begins in the office of Dr. Tschudi, Director of the Jung Institute in Zurich. David Staunton has come to the Institute for help after he, normally the most rational of men, had found himself shouting "Who killed Boy Staunton?" in the midst of Magnus Eisengrim's *Soirée of Illusions* in Toronto's Royal Alexandra Theatre two days before. After a thorough physical examination he is assigned to psychiatrist Dr. Johanna von Haller, and in the balance of the book's opening section he recounts to her the details of the stressful days that had followed his father's death—seeing the body dishevelled on the pier with the pink granite stone in its mouth, dealing with his stepmother's bizarre desire for an "official" funeral, buying the grave, viewing the botched death-mask, recognizing the illegitimate Staunton arms on the coffin, living through the funeral itself, hearing the will read, being appalled by Denyse's desire for a biography and a statue, drinking to excess—all of which had culminated in his shouting at the theatre.

"David Against the Trolls," the book's long middle section, contains the account of his life that David prepared for his sessions with Dr. von Haller and the discussions provoked by it. His life has been dominated by his father, and—although he cannot admit it to himself—his resentment is deep. As a boy he had idolized his father and accepted his authority without question. He had submitted to the weekly purgations deemed essential by his grandfather Staunton during his summers in Deptford. He had accepted his father's decision to give him a smaller allowance than was usual at his school—part of a campaign to "make a man of him"—despite the resulting embarrassments. He had erased from his mind his father's smashing of his "unmanly" Highland doll. He had never assigned his father any responsibility for his mother's attempted suicide. Nor had he blamed his father for his long absences during the years when his mother was fading and finally died. When his father spoke slightingly of the girl he loved, he had swallowed his hurt. When his father arranged his sexual initiation, he had refused to see this as a patronizing act.

But despite his inability to acknowledge or express his resentment, his passivity was not complete. He had chosen to study law, a discipline in which he could demonstrate his worth to his father but which was outside Boy's influence. He had taken great satisfaction in achieving financial independence at the age of twenty-one, through the astute handling of a legacy from his grandfather. On completing his studies he had refused to join his father's company, and had instead become an eminent advocate. But in reaction to his father's interference in his sex life he had refused to involve himself with women. Apparently a successful man, he had remained a profoundly unhappy one—an alcoholic with little understanding of himself or his relationships with those most important in his life. As the section proceeds, and his analyst assists him to reconsider all this, he gradually comes to a better understanding of himself and of his father as well, which permits him to acknowledge the contribution that other paternal figures—Father Knopwood, Dunstan Ramsay and Pargetter of Balliol—had made to his spiritual growth.

The book's brief third section, "My Sorgenfrei Diary," places David in the company of Dunstan Ramsay, Magnus Eisengrim and Liesl Naegeli, all of whom were present when the stage illusion of the Brazen Head responded to his shouted question in the theatre. After each of them has interpreted its enigmatic answer to him, he finally realizes that he had never really known his father, and that Boy had not been "killed"—rather, he had chosen to die. David learns that Magnus made it possible for Boy to end his life without pain, and that the stone in his mouth was the one Boy had thrown in the snowball more than fifty years before.

Davies' first attempt at a title, "Son and Stranger," focused on this central story. He was strongly influenced by the fact that the three men whom he acknowledges as "fathers" had all died within a brief space of time: Rupert on March 11, 1967; Vincent Massey on December 30, 1967; and Tyrone Guthrie on May 15, 1971. (Guthrie's death was reported while Davies was writing the first section of *The Manticore*. He tucked the sheet of brief jottings for his CBC tribute into the notes for the novel in his "Works in Progress" notebook.)

While Rupert was still living, Davies felt inhibited from writing things that might have hurt him, or even from expressing views that might have offended him. But now that both parents were dead, Davies felt that he could express his thoughts with candour. It was the complex feelings and thoughts stirred by Rupert's death that drove the book's powerful opening section.

After his retirement and second marriage, Rupert had established his permanent residence in Toronto at 5 Hawthorn Gardens, Rosedale, and it was in Toronto that the end came. After eighty-seven years of vigorous, healthy life, he became ill at noon one day and died of a heart attack soon after midnight. Brenda, of whom Rupert had become very fond, was the last person he recognized. Davies, who had been kept from the hospital for several hours by a Ph.D. oral, saw him briefly several times in the intensive care unit, when he was labouring and obviously near the end. It seemed to Davies "that things were going on inside him which were inaccessible, but probably something interesting and beyond what we would have understood if we had had access to them" (this perception lies behind his later description of Francis Cornish's gradual separation from life and arrival in the "Realm of the Mothers" at the conclusion of *What's Bred in the Bone*). He was appalled when the doctor told him that Rupert had almost expired at 5:00 p.m. and had been resuscitated by heroic efforts—and would have been nothing but a vegetable had he survived.

Davies and Brenda coped on behalf of Rupert's distraught widow, chose the coffin and settled the details of the funeral at Rosedale Presbyterian Church, whose minister, the Reverend Dr. Eoin MacKay, jointly led the service with the Anglican Bishop F. H. Wilkinson and Canon Robert Dann of St. Paul's Anglican Church (Rupert had toward the end of his life largely reverted to his mother's and second wife's faith). Davies arranged for Rupert to be buried in Toronto's Mount Pleasant Cemetery, in a spacious plot near that of his old Welsh-Canadian friend Leonard W. Brockington, and it was he who chose the inscription for the substantial, polished, gray, granite headstone: Rupert's Welsh dragon crest at the top, his motto at the bottom, and the text:

WILLIAM RUPERT DAVIES
journalist and publisher: born Welshpool
Mont., N. Wales 1879: died Toronto 1967
appointed to the Senate of Canada 1942
High Sheriff of Montgomeryshire 1951

In the letter of January 13, 1971, where he set out his intentions shortly before beginning to write the novel, Davies had asked: "How does a son face the reality of a dominant and successful father?" He continued: "I know something of this, for though my own father was no Boy Staunton (indeed, he detested such people) he was quite sufficiently dominant to have given my life a number of curious twists. So, although the book would be no more autobiographical than was *Fifth Business*, it would have a good lively imaginative springboard."

In establishing what David was like as a son and Boy as a father, Davies drew on some of the facts and feelings of his own experience with Rupert. His own boyhood adoration of his father, his unquestioning acceptance of the indignities of Dr. Tyrrell's Domestic Internal Bath, his experience of being short of money at UCC, his father's love affair with the Old Country (diminished in Boy Staunton to an adulation of the British aristocracy and royalty), his own need for independence as an adolescent and young man—each was adapted to the quite different characters of David and of Boy.

The circumstances of Boy's death make the ensuing decisions and rituals more stressful for David than they had been for Davies. The death is either murder or suicide; David's stepmother is aggressive and unpleasant; and his feelings about his father are ambivalent. Particularly difficult is the moment when David perceives that Denyse has had the Staunton arms, to which his father had no right, embossed on the coffin.

In the matter of arms, Davies turned his own experience upside-down and inside-out. Rupert, when he had become successful, had wanted a coat of arms. Admitting in his application to the College of Heralds that he had no ancestry of any distinction, he had asked that the arms include old-fashioned leather ink-balls to indicate his connection with the printing and publishing business. The College did create new arms for him, starting with a long-disused Davies coat of arms and adding two ink balls to it, with a little Welsh dragon for the crest. Granted in 1940, the arms are described formally thus: "Gules on a Bend Argent between two Ink Balls Or a Lion Passant Sable," and the crest: "On a Wreath of the Colours a demi Dragon Gules supporting a

Scaling Ladder Sable." (This means that the ground colour of the shield is red; the two golden ink balls on it are separated by a silver diagonal band, on which a black lion is walking. The crest is comprised of the upper half of a red dragon supporting a black military ladder with a curved top, both resting on a wreath of silver and red, the two main colours of the shield.) A self-made man, Rupert chose the Welsh motto *A Ymdrecho A Drecha*, literally, "He who comes shall overcome," or, as Davies has it, "He who strives hardest shall conquer." In 1951, when Rupert was High Sheriff of Montgomeryshire, his arms were displayed on banners when he made official appearances, and, of course, the crest and motto appear on his gravestone.

Davies respects, indeed deeply approves of the heraldic tradition, and he applied in 1962 to adapt Rupert's arms for his own use by adding a mullet (a five-pointed star indicating the third son) and by changing the motto to "*Ymwrandawed dyn a'i galon*" ("A man should listen to the promptings of his heart"). He drew the motto, on the advice of the Welsh scholar T. J. Morgan, from *Llyfr y Tri Aderyn* (*The Book of the Three Birds*) by Morgan

Davies' book plate, bearing his crest and arms, and the arms of Massey College

Llwyd, a seventeenth-century Welsh mystic. The application was granted in 1964. The arms appear on his bookplate, on his and Brenda's silverware and in a large piece of needlepoint worked by Brenda for their living-room wall.

In *The Manticore*, Boy Staunton, unlike Rupert, wants "good blood." When he asks his son David to delve into his grandfather Staunton's background, he is hoping to discover a connection with the arms-bearing, long-established Stauntons of Longbridge, Warwickshire. But Adrian Pledger-Brown, the hired genealogical expert, finds bastardy instead—and a cracking good story. David's grandfather proves to have been the illegitimate son of Maria Ann Dymock, a domestic servant at a public house called the Angel in Staunton, Gloucestershire. (Maria's nickname, "the Angel," recalls that of Mary Evans, the second wife of Davies' own Great-grandfather Samuel Davies.) George Applesquire, the landlord at the Angel, had denied paternity, asserting that all Staunton could claim to be the child's father, at which Maria, defiantly christening the baby Albert Henry Staunton, had raised enough money to emigrate to Deptford. Delighted with the story, Pledger-Brown creates a mock coat of arms to represent his friend David's heritage. But, as David anticipates, Boy's interest in family history doesn't extend to his father's bastardy. He tells David: "Pay off Pledger-Brown and tell him to keep his trap shut."

Later, on Boy's behalf, Denyse makes repeated unsuccessful applications to the College of Heralds for the arms of the Warwickshire Stauntons, indignantly rejecting its advice to apply for new arms, and at his death she simply appropriates the coveted arms and has them engraved on his coffin. When their motto, "*En Dieu ma foi*," becomes the theme of Bishop Woodiwiss' funeral oration, it is just one more burden for the much-tried David to endure.

Davies' feelings about his father's last will and testament also had an impact on *The Manticore*. He had known what Rupert intended at least since 1964, when Rupert had created trusts in favour of his seven grandchildren. The trusts held 49 percent of his media interests, consisting of the *Whig-Standard* and the Kingston and Peterborough radio and television stations (by now wholly owned by him). His will had further arranged to leave the bulk of the remainder of his wealth in equal shares to the grandchildren. He provided generously for his widow until such time as she remarried (she never did), made a number of bequests to relatives, employees and charities, and—after his lawyer reminded him in their presence that he had made no mention of his two surviving sons—arranged that they should each receive $10,000 a year for the balance of their lives. Of course, he had already given his sons a major inheritance years before when he transferred ownership of the *Peterborough Examiner* to them on advantageous terms.

In leaving the bulk of his substantial estate to his grandchildren, he was in effect freeing Arthur and Davies to spend their money on themselves. Both were successful; neither needed more inherited wealth. Davies knew all this, and recognized its justice. He was well aware, too, of the tax benefits of this method of dispersing Rupert's fortune. Nonetheless, he could not dispel the feeling that Rupert was declaring his two remaining sons wanting. By placing his confidence in the as yet untried younger generation, it felt as though Rupert had confirmed what Davies had always sensed: that he thought all three of his sons less competent in business than he was himself; and (illogically in the case of Arthur and Davies) that if he hadn't given them good jobs they would not have found satisfactory niches for themselves. Moreover, Davies could not entirely put down the thought that in providing so richly for Miranda, Jennifer and Rosamond, Rupert had pre-empted his own proper role as their father. And it seemed ironic to Davies that he, Arthur and his stepmother, saddled as the will's executors with the task of settling the estate, were largely excluded from its largesse.

David Staunton in *The Manticore* likewise sees his father's will as "the measure of what he thought of me as a man, and as his son." The will made it clear that Boy judged him to be a capable lawyer, an astute manager of money and a suitable chairman for the Castor Foundation, but a disappointment as a son. Like Davies, David is an executor of his father's estate, required to settle matters for the benefit of others.

One of Davies' own executorial tasks was to wind up his father's affairs in Wales—tag the special bequests, arrange for the sale of Leighton Hall and its furnishings, help his stepmother prepare for a different way of life. And so Davies and Brenda came to the great house—the solid embodiment of his father's dream—for the last time, from June 21 to July 6, 1967. They found that it seemed already to have "markedly lost spirit & looks, with the absence of the man who gave it meaning." At Rupert's Welshpool memorial service in St. Mary's Church,

Davies noted the "V. good crowd; muffled peal of bells; red-dragon at half-staff. Good hymns, esp. *Cum Rhondda* heartily sung. Excellent, literate eulogy by the deputy mayor, Elwyn Davies; he recalled WRD as a merry man, wh<u>ch</u> was suitable, & as a great Welshpool partisan. How WRD wd. have been amazed to be thus remembered in 'the Church'—not, be it noted, in the Chapel." He knew all the villagers who served as ushers, which pleased him.

Rupert's friends came to visit and invited Davies, Brenda and Margaret into their homes, where the Wales of Rupert's boyhood came to life for them in keepsakes and pictures they were shown. Seeing photographs (circa 1900) of "poachers, hostlers, messengers, shepherds & bums," Davies reflected: "What clothes! incalculably old, shapeless & dirty; grotesque boots & hats changed by weather into organisms. Faces gnarled, toothless, strangely whiskered. And what a lot of clothes—2 or 3 waistcoats, & mufflers uncounted. Showed us also a real Welshwoman's hat, of fine beaver, most elegantly tapered: oddly coquettish, even to the ribbons under the chin. The Welsh are *not* without looks: around Pool one sees many girls wth. fine straight noses, & beautiful big brown eyes—often wth. good legs—slim, not English. In those hats, & in red flannel cloaks, they wd. be striking."

Between his sessions with guests, estate agents and notaries, Davies listened to his father's old records (among them one of Nellie Melba singing Tosti's "Good-Bye") and saw Fred Anderson, his father's old Welshpool school friend and dealer in antique furniture, who had helped to choose the furnishings for the Hall in the early 1950s. Wanting to be able to call up the detail of this amazing house later, he made extensive notes in his travel diary from the description supplied by the makers of the great hall clock and from the contractor's accounts for much of the original furnishing and decoration. He also wrote descriptions of Leighton's statuary and its pictures. But he was not present when the contents of Leighton Hall were auctioned. In *The Manticore*, Davies used only the description of the hall clock (and his recollection of the gargantuan sideboard his father had had dismantled) in establishing the character of Sorgenfrei, Liesl's extraordinary nineteenth-century Swiss castle. Two decades later, however, he made extensive use of all the notes he had made—including those from a sale of fine English paintings at Christie's—in describing the auction at Rhodri Gilmartin's great Welsh house in *Murther and Walking Spirits*. The "job lot" knocked down at the end of the sale fondly recalls the kind of idiotic purchase he and his father had made at similar auctions during the 1930s—"a hand lawnmower in poor order, a trousers press, a quantity of burlap wrapping, and a zebra-skin rug."

The "Son and Stranger" strand in *The Manticore* was clearly cathartic, allowing Davies to work through a few of the complex aspects of his relationship with his father now that death had intervened between them. But there is little here of the vigorous Rupert who dominated the first twelve years of Davies' life, the man whom he described in a 1972 letter as "composed of the Lord God Almighty, all the bards of Wales, the Devil, Mr. Micawber, Charlie Chaplin, a jeering, tormenting, hateful fellow-boy; a man who was soundly hated by the parents of many of the boys I played with; an innocent who thought that all the e-sounds in French were pronounced 'ay' wherever they occurred; a great comedian; a hypochondriac, and an incorrigible meddler with other people's lives." Nor is there anything of the companionship Davies had enjoyed with his father in Wales, the tact Rupert had exercised as Davies had taken up his post at the *Examiner*, the pride Rupert had expressed at his son's academic accomplishments in *Far-Off Fields* or the deep love, respect and admiration Davies felt for his father. *Brothers in the Black Art*, written two years after *The Manticore*, offers a far more direct evocation of Rupert, as a hard-working, romantic, sober, ambitious, naive, dashingly dressed young man making his way in the printing trade. Davies' introductory note to that television play pays tribute to one of Rupert's sterling qualities: "My father was a very much nicer man than Griff, and never forgot an old friend." Davies would take another long look at his father, and at the background that had shaped him, when he came to write *Murther and Walking Spirits*.

Although the description of a Jungian analysis provides a framework for *The Manticore*'s exploration of the relationship between father and son, Davies had no intention of writing a Jungian primer, nor even to be true to the actual shape of an analysis. On the other hand, since he had found Jung's insights so valuable for his own understanding, he found it a very natural and appropriate device to use in assisting the reader to grasp the characters and their story. In preparation, he read and reread Jung, to consolidate his understanding of the ideas he had been absorbing piecemeal over the previous seventeen years. Zurich Seminar 1925 and the comprehensive overview in Martin's *Experiment in Depth* were particularly useful to him.

To ensure that David's analysis would have the feel not of the library but of a psychiatrist's office, Davies went to Switzerland himself in December 1970. At the appointed hour of 10 a.m., he presented himself at the Jung Institute at 27 Gemeindestrasse in Zurich. It was "not at all as I imagined—large private house & Inst. on 2nd floor: one sec. & Dr. Ribi who is abt 40, pipe smoking, courteous, watchful & obviously wonders what the hell I want: big dog—Alsatian—his companion. He arranges lectures & training courses & recommends patients to analysts—I try to take in all I can of the atmosphere: bourgeois, uncomfortable, pics of mandalas on walls, but not poor or repellent." His observations in this brief encounter animated the convincing scene between David and Dr. Tschudi at the beginning of *The Manticore*.

To ensure that David's analyst, Johanna von Haller, would ring true, he gave her qualities that he had perceived in M. Esther Harding, the New York analyst with whom he had talked for an hour in 1959. Harding had struck him as "splendidly at home in her life; frank, charming, wise, and without being in any way beautiful or young, certainly one of the most fascinating women I have ever encountered." He also gave von Haller the directness, good sense, humour and attractive femininity that he had sensed in Jung's colleague, Dr. Marie-Louise von Franz, from reading her books. (When *The Manticore* appeared, many people assumed that von Haller was a portrait of von Franz, and a number went so far as to send her copies of the book. She wasn't pleased. When she came to Toronto in 1974-75 to address the Analytical Psychology Society of Ontario, there were some stiff moments between her and Davies. But the two of them got onto very good terms in the course of the two or three days she spent as a guest in the Master's Lodgings and at Windhover. Davies treasures the insight she gave him into one of his recurrent dreams. In it he is on stage, acting in a play. His cue has been spoken but he does not know what to say or even what the play is. When he told her that he saw this dream as expressing a desolating inadequacy, she observed: "I would have said that it is an indication to you that you don't go on the stage to say what other people have written, but to say what you have to say yourself" and took him to task for interpreting his dreams in a negative, self-diminishing way.)

Jungians consider that the messages of dreams and visions offer important clues to a person's psychic state. To make David's dreams as authentic as possible, Davies decided to give him some he had had himself, including his boyhood vision of Christ with the globe whirling in the centre of the figure, although he interpreted them in a manner appropriate to David's character and history. One vision actually contributed to the creation of the book. Davies had completed the writing of the first section when, sitting drowsily in Windhover's screened verandah after lunch one day, he suddenly saw before him a gallery with an ancient picture in it, depicting a beautiful woman in classical robes, leading a strange beast on a golden chain: "it had the body and head of a lion, the clawed feet of a dragon, a tail which was barbed as the tails of scorpions are barbed in ancient art, and it

had the anguished face of a man." Consulting a dictionary of mythology, he found it was a manticore, "a thing composed of a man helplessly trapped in the attributes of beings that were less than human." At this, much that he had not

The manticore as pictured on the Davieses' 1974 Christmas card understood about his hero became clear to him.

In order to avoid heavy use of Jungian terminology, Davies hit upon an ingenious device. He gave David, the criminal lawyer, the habit of evaluating his own actions by trying himself in an imaginary court, in which he plays defendant, prosecutor, defence counsel, witness and judge. When David mentions this to Dr. von Haller, she recommends that he use a similar technique in his analysis, presenting his story in briefs for both defence and prosecution and sitting as judge. She herself will assume several roles, unrepresented in David's original fantasy— interested spectator, prisoner's friend, authority on precedent— to make sure that everyone gets his due. This stratagem allowed Davies to translate Jung's ideas into terms more familiar to his readers. Of course, Davies also had at his disposal the hard-won knowledge he had gained from considering the events of his own life in a Jungian light. He knew intimately what projection meant, and about the four types of perception, the persona, the archetypes and so on. As well, he could write from personal experience of what it had been like to be under the enchantment of the anima.

Some time before he began writing *The Manticore*, Davies knew that at the end of the story David would spend some time with Liesl Naegeli, Dunstan Ramsay and Magnus Eisengrim at Liesl's great nineteenth-century house in Switzerland. Its address had been established as "Sankt Gallen" in the postcard Liesl had sent to Dunstan at the end of *Fifth Business*, and so, when Davies travelled to Switzerland shortly before Christmas in 1970 to visit the Jung Institute in Zurich, he also made a brief foray to St. Gall. There, like David after them, he and Brenda settled into the Walhalla Hotel, had dinner at the Metropole, saw Lehár's operetta *Paganini* at the Stadtheater, went over the baroque cathedral thoroughly and visited the Abbey library next door, where Davies noted that it was "odd to find an Egyptian mummy in it, blue-black & linen rags in its eyes (are the gleaming teeth real?): saw their bollandist *Acta Sanctorum* & the great MS. of *Niebelungenlied* & fine illuminations, some of the best Irish—& a nonsense, a pen-pic of J.C. wth. the story of the Passion all written v. small & crinkum-crankum to make his hair, beard, eyebrows & crown of thorns, dated 'nach 1650' & real Counter Reformation *kitsch*." They also bought a gingerbread St. Gall bear to take to Miranda in London and a golden St. Gall thaler with the saint and his bear on it to make a pendant for Brenda.

However, Davies' decision to give David a taste of the rewards of penetrating beyond the personal to the collective unconscious in the final section of the novel appears to have been made very late, the result of a serendipitous discovery in the first volume of Joseph Campbell's *The Masks of God*. Davies already knew the story of St. Gall and his bear; he had made a friendly teddy bear one of the important characters of David's childhood. But it was when he learned from Campbell that the circumpolar paleolithic cult of the bear had left its ancient traces in caves near St. Gall that he made the imaginative connections that resulted in one of the most powerful scenes in the book. Liesl, informed that David must decide whether to remain in Zurich and delve into the primordial contents of the collective unconscious or to return to Canada and take up his pressing obligations, urges him to do both. She points out that, like Freud, Adler and Jung, he can undertake the inward journey alone. To put him on the track she urges him to descend with her into one of the caves where, thousands of years before, primitive man had lived and worshipped the bear. As he returns to the surface he experiences the intense terror and awe of the bear that his primitive ancestors felt, loses control of his bowels and experiences shame so intense that he must dredge up more than personal strength to carry on. He finds the necessary courage by calling upon a much more recent ancestor, Maria Dymock, and emerges from the cave with new confidence and with a much deeper understanding of himself.

The completed novel that Davies' agent forwarded to Macmillan in Toronto and London and to Viking in New York late in February 1972 was as much a product of Ontario as *Fifth Business* had been. A few elements grew out of the Thamesville experience—the look and smell of sugar-beet farming, a Tom Thumb wedding (Davies' brother Arthur had once played the groom)—but the sense of locality was not nearly as strong, because, unlike Dunstan Ramsay, David did not spend the whole of his childhood and adolescence in one village. Boy Staunton's

idolization of the Prince of Wales simply heightened the adulation of British royalty that Davies remembers being shared all
across anglophone Canada in the 1920s and 1930s. The scene of
teenage malevolence was rooted in *Examiner* reports during the
1940s and 1950s of wanton, seemingly purposeless destruction
of cottages in the Peterborough area. The grotesque, botched
attempt to make a death-mask of Boy Staunton was based on a
tale that Davies' own Peterborough dentist had told him. The
"Pittstown cases" that earned young David Staunton his spurs as
a criminal lawyer were all Ontario cases—indeed, the case of the
woman who murdered her brutal, dirty husband in the privy and
was given a very light sentence by a puritanical judge was heard
in Peterborough. (For this reason Davies made no change in his
manuscript when his American editor noted that "this turning of
a case by the lawyer's device of exposing [as it were] the act of fel-
latio to the judge and jury is rather a famous case in the States
and was perpetrated by Samuel Liebowitz and subsequently
chronicled by Quentin Reynolds in a book about Liebowitz
called *Courtroom*.")

   All three publishers liked the book, but not the title "Son and
Stranger," which seemed awkwardly close to C. P. Snow's
Strangers and Brothers (published by Macmillan of London) and
to D. H. Lawrence's *Sons and Lovers*. Almost immediately Corlies
Smith, Davies' editor at Viking in New York, perceived that it
ought to be called *The Manticore*. Davies agreed. It seemed to
him to be "a lucky and organic title," given the seminal role that
his vision of the maiden and the manticore had played in the
conception, and he was astonished not to have thought of it
himself. Although the other two publishers were wary of this
unfamiliar word—Macmillan of London counter-proposed
"Room for Consultation" and "The Dream Prompter"—both
reluctantly yielded to the wishes of their author.

   As is usual when he completes a book, Davies lost confidence
in *The Manticore* for a while. Uncertain that the device of the
Jungian analysis would accomplish its purpose, he worried that
readers might react negatively to the unfamiliar material. He
wrote to his editor at Viking: "If I have succeeded it is a book of
considerable depth but if I have failed it is very probably the

damnedest mess you have ever had on your desk. Unfortunately I am unable to tell which is the case...." One professional, the Toronto psychiatrist Vivian Rakoff, did note a vast difference between real case histories and the tidy, balanced exposition of *The Manticore*. The real ones "are generally confused" and "almost invariably dreadfully written. The subsidiary characters get dismissed in one or two words, they lack symmetry." And he judged Davies' use of "something so spacially real, something in geography, something in the very crust of the earth, something in real time, not personal time [i.e. the episode in the bear cave]" as a sort of *deus ex machina* device to resolve the novel's internal issues. But he accepted Davies' exposition of Jungian concepts without a quibble. June Singer, a Jungian analyst in Chicago who reviewed the book for *Psychology Today*, went further. She was of the opinion that Davies had managed to capture "the feeling tone of a Jungian analysis." Believing that the most important part of a Jungian analysis often takes place outside the consulting room, she saw the episode in the cave as the point where the unconscious finally speaks out and where Davies gathered all the details "into a perfectly formed and consistent whole."

Far from finding the Jungian material tough going, the reviewers simply saw it as yet another manifestation of Davies' unconventional learning. When the book was published in Canada in October 1972, in the United States in November and in Britain in February of the following year, the majority admired it, although a handful found it annoying. Correctly recognizing the book as an extension of the creative act that produced *Fifth Business*, they judged, by and large, that it had sustained the richness and wonder of its predecessor. Once again Macmillan of Canada hosted an imaginative book launch, at which the guests received gingerbread bears imported from St. Gall and a stone with "The Manticore" printed on it. The hardcover sales followed the pattern established by *Fifth Business*—in Canada 6,500 plus 15,000 through the Book-of-the-Month Club, in the United States 18,907, in Britain 2,869. And this time Davies did win the Governor General's Award for fiction (against a field that included Margaret Atwood's *Surfacing*) in a decision that many saw as a belated tribute to *Fifth Business* as well.

As was the case from 1970 onward, the completion of a new novel brought a multitude of demands on Davies' time. Once he had readied the manuscript of *The Manticore* for submission in February 1972, there were editorial queries from all three publishers to be dealt with in the spring, proofs to be read in the summer, publicity tours in Canada and the United States in the fall and winter. In June he and Brenda spent a month in Britain, where they helped the now elderly Elsa move into more manageable quarters in St. Ives, visited Rupert's widow Margaret and saw their old friend Dora Herbert-Jones in Wales. In London they saw Brenda's sister Maisie and her husband Russell Drysdale, took Alexander lessons with Peter Scott and visited Miranda, now established there.

While they were in Britain, Davies' old friend Gordon Roper suffered a grave illness. Roper was indeed more than a friend; he was an academic who had written seriously and insightfully about Davies' fiction and was preparing to write a book on him. He was a man who had lived by "the Spirit and the Word," and Davies was convinced that he could be restored to good health by more of the same. So, through all that summer Davies wrote Roper long letters in which he opened his mind—discussing his writing, the books he was reading and the plays he was seeing at Stratford and the Shaw Festival.

He reported to Roper, too, on the visit of Brenda's mother. (She came in mid-May, went to England with them in June and returned with them to Windhover for the month of July.)

> …the presence in the house of a strong personality, whose ideas and prejudices must not be flouted, makes decided demands, and sometimes results in covert warfare on a midget level. For instance, we have a cork board in the kitchen for bills, reminders and the like, and on it hangs a calendar which Rosamond gave us, of Russian Ikons, one for each month. Now, my Ma-in-law is fiercely atheist— she calls it agnostic but an agnostic is a seeker, and she don't seek—who professes a great regard for something she calls Nature. She was nettled subcutaneously by the ikons, which B. and I both love. And on the cork board there are

a lot of thumb-tacks, which, out of meanness and mischief, I arranged in the form of a small but clear cross.
Every day I would find that my Ma-in-law—for the best of
reasons—found it necessary to disarrange this cross. So I
would make a thumb-tack cross again. Not that I cannot
live without crosses or want them in the kitchen, but out
of sheer Old Nick. The matter of the little cross was never
mentioned, but it was a hard-fought battle, I can tell you. I
think Mrs. N. felt I was dragging her daughter toward
Rome.

   Psychiatry, too, was a bone of contention. Mrs. N. hates
it....

Toward the close of Mrs. Newbold's stay, as was his custom
whenever she came to Canada, he created a remembrance book
of collages, water-colours and drawings for her, and on this occasion he included a portrait of John Barrymore as Svengali, which
he labelled "The Hideous and Ever-Present Threat of
Psychiatry."

World of Wonders

In the midst of all this, Davies already had a new novel simmer-
ing. As described in a letter to Roper on July 3, it was to be centred on a tour of Canada in 1923-24 by an English theatrical
company, a subject that had lain at the back of his mind for
years. The company would be led by an ageing actor-knight and
its repertoire would include melodramas from the Irving tradition, especially those featuring dual roles. The action would centre on a young Englishman, a disciple of Freud, Aldous Huxley
and the Bloomsbury group, who was to prepare a script for the
company containing such a dual role. But the conception was
nothing more than that until after *The Manticore* was published
on October 20, when reviews and readers made Davies aware
that there would be keen interest in another story about the
characters in *Fifth Business* and *The Manticore*. Quite suddenly
(as he wrote on November 6), "the idea came: why not the story
of Eisengrim, with all you have for the novel you have been planning used as a large section of his personal history? And there it

was. Everything seemed to fall into place at once."

Fifth Business had already set forth a considerable portion of Magnus Eisengrim's, or Paul Dempster's, story: his premature birth after the stone-laden snowball thrown by Percy Boyd Staunton strikes his mother; his miserable childhood; his side-show career, and sexual abuse at the hands of Willard the Wizard; the years in Europe with Le grand Cirque under the name Faustus Legrand, doing sleight-of-hand with cards and coins; the tour of South America and Mexico after the Second World War under the name Magnus Eisengrim, doing classical illusions in a show masterminded by the grotesquely ugly Liesl Vitzlipützli; the visit to Toronto in 1968 when he performs at the Royal Alexandra Theatre, until the Brazen Head's clever response to the question "Who killed Boy Staunton?" precipitates Dunstan Ramsay's heart attack and his own speedy exit from Canada.

As the new novel decided "to assert itself," two additional episodes emerged. After the death of Willard the Wizard in 1930, Magnus would join the actor-knight's company and "'double' for Sir John in *Corsican Bros.* & *Lyons Mail* & (most important) in *Scaramouche*, where he must do illusions & sleights: thus he does not appear in program as an actor but as ASM, & he learns what it is to be a Doppelganger & serve a Superior Self: & must also acquire JMH's persona & manner-isms & shed those of WW." During the Phoney War Magnus would go to Switzerland, get employment working on watch and clock works, encounter Liesl and, after the war, create the *Soirée of Illusions* with her. A consequence of this new scheme, of course, was that the young Englishman in the earlier version of the plot became a secondary character.

In the same rush of inspiration, Davies realized that this novel would "complete the story that runs through *Fifth Business* and *The Manticore*," and that together the three would constitute a trilogy. As he told Roper: "It was never my intention to write a trilogy, or even to write the second book. It just happened. The story ran on, and required to be told. I have answered all enquiries about a trilogy with an assured No up to this time. But I have changed my mind."

Through the following winter and spring, Davies gathered his resources, and he began to write on July 2, 1973, working not only in the months that were clear of academic obligations but also for an hour a day during the school year. From Horace Davenport, he got the information he needed to portray Liesl's miseries with acromegaly. From Andrew King, a printer of carnival and circus posters during the first half of the century, he got answers to his questions about the way small carnivals travelled from centre to centre, where they spent the winter, what their financial arrangements were and where their workers came from.

To create the side-show with which Magnus spends his adolescent years, Davies drew on his own memories, a little factual knowledge and a great deal of imaginative insight. He once observed that "There used to be scholars who spent a lot of time insisting that Shakespeare must have been a sailor and a soldier and a lawyer's clerk and a falconer and a variety of other things, because he had such a command of seamanship and military art and law and falconry as revealed in his plays. But this sort of argument is naive. Any writer can mug up enough of the jargon of a special calling to make a good show with it; a few words dropped in here and there and a little common sense works wonders." For his hero's first encounter with Wanless's World of Wonders at the Deptford Fair in 1918, he used his recollections of his own visit in that year to Thamesville's agricultural fair and the all-important side-show tent. Although he had been forbidden to enter it, the five-year-old Davies had been well aware that it held a fire-eater, a fat woman, a snake-charmer, a ventriloquist and an armless man who could write with his feet.

Davies, no insider of the carnival world, made astute use of what he did know about it to give the reader an "insider's" view. He had three important things at his command in addition to the information supplied by Andrew King. From a passage in the *Memoirs of Robert-Houdin* he had gathered a great deal about the operation and construction of an automaton like Abdullah. He had discovered several carnival superstitions, including "kill a monkey—3 people will die" (he jotted this down in his "Works in Progress" notebook), and he knew about the belief of side-show people that natural oddities are morally superior to those that are faked or "gaffed" (he had written about this in "Aristocracy of Freaks"). He placed his information about Abdullah and about show people's attitude toward "gaff" right at the beginning of the side-show section to give the reader a sense of intimacy with the carnival world. But the ensuing detailed account of the show is related largely from an outsider's perspective, depending almost entirely on the sharp eye and retentive ear Davies took to fairs, carnivals and circuses over the years. He used the carny superstition about monkey-killing to give shape to the gradual dissolution of the troupe. When Joe Dark knifes Rango, things begin to fall apart in earnest. And when they do, the show people do not forget the dead "monkey's" curse.

Magnus experiences in an intensified form the wonder that Davies had felt as a boy. His fascination with sleight-of-hand is so great that after watching Willard the Wizard he ends up as part of the side-show. Davies' immense pleasure in being privy to the backstage secrets of Rupert's amateur performances in Thamesville is evident in Magnus, beglamoured by the far more extensive hidden life of the World of Wonders. Davies' enchantment gives the novel tremendous imaginative energy as Magnus watches it all—the acts, the tensions, the eager audiences, the frauds. Davies' awe at Christ's appearance to him in Renfrew is there too, albeit in a negative form. Magnus believes that the Devil walks by his side at the Deptford fair, and that in yielding to him, he consigns himself to hell all through his years with the World of Wonders. He sees himself not only as a bad-luck Jonah but as an abomination lower than a whore.

Davies had little more than the resources of an excellent memory and a very modest amount of insider information with which to create Wanless's World of Wonders. But he had an extraordinary accumulation of raw materials to draw on for Sir John Tresize and his troupe. Having been captivated by Sir John Martin-Harvey and his company as a boy, he had become a collector of the artifacts of Martin-Harvey's personal and professional life—initially newspaper clippings, copies of plays in his repertoire, playbills, and later prompt books, speeches he had delivered in Canada, hundreds of letters, programs, photographs, posters and the like. He had long since absorbed the information in the actor's two books of reminiscences—*The Autobiography of Sir John Martin-Harvey* (1933) and *The Book of Martin Harvey* (1930). He could clearly remember, from his student days at Oxford, the splendour of Martin-Harvey's performance in the title role of Max Reinhardt's production of *Oedipus Rex* in the Opera House at Covent Garden. His seasons with the Old Vic had thoroughly familiarized him with large, well-equipped English theatres of the sort Martin-Harvey used, and of course he was well acquainted with many Canadian theatres. He knew an interesting anecdote, too, about the matinée presented by the actors of England in 1938 in honour of Sir Henry Irving. When Martin-Harvey, resplendent in the robes he had worn as Oedipus, had arrived at the stage door, prepared to speak a verse tribute to Irving, John Gielgud had had the unenviable task of telling him that, through a misunderstanding, he had not been included in the program.

Davies had no intention of writing a narrowly literal historical account of the Martin-Harvey tours, however. For example, he substituted *The Master of Ballantrae*, a "Victorian melodrama" of his own contriving based on Stevenson's novel, for Martin-Harvey's *The Only Way*, and *Dr. Jekyll and Mr. Hyde* for *After All.* In imagining how Sir John Martin-Harvey, his plays, his troupe, the theatres in which they performed, the tours they took across Canada and the humiliation of the Irving centenary matinée would look to Magnus and to the sceptical young Roland Ingestree, Davies drew heavily on his own theatrical experience. At one point, Ingestree provides a vivid description of the "quaint sight" the members of the Tresize troupe present as they assemble on deck for a publicity photograph just before sailing for Canada. Davies not only possesses such publicity photographs, he had been a member of such troupes himself. When the *Love and Libel* company set off from Toronto for Detroit in 1960, for instance, he noted in his diary: "Train call at 8, & we all assemble in the Union Stn. looking like nothing so much as a co. of touring theatricals. The crew are smart in Tyrolean hats & sunglasses, & hard to recognize: Leo Leyden comes as *Le Juif Polonais* in a fur cap & a coat wth. a fur collar; Rob Christie very actory in a raglan & a broad-brimmed hat; Lewin Goff (an 'observer' from Kansas Univ., on a grant to watch T. G. at work) has a brown derby, not worn as a joke but in good sadness; Charmion King wears a honey-coloured coat wth. a very big collar, which has the effect of making her look short-legged, & a Eugénie hat of fur felt, & is a modern Miss Snevellicci. We have a parlour car to ourselves & everybody sleeps, eats, frets about immigration, & Ed Holmes emerges as a great cut-up, as does Gene Saks, who does a turn as a presidential candidate & makes a speech from the back of the train."

For all its imaginative overlay, the account of the Tresize/Martin-Harvey tour is still as accurate in spirit and detail as Davies could make it. In this part of the novel he was performing an act of homage, creating a permanent record of something that had once been immensely moving, not only to him but to audiences across Canada. Even details like the physical appearance of the prompt book prepared by the stage manager— "an interleaved copy of the play, with every cue for light, sound, and action entered into it…and marked…in a fine round hand, in inks of different colours"—could be precise: he possessed at least two of Martin-Harvey's prompt books when he wrote *World of Wonders*.

Since Davies had himself been moved so strongly by the wonder and enchantment of the high chivalric world evoked by Martin-Harvey's romantic productions, it is no surprise that Magnus finds their portrayal of elegant manners, dashing behaviour, adoring love and high-minded self-sacrifice stirring and exhilarating. When the twenty-two-year-old falls worshipfully in love with Sir John Tresize's wife, "Milady," he devotes himself to her service like the knights of old. His devotion is such that he succeeds in doing what she wants, catching Sir John's rhythm and manner thoroughly and "doubling" him perfectly. As a result, the company's audiences receive their own full measure of wonder and delight. Indeed, Magnus goes far beyond what is required of him as Sir John's double: he also changes his off-stage dress, behaviour, carriage and speech, even his values, to meet Milady's standards.

Again the Bible is central to Magnus' experience. Milady suffers from cataracts, and so he reads passages to her that she selects, not the condemnatory verses of the years with Wanless's World of Wonders but encouraging, supportive ones, taken from the Psalms in English and the New Testament in French. His love for Milady makes a Paradise of this period of his life. No longer is Magnus a Jonah; now he represents good luck.

When the Tresizes retire, Magnus has to find a new job, and he becomes a repairer of clocks. Davies had had a long-standing interest in clocks and automata. He had made scrapbooks about clocks and had long been fascinated by the mechanical toys to which the old clockmakers had brought patient and skilful workmanship. He enjoyed the simple automaton that had stood for many years in the foyer of Ed's Warehouse Restaurant on King Street in Toronto—"it was a figure of a gypsy who handed you a printed card upon which was the answer to any question that you murmured into the bell jar in which she was located"—and had parted with twenty-five cents on three separate occasions to consult her, getting "a remarkably effective answer every time." It was probably because she knew of this interest that Brenda's Aunt Elsa gave Davies the Edwardian cane whose monkey head stuck out its tongue at the press of a button. So when Paul patiently repairs old clocks at the Victoria and Albert Museum in London and the Musée d'Art et d'Histoire in Geneva, fixes the monkey stick broken by the little girl at his *pension* and repairs the 120-odd fixable mechanical toys in Jeremias Naegeli's wrecked collection at Sorgenfrei, we experience Davies' own enchantment, not only with the marvel of the clocks and the mechanical toys themselves but with Magnus' superlative craftsmanship.

There is further "wonder" in Magnus' narrative. His story is told as a flood of reminiscence, in order to assist a film crew to understand the inner life that might have lain concealed behind the conventional public mask of Jean-Eugène Robert-Houdin. (Eisengrim is impersonating the great nineteenth-century French illusionist for BBC television.) But as the tale unfolds, the reader gradually realizes that Magnus' experience has indeed made him uniquely capable of portraying this figure from the past. Not only does he command his predecessor's traditional sleights-of-hand, he has also mastered the intricate clockwork needed to recreate Robert-Houdin's Wonderful Bakery, his Inexhaustible

Punch Bowl, his Miraculous Orange Tree and the other illusions. And his years with Sir John Tresize have made him thoroughly familiar with nineteenth-century stage techniques and with the elegancies of manner, carriage, costume and make-up that distinguished Robert-Houdin's *Soirées Fantastiques*. Robert-Houdin was a marvel in the nineteenth century; Magnus' ability to recreate him to the life in the twentieth is an even greater one.

On June 24, 1974, with the first draft just off his typewriter, Davies wrote to Gordon Roper: "I finished the novel this morning, and wish I knew what to make of it. It has been uncommonly tough chewing, because as you know I never intended a trilogy, and so had made no preparation for pulling three books into a unity; attempting to do this without violent warping, or recourse to such passages as…'As my reader will recall, from our earlier volumes'—(which was the method in the Tom Swift books) nor yet chewing the old cabbage twice and even thrice, has been tedious in the extreme. But I think I have managed somehow, if not well, and have even managed a surprise or two."

Fifth Business had told the story of Dunstan Ramsay, one of the three Deptford boys whose lives had been profoundly affected by the loaded snowball. Now, in making *World of Wonders* the story of Paul Dempster, Davies was also inviting readers to see *The Manticore*, at least partly, as the story of Boy Staunton. From the moment he had conceived it, he had meant *The Manticore* not only to deal with David Staunton's reconciliation with himself and his father, but also to tell the story of Boy Staunton's own life as "reflected from his son."

In telling Magnus' story, which covers almost the same time period as *Fifth Business* and revisits many of the events in it, Davies had an opportunity to illustrate how experience is distorted by character and circumstance, as Browning had in *The Ring and the Book*. And in this he was wholly successful. The shift in point of view from one volume to the next is one of the great novelistic accomplishments of the trilogy. Again and again the reader is pleasurably surprised in finding familiar situations and scenes to be newly unfamiliar, seen from a different character's perspective yet ringing just as true. It is satisfying, too, that the narrative method of each book is appropriate to the character of the narrator: the scholarly, secretive Dunstan retires to his study to write the story of his life for posthumous perusal by the headmaster of his old school; advocate David Staunton prepares his tale as a series of "briefs"; and polished performer Magnus Eisengrim presents his as after-dinner reminiscences to a receptive audience relaxing over brandy and cigars.

As important to the unity of the trilogy as the framework of the initiating snowball scene and its consequences is the world-view it presents—a world-view that owes much of its clarity to Davies' reading of Jung. For Davies, the universe is full of wonders, and it has purpose, pattern and meaning. Although the immense forces that brought the universe into being and continue to influence it lie beyond our ken, they do not lie beyond our awareness, and life is only wholly satisfying when we accept this awareness and explore it. For Davies, each stage of life brings its own challenges, which must be confronted if we are not to lose our bearings. Either way, our choices have real consequences that can extend far into the future. To understand our present, then, we must understand what we have inherited from our past: it has much to teach us. The collective unconscious, the deepest level of the mind, is a particularly potent legacy from the human past that we share.

Davies' world-view is woven deeply into the trilogy. We have seen how Dunstan Ramsay and David Staunton in *Fifth Business* and *The Manticore* meet the crisis of middle age, both of them confronting and coming to terms with their shadow and anima. In *World of Wonders*, Magnus, too, successfully reorients himself as he moves into the second half of life. Like Dunstan and David, he begins with very little self-knowledge. When he first joins the acting troupe, he has to be told that the reason Sir John Tresize so dislikes him is that, as "a seedy little carnie, with the shifty eyes of a pickpocket and the breath of somebody that eats the cheapest food," he embodies everything the great actor has taken a lifetime to eliminate from his own character and appearance. In short, he is Sir John's shadow. But, partly to please Milady, he also becomes Sir John's double. Setting out to make himself over in Sir John's image, he wolfishly devours every aspect of his idol, seeking not only to be *like* the actor, but to *be* him—and he succeeds very well. Sir John accepts this only because of the professional advantage it brings: Magnus' uncanny likeness to him onstage makes it possible for Sir John to play dual roles with brilliant effectiveness. But by the time Magnus approaches middle age, and he and Liesl are putting together their magic show, he has understood himself well enough to acknowledge his own wolfish shadow. He takes the stage name Eisengrim—"the name of the wolf in the old fables; but the name really means the sinister hardness, the cruelty of iron itself. I took the name, and recognized the fact, and thereby got it up out of my depths so that at least I could be aware of it and take a look at it, now and then. I won't say I domesticated the wolf, but I knew where his lair was, and what he might do."

As a young man, Magnus also shares with Dunstan and David an inability to achieve a complete relationship with a woman. But in middle age, he successfully makes this passage as well, and Liesl Naegeli again plays a key supporting role. On November 6, 1972, when Davies suddenly realized that the new novel would centre on Magnus, he wrote to Gordon Roper: "It is obvious that sex will appear in this book, as it has done in the two others, as something nearly akin to servitude. Ramsay flees from it; Edward [David] rejects it; Eisengrim is 'used' nastily by Willard. But there is another element. Ramsay finds sex as a fulfilling element in Liesl; so does Edward; so will Eisengrim. But why with such an ugly woman? Because, so far as I can see, she offers understanding, sympathy and a kind of adult sex that is far from the romance of the usual novel. Is this any good? I am puzzled by it, but as it is what I am impelled to write, I write it."

When the young, grotesquely deformed Liesl falls in love with Magnus, the brilliant reanimator of her grandfather's mechanical toys, he politely rebuffs her advances and tells her about his relationships with Willard and Milady, at which she jeers: "From buggery to selfless, knightly adoration at one splendid leap!" They get into a knock-down, drag-out fight, which ends in sexual intercourse, and in time they develop a warm friendship. By the time he came to write this, Davies had realized the answer to his question to Roper. When Liesl describes herself as "the Loathly Maiden in the Arthurian stories," it is clear that in

Jungian terms she is a woman upon whom one cannot hang an anima projection. Each of the men in turn is initially repelled by her hideous appearance, and this allows them to get to know and appreciate her as a person, and eventually to recognize her peculiar beauty as well.

Boy Staunton, in contrast, fails to make the mid-life reorientation. Clinging to the values of the first half of life, he gains neither wisdom nor self-knowledge as he grows older. For him, age brings waning sexual prowess, the offer of a splendid post that carries no real power and finally the desire to "get into a car and drive away from the whole damned thing."

In all three volumes of the Deptford trilogy, Davies portrays myth and fairy-tale as transmitters of the human inheritance. Dunstan, in particular, articulates the view that myth depicts recurring character types, situations and actions. His brief references in *Fifth Business* to Oedipus, Mars, Venus and Ganymede reveal a constant awareness of the "mythical elements" that "underlie our apparently ordinary lives." When Boy shows him a set of nude photographs of his wife, Leola, Dunstan is reminded of the myth of King Candaules, who displayed his Queen in the nude to his friend Gyges. He tells the story, with both its unpleasant endings, to Boy to make him realize that he has carried his ego games into dangerous territory. Boy scoffs, but the myth later proves relevant. Leola does take a fancy to Dunstan, who debates with himself: "Was the story of Gyges and Candaules to have the ending in which Gyges takes his friend's wife? No; upon the whole I thought not." In the second ending, Gyges kills Candaules. Although Dunstan's part in Boy's death is unclear at the end of *Fifth Business*, he certainly shares responsibility for it. Dunstan makes it clear that not only do myths have contemporary relevance, but those who recognize their depiction of deep psychological patterns gain a measure of insight and control over their lives as a result. He outmanoeuvres Boy because he has a deeper understanding of the game that Boy himself has introduced.

David Staunton in *The Manticore* recalls Dunstan's insistence on the importance of myth in his history classes at Colborne College: "The bee in his bonnet was that history and myth are two aspects of a kind of grand pattern in human destiny: history is the mass of observable or recorded fact, but myth is the abstract or essence of it. He used to dredge up extraordinary myths that none of us had ever heard of and demonstrate—in a fascinating way, I must admit—how they contained some truth that was applicable to widely divergent historical situations." At the end of the book, Dunstan recounts the legend of St. Gall, concluding with an observation especially relevant to David: "if we are really wise, we will make a working arrangement with the bear that lives with us, because otherwise we shall starve or perhaps be eaten by the bear." When, in *World of Wonders*, Dunstan suggests that Magnus' initial servitude to and ultimate vengeance on Willard is an instance of the myth of "the man who is in search of his soul, and who must struggle with a monster to secure it," he is drawing a modern parallel with the stories of saints who killed or mastered dragons.

But the Deptford trilogy has more than this to say in urging the relevance of the past to the present. Near the end of *World of Wonders*, Liesl describes the "Magian World View" that, according to Spengler, was embedded in the outlook of the Middle Ages: "It was a sense of the unfathomable wonder of the invisible world that existed side by side with a hard recognition of the roughness and cruelty and day-to-day demands of the tangible world. It was a readiness to see demons where nowadays we see neuroses, and to see the hand of a guardian angel in what we are apt to shrug off ungratefully as a stroke of luck. It was religion, but a religion with a thousand gods, none of them all-powerful and most of them ambiguous in their attitude toward man. It was poetry and wonder which might reveal themselves in the dunghill, and it was an understanding of the dunghill that lurks in poetry and wonder." To Liesl, it is a great loss that "We have educated ourselves into a world from which wonder, and the fear and dread and splendour and freedom of wonder have been banished. Of course wonder is costly. You couldn't incorporate it into a modern state, because it is the antithesis of the anxiously worshipped security which is what a modern state is asked to give. Wonder is marvellous but it is also cruel, cruel, cruel. It is undemocratic, discriminatory, and pitiless."

The capacity for wonder is present in all three of the central characters. Dunstan believes Mary Dempster to be a saint, and tells his friend Padre Blazon about meeting the devil disguised as a woman. David Staunton glimpses the Magian World View on his way out of the bear cave, and Magnus, who is far less a rationalist than either of the others, finds wonder everywhere—in the stories from *A Child's Book of Saints*, in the carnival, in the theatre, in his feelings for Milady, in the great cross-Canada train tour, even in mechanical toys. And he knows the dark side of the Magian world, too, since he allows the Devil, walking by his side at the Deptford fair, to plunge him into a desolating hell of physical and moral degradation. Again and again, Magnus' life has a fairy-tale quality, as when the apelike young Liesl attacks him in his workroom at Sorgenfrei, only to have him deal her a debilitating blow to the diaphragm, bend one of her legs backward, sit on her—and engage her in conversation!

All three novels suggest that it is the role of the artist to make wonders accessible to the rest of us. In *Fifth Business*, Magnus makes it possible for audiences hungry for "romance and marvels" to experience the sense of wonder he himself experiences daily. In *The Manticore*, the analyst tells David that "great myths are not invented stories but objectivizations of images and situations that lie very deep in the human spirit; a poet may make a great embodiment of a myth, but it is the mass of humanity that knows the myth to be a spiritual truth, and that is why they cherish his poem." As the creator of the *Soirée of Illusions* in *Fifth Business*, Magnus presents "such visions and illusions as had nourished the imagination of mankind for two thousand years." As the great magician in *World of Wonders*—"A man who can stand stark naked in the midst of a crowd and keep it gaping for an hour while he manipulates a few coins, or cards, or billiard balls"—he embodies the wizardly aspect of the Wise Old Man.

The trilogy also expresses many of Davies' convictions about the great forces of good and evil and their relation to human life. The characters we come to admire for their breadth and wholeness are conscious of dimensions beyond the merely human, responding to them with awe and wonder and an appreciation of their personal implications. Dunstan Ramsay in *Fifth Business* is

convinced of the saintliness of Mary Dempster and of the mirac-
ulousness of her three interventions into the natural order. He
has a brush with the Devil, and achieves greater self-knowledge
as a result. The much less self-aware David Staunton in *The
Manticore* views worship as a matter of convention—until he
experiences the terror and awe that grip him in the scramble
from the cave. Magnus Eisengrim in *World of Wonders* permits
the Devil to intervene in his life when a boy, and believes himself
condemned to Hell as a result, until he is redeemed by the influence of Milady and later acknowledges and controls his wolfishly
evil streak. Boy, the anti-hero of the trilogy, has a mind closed to
revelation. His religious observance is dictated by society's values
rather than conviction, and in the end he becomes an atheist.
Many of the passages that surround Magnus' narration, introducing speculations about God and the Devil, give direct expression to Davies' own views.

At one time or another Davies considered calling the new book
"A Bottle in the Smoke" or "Merlin's Laugh," but in the end
these became the titles of the novel's main sections. The manuscript he forwarded to his agent on January 17, 1975, bore the
title *World of Wonders.*

Macmillan of Canada published it at the beginning of October
and Viking the following March in the United States. Macmillan
of London refused the manuscript (this was the second time a
British publisher had deserted Davies after publishing two volumes of a trilogy), and W. H. Allen finally brought it out there in
June 1977. The more influential North American reviewers
judged, with some dissenting voices, that Davies' imaginative *tour
de force*, begun with *Fifth Business*, had been vigorously sustained
in the trilogy's final book. *Time* magazine (May 17, 1976) spoke
for many in its opinion that "Davies is not only Canada's finest
active novelist but also one of the most gifted and accomplished
literary entertainers now writing in English." Hardcover sales followed the pattern established by the other two books—14,311 in
Canada, 7,760 in the United States, and 1,200 in Britain.

By now, paperback publication had become very important.
The New American Library had brought out *Fifth Business* in a

Signet edition in 1971, and *The Manticore* had appeared in
Curtis Books in 1974. Solid numbers are elusive—a February
1975 *Toronto Star* article asserts that *The Manticore* had at that
point sold 50,000 paperback copies in Canada alone—but
unquestionably North American sales for both books were
impressive. When in 1976 Penguin acquired the rights to publish all three volumes of the trilogy in Canada, the United States
and the Commonwealth, marketing entered a new phase. By the
end of 1976, cumulative sales of *Fifth Business* in all forms had
reached 145,000.

With the publication of the Deptford trilogy, many Canadians
began to accord Davies the status of a national treasure. This
manifested itself in a startling manner at the opening of the
Stratford Festival in 1977. A crowd of about two hundred people (which included a reporter from the *Globe and Mail*) had
assembled to watch the arrival of the first-night patrons. As
Davies approached the theatre, a large woman lunged out of the
crowd and pulled at his beard:

"Oooh, it's lovely, isn't it?" she said, as her fingers
clutched the learned whiskers.

"Stop that," bellowed the master of Massey College, and
author of *Fifth Business*, "it's extraordinarily rude and vulgar to assault someone like that you don't even know."

There was a moment's pause, and then the woman said:
"But, you're Robertson Davies, aren't you?"

To which Davies responded: "And you, Madam. Who
the devil are you?"

Chapter 14

THE REBEL ANGELS: 1976-81

Enoch relates that after conspiring with one another, two
hundred angels under the leadership of Samiazaz descended to
earth, took the daughters of men to wife, and begat with them
giants three thousand ells long. The angels, among whom Azazel
particularly excelled, taught mankind the arts and sciences. They
proved to be extraordinarily progressive elements who broadened
and developed man's consciousness....
—C. G. Jung, Answer to Job, 1954

MANY COMMENTS IN his journalism imply that Davies hoped
that his sixties, seventies and eighties would be his *floreat*—the
years when, after a lifetime of preparation, he would finally hit
his stride as an author. He was happy to think that his was a calling that could profit from systematic application and long experience. Had not Thomas Mann, a hard worker every day of his
life, published one of his finest books at the age of seventy-nine,
just a year before he died?

Certainly, Davies' own intellectual energy showed no sign of
waning as he moved toward the customary age of retirement. On
November 10, 1977, then sixty-four, he wrote to Horace
Davenport about the continuing urge to spend hours at his desk:

"I have a vast program of work ahead of me, and sometimes I quake and grow pale, for it looks as if the Twilight Years, when I ought to be growing roses and sucking my dentures in peace, are going to be passed in back-breaking toil. But I keep hearing my mother's voice saying 'It is better to wear out than rust out'. That's what a Calvinist upbringing does to you, and not all my fine Anglican prating about Good and Evil really makes any difference."

The three novels that are now known as the Cornish trilogy were the chief result of this sustained burst of energy. Davies published *The Rebel Angels* in 1981, having turned sixty-eight and retired from university work, and the other novels followed in 1985 and 1988. These are big books, sweeping in conception and substantial in length. Davies was still seeing the world through Jungian eyes, but he had now shifted his focus from the psychological development of his characters to much broader concerns, nothing less, indeed, than the nature and the underpinnings of the culture that had nurtured him.

In his early years at the university, while *Fifth Business* was being conceived, Davies knew that he was resented and even mocked in certain academic quarters. But by the time he was planning and writing *The Rebel Angels*, the atmosphere around him was much warmer. During the 1970s, the University of Toronto had finally followed the example of many other Canadian institutions of higher learning and expanded its offerings in Canadian literature. The signal success of the Deptford trilogy in the United States and Canada had brought Davies' writing academic recognition, so that his novels were widely included on the new course lists, and the trickle of academic articles on his work had become a steady flow. Three brief critical books had appeared, and in 1972 Gordon Roper had published an influential article that laid out *Fifth Business'* Jungian foundations and suggested new and challenging ways to approach Davies' writing. Roper gave another boost to Davies' authorial reputation in 1977 with "A Davies Log," in an issue of the *Journal of Canadian Studies* devoted entirely to Davies' work. This year-by-year catalogue of Davies' output as playwright, journalist, reviewer, public speaker and novelist was an astonishment to the many who had known him in only one of his roles. Like Roper's earlier article, the "Davies Log" provided academics with new resources to work with. In the next four years there were two collections of his journalism, a volume of articles on the Deptford trilogy, an annotated bibliography of writing by and on him (which ran to 222 pages) and a special issue of *Canadian Drama* dedicated to his plays.

By the late '70s Davies' strengths had become known and valued in the academic community. A reviewer, commenting in *Theatre History in Canada* on a paper Davies had given in 1978, wrote:

> Robertson Davies' contribution is 'Mixed Grill: Touring Fare in Canada, 1920-1935'. The title is apt: this is a jumble of personal reminiscences and impressions which ought to be vile history, but isn't. Instead it is a goldmine of eye-witnessed greatness, tempting snapshots (oh to see a real Mutt and Jeff show!) and glimpses of the sources of *World of Wonders*. Professor Davies triumphs because his pellucid prose often transcends the Plain Style in flashes of Shavian lightning, but never falls below it, and because he rejoices in our history, with a joy that carries us with him. While the other qualities of a good historian can be acquired, these are conferred by Clio herself. The rest of us must do what we can, with what we have been given.

For a week during June or July in each of 1976, 1977 and 1978, the years when he was gathering his thoughts for *The Rebel Angels*, Davies co-conducted a seminar on fiction at the Wesleyan-Suffield Writers' Conference in Middletown, Connecticut. The experience failed to shake his conviction that good writing, the product of innate ability and application, cannot be taught, except in a very limited sense. In 1977 he also selected twenty-two of his speeches for publication under the title *One Half of Robertson Davies: Provocative Pronouncements on a Wide Range of Topics*. The speeches had been given between 1960 and 1977 to all sorts of audiences—architects, industrial accountants, guests of Massey College, the girls of Bishop

Strachan School, psychiatrists—and they demonstrate Davies' immense skill at making his insights and enthusiasms accessible and interesting. Some of the pieces are slight, but others, like the "Masks of Satan" lectures, which explore the ideas about evil underlying the Deptford trilogy, invite a considered reaction.

Since the trilogy had aroused a good deal of curiosity about Davies the private man, many readers welcomed the personal glimpses afforded by *One Half.* When Macmillan published it in Canada in October 1977 and Viking in the United States in April 1978, most reviewers praised it, but a couple, including the writer Joyce Carol Oates, attacked it and Davies fiercely. She declared him an old fogy of modest talent and expressed indignation that he should be considered Canada's leading man of letters. In his reply to the editors of the *New Republic*, Davies parried skilfully:

> The expression, "Canada's leading man of letters," which Ms. Oates objects to so strongly when applied to myself, pleases me as little as it does her. Not only does it ignore the claims of better men; it is itself a term somewhat out-moded and comic, belonging to the era of spats and piqué vest-edgings. But when it is used of me by people who mean it kindly, am I to be churlish and snarl? No, but I may be grateful to Ms. Oates, who has done so on my behalf.
>
> About her strictures on my personal character it would be foolish for me to protest. We are not acquainted, and as she says she has read comparatively little of my work it must be assumed she has made her discoveries about me by divination. Critics have often laid claim to this power, and when Ms. Oates portrays me as a garrulous, self-delighted mountebank, and a covert undervaluer of women, I can only hang my head in shame, for when has any man known himself as well as a richly gifted observer knows him? ...
>
> Desolated as I am by her opinion, I have some hope that Ms. Oates may not have divined the whole truth about me. She confides to your readers that "Davies is said to regret that public floggings and hangings have been discarded."

Who says it, I wonder? Whence comes this portrait of Davies, the Hangman's Friend? It is true that I sometimes take extreme views on controversial subjects in order to get the goat of campus sorceresses and others who will believe anything they hear, provided it be ugly enough; I have never been able to resist tormenting people who have no sense of humour.

Considering the character that has been ascribed to me by Ms. Oates it would be disingenuous if I were to subscribe myself "Yours sincerely" or "Yours faithfully," so I am content to remain,

Yours, writhing in deserved ignominy,
Robertson Davies
Toronto, Canada

Davies had written the notes and outlines for his plays and novels in his "Works in Progress" notebook since 1952, and forty pages remained unused when he began to plan *The Rebel Angels*. But now he opened a new notebook, even though the five novels he had planned in the old one had taken only fifteen to twenty-eight pages apiece. He obviously anticipated that he would need more space than usual, and so he did. The notes for the Cornish trilogy fill 224 pages in the new 51/2-by-8-inch, three-ringed notebook, 111 for *The Rebel Angels* alone. And from the first entry in August 1976, they took a new form. Davies dropped the character sketches and outlines he had employed in working out *Tempest-Tost* and *Leaven of Malice*, and also the mixture of story outline and brief notation he had used in *A Mixture of Frailties* and the Deptford trilogy. Instead he recorded, in order as he thought of them, items of information and ideas for characters and incidents. On each page he would begin at "a," usually getting to "c," "d," "e" or "f" before beginning the alphabet again on the next page. Sometimes several notes in sequence refer to the same subject, but just as often they bear no relation to their neighbours. Apart from cross-references, there is no overview or synthesis. No one except Davies, who was evolving the complex structure of the story in his head as he moved from note to note, could possibly have imagined the shape *The Rebel Angels* would take from the evidence in the notebook.

The reason Davies needed more space than usual was that he was planning a book quite different in its focus from its predecessors. *The Rebel Angels* was not only to tell the story of a number of characters but would take as its subject one of western civilization's great institutions, the university. He meant the book to be a kind of grand summing up of everything he had come to think and feel about the university since his miraculous admission to Queen's, after his inability to grasp high school mathematics had prevented him from matriculating. Oxford had intensified his sense of privilege, all the more when it had almost slipped through his fingers as a result of his emotional tangle over Eleanor Sweezey. And as the founding Master of Massey College, he had done everything he could to realize his particular vision of academic life, combining the dedication that he had experienced at Queen's with the lightness of spirit that he had encountered at Oxford. Now he wanted to portray the university's complexity: its range, curiosity, idealism and playfulness, its failings and frustrations, its deep medieval roots, the intensity of its intellectual focus and the lack of balance that that could produce. The portrait would be highly coloured, because Davies' university is rife with uncommon interests, zealous pursuits and idiosyncratic individuals. And he was relieved when it turned out that it would not appear in print until after he had retired from Massey College, for even though, as he told his old friends Gordon Roper and Horace Davenport, it was to be "a celebration of what is great in universities" and "a great paean to the learned life," he anticipated that some aspects of the portrait would give offense.

For the most part, Davies' conception of the university is strongly positive. He sees the university as a true community, joined in the pursuit of knowledge for its own sake, the inheritor of a tradition that stretches back to the foundations of medieval Europe. At its heart is its body of learned men and women, for, as one of his academics observes, "the young come and go, but we remain." Ideally, it is the custodian of civilization and sets the intellectual tone of the nation. Its students come there not to get trained but to be educated, to reflect and to feel. "A university," as he observed in a lecture while he was planning *The Rebel Angels*, "ought to be an ocean in which the student bathes, not a tank in which he frantically fishes." At its best, he believes that the life of scholarship demands a selfless commitment, an intensity, a kind of idealism that is truly religious; that its research is undertaken in a hopeful, generous spirit, and that the object of its pursuit is not just knowledge but truth; that the university is genuinely an Alma Mater, dispensing the milk of knowledge and of salvation; that in its search for wisdom, it makes a second paradise of learning. At its best, too, university life is merry, amusing and hospitable.

But Davies also had strong views on the institution's deficiencies, limitations and peculiarities. The university, he believes, has often allowed itself to become cut off from the life of the civilization it serves, and it has often failed to take up the greatest challenges of the day. Many of its members pursue knowledge at the expense of wisdom, and do it in a leaden, plodding and selfish manner. Many students want and are given only training; the balancing search for self-knowledge is often neglected, with the result that non-intellectual capacities are not cultivated and may erupt in undisciplined ways. Diversity of opinion and scruple may, and often do, strangle decisive action. And academics are frequently quarrelsome, spiteful and arrogant.

Particularly at the beginning of his notebook (but also at intervals throughout), he recorded his observations, reflections and ideas about the university and the life within its precincts:

3c What scholarship does to the scholar: 1: to make him merry? 2. to make him gloomy cf. C. Leech & his 'the tragic view is the only possible view': projection of inner content on the world of learning.

3d getting at a man by failing his candidates for Ph.D....

8b Universities formerly dominated by Church & theology: now by government & science: i.e. what lies at the heart of power in their time

9b students 'joyfully frotting & rubbing their bacon together' (check Urq. *Rab.*) & think this Life - & at their age it is.

But: the heart of a Univ. is its body of learned men & it can be no better than that: students come to be warmed at this fire: the scholars preach & sometimes they convert.

9c Univ. not a 'city of youth': is quite as much 'a city of wisdom': intelligent societies have always preserved their Wise Men (not the same as artists) & of course they are sometimes not really wise. BUT: we must not allow the pedants & opportunists to shape our lives & our univs.: nor the scoundrels & thieves to disillusion us - St. Nicholas' clerks - & scholars.

10b When are college flags flown? On the founder's day, or a saint's day. When are university flags flown? When the faculty are being squeezed for the Community Chest or some endowment fund. Those are the holy days of our society.

10d drunks huddled on winter nights in abandoned cars on student parking lot: priest from Newman House seeking them lest they freeze: rookeries owned by Univ. filled with students, filthy, cold & stinking

24f The classroom smell: a Symphony in the Key of Feet, with additions of dirty clothes & sweat.

It is clear from the novel that Davies intended the action to take place at colleges very like Massey and its neighbour, Trinity, and that the large university of which both are part was meant to resemble the University of Toronto. The notes contain phrases like "Master of Coulter" (21a, 24b) or "Coulter High Table" (50d). (The name "Coulter College," like the "Ploughwright" that he eventually settled on, recalls the Masseys' connection with farm machinery.) The personality of St. John and the Holy Ghost, an Anglican foundation like the real-world Trinity College, was also implicit from the start, though it acquired its name bit by bit:

6a College of the Holy Spirit? called familiarly 'Spook'—? Head a Rector? The Rector of Spook. (vide 19-d)

19d 'The College of St. Paul and the Holy Ghost': festal
    day the Conversion of St. Paul. Jan. 25.: Called 'Paul's'
    and 'Spook': head is Rector
98a College of St. John and the Holy Ghost: from <u>Mark</u>
    <u>1</u>: thus 'Spook'

From the beginning, as Davies explained in a letter he wrote
about the time he began to make notes, he intended to include
one or perhaps two murders. As he saw it, the "murder of reputa-
tions and robbing people of their place in the world" were frequent in university life, so that it seemed extraordinary to him
that outright physical murders were so rare. And he actually had
a particular murder in mind, that of the homosexual English
biographer James Pope-Hennessy, whom he had known at
Oxford. (Note 6e is the first reference to it: "The Pope-Hennessy
murder as an example of what may come of 'rough trade.'")
Davies had read in *The Dictionary of National Biography* that
Pope-Hennessy had received a large advance to write the life of
Sir Nöel Coward, and had foolishly advertised the fact, with the
result that "On 25 January 1974 he was brutally murdered by
some ruffianly associates of the unscrupulous youths with whom
he chose to consort. For during his last years an addiction to
alcohol and what Peter Quennell has called the 'denizens of
back-street bars and pubs' led him to take appalling risks of
blackmail and violence." The method of the killing struck
Davies as especially grisly for a man of Pope-Hennessy's delicate
refinement and vivid imagination—a dagger had been thrust
into his cheek and slowly up into his brain. By the time Davies
came to use the material in the book, however, he had moved a
long way from that starting point, though hints of it persist in
the element of homosexuality and in the method.

Two of the main characters in *The Rebel Angels* were to be
partly drawn from particular individuals. One of them was John
Pearson, Davies' friend and fellow "Sterq" from his days at Upper
Canada College. Pearson was for Davies an example of the brilliant student who throws away his initial promise. A multitude
of details from Pearson's life (only a few of them represented in
the notes) provide the background for the renegade monk John

Parlabane: the brilliance that won him prestigious scholarships to the University of Toronto and a year's fellowship at Princeton; a doctoral thesis at the University of Toronto on the history of scepticism from the Greeks to the present, a mother preoccupied with one lost cause or another; a face scarred by hot glue from an exploding pot; weak eyes that made heavy spectacles a necessity; the disdain of the girls to whom he was attracted; his sexual initiation by the wife of a poet during his M.A. year at the University of Toronto; and a slide into dissipation after a glorious homosexual love affair at Princeton that came to nothing. Pearson's story continued with academic appointments that ended amid rumours of homosexual misdoings with students, overeating, drinking and drug abuse. There was a modest inheritance, a dissolute period in the isles of Greece, a letter from the Princeton lover that moved him to join an Anglican order in England, letters appealing to Davies and several other friends (each one believing himself unique) for $500 to finance his exit from the order and an interval back in Toronto, which ended on Hallowe'en in 1958 when he put a shotgun in his mouth and blew his head off. Furthermore, he had named Davies his literary executor for an unpublishable "long philosophical harangue in which he settled scores with everybody with whom he had crossed swords during his unhappy life." Pearson's persuasive tongue, his thorough-going scepticism, his ruined face and his renounced monasticism reminded Davies of Lucifer, the eloquent angel who raised a rebellion in Heaven and who ended, his beauty seared and distorted, by ruling in Hell.

The character of Professor Urquhart McVarish was to incorporate many of the habits and characteristics of Professor W. A. C. H. Dobson, Davies' nemesis at Massey College, although the notebook records only a couple of them. Davies had gathered that Dobson would fuss about his hair and had been known to wear a hairnet to breakfast with the other senior residents of the college. That his hairdresser had been the guest of honour at one of his bi-weekly sherry parties. That he had gloried immodestly in his war record as an officer in a first-class British regiment. That, descended from a Scots laird, he had liked to play the high-born Scot. That his rooms had been graced by objects which, it was rumoured, ought to have been in storage at the Royal Ontario Museum. That he had treated the college staff and some junior Fellows contemptuously, had referred to himself immodestly as an excellent scholar and had given no thought to making his research accessible and interesting to outsiders at general lectures. That instead of guiding his graduate students through the doctoral program and thesis, he had used them as assistants, and that when they had protested that they needed doctorates if they were to get jobs elsewhere, he had asserted that "anybody who had studied with him could go anywhere in the world and get an academic appointment on that qualification alone." That told to mend his ways or step down as head of the Department of East Asian Studies, he had given up the chair but retained the salary and full-time secretary while teaching only one, lightly attended course.

As Davies began to make his notes in August 1976, he wrote to Elisabeth Sifton, his editor at Viking since 1972 and a woman he had come to like and admire, that the new book "might just possibly turn out to be another trilogy. Subject: money, the love thereof and the rich comedy that ensues therefrom. Setting: a university, because nowhere is money, and the greed for benefactions so great." Davies had a good deal of knowledge by now on the subject of benefactors, founders and donors, all the way from Lady Perriam, whose generosity had been acknowledged in the nickname of the Balliol lavatories, to the Masseys and their contemporaries. As a collector and as an author he had himself already been approached by several university libraries interested in acquiring his books and papers. At first he thought he would focus his book on this aspect of university life. A few of his notes concern a character who must find benefactions for Coulter College, and several refer to the university's desire for a great benefactor. A couple consider the perspective of the donors and collectors themselves. But ultimately this became only one of many strands rather than a dominant concern of the novel.

An early note, which proved to be very important in the long run, runs as follows: "[10e]...Douglas Duncan: pictures so thick on the floor one cd. only walk in narrow paths: completely filled three neighbouring apartments pics. thick in bedroom - even in bathroom. Also dressed v. poorly. Sat on floor a great deal." Duncan was a Toronto art collector and bibliophile. At the time of his death in 1968, his collections had taken over three apartments, and although he had made an attempt at imposing order on one of them, the other two, according to an old friend, "still presented an engulfing scene of shelves, stacks, trunks, boxes and cartons—not only of pictures, books, and gramophone records, but also of correspondence, old programmes, Christmas cards going back to childhood, and all the various objects of sentiment as well as art accumulated over many years." For years Duncan had had sole responsibility for the non-profit Picture Loan Society, which encouraged Canadian artists by taking their works on consignment, renting or selling them and arranging exhibitions. However, the Society's records had become increasingly disorganized, and it was not clear at his death which of the pictures in his possession were his own. It had taken the selfless dedication of his sister and three skilled men (including Norman Endicott, whom Davies knew as a fellow professor of English at the University of Toronto) to sort things out. (The most important paintings went to the National Gallery, the fine editions to the Thomas Fisher Rare Book Library at the University of Toronto, and lesser accumulations of art were presented to some forty-four institutions across the country.) Davies richly embroidered the tale when he set Arthur Cornish and Professors McVarish, Simon Darcourt and Clement Hollier to work on the estate of Francis Cornish.

For Davies, the contemporary university descends directly from the foundations of the Middle Ages. In 1961, during the planning of Massey College, he had visited Oxford in England and Coimbra in Portugal to steep himself in those origins. Just when the medieval science of alchemy occurred to him as a way of demonstrating the link between the university's present and its past is not clear. Possibly the seed had been planted late in the 1960s when he read Jung's declaration that "However remote alchemy may seem to us today, we should not underestimate its cultural importance for the Middle Ages. Today is the child of the Middle Ages and it cannot disown its parents." Certainly he made the decision early, because the first entry in the new notebook concerns a book by the alchemist Henricus Cornelius Agrippa.

Davies had long known about the alchemists' search for the elixir of life, the supposed secret of eternal youth, and for the philosopher's stone that could transform base metals into gold. (He had known about it, indeed, since the age of eleven, when he read in Victor Hugo's *Notre Dame de Paris* about the alchemist/priest who lusts after the beautiful Gypsy girl Esmeralda. He read the novel a fourth time in July 1978, while planning *The Rebel Angels*.) From Jung's *Alchemical Studies* (translated in 1967) and *Psychology and Alchemy* (revised and translated in 1968), he had become aware that Jung viewed alchemy not only as the precursor of modern chemistry and metallurgy but also of modern psychology and psychotherapy, since it emphasized the kind of personal development that brought the psyche into balance and wholeness. Jung argued that modern civilization cannot understand itself unless it grasps the nature of the civilization before it, which cannot itself be understood without understanding the medieval science of alchemy. By 1969, when the Stratford Festival performed *The Alchemist* and he spoke at its seminar about "Ben Jonson and Alchemy," Davies had not only chewed his way through these big difficult books, he had made a modest study of alchemy in other sources, including E. J. Holmyard's *Alchemy* and Lynn Thorndike's *A History of Magic and Experimental Science*.

These sources introduced him to the network of connections that had once pertained between the science of alchemy, dung, the physician Paracelsus, Gypsies, Gnosticism and the apocryphal *Book of Enoch*. As he prepared to write his novel, he expanded his understanding of the strands through even broader reading; the notebook makes specific references to thirty-four books, and he evidently absorbed information from many more. Although he would not in the end do as much with the alchemical connections as he had anticipated (and I will consider only a little of what the notebook contains), it is this web that gives *The Rebel Angels* much of its idiosyncratic quality.

Initially, he intended to make the academic whom he eventually called Professor Clement Hollier an alchemist, or, more accurately, a professor whose field of study is alchemy. In 7b he considered possible names for his "alchemist," and on page 14 he wrote:

> Sumner [later Hollier], in his investigation of Alchemy, is a paleo-psychologist - cross appointment to Centre for History of Science & Technology - began as a medieval-ist....

By 17a he was reflecting

> The junk in Templar's [Hollier's] rooms - decor it cannot be called - because things related to Alchemy gravitate to him: globes & astrolabes given: a visitor might laugh thinking it stagey & contrived but it was not - just happened. - His carrel in the Central Univ. Lib. the same: that is where the alchemical bks. are concentrated: but he has some fine ones of his own, bought at great cost. Sold his family's house to buy *Chymical Marriage*? A fine *Cabbala*? with annotations by somebody?

And there are more notes in the same vein.

From the beginning, Davies intended his scientist, Ozias Froats, to engage in the study of human waste products, especially the faeces. This permitted him to develop the alchemical notion, stressed by Jung, that the all-important philosopher's stone or elixir is hard to recognize because it is "thrown out into the street" or "cast upon the dung-heap" or "found in filth." It is "*exilis*" or "uncomely," and so common and ordinary that it may be picked up anywhere. It is (in a quotation from 1 Peter 2:7 that Davies has known all his life) "the stone which the builders rejected, the same is become the head of the corner." Sir William Osler's observation in *The Principles and Practice of Medicine* that there are changes in the bowel movements of people about to come down with tuberculosis, and the great doctor's declaration "that this kind of diagnosis was neglected and that it might prove extremely significant in the future," further encouraged Davies to feel that he could plausibly give Froats a research interest in

human excrement. And of course Davies' own deliberate adult
confrontation of the powerful taboos that had been implanted in
him in childhood was a factor. He had turned his childhood disgust at the filth of the North Ward school in Renfrew into a
source of authorial energy at moments of crisis in *Tempest-Tost*
and *The Manticore*, and, having confronted his own attitudes at
length, he had never been loath to ridicule conventional
Canadians' prudishness on the subject. Here was an opportunity
to do it again and at length.

It was also at the beginning, because of something he had
learned from Holmyard's *Alchemy*, that Davies envisioned
Mamusia, the mother of the brilliant, beautiful graduate student
Maria Magdalena Theotoky, as a Gypsy. The medieval physician
and alchemist Paracelsus had sought knowledge directly from
"physicians, alchemists, astrologers, apothecaries, miners, gypsies,
and adepts of various occult arts." Davies envisioned his own
"alchemist," Hollier, too, as reaching outside the university to
Mamusia for Gypsy lore. Later, in 64b, he saw a further way to
introduce an alchemical connection through Mamusia:

> One of Mamusia's great secrets as a *Luthier* is the *bomari* -
> the poultice of horse dung & wool she wraps 'tired' fiddles
> in to restore them: closely guarded, but MMB [Maria]
> betrays it to Templar [Hollier], who is delighted as this is
> the *bain marie* of the alchemists, reputedly devised by
> Mary of Egypt.

Making Maria herself part Gypsy brought all sorts of personal
associations into play for Davies as well—Hugo's Esmeralda, the
beautiful Gypsy girl that he had spotted sitting on the tilt of a
caravan in Kingston when he was nineteen and the sense of personal loss he had felt in 1945 on reading of the Nazis' campaign
to exterminate the Gypsies of Europe. Once he began his
research, he consulted Jean-Paul Clébert's factual, scholarly,
laconic *The Gypsies* again and again for details that would lend
authenticity to Maria, Mamusia and Mamusia's brother Yerko.

Davies' decision to make extensive reference to the sixteenth-
century alchemist Paracelsus and his writings came fairly late in

the planning of the novel. Jung's two alchemical books and his two essays on Paracelsus in *The Spirit in Man, Art, and Literature* (1967), together with Marie-Louise von Franz's references to him, had whetted Davies' curiosity about this free, questing spirit who had operated outside the university of his day and indeed was repudiated by it. Paracelsus was also a gifted doctor, who knew that there is a link between physique and tempera- ment and was interested in the study of the living body as a whole rather than in formal anatomy. In "Ben Jonson and Alchemy," Davies had gone so far as to characterize Paracelsus as "perhaps the most spectacular alchemist in history." And so, some two years into planning the novel, he read an anthology of Paracelsus' writings and noted down a number of quotations that he might use, including these in 79a:

"The physician does not learn everything he must know & master at high colleges alone; from time to time he must consult old women, gypsies, magicians, wayfarers, & all manner of peasant folk & random people, & learn from them; for these have more knowledge about such things than all the high colleges"
"Medicine rests upon four pillars—philosophy, astronomy, alchemy and ethics"
"The physician should be versed in all branches of philoso- phy, physics and alchemy as well, as thoroughly, as pro- foundly, as possible, & he should not lack any knowledge in these fields.... I praise the art of alchemy because it reveals the mysteries of medicine & because it is helpful in all desperate illnesses...I also praise the art of medicine; but how can I praise those who are physicians and not alchemists at the same time?... Never must knowledge & preparation, that is to say, medicine & alchemy, be sepa- rated from each other." [Davies' ellipses]

Also late was the decision to have the roly-poly Anglican priest and professor, Simon Darcourt, interest himself in Gnosticism— the heresy which holds that salvation can be achieved by knowl- edge rather than by faith—and to have him apply its notion of

"Sophia," the feminine personification of God's Wisdom, to Maria. When reading for "Ben Jonson and Alchemy," Davies had discovered that the philosophical or spiritual side of alchemy was actually a covert form of Gnosticism. And when talking about Gnosticism in that speech, he had observed that "it is a heresy for intellectuals, and not for all intellectuals, at that, for in its highest developments it requires a mystical cast of mind and a degree of psychological insight, and particularly of self-knowledge, that are outside the competence of your run-of-the-mill Ph.D." That being so, a link between Darcourt and Maria and Gnosticism and Sophia was almost bound to occur to Davies as he gathered his ideas for the novel.

Likewise relatively late was his decision to refer to the Rebel Angels described in *The Book of Enoch*. In the Middle Ages, Enoch was thought to have been an astrologer, and the alchemists often referred to him and his story of the Rebel Angels. Davies, who had known the story at least as far back as 1959 when he read Jung's *Answer to Job*, encountered many references to *The Book of Enoch* and to the Rebel Angels as he pursued the threads of his alchemical web, but not until he read Richard Cavendish's *The Black Arts* did he see the possibilities for his novel. Note 69b reads:

> Academics as the Rebel Angels, who lusted after the daughters of men & taught virtually everything for they thought knowledge, rather than virtue is the key to spiritual growth & that knowledge of the universe is synonymous wth its control. Cavendish pp. 255-6.

A few pages later he was considering "The Rebel Angels" as a possible title. And ten pages after that he made notes from the entry on "Angelology" in *The Jewish Encyclopedia* (1901). This, and Jung's *Answer to Job*, provided the information he would use in the novel.

Given his interest in the university's medieval roots, it was inevitable that Davies would make room for Rabelais. The great humorist, humanist, educational reformer and contemporary of Paracelsus had intrigued him since he'd discovered a two-volume edition of his works, illustrated by Heath Robinson, on a family visit to his Uncle Percy in Boston at the age of twelve. He had read bits of the text and studied Robinson's extraordinary pictures attentively, and he was especially struck by a depiction of the country feast at which Gargantua is born, where the peasants exuberantly waved and rolled about as they were "chirping over their cups." For years he had relished the splendid deluge of words in Urquhart and Motteux's famous seventeenth-century translation of *Gargantua and Pantagruel.* By 1961, when he recommended that Massey College take the rule which guides the inhabitants of Rabelais' Abbey of Thélème—"Do what you will"—as its motto, Davies also had on his shelf the illustrated French quarto edition that had belonged to the Toronto theatre and music critic Hector Charlesworth, as well as J. M. Cohen's translation, Samuel Putnam's biography, and, in all likelihood, John Cowper Powys' *Rabelais* and M. A. Screech's *Rabelais.* But it wasn't until December 19, 1969, when he and Brenda saw Jean-Louis Barrault's stunning production of *Gargantua* in Paris that he grasped the sweep of Rabelais' vision and came fully to appreciate his "uproarious big laughter at *bound* people, you know academics, churchmen and citizens—everybody who has got caught in the trap of a way of life."

A loose page of notes that appears to pre-date the three-ringed notebook by several weeks runs:

> Latinist an alchemist?
> Rabelais & alchemy?
> academic executor of
> estate: as N. Endicott
> of D. Duncan: finds notable
> MS.: Rabelais?: shd. go to
> Univ. Lib. but can he
> relinquish it? not his field because
> in Latin.
> or Beerbohm MS.
> or Wilde?
> Can Univ. go to court to get it?

So a possible link between Rabelais and alchemy appears to have been in Davies' mind very early. There are entries throughout the notebook recording odd bits of information on Rabelais and considering how various characters might respond to his writings. Davies quickly realized that Maria's thesis should have something to do with Rabelais; later he saw that it would concern a Rabelais manuscript and the associated papers that would reveal the great man's interest in alchemy.

Once Davies had embarked on his research for *The Rebel Angels*, some items literally thrust themselves upon him.

Horace Davenport, for instance, told him in a letter of a CalTech professor who introduced his course in colloid chemistry by reciting: "They went to sea in a sieve, they did; they went to sea in a sieve," and then floated a sieve on a pot of water— having greased it first so that surface tension would support it. When Horace mentioned that the Vestal Virgins had demonstrated a practical understanding of this principle by carrying water from the Tiber in a sieve, Davies immediately saw that he could use the story to make the point that science has a history.

On June 23, 1977, he and Brenda toured 73 Chestnut Park Road, a large old house in the prestigious neighbourhood of Rosedale in downtown Toronto. Brenda was thinking of buying a duplex or triplex, where they could live after his retirement from Massey, renting out the extra space. (Davies himself was reluctant, envisioning too well the aggravations that accompany landlordship.) But this house had been partitioned into a warren of tiny units. Brenda, repelled by the stench of the catbox that two elderly women had installed in their bathroom and barred from one of the third-floor apartments because its male nurse occupant had just returned from work and wanted to get some sleep, couldn't wait to leave. It was Davies who insisted on going through the place from top to bottom. The sights and smells of 73 Chestnut Park Road turned Mamusia, whom he had previously envisioned as a psychic living in a cluttered flat, into a landlady.

Best of all, two and a half years after he had begun making notes, a letter arrived from a junior Fellow:

19.1.79

Dear Sir,

It is always a good deal easier for me to express myself on paper than *in propria persona*, and so I beg you to accept, in this guise, my thanks for your and the Fellows' invitation to High Table tonight. To a student, even a graduate student, the barrier between the senior scholar and the apprentice often seems discouragingly opaque. However, tonight I sat at dessert with Prof. Stoicheff and, innocent of his academic specialty, began to speak of the Oxford School of the thirteenth century — Grosseteste, Bacon, and the Mertonian mathematicians — and their physical and metaphysical theories about light. The shy delight with which Dr Stoicheff revealed that his own field of study was the physics of light, together with the serious (though scarcely *solemn*) discussion which ensued on what Dante would have thought of the Laser beam, was, without exaggeration, deeply touching. Amidst term papers, seminars, assignments, and the seemingly endless effort to gain mastery of one's beloved discipline, the momentary experience of the sweet fellowship of the life of learning is inspiring beyond description. Remember how S. Augustine characterized collegiate comradeship? "Conloqui et conridere et vicissim benivole obsequi, simul legere libros dulciloquos, simul nugari et simul honestari": "Conversations and jokes together, mutual rendering of good services, the reading together of sweetly-phrased books, the sharing of nonsense and mutual attentions."

With best thanks,
Faith E. Wallis

Davies, deeply moved, entered the quotation, the translation and its source (Augustine, *Confessions*, Book 4, Chapter 8) in his notebook at 75c, thinking it might be an appropriate epigraph for his novel.

Three months later, on April 13, 1979, he began to write *The Rebel Angels*, finishing the first draft on June 30, 1980. The story takes place at a large Canadian university during a single academic year, and its twelve sections are narrated alternately by the twenty-three-year-old Maria Magdalena Theotoky and the middle-aged Simon Darcourt. To distinguish their sections, Davies typed Maria's on blue paper and Darcourt's on white. These were simply the colours he happened to have on hand, but it is not without relevance that he chose blue, the colour associated with the Virgin Mary, for Maria. According to *The Oxford English Dictionary*, her last name, Theotoky, refers to "the divine motherhood of Mary." (It is an association she shares with Mary Dempster, Maria Ann Dymock and Milady Tresize.) When it printed the book, Macmillan of Canada used slightly different typefaces to distinguish the two narrators.

Maria's sections focus almost entirely at first on her life at the university. She believes herself to be in love with her supervisor, Clement Hollier, even though, apart from an unrepeated sexual encounter the previous May, he has given no sign that he views her as anything more than an unusually gifted graduate student. Her thesis is to be based on an important manuscript from the estate of the collector Francis Cornish, and because of it, Hollier moves her into his office in the College of St. John and the Holy Ghost for the academic year. There she is thrown into the disturbing company of the renegade monk John Parlabane, an old school friend of Hollier's and a thorough-going sceptic, who relates his own disastrous personal history to her and invites her confidences in return. It is Parlabane who declares Hollier's office to be "The room of a medieval scholar if ever I saw one. Look at that object on the bookcase; alchemical—even I can see that. This is like an alchemist's chamber in some quiet medieval university. And fully equipped! Here is the great scholar himself, Clement Hollier. And here are you, that inescapable necessity of the alchemist, his *soror mystica*, his scholarly girlfriend, to put it in modern terms. But what's lacking? Of course, the *famulus*, the scholar's intimate servant, devoted disciple, and unquestioning stooge. I nominate myself *famulus* in this little corner of the Middle Ages."

Hollier's specialty—understanding the thinking of medieval people—has him "Rooting about in the kitchen-middens and

trash-heaps of the Middle Ages." He has set Maria to learning
about the intellectual background of Rabelais, and so she is taking a course in Renaissance European Culture with the knowledgeable but dull Urquhart McVarish, and another in New
Testament Greek with the engagingly instructive Darcourt. It is
Darcourt who introduces the quotation from St. Augustine,
writing it on the board at the first meeting of his seminar in
order to establish the spirit in which the group is to work on this
classical language, whose study "can lead in all sorts of directions," including the Middle Ages, when the language was
known in northern Europe only to "alchemists and detrimentals
of that sort."

Since one of Hollier's interests is medieval filth therapy, he
wants Maria to find out whether Ozias Froats' research on
human excrement has revealed why filth therapy worked, observing: "It's astonishingly similar to alchemy in basic principle—the
recognition of what is of worth in that which is scorned by the
unseeing. The alchemist's long quest for the Stone, and the biblical stone which the builders refused becoming the headstone of
the corner...the *lapis angularis* of the Alchemical Cross, and the
stone of the *filius macrocosmi* which was Christ, the Wholly
Good?" For the same reason, Hollier is eager to meet Maria's
mother, Mamusia, whom we now find to be a Gypsy. Maria's life
at the university is a flight from a background of petty thievery,
passionate Gypsy music, gaudy dress, folk wisdom and a rabbit
warren of a house in Rosedale. Mamusia is in the business of
rehabilitating stringed instruments by the medieval method of
burying their wooden cases in a *bomari* of horse manure. It is
Hollier who recognizes the word *bomari* as a Romany corruption
of the *bain-marie* of the alchemists. He tells Maria that her
mother is a living fossil who could have lived anywhere in
Europe during the previous six or seven centuries and reminds
her that Paracelsus had urged physicians to look outside "the
high colleges" and learn from people like Mamusia.

In his sections, Simon Darcourt (who shares Davies' portly figure, his love of ceremony and good fellowship and his pursuit of
self-knowledge) sets out with the energetic curiosity that is "the
lifeblood of universities" to create a record of collegiate life. As he

describes various academic occasions—funerals and a wedding in Spook's chapel, a sherry party, Guest Nights at Ploughwright College—he frequently draws attention to the continuities between medieval and contemporary academic life. It is Darcourt who, at McVarish's cocktail party, hears Maria tell how she describes the Vestal Virgins' practical knowledge of colloid chemistry to her first-year engineering students to convince them that science has a history. And Darcourt, visiting Ozias Froats at the same time as Maria does, hears her making connections between Paracelsus, Froats and the twentieth-century Harvard scientist W. H. Sheldon.

Darcourt joins Hollier and McVarish in sorting out the muddle of Francis Cornish's three apartments. He is thus in a position to comment upon the activities and characters of his fellow academics and of the official executor, Cornish's nephew, the businessman Arthur Cornish. It is Darcourt who reports on the Dobsonesque aspects of McVarish's character. And it is he, too, who notes the competitive instincts of the institutions (including the university library) that hope to benefit from the estate. By the time the estate is finally settled, he and Hollier are certain that McVarish has the missing Rabelais manuscript and three important letters that link Rabelais and Paracelsus and reveal that Rabelais was "if not an alchemist at least a student of alchemy." The first movement of the novel ends with his description of a Guest Night at Ploughwright College, where we hear the Fellows "chirping over their cups" as they entertain their dinner guests with university gossip, odd gobbets of learning and ruminations about medieval and modern collegiate life.

As the year progresses, Maria becomes more and more chilled by Parlabane's all-encompassing scepticism. Parlabane entertains great hopes of getting his long, autobiographical novel published (its title is drawn from Paracelsus' motto) and he cadges more and more money from Maria and Darcourt. Froats is given an important award for his work by the American College of Physicians. Mamusia decides to help Maria marry Hollier and to that end gives an extraordinary, indeed gargantuan, Christmas dinner, at which she tells the fortunes of both Hollier and Darcourt—and watches Darcourt drink the love potion she had intended for Hollier. Darcourt falls in love with Maria, seeing her as Sophia. She tactfully rejects him, but likens him, together with Hollier and other splendidly learned professors, to the Rebel Angels who came to earth and taught men. Meanwhile, gripped by black anger at McVarish for stealing the Rabelais manuscript and letters, Hollier unsuccessfully seeks Mamusia's help in laying a curse on his enemy. These powerful emotions produce a series of startling events—the macabre murder of McVarish, Parlabane's suicide, the recovery of the missing manuscript and the psychological collapse of Hollier.

Extraordinary though university life has been shown to be, the novel has made it clear that it overemphasizes the intellect at the expense of other qualities. Hollier's short-lived passion for Maria, Darcourt's identification of Maria with Sophia and Maria's own obsession with Hollier all spring from the underdeveloped parts of their sensibilities. Now, quite suddenly, Arthur proposes to Maria and she accepts him. This is to be a relationship based on the solid footing of friendship, and, like the marriages that conclude Shakespeare's comedies, it signals a new equilibrium. Maria, who had turned her back on her Gypsy heritage, becomes a barefoot bride, and her necklace of Krugerrands, the bride-price that Arthur has paid to Yerko, is returned as her dowry. By accepting Arthur, who has never studied at the university, she demonstrates her liberation from infatuation with the intellect. Darcourt, who is now Maria's friend rather than her aspiring lover, performs the ceremony, and Hollier proposes the toast to the bride, celebrating Maria's double heritage, from Mamusia, "the *phuri dai*, the Mother of the Earth," and from "the Alma Mater, the bounteous mother of the University." And Arthur gives Maria the Rabelais manuscript, which hints that in the future she will be both wife and scholar. As the novel closes we return to the academics, chirping over their cups on the final Guest Night of the year at Ploughwright College.

Davies takes immense risks in *The Rebel Angels*. He employs a young female narrator, makes a scientist a major character, interrupts the flow of the story with more than thirty pages of academic gossip and esoteric chat at Ploughwright College and

The illustration of the Rebel Angels that Davies pasted
on the title page of his second draft.

marries his heroine to a man the reader has barely met—and yet
he pulls it off, because of the sheer energy that drives the novel's
particular and persuasive vision. Of all Davies' books this one has
the greatest narrative force.

Certainly, the reader is startled to find Maria marrying Arthur
Cornish. Davies provides few prior hints of the match. In fact,
even less provision was made for it in the first draft. Only after
Brenda observed that the reader needed to get to know and care
about Arthur did Davies add several pages to the dinner date
conversation with Maria and two further pages to the proposal
scene. But he wanted, and kept, the emphasis of surprise for the
proposal and marriage.

Many readers have noted that Maria's vocabulary and prose
rhythms are not appropriate for a woman of her age and background. I. M. Owen was right to observe in his review of *The
Rebel Angels* that both Maria and Darcourt "write in the well-
turned periods of the sometime Master of Massey, which come
rather oddly from the 23-year-old Maria." The criticism is not a
new one; from time to time throughout Davies' career, critics
and readers have pointed out that one or another of his characters sounds like their author. Although the minor characters in
his plays and novels speak convincingly from their class, period
and personality, and he is good at flavouring the language and
thought of his major characters with language that reflects their
occupations or deep concerns, it is true that in extended passages, Davies' own distinctive prose rhythms and word hoard are

unmistakable. They certainly dominate the prose of *The Rebel Angels*, whether Darcourt or Maria is in the narrator's chair. In this novel Davies does not manage to create what he so admires in Joyce Cary's two three-decker works, namely, narrators whose expressions, turn of mind and cadences are unmistakably their own. But Owen continued his review: "…it doesn't matter in the least," and indeed the issue is minor.

Another charge concerns Davies' scientist, Ozy Froats. Horace Davenport, Davies' long-time friend and physiologist, has pointed out that his portrayal of the methodology of the physical sciences is unrealistic. Davies was well aware that he might have gotten his science wrong. Shortly after submitting the manuscript in February 1981, he told Davenport: "The scientific passages in it will no doubt have you helpless with mirth, but I done my best, and what can man do more?" He ventured into the area for the same reason he included the evening of academic chat at Ploughwright College—to try to do justice to the breadth of the university.

The Rebel Angels represents a different literary form than Davies has tried either before or since, combining the novel with what Northrop Frye has called "anatomy" or "Menippean satire." If one accepts Frye's fictional categories—novel, confession, anatomy and romance—then the first two Salterton books and parts of the third are primarily novels, because they are concerned with the characters' social interactions. When Davies turned his focus to the inward lives of his characters as the result of his reading of Jung and wrote the Deptford trilogy, he combined romance with confession. (Romance, because the characters are presented as they appear to themselves and there are hints that they have archetypal dimensions. But confession, too, because the characters tell their own stories and because their theoretical and intellectual interests play a leading role.) In the case of *The Rebel Angels*, this kind of theoretical interest—here, in the nature of the university—is no longer attached to a single character but has become a dominant concern of the book as a whole. Although much of *The Rebel Angels* obeys the novelistic impulse, when it focuses single-mindedly on the university it displays the characteristics of pure anatomy. In these patches the characters become stylized carriers of mental attitudes, their conversation is essentially a conflict of ideas and their displays of erudition become catalogues—of the seven deadly sins and the seven virtues, of Sheldon's physical types and their variants, of the medieval words for animal faeces and even of Darcourt's whimsical names for the stools of members of the university community.

The novel appeared in Canada in October 1981, in a peculiarly appropriate jacket. A team from Macmillan had lugged armloads of tarot cards, mortar boards and such around Trinity College, the original of St. John and the Holy Ghost, on midsummer's eve, taking various stagy shots. At 11 p.m., just before leaving, the photographer, Peter Paterson, had snapped the darkened main building with the light of the full moon filtering through the windows of its central tower, a single lamp still burning in an upper room. The result was an "eerie and beautiful" picture that produced "a very elegant jacket" (to borrow the words of Douglas M. Gibson, Davies' editor at Macmillan). Gibson would have liked it even better if he had known that that part of Trinity is known as the Angels' Roost!

The book was published by Viking in the United States in February and by Allen Lane in Britain in April 1982. Critics called it bizarre, esoteric, baroque, whimsical, wicked, esoteric, learned. They commented on the unusual mix of characters, the highly colourful scenes and the preoccupation with academic issues but did not perceive that much of this resulted from the book's unusual form. Although they had trouble characterizing the book, the majority responded warmly to its exuberance and energy and the joy of the writing. Those who disapproved of it wrote of characters "too narrowly bound to their professions," "scenes which seem unrelated to the development of character and plot," a story that "creaks under an excess of intellectual baggage"—in other words, the anatomical aspects of the book.

Two influential reviewers wrote particularly positively, giving Davies' international reputation a substantial boost. The first was the eminent Canadian-born economist John Kenneth Galbraith, who wrote a nicely judged "Appreciation" for the *New York Times Book Review* in which he declared that Davies' novels "will be recognized with the very best work of this century." And in England the novelist Anthony Burgess announced to the readers of the *Observer* that "Among Canadian WASP novelists who have remained loyal to the culture of the Commonwealth, Robertson Davies, at the age of 69, stands out as internationally important and undoubted Nobel material." Burgess subsequently included *The Rebel Angels* in *99 Novels* (1984), his list of outstanding works of fiction written in English since 1939, and in the summer of 1985 he lobbied the Swedish Academy to award Davies the Nobel prize for literature. The hardcover edition of *The Rebel Angels* sold 13,595 copies in Canada, 12,101 in the United States, and 2,959 in Britain.

The academic year 1980-81 was Davies' last as Master of Massey College and Professor of English and Drama at the University of Toronto. At Massey he had successfully established a distinctive college atmosphere that combined commitment to learning with graceful ceremony and leavened it with good fellowship and wit. He had unreservedly committed himself to the college, but the tensions and demands on his energy had been heavy, and by 1981 he was more than ready to step down. He felt strongly that he had done all that he could do there. What was needed now was "a man who can collect some money—a task at which I have been a total failure." He may indeed have been relieved to find that the college had not consumed him entirely, like the graduate student in his ghost story "Dickens Digested" or the visiting scholar in "Offer of Immortality." Brenda, for her part, was eager to make the change. Although she had found outlets in skating, tennis and yoga, in working for the women's volunteer committee at the Art Gallery of Ontario and later in involving herself with an AGO fund-raising group called "Exploring Toronto," she had found little place for her abilities in the college itself, apart from serving as its hostess and one-woman altar guild. Hers was a fish-bowl existence, constantly subject to scrutiny and criticism, and Massey's demands on the Master had cut substantially into their shared private time.

As the day approached, the college community expressed its appreciation in a series of tributes and presentations that reflected Davies' well-known tastes and enthusiasms. In the common room, after his last High Table, the junior Fellows presented Davies, the collector and Victorianist, with the original monthly parts of Dickens' *Little Dorrit*. At a luncheon after his last meeting with the college corporation, the senior Fellows and the college secretary bestowed on Davies, the appreciator of fine silver, a pair of urns engraved with the college crest. At their farewell celebration, the staff gave Davies, the respecter of fine craftsmanship, a handsome walnut lectern made by Norbert Iwanski, with the College crest inlaid on the front by Peter Lapajne. (It stands in his Caledon study today, just the right size to carry his many-volumed *Oxford English Dictionary*.) At a dinner in his honour, the Massey College Singers sang a special program of Victorian songs for Davies, the lover of music, and presented him a folio of the scores. And finally, at a special college dinner at Hart House, to which university dignitaries, former senior Fellows, family and many friends were invited, members of the Drama Centre performed for Davies,

Brian Parker

the theatre enthusiast, "A Masque for the Master." Robert Finch wrote the prologue and epilogue, Ann Saddlemyer concocted the script from Davies' writings, and Keith Bissell wrote the music that the Massey College Singers performed.

All these were things to carry away or to lay up in memory. In addition, the corporation decided to name the college library after him (undoubtedly unaware that years before Davies had mused about this possibility, calling it "the Pedant's Dream")! It also established a "Robertson Davies Library Fund," which was to become a vital resource in sustaining the kind of collegiate life he had established. During his tenure, the college had spent all its income every year. Although the endowment had remained level in dollar terms, its value had been quartered by inflation. Davies' successor in the mastership was J. N. Patterson Hume, a longtime senior Fellow and a distinguished educator in physics and computer science. Hume was determined to maintain the ceremonial life of the college, but to do so he was forced to reduce the portion of his own salary that the college covered, cut some service positions, reduce the number of meals served and raise fees. After 1990-91, however, the income from the fund began to support a portion of the library's expenses, and this freed some of the college budget for other things.

John Leyerle, dean of the School of Graduate Studies, chaired the fund-raising campaign. He had been an ex-officio member of the college corporation only since 1978 and had thus served for a shorter time and in a more peripheral way than most of the other senior Fellows. But he had felt warmly toward Davies since 1966 when the students in his medieval drama seminar had performed *Gammer Gurton's Needle*, and Davies had not only come to a performance but had sent the group fifty dollars by way of encouragement. And when he had begun to serve on the corporation, Leyerle had found among the senior Fellows a degree of loyalty and commitment to the college that was, in his experience of university communities, unique. He led the fund-raising drive in order to honour the man who had overcome the manifest difficulties of creating this sort of cohesion, and to help ensure its survival.

Every one of the thirty-three senior Fellows, past and present, contributed to the Library Fund. One gave $100,000, and a number between $5,000 and $10,000. Their combined gift exceeded $185,000, an extraordinary level of giving. A number of foundations that had refused to support Massey College in its own right were happy to give generously in Davies' name. Although the junior Fellows' donations were much smaller and more selective (not surprising, since relatively few had achieved a high level of discretionary income) the fund had reached $500,000 by 1990, when its earnings began to be tapped.

In the fall of 1981, the University of Toronto made Davies a Doctor of Laws, becoming the fifteenth university in Canada to give him an honorary degree. And in 1982 he was invited to give the university's most prestigious literary lecture series, the Alexander Lectures at University College. This series is usually offered to an academic of stature from another university, and the lectures are always published as a book. Davies elected to speak on the subject he had made his own—melodrama and nineteenth-century theatre—and gave three lively, engaging lectures rooted in the psychological perceptions that had fascinated his students. They were published by the University of Toronto Press the following year under the title *The Mirror of Nature*.

Chapter 15

WHAT'S BRED IN THE BONE:
1980-85

---•---

Monday Aug 3...then to Natl Gallery which was v. crowded &
smelly; took time & looked only at my favourites—Veronese's
Darius & Alexander, some Titians, some Dutch & my never-
failing delight, the Bronzino allegory of *Venus, Cupid, Folly &
Time* whch. I examined at leisure & in detail; had not before
noticed that Venus has her tongue thrust into Cupid's mouth,
or that the Sphinx is so oddly drawn.
　　　　—"Journal of a Journey into Ireland and London," 1959

DURING HIS YEARS at Massey College, Davies had written a
great deal in addition to the novels, and after retirement he went
right on producing short pieces in profusion: speeches, introductions to books, ghost stories, articles and book reviews (the last
primarily for the *Washington Post's Book World* and the *Globe and
Mail*). Hard on the heels of completing the first draft of *The
Rebel Angels* in 1980, he made his selections for *The Penguin
Stephen Leacock* (1981), and the following February wrote the
introduction for it.

In the summer and fall of 1981 he ventured into a new field

with the libretto of a fifty-minute opera for the Canadian Children's Opera Chorus. Derek Holman, who had collaborated with him on several entertainments at Massey College, composed the music, and their altogether charming *Dr. Canon's Cure* was performed at Toronto's Harbourfront in May 1982.

A lively and amusing "young person's guide" to Italian comic opera, its action takes place outside an Italian country inn in the year 1820.

The miserly innkeeper has impounded the musical instruments of an opera troupe that failed to pay its bill. Dr. Canon comes along and saves the day by training the singers to imitate the sounds of the instruments, and introduces them to the canon form as a way to orchestrate the music for their new opera. The opera is then produced, and one by one the familiar characters—chorus, hero, heroine, duenna, father and notary—introduce themselves. Pantalone sings—

> I'm the Operatic Father—
> Stuff and nonsense!
> Bluff and bother!
> Only aim in life for me
> Is to keep my daughter free.
> Huff and puff!
> Grim and gruff!

The action of the opera-within-an-opera is exceedingly brief, and true love quickly triumphs, moving the innkeeper to forgive the company its debts and rekindling his love for his wife. The piece ends with the whole company singing Dr. Canon's praises.

Early in 1982, Davies prepared the eighteen Massey College ghost stories for publication by Penguin Books as *High Spirits*, and that year also he wrote a substantial piece on "The Nineteenth-Century Repertoire" for *Early Stages: Theatre in Ontario: 1800-1914*. In 1983, he created a second libretto for the Canadian Children's Opera Chorus, called "Children of the Moon." Holman found this one unworkably undramatic, however, and although Davies revised it early the following year, he never wrote the music. Davies made no effort to find another collaborator, and the piece has not been produced.

Meanwhile, ideas for the next novel were welling up. Davies had had great difficulty in finishing the first draft of *The Rebel Angels* in June 1980, principally, as he explained to Elisabeth Sifton, "because I was already plagued by ideas for a sequel. Therefore I had to decide whether to turn off the tap sharply and forever on the last page, or leave a few strings dangling—which is what, in the end, I did." During the next two years ideas flooded in on him about the history of the Cornish family, Parlabane's illegitimate son, the Cornish Foundation, the love triangle formed by Maria, Arthur Cornish and Geraint Powell, an unfinished opera about Arthur the Magnanimous Cuckold, Francis Cornish's biography and much more. On August 25, 1981, more than a year into the process, Davies told Elisabeth Sifton that the new book "forces itself into my mind when I am lugging furniture, or pulling weeds, and I have some hopes of it. I often read, with amazement, of people who suffer from Writer's Block; I might enjoy a wee Block, just to have time to catch my breath."

The threads he eventually wove into *What's Bred in the Bone* did not become disentangled from those he used in *The Lyre of Orpheus* until well into the following year. In February 1982, when he wrote to Elisabeth Sifton, he was still conceiving his next novel as a combination of three narratives:

> (1) the childhood of Francis Cornish, explaining what it was that made him a notable connoisseur and collector, despite a Philistine and loveless childhood, and (2) what happens in the marriage of Maria and Arthur Cornish, which runs into some stiffish problems, including a tough illness for Arthur and the complications involved in his determination to be an active arts patron in the world of the theatre, and (3) complications about the publication of Parlabane's horrible novel, arising from the appearance of a terrible fellow who asserts that he is Parlabane's son.

And he was finding that "Getting these threads together into something that makes sense is gnawing at my vitals like the fox

chewing on the Spartan boy." By April, however, he had the list
reduced to two items, and on July 8 he reported that he had the
subject and the method of his new book clear in his mind."

By February 1983, when he and Brenda spent two weeks in
London, he was almost ready to begin writing. By now the book
was forcing itself on his attention almost constantly. He wrote in
his travel diary on February 7: "These nights I wake & plan my
novel: somewhat uncanny, but I am visited by good ideas & clarifications at such hours. Two nights in succession wth. hardly
any sleep & by day I am absent & abstracted. The life of an
author is in some respects the life of a dog." Right after his
return home, he made a beginning, and after two false starts
made steady progress through the book's six parts, completing
the first draft on August 9, 1984, and sending the final typescript
to his publishers the following February.

Three major new elements contributed to the process by which
the material that arose from *The Rebel Angels* grew into *What's
Bred in the Bone.* One of these was Davies' equivalent to Dickens'
hellish childhood experience of being put to work in a blacking
factory. Davies had once observed that this had "burnt itself"
forever into the Victorian novelist's nature, "and he could not be
rid of it, except through the art that was his." Davies' own blacking factory was Renfrew, where he had lived from the year he
turned six until the summer he turned twelve. And as in
Dickens' case, art was Davies' means of coming to terms with it
all. Talking about his Renfrew experiences while he was preparing to write *What's Bred in the Bone,* he observed, "in my next
novel I'm going to get into this, because I've got to get it out of
my system." However, although Davies made direct use of his
most vivid recollections, and drew extensively on his broad
knowledge of Renfrew in drawing Blairlogie, Francis Cornish
grows up in a religious and aesthetic context quite different from
the one Davies knew.

The second major element was indignation. "One of the things
that burns me furiously is that some reviewers say that I'm an
old-fashioned novelist and never do anything that's new." An
instance to which he has recurred again and again is William
French's review of *Fifth Business* in the *Globe and Mail*:

"...Davies is so heroically old fashioned, so impressively erudite, so puckishly disdainful of current fashion, that he will not only dazzle his faithful admirers, but may successfully woo the uncommitted." Others might have considered this high praise, but Davies was ultra-sensitive to the implication that he was trying nothing new as a writer. So he met the fancied challenge head-on in *What's Bred in the Bone*, creating as his major character an artist who exercises his genius in the style of a period much earlier than his own. This subject provided Davies with the added advantage that it allowed him to explore further his long-standing interest in the subtle relationships between art, deception and truth. He had written on this topic as early as 1955, in reviewing Thomas Mann's *Confessions of Felix Krull, Confidence Man* for *Saturday Night*, and, of course, he had already explored it at length in *World of Wonders* with the story of Magnus Eisengrim, master illusionist.

A third, lesser factor underlying the creation of the new novel was the peculiar experience of being himself the subject of a biography. Davies had done a lot of thinking about biographies, particularly those of artists. As literary editor of *Saturday Night* during the 1950s he had reviewed a few that had admirably captured the quality of the life at hand, and many more that lacked the requisite breadth of spirit, scholarship, professionalism, enthusiasm or skill. In the Deptford novels he had set out to catch the shape and the essence of individual lives himself, and in *The Rebel Angels* he had raised the spectre of an official biography of Francis Cornish, which, although based on multitudinous papers, would fail to explore anything that mattered. When Davies began to plan his new novel, he speculated about a Cornish family history and a life of Francis Cornish as possible components of the story. The intrusion of a biographer into his own life, and his more than half serious apprehension of an "anticipatory embalming," gave him the impetus for a new say on the subject. As he explained to Elisabeth Sifton early in the process:

...I have been seeing a woman regularly who is going to write a biography of me!

This is partly flattering, partly awesome, for she is good at that kind of job, but she is an academic and sees me through academic eyes, which means that nothing I have ever done is without significance in terms of what I have written, and nothing I am or have been is beyond the range of academic explication. I do not think I am more vain than most authors, but really I think academics have a lot of gall, in their firm belief that they can comprehend and explain writers, musicians, painters and so forth, better than these creatures can explain themselves in their work....

But amidst all this tohubohu and brouhaha I have been planning my next novel, which will not be a sequel but what I believe is called a 'linked book' with *Rebel Angels.*

As the novel begins, Arthur Cornish is insisting that Simon Darcourt stop writing his uncle's biography. Darcourt is himself in despair over the book. After eighteen months of research he has many unsubstantiated suspicions and there are important gaps in his knowledge—not least his inability to learn anything about Francis Cornish's formative years in Blairlogie.

With Darcourt unable to proceed, Davies introduces the Lesser Zadkiel, a member of the staff of the Recording Angel whose special concern is biography, and Maimas, Francis' "daimon" or guardian spirit. Zadkiel sets the record of Francis' life going for Maimas' amusement, and at intervals the two discuss what it reveals. The reader thus becomes privy to all the things that Darcourt had not been able to discover about Francis' life, starting with the character of Blairlogie, the town that so resembles the Renfrew of Davies' memory.

The record explores the things that have conditioned Francis' artistic bent: his innate responsiveness to beauty, the often brutal local schools, his aunt's Catholicism, Victoria Cameron's Calvinism, Dr. G. Courtney Upper's lectures on sex, his absent father's involvement in the British Secret Service, his fashionable mother's chilly remoteness, the family's wealth. And we also see how his exceptional talent impels him to begin to come to terms with his anima and his shadow, and stimulates his interest in the camera technique of the movies, his grandfather's photography, his aunt's pictures and her books about art, and the bodies (including that of the dwarf tailor) in the embalming room of the local undertaker.

At Colborne College the Grail myth grasps Francis' imagination. By the time he arrives at Oxford, the record is already beginning to demonstrate that "what's bred in the bone will not out of the flesh." And what is bred in the bone appears to be a strong sense of what is "right and proper," as opposed to what would best serve his talent. He falls in love with his cousin Ismay, and when she turns up pregnant both the Catholic and the Calvinistic strains of his upbringing make it impossible for him to countenance an abortion. So he marries her. But he does manage to resist her family's attempts to gain control of his inheritance, and he gets clear of the situation when he finds out that the child is not his and that his wife has run off to her lover.

By this time Francis wants to become a painter. Although fascinated by Tancred Saraceni, he does not want to apprentice himself to the great art restorer, preferring to develop a style of his own. Nonetheless, following his father's example, he capitulates to the British Secret Service's desire that he go to Schloss Düsterstein in Lower Bavaria as Saraceni's assistant, in order to report on train movements to a nearby concentration camp. Already practised in the Renaissance manner of drawing, he now learns the craft and spirit of painting prior to the year 1700 and absorbs the more morally ambiguous skills involved in making a new or inferior old painting appear genuinely old and valuable. He executes two, deeply personal "old" paintings of his own, one a portrait of the Blairlogie dwarf, which comes to be called *Drollig Hansel,* and the other a triptych depicting the meaning of his own life as *The Marriage at Cana.* With Saraceni, he also "enhances" inferior old works. The Gräfin of Düsterstein's cousin, Prince Maximilian, then conveys these to an art dealer in London, who palms them and *Drollig Hansel* off on the Nazis as distinguished Old Masters, the resultant money returning to the Gräfin to restore the family's fortune (and, it transpires later, to Saraceni). Sent to judge the authenticity of a recently discovered painting, purportedly by Hubert van Eyck, he is able to state authoritatively that it is a fake, thus winning a reputation in the field. At Düsterstein Francis meets a woman he likes and loves: she casts his horoscope (which adapts the one that Hugh McCraig cast for Davies in 1958) and interprets it with great insight.

He spends the Second World War in England working for counter-intelligence, and in that period loses the woman he loves in an air-raid. After the war, he returns to Blairlogie briefly to settle his affairs. Now, seeing the people who shaped him through mature eyes, he comes to understand more clearly his adolescent struggles to understand his anima (by secretly dressing as a girl) and his shadow (by drawing his imbecile older brother). He then serves on the Allied Commission on Art, whose task it is to return the paintings that had fallen into Nazi hands to their rightful owners. He comes to love his assistant, the stunningly handsome, self-centred Aylwin Ross, not physically, but for his personification of youth. When *Drollig Hansel* and *The Marriage at Cana* turn up among the paintings to be returned, the conscience that was bred in his bone in Blairlogie torments him as he fails to acknowledge that they are his. But the issue of right and wrong is tangled with personal loyalties. Claiming ownership would expose the wartime fakeries of the Gräfin of Düsterstein and Saraceni, and later it would deprive Ross, who has written a clever article about *The Marriage at Cana*, of a chance to advance his career. These conflicting scruples are exacerbated by the mercurial side of his nature that delights in having perpetrated a good hoax. The same scruples prevent him from continuing to paint in the style that is so peculiarly appropriate to his genius.

When Saraceni dies, Francis finds himself heir to an astonishing fortune that allows him to become an influential art collector in Canada. Aylwin Ross, now director of the National Gallery in Ottawa, announces the purchase of six important European paintings for the Gallery, but his minister repudiates the purchase, and Ross attempts to persuade Francis to buy one of them—*The Marriage at Cana*—to rescue his reputation. When Francis refuses, Ross commits suicide.

In his final years, Francis gradually comes to terms with his life, and so he leaves behind a clue that will reveal that it was he who painted *The Marriage at Cana,* making it possible for his artistic genius to be recognized posthumously. At the book's close, Francis, on his deathbed, withdraws from life into the archetypal "Realm of the Mothers," the source of his creativity. Arthur Cornish decides that Simon Darcourt should go ahead with Francis' biography.

By the time he began writing *What's Bred in the Bone,* Davies and I had completed almost a year of the interviews that laid the foundation for this biography. Whereas Darcourt's subject was dead, and could not be asked to recall his childhood in Blairlogie or to fill in the gaps in the public record of his life, Davies, very much alive, took exuberantly to the task of recalling the past at my urging, in hour-and-a-half, once-a-week sessions whenever he was in town, starting in April of 1982 and continuing for the next two years.

Despite his willingness to participate in the exercise, Davies retained his conviction that biography cannot really catch the actuality of a life, no matter how far the biographer's resources and strategems may carry her. As far as he is concerned, the ideal biography, in which the shaping power of a particular childhood context has been thoroughly understood, and the inner life of the subject is completely exposed, is possible only in fiction—or in the records of the Recording Angel. His account of Francis' life is to be seen as a model of this unachievable ideal. Indeed, Davies was sufficiently worried that I might take Darcourt's impasse as a criticism of my own endeavours that, in March of 1983, soon after he had written the opening section (which ends with the introduction of the Lesser Zadkiel and the Daimon Maimas), he read it aloud to me, with the assurance that I should not take its implications personally.

Many of Davies' resources for telling the story of Francis Cornish lay well below the surface. The Blairlogie sections in particular were so emotionally weighted for him that he had trouble staying at his desk. Soon after beginning the book's second section, in July 1983, he explained to Elisabeth Sifton: "I keep pushing it into the background because I am finding it very heavy and exhausting work. It has roots in my own childhood—in the emotions, not in the actualities—and is painful to drag out of the past. I do not suppose that as a child I suffered more than any reasonably intelligent child, but I felt it keenly, and feel it now, and as I write I feel that I am the Scriptural dog returning again to his vomit, and the sow that was washed to her wallowing in the mire—only in the past sixty years the dog and the sow have lost their taste for vomit and mud. But I drive myself forward. The pace is so slow that I think the book may be ready for Autumn 1985, but not before—not if it is to be any good, and I still hope it may be good."

Davies had had to wait until he was seventy before he could make use of this painful raw material in his writing. The Deptford books, with their powerful statement of his deepest convictions, had not been possible for him until he had passed through the crisis of middle age and had thoroughly reoriented his outlook on life. And this cankered part of his past had resisted him until he had reached the age of retirement and entered the years when, as he sees it, a man must explore his soul and face everything his life has been. But his growing success as a writer provided him with reassurance that what he found when he dug deep would find public acceptance.

The fact that the new novel was rooted in painting was another aspect of the "very heavy going." It is not that he knows nothing about art. He is familiar with many of the major public collections in Canada, the United States and England. When travelling he always spends time in art galleries and pays attention to the pictures and statuary in churches and cathedrals and monasteries. He is especially knowledgeable about religious pictures and made himself encyclopedic about the symbols associated with various saints while writing *Fifth Business*. In galleries, he takes particular interest in portraits for their psychological insights and judgments. He has a long list of favourites: the primitives, Rembrandt, Titian, Raphael, Rubens, Dürer, Holbein, Vermeer, Bronzino, Arcimboldo, Goya, Hieronymous Bosch, Brueghel (both Old and Young), Altdorfer, Murillo, Augustus John, Tiepolo. He is fascinated by the dark, visionary art of Fuseli, and drawn to ikons of the Novgorod school for the way they "speak resonantly and without illusion of faith and the shackles of the flesh, and the nobility that triumphs over death." Veronese's *Family of Darius before Alexander*, Vermeer's *The Painter in His Studio* and Bronzino's *An Allegory* are especially important to him.

His response to painting does not rest primarily on "painterly" qualities or aesthetic considerations. Speaking to the Royal Canadian Academy of Arts in 1973, he declared, only partly tongue-in-cheek: "...I dearly love a picture that tells a story, and has some thrilling title like *The Last Day in the Old Home*, or *And When Did You Last See Your Father?* It was my good fortune to marry into a family that contains rather more than the statistical average of painters, and they have done something to raise my level. But my wife has made what I consider the most perceptive judgement about my attitude toward pictures: she said, 'You don't really see pictures, you read them.' And that is true. My cast of mind is incorrigibly literary."

His cast of mind is also associative, symbolic, religious and theatrical—the qualities that led to the selection of the pictures that hang on the walls of Windhover and the condominium in Toronto. He and Brenda have a number of paintings by her brother-in-law, Sir Russell Drysdale, which he recognizes as "plainly the work of a fine painter," but they say little to him. Many of their pictures are illustrations of the theatre of the eighteenth and nineteenth centuries, and a good part of Davies' pleasure in them derives from his familiarity with the play, or the theatre where the performance took place, or the life of the actor or actress in question. He particularly prizes a scene from the first production of Goldsmith's *She Stoops to Conquer* in Covent Garden, painted in 1774 by Thomas Parkinson. It calls to his mind the lines that the characters are speaking at that point, lines that he himself memorized—along with the rest of the play—at the Old Vic; it evokes the performances he has attended (he has seen at least four); and it reminds him of Goldsmith's marvellous capacity to create character through dialogue and comedy in situation. It gives him further pleasure to know that the picture is the original of two engravings frequently reproduced in theatre histories. Having bought it in London in 1964 as a dirty and misshapen canvas, he had it cleaned and authenticated, and in 1983, just before he began to write *What's Bred in the Bone*, it was hung in the Royal Academy in a show celebrating the 250th anniversary of the Royal Opera House, Covent Garden.

Nonetheless, Davies' knowledge of painting falls far short of his grasp of music, literature or drama, and so he did a great deal of research to underpin what he did know and to avoid errors. While he was developing his ideas for *What's Bred in the Bone* he put himself into the company of art experts by going on two two-week trips sponsored by the Art Gallery of Ontario—one to Vienna, Budapest and Prague and the other to Bavaria. These turned out to be productive in tangential but important ways. Harrach Castle near Vienna gave him a starting point for Schloss Düsterstein and for the Gräfin and her granddaughter: "the Countess received us & we saw the collection, now maintained by some arrangement wth. the State. Mixed, but a fine Brueghel, a fine Bosch of the Harrowing of Hell, a fine Cranach, & a group of three huge processional pictures of a type I had never seen.... Was delighted in the private apts. - to which we were admitted—to see a long range of family portraits & in the room wth. them the Countess's grand-daughter, a girl of abt 16, wth. the *same face*, but living, gentle & distinguished. How long it is since I saw a girl of such manifest breeding! We were given cakes & wine & Jane Zeidler gave the Countess flowers, & she was v. charming in return—an aristocrat who survived great reverses in the war &, in the finest sense, a gutsy old broad." He gave the Schloss a grotto room similar to the one at Weisenstein Castle, "in which all the minerals on the walls had 'died' with depressing effect." Seeing a suit of armour for a dwarf jester at Veste Coburg castle stirred his imagination with its suggestion of "boundless cruelty." This may have been what moved him to include the suicide of the dwarf tailor in Francis' Blairlogie years; it certainly lies behind the inclusion of such a suit in *The Marriage at Cana*. And Davies' reaction on seeing the Grail Hall at Neuschwanstein probably entered into his depiction of Francis' fascination with the Grail myth: "I sympathise deeply with Leopold & his longing for something wholly beyond the common. This visit is important to me: it crystalizes something within me. Oddly reminiscent of Leighton, though Leighton was built almost 20 years earlier. But the same unappeasable romanticism was at work there, the yearning for the light that never was on sea or land."

Brenda's relatives provided Davies with several resources for Francis' education as an artist. Her grandfather, Richard Larking, who doted on his daughter Mimi, delighted in taking photographs. Davies made Francis' grandfather, whose great love was his elder daughter, a keen amateur of the camera who pursued "the many sorts of light the Canadian seasons afford" in photographs he called "Sun Pictures." Brenda's Aunt Elsa, like many other artists, had chosen to live in St. Ives, and so Davies viewed Cornwall as a good place to send an artist. (He had other reasons for Francis to be there too: as the name suggests, the Cornish family estate is there, and the Grail legends are based there as well.) Maisie's two husbands, Pete Purves-Smith and Russell Drysdale, had, in the late 1930s, studied under Othon Friesz at La Grande Chaumière in Paris, and Drysdale in particular had told Davies something of what he had learned there. So Davies knew that that was a good place to send his budding artist to learn the technique of oil painting.

But Davies found most of the basis for Francis' artistic life in his own experience. It gave him a rough guide for what Francis might plausibly brush against during a life that occupied roughly the same time and places, and it afforded events that could be tailored to fit a medium of expression very different from his own. The borrowing and reinterpretation begin virtually as Francis steps on stage. Davies gives his own first recollection— the encounter with a deep-red peony—to Francis, and uses the incident to mark the advent of consciousness and the first recognition of passionate, entrancing, unchaste beauty, the delight and bedevilment of his hero's life as a man and as an artist.

As a child, Davies was an extraordinarily retentive observer, a capacity which has been of the utmost importance to his art; Francis too is "a noticer" from a very young age. In Renfrew, Davies spent many Saturday afternoons at the movies; he was aware that the local undertakers did crude embalming; he was accused of hiding a lunatic relative or hideous freak in the attic; he read Harry Furniss' *How to Draw in Pen and Ink*. Davies refocused these experiences to become stimuli for Francis' sort of artistic sensibility. At films, Francis is aware of the backgrounds and camera angles; at the local undertaker's he learns much about human anatomy, the dwarf tailor's included. He sets his foot on the all-important road to self-discovery when, again and again, he draws his idiot brother, the personification of his shadow, whom he discovers hidden in the attic. He studies Furniss' book and follows his advice about drawing. At UCC, Davies had given a speech *extempore* criticizing the portraits of school dignitaries in the Prayer Hall, an indiscretion that prompted the headmaster to give him some advice—the same advice that Francis is given by the Head of Colborne College. Where Davies had spent his prize money on books like Shaw's prefaces and plays and Browning's *The Ring and the Book*, Francis uses the money slipped him by the headmaster to purchase Burckhardt's *History of the Renaissance* and Vasari's *Lives of the Painters* (Davies read them in preparation for writing the novel).

While a student at Oxford, Davies had seen the miserable state of the Pre-Raphaelite murals in the Union. In *What's Bred in the Bone,* he used this as a reason for the Union (of which Francis is a member) to seek the advice of Tancred Saraceni, and thus for Francis to meet him. The marvellously vivid Saraceni, with his treasure-packed apartment in Rome, his estrangement from his wife and his Evil Eye, got his own start later, in a few things that Davies had learned about the famous Italian scholar Mario Praz—things that were omitted, as he explained in a letter to the editor of the *Times* of London, from that newspaper's obituary of Praz, which appeared in 1982 while he was making notes for *What's Bred in the Bone.*

The first was his stature as a great collector of European furniture of the Napoleonic era. His description of his dwelling and his furniture in *La Casa della Vita* (published 1958, translated as *The House of Life* 1964) is a moving and also a somewhat alarming description of the collector's mania. It was said that Professor Praz sacrificed his marriage to his collection, but I have no way of verifying the truth of this statement.

The second important thing of which no mention was made is that for many years it has been discussed, half jokingly and half in awe in academic circles on two continents, as to whether or not Professor Praz really possessed the Evil Eye. Stories went round of visitors to the House of Life who had not pleased the Professor and who, on leaving, fell down the stairs and broke a leg. Other stories told of those who attempted to contradict him in public only to find that their senses swooned and their voices sank to an incomprehensible croak. Unfavourable critics of his work encountered strange misfortunes....

Even before he went to Oxford, Davies had been fascinated by Bronzino's *An Allegory*, which presents Venus, framed by a number of allegorical figures, in incestuous embrace with her son Cupid. He had hung a reproduction of it in his rooms at Balliol and visited the original regularly thereafter at the National Gallery in London. It is very much a picture which asks to be "read," but to understand even part of its message one must know a great deal about Renaissance iconography, or approach the painting (as Davies did) with the help of a commentary, like the one Erwin Panofsky offers in *Studies in Iconology: Humanistic Themes in the Art of the Renaissance*. Even so, the full meaning of the painting yielded itself only slowly, and some physical details remained obscure to him for years. Not until 1959, for example, did he notice that Venus has her tongue thrust into her son's mouth. In 1983, just before he began to write *What's Bred in the Bone*, he came to have a good look at it.

...to the Ntl. Gallery to see the Bronzino *Allegory* & spent 45 mins contemplating it as well as I could while shoals of schoolchildren aged 8 or so rushed & chattered around me. They were doing a 'class' & had writing-boards & pencils & forms to fill in. The first query abt. the Bronzino was 'Do you think this picture is rude?' Rude in what way, I asked a teacher. 'The lidy is niked', said she. The children all said No save for one black child who had the guts or the perception to say Yes! 'You recognize that

this is one of the most subtly erotic pictures in the Gallery'
said I. 'Yes, but they don't know what erotic is', said the
teacher. 'A mother is seducing her son' said I. 'Aoh, I didn't
know *that*' said she. She seemed a very decent woman but
no Kenneth Clark. One boy identified the honey comb
held by Fraude as a grater - a reasonable guess but he was
not told otherwise. But at last I was able to see it untrou-
bled save by a tedious foreigner - Scandinavian I guessed -
who wanted to inform me about how 'sick religion' had
demanded modest overpaintings at one time.

The Bronzino is Francis Cornish's favourite picture, too. Like
Davies, he discovers it before he goes to Oxford, and like Davies,
he can do little more at that stage than to describe its various
puzzling characters. But when he meets Saraceni, he is given the
benefit of the restorer's knowledge of Renaissance painting (courtesy of Panofsky) and thus learns that the painting is about
Luxury, whose sensual pleasures mask jealousy, bitterness, beastli-
ness, madness. Saraceni pushes Francis to see that its central figures represent the erotic potential in the relationship between
mothers and sons, suggesting that he probably has knowledge of
this from his own relationship with his mother. Francis resists
this, but the reader knows that Francis' mother *did* flirt with
him. (Was Davies himself drawn to the painting by a somewhat
different possibility—that the central figures suggest the possessive, competitive love that had so bedevilled the period when he
was growing up and moving beyond his mother's orbit into relationships with girls of his own age?)
     There was one figure in the painting that particularly intrigued
Davies when he hung a reproduction of it in his rooms at Balliol
in 1935—that of Fraude. Her face reminded him of Eleanor
Sweezey's. It was a connection he continued to make whenever
he saw the picture, as he noted in 1985: "Impressed as always by
the facial resemblance of the figure of Fraude with EAS when
first I met her when she was seventeen. And Fraude she was to
me, with the honeycomb & the sting." Francis has his own
encounter with Fraude—whom Saraceni describes as having "a
wistful, appealing face, a rich gown that might almost blind us to

her lion's feet, her serpent's sting, and her hands that offer both a
honeycomb and something beastly"—in the shape of his cousin
Ismay, who tricks him into marrying her to legitimize her lover's
baby, then deserts him and the child to join her lover in Spain.
Like Davies' own brush with Fraude, this episode puts an end to
Francis' youthful, dreamy romanticism.

Davies turned an embarrassment to advantage when he used a
monkey to establish Francis' credentials in the realm of art. As a
writer, he goes to great lengths to get his facts right—consulting
experts to find out whether a monsignor wears violet socks, or if
owls ever attack women's heads, or how to address a judge in
Holland—and it grates on him painfully to be caught in an
error. In *World of Wonders* he had given the orang-outang Rango
a tail, and when his readers informed him that orang-outangs are
tailless, he checked into the matter and found to his chagrin that
apes are indeed tailless, and that while some Old World monkeys
have tails, only those from the New World have ones that are
prehensile or grasping. However, he was able to capitalize on the
experience when he discovered, reading up his iconography for
What's Bred in the Bone, that medieval paintings like Hubert van
Eyck's *Annunciation* used a fettered ape or monkey to symbolize
the fallen state of the world before the coming of Christ. This
allowed him to establish Francis' expertise in a satisfyingly dramatic way. Saraceni's arch-rival Letztpfennig produces a splendid
painting of *The Harrowing of Hell* and claims it to be by van
Eyck. The experts smell a fake, but can't prove it. When Francis
is sent by Saraceni to uncover the fraud, he spends a few hours at
the zoo, and there he spots what he needs to know. He then bests
the experts by pointing out that the monkey hanging by its tail
in the upper left-hand corner of *The Harrowing of Hell* cannot
have been painted by van Eyck, who died in 1426, since monkeys with prehensile tails were unknown to Europe before the
sixteenth century!

Davies had been acquainted with Alan Jarvis—upon whom he
based Aylwin Ross, Francis' last great love—since the 1930s. As a
newspaperman, he had watched the Oxford-educated, socially
adept, extraordinarily handsome Jarvis soar to prominence in
Canada as director of the National Gallery from 1955 to 1959,

and he was well aware of Jarvis' ambition to build the Gallery's collection to world stature, as well as of the clash that resulted in his disgrace, alcoholism and eventual death. When John Diefenbaker came to power in 1957, Jarvis found that the position of secretary of state (to which he reported) had gone to Ellen Fairclough, reputedly rabidly opposed to giving homosexuals positions of prominence. When Jarvis made himself vulnerable by committing the Gallery to the purchase of several expensive European paintings without first getting the government's approval, Fairclough refused to back him and had him fired.

In creating Ross, Davies deliberately immortalized an exceptional Canadian. The journalist Robert Fulford, who knew Jarvis well, published an article after *What's Bred* appeared in which he delineated the parallels between the man and the fictional character. He judged that Davies had described his friend "with insight and imagination," and had caught the very tone of his voice. But he also noted an absence of sympathy: "On his best days Jarvis reached for a certain nobility of spirit; he had a marvellously spontaneous gaiety; and he could inspire others to their best efforts." In fact, Davies and Jarvis, rival lions on the Canadian cultural scene, were never at ease with each other. When they met, as Davies once frankly admitted, Jarvis always tried "to take the mickey out of me and I was equally determined to deflate him." Also, as Davies imagined the relationship between Francis Cornish and Aylwin Ross it was important that the latter be the less admirable character. In a work of fiction he was free to make use of the qualities that served the needs of his story and to ignore those that did not.

Most important, Davies gave Francis and his mentors his own artistic convictions. Like Davies, Francis believes that an artist must find his own way, and that no one else can teach it to him. Like Davies, too, Francis believes that an artist must open himself to the world in all its extravagance and must not permit conventional attitudes to limit his perceptions. Aunt Mary-Ben shares Davies' view that one function of art is to make people appreciate and see what lies around them. And Saraceni assures Francis that "art is a way of telling the truth," even when its inherent deceptiveness is manipulated in ways that verge on the criminal.

Modern painting for the most part does not interest Davies. It is not that he views contemporary painters as being less capable or honest or inspired than those of earlier generations. As he explained in a speech about "Painting, Fiction and Faking," which he gave at the Museum of Modern Art in New York in 1988, he believes that they have lost access to an important resource, that is, the shared myth and religion whose wisdom has captured imaginations and commanded belief across the western world from the time of the ancient Greeks until the present century. The stories of the classical and Judaeo-Christian heritage gave earlier artists a vocabulary that their viewers understood, in which they could frame their most profound insights. Lacking this shared language, modern artists paint the things that arise from their unconscious in a multitude of private forms. In such circumstances it is easy for an artist to fake inspiration, while the viewers, confronted with this multiplicity of new symbols and forms, are faced with an extraordinary challenge.

This is in essence the view of the moderns that Saraceni propounds to Francis:

> The best of them are doing what honest painters have always done, which is to paint the inner vision, or to bring the inner vision to some outer subject. But in an earlier day the inner vision presented itself in a coherent language of mythological or religious terms, and now both mythology and religion are powerless to move the modern mind. So—the search for the inner vision must be direct. The artist solicits and implores something from the realm of what the psychoanalysts, who are the great magicians of our day, call the Unconscious, though it is actually the Most Conscious. And what they fish up—what the Unconscious hangs on the end of the hook the artists drop into the great well in which art has its being—may be very fine, but they express it in a language more or less private. It is not the language of mythology or religion. And the great danger is that such private language is perilously easy

to fake. Much easier to fake than the well-understood language of the past.

It is also the view that Francis himself reaches when he begins to
use his wealth to encourage contemporary Canadian art, an
experience that proves to be "like that of a man who bites into a
peach and breaks a tooth on the stone."

Davies was once told by Gilbert Bagnani, a colleague in classics
at the University of Toronto, that he is "a Mannerist writer"—an
observation he accepts as insightful. In the history of painting
the term "Mannerism" describes a movement dominant between
1520 and 1600, primarily in Italy, that included Pontormo,
Parmigianino, Vasari, Arcimboldo, Bronzino and El Greco. For
Davies, it "means something between Classicism and Baroque—
not rigidly austere, or Papist Profusion but with a bit of El Greco
distortion, used as a way of presenting truth more sharply than
strict representation can do. Truth is not always or invariably
what the dullest wit or the most unimaginative eye can discern.
Mannerists in literature? Meredith, I suppose, but the king of
them all was Rabelais, and after him and very different, Byron—
which is why he hated the leaden virtue of Wordsworth. In art,
perhaps my favourite is Bronzino, whose Allegory of Love
(Venus, Cupid, Folly and Time) I used as one of the underprops
for *What's Bred in the Bone*."

When Davies talked about Bronzino's *An Allegory* and his
Madonna and Child with St. John the Baptist in his speech
"Painting, Fiction and Faking," he focused not on their painterly
qualities—the crowding of the figures into the foreground plane,
the attenuated proportions, the twisting yet graceful poses of the
figures—but rather on their subject matter, and particularly on
Bronzino's capacity to portray important truths about human
behaviour through the symbols of classical and Christian myth.
In that speech his consideration of Bronzino led him to declare
that Mannerism "is not a technical style of painting; it is a way
of feeling and thinking about life, the way of the moralist who
sees and records and reminds, but who does not insistently
judge."

Certainly Francis Cornish is a Mannerist painter, both as the world of art and as Davies understand the term. Confronted with Francis' *The Marriage at Cana*, the experts of the Allied Commission on Art in *What's Bred in the Bone* comment on "the distortion of some of the figures and the *grotesquerie*" and they observe that the painting has "Italianate, Mannerist features." The story makes it amply clear that *The Marriage* is the work of a moralist who has seen himself and the important figures in his life with clear eyes. It does not shout its message, but, like Bronzino's *An Allegory*, unfolds it gradually to the viewer's contemplation.

All this being said, the connection between Mannerism and Davies' work would be obscure in the absence of his interpretation. When art critics talk of Mannerism, they usually have in mind the technical, painterly elements that Davies downplays, and their assessments of Bronzino typically see a cool worldliness where he sees subtlety and penetration to the archetypes. If one were trying to find painters to compare with Davies—a pleasant, if ultimately unsatisfying game—then one might with comparable justice consider Hieronymus Bosch's depictions of Hell, Earth and Paradise, Goya's dark confrontations with the shadow or his sharply observed depictions of the Spanish royal family, Titian's knowing portraits, Rembrandt's self-revelations, Degas' circus performers or Dutch genre painting.

Though he thought of himself as not knowing much about painting, Davies proved to have amply broad resources once he put his mind to the subject. Davies' annoyance with the critics who accused him of being old-fashioned led him to create an artist whose genius is to paint in the manner and with the technique and materials of the sixteenth century, and the result is a portrait of an artist that is individual and compelling.

Shortly after completing the first draft of *What's Bred in the Bone*, Davies wrote a brief progress report to Douglas M. Gibson, then his editor at Macmillan of Canada. "The book, as I think you know, is linked with RebAngs, but is not a sequel; indeed the action is anterior to the first book and is the life of Francis Cornish, the art connoisseur whose great collections set off the action in the first book. This is bad chronology, I know, but the fact is that I do not write trilogies, all neatly planned to follow in sequence: I write about groups of characters, and their stories get mixed up and sometimes cause some awkwardness. I am no Henry James worker in exquisite marquetry: my stuff is often very badly shaped." This is unnecessarily modest. The sudden shifts in time and perspective from one volume of the trilogy to the next is one of its pleasures. And the individual volumes are linked by far more than their common characters. Mamusia's restoration of old stringed instruments anticipates Saraceni's enhancement of old paintings, and both of them emphasize the element of deception that is present in all art. In both books, past and present are made to approach each other: in *The Rebel Angels*, the characteristics of medieval universities persist in their contemporary descendants; in *What's Bred in the Bone*, a modern artist so thoroughly absorbs the techniques and manner of an earlier day that his works are mistaken for those of an Old Master. The medieval science of alchemy is important for both novels, determining the interests of several characters in the one, and providing the basis for the interpretation of *The Marriage at Cana* in the other, which results in the "unknown" painter coming to be known as "The Alchemical Master." Angels make an appearance in both books: in *The Rebel Angels* in the guise of learned professors and in *What's Bred in the Bone* in the custodian of the record of Francis Cornish's life.

What's Bred in the Bone was published by Macmillan in Canada in October 1985, by Viking in the United States in November and in Britain the following February. Although there were a handful of condemnations of the book as "pretentious" (the *Peterborough Examiner*), "interminable" (the *Boston Globe*) and cobbled together with "too improbable" coincidences (the *Times*), the prevailing view was that the book was vintage Davies, indeed his best novel since *Fifth Business*. For the first time he was taken seriously in Britain, and was given the lead spot in those reviews that dealt with several new novels, or in some cases an extended solo treatment. The *Times Literary Supplement* credited him with "five brilliant novels" over the past fifteen years, the *Daily Telegraph* saw him as "Canada's cleverest novelist" and the London *Sunday Times* called him "one of the great modern novelists, and probably the most important to have emerged in Canadian fiction."

This was heady stuff. It put the novel on the Canadian best-seller lists in *Maclean's* magazine for thirty-two weeks and in the *Toronto Star* for thirty, and on those published in the *New York Times* and the *Washington Post* for nine and fourteen weeks respectively. This translated into hardcover sales of 21,795 in Canada, 40,759 in the United States, and 5,995 in Britain.

As he was readying *What's Bred in the Bone* for publication, Davies put some time into a revival of his old literary persona, Samuel Marchbanks. Clarke, Irwin had published the first two Marchbanks books years before, but during the 1970s, to his frustration, it had allowed those books and the plays to go out of print. He was also unhappy with the company's handling of *Tempest-Tost* and *Leaven of Malice*. Although it continued to sell substantial numbers of both novels in Canada, it had made no move to develop an American or international market for them. Davies tried various stratagems to recover the rights. He encouraged his agent to approach the publisher with Canadian and American paperback offers and supported the efforts of at least three other houses (Macmillan of Canada, McClelland and Stewart and Penguin Books Canada) that wanted to republish the Salterton novels and the Marchbanks books. He set lawyers, agents and publishers to examining the contracts for loopholes, but they found none. However, Clarke, Irwin's financial difficulties accomplished what his efforts had not; Penguin Books was finally able to acquire the rights to *Tempest-Tost* and *Leaven of Malice* in 1979, and republished them in 1980, along with *A Mixture of Frailties*, for the Canadian, American and Commonwealth markets. After Clarke, Irwin went into receivership in 1983, Davies' agent struck a satisfactory deal with the company that purchased its assets—The Book Society of Canada Limited, subsequently renamed Irwin Publishing Inc.—to do a Marchbanks omnibus volume.

The idea of putting all of Marchbanks in a single volume had been in the air since 1977. All three publishers had pursued it, but it was Douglas Gibson at Macmillan who came up with an approach close to the one Davies decided to use. Noting Davies' concern about the advisability of bringing out "a book of warmed over material when I seem to be in the process of establishing a serious reputation as a novelist," Gibson had replied:

> I believe that your reservations about the book's reception would be perfectly justified if we merely threw together a slap-dash collection of material from the three previous books and presented it as new. The key, I believe, lies in making a careful selection, organizing it well and—as you suggested at one point—linking it with new writing in the form of a running commentary, notes or what have you. You might even like to consider the idea of the current R.D. treating the task seriously and writing in the role of editor of the works of the now-deceased and unjustly-neglected Marchbanks.

And so, in November and December 1984 and the first four months of 1985, as he readied the final typescript of *What's Bred in the Bone* for submission to his publishers and responded to their editorial queries, Davies reframed and reorganized the 1947 *Diary*, the 1949 *Table Talk* and the 1967 *Almanack* into *The Papers of Samuel Marchbanks*, a "scholarly edition" prepared by Marchbanks' old academic friend and look-alike, Robertson Davies.

This was a new stage in the long history of playfully intertwined relations that had begun in 1940. Up to 1953 Marchbanks had regularly claimed authorship of the plays that were published under Davies' name, and made a habit of reporting to the *Examiner* on the various regional and national competitions of the Dominion Drama Festival at which they were performed. In 1954, the year after his column ended, Marchbanks provided biographical sketches of himself and his *doppelgänger*, Robertson Davies, for the readers of *Liberty* magazine, acknowledging Davies' activities as a playwright and newspaperman but claiming for himself the novel *Tempest-Tost* and, of course, the Marchbanks books. In the Introduction to the *Papers*, Marchbanks appropriated Davies' journalistic career to himself as well, leaving Davies to figure only as a university professor.

Davies, for his part, enjoyed his role as the scholarly editor of the *Papers*. He used a number of different methods to reduce the three original volumes to one. In the case of the *Diary*, he took little tucks here and there in the individual entries and made major changes in only a couple. With the *Table Talk* he changed the placing of half a dozen entries, shortening or cutting out many more. On the initial run-through he gave the *Almanack* the same light editorial treatment, but then decided to excise seventy-nine manuscript pages of almanack apparatus, letters and entries, and rearranged what remained into "Marchbanks' Garland." Throughout, he took immense pleasure in comporting himself in the "real academic style—correcting the author, throwing doubt on his memory and veracity, and generally trampling him beneath my feet," as he cheerfully told Horace Davenport. The scholarly notes often smack of Marchbanks, however, which is a puzzle that may vex the latter's biographer, when one appears.

Critics greeted the volume with enthusiasm when Irwin Publishing brought it out in Canada in the fall of 1985, followed by Viking in the United States in July 1986 and in Britain in May 1987.

Chapter 16

The Lyre of Orpheus: 1984-88

—————◆—————

...Giles' ring was one of these—a green stone in which was
engraved a figure of Orpheus bearing his lyre. The naked god
was incised, and could be transferred to wax, as a seal.
                                              —*A Mixture of Frailties*, 1958

THE FALL OF 1986 brought two clear indications that Davies
had achieved international renown, and at the same time introduced him to some of the more trying aspects of fame. He had
been looking forward to a Scandinavian tour in September during which he was to be the guest of the Canadian government in
Copenhagen, Oslo, Helsinki and Stockholm and guest of honour at literary lunches and dinners given by his publishers in
each country. He had long felt that Canadians have much in
common with the peoples of Scandinavia and Russia, and it
pleased him to know that his books were selling well in
Denmark, Norway, Finland and Sweden. The tour was to last
seventeen days, and then he and Brenda were to go on to
London for a month's vacation. But he had hardly set out when
he heard that he was one of the eight writers on the short list for
the Nobel Prize for literature and that he had been on it in 1985
as well. This was stunning news: whether he won or not, he was

being viewed as one of the world's leading writers.

The Nobel Prizes (except for the peace prize) are awarded by an international committee based in Stockholm, and Davies found the Scandinavians preoccupied with the subject. For the first time he found himself the object of attention from female literary groupies: after one good-looking blonde made "a dead set" at him, he reflected: "Wd. once have been flattered: now wish she wd. restrain herself." Everywhere he went the prize was a topic of conversation, albeit an uncomfortable one, since people would acknowledge that he was in the running and then invariably point out that he wasn't expected to take it. Davies himself was certain that he wouldn't win and was inclined to accept the prevailing wisdom that the prize would go to an African for political reasons. Nonetheless, he found himself reflecting: "I know it is absurd, but I cannot put it out of my mind or utterly relinquish hope until I hear the result. What wd. it really do for me? Give me much-desired reassurance & a bulwark against that Canadian 'interesting but flawed' criticism. Let those who think it foolish consider what they would feel if such a stamp of value hovered like a phantom in their own careers. Much energy is wasted in this torment."

After the tour ended Davies and Brenda spent a couple of days in Amsterdam. The Nobel was still up in the air and would not be settled for several more weeks. While there, they learned that *What's Bred in the Bone* had been nominated for the Booker Prize, the most prestigious award for fiction in the English-speaking world. Davies, the oldest person ever to have been nominated, observed in his travel diary: "Try not to allow vaulting ambition to unseat my reason, with only limited success." And two days later, after a bad night, he wrote, "the Booker & the Nobel have stuffed my pillow with thorns: I shall know no peace until both are decided. I am reconciled to getting neither, but while a hope remains I cannot abandon it. No Stoic, I."

Worn out, he looked forward to enjoying some peace and quiet in London. But when he arrived, on September 27, he was swept into the hype associated with the Booker, a four-week marathon of book-signing sessions and interviews (the latter often three a day), and his periods of rest became less and less effective against a weary spirit and an exhausted body. At his daughter Miranda's house on September 28 he got out her copy of the *I Ching* and "cast for the Nobel & the Booker: hexagrams 15 & 34 respectively wth. the counsel of which the I Ching is so fond: patience & honourable conduct bears good fruit, which is not very revealing in the circs." At St. Paul's, Covent Garden a couple of days later he "looked at the memorials & was saddened by the number of players I admired who have gone. Even Michael Benthall, my Oxford & OUDS friend. Was almost in tears before the tablets to Dame Sybil & Sir Lewis. Prayed that I might have the grace to accept whatever happens—Nobel & Booker—in a proper spirit, neither inflated nor cast down. God, what a bred-in-the-bone Calvinist I am!"

When the time came, he did accept the results with calm. On October 17, when he learned that the Nobel had gone to the Nigerian Wole Soyinka, he concluded: "So that is that, I should think, forever." (He was wrong: he was short-listed again at least once more, in 1992.) And after he found on the 22nd that Kingsley Amis had pipped him for the Booker in a close contest, he observed: "To bed at last, & that is over. I never thought I wd. win & am glad to have given Amis such a close run.... The opinion of the publishers is that this shd. at last establish my work in the U.K.—So, if I'm spared, as Grandmother McKay used to say, I must do something good with the next book. I have won no prizes but, as Thwaites [the chairman of the judges] said, I have a chance of being read in 100 years and that is really what it's all about." So ended a trip that Davies felt to have been "the most unremittingly stressful & demanding period in my recent years—continual outpouring."

The surge of ideas that had overwhelmed Davies in the first two years of preparation for *What's Bred in the Bone* kept driving him along. In the fall of 1984, before the final draft of *What's Bred* was off his desk and before he settled down to creating *The Papers of Samuel Marchbanks*, he started note-making again, and by the end of a short vacation in London over Christmas (during which he and Brenda stayed in the time-shared apartment at 46 Pont Street that they had purchased in 1983), he had "laid the keel of the 3<u>rd</u> bk. in my current trilogy." He continued to make notes during 1985 as he completed *What's Bred* and *Marchbanks*, publicized the two books, and spent a month in London, Florence and Rome with Brenda.

The year 1986 brought its share of distractions as well. In January, he was among the specially invited guests at the week-long 48th International PEN (Poets, Playwrights, Editors, Essayists, and Novelists) Congress in New York, where his snowy hair and beard caught the eye of the cartoonist for *New York* magazine, and he enjoined his fellow writers: "A week of collegial fraternity every few years is quite enough. On Saturday—back to your ivory towers!" In August, he spent a week at the Banff Centre School of Fine Arts in Alberta, as the winner of the school's National Award. And, of course, it was that autumn that brought the Scandinavian tour, the London "vacation" and the emotional roller-coaster of the Nobel and Booker near-misses. On his return from London he wrote "The Harper of the Stones," a ghost story for children, set to music by Louis Applebaum and performed (with Davies himself reading the story) at the Young People's Theatre the following May. During 1985 and 1986 he also gave the occasional speech and wrote a few reviews and articles.

By January 1, 1987, he was ready to begin writing, and a year later *The Lyre of Orpheus* was completed, revised and off to his publishers. He drew his title and epigraph—"The lyre of Orpheus opens the door of the underworld"—from E. T. A. Hoffmann's criticism of Beethoven's Fifth Symphony. Two projects provide the basis for the action—the completion and production of the opera *Arthur of Britain*, left unfinished by Hoffman, the composer, nov-elist, critic and conductor, at his death in 1822, and the writing of the biography of Francis Cornish.

Davies had plenty to work with in taking up the subject of opera. He had a lifetime of opera-going behind him (in 1989 he reported that he had seen between eighty and ninety, a number of them many times) and has always been tremendously suscep-tible to its enchantments. For him, "Opera gives us the great big basic emotions of life itself. It strikes at once on your feelings because music is the very language of feeling." More, as he observed in a speech given in 1989, "Opera in a splendidly direct way takes us into the world of archetypes, and music has its own overmastering way of making archetypes palpable to us.... In great opera, as in great painting and great literature, we meet these possibilities of ideas given an immediate and comprehensible form, and we are seized by them because what we see and hear from the stage speaks directly to things that lie very deep in our nature."

Of the three great composers of opera, Mozart, Verdi and Wagner, Mozart is Davies' special favourite. He savours the composer's deft musical comments on the libretto in *The Marriage of Figaro* and his masterful evocation of the stages the hero passes through in *The Magic Flute* on his way to becoming a complete and unified human being. High on Davies' list are the sweeping melodrama and psychological perception of Tchaikovsky's *Eugene Onegin*, the bittersweet charm of Strauss' *Der Rosenkavalier*, the audacious mingling of comedy and tragedy in his *Ariadne auf Naxos* and the great theme of remorse in Mussorgsky's *Boris Godunov*. He also has a soft spot for Sir Julius Benedict's *The Lily of Killarney* and Balfe's *The Bohemian Girl*, because Rupert sang some of their songs. But his interest in opera is broad and adventurous.

For Davies, opera's potential is only satisfactorily realized in live performance, where the spectacle, the music, the singing and the acting can build on the shared excitement of the audience. He believes too that opera works best when the libretto is built around a single idea, a well-drawn plot and broadly conceived characters. These convictions became part of *Lyre*, whose opera-in-the-making is based on the Arthurian legends. Geraint Powell, the opera's producer, understands very well that the piece "must above all have a strong narrative that can carry the weight of music." And when he outlines a clear, but emotionally and symbolically powerful, story-line for the libretto of *Arthur of Britain*, he makes sure that it affords ample opportunity for spectacle. With the support of Dr. Gunilla Dahl-Soot, an experienced operatic conductor, he firmly turns aside all suggestions that would blur the tale's clarity, or that might be theatrically impractical, no matter how true they might be to Malory's *Morte Darthur*. In one of the novel's climactic scenes, Davies makes us see and feel the enchantment as the story, the music, the spectacle and the glorious singing grip the opera's audience.

In *Lyre*, Davies is particularly interested in three elements in the creation of a work of art, whether opera or biography. One is the flash of audacious imagination; another is the recondite skill of the practitioner; the third is the human drama. As the story begins, Arthur Cornish dares the directors of the Cornish Foundation, audaciously enough, to take a major risk—to support a nineteen-year-old composer, Hulda Schnakenburg, in her project of completing Hoffmann's opera (the project will fulfil one of the requirements for her doctorate in music), and then, if her work is satisfactory, to underwrite the cost of mounting the opera and giving it a public performance. Guided by her supervisor, the respected musicologist, composer and conductor of opera Dr. Gunilla Dahl-Soot, "Schnak" sets to work, learning everything she can about Hoffmann's music and his intentions for the opera and about contemporary operatic conventions and conditions, and she manages to develop Hoffmann's scraps and pieces into an effective and organic whole. She is assisted as well by Simon Darcourt, who writes a fine libretto to replace the inappropriate original one by James Robinson Planché. Like her score, the libretto is the product of an historical imagination: Darcourt searches out a poet from Hoffman's period and adapts his verses and poems to fit their new context, writing congruent *recitativo* passages himself. Schnak's third professional supporter is the producer Geraint Powell. With dynamism, vision and practicality he conceives the basic outline for the libretto, hires the right singers, finds a sympathetic designer, approves a claque (led by Maria's uncle Yerko) and succeeds in giving the opera an imaginative period staging. Despite a tragicomic doctoral examination at which a blinkered pedant fails to appreciate Schnak's genius and upsets the balance of her finely tuned work of art, the opera's first performance is a magical experience.

While work is proceeding on the opera, Darcourt solves the problems that had prevented him from completing the biography of Francis Cornish in *What's Bred in the Bone*, through a combination of careful hard work, a few imaginative leaps and a dash of chicanery. Leafing through a copy of *Vogue*, he recognizes an Old Master drawing in a cosmetics advertisement as Francis' work. He follows the lead to New York and to the owner of the drawing, Princess Amalie, daughter of the Gräfin of Düsterstein. She agrees to tell him about the missing middle years of Francis Cornish's life, if in return he will acquire for her the preliminary studies for the drawing, since she is worried that it may be exposed as a fake. So Darcourt, turning thief, steals some of Francis' as-yet-uncatalogued drawings from the university library and substitutes them for the (also uncatalogued) preliminary studies at the National Gallery. On his return to New York, the Princess and her husband tell him of Francis' activities as a spy, his apprenticeship under Saraceni, his exposure of the Letztpfennig fraud and the creation of *Drollig Hansel*. In their apartment Darcourt sees *The Marriage at Cana* and privately suspects the true identity of its painter. In time he confirms his suspicions and goes on to puzzle out much of the meaning of the painting, identifying most of the figures in it and coming to understand the roles they had played in Francis' life.

Although much of Francis remains elusive, Darcourt has the insight to grasp his essence, and so the biography rings true. It reveals that Francis is The Alchemical Master of *The Marriage at Cana*, and thus establishes him as a painter of genius, finally winning for him the recognition that, to his daimon's despair, he had scrupled to claim. In *Lyre*'s final section, Darcourt persuades the Princess, the Cornish Foundation, the university library and the National Gallery to place *The Marriage at Cana* and its related sketches, studies and "Sun Pictures" on display in the Francis Cornish Memorial Gallery, so the public will be able to see and appreciate Francis' great achievement.

As always with Davies' novels, real life energized *Lyre* in diverse ways. By the time he began to write in 1987, I had been hard at work for five years, and he was aware of much of my activity. Our interviews had continued at a rate of two or three a year after the first two years. We had discussed a list of additional prospective interviewees, and he knew that I had been making notes from his family and academic records, speeches, travel and theatre diaries, notebooks, favourite melodramas, publishers' and agents' files. He was aware that I had scanned the relevant years in his father's three newspapers and in the *Peterborough Examiner.* And he had agreed that I might see the working notebooks for *The Rebel Angels* and *What's Bred in the Bone.*

But all this activity on my part was stirring a complex response. When I reminded him about the notebooks, he replied on April 7, 1986, with a letter which proved to be something of a writer's manifesto:

When you asked to see my notes for *The Rebel Angels* and *What's Bred in the Bone* I agreed, but since then I have been looking over those notes, and a very strong feeling which I dare not ignore comes over me that I should not let them out of my hands. There are three reasons. First, the two novels are so linked with the one on which I am now working and which will complete this trilogy that I need the notes for checking and reference, because they contain matter important for the third book, on which I am now hard at work. That is the *least* of the reasons. The second is that the notes contain references to people and incidents that are clear to me but which might be misunderstood even by so perceptive a reader as yourself—references to living people, real incidents and matter which could be construed as libellous. Like every novelist I protest that my characters and incidents are without any relation to real people or happenings, and like every novelist I know that this is true only in the sense that real people and incidents are the spark of something which is changed totally in quality when it appears as fiction, but which can be misunderstood if the fictional process is somehow overlooked. Such revelations could give pain, and I do not want that to happen even in the consideration of so judicious a reader as yourself. Like most novelists I know a great deal about people whom I know only slightly, because of gossip or indiscreet revelation from other sources; such material is suitable for fiction but it is troublesome if it becomes confused with reality. That is the *sec-*

ond reason and a good one. But the third reason is the real one: I am, I suppose, superstitious, which I interpret as meaning 'heedful of omens' and I feel in the deepest marrow of my bones that to open the workshop, or the butcher's shop, before all the work is done there—to admit even a guest like yourself to the kitchen—is unlucky in the most profound sense....

My books are works of imagination. Every time one appears I receive letters explaining to me that I have made mistakes about this, that and the other, as though historical accuracy were my principal aim. Of course I try not to make mistakes in matters of fact, but if I were a better historian I would be a lesser novelist. The imagination is a cauldron, not a filing cabinet. But in most of the criticism of my work I read I find that imagination is the quality that appeals least to the majority of critics. To compare small things with great, I would infinitely rather have *Twelfth Night*, in which Illyria has a seacoast, than Hakluyt's *Voyages*. Imagination is all I have to work with; take it from me, and I am rotten meat for any critic with a pocket-knife.

Imagination is in short supply in Canada. Whenever I meet with students I invariably hear the question: 'Where do you get your ideas from?' and whenever I read criticism I know that many of the critics will be hog-wild for *research* and consider imagination a rather sneaky trick. It is the NOTHING BUT attitude toward literary art.... Admittedly I try, like a good conjuror, to persuade my readers, for as long as they read, that I am offering them reality. I bring in Sir Wilfrid Laurier and King George V as front-men for illusion. But in the end the illusion is the best I have to offer.

Of course, Davies was well aware that the province of the biographer is not illusion but fact, personal history and interpretation. He also knew that the biographer of an artist must concern herself with the process of creation as well as with its results, and so has a natural interest in the workshop, the butcher's shop or the kitchen. Actually he placed a certain value on the contents of the workshop himself, having carefully preserved his notes, out-lines, manuscripts, pages of revisions and the like, and in the final analysis he accepted that such records should be drawn upon in any recounting of an artist's life. After he completed *The Lyre of Orpheus*, he gave me access to the notes for all three books of the Cornish trilogy.

The fact that his own biography was in process as he prepared to write *Lyre* reminded him of the sorts of things a biographer might spend her time doing, and he made some use of this sort of detail in his portrayal of Darcourt's activities. The experience of being the subject of an intense investigation is probably reflected in declarations such as "Darcourt yearned for that infor-mation with the feverish lust of a biographer" and "he was wholly in the grip of the biographer's covetous, unappeasable spirit." Davies also explored some of the comic possibilities of the-interview-that-yields-nothing in the scene in which Darcourt, lunching with Francis' "daughter" Charlotte in the hope of discovering something about the missing years of his subject's life, is treated instead to a lengthy rant on ponies and grooms.

Arguably, in Darcourt, Davies himself steps imaginatively into the biographer's shoes. Darcourt's mind works like Davies' own. He reaches important decisions, not through logic but "as a gifted cook makes soup: he threw into a pot anything likely that lay to hand, added seasonings and glasses of wine, and messed about until something delicious emerged." His random "hums" are a key to what is going on in his mind below the busy level of conscious thought. Darcourt's methods, too, are certainly Davies'. The way he discovers *The Marriage at Cana*, and then learns how to interpret it, reflects what often happens when Davies is preparing a novel. Davies often comes upon crucial bits of information by chance, in conversation or from television or newspapers, even as he is making extensive use of reference sources and doing a great deal of very specific reading. Also, the kind of discovery that Darcourt makes about himself has its par-allel in Davies' own life (one Davies himself drew to my atten-tion). Early in the novel Darcourt recognizes that he is a mere factotum of the Cornish Foundation. Then, "without particularly changing the externals of his life, he takes an entirely different attitude toward it and it makes him a different kind of man, and he is freed from the sense of being somehow or other at the beck and call of others." Davies feels that he himself had lived a life in which he was "always having to do other people's bidding—my father's bidding or the bidding of the Massey family," and that like Darcourt he had "had to find a way of doing it without losing myself and just becoming a sort of functionary." Finally, Darcourt's conception of his biography is in the spirit that Davies hoped his own biographer would entertain. Darcourt views Francis' life "as a great artistic adventure. And a very Canadian sort of adventure, what's more." Asked once what he would himself choose as a title for his biography, Davies replied, "The autobiography, the title of which I like best, is Hans Andersen's *Eventyr—An Adventure.*"

The story of the gradual reconstruction of *Arthur of Britain* draws a great deal from Davies' academic and theatrical experience. Articles and reviews about the careers of women composers and the completion of unfinished musical works (gathered from the London *Times*, the *Toronto Symphony Magazine* and an LP's liner notes) reassured him that what he envisioned was credible. His twenty years as a professor and Master gave him intimate knowledge of the process that Schnak is put through to win her doctorate in music. (However, the Cornish Foundation, with its avowed interest in genius and its willingness to underwrite a proposal that "is crack-brained, absurd, could prove incalculably expensive, and violates every dictate of financial prudence," takes a far greater risk than any of the foundations to which Davies was exposed during his years at Massey College.) Schnak's parents, with their limited vision of life's possibilities, are the type of all those whom Davies had met at Massey College whose children had soared into realms beyond their comprehension. Schnak's own dirty sweater, filthy jeans and worn-out running shoes make a statement that Davies had often witnessed at the university and personally abhorred as a mark of disrespect for the institution. Al Crane, the graduate student who records the aspects of the opera's production for his doctorate in theatre, exemplifies the kind of laborious, uninspired tracing of influences that Davies had warned his students to avoid. And among the academics, Hollier demonstrates the kind of fussy pedantry about the opera's libretto that had exasperated Davies from time to time when he was at the university. The external examiner who causes Schnak such trouble at her oral is also a type that Davies had occasionally encountered, great in reputation and in his own opinion, biased on narrow grounds against the examinee, unfair in his questioning. But Davies also draws academics of a different stripe, nourishers of Schnak's talent, who import a supervisor of genius to guide her work, who make the effort to unearth Planché's libretto in the British Museum, who provide an insightful and learned introduction for Darcourt's biography. They represent the fine teaching, skilled research and authoritative scholarship that Davies respected in many of his colleagues.

A little of the depiction of the staging of *Arthur of Britain* draws on Davies' Old Vic experiences—the way scenery was painted, his own enchantment with the theatrical tales of old Ben Webster and the competence that Brenda, as stage manager, had brought to a multitude of details (Davies gives his SM the last name of Brenda's mother). A more pervasive, and more subtle, source of hints, ideas and connections for the story of the creation of the fictional opera lies in Davies' encounters with Tyrone Guthrie over *Love and Libel*. The uneasy moment in Ireland when Guthrie, nude, entered the bathroom and talked while Davies was in his bath, for example, is in the background when Dr. Gunilla Dahl-Soot bathes and seduces Schnak. Similarly, Davies' frustration at the endless rewriting of the script of *Love and Libel* underlies Darcourt's conviction that a librettist leads a dog's life. And Davies pays homage to Guthrie's directorial dynamism, imagination and forceful practicality in the character Geraint Powell.

Davies' decision to have his fictional opera produced in what is clearly the Avon Theatre in Stratford was probably also the result of an association with Guthrie—not in his role with the Festival during its initial years in the great tent, but rather as the director of *H.M.S. Pinafore* in the Avon in 1960, the summer before *Love and Libel* went into production. And the scene in Darcourt's study at Ploughwright College when Geraint Powell, in a whirl-wind of "Shakespearean *brio*," describes the "gigantic obstacle race" that lies before them if the opera is to be mounted the following year, compels Darcourt's agreement to a character list and assigns him the task of preparing the libretto probably owes a good deal to Guthrie's descent on Davies in his Massey College study when the two were planning "The Centennial Spectacle."

Powell also recalls the matinée-idol handsomeness of Robert Goulet, the actor who had played Lancelot in the Lerner and Loewe musical *Camelot. Camelot* had opened in Toronto when *Love and Libel* was going into rehearsal, and it succeeded in New York when Davies' play failed. *Camelot*'s deficiencies, diagnosed in Davies' "Theatre Notes" after the première at the new O'Keefe Centre in 1960, were probably a factor that helped to set the creative juices flowing for *Arthur of Britain*: "The piece is said to be founded on T. H. White's *The Once And Future King*, but all his wit, fantasy, knowledge of chivalry & love of Malory were missing: instead, American 'manlydom', mockery of Lancelot for his purity (Robt. Goulet) & a prissy Guenevere (Julie Andrews) & an Arthur who is an idealistic cuckold (Richard Burton). Tons of handsome, rather too garish scenery by Oliver Smith, & costumes which, rich as they were, did not suggest anything. Everything heavy, slow-moving & repetitious: Hart's production uninventive. Music commonplace: not one tune remains."

As Davies presents it, *Arthur of Britain, or the Magnanimous Cuckold* is a far more satisfying experience than *Camelot*. It is essentially a product of the nineteenth century and, like the great ballets and operas from that period, "a great dream which is of importance to the tribe." Davies chose Hoffmann as its composer, after considering Handel and Purcell, partly for his influential role in the Romantic movement, but also because he had long felt a personal affinity with him. At Queen's he had written a Gothic horror story in the Hoffmann manner, and shortly after completing *Fifth Business* he observed that "if I had to name an author who had strongly influenced me, and whom I admire, it would probably be E. T. A. Hoffmann, whose mingling of the uncanny, the commonplace and the funny I think masterly." Darcourt borrows much of the libretto of the opera (apart from the old ballad at the start and the love lyric from Sir Walter Scott's *Lay of the Last Minstrel* at the climax) from Thomas Lovell Beddoes, partly because his poetry was from the right period and appropriate to Hoffmann's music, but also because Davies himself much enjoys his verse. (To test the critics, Davies decided not to name Beddoes in the text. He was certain that none of them would recognize his poetry, and he was right. None of the reviewers that I read came up with the name.)

Davies' decision to give the opera a production similar to those of Hoffmann's day permitted him to introduce his readers to the special delights of his beloved nineteenth-century theatres. A pair of backstage visits just before he began to write sharpened his long-held convictions about the advantages of earlier methods of staging. In August 1986 he toured the up-to-the-minute opera house in Banff, where everything was electronically controlled, and learned to his surprise and disappointment that it used very little scenery because of the expense. He also learned that if anything went awry, ordinary mortals could be stymied; the circuitry was too complex to put right in a hurry. It was a different story in September, when he and Brenda visited the eighteenth-century Drottningholm Theatre in Sweden. Here there was lots of scenery, painted backdrops and wings, all of it pulled into place and removed by hand. Observing the great windlass under the stage and the huge coils of thick rope once manned by a large stage crew, Brenda said, "This is perfect. You've got *people*. You can rely on *people*. You can tell *people* what to do. But you can never depend on those damned machines." *Lyre* presents the effects that people can achieve, as "with no interfering curtain, and the barest minimum of mechanical sound, the scene changed visibly from Arthur's Court to a nearby chapel, where Morgan Le Fay and her son Modred were plotting the theft of the scabbard of Caliburn. What happened, if you knew, was that the twelve wings that flanked the court scene were drawn silently back out of sight, and wings suited to the ruin were left in view; at the same moment a drop scene was lowered at the back of the stage, and the great hall seemed to have melted imperceptibly into its successor."

Not only does *Arthur of Britain* appropriate the success of

Camelot, the production that had succeeded opposite his own Broadway failure, it goes it one better. Davies thus takes a private opportunity to redress the public failure of *Love and Libel*. It is not coincidental that Geraint Powell, the masterful Guthrie-like producer who gives *Arthur* an enchantingly sympathetic production, also plays Lancelot the betrayer, recalling Guthrie in his role as betrayer of Davies' original conception of *Leaven of Malice* with his rambunctious production of *Love and Libel*.

At the time that Davies "laid the keel" of *Lyre*, late in 1984, he was also working on *The Papers of Samuel Marchbanks*. The act of resetting the columns he had written thirty to forty years earlier moved him to consider "what that was and why it was and who Marchbanks was." And the conclusion he reached was that Marchbanks represented a small but vital part of his own character, an aggressive, extroverted side "that nags me and lives in me [and] which demands that kind of utterance—a rather irreverent, derisive sort of slapstick."

Lyre likewise compelled a reassessment. Davies had reached the age of seventy-four when he wrote the last Cornish volume, and although he did anticipate another book or two, he did not envision any more trilogies. So it is not surprising that he decided, in planning the novel, to gather, restate and expand some of the themes and ideas of his earlier books. He used the notion that recurrent patterns underlie the surface variety of experience to give himself the opportunity to do so. Darcourt introduces it with the observation: "It's been said since—well, at least since Ovid. He says somewhere—in the *Metamorphoses*, I think—that the great truths of life are the wax, and all we can do is to stamp it with different forms. But the wax is the same forever—." He expands on this idea several times later in the story—myth is the unchanging wax, our individual lives are the infinite variations; the basic patterns are relatively few, recurring again and again as the basic plots of literature and life; what is "amazing, and humbling" is "how we tread the old paths without recognizing them." "A Man's life of any worth is a continual allegory—and very few eyes can see the Mystery of his life—a life like the scriptures, figurative," as the quotation that Darcourt places on the wall above

Francis Cornish's painting in the National Gallery says.

Some of the characters perceive the underlying patterns, and others do not. One who does is Francis Cornish, who paints the biblical story of the marriage at Cana as a symbolic representation of his life. Another is Mamusia, who uses the tarot pack to interpret the life of the person before her. But the most conspicuous instance of mythic patterning is the repetition by Arthur, Maria and Geraint Powell of the love triangle in the legends about King Arthur, Queen Guenevere and Lancelot, and in this case Arthur refuses to accept the parallel, even when it is drawn to his attention.

The reader is reminded of the details as Powell explains his ideas for the libretto of *Arthur of Britain, or the Magnanimous Cuckold,* and the parallels of character and situation are drawn to our attention at intervals throughout the story. Like his great namesake, Arthur Cornish has a round table, around which the directors of the Cornish Foundation meet. He is a man of high purpose on a quest to retrieve something very special that was lost in the past. And when he is cuckolded, like the Arthur of old, Darcourt advises him to make a good job of living out the pattern that fate is weaving—to "take a hint from this opera that has brought about the whole thing, and decide to be the Magnanimous Cuckold." Maria, who, as Darcourt tells Arthur, may have "a destiny that needs this fact that you call an infidelity," plays out the role of Guenevere, allowing herself to be seduced by a man who comes to her in the middle of the night wearing the dressing gown she made for her husband. At a deep level she knows it is not Arthur, but this is (as she recognizes) an instance of being deceived "because we will our own deception. It is somehow necessary to us. It is an aspect of fate." And Powell, who seduces Maria and subsequently goes briefly mad (repeating the pattern of Lancelot's betrayal of Arthur and his later insanity), claims that he has acted "in the grip of a great archetypal experience," stirred up by his intense involvement with the opera and by rereading Malory. Both Maria and Powell recognize and accept the connections between their own actions and the legend, but Arthur refuses to do so—which Maria accepts as right for him. "Of course you don't see it. It's not the nature of heroes of myth to think of themselves as heroes of myth. They don't swan around, declaiming, 'I'm a hero of myth.' It's observers like Simon and me who spot the myths and the heroes. The heroes see themselves simply as chaps doing the best they can in a special situation."

All this business about the wax and the forms restates, of course, what Davies has had Dunstan Ramsay say in the Deptford trilogy about myth as the essence of history. But here the notion of life being fated rather than freely chosen (an idea also expressed earlier by Dunstan) is connected with myth, indeed felt to be the driving force that produces mythic pattern in individual lives.

In addition, there are instances of characters living out variations of patterns described in Davies' earlier novels—a correspondence that is not too surprising if the contention is valid that "there are not more than nine plots in all literature." It is suggested, for example, that Simon Darcourt is "a good old Merlin," and thus "Fifth Business," since that is the role that Merlin plays in the legends about King Arthur. Early in the novel, Darcourt views this personal myth negatively, seeing himself as little more than "an educated upper servant...a confidential secretary, intermediary, and fixer." But later, with Mamusia's help, he recognizes that he is the Fool in the tarot pack, and thus that he brings an adventurous, self-respecting, intuitive and aggressive approach to the role of fifth business.

The most startling example of a character playing out a pattern from an earlier Davies novel is Hulda Schnakenburg. Although Davies never mentions the parallel, the pattern (that of the development of an artist, her unsympathetic background, discovery, training, experience and success) is repeated from *A Mixture of Frailties*. (Indeed, while he was planning the novel, Davies had thought of making Sir Benedict Domdaniel and Monica Gall characters in *Lyre*.) In the earlier novel, the Bridgetower Trust wishes to underwrite the training of a young woman in the arts. It receives wildly unsuitable applications before finally settling on Monica Gall. A factor inhibiting Monica's development is the limited outlook of her parents and the narrow Protestant sect to which they belong. The Trust does what it can to allay the suspicions of her parents, but without complete success. Once embarked on her training, she has an affair with one of her teachers and learns a great deal from it. Her training extends far beyond the realm of music to embrace manners, dress and general cultivation. When a new opera is mounted with the Trust's money, she plays a prominent part in it. The opera house's claque skilfully controls the audience's responses. Roughly parallelling the opera's conception and eventual production is the conception and birth of a child.

In *The Lyre of Orpheus*, the Cornish Foundation for Promotion of the Arts and Humane Scholarship receives wildly unsuitable applications. It decides to support Hulda Schnakenburg. She has rebelled against her parents and the narrow Protestant sect to which they belong. The Foundation attempts to allay her parents' concerns, but without complete success. Once embarked on completing the opera, she falls in love with the woman who is her supervisor and has an affair with her that teaches her much. Among other things, she improves her manners, dress and general cleanliness. When the opera is mounted, she figures both as composer and as off-stage conductor. And when the audience is not quite sure when to applaud, Yerko and his European claque manage its reactions with great subtlety and authority. Through the period that the opera is undertaken and staged, two children are conceived and are born, the one a parallel of the artistic creative act, the other an unhappy parody. (Of course, the situations of Monica and Schnak are not entirely similar. In particular, there had been great advances in Canada's artistic life since Davies wrote *A Mixture of Frailties*. Whereas in the earlier novel the Bridgetower Trust sends Monica to England for her training, in *Lyre* Schnak takes advantage of the fine music department in a Canadian university, the excellent theatre at Stratford and a talented pool of Canadian performers.)

Another pattern that Davies repeats—and varies—comes from *Tempest-Tost*. Davies has made the point often that a powerful work of art can stir uncontrollable feelings, especially in those who are emotionally stunted or immature. In *Tempest-Tost*, it is the repressed, middle-aged high school mathematics teacher Hector Mackilwraith, playing the part of Gonzalo in an amateur production of Shakespeare's *The Tempest*, who loses his emotional balance. During the opening night performance, despairingly attracted to the girl who has the part of Ariel, he makes a half-hearted attempt at suicide. *Lyre* likewise describes the preparations for a first performance, but this time the preparations are on a level far beyond the capacity of all but the professional director in *Tempest-Tost*. Nineteen-year-old Schnak, falling hopelessly in love with the opera's producer, Geraint Powell, despairs when she hears a cruel remark, and she too makes a feeble attempt at suicide. Like Mackilwraith's botched attempt, this comes as a surprise, but where Mackilwraith's motivations are murky, and the ensuing resolution is dealt with only briefly, Schnak's bid for attention is thoroughly explored.

In completing the Cornish trilogy, *The Lyre of Orpheus* keeps before our mind's eye the concerns of the earlier volumes. Characters refer easily and casually to matters like alchemy and angels and Gnosticism that engaged attention in *The Rebel Angels*. And Davies expands his earlier portrait of academe as he presents one of its central rituals, the preparation and examination of a student for her doctorate. In like manner, the kind of painting that had absorbed so much of Francis Cornish's creative energy in *What's Bred in the Bone* is under consideration again as Darcourt learns about the missing years in Francis' life. The theme of deception in art returns in Schnak's interweaving of old and new in the score of the opera, in Darcourt's borrowings for the libretto, in Powell's choice of artistic over literal truth in his production and in Darcourt's exercise of imagination as he writes the life of Francis Cornish. *Lyre* also neatly ties off the strands of plot left hanging in the earlier novels. As we are led to expect at the end of *The Rebel Angels*, the marriage of Arthur and Maria does get into trouble, but by the close of *Lyre* it is stronger than before. And Darcourt finally writes his biography of Francis Cornish. In a few cases the reader is treated to unanticipated developments, as when Wally Crottle demands compensation for the suppression of "M'dad's book," and Charlotte Cornish comes from Cornwall to be a judge in the pony division at the Royal Winter Fair.

But *Lyre* is also a free-standing work. In taking opera as a focus, it engages with yet another of the great achievements of western culture. Its many themes are stated, reiterated, parodied and interwoven with skill and clarity. Throughout there is a feeling of amplitude and leisure, allowing the forward narrative momentum to pause from time to time for a fully dramatized scene. Davies has always been good at these, and this novel adds several—the lawyer Mervyn Gwilt presenting Wally Crottle's case, Charlotte Cornish talking about the farrier groom, Schnak's doctoral examination—that are as vivid as the comic descent of the clergy on Dr. Savage's library in *Tempest-Tost*, or the parade and the evening of entertainment and oratory with which the village of Deptford welcomes Dunstan Ramsay home from the First World War in *Fifth Business*, or Mamusia's lavish Christmas dinner in *The Rebel Angels*.

As a whole, the Cornish trilogy celebrates the fruitfulness of our heritage. *The Rebel Angels* demonstrates Davies' conviction that the medieval roots of the university still nourish the institution we know today. In *What's Bred in the Bone* the hero succeeds because he masters the art and the craftsmanship of the Renaissance. In *The Lyre of Orpheus*, because of an ingenious narrative device, the commerce between past and present flows both ways. The composer, librettist, producer, designer and stage manager of the present day all reach back in time to produce their early nineteenth-century opera, and as they do so their activities are described to us by an omniscient narrator usually stationed at Simon Darcourt's shoulder. At the same time E. T. A. Hoffmann himself, speaking to us from Limbo at the end of each of the first seven sections of the novel, reaches forward to comment on their twentieth-century lives and gives his reactions to the manner in which they are completing his unfinished work.

Macmillan published the novel in Canada and Viking in Britain in September 1988, and Viking brought it out in the United States that December. With some exceptions, the reviewers celebrated it as a fitting finale to one of the great fictional enterprises of the decade. In the United States, Andrew Porter (then the

music critic for the *New Yorker*) felt complimented, as he told
Davies when they met at the St. Louis Opera Festival the following year, to find himself portrayed in *Lyre* as Robin Adair, whom
Darcourt entertains at dinner before the première of *Arthur of
Britain*. (Porter also correctly identified the other critic at the
dinner as Clive Barnes, the drama critic for the *New York Post*.)
In England, the magic of the Booker nomination had done its
work, and reviewers, who had by now familiarized themselves
with Davies' earlier fiction, gave the book extended, appreciative
treatment. Hardcover sales soared to a new high—31,943 in
Canada, 53,916 in the United States, and 6,609 in Britain. The
book moved quickly to best-seller status, staying on the *Maclean's*
magazine list in Canada for thirty-three weeks, on the *Toronto
Star's* for thirty-six weeks, the *New York Times'* for eight weeks
and the *Washington Post's* for ten weeks.

Selling the book involved Davies in his most arduous efforts to
date. Now there was Britain to deal with as well as Canada and
the United States, and at seventy-five, he tired more easily than
he had before. As always, he rebelled in a corner of his mind
against the notion that it was the author's (rather than the publishers') job to sell the book. When in the summer of 1988 he
contemplated the busy days of readings, book-signings and interviews his three publishers had projected for that fall and winter—

September 6-9 in Toronto and Ottawa
September 11-21 in Western Canada
September 23-October 2 in London, England
November, a dozen readings scattered through southern
Ontario
January 22-28 in Los Angeles, San Francisco, Chicago,
and Milwaukee
February 5-9 in New York, Boston and Washington—

he seems to have been seized with a fit of amusement at the
entire exercise and his own role in it. At any rate, for the first
time he kept a diary of his promotional travels, titling them:
"Publicity Journey for *The Lyre of Orpheus* or: The Great Dog &

Pony Show (1988)," "The Great Dog & Pony Resumed…1989" and "The Last Leg of the Great Dog & Pony."

All the predictable annoyances of a demanding schedule occurred—meals grabbed on the run, hotel rooms not ready on arrival, unexpected delays, sleepless nights, signings where there was no desk, readings where the light was so poor he could barely see his text. Signing books (often as many as 200 or 250 at a crack) he found the least rewarding of his tasks, but his irrepressible imagination sometimes gave a lift to the enterprise, as when the Penguin Books shop in Covent Garden had him "sign outside amid racket of street performers—attractive girls bellydancing & much music. V. 18th cent. & I am tempted to cry: 'Buy a book, of your charity! I have a sick wife & twelve children in the Marshalsea! Pity the poor scribbler!'" He did his best for interviewers, but by the last day, when an interviewer grilled him for a full fifty minutes "abt. Free Trade, racism, Jung, the coming millennium & God knows what not," he was thoroughly envious of Brenda, who had the good fortune to "go for a walk in the grounds & breathe the pure air of freedom."

Readings were another matter. For these he rehearsed carefully. He took great pleasure in giving a section of the book a good performance for the fans, who filled lecture halls and theatres to the brim. An astonishing and pleasant result of the trekking about was the unexpected appearance of people he had not seen for years—contemporaries from Upper Canada College, acquaintances from Peterborough, a friend of a woman he had dated at Queen's, John Espey from Oxford, erstwhile Massey College students, a Canadian diplomat encountered earlier in Scandinavia—all scattered along his path in places remote from where he had first known them. The fan whose presence pleased him most was his eldest grandson, Christopher, who came up from Queen's and lined up for two hours with several friends to hear him read in Hart House at the University of Toronto.

These travels did not complete his exertions on *Lyre*'s behalf. For a hefty fee, he also wrote a "special message" and signed 9,600 sheets for inclusion in the Franklin Library's first edition of the novel.

As each volume of the Cornish trilogy appeared, Davies' reader-ship expanded. Not only did hardcover sales increase dramati-cally from one to the next, but paperback sales burgeoned too. Penguin Books continued the process it had begun in 1976 by acquiring the rights to the Deptford trilogy and through the lat-ter 1970s, the 1980s and early '90s republished all Davies' novels in individual volumes, as well as *One Half of Robertson Davies, High Spirits, The Enthusiasms of Robertson Davies* and *A Voice from the Attic*. In addition it published each of the trilogies in its King Penguin editions. This made Davies' work newly accessible to readers throughout the English-speaking world. Comprehen-sive figures are not easily come by, but early in 1989, the *Boston Globe* reported that paperback sales of the Deptford novels and the first two volumes of the Cornish trilogy had amounted to 580,000 copies in the United States alone.

In the same period, foreign language sales of his work mush-roomed. There had been German and Dutch translations of *A Mixture of Frailties* in the early 1960s, a Polish *Fifth Business* in 1973, a French *Fifth Business, The Manticore* and *World of Wonders* later in the 1970s. But from 1980 on, the pace of trans-lation picked up, the result not only of astute management of Davies' interests by Curtis Brown in New York but of increased international awareness of Canadian literature generally. (Literary agents had begun to flourish in Canada late in the 1970s, mak-ing it their business to bring Canadian literature to the attention of foreign publishers.) By 1988, Davies' novels had been trans-lated into a dozen languages—German, Dutch, Polish, French, Norwegian, Swedish, Finnish, Danish, Spanish, Italian, Portuguese and Hebrew—and by 1992 into Japanese, Greek, Estonian, Hungarian and Czech as well.

Only once has Davies' pleasure at being so widely translated cooled slightly. In 1987 he discovered that several sentences and a long passage about popular attitudes toward saints had been cut from the 1973 Polish translation of *Fifth Business*, with the claim that they offended Catholic and Soviet sensibilities. When the publishers made it clear that the new edition in preparation would have the same omissions, he resigned himself to the inevitable, not without commenting that he thought the excisions weakened the book.

Occasionally translators sought Davies' help. Here are excerpts from letters to his Portuguese translator in Rio de Janeiro, first concerning *Fifth Business* and then *The Rebel Angels*:

> Many thanks for your letter of May 29th which has just reached me. I am delighted that you have translated *Fifth Business* into Portuguese and I can understand that you would have met with some difficulties, as there are expressions in it which are peculiar to Canada, and especially to the province of Ontario, which is a very old English settlement.
>
> Now a Calithumpian parade would be very familiar to you if you saw it as it is a sort of Carnival parade in which people wear grotesque costumes and often great heads made of papiermache. It used to be customary when a very dignified parade had been organized to have it followed by the Calithumpians, as a sort of counter-balance to the solemnity of what had gone before. In a village like Deptford it would have been very simple in nature but would undoubtedly give immense pleasure....

And—

> Thank you for your letter of September 23rd. I am not surprised that you had trouble finding a Portuguese equivalent for Ozy Froats and Dozy Doats and Little Lambsie Divy. The explanation is long and may seem to you rather silly, but here it is.
>
> In the nineteenth century there was a trick that older people played on children, saying to them, very rapidly
>
> > Hareseathay
> > Mareseathay
> > Sheepeativy
>
> As you see, it means, Hares eat Hay, Mares Eat Hay, Sheep eat Ivy, but it is puzzling when spoken quickly. In the late '40s or early '50s of this century there was a popular song founded on this catch, which went—Maresy doats

and dozy doats and little lambsie divy—which is the same sort of thing: mares eat oats, &c. Because Ozias Froats had that strange name his football supporters adapted the song in his honour.

I think that your best plan in a translation would be simply to say that the crowd sang a popular song in which they had adapted some of the words to suit the name of Ozy Froats....

Translation was not the only thing that kept Davies' past work before him. From 1972, one film-maker after another had taken options on his books—*Fifth Business* for the entire period, *A Mixture of Frailties* since 1982, *World of Wonders* since 1985, *Leaven of Malice* since 1987 and *What's Bred in the Bone* (for a television miniseries) since 1987. To date, no films have emerged from this interest, but Davies' letters in reaction to proposed scenarios reveal him as an astute man of the theatre and a good critic of his own work. Here is part of a response written early in 1989 to a movie script for *Fifth Business*:

...I like the narrative line which is clear and direct. I wish you could see your way to use the material about Ramsay's return to Deptford—the village parade, the presentations in the town theatre, and the burning in effigy of the Kaiser, which is symbolically important to Ramsay's character—he is the only person present who knows what it is like to be burned. And I suggest that at the end of the picture the children should be engaged in a snowball fight—not tobogganing—as a sign that the story of Ramsay's life may be repeated many times.

I have a few other comments....

— Be careful about language. In 1912 Leola would not say 'Hi'; she would say 'Hello'; little things like this endanger the period quality of the film. Just so on page 43 Dunny tells Milo to 'piss off'—an expression not in general use until fairly recently. Dunny should say 'bugger off', although in Deptford that would be considered very dreadful.

— P. 16: the child of a Baptist minister would not have toy cars, which cost money; more likely he would be playing with spools and string.

—The scene in the gravel pit must be dark, as you have made it. But I see that you have made the scene of throwing the snowball (P. 6) a Day Scene, and it most decidedly should be night, and clearly identified as at Christmastime, as this has a glancing reference to the Birth of the Miraculous Child—which is what Paul is to Dunny.

—Nobody spoke of 'tetanus' in 1914—always 'lockjaw'....

—If Liesl...is to make her mark in the story she must be *hideous*, not just an 'interesting-looking woman with a radiant smile'; she is the Loathly Damsel of romance, who proves to be the woman who reveals great things to the Hero when once he has overcome his repulsion. I know you shrink from this but it is vital if you are making a film of *Fifth Business* and not of some other book of your own invention. She and Old Blazon are revelations to Dunny, and Liesl must astonish and shock the audience until they fall in love with what she really *is*. She should have an exceptionally beautiful voice, and not the usual Hollywood scissors-grinder snarl.

—P. 93: please don't show Ramsay stuffing ice down Faustina's bosom and playing the fool; he *adores* her but he dares not say so, and that is why he spies on her. He is a schoolboy in his love, and that is why Liesl comes to his rescue....

—I think it is a pity to lose the postcard calling Ramsay to Switzerland at the end of the film; this opens new life to him when he thought his life was over. He should *not* say: 'After all, it was only a snowball'. The whole book tells us that a snowball may influence lives in the most important way, for many years, and that *nothing*—repeat *nothing*—is unimportant....

Chapter 17

MURTHER AND WALKING
SPIRITS: 1988-91

Mary Jones Gage gathered the few possessions she could save
into a canoe and made her way along the old time water route
to Canada; she therefore traveled up the Mohawk, past Fort
Stanwix, across the short portage to Wood Creek, down Oneida
Lake and the Oswego River, and thence along the Southern
shore of Lake Ontario to Niagara and the Head-of-the-Lake at
Stoney Creek. With her were her two children, James, born in
1774, and Elizabeth, born in 1776.
     —Stanley Mills and John Pierce Langs, "Our Gage Family,"
          Genealogical and Historical Records of the Mills and
                              Gage Families 1776-1926, 1926

Shortly after that, the decision that Percy and I should go to
Canada was reached.... We sailed on September 13, 1894....
Percy and I, with our two cabin companions, and twenty other
men, had been herded into a small cabin.... It was horrible. We
just slept in our clothes with a board about nine inches high
dividing us.
                              —W. Rupert Davies, *Far-Off Fields*, 1962

As A BOY, Davies had felt pulled in two directions by his father's Welsh stories and his mother's tales of her Loyalist ancestors. What *he* was, and where he belonged, was unclear. It took him until 1948 and the writing of *Fortune, My Foe* to accept that he was Canadian, and to acknowledge fully his allegiance to the country of his birth. Understanding what it meant to be a Canadian occupied him for a much longer time. Indeed, it turned out to be a task of a lifetime, and his tentative answers changed as he grew older and as the country itself grew up.

In his youth, English-speaking Canada, if no longer a British colonial possession, nonetheless constituted a cultural colony of Britain and of the United States. Most of its books and magazines were imported; almost all its professional dramatic performances were given by British or American touring companies; most films came from the States. Only in music was there a vigorous indigenous professional tradition. As a boy, Davies accepted the situation, but he felt he must be missing something: the stories he read about British private school boys or patriotic American lads made it clear that their milieux were very different from his own. And once he became interested in an acting career, he found the position he was in, so far from the centre of things, increasingly frustrating. His visits to England with Rupert in 1924, 1932 and 1934, and his time at Oxford and the Old Vic, gave him firsthand experience of what it was like to live at the centre.

In the editorials, articles, reviews and plays he wrote during the 1940s, Davies characterized his fellow Canadians as serious, cautious, unenthusiastic, slow to laugh, indifferent or antagonistic to the arts, unreceptive toward new ideas. These traits, he considered, arose variously from the harsh climate, from early religious attitudes, from the fact that most of Canada's immigrants had been uprooted from their mother countries and from the country's materialistic political and economic history. He perceived that Canadians were similar in outlook to other northern peoples, particularly the Russians, Scandinavians and Scots. He saw the works of Chekhov and Ibsen as relevant to Canada. He yearned to see vigorous Canadian artistic and intellectual accomplishment, but *Hope Deferred, Overlaid* and *Fortune, My Foe* reflect his rueful view that few of his fellow citizens shared this concern.

Nonetheless, he did not despair. He sensed in this period the tentative beginnings of Canadian artistic independence, and each year he charted the gains, pointing, for example, to one or two books that he thought would become lasting additions to the nation's literature. He predicted that as the arts matured in Canada they were likely to have a regional focus, that they would reflect the life of the towns and cities rather than the rugged backwoods, and that they would present a hybrid outlook, as befitting a people of mixed origins. Indeed, he opposed the notion of a narrow nationalism in subject matter, since the country's artistic heritage drew, after all, on the entire breadth of western culture. He hoped for a time that he would be the means of establishing a Canadian foothold on the English stage, but neither the plays he set in Britain ("The King Who Could Not Dream," *King Phoenix*, *A Jig for the Gypsy*) nor the plays he gave Canadian settings found producers in the West End. It was not for him to unlock that door. Drama in the 1940s still flowed from the Old Country, and Canada was still perceived abroad as a dull, provincial place.

During the 1950s, when many of Canada's major cultural institutions were founded (the National Ballet of Canada, the Canadian Opera Company, the Stratford Festival, the Canada Council, the National Library, the New Canadian Library), Davies again and again chastised his fellow Canadians for their indifference to the arts. "Unwilling though some of us may be to face the fact, other nations judge us by our learning, our arts and letters. They buy what we produce, of course, and they sell us what they produce themselves, but buying and selling alone cannot make a great nation. Only greatness in the things of the mind and spirit brings lasting reputation." Only by fostering learning and the arts could Canada become something more than "a nation of wealthy, law-abiding, hard-working, lucky savages." *Tempest-Tost* and *A Mixture of Frailties* both sprang from Davies' respect for the highest standards of artistic performance and from his frustration with the indifference that so many Canadians displayed toward them. For the first time he began to decry the country's "anti-intellectual" system of education. At the end of the 1950s, in a review of Hugh MacLennan's *The Watch That Ends the Night*, he made the first of many references to a metaphor that his old friend Douglas LePan had used in one of his poems:

> Our climate sets its mark on us, making some of us moody and introspective in a fashion which is akin to the Scandinavians, or the Russians, and when we dig deep into ourselves we find matters which are very much our own. We are superficially a simple people, but our simplicity is deceptive.... For every man who recalls his own childhood in terms of the boys in Ernest Thompson Seton's *Two Little Savages*, there is another who sees himself in the worrying, raw-nerved Harold Sondern, in Ralph Allen's *Peace River Country*. If Canada gets another hundred years in which to present herself to the world through her books, this aspect of the Canadian character will become widely known, and will find affectionate understanding in the rest of the literate world. "Wild Hamlet with the features of Horatio," said Douglas LePan of the *coureur de bois*; never did anyone pack so much insight into the Canadian character in a single phrase.

As Canada moved toward its centennial in 1967, Davies' thoughts turned to the country's political beginnings. Its birth in an act of political goodwill and compromise struck him as "a favoured, but not heroic, origin." Canadians, as he saw it, distrusted beauty, elegance and eloquence, an attitude they had inherited from the pioneers. "We are still apt to confuse beauty with immorality. But don't you think it is time we got over all that nonsense? It comes to us from pioneer days, when dressing well, and speaking like a person of education and taste, was enough to mark a man as a stranger and probably a crook.... But not all our pioneer ancestors lived in this state of innocence. The people who made things happen rose above the frontier ideal of ungrammatical virtue. The Fathers of Confederation were excellent grammarians, every one of them, and most of them were pretty good at Latin, too."

As Davies and Tyrone Guthrie prepared to present Canada's history in a gigantic "Spectacle," he berated Canadians—as he would many times again—for shunning introspection, for flinching from poems or novels that exposed reality, for taking Horatio-like appearance at face value, ignoring the Hamlet underneath. By now, the country did not lack for writers who could penetrate deep into the national psyche, but the truths they unearthed were broadly—although not wholly—disregarded. He did admit that some Canadians had begun to turn an observant view upon themselves. And, of course, this was the decade when he himself was preparing to exhibit the wild, passionate, extraordinary man under the bland Canadian exterior in the novels of the Deptford trilogy.

In centennial year Davies hit upon a new metaphor for Canada, and he elaborated it during the next decade. Now the country was the Good Daughter Who Stayed at Home to Help Mother, first in 1776, when the naughty daughter Columbia independently set up housekeeping for herself, and again in 1812, when the United States mistakenly thought Canada might like to leave home and join her. Canada's reward for her loyalty was to be taken for granted. Mother found her boring, while Columbia's prosperity attracted Mother's affection. But Canada was far from boring! By the end of the 1970s, Davies believed that his country was engaged in a protracted struggle for its soul, a struggle as profound as the Civil War had been for the United States—a tussle between francophone and anglophone, between provinces and central government, between rich and poor, between the industrial East and the newly rich West. Douglas LePan's poem with its metaphor, "Wild Hamlet with the features of Horatio," now struck him as a challenge. The Canadian, the *coureur de bois*, must understand the savage land of the spirit. The voyage he must take is the voyage within. He may appear to be no more than the hero's friend and confidant, but if he has the courage, he "may be a hero, and a new kind of hero, a hero of conscience and spirit, in the great drama of modern man." In his play *Question Time*, in which Canada's prime minister crashes in the Arctic and makes the inner voyage with the help of a shaman, Davies presented the challenge in dramatic terms.

In the late 1970s and through the '80s, Davies was heartened by what he saw as a major shift in the international assessment of Canada. He had come to believe that the country had outgrown the role of the unfashionable, dutiful daughter and was making valued contributions to western culture. In several long articles and speeches, he set the earlier period of cultural dependency in a new light. He contended that, in the nineteenth century and the early years of the twentieth, Canadians had been demanding, intelligent consumers of western culture, keeping themselves abreast of theatrical offerings in London and New York—new plays, classics, entertainments, the lot—through travelling companies; but now, after several difficult decades, he argued, the transition had been made from consumer to participant. He pointed to the success of the Stratford Festival and to the establishment of centres for Canadian studies in universities all over Europe. Davies' novels of this period—*The Rebel Angels, What's Bred in the Bone* and *The Lyre of Orpheus*—all celebrate this cultural coming of age and show Canadian artists and academics as full participants in a shared civilization.

In the 1980s Davies also gave a good deal of attention to the contrast between Canada and its neighbour to the south. Canada, the "socialist monarchy," differs fundamentally from the democratic republic on its border. The American national character is extroverted, the Canadian introverted, largely because of the contrasting outlooks of their early settlers. The United States, whose "psychological energy is directed outward, toward the world around" and which "assumes that it must dominate, that its political and moral views are superior to all others, and that it is justified in interference with countries it thinks undemocratic," was initially settled by Puritans and by a small but influential number of British aristocrats. The Puritans were convinced of the rightness of their chosen way of life, and the aristocrats were accustomed to rule. Together, as Davies told an American audience, they "established your national spirit, your dominant psychological strain, and virtually all of your people have adopted it and regard it as the way life is at its best."

Canada, on the other hand, whose "psychological energy turns inward" and which "feels no impulsion to spread its domination beyond its own boundaries," was settled by exiles and refugees, who felt their betrayal and their loss of patrimony deeply, and by United Empire Loyalists, who maintained a dogged loyalty to the British Crown. Here Davies drew on his own family for his examples, noting that his Grandfather McKay's forbears had been exiled Scots crofters, that his father's family had been economic refugees, and that Captain John Gage had died fighting for the British in the American War of Independence, leaving his widow and her children to come to Canada as United Empire Loyalists. But, he emphasized, "It is not simply my story but that of many thousands of Canadians whose character and outlook has been determined by it." He urged Canadians to undertake the rigorous self-examination that would result in recognition of their national psychological direction, instead of thoughtlessly aping the extroversion of their powerful neighbours and thereby putting their own distinctive culture at risk.

Five decades of mulling over what it meant to be Canadian had led Davies back to his parents' family stories. But it took him some time to recognize that they should serve as the basis of the central sections of his next novel. Earlier, whenever he had been tempted to incorporate them in a book, he had always rejected the idea, thinking, "No, if you start to write loads of stuff like that, it'll be dull as ditchwater. I wouldn't be able to do it. It's got to come through something else and come from somewhere else."

It did "come through," emerging in spurts in the course of a fall and early winter otherwise occupied largely by publicity for *The Lyre of Orpheus* and an ensuing year cluttered with seven major speeches on diverse topics, half a dozen pieces of writing and eleven weeks of travel. The first idea that came to Davies developed out of a kind of memoir that he had been considering writing for some time. He noted it in his travel diary on June 3, 1988, while he was in Britain to give one of the lectures in which his own forbears figure as examples of those who settled Canada. "I am haunted by a notion for my Three Father book: a novel: a Candn living in England, is invited to adjudicate the finals of the

Dominion Drama Festival. As he sees the eight plays: Ibsen, Chekhov, Th. Wilder, Racine, Moliere, N. Coward, etc. he reflects on their application to his own life - The Three Fathers. Each section treated in the mode of the playwright. The problem is to avoid too much reflection. But it is a notion v. much in my line & wth Joycean possibilities of parody." The fathers he had in mind were Rupert Davies, Tyrone Guthrie and Vincent Massey, the three men whom he acknowledges as standing in paternal relation to him, the men who had influenced him to give so much of his life to journalism, the theatre and the university, the fields that gave him so much subject matter for his writing.

Almost immediately, as the first page of the notebook he kept for this novel reveals, he knew that his adjudicator had earlier been a journalist, that his wife has left him, and that as he watches the plays he is to do so in the spirit of a quotation from Francis Quarles' *Emblems*:

> My soul, sit thou a patient looker-on;
> Judge not the play before the play is done:
> Her plot hath many changes; every day
> Speaks a new scene: the last act crowns the play.

By the second notebook page, probably written before July 13 when Davies mentioned some of its contents to me, the three fathers had been augmented by some ideas about the adjudicator's mother. And by the third, which was probably written before December 7, he had considerably more: a title ("The Revenger's Comedy"), the notion of using a ghost as the narrator, a good idea for the opening line—"It came as a dreadful shock when ——— quite uncharacteristically produced a gun & shot me dead"—and a further thought about the weapon: "Shd. the murder weapon be a loaded cane? Pull leaden weight on spring out of top? Then murderer must keep it always with him…." Shortly after that, the "fathers" notion had broadened, as he speculated: "Forty days after death [the ghost] wanders in a labyrinth where he encounters his forbears, his influences & Fathers as prompted by the plays the Critic is witnessing. Meets the god, or the Minotaur, at last & must choose between Revenge & Forgiveness."

Thereafter the focus shifted wholly to forbears rather than the Three Fathers, the plays became films, and the novel gradually assumed its final shape. After June of 1989, when *The Revengers' Comedies* opened in London and Davies discovered that the British playwright Alan Ayckbourn had pre-empted his title, the search for a replacement caused him considerable trouble. He entertained at least nine possibilities ("Where All the Ladders Start" and "Afterlife in the Fun Shop" among them) before finally settling on *Murther and Walking Spirits*. The actual writing commenced on November 20, 1989, and was finished a little over a year later.

The story opens with a double surprise. Connor Gilmartin is surprised to find his wife, Esme Baron, in bed with her lover, Randal Allard Going, and has just been struck down by Going with a metal cosh concealed in his walking stick. The reader is surprised in turn to find that Gilmartin's ghost is telling the story.

The participants in the love triangle all work for the *Colonial Advocate* in Toronto, the late Gilmartin as entertainment editor, Going as a drama critic in his department and Esme as a columnist on women's affairs. Esme cool-headedly organizes her lover on his way, tidies up and concocts a plausible story for the police. She behaves in a calculatedly moving fashion at the funeral, and exploits her situation in articles and plans for a "how-to book for widows." Going, for his part, is miserable, throws up, weeps and wishes the deed undone. Gilmartin's ghost, alternately admiring and despising his wife's behaviour, is eager to revenge himself on Going. He is also curious about his new existence, assessing his capacities and feelings and recalling conversations he has had on the subject with his philosophical friend, Hugh McWearie.

When Going attends a week-long film festival, the ghost discovers that he must go along. But while Going is viewing cinema classics, the ghost finds himself watching films, private to himself, about the lives of his forbears. In the first, his ancestors, Major Gage and Anna Vermuelen, are observed living in the city of New York in the years prior to the American War of

Independence. The Major dies fighting on the British side, and several years later the widowed Anna flees up the Hudson by canoe with her children, Roger, Elizabeth and Hannah, reaching Canada, where they become United Empire Loyalists. In the next film, set in Wales at about the same time, the Wesleyan Methodist preacher Thomas Gilmartin, seeking shelter from a storm in a rough country inn, mesmerizes its inhabitants with an ancient tale. The film explores the lives of the four generations that succeed Thomas and ends, toward the end of the nineteenth century, with the emigration of his descendants, Lancelot and Rhodri Gilmartin to Canada.

The third film takes up this tale a few years later, with a ghastly confrontation between Rhodri, now married to Malvina McOmish, and his father-in-law, William McOmish, in the latter's dark, empty house. As McOmish tells his life story, we find that he has made a disastrous marriage to a descendant of Anna Vermuelen, that his career in the building trade has ended ignominiously in the poorhouse, and that Malvina's life has been warped irretrievably by her parents' conflicts.

In the next movie the ghost is presented with a domestic scene in the library of Rhodri and Malvina Gilmartin's house in Salterton, some thirty or forty years later. The ghost finds himself privy to the thoughts and feelings of the four people in the room: his great-aunt Minerva McOmish, his invalid grandmother Malvina Gilmartin, his grandfather Rhodri Gilmartin (by now wealthy and successful) and his father Brochwel, a student at Waverley University.

In the last day's film, the ghost watches Brochwel, now in the Allied Armies, in Italy in March 1944. While sheltering from German bombs near Monte Cassino he reviews his beliefs concerning civilization and faith. The scene then shifts to Wales about twenty years later, where Brochwel is dealing with the dismantling of Belam Manor, his father Rhodri's great dream-house. Midway through the auction of furnishings, he recalls a conversation of five years earlier in which Rhodri had finally revealed to him the lie that had drained the love from his and Malvina's marriage, and he had himself been moved to confess how as a child he had felt torn between Rhodri's love for Wales and Malvina's for Canada. The exercise of settling his father's affairs in the Old Country leads him to muse about his parents' lives and those of his forbears, and draws the totality of his—and the ghost's—Welsh heritage to his mind as the films end.

Throughout the long festival, we are told that Gilmartin's ghost has been more than just a patient looker-on. These personal films have forced him to smell, to feel, to live the lives of his ancestors with them. He is moved to laugh and to love them, to pity and admire them, and to ponder the sort of love that encompasses both charity and forgiveness.

Returned to time present, he discovers to his joy that Esme is pregnant with his child, and he does his best to co-operate when her agent, eager for an unconventional quotation to promote her book, employs a Swedenborgian medium to get in touch with him. Going, meanwhile, is dumped by Esme and tries unsuccessfully to slough off his burden of guilt by confessing to his crime. But the ghost, for his part, wins a measure of self-knowledge and self-acceptance. Finally, after a lifetime of struggle, he has reached a state of ease with his inner self, and he recognizes this in a concluding conversation with his anima.

Davies once observed: "death means the cessation of the ego, the cessation of the person that you recognize as you, the disappearance of your face from the mirror, and the end—or the fear of the end—of contact with a world that perhaps has grown very dear to you." With regard to life after death, he is more tentative. He does believe in a persistence of some sort and has often argued that each individual existed as a "possibility" before birth. After "blooming" in this life, "it is absurd to suppose that there is not a life after death." Sometimes he uses a different argument and roots his own belief in the observation that mankind has a seemingly ineradicable expectation of resurrection.

As to the form life will take after death, he imagines that some part of the energy or spirit that animates us will persist, referring to two near-death experiences—one recounted by a patient in the Toronto General Hospital to his doctors and the other by C. G. Jung in *Memories, Dreams, Reflections*—in which the patients viewed their bodies from a distance. But he is not certain of the specifics: "I haven't any notion of what I might be or whether I'll be capable of recognizing what I've been, or perhaps even what I am, but I expect that I shall be something." With regard to the traditional belief in reward or punishment after death, Davies speculates: "I thought at one time that people had their reward and punishment here on earth. But I am not perfectly certain that is necessarily the case. I begin to wonder whether an afterlife is necessary to sort of even things out…. The idea that the after-life is totally free from pain or from experience of one sort and another, or involves some complete illumination, I cannot believe. But I think it is going to be uncommonly interesting."

Are ghosts a plausible shape for psychic energy to take after death? Davies once said: "I believe in them [ghosts] precisely as Shakespeare believed in them"—implying openness to the possibility that they exist, mixed with scepticism. He quotes Samuel Johnson: "It is wonderful that five thousand years have now elapsed since the creation of the world, and still it is undecided whether or not there has ever been an instance of the spirit of any person appearing after death. All argument is against it, but all belief is for it." He accepts that many people believe that they have seen ghosts, so that there is at least a kind of psychic necessity to them. Ghosts in stories, he notes, are usually in search of something—"something has been lost, or some revenge or justice is sought, and the spirit cannot rest until this unfinished business is concluded." Thus "they are a manifestation of the deeply rooted notion that somehow and somewhere, every living creature should have his due, and if he cannot get it before death he may return to demand it after death."

By the time he came to write *Murther*, Davies could draw on over seventy years of affectionate familiarity with the ghost story. One of his earliest attempts at fiction, "Mr. Paganini Complies," was one, and of course he had created a new one every year while he was Master of Massey College. The Massey *High Spirits* are highly traditional in many ways, making use, for instance, of the most time-honoured means of communication between the dead and the living—table-tapping, astrology, alchemy, chalk circles, the evil eye, mysterious corked bottles and the like. These tales are set at traditionally propitious times—at night, on All

Hallows' Eve, or at times with special associations for the spectre at hand. The ghostly sometimes expands into the more general province of the supernatural—a character is translated into a frog, Satan pays a visit, a monster cat is created, an academic arrives who has lived for more than four centuries. But the stories were not meant to chill and terrify. Rather, they aimed to warm and charm, and to draw the College Fellows, as they listened to them at Gaudy Night, into closer community. The spectres are presented from the perspective of Davies himself, a Davies who is timorous, learned, resourceful and ultimately undaunted. They make contact with all his senses. He hears them rustle or tap, talk or play music. He scents the aroma of a pipe or cigar. A mauve or bluish light flickers; the ghostly visitors wear full historical costume; their translucency catches his eye. A chill hand or a fawning rub alert his touch. A banquet or drink stimulate his taste. In story after story, the ghosts reveal themselves to be uncannily human as they confide to him their concerns, desires and feelings.

Davies continued to write of ghosts after he retired as Master. In 1988 he wrote a "Twenty-Fifth Anniversary Ghost Story" for Gaudy Night, glancing back at the turbulent early years of the college and paying tribute to those, no longer living, who had served it well. In the last ghost story he wrote as Master, in 1980, he disavowed the intention of becoming a college ghost, but in 1989 he teasingly raised the possibility again, speaking at a party in honour of donors to the Robertson Davies Library: "While I was Master I made an attempt—half jesting but not wholly in jest—to provide this College with a number of ghosts. If in the future I find that I am haunting this Library, I hope that it will be a Library in which a ghost may take real pride."

When he read his "Twenty-Fifth Anniversary Ghost Story" to the Gaudy Night audience in December 1988, Davies already knew that his next novel would be a ghost story. But it would be unlike any he had ever read or written. Because it was to be told by the ghost, it would be "technically tricky because you've got to consider what also the limitations and freedoms of a ghost are." To a large degree, the tale is rooted in Davies' own personal convictions. He explored a wide variety of sources (*The Oxford*

Book of Death, Tourneur's gloomy, intense *Revenger's Tragedy*, Joseph Campbell's *The Power of Myth*, Maud Bodkin's *Archetypal Patterns in Poetry*), but in the event, the opening and closing sections of *Murther* make use of ideas culled primarily from *The Tibetan Book of the Dead* (the prefatory material in the edition Davies used includes references to the Buddhist belief in reincarnation, the *Bhagavad Gita* and Emanuel Swedenborg), with which he had long been familiar.

The novel's opening scene draws on descriptions of near-death experiences in which people have recalled looking at their bodies from a distance. Davies had used this device once before, in "The Xerox in the Lost Room," where, as the ghost of the Poor Relation explains, the butler "picked up a pewter tankard and hit me over the head, and to my surprise and indignation I fell to the floor, dead as a nit." The Poor Relation had then found himself "about nine inches above the ground, watching everything— myself stretched out on the floor, the cook trying to staunch the blood from my head with a towel, all the maids in hysterics, the footman saying he knew it would come to this some day, and the butler, as white as a sheet, blubbering: 'Oh zur, come back I beg 'ee. I never went fur to do it, zur. Come back and I'll go light on the brown sugar as long as I live, indeed zur, I will.' But it was hopeless. I was gone, so far as they were concerned." In the opening lines of *Murther and Walking Spirits* the ghost of Connor Gilmartin explains how he came to be "Roughly Translated" from this life to the next: "I was never so amazed in my life as when the Sniffer drew his concealed weapon from its case and struck me to the ground, stone dead. How did I know that I was dead? As it seemed to me, I recovered consciousness in an instant after the blow, and heard the Sniffer saying, in a quavering voice: 'He's dead! My God, I've killed him!'... Where was I? I was surveying the scene at close range but I was not in the body that lay on the floor. My body, looking as I had never seen it in my life."

Consistent with Davies' belief in the persistence of the animating spirit, Connor Gilmartin's ghost observes, reacts, thinks, feels and remembers, still possessing the personality he had in life. And, as Davies had once speculated, Gilmartin's afterlife is not "totally free from pain or from experience of one sort and another." Almost immediately the ghost begins to make discoveries about the possibilities and limitations that accompany his new state. When startled into laughter at Going's farcical fright, he realizes that neither Going nor Esme can hear him. He experiences "a strong charge of erotic feeling" as he watches Esme, nude, tidying the scene of the crime. He feels hunger, but this sensation ceases when his corpse is carried away. Finding that he can remain at the scene, he does so, to satisfy his curiosity about how Esme will handle the police. Then, eager to see what Going is up to, he discovers that he can join him simply by wishing to do so. But after the film festival begins, he finds that his freedom is not absolute: he is tied to Going for the duration. He finds himself disconnected from the rhythm of day and night: since he has no substance, he does not feel fatigue. But his powers of observation remain acute, his emotions keen. And he is intensely lonely, since there is no one to share his mode of existence.

Like many ghosts who "cannot rest until this unfinished business is concluded," he decides that "in so far as my unaccustomed condition would permit, I would hound him [Going] down, and revenge myself upon him in any way I found possible." But he doesn't know what resources he brings to the task. Can he haunt his enemy, as ghosts have been wont to do in stories? Can he invade his mind, as Henry James imagined? He yearns to be able to discuss these matters with his friend Hugh McWearie.

As a young man McWearie had been ordained a Presbyterian minister, and he later became a journalist on religious topics and a student of metaphysics. McWearie holds many of Davies' views. He sees the essential journey as solitary and inward and is convinced that the antiquity of an idea does not invalidate it. On matters of the spirit, he maintains what he thinks of as "the Shakespearean cast of thought. That is to say, a fine credulity about everything, kept in check by a lively scepticism about everything." He is cautious about the value of eastern religious ideas to westerners, who are conditioned by a quite different "geography and race." He is convinced that God has a feminine component. He talks about "one's personal drama," in which all others are supporting players. And he is familiar with Jung's conception of the animus and anima.

While Gilmartin was alive, he and McWearie had talked about near-death experiences in which people felt themselves to be outside their bodies and looking at them; they had talked about reincarnation; and McWearie had told Gilmartin of the Buddhist belief, shared by the western philosopher Swedenborg, that there is a period of waiting after death. McWearie had imagined that Swedenborg and his follower, the poet William Blake, would have been interested in the description of this period of waiting in the *Tibetan Book of the Dead*, but he hoped that when it came their turn to wait, Celts like himself and Gilmartin would encounter beings appropriate to their own heritage—perhaps one of the Celtic goddesses.

In Davies' mind (though he did not draw attention to the connection in the novel he wrote), ghosts were one of the bridges linking the opening situation of *Murther* with the sections dealing with Connor Gilmartin's ancestors. In a speech written just before he began to write the novel, he observed:

> I have…been aware of the existence of ghosts where most people refuse to see them. I assure you that I do not mean spooks in white sheets; no, I mean the persistence after death of the influences of people who cannot be forgotten or discounted as influences in the lives of their children. Hamlet's father's ghost is no outmoded dramatic device in a play which is now nearly four hundred years old. It is a part of Hamlet's soul. There are many of you here who have not freed yourselves from the ghosts of your fathers, and perhaps more particularly of your mothers, and because they haunt you, they also haunt your children, your lovers and sometimes even your friends. That is part of what heredity means, and it deserves careful attention. I try in my novels to come to terms with aspects of life which many people do not observe, or choose not to observe, but which I feel are determining elements in what we do with our lives.

In evoking the ghosts of his own ancestors in the five long middle sections of the novel, Davies felt that he was helping his fellow Canadians to better understand the ghosts who shaped their own lives. However, in making use of his family stories he did not feel himself "bound to fact or literal interpretation," but rather to "the totality of it" as it came to him.

In calling up Major Gage and his resilient widow in "Cain Raised" to exemplify the qualities of spirit that the United Empire Loyalists brought with them to Canada, Davies had very little to go on beyond the name of the village where the Gages had lived on the Albany River, the knowledge that Captain John Gage had died fighting on the British side in the American War of Independence and the possibility that the Captain may have had a family connection with Thomas Gage, the commander-in-chief of the British forces in North America. He knew that the Captain's widow and her two children had come to Canada either by horse or by canoe, and if the latter, as the family history quoted at the head of this chapter declares, that they had made their way along "the old time water route to Canada." He knew that Augustus Jones, the widow's brother, had already established himself in Stoney Creek as a surveyor for the government of Upper Canada.

Davies fleshed out these few facts in such a way as to incorporate more of his mother's American background. To represent the "Dutch" Langses, he introduced Anna Vermuelen as the wife of his fictional Major Gage (in place of the historical Mary Jones, with her Welsh background) and settled the pair in the city of New York, originally a Dutch colony, a move that lengthened the epic canoe trip dramatically. He established the look and feel of life as the wealthy Gages had lived it in the years leading up to the war in order to throw into sharp relief their subsequent ostracization, the tarring and feathering of one of their servants, the sequestration of their property and their eventual flight. He made use of military and popular songs of the period, and he expanded the family to include a third child, Hannah, in order to justify the inclusion of details about the physical ills and nostrums of the day, particularly the widespread use of laudanum for pain, since he wanted to establish addiction to opiates as a recurrent hazard in the eighteenth and nineteenth centuries. He made the Gages Anglican and emphasized the centrality of the Bible, *The Book of Common Prayer* and *The Pilgrim's Progress* in their lives. Anna and her two older children, Roger and Elizabeth, grow in spirit and mind as they cope with the difficulties of the great canoe journey through the wilderness. Endurance, resourcefulness, fortitude and dogged loyalty are the legacy they leave to Canada.

To portray the Welsh heritage that brought the Gilmartins to Canada as economic exiles in "Of Water and the Holy Spirit," Davies had ample resources in his father's stories. He knew of his Great-grandfather Samuel's rise to prominence as the owner of several tailoring shops and as the first Nonconformist mayor of a Welsh borough. And he knew that Samuel had spread his assets thinly among various enterprises, and how the coming of the railways and the decay of the aristocracy had reduced the amount of business for the local tailors. What had precipitated Samuel's ruin, however, was his penchant for raising and backing racehorses, coupled with his decision to guarantee a fairly large note for a fellow Wesleyan that the latter could not meet. Although a heart attack was the stated cause of Samuel's death, family tradition had it that he died of shame. At that time, bankruptcy was seen as the ultimate humiliation: the citizens of Welshpool even had a special phrase for it—"having to go up the town hall steps." Samuel died just three days before that humiliation.

Davies also knew about Samuel's son David, who had been trained to take over the tailoring business but proved a drunken ne'er-do-well, and about David's brother Walter, a brilliant student who had abandoned his dream of a civil service career at his dying mother's request in order to help his father in the business. He knew of the saintliness of Walter's wife and of the impractical nature of her brother, John Robertson, who married Walter's sister Polly. And, as we have seen, he had absorbed many stories about the family's radicalism, about his father's boyhood in Wales and about his emigration with his brother Percy to Canada.

What patterns to draw out of this mass of material? It seemed to Davies that Wesleyan Methodism had been a central influence for generations of his Welsh ancestors, and for this reason he made Thomas, the earliest forbear Rupert could trace, a lay preacher, and he added a second preacher to the family tree for good measure in the shape of Thomas' fictional adopted son, Wesley. (He knew as he did this that another Samuel Davies, a co-founder of a Wesleyan Methodist chapel in Meifod early in the nineteenth century, might also have been his forbear.) In creating these lay preachers, Davies drew on Welshpool tradition, and on the spirit of the family stories told by and about his cousin Robert Grindley, a Welshpool baker. Grindley, an old man when Davies knew him in the 1930s, was a plain, simple preacher who spoke from personal experience of God's work in his life and the lives of others. A favourite story—known to the family as "Bob Grindley and the vision in the bakehouse"—told how he had taken up preaching. One day, as he opened the bake oven, a great blast of heat had issued forth, and a voice asked him: "Bob Grindley, where are you going?" It was the Lord's voice, as it seemed to him, and he decided that he had better do the Lord's work.

Davies chose to introduce the family gift for story-telling through Thomas Gilmartin, the first of the lay preachers, by having him mesmerize the ruffian descendants of the Red Banditti with one of the great Welsh myths collected in *The Mabinogion*. And he engaged Thomas and his adopted son Wesley in the Robertson "Scotch trade," modifying the meaning of the term to suit his ends.

He strengthened the mythic quality of the story by repetition of important points. He anticipated Walter's promise to his dying mother by making the young Wesley, in the previous generation, promise *his* dying father to continue his evangelical work. For the same reason he established a pairing of feckless and faithful brothers in the generation before David and Walter by giving Samuel a scapegrace brother Thomas. (In making this Thomas a servant, Davies was able to draw on notes he had written in 1961 when his London publisher, Frederick Warburg, challenged him to write an autobiography of a Victorian butler.) The legacy this family leaves to Canada is its gift for story-telling, its faith and simple goodness and its sense of betrayal—as well as a grim determination to rise above failure.

In telling the story of William McOmish, descendant of the exiled Scottish crofters, in "The Master Builder," Davies had only a little to go on. He had known the man upon whom he based McOmish—his mother's father, William H. McKay—only as a dour figure in a coffin. His father had described him in *Far-Off Fields* in a single phrase as "a contractor and builder." His mother and her sisters had been so mortified by their father's behaviour and ignominious end that they refused to speak of him. (The blackest day in the life of one of his aunts had come when she saw her father driving the poorhouse wagon into Brantford.) Davies heard about McKay primarily from Rupert. The latter had visited the old man from time to time and told him that McKay kept up with the newspapers and gave talks to the other paupers on the building trade and the Russo-Japanese war.

The Highland heritage was only a guess, and information about other aspects of McKay's descent was fragmentary and contradictory. Davies had been told, for example, that McKay had been orphaned young and then raised by a German family. But Florence had spoken of visits to her grandmother McKay (who would have been William McKay's mother, so how could he be an orphan?) at a tavern with a taproom circled by low cupboards in which she crawled around the room, re-emerging where she entered. He knew that McKay had been respected for his ability to cast stairs and for his fine cabinet work, and that the houses he constructed were distinguished by large, horseshoe-shaped, plate-glass front windows. He had heard it whispered that McKay had become an "opium-eater," addicted to the morphine prescribed by his doctor brother-in-law for asthma; that "the old devil" had chased his wife with a carving knife while under the influence of the drug; and that his troubled marriage to Lavina Langs had been worsened by the spitefulness of her sister and confidante, Cynthia. Embittered by a lame leg, and later by the defection of her husband, the bluff, jocose Daniel Blaisdell, Cynthia flayed everyone, and especially her brother-in-law, with her sharp tongue.

Of the deciding events of McOmish's career—the building of Mrs. Long-Pott-Ott's mansion and the Wesleyan Methodist church, the elders' decision not to pay him in full, the Wesleyan bankers' refusal of a loan, Mrs. Long-Pott-Ott's offer to become a sleeping partner in his business, his drug addiction and descent into the local poor farm—only the last two are rooted directly in fact. Davies added the rest to lend substance to a career he knew only in outline. He included the church and its hypocritical elders to carry the mixed influence of Wesleyan Methodism down another generation. He introduced Mrs. Long-Pott-Ott to pay tribute to a long-sighted, generous woman of that name in the Brantford of William McKay's day, although she had no particular connection with his grandfather. The confrontation between McOmish and his son-in-law Rhodri Gilmartin, which Davies used to introduce his story with a flash of drama, did have roots in real life, however. A few years after Florence and Rupert married, Florence's mother and her sisters had left McKay in possession of the family house and retreated to a smaller one owned by one of her maternal uncles, taking most of the furniture with them. They then sent Rupert to persuade his father-in-law to sign the papers to effect a legal separation—"a gruesome business," he told Davies, "because McKay was as mimsy as a borogove." It was during this difficult encounter that Rupert gained some understanding of why the man had lashed out at his wife in his drug-induced fits. The father of four daughters, he had had sex with Lavina no more than ten times during their long marriage, because she thought it was wrong.

The telling of McOmish's story includes glances at his wife Virginia's forbears, in the first instance a thumbnail sketch of Anna Vermuelen's successful life in Canada, her daughter Elizabeth's marriage to Justus Vanderlip and their eleven children, including Nelson, Virginia's father (all this drawn, with a little variation, from the lives of Davies' own Gage and Langs forbears). As one might expect, Davies based Virginia on his maternal grandmother, Lavina Langs McKay. McOmish's account of what his wife was like at sixteen makes use of a detail from this grandmother's girlhood. She had grown up at a time when, as Davies commented in a 1943 article, "aids to beauty were regarded with horror," but she "had sometimes crushed berries to her lips to give them colour...[while] an abandoned cousin of hers had chewed a piece of pink ribbon and pressed it to her cheeks to simulate the blush of health and innocence." And so McOmish catches a glimpse of his future wife with several other girls, sitting on the bank of Fairchild's Creek, chewing something. "And do you know what it was? A ribbon. A pink ribbon and she was chewing it to make it wet and then she was dabbing her mouth with it, to make her lips a pretty pink! The Devil! And I thought that's the one for me, the girl with the Devil in her!"

Further along in McOmish's long harangue, Davies introduces a photograph taken at a reunion of the Vanderlip-Vermuelen-Gage family, a ploy that allows for the inclusion of odd nuggets that convey the peculiar quality of this family. Some of the Langses' tall tales, including those about Granny Sands and Bug Devereux, get told here. Here too, in describing the matriarch Elizabeth Gage Vanderlip, Davies includes a vignette from a reminiscence of his mother's about her grandmother, Sarah Westbrook Langs—of watching her in old age, sitting in the parlour with a snuff-box and a little box of peppermints, alternating a pinch of snuff with a peppermint all day while her unmarried daughters managed the house.

Davies also uses the photograph to shift the focus from William McOmish to his eldest daughter, Malvina, basing the description of her childhood and youth on the stories Florence had told him about herself. In July 1988, when he had just begun to plan the novel, he had worried that he would not be able to be fair to his mother, since the negative feelings that had bedevilled his relationship with her from adolescence onward still lurked near the surface. While he was writing *Murther* in 1990 they continued to make themselves felt. Abroad that summer, he recorded a confrontation with her spirit, "whose travelling complaints about cobblestones, foreign food, lack of elevators, dirt & probable cheating, ring in my mind's ear & spoil my pleasure. I sit her down before me and demand to know why she plagues me. She has no answers but her fears of the unknown & inbred suspicion. Tell her it won't do. Knock it off, Flo. Are many men so haunted, I wonder? Can I deliver myself by this Jungian technique of Active Imagination? The Great

Mother in her negative form. The Dragon, Gorgon, emasculator...."

But his portrait of Florence/Malvina is generous. He presents her reaching out toward drama and theatre—delighted at seeing General Tom Thumb, the splendidly dressed daughters of Chief Johnson, the plays starring Ida Van Cortland—and involving herself at the Wesleyan Methodist church in the choir and in amateur entertainments. He shows her pride in her achievements as a working girl, her attraction to the dashing young Rhodri Gilmartin, who sings so movingly and talks so well about books and music and theatre, and her courage in seizing her chance to escape her family through marriage. In his account, the shadows that loom over the picture of her are cast by her parents; indeed, Davies goes so far as to have Gilmartin's ghost hypothesize that the poisonous atmosphere between them had marked her in the womb: "Malvina had been begotten in a world without love and, whatever her aspirations nurtured in the theatre and in happier circumstances, would never truly be at ease in a world where love in its manifold forms is the begetter of all that makes life sweet. Malvina might yearn for love, might try her best to engender love and stimulate it in her own life, but would never be free to trust love or give herself to love without fear." Canada's inheritance from the McOmishes is defeat, bitterness, despair, meanness and thwarted love.

In "Scenes from a Marriage," the revealing, rambling thoughts of Minerva McOmish, Malvina and Rhodri Gilmartin, and their son Brochwel, all of them blighted by the emotional snarl inherited from McOmish and his wife Virginia, draw on Davies' memories of his maternal aunt Martha, of Florence, of Rupert and, in part, of himself while a student at Queen's. Davies had known his mother's sister Martha very well, having visited her and her sister Cynthia at their home in Brantford on occasional weekends when he was a schoolboy and having seen her when she came to stay for long periods when his mother was unwell, while he was at Queen's and later. He remembers her as a charmer who was pretty in the fashion of the day—big bosom, tight waist, big hips, round, rosy face, nice hair. As a young girl she had been apprenticed in millinery, became a buyer at Ogilvie's ladies' ready-to-wear store in Brantford and later, with Rupert's help, set herself up in business as "The Home of the Hat Beautiful." But she was subject to attacks of *petit mal* and eventually had to give up the business to keep house for her mother and sister. For many years there had been romance in her life. Her fiancé was an optician who wore pale violet pince-nez and introduced the tinted lens to Brantford. He gave her a little dog whose name was Captain, Cap for short. But since his mother was determined that they shouldn't marry until after her death, they waited. Finally she did die, but then Lavina demanded equivalent treatment. They waited longer. Finally, during the year of mourning after Lavina's death in 1924, he took ill himself and died. He left her everything he had but himself. Davies used details from her story not only for Minerva, but also as background for Monica's Aunt Ellen in *A Mixture of Frailties*.

While Minerva is ruminating about her long-dead fiancé and her beloved hat business, Malvina reflects on her early life, her long marriage to Rhodri (their romance, her pride in his success, their estrangement, her jealousy, her hatred of Wales), her thwarted imagination, her unease with her son, her spells of black hatreds, her illnesses. Davies' other maternal aunt, Cynthia, makes an appearance here as Caroline McOmish, the sister Malvina recalls as Carry. Davies himself remembers Cynthia as a plain woman, almost saintly in her devotion and kindness to her mother. As a young woman (as Malvina recalls) she had been a good pianist, capable of playing period favourites, like fantasies on airs from one or another grand opera. After Florence's marriage, Cynthia had become the family's financial mainstay and gradually worked her way up from a secretarial position to become the chief accountant at the head office in Brantford of the Canadian Order of Foresters, an insurance company.

For his part, Rhodri casts back to his family's failure in Wales and to the humiliating years when he began to carve out his career in Canada, and also to his wife and the kind of solid partner she has been in spite of their estrangement. Here Davies harks back not only to Rupert's early experiences as a printer's

devil at the *Expositor* in the fall of 1894, but to the equally trying period the following year when Walter and Jessie Davies
arrived in Brantford with their three youngest children in the
midst of the depression of the 1890s. There had been less money
than there ought to have been for them to establish themselves:
Percy and Rupert had turned most' of their wages over to their
Uncle John to hold for their parents, only to find that he and
Polly had spent it on furniture. Desperate to find a job, Walter
placed an advertisement in the *Expositor*: "Bespoke tailor desires
employment. Eighteen years experience as cutter and fitter.
London (Eng.) training." This was one of the times when Jessie
Robertson's faith counted. Every night before the meagre evening
meal she made the family pray for God's help in this new land.
One evening in December, while they were all on their knees,
Percy burst in with the news that there was a notice for an
accountant in the window of Goold, Shapley and Muir. God had
responded! Walter Davies dashed off and got the job, and from
then on all the family said that Jessie Robertson had "prayed
them out of poverty in the new country." At a family gathering
in 1959 to celebrate the sixty-fifth anniversary of their coming to
Canada, Rupert and Percy wept like children as they reminisced
about their mother. She died before Davies was born, but not, he
observes wryly, without leaving him the legacy of the Robertson
weak throat and lungs. Tuberculosis was rife in her family.

Finally, Brochwel's thoughts expose youthful romanticism and
a mixture of sharpness and muddle in his assessments of his professors, a fellow student and a girl with whom he is despairingly
in love.

Davies' decision to provide a musical accompaniment for each
of the four thought streams in "Scenes from a Marriage" probably sprang from reflections like this, written while he was planning the book in 1989: "My inner music—what plays in my
head if I am not thinking of anything in particular, is ballad
trash from my youth: *Just A-Wearyin' For You, My Ain Folk,
Husheen, Absent* & all the sweet gush of Carrie Jacobs-Bond, &
Guy d'Hardelot. Is this my mother's music, that she was playing
in my dream of Saturday? She seems much in my mind, just
below the level of consciousness." The legacy of these people is

thwarted love and imagination, ill health and faith, and success wrestled from the teeth of failure.

The scene at Monte Cassino during the Second World War in "The Land of Lost Content" is entirely invention, but the conclusions Brochwel reaches there about the unconquerable, questing spirit of western culture, the negativism of those who attack faith and the ideas of the Manichees are certainly Davies' own. The second part of this section, in which Brochwel makes arrangements for the sale of Rhodri's great Welsh house and attends as its furnishings fall to the auctioneer's hammer, draws skilfully on the notes Davies had amassed at Leighton Hall in the summer after his father died. For the revelation of Malvina's lie about her age and its effect on her marriage with Rhodri, Davies made use of one last family story and of his own experience of a home full of tension, where the Loyalist heritage of his mother was pitted against the Welsh inheritance of his father and he felt himself torn between the two. Like his character Brochwel, Davies himself eventually chose "Both. Or neither." His world extended beyond Old World Wales to embrace all of western culture. Although he could not love Canada as his mother did, he had to accept that, willy nilly, he was Canadian. As Brochwel observes, "You don't love Canada; you are part of Canada, and that's that." Canada is "like a family—various, often unsympathetic, sometimes detestable, frequently dumb as hell—but inescapable because you are part of it and can't ever, really, get away." The legacy here is engagement in western culture, willingness to believe, openness of mind.

Davies has speculated on the one hand that people receive their reward and punishment on earth, and on the other that an afterlife may "even things out," effecting a poetic justice of its own. *Murther* presents us with both possibilities. The ghost has been deprived of the balance of his natural life, possibly thirty or forty years of it, but in place of a future he is united with his past. As he watches the lives of his forbears he comes to feel their weight and solidity and courage, as David Staunton had before him in *The Manticore*. Often a reluctant witness, he is embarrassed at his intrusion into their privacy and misery, but he must endure it all, and the resulting "even-ing out" becomes much more than an exchange. A man who had approached life rationally and coolly, he finds that the movies force him, in death, to feeling. In life, he had starred in his own drama; in death, he is able to participate in others' perspectives. In life, he had studied history and psychology; now, presented with his heritage in an artistic form that exposes its underlying patterns, he gains a deeper comprehension of his forbears, one indeed that is better than their own. He admires, pities and loves them, and in doing so, he comes to recognize that he had failed during his life to love himself. He yearns to be remembered in his turn with the same charitable, forgiving love.

In the concluding section of *Murther*, Randal Allard Going receives poetic justice as well, although it comes in a manner that Gilmartin's ghost does not anticipate. The latter does his best to exact vengeance. At the seance arranged by Esme's agent he makes every effort to reveal the identity of his murderer, but, unlike the Massey College ghosts, he fails to make contact. He then seeks out his enemy and, in a scene that recalls Humphrey Cobbler's zany song and dance for Professor Vambrace in *Leaven of Malice*, sings "The bells of Hell go ting-a-ling-aling" in Going's ear. He manages to intensify the latter's unease, and by hounding his enemy's footsteps he succeeds in making Going feel his shadowy presence. But when Going tries to relieve his troubled conscience by confessing, first to Father Martin Boyle and then to Hugh McWearie, they rebuff him. Neither Boyle nor McWearie will let him off so lightly. He is to have no relief in this life from misery and guilt. As the voice that spoke at the séance had said: "Vengeance is of the world that I have left behind.... The man must live with his own soul. Do not rejoice in the burden of another's soul."

Things also even out for Gilmartin's ghost. He finds the charitable and forgiving love that he yearns for in McWearie's remarks to Going, for everything in them springs from a generous, loving appreciation of the person he had been. McWearie even suggests that Gilmartin may be being readied for rebirth, perhaps as Esme's child (a reversal of the Massey ghost story "The Pit Whence Ye Are Digged," where the guests at High Table, all reincarnations of their own forbears, suddenly turn into their eighteenth-century ancestors). And suddenly, in the novel's closing pages, the ghost discovers a dear companion in his anima, "the woman in the man," in a kind of poetic justice similar to that which Davies' character Casanova had won by confronting and accepting the component elements of his psyche in *General Confession.* Seeing the movies of his heritage, the ghost has come to understand that his wife's betrayal of him is only the latest of a series of wounding relationships, beginning with that of William McOmish with his wife Virginia and extending through Rhodri Gilmartin's with his wife Malvina, to Brochwel's with Julia. Brief references in "The Land of Lost Content" make it clear that Brochwel's marriage to Nuala represents the first break in this painful chain, for she "had healed the wound left by Julia, though nobody could erase the scar." (Here, Davies pays tribute to the warmth, love and balance Brenda had brought into his life, but preserves her privacy, assigning Nuala none of his wife's qualities or history.) Now, with the recognition that his anima is his friend, Gilmartin's ghost takes a great stride in self-recognition and acceptance, and with it ends the series of destructive relations between the sexes, fulfilling McWearie's conviction that "it is the Eternal Feminine that leads us aloft, as Goethe very finely said."

If we are to go by the stories in *Murther,* the ghosts that haunt Canadians are complex, watchful, resourceful, dogged, wary— and yet open to belief and love. In March of 1991, about a month after he submitted the manuscript of *Murther and Walking Spirits* to his publishers, Davies was asked by a reporter for the *Toronto Star* to describe the book's theme. He replied: "How people become Canadians." He had in mind not only the characters who come to Canada as refugees and exiles, but also Brochwel, who is born here and eventually comes to accept that he is Canadian, whether he wants to be or not. When thinking about one of his dreams, Brochwel draws the connection Davies often makes between climate and psychology: "Why has this dream so strong a Russian atmosphere, and why does it seem to belong in the nineteenth century, although all the people in it are of today? The intensely northern atmosphere of Canada, I suppose. We have hot summers and resplendent autumns, but it is winter that establishes the character of our country and our psychology. The Canadian mood. Canadian love, not cold but certainly not Mediterranean, as so many people expect love to be. Is it because I have been reading so many Russian novels and found myself in them as I never do in novels about the south?" And it is Brochwel, again, who makes a fresh application of Davies' belief that Canada is watchful and introverted by nature rather than assertive and extroverted. He reflects that Canadians are provincials, and that, as such, they have a place, "and an important one, for we are not beguiled by the notion that the fate of mankind and of human culture lies wholly in our hands. These others—the French, the English and even the Poles— probably enjoy some such delusion. The Americans certainly do, for they are natural-born crusaders, forever in the right, even when they are least aware of what they are crusading about. But we provincials, who are compelled by a dozen reasons, some of them not wholly mistaken, to tag along in such crusades as this, are also in our way the patient lookers-on in these political and cultural convulsions, and perhaps we have cooler heads when it comes to weighing the importance of what is being done."

After *Murther and Walking Spirits* appeared in the fall of 1991, Davies said that he thought he "had rather made a muddle of the book...it starts off with a slightly farcical tone and I had hoped that...gradually it would become more serious and that the reader would feel this. But a lot of readers have just carried over the almost comic murder through the book." Certainly there is a disjunction between the book's framing sections and its middle. But there is another reason why it does not, in the end, reach the level of masterworks like *Fifth Business*, or *The Rebel Angels* or *What's Bred in the Bone*. The central sections include some of Davies' most powerful writing. William McOmish, to take a conspicuous example, is a magnificent creation. The macabre scene where he fixes Rhodri Gilmartin with his glittering eye and forces him to listen to his tale, like a gaunt Ancient Mariner to a latter-day reluctant Wedding Guest, and the spellbinding scene in which Thomas Gilmartin bests Cursing Jemmy with one of the great tales of the *Mabinogion* are among Davies' most vivid. But since the central sections dramatize the ghost's inheritance, he should strike us as their sum. Yet this ghost is (literally) thin and bloodless; he feels far less real to the reader than his philosophical, opinionated friend McWearie.

The individual who does incorporate the full complexity and colour of this heritage—the imagination, the asthma, the gift for story-telling, the reluctant Canadianism, the openness to belief, the lot—is, of course, Davies himself. It is he whose engagement in the ancestral stories is rich and complex. He was no patient looker-on in the writing, but reviver, creative collaborator, imaginative conspirator. He strove to penetrate to the heart of their meaning for himself as he entered into the lives of those who had gone before. Where the disembodied ghost reports that he cannot weep at the pity of Malvina's inability to give herself to love, Davies himself could and did. This was the book that he felt most deeply as he was writing it, and for this reason he dedicated it to Brenda.

This added a special edge to the pain he felt when "some people were nasty about it." His publishers—Douglas Gibson–McClelland and Stewart in Canada (Davies had followed Gibson, his editor for several books at Macmillan, to M & S), Viking in New York and Sinclair-Stevenson in Britain—brought the book out in the fall of 1991. In Canada, many of the key critics were abrasive. George Woodcock set the tone: "Robertson Davies's theatrical past hangs heavy over his novels, which tend to combine saucily implausible plots with a good deal of creaking stage machinery, a romantic realist manner, and a shameless display of knowledge in some mildly esoteric field." He announced that in *Murther and Walking Spirits* "the machinery is so absurd that I am no longer willing to suspend my disbelief."

The U.S. critics gave it important and thoughtful appreciations, most notably in the *New York Times*, the *New York Times Book Review* and the *New Yorker*, although there were also influential negative responses, one in particular in the *Washington Post's Book World*. In Britain, Davies was now accorded the status of a major writer. After the short list for the Booker Prize was announced, one of the five judges, Nicholas Mosley, resigned in protest because Martin Amis' *Time's Arrow* had been included and *Murther* had not. The critical response there was either mixed or positive, the tone was respectful, and the reviews were meaty. Negative points were introduced regretfully, with observations like John Melmoth's in the *Sunday Times*: "It seems almost churlish to note that the novel does not cohere...." Positive assessments were sweeping, as with the conclusion reached by Valentine Cunningham in the London *Observer*: "It's hard to doubt that the sober, wry, compassionate touch for human frailties as they manifest themselves in the large, transcontinental shifts of family, fortune and faith will recruit huge numbers of new readers to the Davies fan club."

The harsh critical response appears to have interrupted the upward surge of Davies' hardcover sales in Canada. Although *Murther* stayed on *Maclean's* best-seller list for twenty-eight weeks and on the *Toronto Star's* for twenty-two, its sale of 25,000 copies fell short of the figure achieved by *The Lyre of Orpheus*. In the United States, *Murther* spent eight weeks on the *Washington Post's* list, but never made it onto the all-important one in the *New York Times*, and hardcover sales, at 40,638, retreated to the level attained by *What's Bred in the Bone*. In Britain, the substantial, thoughtful reviews may have kept sales at the level achieved by *Lyre*, but only preliminary figures are available so far.

Soon after the novel appeared in Canadian book stores, the *Globe and Mail* reported that "Davies has said *Murther* is his last novel." But Davies could no more stop writing than he could voluntarily stop breathing.

Chapter 18

ENDINGS AND BEGINNINGS

My desire is to die in my own bed, leaning back on a heap of
pillows, wearing a becoming dressing-gown and a skull-cap,
blessing those of whom I approve, gently rebuking my enemies,
giving legacies to faithful servants, and passing out clean
handkerchiefs to the weepers; I should also like a small choir
to do some really fine unaccompanied singing within earshot.
But will I be able to stage such a production in a hospital?
Never! I'll be lucky if the nurse answers the bell in time to jot
down my last words.
> —Samuel Marchbanks, "Diary of Winter Depression,"
> 6 March 1948

By preparation for death I don't mean folding your hands or
going around forgiving a lot of people you don't want to forgive:
it's preparing for a richness, a good and glorious end.... You
have to come to terms with yourself and your place in the
scheme of life—something a good many people don't want to
do. In the last century we have extended the normal life-span.
Many seem to believe that this means we have extended the
period when they should enjoy the things they enjoyed in youth.
But, I don't think they realize that we've also expanded the

period of life when we can learn to think, feel, and experience the largeness and the splendor of life.

—"You Should Face Up to Your Death, Says Author," *Toronto Star*, 15 November 1975

Davies WAS INTERESTED in death as a central event in life from the moment he began to write plays and fiction. Over the years his *alter ego*, Samuel Marchbanks, ruminated whimsically on the subject, writing of arranging his own funeral, of framing satisfactory last words, of dying where he wanted to (in his own bed at home, not in hospital), of putting interesting surprises into his will, of recording a eulogy to be played at his funeral, of memorializing himself in an epitaph. Sometimes in Davies' plays and novels a death starts the plot rolling, and sometimes it is the conclusion toward which everything leads. Davies' characters not infrequently seek to take their own or someone else's life, and often they manage to do so. The dead reach out of the grave in his books, entangling the living and attempting to impose their will upon them.

The prospect of his own death holds no terrors for Davies. He contemplates the end of his life with equanimity, partly because he does not regard it as the absolute cessation of all that he has been, and partly because he has been actively preparing for it since his forties. He talks easily about winding up his earthly affairs. He envisions a quiet, very private funeral, followed at an interval by "a good beano" with lots of food and drink and music supplied by a small, unaccompanied choir. Among other things, he imagines the choir singing an anthem that was a favourite of the Massey College Singers, an adaptation of Psalm 39 set by the eighteenth-century composer Matthew Locke:

> Lord, let me know mine end, and the number of my days: that I may be certified how long I have to live.
> Behold, thou hast made my days as it were a span long, and mine age is ev'n as nothing in respect of thee; and verily ev'ry man living is altogether vanity.
> For man walketh in a vain shadow, and disquiets himself in vain; he heaps up riches, and cannot tell who shall

gather them.

And now, Lord, what is my hope? Truly my hope is ev'n in thee.

When thou with rebukes dost chasten man for sin, thou mak'st his beauty to consume away, like as it were a moth fretting a garment. Ev'ry man therefore is but vanity.

Hear my pray'r, O Lord, and with thine ears consider my calling; hold not thy peace at my tears. For I am a stranger with thee, and a sojourner, as all my fathers were.

O spare me a little, that I may recover my strength, before I go hence, and be no more seen.

Surprisingly, given that he frequently searches out the graves of forbears, friends and the great, he does not want to be buried in a cemetery. In 1972, in Llanfair Caerinion, Wales, he tumbled through "hay & broken tombs to the gravestone of William Robertson which Mgt. [Margaret, Rupert's widow] has had cleaned up. Vowed there to be cremated: how sad these old graves are & what a nuisance to the survivors! None of that for me." Instead of being consigned to "some miserable plot in a rather creepy bourgeois garden," he wants his ashes to be distributed in the garden at Windhover, and he would like a brief commemoration on a plaque.

Although death itself does not terrify him, Davies does fear the loss of his faculties—"oblivion in this life." Over the last decade or so, ailments have pressed more heavily upon him. Early in 1982, when he was sixty-eight, a cataract began to cloud his right eye, which was probably a factor in an accident shortly before Christmas in 1983, when he stepped into the path of a car in the dark and was knocked down. Fortunately the car was moving slowly, and the driver (a fan who had always wanted to meet Davies, but not in these circumstances) helped him to his feet and took him home. He wore glasses with one darkened lens for a couple of years until surgery removed the cataract in 1986. (The other eye was operated on successfully as well in 1992, a year or so after he gave himself a black eye by misjudging a curb.) During the 1980s, the colds, bronchial ailments and asthma that have plagued him all his life became increasingly tenacious. In 1987 he finally put himself in the care of a specialist, and on the latter's recommendation he stopped smoking the single cigar or pipe he had enjoyed each day. Early in 1988 he gave his chest a respite from the Canadian winter with a vacation in Arizona. In spite of these precautions, however, in Sweden the following year he suffered an attack of asthma so severe that Brenda feared for his life, and he himself worried that he might no longer be capable of travel, or even of living effectively. More recently, in December 1992 and January 1993, he had two minor heart attacks.

Nonetheless, despite the moments of sharp despair that these episodes brought, their primary effect was to reinforce his resolution to resist senility and feebleness. He hates the thought of turning into the archetypal Senex, resigned to physical decline, to hardening of the mental arteries, to stupidity and old-fogydom. Given a chance to choose among the many faces of old age, Davies would himself select the Chinese "Old Rogue" or the merry old man in the Welsh folk song "*Yr Hen Wr Mwyn.*" But although he often emits roguish sparks, he has actually become a "Wise Old Man," magical in his great experience and knowledge. He sees curiosity as the key to making "old age...a delight. One has seen so much, and one is eager to see more. One has reached a few conclusions. The twilight years [a phrase he hates] are a glorious sundown." Not only has he himself retained curiosity in abundance, he has managed to round his life to the sort of conclusion he described in the second of the quotations that head this chapter. He has come to terms with himself and his place in the scheme of things and has capitalized on the years beyond the normal biblical span "to think, feel and experience the largeness and splendor of life."

In almost all the activities of Davies' late years, there are indications of his intention to summarize what he has learned from life and to pull his experience into a coherent whole. Although the Cornish novels drew together a great deal of Davies' thinking on a number of subjects, he continued to consider them and reach fresh conclusions. He remained in close touch with the university in the years after *The Rebel Angels* appeared, and he used the

This calendar amused me for the whole of 1989 for I had augmented it to include dates literary, theatrical & personal that had significance for me.

Robertson Davies

JUNE

MONDAY	TUESDAY	WEDNESDAY	THURSDAY	FRIDAY	SATURDAY	SUNDAY
			1 — Christopher Marlowe d. 1593	2 — de Sade b. 1740 / E. Elgar 1857 — Thomas Hardy b. 1840	3 — Kafka d. 1924	4 — Casanova d. 1798
5 — Dame Ivy Compton-Burnett b. 1884 — Stephen Crane d. 1900, Adam Smith b. 1723	6 — Tho: Mann b. 1875 / C.G. Jung d. 1961 — Alexander Pushkin b. 1799, Pierre Corneille b. 1606	7 — E.M. Forster d. 1970	8 — R. Schumann b. 1810 / Sarah Siddons b. 1951 — Gerard Manley Hopkins d. 1889, George Sand d. 1876	9 — Dame Sybil Thorndike d. 1976 — Charles Dickens d. 1870	10 — F.D. d. 1901	11 — Ben Jonson b. 1572
12	13 — W.B. Yeats b. 1865	14 — G.K. Chesterton d. 1936	15 — Edvard Grieg b. 1843	16 — Bloomsday Memorial	17 — J.C. Page d. 1963	18 — Samuel Butler d. 1902, William Cobbett d. 1835
19 — J.M. davis d. 1937 — Blaise Pascal b. 1623	20 — Offenbach b. 1819	21 — Inigo Jones d. 1652	22 — W. de la Mare d. 1956 — Niccolò Machiavelli d. 1527	23 — Carl Shappe d. 1924	24	25 — ETAH d. 1822
26 — Madame de La Fayette d. 1683, Gilbert White d. 1793	27	28 — L. Pirandello b. 1867 — Jean-Jacques Rousseau b. 1712	29	30 — John Gay b. 1665		

Annotations on Davies' copy of the 1989 Penguin Classics Calendar.

opportunity of a series of convocation addresses to revisit his views on the centrality of the humanities in the university and on the value of a university education. Similarly, after finishing *What's Bred in the Bone*, he took another Art Gallery of Ontario tour (this one to Florence and Rome). When the Metropolitan Museum of Art in New York asked him to talk about "Painting, Fiction and Faking" in 1988, he expanded on the personal convictions that underlay the novel. After *The Lyre of Orpheus* was completed, he and Brenda gave more time than usual to opera, continuing to attend most of the Canadian Opera Company's performances at the O'Keefe Centre in Toronto, taking in the St. Louis Opera Festival three times, making a pilgrimage to Bayreuth to see *The Ring*, feasting on Mozart in Vienna and visiting the Aldeburgh Festival.

As he had several times earlier, Davies wrote a commentary for one of the Canadian Opera Company's programs, and in two separate speeches he expanded his thinking about the nature of opera and drew it into relation with his other major concerns. In "Opera As Related to Literature," he discusses some of the personal experiences underlying *Lyre* and contrasts a number of operatic librettos with the literary works from which they were drawn.

In "Opera and Humour," he dismisses Freud's attempt to define humour (in *Wit and Its Relation to the Unconscious*), restating his own oft-stated view that Freud's pessimism and tragic outlook typify a rigid, reductive approach to life. In developing his own definition of humour, Davies turns to certain ideas of the ancient Greek philosopher Heraclitus that had been fundamental to the thinking of Jung and that had impressed him when he first began to read the great psychologist—that the world is united through the combination of opposites, that "Everything flows: nothing stands still," that anything pursued to extremes turns into its opposite. (Davies had the quotation inscribed in Greek on the porringer that he and Brenda gave to Robertson Davies Davenport, Horace's son, in 1955, and made Heraclitus' idea that anything pursued to extremes turns into its opposite into a leitmotif in *Murther and Walking Spirits*.) The notion of the reconciliation of opposites leads him to the argument that life is best lived "with one eye cocked toward Comedy and the other eye skewed toward Tragedy," and that "out of this feat of balanced observation emerges Humour, not as a foolish amusement or an escape from reality, but as a breadth of perception."

Davies views this profound sort of humour as an archetype—a notion he first advanced in a lecture in 1980. He now calls it the "Janus Archetype," after the two-faced Roman god who looks both ways at once. Drawing on his lifelong interest in melodrama, he goes on to argue that the great melodramatic operas rarely incorporate this powerful sort of humour. Only a few masterworks—John Gay's *The Beggar's Opera*, Vaughan Williams' *Sir John in Love*, Mozart's *The Marriage of Figaro* and *The Magic Flute* and Richard Strauss' *Ariadne Auf Naxos*—have the power to make audiences experience what G. K. Chesterton once described as "the mysticism of happiness." In introducing this phrase to stand for "the sense of splendour and illumination and rich enlargement of the spirit," Davies makes a fresh application of a quotation that he had used at intervals, at least since the 1960s, to describe his most exalting evenings in the theatre.

Education, art and opera were not the only interests that Davies continued to pursue in his "retirement." He and Brenda travelled a great deal, often planning a trip around one or another of his professional obligations—publicity, speeches, readings and the like. Almost all their expeditions to Europe began or ended with a stay in London, "the city of our youth...full of memories & sacred places." In London and Oxford their pattern was much what it had always been, and, when something altered, Davies felt it keenly. In Oxford in 1988, he noted: "B. & I go out to walk & to the pen shop to get my nibs ground, but alas! they no longer do it & say the people in Bush House in London are the only ones who do. Feel this change with absurd intensity—but the pen shop was one of my Oxford bastions."

Increasingly, the connections that he and Brenda had always sought out when they travelled brought with them now a sense of termination and closure. In Edinburgh, Davies asked after his Queen's professor James A. Roy and learned that in his later years he had become the "Club Bore" at the Edinburgh Arts Club. At

Balliol he learned that his tutor M. Roy Ridley had years ago been deprived of his fellowship for taking up with the master's secretary, had been divorced by his wife and married the secretary, and had spent the balance of his life eking out a living in Bristol as a reviewer and examiner. At Buxton, they toured the Opera House ("and a pretty old house it is, & a fine large stage"), saw the hospital where Davies had filled sandbags in the earliest days of the war and viewed the garden and pavilion where they had become engaged ("sadly fallen—a mini-railways in the former & a display of hearing-aids in the latter"). In London, revisiting the church where they had been married nearly fifty years before, they found it rebuilt but chilly; the vicar, barely audible, was christening a child named Miranda.

In Ireland they made a special expedition to Annagh-ma-Kerrig, once Tyrone Guthrie's home, now a centre for painters and writers, and had a good gossip with the custodian over an excellent dinner in what was once the kitchen ("now wholly revised & unrecognizable as the filthy witches' cavern it was"). The next day they searched out the graveyard where Guthrie and his wife Judith "are buried in an enclosed plot with a couple of centuries of forbears—but *not* Tony's father. Graves utterly neglected under grass & weeds: two large yews grow in the plot. Names on a dark grey Victn stone. Sad, but probably for the best. Tony, a lifelong Oedipus, lies at last wth. his mother." At the Theatre Museum in London there was a trove on display— "Lilian Baylis's desk! B. had stood by it often when The Lady had it heaped with papers. Irving's swords for Lear & Macbeth delighted me; Chaliapin's costume for the Coronation Scene in *Boris*; Martin-Harvey's shoes from *The Shrew*; Irving's 'invisible' spectacles for stage use (& how invisible were they really?)."

The Davieses, now attending on average about thirty theatrical productions a year, continued to take full advantage of the Stratford Festival, the Shaw Festival in Niagara-on-the-Lake and the London theatres. But his "Theatre Notes" increasingly reflected a sense of conclusion or rounding-up. When plays that he knew from their first production were revived, he often commented not just on the direction, staging and performance but on how well the play itself had held up. And at productions of the classics he frequently recalled his earliest experiences of them. His note about Farquhar's *The Beaux' Stratagem* at the Stratford Festival begins: "How often have I seen this play? First, certainly, at the Oxford Rep. where Stanford Holme was a memorable Sullen." His entry about *John Bull's Other Island* at the Shaw Festival closes with the observation: "I first saw this play done by Maurice Colbourne (Broadbent) & Barry Jones (Keegan) as a schoolboy in 1929 at the Royal Alec. Margaret Rawlings an irresistible Nora. Jones was v. fine as Keegan & his final speech deeply moving."

Again and again the "Notes" suggest that he was summing up in his mind his experience of a particular play. Occasionally he unfolded his thoughts more fully to an actor or actress after a particularly fine performance. Here is the letter he wrote to Domini Blythe after he saw her in Wycherley's *The Country Wife* at the Stratford Festival:

Dear Miss B.

Congratulations and warm admiration for your Margery Pinchwife; my wife and I agreed it was quite the best we have ever seen.

So what have you seen, sez you? Well, to begin, the first modern revival of the play that Sydney Carroll did in London in 1934, in which Lesley Wareing as Margery was quite obliterated by Athene Seyler as Lady Fidget. Then the Old Vic production in 1936, in which Ruth Gordon played Margery, but was (in the director, Tyrone Guthrie's, words) "acted right off the stage and out into the alley" by Edith Evans as Lady F. Ruth G. was too cunning, too foxy, too knowing, for the part. Then in 1959, Julie Harris's undistinguished venture in New York, in which nobody shone; a common grayness silvered all. Then the Stratford production in which Helen Burns was very good as Margery, but the teeniest bit too much the simpleton, the witling. Where you scored heavily was in making Margery an innocent, rather than a fool—a good-hearted determined, sensible girl. It was sensible of the director to make the relationship between Pinchwife and Margery not all disagreeable; he shows some affection, and she some compliance. This is so much better than the usual cat-and-dog affair between a brute and a scheming yokel....

So—once again we are greatly in your debt for a very fine performance, and as we have seen all the important productions of the play since it rejoined the repertoire (the Victorians simply couldn't endure it) I hope that gives you some satisfaction.

Sincerely

Robertson Davies

As Davies discovered when he was a finalist for both the Nobel and the Booker Prizes in 1986, being lionized was often an uncomfortable and exhausting business. Even when he enjoyed it greatly, as he did at a series of lively literary dinners in London during June of 1988, he found it a "strange sensation." And later that year, after a Canadian interviewer informed him that he was "an ikon of Canada," he reflected ironically: "Astonishing how I have been suddenly promoted to this status as an ancient monument." On a publicity tour for *The Lyre of Orpheus* he was incredulous at the warmth of the welcome he received in the United States: readings sold out halls designed for eight hundred or a thousand, hundreds lined up to get their books signed, fans recognized him in the street, and everywhere he was "Acclaimed as a writer of world significance." He found most of it "a very nervous-making experience. I don't truly believe it. I don't bask in it. I don't find it feeds or nourishes me and neither does Brenda. We both find it slightly embarrassing."

On the other hand, some of the honours bestowed on him were a source of great and deep satisfaction, particularly his country's decision to make him a Companion of the Order of Canada in 1972, the American Academy and Institute of Arts and Letters' to make him an Honorary Member in 1980 (the first Canadian to be so recognized), the *Paris Review*'s to include him in its prestigious series of literary interviews in 1986, and Balliol College's to confer on him an Honorary Fellowship in the same year. Since he holds universities in high esteem, Davies was always pleased to receive honorary degrees, but particularly so when an institution of the antiquity, reputation and associations of Trinity College, Dublin, or Oxford gave him a D. Litt. As he observed in his travel diary at the conclusion of the "immensely complimentary day" on July 6, 1990, at Trinity College, Dublin: "I now have a link—gossamer-like, spiderweb-like—wth. Swift, Congreve, Goldsmith & Wilde. Or so I like to think." Such honours consume a surprising amount of time in writing letters, making arrangements and travelling, preparing speeches, attending the ceremony and the like, but Davies does not begrudge it, not only because he believes in the importance of ceremony but also because he makes such occasions fruitful for himself in one way or another.

The day-long affair at Oxford in 1991 will serve for all. "First everybody involved goes to St. John's College where many long years ago some benefactor endowed a little refreshment for degree giving which was strawberries and champagne and so the hall was packed with people having strawberries and champagne and a rather smashing looking outfit because they were all got up very handsomely and there was a Cardinal present and the Cardinal was being, in an Italian manner, extraordinarily affable to everybody. So I had some strawberries and a glass of champagne. Then along came a man of high university rank, as I could tell from his garb, and offered me some more champagne. I said: 'No thank you. I think one is enough.' And he said: 'Wise man. Long time 'til the next leak.' A very Oxonian touch. Realism breaking in upon grandeur." Then, as Davies walked in the procession from St. John's along Broad Street to the Sheldonian Theatre, he was annoyed to find Josef Brodsky, the Russian poet now living in the United States, with whom he was paired, pooh-poohing the whole affair and behaving inappropriately, smoking and joking with the crowd and refusing to attend the Chancellor's lunch. He noticed, however, that Brodsky's publisher's representative did come to the lunch. "And who do you think his representative was?—Jackie Kennedy! And she was there, doing the polite. I have met her once or twice and she is a really charming and gracious sort of person and she was charming the socks off everybody. But not Brodsky. He was too fine.

He had too big a soul to be involved in anything like that."

Besides Brodsky and Davies, the honorees that day were Sir Robin Cooke, president of the New Zealand Court of Appeal (in a dither about whether or not to bow to the chancellor) and Cardinal Casaroli ("who never went anywhere without a little clerical stooge right behind him in case he wanted his hanky"). As the impressive ceremony proceeded, Davies thought to himself: "I am a very queer character in the midst of all these grandees—politicians and theologians and this, that and the other. Then I thought of a tale which I have always enjoyed, which was that toward the latter part of his life, Richard Brinsley Sheridan was granted an honorary doctorate at Oxford and then at the last moment they nixed it and said No, he couldn't have one. But he went anyway and sat in the audience, and the students set up a great outcry and cried: 'Sheridan among the doctors! Sheridan among the doctors!' And so they had to give him the degree and Sheridan was ushered up and seated among the doctors." And so Davies, too, took his place among the doctors.

He accepted only a few of the flood of requests for interviews, speeches, introductions to books, articles, book endorsements. But some were special. When he received an invitation to address the Jung Institute of San Francisco (1979 and 1982), or to give the Neil Gunn Memorial Lecture at Edinburgh University (1988), the Tanner Lectures at Yale (1991) or the Prince of Hesse Memorial Lecture at the Aldeburgh Festival (1991), it was recognition that he respected and valued.

When the Stratford Festival, which was presenting thirty-three performances of Elliott Hayes' appropriately theatrical adaptation of *World of Wonders* in the Avon Theatre between May 16 and August 9 in 1992, asked him to give a lecture about the novel and the adaptation, he was pleased to comply (and delighted when both speech and production drew good houses). And when impresario (and old friend) Nicholas Goldschmidt approached him to create a libretto for an oratorio to be part of an international choral festival, he interrupted the writing of *Murther* to do it. The Old Testament story of Ahab, Naboth, Jezebel and Jehu had been a great tale of wonder for him since he had first encountered it in Sunday school as a boy, and he quickly determined to use this as his subject. His libretto, cast in the language of the King James Bible, is powerful and sure. On June 3, 1993, the Toronto Symphony, the Toronto Mendelssohn Choir and eight soloists gave *Jezebel: The Golden Tale of Naboth and His Vineyard, and of King Ahab and His Wicked Queen*, with music by Derek Holman, a première performance at Toronto's Roy Thomson Hall. Both the audience and the critics gave it a warm reception.

Other invitations provided Davies with opportunities to reflect on various aspects of his life. The titles of two of these pieces— "A Chapter of Autobiography" (for the UCC *Old Times*) and "My Early Literary Life" (for *Saturday Night*)—make obvious the strength of Davies' impulse to review his life. In 1989, on the occasion of the "Robertson Davies Tribute" at the Wang International Festival of Authors in Toronto, he addressed the audience, tongue in cheek, on "Why I Do Not Intend to Write an Autobiography." After revealing that several publishers had urged him to write such a book, he claimed that a dream had convinced him not to do so. In the dream, Samuel Johnson and his biographer James Boswell gave him many reasons to forbear: he has done nothing but write all his life, so there is nothing to tell of; his childhood had lacked in wondrous events; his happy marriage could not be explored without violating Brenda's privacy; he has no military exploits to relate; no great fortune has been acquired; although he *has* written indiscreet letters to women, he is unlikely to get his hands on them, since the women hope to sell them later for profit. At this point Anthony Trollope, writer of an immensely successful *Autobiography* of his own, arrives, and it is recalled that Trollope had died laughing. "Perhaps," Boswell observes, "Davies wishes to die laughing at the autobiographies of his contemporaries…. He is known to have a keen appreciation of irony. Perhaps that is why—if I may change my ground in this argument—he would do well to remain silent about himself." With this, the dream ended.

The speech kept a packed audience of fans in delighted thrall throughout. It was Davies in the role of Magnus Eisengrim, "A man who can stand stark naked in the midst of a crowd and keep it gaping for an hour while he manipulates a few coins, or cards,

or billiard balls," throwing out hints, raising expectations, weaving from one to the next in an entertaining and recondite manner, never letting the mask drop."

In 1981, before telling Davies of my interest in writing a biography of him, I asked whether he intended to write his own. He
said no. It wasn't his *métier*. Facts—even his own facts—do not
come alive for him until they are transformed by imagination.
Striking the balance, establishing a distanced context, checking
for accuracy—such exercises hold little appeal for him. Later, as
we talked our way through his life over the next couple of years,
it became clear to me that another reason was his instinctive
dread of confronting painful episodes in his past. By then I had
realized that his memory is exceptionally vivid, and that he didn't
wish to reopen passages like the despairing year at Oxford or the
dark winter of the diagnosis of Hodgkin's disease. Of course, one
might argue that he was actually writing an autobiography of the
most powerful, persuasive, enchanting sort in the guise of his
novels and plays, each of them constituting an indirect record of
part of his life's spiritual voyage.

From the beginning, Davies understood that writing demanded
a special sort of honesty, an ongoing soul-scrape. By the late
1950s, and probably earlier, he had come to believe that the
inner voyage not only yielded self-knowledge but helped him to
grasp aspects of the nature of God. By 1968, his ideas about the
unconscious, the source of a writer's most powerful perceptions,
had been strengthened by his reading of Jung. As he moved
toward and past retirement in the late 1970s and through the
1980s, he became able to speak with greater frankness than
before about his personal experience of the process of creation
and self-discovery. He tackled the topic initially for the Jung
Institute of San Francisco, an audience distant from his ordinary
context and one likely to be open-minded about what he had to
say. There, in 1979, he spoke for the first time in public about
his recurrent vision of the throwing of the fateful snowball, the
starting point for the Deptford trilogy.

Eleven years intervened, and then, in "Jung and the Writer,"
the speech he wrote for the Gothenburg book fair in 1989, he

revealed how his unconscious had gradually persuaded the conscious to its view. The initiating snowball scene, appearing and reappearing to him, had finally moved him to think about it carefully and to make some rough notes. But he had still not fully understood what the vision had to tell him. When he came to prepare a detailed plan of *Fifth Business*, he found that it took a different direction than he had anticipated, and later, when the writing was actually under way, he found himself learning new things about the story all the time. His experience was similar in the case of *The Manticore*, where a full understanding of his hero did not come until after he had begun to write the story, and the maiden and the manticore appeared to him in a waking dream.

Later in 1989, in a speech which was given not at a safe distance but on his home ground at the University of Toronto, Davies gathered his thoughts on many subjects—magic, the desire for marvels, religion, archetypes, Freud and Jung, evil, comedy and tragedy. By now he could declare: "It is here that I have to tell you one or two things which I have not spoken of in public, because I thought they would be misunderstood. But I have now come to a time of life when I really don't care very much whether people understand me, because I have spent my life trying with my best efforts to understand myself." He had just said that his novels had been criticized for elements that were termed "supernatural." Now, to demonstrate that such things were actually "psychological," he described his childhood visions of Christ and of the evil witch in the cupboard, his adult dream in which he shook hands with the witch, and his waking dream of the maiden and the manticore. He also argued (as he had in "Jung and the Writer") that he, like all serious writers, is a religious man—taking the meaning of "religious" not from the Latin *religare*, "to tie, to fasten, to assume a yoke" and hence to adhere to a system of belief, but from *relegere*, "to consider, to ponder, to examine" and thus "to examine and reflect upon every sort of experience in a personal way"—and that writers provide an example of "the exploration and the coming to terms with the inmost self" that he sees as one of the great adventures of mankind in the future.

Since retiring from his university appointments in 1981, Davies has lived the life of a full-time writer, and he and Brenda have adopted a new rhythm of life. For much of the year they spend four days of the week at Windhover, where Davies writes in the morning and rests after lunch, keeping the balance of the day free for other activities. Brenda gardens (taking special pleasure in creating walks to points that overlook pleasant vistas) and manages their two homes. Their Toronto residence is a condominium in The Oaklands at the bottom of the Avenue Road hill, a brisk twenty-minute walk from Massey College. They have a busy social life in the city and are frequent film-goers. He has an Alexander Technique lesson every week, Brenda one less frequently. Brenda still plays tennis at her club, does the shopping and cooking herself and, as always, all the driving.

Davies keeps rooms in Massey College, where he attends to the business side of authorship: responding to correspondence, keeping in touch with agents and publishers, giving interviews, proofreading typescripts and the like. His long-time secretary, Moira Whalon, has continued with him on a part-time basis. His study is a pleasant room located in the northeast corner of the College, with windows overlooking both Devonshire Place and the quad. It has a fireplace, commodious bookcases housing the books he used as a teacher of drama, a low table, two easy chairs and a large desk acquired from his father, who had prized it as the oldest newspaperman's desk in Canada. (It was made in 1837 for Edward John Barker, the founding editor of the *Kingston British Whig*, and was used by every succeeding editor of the *Whig* down to Rupert.) On the walls are a caricature of Angelica Catalani, the early-nineteenth-century Italian diva, and her lover, the Bishop of Limerick, escaping down a ladder while a Cambridge don admires her legs; an old print of Balliol; Rupert's crest, as modified for Davies' use; the Oxford Almanack (a large sheet with a picture, a calendar and information about saints' days and the like); and three playbills from the history of his and Brenda's beloved Old Vic. On or above the mantel is an everchanging clutter—in the late 1980s a map of Montgomeryshire, the crest of Oxford University, a leering satyr's head that had once belonged to John Pearson, several small Palm Sunday crosses, a drawing of Henry Irving as Cardinal Richelieu, a school bell, a reproduction of a painting of Christ riding the ass into Jerusalem and a picture of Shakespeare.

No marital partnership escapes trials. It is likely that Davies spoke from personal experience when he observed once that "we love in terms of what we are and in even the most profound love are pools of loneliness—feelings unrequited, needs unfulfilled, and tendernesses proffered in vain, because there are no two people perfectly suited to one another." But all the evidence suggests that Davies and Brenda have created a marriage close to their personal ideal. In one of his many travel diaries, Davies wrote, "We lunch...& talk abt. our special happiness, in whch we take so much delight." Together they have enjoyed a lifelong, spirited conversation, like the one that Davies had observed between W. L. Grant and his wife at UCC. They talk at length, about anything and everything—theatre, friends, people, psychology, religion. After an evening of theatre followed by a light supper and discussion of the play, Davies noted: "This has always been one of our great pleasures—the theatre *post mortem*." They have shared many ventures over the years—play productions in Peterborough, Alexander Technique lessons, absorbing Jung's ideas, the challenge of Massey College and, since the early 1980s, publicity tours (Brenda providing companionship and organizational skills).

Over the past ten years or so, their family life has fallen into a pattern. There is a gathering at Windhover at New Year's which includes Jennifer and her husband Tom, and Rosamond and her children, Christopher, Piers, Erik and Cecilia. In April there is a second to celebrate the birthdays of Tom, Rosamond, Piers and Cecilia. Most years a trip to the Stratford Festival in August marks Davies' and Christopher's birthdays, and shortly before Christmas there is another theatre outing for the grandchildren. They visit Miranda almost every year in London; the rest of the time Brenda keeps in touch with her by letter. Both Miranda and Brenda's sister Maisie visit from time to time.

They continue to expand their circle of friends. Both Davies and Brenda are good at writing occasional notes and at getting in touch with far-flung acquaintances when they are near enough for a visit, and their contact with such people continues to be vital and warm.

On February 2, 1990, Davies and Brenda celebrated their fiftieth wedding anniversary, inviting some sixty or so nearby friends and family members, ranging in age from eleven to ninety, to a black-tie dinner at the York Club. Claude Bissell in his toast spoke wittily on marriage, using passages from Davies' own writing. In reply the author, by now a little shorter than his original six feet but still unstooped, an arresting, slightly puckish figure in formal dress and silver-white hair, spoke of the ingredient that keeps a marriage vital—good talk. Brenda—elegant, quick of manner, sharp of feature—expressed their pleasure that so many friends had gone to such great lengths to be present.

I leave Davies in his study at Windhover, in September 1993, working on his new novel, *The Cunning Man.* It has presented itself to him in the usual "mass of incident and narrative and scenes" that always makes him wonder whether he will ever be able "to get them down on paper in a way which will appear coherent and not just a terrible one thing after another in a ridiculous fashion." He does most of his writing here, surrounded by objects of special significance on the few patches of wall and the tops of the bookcases. None of them is there to remind him of Brenda, however. She is the companion of the lived—rather than the imagined—life. She is omnipresent in the house and the life that surrounds the study—as the first person consulted about an emerging book, as Katherina on the wall of the living room, as the spirit of the house.

The Karsh photograph of Jung—"the picture of the great doctor looking wise"—that hung over his desk during the writing of *The Manticore* is still there, although on a different wall. For Davies it is "a thing which feeds me. I have a sense of touching base." The handsomely painted Punch that he acquired in 1961 is there too, perched on a bookcase, reminding him of the Old Adam in all of us. The coloured print of an Oxford scholar in his robes that Davies sent to his mother when he got his B. Litt. is there, and so is Max Beerbohm's caricature of "Dante at Oxford," showing Dante in the street past midnight, being confronted by the proctors demanding "Your name and college?"

The piece of the oak beam from the Welshpool house in which his father was born is still fixed over the window, providing "something of Wales, and a very strong reminiscence of my father." There are three items on display from his Martin-Harvey collection—the proof copies of the posters used to advertise *The Only Way* and *Scaramouche*, and a design by Charles Buchel for a poster (never used) for *The Lyons Mail*. The last, illustrating Martin-Harvey's double role, speaks to Davies very powerfully. "Nice Guy" Leserques, in profile, sees his shadow, the evil Dubosc, leering back at him from the mirror, a reminder to Davies that "if I were just Mr. Nice Guy I would never be a novelist."

There is a fine engraving of Paganini. The great actor-manager Henry Irving—who is also present in a small alabaster bust—was said to have had a very strong whiff of Paganini about him. For Davies, Paganini "sums up an enormous amount of nineteenth-century virtuosity and that stylish fashion of presenting art which has become very much out of fashion now and which we probably wouldn't like if we could hear it, but it's fascinating to think about it.... Rumours circulated that Paganini had been taught to play the violin by the devil.... And he was indeed a very curious man. He had a very peculiar walk. He was tall, extremely thin and emaciated.... All those things interest me. They warm me. They give a vivid sense of the past which is also the present. I feel that as long as I remember these things, those people are not gone."

On the wall behind the desk is Rupert's grant of arms from the College of Heralds. As Davies once explained in an article on "Jung and Heraldry," the dragon on the crest stands as "a reminder of the incalculability, the might and the chthonic force of the Unconscious; he is a perpetual adjuration to seek below the surface for the truth of things; he is a counsellor that instinct is often the surest guide in important human affairs. His wings give him power to soar: he is no creeping thing. He is the Old Saurian who possessed the earth before the johnny-come-lately Man seized it and proceeded to mess it up with his cleverness. The dragon says: Trust Nature but do not fear to fly above Earth, and Remember Me. The dragon frees the mind from the present, for he is very old, and he frees the spirit from commonplace considerations, because he has wings. And the dragon, looked at in this light, is a dear companion indeed, a Wise Animal, A Counsellor that only a fool would neglect."

Abbreviations Used in the Notes

Davenport   Horace W. Davenport
Examiner   *The Peterborough Examiner* and later *Peterborough Examiner*
Herald   the *Herald* and later the *Thamesville Herald*
Mercury   the *Renfrew Mercury*
RD   Robertson Davies
Robertson   R. W. W. Robertson
Roper   Gordon Roper
Ryerson   Donald Ryerson
Sifton   Elisabeth Sifton
SN   *Saturday Night*
Star   the *Toronto Daily Star* and later the *Toronto Star*
Sweezey   Eleanor A. Sweezey
Whig   the *Kingston Whig-Standard* and later the *Whig-Standard*

Books and Writings Cited in More Than One Chapter:

"¿Aca nada?"   "¿Aca nada?" *Times Literary Supplement* 30
                        Sept.-6 Oct. 1988: 1070+.

Aesop   *A Masque of Aesop*. Toronto: Clarke, Irwin,
                        1952.

Almanack   *Marchbanks' Almanack*. Toronto:
                        McClelland and Stewart, 1967.

Angels   *The Rebel Angels*. Toronto: Macmillan,
                        1981.

"Autobiography"   "A Chapter of Autobiography," *Old Times*
                        Jubilee issue [1979-80]: 14-17.

"Ben Jonson and Alchemy"   "Ben Jonson and Alchemy." *Stratford
                        Papers: 1968-69*. Ed. B. A. W. Jackson.
                        Hamilton, Ont.: McMaster U Library P,
                        1972. 40-60.

Boy Actors   *Shakespeare's Boy Actors*. London: Dent,
                        1939.

Bred   *What's Bred in the Bone*. Toronto:
                        Macmillan, 1985.

Brothers	*Brothers in the Black Art: A Play for Television.* Vancouver, B. C.: Alcuin, 1981.
Centennial Play	With W. O. Mitchell, Arthur L. Murphy, Eric Nicol, and Yves Thériault. *The Centennial Play.* Music by Keith Bissell. Ottawa: Centennial Commission, 1966.
"Christmas Carol Reharmonized"	"A Christmas Carol Reharmonized." *Book World* [*Washington Post*] 28 Nov. 1982: 4+.
"Delusions of Literacy"	"Delusions of Literacy: The Lahey Lecture of Concordia University," *McGill Journal of Education* 13 (1978): 250.
Diary	*The Diary of Samuel Marchbanks.* Toronto: Clarke, Irwin, 1947.
"Double"	"The Double Life of Robertson Davies." *Liberty* Apr. 1954: 18+.
Enthusiasms	*The Enthusiasms of Robertson Davies.* Rev. ed. New York: Viking, 1990.
Eros	*Eros at Breakfast and Other Plays.* Toronto: Clarke, Irwin, 1949.
Fifth	*Fifth Business.* Toronto: Macmillan, 1970.
Fortune	*Fortune, My Foe.* Toronto: Clarke, Irwin, 1949.
Frailties	*A Mixture of Frailties.* Toronto: Macmillan, 1958.
"Harp"	"A Harp That Once." *Queen's Quarterly* 50 (1943): 374-81.
Heart's	*At My Heart's Core.* Toronto: Clarke, Irwin, 1950.
Hunting	*Hunting Stuart and Other Plays.* Toronto: New Press, 1972.
Jig	*A Jig for the Gypsy.* Toronto: Clarke, Irwin, 1954.
"Keeping Faith"	"Keeping Faith," *SN* Jan. 1987: 187+.
Leaven	*Leaven of Malice.* Toronto: Clarke, Irwin, 1954.

Lyre	*The Lyre of Orpheus.* Toronto: Macmillan, 1988.
Manticore	*The Manticore.* Toronto: Macmillan, 1972.
Marchbanks	A column, variously titled, written under the pseudonym Samuel Marchbanks, initially three times a week, then twice, and finally once, in the years 1940 to 1953.
Mirror	*The Mirror of Nature: The Alexander Lectures 1982.* Toronto: U of Toronto P, 1983.
"Mixed Grill"	"Mixed Grill: Touring Fare in Canada, 1920-1935." *Theatrical Touring and Founding in North America.* Ed. L. W. Conolly. Westport, Conn.: Greenwood, 1982. 41-56.
Murther	*Murther and Walking Spirits.* Toronto: McClelland and Stewart-A Douglas Gibson Book, 1991.
"Nineteenth-Century"	"The Nineteenth-Century Repertoire." *Early Stages: Theatre in Ontario 1800-1914.* Ed. Ann Saddlemyer. Ontario Historical Studies Series. Toronto: U of Toronto P, 1990. 90-122.
One Half	*One Half of Robertson Davies: Provocative Pronouncements on a Wide Range of Topics.* Toronto: Macmillan, 1977.
Papers	*The Papers of Samuel Marchbanks.* Toronto: Irwin, 1985.
Punch	*A Masque of Mr Punch.* Toronto: Oxford UP, 1963.
Question	*Question Time.* Toronto: Macmillan, 1975.
"Rake"	"A Rake at Reading." *Mosaic* 14.2 (1981): 1-19.
Revels	"Playwrights and Plays." *The Revels History of Drama in English.* 7 vols. London: Methuen, 1975-83. 6: 147-286.
"Rhetoric"	"A Return to Rhetoric: The Brockington Lecture" *Queen's Quarterly* 87 (1980): 183-97.
Spirits	*High Spirits.* Markham, Ont.: Penguin, 1982.
Stephen Leacock	*Stephen Leacock.* Canadian Writers Number 7. Toronto: McClelland and Stewart, 1970.
Table Talk	*The Table Talk of Samuel Marchbanks.* Toronto: Clarke, Irwin, 1949.
Tempest-Tost	*Tempest-Tost.* Toronto: Clarke, Irwin, 1951.
"Theatre in Canada"	"Fifty Years of Theatre in Canada." *U of Toronto Quarterly* 50 (1980): 69-80.

Thirty Years at Stratford	*Thirty Years at Stratford: A Lecture Given by Robertson Davies for the Stratford Shakespearean Festival. August 29, 1982, Festival Theatre.* N.p.: Stratford Festival, 1982.
Voice	*A Voice from the Attic.* New York: Knopf, 1960.
WD	"A Writer's Diary," a weekly column written for the Toronto Star syndicate 1959-62.
Well-Tempered	*The Well-Tempered Critic: One Man's View of Theatre and Letters in Canada.* Toronto: McClelland and Stewart,1981.
Wonders	*World of Wonders.* Toronto: Macmillan, 1975.

Principal Sources of Unpublished Material:

The unpublished material is diverse and lodged in many places. Most of Davies' letters remain in the hands of their recipients. Davies himself has many diaries, scrapbooks, typescripts of some articles and speeches, and copies of his voluminous correspondence insofar as it has passed through the hands of his secretary, Moira Whalon. He also has the selective typescript he made in 1983 of the letters he wrote between 1934 and 1937 to Eleanor A. Sweezey. When referring to this typescript, I supply such dates as Davies included and the number of the typescript page. I have corrected misspellings and expanded contractions. References to the few letters still in her possession do not carry a typescript page number.

Many of Davies' literary papers (notes, outlines, notebooks, manuscripts, typescripts) are in forty or so boxes in the National Archives of Canada where they have the number MG 30, D 362. My references to this material include the word "Archives" and a number like 36.3, "36" referring to the box and "3" to the particular file in that box. Materials more recently donated to the Archives are referred to as "Archives 92/152."

Several bodies of material are in public hands. Curtis Brown, Davies' New York agent, has lodged some of its papers at Columbia University. McMaster University has acquired the editorial files of Clarke, Irwin, Davies' first Canadian publisher, and some of the files of McClelland and Stewart and Macmillan of Canada, his later Canadian publishers. Upper Canada College has correspondence connected with the plays Davies wrote for his old school.

In addition, a few of Davies' literary papers are now in the collection of Dr. Richard C. Davis in Guelph, Ontario. Its primary focus is first editions, clippings and articles by and about Davies.

Interviews with Davies and others are an important source. With a very few exceptions (when I took notes by hand) my own interviews were taped, then transcribed. I was also given access to tapes of a number of uncut interviews conducted for the Canadian Broadcasting Corporation.

For the Oxford years, Horace Davenport's letters to his mother, Elizabeth Langendorf Davenport, are a valuable source. She made a typed copy of his letters. It is to this copy that the page references in the notes refer. I have corrected occasional misspellings.

For the Massey College years, Vincent Massey's diary and his correspondence with Davies were helpful. The Vincent Massey Papers are on deposit from Massey College in the University of Toronto Archives.

Archives	National Archives of Canada: Manuscript Division, Ottawa, Ontario.
Columbia	Robertson Davies Papers, Curtis Brown Collection, Rare Book and Manuscript Library, Columbia University Libraries, New York.
Davis	Collection of Dr. Richard C. Davis, Guelph, Ontario.
McMaster	Mill Memorial Library, McMaster University, Hamilton, Ontario. Clarke, Irwin is abbreviated as CI, and Macmillan of Canada as Macmillan.
PI	Personal Interviews with Robertson Davies conducted by the author. The same abbreviation is used for personal interviews conducted by the author with other interviewees, except that the person's name is cited, as in "Douglas LePan, PI...." An interview conducted by someone else is noted as such.
Theatre	"Theatre Notes." A series of notebooks in Davies' hand begun in 1957 or 1958 and kept up until the present (except for a four-year intermission between September 1970 and August 1974 when he had trouble with writer's cramp), in which Davies records theatrical experiences. In 1962 it became a theatrical diary.
Travel	Travel Diary. For many years Davies has kept a handwritten record of his travels. His notes on each trip begin with a descriptive heading like "Journal of a Family Excursion: 1958" or "A Diary of a Journey into the Netherlands, Denmark, the Shetland Islands, the Highlands of Scotland, North Wales & England:1963."
UCC	Upper Canada College, Toronto, Ont.

Published Sources Cited in More Than One Chapter

An Appreciation   Elspeth Cameron, ed. *Robertson Davies: An Appreciation.* Peterborough, Ont.: Broadview, 1991.

"Art of Fiction"   RD. "The Art of Fiction CVII: Robertson Davies." With Elisabeth Sifton. *Paris Review* 110 (1989): 35-60. (Rpt. in *An Appreciation* 9-33.)

Arts National   RD. Interview. "Arts National." CBC Radio. 23 Dec. 1983.

"Beard"   June Callwood, "The Beard," *Maclean's* 15 Mar. 1952: 17+.

"Charm of Kingston"   RD. Interview in "The Charm of Kingston." *CBC Tuesday Night* series. CBC-FM Radio. 11 Dec. 1973.

Conversations   J. Madison Davis, ed. *Conversations with Robertson Davies.* Jackson: UP of Mississippi, 1989.

Explorations   RD. Interview. *Explorations.* With George Grant. CBC Television. 5 Mar. 1959.

Far-Off   W. Rupert Davies. *Far-Off Fields.* N.p.: privately printed, [1962].

Fetherling   Douglas Fetherling. *A Little Bit of Thunder: The Strange Inner Life of the Kingston Whig-Standard.* Toronto: Stoddart, 1993.

Green Pastures   Arthur L. Davies. *Green Pastures: A Sequel to Far-Off Fields.* N.p.: Estate of W. Rupert Davies, [1974].

Historical Records   Stanley Mills, ed. *Genealogical and Historical Records of the Mills and Gage Families 1776-1926: 150 Years.* Hamilton: Reid, 1926.

Jung   C. G. Jung *Collected Works.* Ed. Herbert Read et al. Trans. R. F. C. Hull. 20 vols. Bollingen Series 20. London: Routledge & Kegan Paul. 1953-79.

McInnes   Graham McInnes. "An Editor from Skunk's Misery Is Winning Fame for Peterboro'." *SN* 26 Apr. 1947 14-15.

Memories, Dreams, Reflections   C. G. Jung. *Memories, Dreams,*
                                  Reflections. Ed. Aniela Jaffé. Trans.
                                  Richard and Clara Winston. 1963. New
                                  York: Vintage, 1965.

Peterborough   Ronald Borg, ed. *Peterborough: Land of Shining*
                        Waters. 2nd ed. Peterborough, Ont.: City and
                        Council of Peterborough, 1967.

Ross   Val Ross. "Alchemist, Trickster...Ugly Duckling?"
                        Globe and Mail 28 Sept. 1991: C6.

Ryrie   John Ryrie. "Robertson Davies: An Annotated
                        Bibliography." *The Annotated Bibliography of Canada's*
                        Major Authors. Ed. Robert Lecker and Jack David. 7
                        vols. to date. Downsview, Ontario: ECW, 1979- . 3:
                        57-279.

Rubin   RD. Interview. Ontario Historical Studies Series.
                        With Don Rubin. Archives of Ontario. 8 June 1976.
                        ts. 1-50.

Stage   RD. "Robertson Davies." *Stage Voices: Twelve*
                        Canadian Playwrights Talk about Their Lives and
                        Work. Ed. Geraldine Anthony. New York: Doubleday,
                        1978. 62-79.

Stone-Blackburn   Susan Stone-Blackburn. *Robertson Davies, Playwright:*
                        A Search for the Self on the Canadian Stage. Vancouver:
                        UBC Press, 1985.

Studies   Robert G. Lawrence and Samuel L. Macey, eds.
                        Studies in Robertson Davies' Deptford Trilogy. Victoria,
                        B.C.: U of Victoria, 1980.

Welshpool   William Rupert Davies. *Welshpool Sixty Years Ago:*
                        Some Reminiscences of a Town in Montgomeryshire
                        which received its charter from Griffith ap
                        Gwenwynwyn, Prince of Powys, in 1263. N.p.:
                        privately printed, [1954].

Writers and Places   RD. *Writers and Places.* BBC2-TV. 7 Aug. 1983.

Chapter 1—Thamesville: 1913-19

1   "I can," *Almanack* 195. For the date of this passage in *Almanack*, see 437.

1   "DR. VON HALLER," *Manticore* 78.

2   "It was," *Bred* 62.

2   first recollection, *Conversations* 216 and PI, 21 Mar. 1984.

2   "hard words" and "brace up," RD, interview, with Ann MacMillan for CBC-TV, 26 July 1984.

2   until May, "Presented With Fountain Pens," *Mercury* 23 May 1919: 5.

3   "which was," PI, 4 May 1982.

3   "appalling," "high old" and "All Welshmen," PI, 14 Apr. 1982.

3   Reading aloud to, Davies recalled some of this early reading in "Rake" 2.

4   "bloody old," PI, 26 Nov. 1987.

4   "a pack" and "Now, you're not," PI, 12 May 1982. Kingsley's attack on the Welsh, which comes well along in *The Water-Babies*, runs as follows: "Or was it like a Welsh salmon river, which is remarkable chiefly (at least, till this last year) for containing no salmon, as they have been all poached out by the enlightened peasantry, to prevent the *Cythrawl Sassenach* (which means you, my little dear, your kith and kin, and signifies much the same as the Chinese *Fan Quei*) from coming bothering into Wales, with good tackle, and ready money, and civilisation, and common honesty, and other like things of which the Cymry stand in no need whatsoever?" ([1886; New York: Garland, 1976] 132-33).

4   "Nell Cook!!" see *One Half* 232-34.

4   "he'd give," PI, 14 Apr. 1982.

4   "something," PI, 19 Oct. 1983.

4   Presbyterian Church, Rupert and Florence had earlier been Congregationalists, but joined the Presbyterian Church in Thamesville as the village had no Congregational Church and Rupert was asked to direct the St. James choir.

5   "a thin" and "like kine," *Enthusiasms* 98. In this column Davies
      mistakenly substituted Alma Gluck for Louise Homer (RD, let-
      ter to Edward Emerson, 14 June 1962).

5   "Stop Your," Arthur L. Davies, interview, *Ideas*, CBC Radio, 31
      Oct. 1988. Other records in the family collection then or very
      soon after were "The Wedding of the Winds," "Alexander's
      Ragtime Band," "Cohen on the Telephone," selections from
      Harry Lauder, Alma Gluck singing "Carry Me Back to Old
      Virginny," Caruso singing "M'Appari," the Overture to *William
      Tell*, Arthur Pryor playing "The Lost Chord" on the trombone,
      and the ragtime waltz "Poor Butterfly." For these see RD, "The
      Sound of a Voice That Is Still," *SN* 26 Nov. 1955: 12;
      Marchbanks, *Examiner* 20 Jan. 1951: 4; RD, "The Last of 'Poor
      Butterfly,'" editorial, *Examiner* 20 Dec. 1954: 4.

6   "vividly," Rubin 2.

6   "the very," *Enthusiasms* 292.

6   "far more," *Enthusiasms* 291.

6   Cuneo's portrait, he got this on the jacket of Eric Jones-Evans,
      Henry Irving and The Bells (1980).

7   "chewed," PI, 21 Mar. 1984.

7   "tapped Fred's," *Green Pastures* 40.

7   "some sort," PI, 6 Feb. 1985.

8   "It was," *Manticore* 77.

8   "old Ontario" and "cut you," PI, 11 Apr. 1984.

8   "as having," Douglas LePan, PI, 2 Aug. 1983.

8   her metaphors, PI, 4 May 1982.

8-9 references to vomit and "emerods," "Rake" 16 and *Conversations*
      228.

8   "As a dog," used in *Angels* 12.

9   "If you said," PI, 28 Apr. 1982.

9   "took a," "Broadcast Talk on Stephen Leacock," recorded for CBC
      Radio 3 Feb. 1956, ts. 1-2, Archives 26:12.

9   "And who do" and "Your esteemed," *Conversations* 11.

9   "Oh Lord," PI, 28 Mar. 1984 (Davies used this quotation in
      Tempest-Tost 358 and again in *Fifth* 57).

9   "properly," "there was," "a delight" and "would not," RD,
      "Convocation Address," Mount Allison University, Sackville, N.
      B., 19 Oct. 1973, ts. 6, Archives 31.55.

10   "Two electricians," RD, "Education and Literacy," Tenth
      Anniversary Lecture Series, Ontario Institute for Studies in
      Education, Toronto, 14 Nov. 1974, ts. 10, Archives 34.5.

10　"Speak, Lord," for a use of this quotation, see *Bred* 101.

10　of the *Herald,* when Rupert succeeded to the paper on 2 April
　　1908, the paper was called the *Herald.* He retitled it the
　　Thamesville Herald later.

11　"I want to go to Annie," interview, with Ann MacMillan for CBC-
　　TV, 26 July 1984.

11　Aunt Ellen Mcfarlane, PI, 4 May 1982.

11　Albertson family, PI, 15 Sept. 1982.

11　Miss Causgroves, Cryderman ménage and a little girl, PI, 4 May
　　1982.

12　"for copulating," PI, 4 May 1982.

12　"Jeez the," *Fifth* 118-19.

14　"under a," PI, 21 Mar. 1984.

14　"Numbah" and "Well, there's," PI, 4 May 1982.

14　son of the preacher, PI, 4 May 1982.

14　conception of God, *Explorations.*

15　"like big," PI, 12 Dec. 1984.

16　"made his," "Isis Idol," *Isis* 17 Nov. 1937: 7.

16　"He first," "Double" 55-56.

16　"In this same," Theatre 1 [2].

17　The pages of the *Herald,* "'Queen Esther' A Big Success," *Herald* 3
　　Apr. 1919: [5].

17　"The Rose That Blows," see, for example, RD, "Speech for the Gra-
　　duation Ceremony of the Atkinson School of Nursing," Toronto
　　Western Hospital, Toronto, 7 June 1965, ts. 2, Archives 33.5.

17　Snarey orchestra, PI, 21 Sept. 1983.

17　"long and loud" and "If he," PI, 30 Mar. 1983.

17　"with a great," PI, 4 May 1982.

18　"a picture," PI, 4 May 1982.

18　"it was to defeat," *Enthusiasms* 253.

18　"With the axe," *Enthusiasms* 254-55.

18　like Dunstan, RD, "Robertson Davies: Part II," with Peter Gault,
　　Ontarion 20 Feb. 1979: 21.

18　"A boy is," *Fifth* 9.

19　"First came," "Thamesville Celebrates Peace and Victory," *Herald*
　　14 Nov. 1918: [1].

20　"medley," "short" and "The Kaiser," "Thamesville Celebrates" [1].

20-21　"Six of Our" and "a handsome," "Public Welcome Given to Six
　　of Our Returned Men," *Herald* 13 Mar. 1919: [1]. See also
　　"Opera House Monday Night," *Herald* 6 Mar. 1919: [1].

Chapter 2—Family History

23 "'Have you a name?'" *Murther* 107.

23 "threshing," PI, 27 Mar. 1986.

23 "Born," *Herald* 4 Sept. 1913: [5].

24 **about seven or eight**, RD, letters to Nora R. Safran, 16 Mar. 1983 and to Erin Sullivan-Seale, 3 Mar. 1987, and "Profile," *Quill and Quire* 6 Nov. 1970: 4.

24 **Dr. George K. Fraser**, probably the Dr. R. N. Fraser often referred to in the *Herald*.

24 **"within two,"** PI, 4 May 1982.

24 **"got along fine"** and **"this red, wrinkled,"** Arthur L. Davies, PI, 30 Aug. 1982.

24 **William Robertson was**, PI, 19 May 1982, also PI, 26 Nov. 1987, and RD, letter to Sweezey, 16 Apr. 1934, ts. 3.

24 **"Despaired Of,"** RD, letter to Roper, 31 Aug. 1972 and PI, 12 May 1982.

24 **"to what"** and **"to work,"** PI, 12 May 1982.

24 **"make sure,"** Arthur L. Davies, PI, 30 Aug. 1982.

25 **"We took,"** PI, Arthur L. Davies, 30 Aug. 1982.

25 **"The usual,"** Marchbanks, *Examiner* 4 Jan. 1947: 4.

26 **modest quarters** and **Liz Duckett**, compare *Murther* 140 and 315.

27 **"equipped,"** *Far-Off* 19.

27 **"could stick on,"** *Far-Off* 69.

27 **"unceasingly"** and **"the real,"** PI, 14 Apr. 1982.

27 **"shuts,"** compare *Murther* 124 and 315.

28 **"I knew,"** *Far-Off* 53.

28 **"see somebody,"** PI, 14 Apr. 1982. Compare *Murther* 154.

28 **to send the two oldest**, compare *Murther* 154.

28 **S.S. *Vancouver***, compare *Murther* 155.

29 **"the weather,"** *Far-Off* 72.

29 **the *Expositor***, this paper was retitled the *Brantford Weekly Expositor* in 1900.

29 **started the next day**, compare *Murther* 241.

30 **"But...woe betide,"** Rupert Davies, "Happy, Hand-Set Days," *Examiner* 2 Sept. 1950: 4.

30 **"SCOTTY: God damn,"** *Brothers* 3-4. One long stage direction has been omitted.

31 **night school**, compare *Murther* 245.

31 **"Scotch trade,"** *Far-Off* 7; in *Murther* 109-10 Davies appears to

have given his own meaning to this term.

32   "My great-aunt Isobel," RD, "The Fiction Habit," *SN* 4 Sept. 1954: 11.

32   "See something," Travel 24 July 1964.

32   Speaking to a, RD, "Speech for the Graduation Ceremony of the Atkinson School of Nursing," Toronto Western Hospital, Toronto, 7 June 1965, ts. 2, Archives 33.5.

33   "in Church," Travel 24 July 1966.

33   Thomas Davies, *Far-Off* 28-29.

33-34   got a character, see *Spirits* 123-24.

34   a shepherd, PI, 6 Feb. 1985.

34   "Angel Sam," *Far-Off* 33.

34   Mary Evans the Angel, PI, 21 Mar. 1984.

34   Maria Ann Dymock, *Manticore* 211; and see *Murther* 122.

34   Samuel Davies, *Far-Off* 43-52 and compare *Murther* 119-32.

35   painted…on the sidewalks, *Far-Off* 17 and compare *Murther* 149-50.

36   "I know you," *Jig* 57 and compare *Murther* 138.

36   deathbed promise, *Far-Off* 53-54.

37   "There was," *Far-Off* 77.

37   "I wanted," quoted in PI, 14 Apr. 1982.

37   jilted, compare *Murther* 228, 247 (the name of the girl who jilted Rupert was not Elsie Hare).

37   Into this vacuum, compare *Murther* 212-14.

37   McKay, in family and official records, this name is spelled variously McKay, Mackay, MacKay. I have standardized to McKay.

37   "just pestered," PI, 14 Apr. 1982.

38   Jacob Langs and his son, Langs 3-5.

39   Battle of Stoney Creek, *Historical Records* 83, 85, 87, 88.

39   "in the only," RD, "But Why Do You Call It Canadian?" The Spencer Trask Lecture Series, Princeton University, 16 April 1985, ts. 18, Archives 35.16.

39   "He was," "Harp" 374 and compare *Murther* 176.

39   "[they] possessed," RD, "How to be Wise without Tears," *SN* 14 May 1955: 22.

40   "there; let 'em," "slopdolly," "she's got" and "independent as," *Frailties* 75, 84, 148, 287.

40   expressions that flavour, *Lyre* 9,150, 265, 277, 289, 308, 374, 464. In addition, "as conceited as if she'd cut a dead dog in two with a

dull knife" surfaces in the mouth of Phelim Brady (*Heart's* 86) and "tighter than the bark to a tree" in that of one of Solly Bridgetower's uncles (*Frailties* 9).

40   **They figure again**, see, for example, *Murther* 206 and 207.

41   **"grim lot"** and **"suspected,"** RD, "Profile of Robertson Davies," "Take Thirty," CBC-TV, 4 Jan. 1972.

41   **Uncle Nelson**, PI, 6 Feb. 1985; and compare *Murther* 194-95.

41   **"it swelled"** and **"he had to be,"** PI, 6 Feb. 1985 and compare *Murther* 195.

41   **"clanking and clinking,"** and **"it was as though,"** PI, 21 Apr. 1982.

42   **"as I understand,"** PI, 7 Apr. 1982.

42   **Davies suspects**, compare *Murther* 168-70.

42   **"gaunt, tall,"** PI, 28 Apr. 1982.

42   **subject to asthma**, for this affliction and its consequences, see *Green Pastures* 37.

42   **"furious whaling"** and **"whaled royally,"** PI, 28 Apr. 1982 (compare *Murther* 233 and 199-200).

43   **"felt faint,"** PI, 7 Apr. 1982. (I cut five "ands" from this quotation.) Compare *Murther* 203-4.

43   **When Florence was**, PI, 28 Apr. 1982.

44   **"She, and,"** "Mixed Grill" 42.

44   **the visit to**, "Nineteenth-Century" 118 and compare *Murther* 201.

44   **the sight of**, RD, interview, *Judy*, with Judy Lamarsh, CBC Radio, 28 Oct. 1975 and compare *Murther* 201.

44   **"a sense,"** RD, "Speech for the Opening of the Thomas A. Stewart and Auburn Vocational Schools," Peterborough, 30 Nov. 1967, ts. 8-9, Archives 33.9.

44   **Pitman's shorthand**, compare *Murther* 236.

44   **"It meant,"** PI, 28 Apr. 1982. (There *was* a confectioner called Alfred Tremaine who ran a "candy kitchen" according to contemporary Brantford directories.) Compare *Murther* 231.

45   **"Now, Miss Florence,"** quoted in PI, 28 Apr. 1982 and compare *Murther* 198.

45   **little for housework**, compare *Murther* 235.

45   **stillborn**, compare *Murther* 299.

46   **had substantially misled**, compare *Murther* 299-301.

46   **"he never,"** PI, 14 Apr. 1982. Note that in *Brothers* 14, it is said of the characters who are partly based on Rupert Davies and Florence McKay: "Griff was twenty-two and Lou, believe it or not, was thirty, though she didn't admit to it."

46-7 **"a pitiful,"** **"It may,"** **"a very,"** **"parents who"** and **"took on an,"** PI, 14 Apr. 1982.

47   **"an unintentional,"** **"a wildly,"** **"ill-used"** and **"fearful,"** PI, 14 Apr. 1982.

47   **"My deep buried,"** Travel 1 Aug. 1966.

48   **"He is, like,"** "Double" 54.

48   **pulled in contrary,** compare *Murther* 301-02.

Chapter 3—Renfrew: 1919-25

49   **"To begin,"** *Bred* 20.

50   **"Altogether,"** W. E. Smallfield, "A Short History of Renfrew," *Mercury* 14 Sept. 1923: 2. See also "Renfrew's Industrial Expansion," *Mercury* 14 Sept. 1923: 10.

50   **"bleak"** and **"a bitter,"** PI, 14 Apr. 1982.

50   **"troglodytes"** and **"Lord, what"** PI, 7 Mar. 1984.

51   **"The Better 'Ole,"** see *Murther* 271.

51   **"a lunatic,"** RD as quoted in Rebecca Wigod, "Robertson Davies," *Times-Colonist* [Victoria, B.C.] 29 Nov. 1985: C1.

52   **"a budding"** and **"she had eaten,"** PI, 20 Feb. 1985.

52   **closed community,** see, for example, Isobel Ferrier, PI, 20 Dec. 1983.

52   **"very withdrawn,"** Lillian Handford, PI, 19 Dec. 1983.

52   **"high hat,"** John Ferrier, PI, 20 Dec. 1983.

52   **"overshadowed,"** D. W. Stewart, telephone interview, 20 Dec. 1983.

52   **"self-sufficient,"** Allie Clements McCallum, PI, 20 Dec. 1983.

53   **"stuck up"** and **"the salt,"** Arthur L. Davies, PI, 30 Aug. 1982.

53   **"lacked the,"** John Ferrier, PI, 20 Dec. 1983.

53   **"The beds,"** RD, "Tales of Our Wayside Inns," *SN* 4 Jan. 1958: 22.

54   **"In the regularity,"** W. E. Smallfield, "The Newspapers of Renfrew," *Mercury* 14 Sept. 1923: 22.

54   **thirty-six-page,** in *Far-Off* 86 Rupert said that this issue ran to forty-eight pages, but the paper itself reveals otherwise.

54   **the town's respect,** Handford, PI, 19 Dec. 1983.

54   **"bringing the *Mercury*"** and **"felt himself,"** D. W. Stewart, telephone interview, 20 Dec. 1983. John Ferrier, PI, 20 Dec. 1983, was another who saw Rupert Davies as pompous.

55   **"a three-layer,"** PI, 14 Apr. 1982.

55   **"The best,"** *Bred* 20.

55 **As a broad**, Babe Stacey, telephone interview, 10 Sept. 1986; and "The Ethnic Mosaic," Heritage Renfrew, *The Story of Renfrew*, ed. Carol Bennett (Renfrew, Ont.: Juniper Books, 1984) 215-27.

56 **Mrs. Low** and **mix-up**, John Ferrier, PI, 20 Dec. 1983.

56 **"to see,"** PI, 28 Apr. 1982.

56 **"life a burden,"** PI, 20 Feb. 1985.

56 **"took a volume,"** "Rake" 3.

56 **"the most kind,"** PI, 28 Apr. 1982.

57 **"lemon-coloured,"** PI, 30 Mar. 1983.

57 **"a good," "a lot of"** and **"You could always,"** Allie Clements McCallum, PI, 20 Dec. 1983.

57 **"froggies"** and **"Mr. Bullfrog,"** "Health Concert Given By Pupils," *Mercury* 3 Dec. 1920: 4.

57 **"If Santa,"** "Kindergarten Classes Give Concert," *Mercury* 24 Dec. 1920: 5.

57 **"cheap and nasty"** and **"'Feet flat on,"** RD, "History of Handwriting: Part Three," ts., 7 May 1956, 1, Archives 29.17.

57 *Ontario Primer*, Davies used *The Ontario Readers: Primer* (Toronto: Eaton, 1920).

57 **"the Little Red Hen was,"** "Rake" 3.

58 **"I don't know,"** PI, 7 Mar. 1984.

58 **"a little, bumpy,"** PI, 19 May 1982. For the witch in the attic, see also RD, "The Wiegand Lecture," Dept. of History, U of Toronto, Toronto, 8 Nov. 1989, ts. 42-43, Archives 92/152.

58 **"liver and,"** *Table Talk* 207.

58-9 **Rosamond was afraid**, RD, "Robertson Davies: Beyond the Visible World," with Terence M. Green, *Twilight Zone* July 1982: 22.

59 **"of God"** and **"this was,"** PI, 27 Mar. 1986.

59 **"and right,"** PI, 30 Mar. 1983; Davies also talked about this vision in PI, 2 June 1982 and 12 Dec. 1984.

59 **"In the Orphanage,"** Travel 10 July 1964.

59 **"a vision of,"** "Wiegand" 42 and *Manticore* 88.

60 **"oak &"** and **"with a rushing,"** Theatre 1 [3].

60 **newspaper bears out**, "Local Talent Present 'In Sunny France,'" *Mercury* 27 Feb. 1920: 1.

60 **"These musical,"** "Mixed Grill" 44-45.

61 **1850s until**, "Exit Uncle Tom's Cabin," *Whig* 6 Mar. 1930: 4.

61 **"was still,"** "Mixed Grill" 44.

61-2 **"just barely"** and **Murray Dagg** story, PI, 19 May 1982.

62 **tricks of stagecraft**, PI, 3 Nov. 1982 and RD, "Good-Bye, Dear

Uncle Tom," editorial, *Examiner* 12 June 1951: 4.

62   **"two Lawyer,"** RD "Aspects of Comedy," The Shakespeare
     Seminars, Stratford (Ont.), 27 July 1975, ts. 6-7, Archives 28.9.

62   **"neither the house,"** Arthur L. Davies, PI, 30 Aug. 1982.

62   **"very considerable,"** PI, 19 May 1982.

63   **"Many years ago,"** *Table Talk* 61; this story is dramatized in *Bred* 84.

63   *The Unwanted Child*, advertisement, *Mercury* 21 Mar. 1924: 8.

64   **"Bobby, it,"** quoted in PI, 19 May 1982; Davies also told *The
     Unwanted Child* story in Theatre 1 [3] and "Mixed Grill" 44; see
     also *Bred* 82.

64   **and transferred,** Davies was certainly still at the Central School in
     April 1921 because he has a vivid recollection of Miss Eva
     Millar's hair turning white in the fortnight after her teenage sis-
     ter was killed ("Margaret Millar, Student, Is Dead As Result of
     Accident," *Mercury* 22 Apr. 1921: 1); he was not listed as partici-
     pating in a concert at the North Ward school in May 1921
     ("Health Entertainment in Victoria School," *Mercury* 13 May
     1921: 4) so he was probably not transferred until September
     1921—the month when a school might sensibly ascertain
     whether its students came from its district.

64   **"It was like,"** PI, 30 Mar. 1983.

64   **a rough affair,** Lillian Handford, PI, 19 Dec. 1983 and Allie
     Clements McCallum, PI, 20 Dec. 1983.

64   **some contemporaries,** John A. M. Austin, telephone interview, 13
     Jan. 1984, and John Ferrier, PI, 20 Dec. 1983.

64   **common practices,** John Ferrier, PI, 20 Dec. 1983.

65   **"two lickings,"** John G. McNab, PI, 19 Dec. 1983.

65   **"went to work,"** PI, 12 May 1982.

65   **"a war whoop,"** Lillian Handford, PI, 19 Dec. 1983.

65   **"some cringing"** and **"The trouble,"** PI, 12 May 1982. A slightly
     different version of this story appears in RD, "As Others See Us,"
     10 May 1978, ts. 2.

65   **teaching him for three years,** *Enthusiasms* 266.

66   **"A summer,"** *Diary* 131-32.

66   **"sewn into"** and **"they became foul,"** PI, 14 Apr. 1982.

66   **"Same old,"** quoted in D. W. McCuaig, telephone interview, 20
     Dec. 1983; Davies has no recollection of the Gays; he remem-
     bers taking himself around the school.

67   **"bloody-minded,"** PI, 14 Apr. 1982.

67   **A contemporary,** John Ferrier, PI, 20 Dec. 1983.

67   **the usual "honours,"** "Public School Promotion Lists," *Mercury* 2
     July 1920: 5; "Renfrew Public School Promotion List," *Mercury*
     8 July 1921: 5; "Renfrew Public Schools Promotions," *Mercury* 7
     July 1922: 4; "Results of Renfrew Public School Promotion
     Exams," *Mercury* 6 July 1923: 1; "Renfrew School Promotions,"
     Mercury 4 July 1924: 1 (Davies was in Europe during examina-
     tions); and "Public School Promotion Results," *Mercury* 3 July
     1925: 4.

68   **"who stand"** and **"because their,"** PI, 12 May 1982.

68   **"Hullabaloo,"** Marchbanks, *Examiner* 4 Aug. 1945: 4 (rpt. *Diary*
     129-30).

69   **"was laid,"** RD, preface, *Four Favourite Plays* (Toronto: Clarke,
     Irwin, 1949), v.

69   **a concert,** "Milk Fund Augmented By Concert Proceeds," *Mercury*
     27 Apr. 1923: 1.

69   **"'Press' Prize,"** "Victoria School Holds Christmas Concert,"
     Mercury 29 Dec. 1922: 5; for additional recollections of dia-
     logues see WD, *Star* 11 Nov. 1961: 29.

69   **"Now children,"** quoted in PI, 12 May 1982.

70   **"the fund which,"** "North Ward School Health Entertainment,"
     Mercury 14 Apr. 1922: 5.

70   **"Flag Salute,"** "North Ward School Health Entertainment" 5.

71   **whitewashing episode,** John G. McNab, PI, 19 Dec. 1983.

71   **"wrote the most,"** Lillian Handford, PI, 19 Dec. 1983.

71   **her most outstanding,** Roper (who talked to Eva Millar in the mid-
     1960s), letter to the author, 20 Nov. 1986.

71   **and often talked,** Allie Clements McCallum (who knew Eva Millar
     for most of her life), PI, 20 Dec. 1983.

71   **"Mrs. Easton"** and **"was coming right,"** Arthur L. Davies, PI, 30
     Aug. 1982.

71   **The readers,** besides the *Primer,* Davies used *The Ontario Readers:
     First Book, The Ontario Readers: Second Book* and *The Ontario
     Readers: Third Book,* all (Toronto: Eaton, 1909). For Junior
     Fourth, he used *The Ontario Readers: Fourth Book* (Toronto:
     Eaton, 1909), and for Senior Fourth probably the 1925 edition.

71   **"tough"** and **"splendidly,"** WD, *Star* 17 June 1961: 29.

72   *Fourth Reader,* I can find the Jonson ode only in a long outdated
     text, *The Ontario Readers: Fourth Reader* (Toronto: Gage, 1885),
     42, where it appears under the title "Good Life, Long Life."

72   **"educational time,"** "Rake" 4. Davies also discussed the readers in
     "Remembering Old Readers," editorial, *Examiner* 9 Oct. 1956:

4; he quoted the Jonson poem in "Delusions of Literacy" 245.

72   "a coherent," "Rake" 5.

72   **did not...influence**, Davies does not share Graham Greene's belief
      that the books that have the greatest influence are those read
      before the age of fourteen (WD, *Examiner* 16 June 1962: 4).

73   "**to get the full**," Theatre 1 [3]. Davies discussed much of this early
      reading in PI, 12 May 1982, 19 Oct. 1983, 9 Nov. 1983, 12
      Nov. 1986, 26 Nov. 1987, 7 June 1989 and in "Rake" 8. For
      reassessments of early reading, see *Table Talk* 182 (*Peck's Bad
      Boy*); WD, *Star* 18 Feb. 1961: 28 (*The Swiss Family Robinson*);
      RD, "Speaking of Books," *New York Times Book Review* 14 Jan.
      1962: 2 (*Sir Aylmer's Heir*); and *One Half* 231-35 (*The Ingoldsby
      Legends*).

74   "**supposedly**" and "**Is Nudity**," "Rake" 7. Davies also discussed the
      magazines he read in PI, 12 May 1982.

74   **His mother**, RD, "The Personal Art: A Series of Three Lectures"
      Trinity College, University of Toronto, Toronto, 31 Jan. 1961,
      ts. 2.21, Archives 32.16. Davies mentioned this system face-
      tiously in "You, Too, May Punctuate," *SN* 12 Dec. 1953: 22 and
      he discussed it in PI, 16 June 1982.

75   "**A Visit**," PI, 12 May 1982.

75   "**and made it**," PI, 26 May 1982. See also PI, 26 Jan. 1983 and
      "Robertson Davies: An Honest Exponent of his Art," *Hamilton
      Spectator* 9 Jan. 1971: 28.

76   **Another piece**, "Our Boarding House" started appearing in newspa-
      pers in 1923 so Davies probably did not create his little drama
      until 1924 or 1925.

76   "**about people**" and "**an exposition**," *Stage* 62.

76-7 "**his hair**," "**his manner**," "**richly**" and "**Before it**," *Enthusiasms*
      245-47.

77   **1921 or 1922**, these were the years during the Davieses' stay in
      Renfrew that Chautauqua brought its program of music, lectures
      and drama to the town. It began on Lake Chautauqua in New
      York State, was active across Canada from 1917 to 1935, and
      represented a cultural lifeline for many communities across
      North America.

77   "**knew that**," "**hurled themselves**" and "**I did not**," *Enthusiasms*
      256, 258.

78   **Percival Kirby**, Kirby was not Davies' only piano teacher in
      Renfrew; he also took lessons briefly from a teacher in a convent.

78   "**on the piano**," RD, "Speech," Royal Conservatory Convocation,
      Toronto, 14 Nov. 1962, ts. 2-3, Archives 32.19. The collection

of piano pieces named for flowers was called *Graham's Music Made Easy*. Davies told a variant of this story in RD, speech, Royal Conservatory of Music Annual Convocation, Toronto, 12 Nov. 1975, ts. 7-9, Archives 34.7.

79   **He remembers seeing**, these films came to Renfrew on the following dates: *Orphans of the Storm*, 24-25 Aug. 1923; *The White Sister*, 17-18 Sept. 1924; *Tol'able David*, 5-6 Jan. 1923; *Sonny*, 5-6 Feb. 1923; *The Bright Shawl*, 29-30 Aug. 1923; *Way Down East*, 12-13 Sept. 1923; *Lorna Doone*, 5-6 Sept 1923; *The Hunchback of Notre Dame*, 22-23 and 29-30 Oct. 1924.

79   **"talking about,"** PI, 19 May 1982.

80   **"that they,"** *Enthusiasms* 248.

80   **"were always,"** *Conversations* 172.

80   **"some of the,"** W. Rupert Davies, *Pilgrims of the Press: The Story of the Tour of the Canadian Weekly Newspaper Editors and Their Wives to Europe in 1924* (Kingston: British Whig, 1925) 2.

81   **"so bitter,"** Travel 24 July 1964.

82   **"a sleeve-waistcoat,"** RD, "Forty Years On: Speech for Shaw Festival Seminar," Niagara-on-the-Lake, Ont., 28 July 1970, ts. 15, Archives 33.17, and see also *Bred* 28.

82   **"Hello, Lennox,"** PI, 19 May 1982 and see also *Bred* 173.

83   **"truly formative,"** Travel 26 July 1967.

83   **by the episode**, Book 2, chapters 4-7.

83   **"they hung the,"** PI, 19 May 1982.

84   **"of course"** and **"came and said,"** Arthur L. Davies, PI, 30 Aug. 1982.

84   **"from whose mouth,"** Theatre I [6]; Compare Puck, *Tempest-Tost* 47.

84   **"was fixed,"** *Far-Off* 87.

85   **"of a woman,"** PI, 12 May 1982.

86   **"of women,"** Travel 24 July 1964.

86   **His book**, Arthur W. Beall, *The Living Temple: A Manual on Eugenics for Parents and Teachers* (Whitby, Ont.: Penhale, 1933).

86-7 **"The Devil's Dump," "God's Honor Roll"** and **the triangle-motto**, Beall 38-39, 42.

87   **"For on the day,"** Beall 53.

87-8 **"When they," "***The Third Function***"** and **"a new baby,"** Beall 65, 70-71.

88   **"Those were the sunset,"** *Wonders* 98.

89   **"My father,"** *Fifth* 34-35.

89   **Like his brothers**, PI, 6 Dec. 1989.

89   **"Honour thy,"** compare *Frailties* 69 and *Murther* 136, 200, 223.

89-90   **"heavy-headed"** and **"they would chase,"** PI, 14 Sept. 1983. This story may not be true, though Davies certainly believes it to be fact. John Ferrier had been told quite a different story about the tailor's death (Letter to the author, 28 Nov. 1986).

91   **"...what a compilation!"** RD, letter to the author, Feast of Stephen [26 Dec.] 1986. For the confusion of F. X. Boucher with Mr. Pausé, see Heritage 232. The words "their daughter" and "who was my age" have been added to the second sentence of the "P.S."

Chapter 4—Kingston and Upper Canada College: 1925-32

93   **"As they are,"** *Examiner* 4.

93   **"It has long,"** "Autobiography" 14. I follow Davies' original typescript ("A Chapter of Autobiography," 19 Sept. 1979, 1, Archives 30.43) as several errors crept into the printed version.

94   **"investments,"** *Far-Off* 93.

95   **"the melancholy,"** *Writers and Places.*

96   **and his contemporaries**, A. H. Young, "The Rev'd. George Okill Stuart, M.A., LL.D.," *Ontario Historical Society Papers and Records* 24 (1927): 515. Archdeacon's Folly and similar nicknames (Okill's Folly, Stuart's Folly, Archdeacon's Great Castle) have attached themselves to Summerhill in recent Kingston guides.

96   **"four houses,"** *Tempest-Tost* 14.

97   **One marvellous**, Miranda Davies, PI, 3 Jan. 1983. Jennifer Davies Surridge also remembers this incident, PI, 10 and 13 Mar. 1983.

97   **"Gardening is,"** Marchbanks, *Examiner* 20 July 1946: 4 (rpt. *Diary* 120). See also Marchbanks, *Examiner* 29 Sept. 1945: 4 (rpt. *Diary* 145).

97   **three ghosts**, RD, letter to Sweezey, 7 May 1934, ts. 4-5. See also *One Half* 224; *Writers and Places*; and RD, letter to Flora Douglas Betts, 11 Mar. 1987.

98   **"a groom,"** PI, 26 May 1982.

98   **"who had,"** "Charm of Kingston."

98   **most beautiful girl**, PI, 12 Nov. 1986.

98   **"A gypsy,"** Marchbanks, *Examiner* 21 May 1949: 4.

99   **"touched up"** and **"painted,"** RD, letter to Sweezey, 12 June 1934, ts. 6.

99   **English Singers**, "English Singers at Grant Hall," *Whig* 28 Nov. 1927: 2 and RD, "Death of a Great Singer [Cuthbert Kelly, the leader of the English Singers]," editorial, *Examiner* 8 May 1948: 4.

100   **"Edward Johnson did,"** *One Half* 25.

100   **"She performed,"** *Frailties* 306.

100   **"appearance,"** rev. of *The Mikado*, RD, *Scrapbook Begun Christmas 1927* [28].

101   **"absolutely rigid,"** PI, 4 May 1983.

102   **"because I knew,"** PI, 12 Nov. 1986.

102   **"a young man"** and **"Oh, I know,"** PI, 11 Apr. 1984.

102   **"that she was,"** PI, 21 Sept. 1983.

102   **"in an immensely,"** PI, 14 Apr. 1982.

103   **"I wish you,"** quoted in PI, 15 Sept. 1982.

103   **"mollycoddle,"** quoted in PI, 14 Apr. 1982.

103   **"an absolute,"** PI, 12 Nov. 1986.

104   **"big softie,"** **"the pictures,"** **"throw up"** and **"terrific,"** PI, 12 Nov. 1986.

105   **"when Robertson,"** Jackson Telgmann, letter to the author, 10 Oct. 1984.

105   **The classmate remembers**, Jackson Telgmann, telephone interview, 21 Nov. 1986.

105   **The class performed**, "K.C.I. Pupils Give Fine Programme," *Whig* 2 Apr. 1927: 2 and "A Fine Event at Macdonald School," *Whig* 7 May 1927: 2. Davies was in class 1G.

105   **The first, presented**, "'Romance of Canada' Given at St. Andrew's," *Whig* 25 May 1927: 3.

106   **"The Romance of Canada,"** "2,000 Children in Pageant Stir Large Audience," *Whig* 2 July 1927: 1, 16. For these pageants see Marchbanks, *Examiner* 2 June 1951: 4.

106   **"liked the"** and **"kids dressed,"** PI, 24 Oct. 1984; article on, "Famous Canadian Stories: Story XLV—Arms and Emblems of Canada," RD, *Scrapbook Begun Christmas* 1927 [7]. Florence filled the first fifteen pages of this scrapbook, then Davies carried on himself.

106   **"phoney Indianry,"** PI, 23 June 1982.

107   **Augustus Bridle** story, PI, 16 Sept. 1982.

107   **"A few suggestions,"** "The School for Scandal," *Whig* 5 May 1928: 2.

107   **"A very queer,"** PI, 26 May 1982.

107 "Teacher of Piano," "Talented Pupils Gave Interesting Recital," *Whig* 26 Apr. 1928: 2.

107 "to talk," PI, 26 May 1982.

107 second in the story, "K.C.I. Honors Prize Winners," *Whig* [1927-28].

107-8 second in the...poem, "Prizes Given at Collegiate," *Whig* 2 June 1928: 3.

108 first in his class, "Essay Contest Prize Winners," *Whig* 19 July 1927: 2.

108 twenty-five-dollar, "Prize Winners Named in Contest," *Whig* 2 June 1927: 9. Davies recalls this prize-winning essay as being on the subject of Sir John A. Macdonald (PI, 24 Oct. 1984). Possibly there were two essay contests.

108 "One day there," "The Hero Worshipper," *Times: K.C.I.* May 1928: 59.

109 "He arrived," "Beard" 31.

109 "spats," "Viscount" and "cruder," Ryerson, PI, 9 Dec. 1983.

110 "...he made," "wonderful," "marvellous" and "brilliant," Arnold Smith, PI, 21 Dec. 1983.

110-11 "One fine" and "entered," "Autobiography" 14.

112 "Here is," PI, 16 June 1982.

113 "You go through," PI, 21 Apr. 1982.

113 had started smoking, RD, letter to the author, 23 Oct. 1991.

113 so pasty, Ryerson, PI, 9 Dec. 1983.

113 "was at once," WD, *Star* 24 Sept. 1960: 30.

114 1926, signature from flyleaf of one of Davies' books.

114 1930, libretto of an uncompleted operetta.

114 1933, letter to Ryerson, 18 June 1933.

114 1937, "Three Gypsies" ms., 46, Archives 8.15.

114 1947, letter to Robertson, 21 Sept. 1947, CI, McMaster.

114 1954, letter to W. H. Clarke, 10 Oct. 1954, CI, McMaster.

114 1963, Travel 4 July.

114 1987, Theatre 20 Jan.

115 "like an actor," Jackson Telgmann, telephone interview, 21 Nov. 1986.

115 "Do you talk," RD, "Speech to Honour Students Banquet," Stratford, Ont., 10 May 1962, ts. 8, Archives 32.21.

115 "in the head," "Rhetoric" 192. Compare *Conversations* 18.

115 *Antic Hay*, Davies has often written and spoken about the joy of

discovering this book. See, for example, *Enthusiasms* 258-59;
WD, *Star* 26 Nov. 1960: 36; and PI, 26 Nov. 1987.

116 "His words came," Ryerson, PI, 9 Dec. 1983.

116 "Cut out," "Speech to Honour Students Banquet" ts. 8.

116 "To be apt," WD, *Star* 1 Oct. 1960: 30.

116 "pretty" and "'Well, no,'" quoted in PI, 23 June 1982.

117 "that he," Ryerson, PI, 9 Dec. 1983.

117 "tone itself," RD, "Modern Advertisement," *College Times*
Christmas 1929: 49.

117 "It is our," RD, "I," *In Between Times* 1931: 27-28.

117 "Scholasticum," *In Between Times* 1931: 5-10.

118 The second of, "Saltatiuncula," *In Between Times* 1932: 7-11.

118 rather ashamed, PI, 2 June 1982.

119 outdated and silly, RD, editorial, *College Times* Christmas 1931: 5.

119 wounded the feelings, RD, "40 Years Later," *College Times* Easter
1972: 56.

119 "like a," Sydney Hermant, PI, 18 Nov. 1982.

120 "W. R. Davies'," Yenmita [Edward W. Wodson], "Music Notes:
U.C.C. Boys Good Actors," *Evening Telegram* [Toronto] 22 Apr.
1929: 36. See also "The Pirates of Penzance," *College Times*
Summer 1929: 41-42.

120 in reviews that, see, for example, "H.M.S. Pinafore," *College Times*
Easter 1930: 37-42; Yenmita [Edward W. Wodson], "Music
Notes: U.C.C. Boys Sing 'Pinafore,'" *Evening Telegram* [Toronto]
5 Apr. 1930: 45; R. Duff, "The Mikado," *College Times* Easter
1931: 28-30; "Boys of U.C.C. Score in Staging 'Mikado,'" *Star*,
23 Mar. 1931: 9; "Upper Canada Boys Give Light Opera 'The
Mikado,'" *Mail and Empire* [Toronto], 20 Mar. 1931: 6; "Upper
Canada Students Play 'The Mikado,'" *Evening Telegram*
[Toronto], 21 Mar. 1931: 19.

120 "The work of" Yenmita [Edward W. Wodson], "Music Notes: U.C.C.
Boys Score a Hit in 'Iolanthe,'" *Evening Telegram* [Toronto] 19
Mar. 1932: 19. See also Augustus Bridle, "Lyrical Triumph Is
U.C.C. Iolanthe," *Star* 19 Mar. 1932: 29; and E. V.[ivien]
R.[eynolds], "Iolanthe," *College Times* Summer 1932: 31-32.

120 "gorgeously," Arnold Smith, PI, 21 Dec. 1983.

120-21 "magnificent" and "I feel," Ryerson, PI, 9 Dec. 1983.

121 "superior to," quoted in W. L. Grant, letter to Rupert Davies, 11
Dec. 1930.

121 "with a," "Anti-Romance in Shaw's Play," *Evening Telegram*
[Toronto] 5 Dec. 1931: 21.

121 **Critics attending**, see, for example, "Anti-Romance in Shaw's Play" 21.

122 **"He was quite,"** Alison Grant Ignatieff, PI, 9 Nov. 1982.

122 **"much has,"** PI, 26 May 1982.

122 **"Live in,"** quoted in RD, "Some Reminiscences of W. L. Grant," written 3 Apr. 1969 for the W. L. Grant Fellowship brochure, Ontario Institute for Studies in Education, ts. 3, Archives 30.16. This story is a favourite. Compare RD, "A Matter of Morality," *SN* 28 Apr. 1956: 20; WD, *Star* 12 Dec. 1959: 28; and RD, "Notes" for speech, ts., 48th International PEN Congress, New York City, 15 Jan. 1986, 5-6.

122 **Ripon**, *Frailties* 239.

122 **"a long,"** "Some Reminiscences of W. L. Grant" ts. 5.

122 **Grant took him aside**, PI, 20 Feb. 1985 and 14 June 1990.

122 **Cornish in**, *Bred* 160-61.

122 **"The Headmaster,"** "Some Reminiscences of W. L. Grant" ts. 2-3.

123 **"absolutely knocked,"** PI, 19 Apr. 1983.

123 **"another world,"** PI, 2 June 1982. The details of this story vary in other tellings. In a letter to Dr. Charles Peaker, 30 Nov. 1964, for example, Davies said that the music he heard at St. Paul's was César Franck's.

124 **Harold Packer**, RD, letter to the author, 4 Sept. 1986; also RD, "Speech," Royal Conservatory Convocation, Toronto, 14 Nov. 1962, ts. 5-6, Archives 32.19; and RD, speech, Royal Conservatory of Music Annual Convocation, Toronto, 12 Nov. 1975, ts. 9-10, Archives 34.7. Davies also took lessons in Kingston briefly from a Miss Grace Clough.

125 **"the Master"** and **"never heard,"** PI, 2 June 1982. Davies told a slightly different version of this tale in RD, speech, 12 Nov. 1975, ts. 22-23. There should probably be one more "master" in the sequence stretching back from Tattersall to Chopin, namely Czerny, who taught Leschetizsky and earlier played duets with Chopin.

125 **In *World of Wonders***, see *Wonders* 311-12.

125 **"Organist,"** quoted in PI, 2 June 1982.

125 **bought Percy**, RD, "In Compliment to the Young," *SN* 4 Dec. 1954: 19.

125 **plays** and **sight-reads**, WD, *Star* 29 July 1961: 24.

126 **follow the score**, RD, letter to Heather Kipkie, 10 Jan. 1966.

126 **"You lead,"** Conversations 119.

126 **"the concentration,"** RD, "Speech," 14 Nov. 1962, ts. 14-15.

126 **David Staunton,** *Manticore* 144.

127 **"the descriptions," "sophisticated"** and **"neither," "Rake"** 9.

127 **invited Alison Grant,** Davies recalled this occasion in PI, 2 June 1982, and Alison Grant Ignatieff put down her memories of it in "Growing Up at UCC: the 1920s," *Old Times* Jubilee issue [1979-80]: 3-4. I follow Davies' version for the most part. The quotations are Davies' except for "rather scared," which is Alison's.

128 **"hardly a,"** RD, letter to Roper, 5 Oct. 1972.

128 **"those shits,"** PI, 18 Mar. 1987.

128 **"just couldn't,"** PI, 21 Sept. 1983.

128 **One observer,** Mrs. Noreen Kahn, telephone interview, 31 Jan. 1983.

129 **"were eating,"** PI, 21 Sept. 1983.

129 **"in a voice"** and **"with the air,"** letter to Sweezey, 15 June 1934, ts. 6.

129 **in his dreams,** "Speech to Honour Students Banquet" ts. 2-3, Travel 13 Aug. 1964 and Travel 22 July 1966.

130 **"...there's got,"** PI, 3 Nov. 1982.

131 **Hector Charlesworth,** "Music and Drama: The Theatre," *SN* 15 Sept. 1928: 6. Davies recalled more details about Robey at the time of the comedian's death in RD, "A Master of Hearty Humour," editorial, *Examiner* 7 Dec. 1954: 4.

131 **"he's very,"** quoted in "Theatre in Canada" 69.

131 **fifty conversations,** RD, letter, *SN* 26 Apr. 1947: 4; see also RD, letter to Percy Ghent, quoted in Percy Ghent, "In The Spotlight: Dramatist Robertson Davies Discusses Sir Henry Irving," *Telegram* [Toronto] 23 Oct. 1952: 6.

133 **"a single," "Mixed Grill"** 48.

133 **never judged,** an exception to Davies' usual opinion of Mason appears in *Well-Tempered* 132.

134 **"fossil theatre"** and **"dry of voice," "Mixed Grill"** 48, 46.

134 **"Boys, you must,"** quoted in RD, "Gilbert and Sullivan," *Performing Arts in Canada* 1.2 (1961): 5.

134 **"Well, children,"** quoted in PI, 2 June 1982.

135 **"without appearing,"** "Nineteenth-Century" 97.

135 **curtain calls,** "Mixed Grill" 56.

135 **"We have played,"** quoted in PI, 28 Mar. 1984.

136 **"I felt,"** *Far-Off* 138.

136 **Fronfraith,** this is an anglicization of the Welsh spelling which is

"ffronfraith." Other variations include Fron Fraith, Fron-fraith and Fron-Ffraith. According to Davies, a ffronfraith is a thrush; the word means "speckled breast" and, applied to the Hall, refers to the sun-flecked hill upon which the house stood (letter to the author, 20 Aug. 1991).

136   "I cabled," *Far-Off* 138.

137   "...he faced," "Ben Jonson and Alchemy" 46-47.

138   As at Stratford and Malvern, see RD, "The Shakespeare Festival," *Whig* 22 Aug. 1932: 2; RD, "Malvern Dramatic Festival," *Whig* 10 Sept. 1932: 2; and RD, "The London Theatre," *Whig* 24 Sept. 1932: 2.

Chapter 5—Queen's: 1932-35

139   "'I suppose,'" *Tempest-Tost* 57.

139   "It was because," *Tempest-Tost* 17-18.

140   "protests against" and "Mathematics," *Whig* 17 June 1932: 4.

140   "There are," quoted in RD, "Robertson Davies in Conversation with Michael Hulse," *Journal of Commonwealth Literature* 22.1 (1987): 127-28.

141   "perfectly gorgeous," Sweezey, PI, 2-3 Nov. 1983.

141   "why embrace" and "I didn't want to," PI, 12 Dec. 1984.

141   he took: In 1932-33: English 3 "Advanced Pass English" (82%: A); English 18 "Shakespeare" (90%: A); Philosophy 1 "Introduction to Philosophy" (59%: C); History 2 "British History Since 1714" (67%: B).

In 1933-34: English 20 "English Literature from 1780 to 1832" (72%: B); English 22 "The Victorian and Georgian Periods" (83%: A); Philosophy 2 "Psychology" (71%: B); History 12 "Mediaeval European History, 300-1453" (74%: B).

In 1934-35: English 19a "The Classical Age" (77%: A); English 16b "Spenser and Milton" (84%: A); English 14a "Old English" (45%: F); English 14b "Middle English" (68%: B); Philosophy 24a "Abnormal Psychology" (75%: A); Philosophy 26b "History of Psychology" (60%: C); History 24 "The Renaissance" (78%: A).

142   "absolutely splendid," PI, 23 June 1982.

142   "at the top," WD, *Star* 7 March 1959: 30.

142   "full-packed," PI, 23 June 1982.

142   "entrapped," *Enthusiasms* 293.

142   "You have to recognize," quoted in RD, "History, Freud and a 'Symphonic Treatment' of Sexual Life," *Globe and Mail* 17 May 1986: D20.

143 **first marriage** and **choral speaking group**, RD, letter to H. J. Hamilton, 4 Jan. 1974.

143 **"I am seriously,"** RD, "The Bookshelf: Old English Works," *Queen's U Journal* 1 Feb. 1935: 7.

143 **"...it is a question,"** PI, 12 May 1982.

143 **"couldn't refrain,"** PI, 12 May 1982.

144 **"forty-eight"** and **"sitting in a,"** letter to Sweezey, 25 Jan. 1934, ts. 2-3.

144 **Solly Bridgetower,** *Leaven* 190-91.

144 **"odds and ends,"** PI, 15 Sept. 1982.

145 **"writing a sonnet,"** letter to Ryerson, 17 Aug. 1933.

145 **"impudent,"** PI, 15 Sept. 1982.

145 **advising incoming students** and **"intimately acquainted,"** RD, "The Bookshelf," *Queen's U Journal* 2 Oct. 1934: 5 and 6 Nov. 1934: 5.

145 **published reminiscences,** see for example, "Rake" 9-11.

146 **"And the stench,"** PI, 15 Sept. 1982.

146 **"felt the monotony,"** "Ottawa Drama League Won Festival Honors," *Whig* 27 Feb. 1933: 2.

146 **"But the thing is,"** PI, 11 Oct. 1982. It is possible that Davies here simplifies what happened in order to make a point. When the *Whig* announced the "Cast of Characters for Galsworthy Play" a few days before the performance, it listed "D. Miller" as playing "the Girl of Town" (15 Apr. 1933: 3), and when the *Whig* reviewed the play, it commended Mrs. Miller for her performance in the role ("Drama Group Gave Galsworthy Play," *Whig* 20 Apr. 1933: 16).

147 **"The production,"** RD, letter to Ryerson, 19 May 1933.

147 **to create an operetta,** this was their second attempt. The first, from the summer of 1930, survives only in fragments. It had as characters Oliver Goldsmith, David Garrick, Sir Joshua Reynolds, Dr. Johnson, James Boswell, Charles Richmond, Godalming, Pendlebury and Warboys.

149 **"which had the beauty,"** "Charm of Kingston."

149 **"Still is the Night,"** Heinrich Heine, *Heine's Book of Songs*, trans. John Todhunter (Oxford: Clarendon, 1907) 147-48.

149-50 **"she had"** and **"apt to,"** RD, "From Notes Made After I had Known the Family Three Months," letters to Sweezey, ts. 2.

150 **"utterly,"** RD, letter to Ryerson, 14 Feb. 1934.

150 **"began to,"** Sweezey, PI, 2-3 Nov. 1983.

150 **"bejesus awful,"** PI, 15 Sept. 1982.

150 "wood-carver," "Queen's Dramatic Guild Won Regional Festival,"
     Whig 12 Feb. 1934: 3.

151 "one of the loveliest," RD, letter to Ryerson, Feast of St. Valentine
     Bishop and Martyr [14 Feb.] 1934.

151 "You think you're," RD, "St Valentine's Day February 14th.," edi-
     torial, *Examiner* 14 Feb. 1951: 4. See also Marchbanks,
     Examiner 13 Feb. 1941: 4; Marchbanks, *Examiner* 10 Feb. 1945:
     4 (rpt. *Diary* 24); and RD, "What, No Comic Valentines?" edi-
     torial, *Examiner* 16 Feb. 1946: 4.

152 "your halo," Sweezey, PI, 2-3 Nov. 1983.

152 she never forgave, Sweezey, letter to the author, 24 Dec. 1983.

152 "most thrilling," RD, letter to Ryerson, 13 Mar. 1934.

152 "Well, I don't want to go," quoted in PI, 23 June 1982.

153 theatre-going, RD, "The Ludlow Pageant," *Whig* 20 July 1934: 12;
     RD, "Shakespeare Festival," *Whig* 17 Aug. 1934: 12; RD, "New
     John Drinkwater Play 'A Man's House' Is a Flop," *Whig* 31 Aug.
     1934: 2, 10; and RD, "The London Theatre," *Whig* 22 Sept.
     1934: 2.

153 pages of his letters, RD, letters to Sweezey, summer 1934, ts. 8-9,
     12-14.

156 "above a," PI, 23 June 1982.

156 "practically," PI, 23 June 1982.

157 "that the Greeks," "the dénouement" and "usually just," PI, 23
     June 1982.

157 "you couldn't get," PI, 23 June 1982.

157 "outdid" and "The startling," "Brilliant Acting and Intelligent
     Directing Displayed in 'Oedipus King of Thebes,'" *Queen's U
     Journal* 4 Dec. 1934: 1, 5.

158 "a relief," "Shakespeare Festival" 12.

158-9 "Clarkey" and "They are so," RD, letter to Sweezey, 30 Apr.
     1935.

159 "in a kind of," PI, 23 June 1982.

159 "it was some," PI, 15 Sept. 1982.

159 "thrilled" and "Lavish," H. J. H., "A Midsummer Night's Dream,"
     Whig 30 May 1935: 2.

159 "lying about," RD, letter to Ryerson, 8 June 1935.

159 a door opened unexpectedly, PIs, 26 Nov. 1987 and 6 Dec. 1989.

Chapter 6—Oxford: 1935-38

161 "The meeting was," RD, "A Forest of Feathers," ms. 69, Archives

23.8.

161 "DR. VON HALLER," *Manticore* 143.

162 "a cape" and "For all my," Travel 10 Sept. 1965.

162 "amazed," J. Max Patrick, letter to the author, 12 May 1984.

163 "Well, last night," PI, 19 May 1982.

163 "rabble" and "undersized," RD, letter to Sweezey, Sept. 1935, ts.
      14. For another story about this voyage and Villeneuve, see
      Marchbanks, *Examiner* 25 Jan. 1947: 4.

163 "a little emblematic," Douglas V. LePan, PI, 2 Aug. 1983.

163 "sun shining," Travel 14 Oct. 1985.

163 No. 8. Staircase XXII, Travel 7 Aug. 1963. Since Davies revisited
      the rooms on this trip, the number seems more likely to be cor-
      rect than the alternative "Staircase XXII - 7" in Note 14
      appended to his typescript of his letters to Sweezey in 1983.

163 There was a, RD, letter to Sweezey, Oct. 1935, ts. 15-16.

163 *Allegory of Time*, this painting is now called *An Allegory*.

164 "no form of heating," RD, letter to Sweezey, Oct. 1935, ts. 15-16.

164 "Lady" and "A poor requital," Travel 13 May 1961.

164 "the next man," RD, letter to Sweezey, 17 Oct. 1935, ts. 17. (One
      word has been omitted from this quotation.)

165 "Pickwick," RD, letter to Sweezey, 26 Nov. 1936, ts. 23.

165 "enjoying it," "velvet bands," "Are you a member" and "a severe
      warning," RD, letters to Sweezey, 10 Nov. and circa 17 Nov.
      1935, ts. 20-21.

165 "soother than the creamy curd" is from Keats' "The Eve of St.
      Agnes." For a later use of the same quotation see *Fifth* 146.

166 "Not a good," Kenneth Garlick, PI, 16 Feb. 1983.

166 "No, because," W. F. A., "Round the Senior Common Rooms: No.
      8. Rev. M. R. Ridley, Fellow of Balliol," *Isis* 6 May 1936: 5.

166 this incident, "How Rick-Victim Met His Death," *Oxford Mail* 18
      June 1935: 1; also RD, letter to Sweezey, May 1936, ts. 35-36;
      and PI, 20 Oct. 1982.

168 "shaking," RD, letter to Sweezey, Oct. 1935, ts. 17.

168 "about whether," RD, letter to Sweezey, Oct. 1935, ts. 16.

168 "very bouncy" and "a species," RD, letter to Sweezey, Nov. 1935,
      ts. 23.

168 "Unfortunately," Davenport, letter to his mother, 10 Jan. 1937, ts.
      310.

168 "when you" and "when a girl," RD, letter to Sweezey, Oct.-Nov.
      1935, ts. 19.

169 "college homos," RD, letter to Sweezey, Nov. 1935, ts. 22.

169 "Oh, yes," PI, 1 Dec. 1982.

169 "the Havelock," RD, letter to Sweezey, Jan.-Feb. 1936, ts. 26.

170 "And what were," see Alicia Craig Faxon, *Dante Gabriel Rossetti* (N.Y.: Abbeville, 1989) 107-9 for a discussion of both mural and cartoon.

170 "Once, when I," Marchbanks, *Examiner* 4 Aug. 1945: 4 (revised and rpt. *Diary* 131).

170 "We had to get up," Davenport, letter to his mother, 1 Mar. 1938, ts. 457.

171 "Ah, there," quoted in PI, 19 Oct. 1983.

171 "mint julep," RD, letter to Sweezey, 18 May 1936, ts. 36.

171 "somewhat of," Davenport, letter to mother, 19 May 1936, ts. 190.

171-2 "...it is against" and "Cabot was," RD, letter to Sweezey, 18 May 1936, ts. 36.

172-3 "A positive old," "Because you see," "that fabled" and "Miss L. swears at," RD, letter to Sweezey, Feb. 1936, ts. 29.

173 "frightful breath" and "a privy," PI, 27 Mar. 1986.

173-4 "sit on the book" and "How does he," RD, letter to Sweezey, Jan. 1936, ts. 26.

173 about Gielgud, RD, "Directors for Canadian Theatres," *Theatre Canada* 1.1 (1951): 8, 10.

174 "This is considered," RD, letter to Sweezey, Feb.-Mar. 1936, ts. 29.

174 "the most obscene," "had a habit," "in a great state," "to be sick" and "there is a very," RD, letter to Sweezey, Mar. 1936, ts. 31-32.

175 "Back stage is," Davenport, letter to his mother, 19 June 1936, ts. 207.

176 "a severe nervous," RD, letter to Sweezey, 25 June 1936.

177 "put me to work," RD, letter to Sweezey, Feb. 1936, ts. 28.

177 "And this got," PI, 11 Oct. 1982.

177 "about as musical," Sweezey, PI, 2-3 Nov. 1983.

178 had cut an eccentric, PI, 9 Nov. 1983 and *Spirits* 3-4.

178 "in a great," "some woman" and "Could there," PI, 9 Nov. 1983.

179 "I'm 6 feet 4," J. Max Patrick, letter to the author, 12 May 1984.

179 "depressed in soul" and "As for you," J. Max Patrick, letter to Sweezey, 18 Apr. 1936.

180-1 "say with sincerity," "what a false" and "change his," J. Max Patrick, letter to Sweezey, 18 Apr. 1936.

181 "Penillion for Davenport," Davenport, letter to his mother, 2 Aug. 1936, ts. 229.

182 "I can't describe," Davenport, letter to his mother, 5-8 Aug. 1936, ts. 231-32.

182 "pleasant and" and "first-class hammer," Davenport, letter to his mother, 8 June 1936, ts. 203.

182 "I continued," Davenport, letter to his mother, 5-8 Aug. 1936, ts. 232.

183 "a thrilling experience," RD, letter to Sweezey, 22 Sept. 1936.

183 "undergoing that," RD, letter to Sweezey, 2 Nov. 1936.

183 By mid-November and Formal permission, Davenport, letters to his mother, 15 Nov. 1936 and 2-6 Dec. 1936, ts. 276, 289.

184 "You know" and "Whew!" PI, 9 Nov. 1983.

185 "Well, of course," PI, 20 Oct. 1982. Davies used the first part of this quotation several times in his writing. See for example *Lyre* 309.

185 remembered despair, RD, letter to the author, 29 May 1987.

185 to write *World*, RD, letter to Roper, 23 Aug. 1972.

186 "I can say," RD, letter to Sweezey, 2 Nov. 1936.

186 whom he still regards, RD, "Read Twain, or Sir Thomas Browne, and Call Me in the Morning," *Johns Hopkins Magazine*, 36.3 (1985): 30-31.

186 ideas from them, Georg Groddeck, *The Book of the It*, trans. V. M. E. Collins (1923; New York: International Universities, 1976) xii, 86, 208.

187 In one part of, and In another section, Groddeck, *The Book of the It* 25-35, 6-11.

189 "What with my," Davenport, letter to his mother, 7 Mar. 1937, ts. 333.

189 "a delectable," RD, "A Forest of Feathers" 73.

189 "An Apostrophe," "Oxfords Helicon: The Collected Papers of The Long Christmas Dinner Club: 1938," ms. In spite of the use of "Club" in this title, Davies and other members habitually refer to the association as a "Society."

190 "very frail," PI, 11 Oct. 1982.

190 "What asses," Travel 29 Apr. 1977.

190 "ghosts, magic," letter to Sweezey, 22 Apr. 1937, ts. 34.

191 "Peers and," RD, letter to Sweezey, May 1937, ts. 37.

192 "were fulfilling," and "I would," RD, "A Kingstonian Views the Crowning," *Whig* 26 May 1937: 4.

192 He is still, see "?Aca nada?" 1070 and RD, letter, *Globe and Mail* 23 Apr. 1991: A14.

192 **"The O.U.D.S. production,"** "O.U.D.S. in 'Twelfth Night.'" The clipping in one of Davies' scrapbooks is labelled *Sunday Times* 20 June 1937, but I cannot find it there.

192 **Oxford and London reviewers,** see W. A. Darlington, "Shakespeare in a College Garden," *Daily Telegraph* [London] 16 June 1937: 12; B. H. de. C. I., "Oxford Finds a Great Malvolio," *Oxford Mail* 16 June 1937: 3; Walter Andrewes, "O.U.D.S. Production of 'Twelfth Night,'" *Isis* [Oxford] 16 June 1937: 3-4; S., "O.U.D.S. in 'Twelfth Night,'" *Oxford Magazine* 17 June 1937: 762; B. D., "O.U.D.S.: 'Twelfth Night,'" *Cherwell* [Oxford] 19 June 1937: 176; Ivor Brown, "O.U.D.S. Twelfth Night," *Observer* [London], 20 June 1937: 17.

192 **"with brilliance,"** Rachel Kempson, *Life Among the Redgraves* (New York: Dutton, 1986) 126.

193 **"rather impressed"** and **"was even more impressed,"** Tyrone Guthrie, "Introduction to Robertson Davies' Plays," ts., July 1948, CI, McMaster.

193 **brief comment,** H. H., "O.U.D.S., Arts, 'Magic,'" *Observer* [London] 18 July 1937: 15; K. A. B., "Magic," *Sunday Times* [London] 18 July 1937: 6.

194 **a letter in August,** RD, letter to Sweezey, 9 Aug. 1937, ts. 33. On the other hand Davenport was under the impression that the play Davies wrote that summer was his first (Letter to his mother, 13 Sept. 1937, ts. 411).

194 **in a scene that,** RD, "Three Gypsies: A Comedy," ms., 40-45, Archives 8.15.

195 **the ballad,** quoted in RD, "Folksong: A Lost World of Archetypes," The Analytical Psychology Society of Ontario, Toronto, 5 May 1986, ts. 15-16, Archives 36.1.

195 **"got a pretty,"** Davenport, letter to his mother, 21 Feb. 1938, ts. 456.

195 **the *Isis* and the *Cherwell,*** "Passing Hour: Victorian Revival?" *Isis* 28 Oct. 1936: 3; "Social News: Confirmations and Denials," *Isis* 10 Mar. 1937: 4; "La Gazette: Twelfth Night Anxieties," *Cherwell* 29 May 1937: 101; "The Passing Hour: Mr. Robertson Davies," *Isis* 26 Jan. 1938: 3.

195 **"Unless someone,"** "Isis Idol: No. 922: W. Robertson-Davies," *Isis* 17 Nov. 1937: 7. (Oxonians regularly hyphenated Davies' middle and surname.)

196 **"neat,"** D. G. C. "The O.U.D.S. One-Act-Plays," *Isis* 24 Nov. 1937: 12.

196 **good performance,** John Short, "The Merton Floats," *Cherwell* 4

Dec. 1937: 182, 184.

196 **an article for**, RD, "Dramatic Suicide," *Light and Dark* Dec. 1937: 7, 9.

196 **rushed to the defence**, Leslie French, letter, *Isis* 9 Feb. 1938: 11.

196 **amusing reply**, RD, letter, *Isis* 9 Feb. 1938: 11.

196 **"the best and most,"** Nevill Coghill, "'Much Ado About Nothing' Presented by the O.U.D.S.," *Isis* 16 Feb. 1938: 10-11.

199 **"all dolled up,"** PI, 22 Sept. 1982.

199 **"I die, I faint, I fail"**—a favourite quotation of Davenport's from Shelley's "The Indian Serenade."

199 **coloured print**, this was the illustration of the "Bachelor of Laws" robes (later the B. Litt robes) from R. Ackermann's *A History of the University of Oxford* (1814).

200 **"must never be,"** PI, 22 Sept. 1982.

Chapter 7—The Old Vic: 1938-40

201 **"I think the,"** *Angels* 304.

202 **"Forty-five,"** PI, 22 Sept. 1982.

203 **play bills** and **tinsel pictures**, Marchbanks, *Examiner* 14 June 1944: 4.

203 **"the most useful,"** "Boys on the Elizabethan Stage," *Times Literary Supplement* 4 Feb. 1939: 74.

204 **"It appeared,"** *Table Talk* 236. In 1941 and 1964 there were reprintings of the book in the United States, both surprises to Davies, but neither made any stir.

204 **some sketches and lyrics**, see Archives 8.17 [Davies has mis-labelled them "Material for the OUDS Smoker"].

204 **insufficient weight**, Travel 5 Jan. 1971.

204 **"ALAN HAY presents,"** John Stead, PI, 18 and 20 Nov. 1983.

205 **"P. J. Stead's Uncle,"** RD, Cornish trilogy three-ringed notebook, 184d, Archives 37.

205 **"Have you had,"** quoted by Philip John Stead, PI, 18 and 20 Nov. 1983.

205 **"Would you like,"** PI, 10 Nov. 1982. This landlady and her monkey surface briefly in Marchbanks, *Examiner* 18 May 1946: 4 (rpt. *Diary* 82).

205 **and lit into**, RD, "On the Margin: For Theatre Lovers," rev. of *Mr. Punch*, by Philip John Stead, *Examiner* 10 Jan. 1951: 4.

206 **The theatre itself**, "Old Vic Theatre," *The Oxford Companion to the Theatre*, 4th ed. (Oxford: Oxford UP, 1983), and RD, "The Old

Vic Shines Again," editorial, *Examiner* 16 Nov. 1950: 4.

206 **imaginatively Victorian**, see *Well-Tempered* 70.

207 **"'Why, cocky, you're,'"** RD, "A Link with the Past," editorial, *Examiner* 14 June 1948: 4. See also Marchbanks, *Examiner* 8 Mar. 1947: 4 and *Well-Tempered* 44-45.

207 **Tyrone Guthrie**, RD, "The Genius of Dr. Guthrie," *Theatre Arts* Mar. 1956: 28-30, 90.

208 **pillorying old Ben**, Travel 9 May 1961.

208 **"Every Friday,"** quoted in Birgitta Rydbeck Heyman, letter to the author, 14 April 1987.

209 **Bertie Scott** wrote a book called *The Life of Acting* (N.p.: n.p., 1964).

209 **"all a singer,"** PI, 19 Oct. 1983 and *Frailties* 111.

209 **"spit y'up a,"** Brenda Davies, PI, 3 May 1983 and *Frailties* 119.

209 **"breathe the muhd,"** PI, 19 Oct. 1983 and Brenda Davies, PI, 3 May 1983 and *Frailties* 128, 141 and 149.

209 **"He can't resist,"** PI, 18 Oct. 1983 and *Frailties* 260.

210 **"My God, I think,"** quoted in PI, 28 May 1987.

210 **"This is not a"** and **"we have made,"** quoted in Birgitta Rydbeck Heyman, letter to the author, 14 Apr. 1987.

210-11 **"*wonderful*,"** **"unbelievably entertaining,"** **"fairy-prince,"** **"a sort of symbol"** and **"I think Rob was,"** Birgitta Rydbeck Heyman, letter to the author, 14 April 1987.

212 **"formal"** and **"pushy,"** Brenda Davies, PI, 3 May 1983.

212 **"It's tuppence to,"** quoted in RD, letter to the author, [Oct. 1991].

212 **Guthrie directed her**, the Mendelssohn music story is a favourite and has been told with many minor variations over the years. I follow the version Brenda Davies gave in an interview on "Ideas," CBC Radio, 7 Nov. 1988, except for the number of bars counted which depends on RD, letter to the author [Oct. 1991].

212 **"throwing a stone,"** PI, 1 Dec. 1982.

212 **"Oh, where did"** and **"You don't believe,"** quoted in PI, 4 May 1983.

213 **"passionately keen,"** Brenda Davies, PI, 3 May 1983.

214 **"the only drinkable,"** quoted in Brenda Davies, PI, 15 Sept. 1987.

214 **"Admonitory Lines to Pete,"** this is the second of three verses and is quoted from a ts. copy made by RD for the author, 30 May 1987.

215 **"very personal,"** **"revealing"** and **"so beautifully,"** Birgitta Rydbeck Heyman, letter to the author, 14 Apr. 1987.

215 "**What the hell**" and "**Oh, I don't think,**" quoted in RD, speech, Second Arts and Media Conference, National Arts Centre, Ottawa, 15 July 1976, ts. 3, Archives 34.13.

215 **his long-term ambition,** in her diary, Jan. 1939, Birgitta Rydbeck wrote "His goal in life is becoming an author of drama," quoted in Birgitta Rydbeck Heyman, letter to the author, 14 April 1987.

216 "**Hell Hall,**" named with reference to Beerbohm's *The Happy Hypocrite.*

217 "**Tell me it,**" quoted in PI, 1 Dec. 1982.

217 "**the danger,**" "Theatres in an Emergency," *Times* [London] 30 Aug. 1939: 8. See also "The Theatres: Emergency Plans," *Times* [London] 4 Sept. 1939: 6.

217 "**less vulnerable,**" "London Sandbags: The Technique of Packing," *Times* [London] 18 Sept. 1939: 4.

218 "**when you put some,**" PI, 10 Nov. 1982. (I cut half a dozen "ands.")

219 "**...marriage with,**" *Angels* 305.

219 "**B. gets,**" Travel 30 May 1984 (Davies' italics).

221 "**this ancient scandal,**" Travel 26 July 1963.

221 "**just sheer invention,**" PI, 28 May 1987.

221 "**how glad one is,**" Travel 26 July 1963.

222 **supported his mistress,** Ben Pimlott, *Hugh Dalton* (London: Cape, 1985) 122-23, 197-98; Davies made notes about Arthur Peterson and his ménage from this book, Travel 14 Oct. 1986.

222 **Valentine Fox played hostess,** when she was herself a very young student, Brenda's aunt, Elsa Larking, saw her do so (RD, letter to the author, [Oct. 1991]). Presumably Pimlott was reporting on a later period, when he said that Valentine would make the preparations for parties, then retire, forcing her daughter into the unwelcome role of hostess (Pimlott 123).

222 **implication was** and "**I say, Arthur old,**" PI, 28 May 1987.

223 "**No daughter**" and "**No granddaughter,**" Brenda Davies, PI, 3 May 1983.

224 **obliterate the memory,** Brenda Davies, PI, 21 Feb. 1990.

224 "**warmth & flow,**" "**a tall, heavy**" and "**a psychological,**" Travel 28 July 1958.

225 "**Malacca, with**" and "**Elsa's monkey,**" Travel 28 Dec. 1969 and 1 Jan. 1970.

225-6 "**a play,**" "**v. much B's occasion,**" "**palm-tree,**" "**ghostly-grey**" and "**with hair tossed,**" Travel 8 July 1968.

227 "**associating with,**" quoted by James Forsyth (Tyrone Guthrie's

biographer), letter to the author, 12 Oct. 1982.

227 "**very fine**" and "**everybody spoke,**" quoted in PI, 16 Nov. 1982.

229 "**Well, Mrs. Davies,**" quoted in PI, 16 Nov. 1982; Brenda Davies told the same story in slightly different words, PI, 15 Apr. 1986 and 15 Sept. 1987.

Chapter 8—Editor and Journalist: 1940-63

231 "**To be an editor,**" *Leaven* 19.

231 "**No man's newspaper,**" *Examiner* 4 (rpt. *Table Talk* 226).

232 **and editorialized,** RD, "What Are a Housewife's Wages?" *Examiner* 8 Nov. 1943: 4.

232 "**I think any,**" Amelia Hall, PI, 3 Jan. 1984.

233 **Arthur, who felt free,** PI, 9 Dec. 1982. Arthur does not recall his brother's stint at the *Whig* at all (Arthur L. Davies, PI, 22 Apr. 1988).

236 "**in classroom,**" Robertson, PI, 23 Mar. 1984.

236 "**one of the most,**" B. K. Sandwell, "'Squeaking Cleopatras,'" *SN* 18 Mar. 1939: 21.

236 **an apprenticeship,** see RD, "My Early Literary Life," *SN* Aug. 1988: 32-39 for reminiscences of this period.

237 "**a liberal**" and "**a man whose,**" RD, introduction, *The Diversions of Duchesstown and Other Essays,* by B. K. Sandwell (Toronto: Dent, 1955) xi. See also RD, "Honour to B. K. Sandwell," editorial, *Examiner* 27 July 1954: 4, and Rubin 18.

237 **diverse talents,** John W. Lennox, "New Eras: B. K. Sandwell and the Canadian Authors' Association, 1919-1922," *English Studies in Canada* 7 (1981) 95-97.

237 "**cut a man's,**" RD, introduction, *Diversions* x-xi.

238 "**plump, with,**" quoted in Claude Bissell, letter to the author, 20 June 1983.

238 "**sweet, genial**" and "**was wearing,**" RD, "How to Keep the Mind Alive," Canadian Authors Association and Simpsons Literary Luncheon, Sheraton Centre, Toronto, 23 Feb. 1978, ts. 14 and 14-15, Archives 35.2. The "small metal airplane" reappears in *Tempest-Tost* 256.

239 **Graham's family,** RD, introduction, *The Road to Gundagai,* by Graham McInnes (London: Hogarth, 1985) [4].

240 "**If Robertson,**" quoted by Garner's son W. L. Garner, PI, 7 Dec. 1982.

241 "**the Old Families,**" RD, foreword, Peterborough vii.

241 **rarely socialized**, Margaret Heideman (author of "Envoi: Living in Peterborough Today," *Peterborough* 513-14), letter to the author, [Dec.-Jan. 1984-85].

241 **"Oh, you must,"** quoted in Brenda Davies, PI, 14 Apr. 1984.

242 **"Well, I suppose,"** quoted in PI, 24 Nov. 1982.

242 **"And who were you,"** quoted in Brenda Davies, 15 Apr. 1986.

242 **"You know, if you,"** quoted in PI, 24 Nov. 1982.

242 **"a man of your education,"** Bronwyn Drainie, "Profile: The Old Master," *Books in Canada* Aug./Sept. 1985: 9.

243 **"sneaking fondness"** and **"a man without,"** Marchbanks, *Examiner* 17 Sept. 1942: 4.

243 **"Hey, Davies!"** quoted in Miranda Davies, PI, 3 Jan. 1983.

244 **"Don't you know,"** quoted in Moira Whalon, PI, 17 Dec. 1985.

244 **"rushed,"** PI, 21 Sept. 1983. See also *Papers* 53-54.

244 **"screw,"** Brenda Davies, PI, 14 Apr. 1984.

244 **"Some Aspects,"** see "Theatre Helps People Forget Unhappy Lives," *Examiner* 4 Nov. 1944: 10.

244 **"How to Read,"** see "Robertson Davies Addresses W. A.," *Examiner* 9 Nov. 1944: 12.

244 **not yet as effective**, Brenda Davies, PI, 15 Sept. 1987.

245 **a university professor**, Roper, PI, Sept. 1981.

245 **classes at the YWCA**, "So-Ed Classes Are Ready to Start Work," *Examiner* 4 Nov. 1943: 11 and "83 Registered in So-Ed Courses," *Examiner* 26 Oct. 1944: 9.

246 **Roper loved**, Roper, PI, Sept. 1981.

246 **Breyfogle remembers**, Elizabeth Breyfogle, letter to the author, [June-July 1984].

246 **"Rise at 7.30,"** RD, "Answers to Lloyd Lockhart's Questions," ts., 6 Mar. 1957, 7, Archives 29.20.

247 **He told Graham**, McInnes 15.

247 **was still**, Antony Ferry, "12,000 Words Every Week Robertson Davies Average," *Star* 15 Oct. 1960: 21.

247 **"Now, remember,"** quoted in PI, 9 Dec. 1982.

247 **"You must,"** quoted in PI, 6 Jan. 1983.

247 **"that a newspaper,"** Ralph Hancox, speech, Robertson Davies Tribute, Wang International Festival of Authors, Harbourfront, Toronto, 19 Oct. 1989, ts. 4.

247 **"Wealth,"** *Examiner* 1 Nov. 1941: 4.

248 **very hoary**, see RD's editorials "The Longevity of Jokes," *Examiner* 28 July 1944: 4; "No Timely Joke," *Examiner* 11 Nov. 1950: 4;

"Old Morning Smile," *Examiner* 10 Nov. 1951: 4.

249 **"bread and butter,"** Tom Allen, PI, 1 Oct. 1982.

249 **"outside the usual,"** RD, "Our Third Column," editorial, *Examiner* 30 Sept. 1942: 4.

253 **Marchbanks records,** see page 4 of the *Examiner* for 19 July 1947, 6 Sept. 1947, 20 Sept. 1947, 27 Sept. 1947, 11 Oct. 1947, 1 Nov. 1947, 15 Nov. 1947, 22 Nov. 1947, 19 June 1948, 3 July 1948 and 25 Sept. 1948. Readers of *Table Talk,* which draws on columns from 1947 and 1948, had even less chance of perceiving the links between Marchbanks' and Davies' ill health since it is selective and departs from chronological order. See *Table Talk* 7-10, 73-74, 162-63, 165-66, 191-93, 195-96.

255 **had the numbers,** RD, "Does Anybody Read the Bible Message?" editorial, *Examiner* 26 Mar. 1951: 4 and RD, "Strong Support for the Bible Message," editorial, *Examiner* 4 Apr. 1951: 4.

255 **successfully argued,** RD, "Why the Bible Message Has Gone," editorial, *Examiner* 14 Jan. 1956: 4.

255 **often drawn,** Davies reviewed Bartlett's *Familiar Quotations* in "Cap and Bells," *Examiner* 4 Mar. 1941: 4; *The Oxford Dictionary of Quotations* in "'...As the Fellow Says...,'" *SN* 6 Dec. 1941: 28; and *A New Dictionary of Quotations* in "The Mind of H. L. Mencken," *Examiner* 16 May 1942: 4.

256 **"I am interested,"** RD, "The Examiner's New Heading," editorial, *Examiner* 14 July 1950: 4.

256 **flourished briefly,** "Dolly Gray Replies," *Examiner* 21 Sept. 1957: 5; "Dolly Gray Advises," *Examiner* 17 and 31 May 1958 and 7, 14, and 26 June 1958: 5.

257 **being ticked off,** Jan Rubes, PI, 12 Oct. 1985.

257 **"We must smile,"** RD, "Fine Quality Musicianship, Understanding in Jan Rubes," *Examiner* 9 Nov. 1954: 9.

258 **"Well, it's for,"** quoted by Ralph Hancox, PI, 27 Oct. 1982.

258 **began to quote,** "On Being Quoted," editorial, *Examiner* 10 May 1945: 4; "Spreading the Name and Fame of Peterborough," editorial, *Examiner* 7 Nov. 1945: 4; "About Being Quoted," editorial, *Examiner* 23 July 1952: 4; "About Being Quoted," editorial, *Examiner* 19 July 1954: 4; "Honor General Manager On Eve Of Retirement," *Examiner* 13 Dec. 1957: 19; "Employees Told Examiner Often Quoted," *Examiner* 14 Dec. 1959: 13.

258 **"a nice manner,"** Margaret Rodney McCauley, PI, 6 Dec. 1982.

258 **"etiolated,"** Christopher Gledhill, letter to the author, 13 Oct. 1983.

259 **On October 3,** RD, "Why Not Call It Eugenics," *Examiner* 3 Oct.

1942: 4.

259 "[He] planked himself," PI, 6 Jan 1983. There is no sign of the second editorial in the *Examiner*.

260 **had not expected**, Douglas Vaisey, PI, 1 Oct. 1982, and Dr. Thomas Currier, PI, 5 Dec. 1982.

260 **"the old hand,"** PI, 6 Feb. 1985.

260 **Not unusually**, letters, *Examiner* 1 May 1950, 26 Mar. 1951, 4 Dec. 1951, and 12 Dec. 1953: 4.

260 **"some awful"** and **"chewing their nails,"** Tom Allen, PI, 1 Oct. 1982.

261 **quatrains** and **heroic couplets**, "Local Poetasters on the Royal Wedding," *Examiner* 20 Nov. 1947: 4.

261 **"prime the pump,"** Ralph Hancox, PI, 27 Oct. 1982.

261 **"Mother of Three,"** Tom Allen, PI, 1 Oct. 1982.

261 **Londerville...took issue**, see RD, "Rationing the Liberal Arts," editorial, *Examiner* 12 Jan. 1943: 4; "More about Universities," *Examiner* 15 Jan. 1943: 4; John Londerville, letters, *Examiner* 15 and 19 Jan 1943: 4.

261 **sometimes twenty**, RD, "This Country in the Morning," with Peter Gzowski, CBC Radio, 27 Sept. 1973.

261 **"almost 1,500,"** RD, "An Editor, His Newspaper, Its Community," *Examiner* 8 June 1963: 4. (The latter is more accurate according to Moira Whalon, Davies' secretary during his last seven years with the *Examiner* [Random notes about Judith's MS, April 1994].)

262 **"What colour,'"** Marchbanks, *Examiner* 16 Oct. 1948: 4.

263 **came to naught**, PI, 9 Dec. 1982. Arthur recollects neither his father's proposal nor his opposing it (PI, 22 Apr. 1988).

263 **When the post**, for a description of the way Davies approached Edinborough about the editorship on his father's and brother's behalf, see *Arnold Edinborough, An Autobiography* (Toronto: Stoddart, 1991) 65-66.

263 **Cooke...approached Davies**, see Hugh Garner, *One Damn Thing After Another* (Toronto: McGraw-Hill Ryerson, 1973) 118-19.

263 **Thomson dangled**, RD, PI, 9 Dec. 1982.

263 **probably in 1955**, Russell Braddon, *Roy Thomson of Fleet Street* (London: Collins, 1965) 225.

263 **"an absolutely,"** PI, 9 Dec. 1982.

264 **in July 1946**, reader's report, 2 July 1946, CI, McMaster.

264 **wanted the cachet** and **usually made back**, Robertson, PI, 23 Mar. 1984.

264   **on March 7**, the date is noted on the folder containing a carbon ts. of the submission ms., Archives 10.8.

265   **a few modest excisions**, for the dedication and the mock verse quotations see Archives 10.6-7.

265   **"(a) They add,"** Robertson, letter to RD, 19 Sept. 1947, CI, McMaster.

265   **"I disagree,"** RD, letter to Robertson, 21 Sept. 1947, CI, McMaster.

267   **on May 12**, see RD, letter to Robertson, 12 May 1949.

267   **On May 30**, see RD, letter to Robertson, 30 May 1949.

267   **"very good"** and **"clean books,"** Robertson, PI, 23 Mar. 1984.

267   **"Worked on my,"** Marchbanks, *Examiner* 28 May 1949: 4.

267   **6,000 copies**, see the note in the Clarke, Irwin files concerning sales of the *Diary*, and W. H. Clarke, letter to RD, 3 Apr. 1950, CI, McMaster.

268   **"the crusty"** and **"the real,"** Robertson, "Report on Manuscript [of "The Correspondence of Samuel Marchbanks"]," 8 Feb. 1952, CI, McMaster.

268   **"The Secretary of,"** included in letter to W. H. Clarke, n.d. [but shortly before 28 Mar. 1953 when Clarke replied], CI, McMaster.

269   **"Almanack," "Secretary"** and **"would be divided,"** RD, letter to W. H. Clarke, n.d. (but shortly before 28 Mar. 1953 when Clarke replied), CI, McMaster.

269   **Clarke, Irwin's reader**, E. D. M., "Comments on Marchbanks' Almanack," 26 May 1953, CI, McMaster.

269   **almanack-like additions**, Archives 11.5.

269   **"on the ground,"** RD, letter to Willis Kingsley Wing, 23 Jan. 1958.

269-70 **"a really"** and **"We're having,"** PI, 11 May 1983.

270   **"'You know'"** and **"rolled around,"** PI, 11 May 1983; see also RD, "Can Carlyle Be Resurrected?" *SN* 31 Oct. 1953: 16-17.

272   **"The theme,"** RD, letter to Alfred A. Knopf, 6 Nov. 1958.

272-3 ***"AT LARGE"*** and **"more and more,"** RD, letter to Alfred A. Knopf, 15 Oct. 1958.

273   **"Yes, I am,"** Patrick Anderson, *The White Centre* (Toronto: Ryerson, 1946) 43.

273   **cuts of about 3,500**, there is a trace of this material in the Contents pages of Secker and Warburg's English edition, *The Personal Art: Reading to Good Purpose* (1961)—the headings "Digression on Victorian Song" in part IV and "Failed Playwrights," "A Playwright for the Few" and "Further Failures" in part V. For this

edition Davies cut forty-seven sub-headings from the text, made a few modest changes in wording and wrote a new Prologue. See Archives 25.2.

274 **"It seems obvious,"** RD, letter to Willis Kingsley Wing, 15 Dec. 1958.

274 **"a chatty,"** W. B. Spears, letter to RD, 25 Oct. 1958.

274 **"using the,"** RD, letter to W. B. Spears, 29 Oct. 1958.

275 **"a mythic,"** WD, *Star* 3 Jan. 1959: 26.

275 **"What I wanted,"** RD, letter to Raleigh Parkin, 26 Feb. 1959.

275 **"the best,"** WD, *Star* 7 Feb. 1959: 30.

275 **sold the column,** this list is drawn from J. F. Cherrier (manager of the Toronto Star Syndicate), letters to RD, 4 May, 31 May and 30 June 1962, and checked in the papers themselves. Ryrie 79 mistakenly lists the Saskatoon *Star-Phoenix* and omits the *Montreal Star*.

275 **"It pays,"** RD, letter to Arnold Edinborough, 21 Aug. [1961].

276 **found satisfaction,** Travel 16 and 26 Aug. 1965.

277 **$3.1 million,** Fetherling 262.

277 **"Their word,"** Arthur L. Davies, 22 Apr. 1988; Arthur also discussed the sale of the *Examiner* in *Green Pastures* 44-45.

277 **"didn't give,"** PI, 12 Dec. 1984. See also PI, 12 Jan. 1983.

Chapter 9—Playwright and Director: 1940-50

279 **"...I think that,"** *Examiner* 4.

280 **"Clippings Relating,"** WD, *Star* 10 Sept. 1960: 30.

280 **a neighbour,** Gwen Brown, PI, 30 Sept. 1982.

280 **the following exchange,** quoted in Amelia Hall, PI, 3 and 27 Jan. 1984.

281 **"That, dear girl,"** quoted in Ellen Matthews McDonald, telephone interview, 14 Aug. 1989.

282 **"Twine,"** quoted in Miranda Davies, letter to the author, 31 Dec. 1991.

282 **They delivered Purcell's,** James Cunningham, interviewed by Martin Hunter, 1987-88.

282 **"to know," "pretty tricky"** and **"a very mercurial,"** Miranda Davies, PI, 3 Jan. 1983.

283 **"eventual aim,"** RD, letter to W. H. Clarke, 17 Sept. 1944, CI, McMaster.

283 **made it his goal,** McInnes 15.

284 **a light-hearted 1948 talk,** "Dramatist 'Embalms' Ideas as Soon as

They're Born," *Star* 19 Oct. 1948: 25.

285 "You don't. The," *Conversations* 116.

285 "It is this," RD, "Jung and the Writer," Gothenburg Book Fair, Gothenburg, 7 Sept. 1989, ts. 26.

285 "by gaining knowledge," *Explorations*.

286 "O Mister Paganini," RD, "Mr. Paganini Complies," ms. 2, Archives 9.3. Davies noted the date of composition at the top of the first page.

287 Davies endowed, RD, letter to the author, 27 June 1992.

287 begun on November 15, Davies noted the date at the top of his first page, Archives 23.8.

287 "set on the" and "a measure of," "A Forest of Feathers," ms. 1, Archives 23.8.

287 "too autobiographical" and "too Oxford-enchanted," see Davies' note on the folder containing "A Forest of Feathers."

287 The King in question, he drew much of this detail from *The Dictionary of National Biography*, which he already owned; he has drawn upon it and its supplemental volumes ever since.

288 "…we must," "King and Caliph," ts., act 3, page 83.

288 scripts for the VON, "V.O.N. Broadcast First Radio Show to Be Presented Entirely by Local People," *Examiner* 15 Mar. 1944: 9; "Early Nurses Drunken Lot," *Examiner* 22 Mar. 1944: 14; "Third V.O.N. Broadcast Scheduled for 8:45 This Evening over CHEX," *Examiner* 29 Mar. 1944: 9; "Final Broadcast of VON Tonight," *Examiner* 5 Apr. 1944: 2.

289 "strabismus," PI, 9 Dec. 1982. A Novachord was an electronic organ.

289 "put everyone," "Enjoyable Play Presented in Aid of Victory Loan," *Examiner* 10 May 1944: 12. See also "Cast of Victory Loan Show," *Examiner* 28 Apr. 1944: 9; "Plan Concert Tuesday Night," *Examiner* 6 May 1944: 9; "Victory Loan Plays Planned," *Examiner* 23 Apr. 1945: 9.

289 "you could," PI, 24 Oct. 1984.

289 "a one-act," RD, letter to W. H. Clarke, 17 Sept. 1944, CI, McMaster.

290 Between July 23 and September 30, these dates are noted on the verso of the front cover of the notebook which contains plans and the first draft of the play, see Archives 3.28.

291 "bohemian set," *Eros* 84.

291 "I'd go to New," *Eros* 89-90. As there are only minor differences between the published play and the manuscript of "Intermission

Time" (Archives 3.5) I quote from the more accessible source.

292 **"A headstone,"** *Eros* 98.

293 **an extra Marchbanks,** "A Reconsideration of Belief," rev. of *What Can a Man Believe?* by Rev. Dr. J. D. Smart, *Examiner* 25 Apr. 1944: 4.

293 **"These good men,"** *Eros* 76.

293 **"There's a special,"** *Eros* 100.

293 **In fall 1946,** the notebook containing a brief scenario titled "Love at Breakfast," and the original draft of *Eros at Breakfast,* has the date November 18, 1946, on the verso of the front cover, but whether this is a starting or finishing date is unclear (Archives 2.23).

293 **"*a hussar's*"** and **"*an indoor,*"** *Eros* 15, 3.

293 **"ARISTOPHONTES,"** *Eros* 13.

294 **Reading Geoffrey,** "Author's Note" to *King Phoenix* in *Hunting* 105.

295 **Davies gave him,** although his "Author's Note" says that "the play was given flattering consideration by two famous English actors," Davies has no recollection of any English actor besides Gielgud seeing it. In particular he is certain that Ralph Richardson, with whom he had no contact, never saw it (PI, 13 Mar. 1991), contrary to what Michael Peterman says in *Robertson Davies* (Boston: Twayne, 1986) 52.

295 **a mythic,** Stone-Blackburn 48.

295 **under the pseudonym,** see the title page of the typescript copy of *Overlaid* in Archives 3.6.

295 **"one of the finest,"** "Proclaims *Examiner* Editor's One-Act Play One of 'Finest' Ever Written in Canada," *Examiner* 30 Oct. 1946: 9.

295 **"A hilarious"** and **"a concocter,"** RD, letter to Tyrone and Judith Guthrie, 27 May 1946; there is a later version of this story in *Stage* 66.

296 **"distasteful,"** quoted in PI, 19 Oct. 1983.

296 **"the possibility,"** RD, introduction, *Renown at Stratford,* Special Memorial ed. (Toronto: Clarke Irwin, 1971) n.p.

296 **"water in a,"** RD, letter to Tyrone and Judith Guthrie [October 1946].

296 **"so poignantly,"** Marchbanks, *Examiner* 3 July 1946: 4.

297 **greatest playwright,** RD, "Canada's Great Playwright," editorial, *Examiner* 24 May 1956: 4 (rpt. *Well-Tempered* 86).

297 **Everyman's Library edition,** "The Coventry Nativity Play of the Company of Shearmen and Tailors," in *"Everyman" with Other*

Interludes including Eight Miracle Plays (London: Dent, 1909) 74-98.

297 his own adaptation, "A Play of Our Lord's Nativity: Adapted from the Medieval Pageant of Shearmen and Tailors," Archives 7.3-7.

297 *God's Promises* is in *"Everyman" with Other Interludes* 153-82.

297 sketched the settings and, two of these are now in Archives DAP, Accession 1992/395.

297 to guide, Rita Oates, "Fond Memories of 1946 Christmas," *Examiner* 15 Dec. 1982: 10.

297 "an apparition," Roy Boyd, "Unusual Treatment Given Nativity Play By Guild," *Examiner* 16 Dec. 1946: 16.

298 "as a service," "Plan to Present Nativity Play at St. George's," *Examiner* 5 Dec. 1946: 15.

298 "to step out," John Londerville, PI, 18 Nov. 1982.

298 it was sheer, Miranda Davies, PI, 3 Jan. 1983.

299 "could have," PI, 28 Apr. 1982.

299 "utter ferocity," "like something" and **And I thought,** PI, 28 Apr. 1982.

299 "tried to kill," RD, Speech for the Arts and Letters Club, 1 April 1967, ts. 14, Archives 33.10; see also *One Half* 224.

299 "The ghost is," *Conversations* 223.

300 "immediately recognized," RD, letter to the author, 20 Aug. 1991.

300 At the funeral parlour, PI, 6 Feb. 1985.

301 "an original" and "drama is at," "Examiner Editor Repeats with 'Smartest' Play Yet," *Examiner* 19 May 1947: 9.

301 "try something," John Londerville, PI, 18 Nov. 1982. In addition to interviews and sources noted below, my account of the Little Theatre's beginnings draws on several articles from the *Examiner*: "Little Theatre Group Plans To Present Three Plays," 10 Jan. 1948: 13; "Have Missed Much without a Little Theatre," 16 Jan. 1948: 14; T. J. Allen, "Modern Sets for 3 Plays Leave Imagination Free," 20 Jan. 1948: 9.

302 "*Tonight we are*," quoted in RD, "Introduction to the History of the Peterborough Little Theatre," ts., 2 June 1989, 2.

303 "the acceptance," T. J. Allen, "Little Theatre Makes First Presentation In City," *Examiner* 21 Jan. 1948: 11.

303 "oranges," Musa Cox, PI, 6 Dec. 1982.

303 "came on playing" and "a dancing bear," Fern Rahmel, PI, 1 Oct. 1982.

303 "pertly vulgar," Allen 11.

303 "The Marchbanks," Marchbanks, *Examiner* 8 May 1948: 4.

304 In a striking, "Davies' Overlaid Corners Openings," *Globe and Mail* 24 Jan. 1953: 10.

304 "like chewing," RD, letter to Robertson, 9 June 1948, CI, McMaster.

304 Titled "The Man," see the notebook in Archives 8.24.

305 "They're the voice," quoted in PI, 4 May 1983.

305 an important nationalistic, David Gardner, PI, 4 Feb. 1983.

305 "Canada was a garden," Donald Davis, PI, 15 Apr. 1983.

305 more than a hundred, RD, letter to Nathan Cohen, 24 Nov. 1967.

306 "have a," *Fortune* 96.

306 "If you can stay," *Fortune* 98.

307 "...across the" *Fortune* 3.

307 an original in Kingston, note that Franz Szabo was inspired by the merry bohemian artist Walter Trier.

307 James A. Roy, see Marchbanks, *Examiner* 7 Jan. 1948: 4.

307 recognized and appreciated, see Forrest Johnston, "'Fortune, My Foe' Gets Premiere before Enthusiastic Audience," *Whig* 1 Sept. 1948: 3.

307 Elizabethan song, for the original wording and melody, see Edward W. Naylor, *Shakespeare and Music* (1896; London: Dent, 1931) 75 and 189.

308 "an everchanging," Johnston 3.

308 "the much," "Robertson Davies Play Makes Stage 49 Debut," *CBC Times* week of 17 Oct. 1948: 4.

308 "any grace," Robertson, "Report on Manuscript [of *Fortune, My Foe*]," 28 Oct. 1948, CI, McMaster.

308 Davies' displeasure, PI, 19 Oct. 1983, and see "Theatre in Canada" 77.

308 "Sure," John Londerville, PI, 18 Nov. 1982.

308 "understood what," PI, 4 May 1983.

309 especially relished, Miranda Davies, PI, 3 Jan. 1983.

309 "like clear," James Cunningham, interviewed by Martin Hunter, 1987-88.

309 She herself, Brenda Davies, PI, 3 May 1983.

309 "just threw away," Musa Cox, PI, 6 Dec. 1982.

309 "a brilliant production" and "well-drilled," quoted in Lauretta Thistle, "Best Play Is Produced by Ottawa Drama League," *Citizen* [Ottawa] 21 Feb. 1949: 7.

309 "quicksilver," Arnold Edinborough, PI, 1 Dec. 1983.

310 **"Author,"** Molly DeProse, "Ottawa Drama League Entry Sets High Mark," *Citizen* [Ottawa] 29 Apr. 1949: 16.

311 *Saturday Night's*, see Lucy Van Gogh [B. K. Sandwell], "Writing, Acting, Devotion Marked '49 Festival," *SN* 17 May 1949: 10.

311 **In the audience**, David Gardner, PI, 4 Feb. 1983.

311 **Tom Allen recalled**, Tom Allen, PI, 2 Oct. 1982.

311 **"your husband,"** RD, "Advice to a Bride," *Mayfair* May 1948: 95. Compare the view Brenda expressed in "Beard" 32-33.

312 **at the opening**, this is where Davies places the initial encounter (PI, 19 Apr. 1983). A newspaper account closer to the event sets it in the Royal Alexandra Theatre in Toronto where Sadlier was acting (Mackenzie Porter, "Canada's New Showmen," *Standard Magazine* [Montreal] 14 July 1951: 11.

312 **Over the next four years**, in 1950 Brenda played Mrs. Montgomery in *The Heiress*, 8-13 August, and Davies directed her in the role of Mrs. Stewart in *At My Heart's Core*, 28 Aug.-2 Sept; in 1951 neither was involved; in 1952, Davies directed *The Silver Whistle*, 23-28 June (with Brenda as Mrs. Sempler and himself as the Bishop), also *East Lynne*, 21-26 July (with Brenda as Lady Isobel Carlyle), also *Arms and the Man*, 4-9 Aug. (with Brenda as Catherine Petkoff); in 1953 Brenda played Mrs. Winslow in *The Winslow Boy*, 6-11 July, and Davies directed *Pygmalion* (with Brenda as Mrs. Higgins), 20-25 July, also *Ten Nights in a Barroom* (with Brenda as the drunkard's wife), 3-8 Aug.

312 **"I learned to,"** Jennifer Surridge, PI, 10 and 13 Mar. 1983.

312 **Miranda, too**, Miranda Davies, PI, 3 Jan. 1983.

313 **generous hospitality** and **slight nervous breakdown**, William Needles, PI, 18 Oct. 1983.

313 **"good-natured"** and **"But the *spirit*,"** Theatre 31 July 1985.

314 **collected in**, *Almanack* 4-15, 20-28, and later in *Papers* 387-405.

314 **His reports**, RD, "Enthusiastic Edinburgh Applause Given to Canadian Play and Actors," *Globe and Mail* 6 Sept. 1949: 17; and "Canadian Cast Anxious to Impress Edinburgh," *Globe and Mail* 10 Sept. 1949: 10.

314 **"slight but highly,"** Philip Hope-Wallace, "Canadians Merit More Than Edinburgh Gives," *Globe and Mail* 17 Sept. 1949: 10.

314 **were impressed**, RD, "Festival Enthralls Canadian Players," *Globe and Mail* 13 Sept. 1949: 9 and *Well-Tempered* 71.

315 **Letters of outrage** and **rebukes**, see "Letters to the Editor," *Examiner* 23 Feb. 1950: 4 and Fern Rahmel, "The Theatre,"

Peterborough 389.

315 *United Church* and **Baptist minister**, RD, letter to Rev. K. C. Bolton, 13 Apr. 1951.

315 *At My Heart's Core,* Davies prepared for the writing of this play by reading books by Catharine Parr Trail, Susanna Moodie, Frances Stewart, Samuel Strickland, Thomas Need, Anne and John Langton, as well as Alexander Neil Bethune's *Memoir of the Right Reverend John Strachan, D.D., LL.D., First Bishop of Toronto,* Henry Scadding's *The First Bishop of Toronto: A Review and a Study* and M. A. FitzGibbon's *A Veteran of 1812.* He made notes from Traill's *The Backwoods of Canada* with an introduction by Edward S. Caswell, Moodie's *Roughing It in the Bush,* Stewart's *Our Forest Home* and Edwin C. Guillet's *Early Life in Upper Canada* (see RD, "Epilogue by the Author" and "Notes: *At My Heart's Core,*" *At My Heart's Core [and] Overlaid* [Toronto: Clarke, Irwin, 1966] 111-21 and Davies' notes in Archives 4.16).

315 **January 17 and April 7,** Davies noted these dates on the verso of the front cover of his *Tempest-Tost* notebook, Archives 11.13.

315 **Cantwell is based,** see *Our Forest Home,* ed. E. S. Dunlop, 2nd ed. (Montreal: *Gazette,* 1902) 125.

315 **Phelim Brady, recalls,** PI, 11 May 1983.

316 **"a tight, snug,"** *Heart's* 83.

316 **the role he had,** Davies had particular actors in mind for two other characters too—Amelia Hall for Mrs. Traill and John Primm for Edmund Cantwell, see L. T., "Brenda Davies Finds CRT Works with Great Speed," *Citizen* [Ottawa] 8 Jan. 1951: 3.

317 **"Canada's best-known,"** "Local Ladies in the Bush," *Telegram* [Toronto] 2 Dec. 1950: 33.

317 **"Canada's leading,"** S. Morgan Powell, "Robertson Davies' New Play Set in Canadian Backwoods," *Montreal Star* 2 Dec. 1950: 25.

317 **"Canada's foremost,"** "The Arts and Humanities," *Edmonton Journal* 9 Dec. 1950: 4.

317 **"rapidly becoming,"** "Herald Book Reviews," *Calgary Herald* 24 Feb. 1951: 4.

317 **By the early months,** "Beard" 30.

317 **performed across Canada,** Antony Ferry, "12,000 Words Every Week Robertson Davies Average," *Star* 15 Oct. 1960: 21.

317 **Davies' submission,** "A Dialogue on the State of Theatre in Canada: 1951," *Well-Tempered* 39-64.

318 **"You must realise,"** quoted by RD in Simon Hoggart, "Master of

Myth and Magic," *Observer* [London], 23 Feb. 1986: 28. Davies told this story a little differently in "Theatre in Canada" 77.

319 **"stupefying" and "Oh, you know that,"** RD, Speech to the Royal Canadian Academy of Arts, 17 Nov. 1973, ts. 21, Archives 33.25; for other tellings of the story see Rubin 46 and "Theatre in Canada" 76.

319 **Ottawa Drama League,** RD, letter to H. S. Southam, 15 Jan. 1951.

319 **"Well, here we,"** RD, letter to Roper, 21 July 1972; see also Rubin 46-47 and "Theatre in Canada" 77.

319 **"Its reception,"** Robertson, "Report on Manuscript [of *King Phoenix*]," 6 Oct. 1950, CI, McMaster.

320 **"Moments of" and "the libretto,"** "Ottawa Carries Off Most Drama Awards," *Examiner* 19 Jan. 1953: 12.

320 **visibly distressed,** Gertrude Cox, PI, 6 Dec. 1982.

320 **smug pleasure,** Bruce Swerdfager, PI, 8 Aug. 1983.

320 **"Playwright's Plight"** (Archives 8.12) was probably written in 1950, the year Davies gathered his thoughts on the state of theatre in Canada for the Massey Commission. Apollo Fishorn made his first public appearance in Marchbanks, *Examiner* 4 Mar. 1950: 4.

321 **"They adopt,"** RD, letter to R. S. Southam, 15 Jan. 1951.

Chapter 10—The Salterton Trilogy: 1950-58

323 **"He has written,"** McInnes 15.

323 **"By the development,"** RD, "The Individual and the Mass" 26.

324 **occasion remembered best,** Dr. Thomas and Sheila Currier, Scott Young, Robertson and Brenda Davies, Miranda Davies and Jennifer Davies Surridge all described this party.

324 **The script,** for the script and an expanded six-page version (a reference to Sputnik places it in or soon after 1957) see Archives 7.8-9.

324 **a minor demon,** RD, letter to Gerhard Dusterhaus, 11 Nov. 1988.

325 **When Porter advertised,** Ralph Hancox, PI, 27 Oct. 1982. Porter and his wife, however, recall the letter as being from a Rhodesian woman asking "Bwana" Porter for support for the fruit of his loins, namely the two cherubic children depicted in an enclosed photograph (Robert B. and Valerie Porter, PI, 30 Sept. 1982).

325 **more elaborate hoax,** see Robert B. Porter, PI, 30 Sept. 1982; Ralph Hancox, PI, 27 Oct. 1982; and PI, 12 Jan. 1983.

326 **on September 18,** see Davies' note on the verso of the cover of his *Tempest-Tost* notebook, Archives 11.13.

326 **in June 1950**, RD, letter to W. H. Clarke, 20 June 1950, CI, McMaster.

326 **"To hell,"** quoted in PI, 21 Sept. 1983.

326 **indifference and**, RD, letter to Anthony Quayle, 8 Jan. 1957.

327 **"A Shakespeare play,"** RD, "Proposed Play," ms. [1], Archives 11.13.

327 **In his recent,** *Well-Tempered* 50-51.

328 **article about the city**, the *Maclean's* piece was called "Kingston: A Mature Charmer" (Archives 29.14). The section that depends on it begins: "Like Quebec and Halifax, it is a city which …" and concludes: "…the knack of building houses which have faces, as opposed to grimaces, is retained by few builders" (*Tempest-Tost* 11-14).

328 **to produce** *The Tempest*, in his play notes Davies had imagined his Little Theatre preparing *Twelfth Night* and in his novel notes either *Twelfth Night* or *As You Like It*. It is likely that he changed to *The Tempest* when he and Brenda decided to do *Twelfth Night* with the Peterborough Little Theatre the following February. Davies' declaration (in RD, letter to David Webster, 30 Oct. 1972) that he had originally intended to use *A Midsummer Night's Dream* would appear to be a misremembrance.

329 **"members of,"** PI, 21 Sept. 1983.

329 **"By half-past,"** *Tempest-Tost* 259.

330 **"a light,"** RD, letter to W. H. Clarke, 20 June 1950, CI, McMaster.

330 **"Hector was,"** PI, 21 Sept. 1983.

331 **"The Life, Pathetic,"** noted on the verso of the cover of Davies' *Tempest-Tost* notebook and quoted from memory as "The Strange Love, Tragical Death and Glorious Resurrection of Hector Mackilwraith, B. A." in RD, letter to Harold Raymond, 28 July 1951, CI, McMaster. In this letter Davies explains that he had originally wanted to use this phrase as the book's subtitle.

331 **"It may seem,"** RD, letter to Robertson, 16 Nov. 1950, CI, McMaster.

331 **He did recommend**, Robertson, letter to RD, 22 Nov. 1950, Archives 11.13.

332 **"I hardly,"** RD, letter to Robertson, 6 June 1951, CI, McMaster.

332 **"At the instant,"** "Tempest-Tost," ts. 162, Archives 12.6.

333 **"unworthy," "best self"** and **"take out,"** quoted in PI, 26 Jan. 1983.

333 **Chatto and Windus…objected**, W. H. Clarke and Robertson, letters to RD, 23 July 1951, CI, McMaster.

333 **"mistaken my,"** RD, letter to Harold Raymond [Chatto and Windus], 28 July 1951, CI, McMaster.

333 **to replace**, the substitution runs: "and to creak as though in an uneasy slumber" (*Tempest-Tost* 199-200).

333 **cut out two chunks**, the first was a single paragraph preceding the paragraph that begins "Because Hector was a growing boy" in *Tempest-Tost* 101 and the second, two and a half paragraphs just before the paragraph that begins "Hector did not want money" in *Tempest-Tost* 113. For the cut passages see the paragraph beginning "The family diet did nothing to relieve the family gloom" and the passage beginning "It was not long after the distressing" and ending "Hector was glad that this scheme had turned out badly" ("Tempest-Tost," ts. 81-82 and 93-94, Archives 12.6).

333 **"wit, humour and,"** L. F. C., "His First Novel Has Wit, Charm," *Hamilton Spectator* 20 Oct. 1951: 14.

334 **"no more than,"** W. A. D., "Little Theatre Produces Play," *Globe and Mail* [Toronto] 24 Nov. 1951: 11.

334 **5,000 hardcover**, see PI, 15 May 1991; also J.M.G., memorandum to Mr. Frank Upjohn, 16 Sept. 1958, Macmillan, McMaster; also Donald M. Sutherland, letter to Professor E. Buitenhuis, 18 June 1971, Macmillan, McMaster.

334 **High Sheriff**, the best account of Rupert's post is "Canadian Senator Is High Sheriff of County in Wales," *Mayfair* July 1951: 26-31, 71.

334 **1851** and **Liverpool banker**, Eva B. Bredsdorff, *Welshpool in Old Photographs* (Stroud: Alan Sutton, 1993) 158.

334 **great hall**, described in RD, "In a Welsh Border House, The Legacy of the Victorians," *New York Times* 29 Nov. 1984: Cl and C12, with additional details from Travel 24 June 1967.

335 **"*My Father*,"** Travel 5 July 1967.

335 **"Would you,"** RD, "In A Welsh" C:12.

335 **"(1) everybody is,"** Marchbanks, *Examiner* 2 May 1953: 4.

336 **An observer in Renfrew**, John Ferrier, PI, 20 Dec. 1983.

337 **threatened to cut**, Jennifer Surridge, PI, 10 and 13 Mar. 1983.

337 **"when his car,"** "Fred R. M. Davies to Be Buried in Toronto," *Examiner* 9 Mar. 1954: 9.

337 **By March**, RD, letter to an unidentified recipient, 21 Mar. 1952.

337 **"have as its centre,"** RD, letter to G. H. Clarke, 27 May 1952.

337 **intended to call**, "Report on Manuscript [of the first third of *Leaven of Malice*]," 3 Dec. 1952, CI, McMaster.

337 **titles for the book's**, "Works in Progress" notebook 17, Archives 23.9.

337 **"fretting scall,"** RD, letter to Tyrone Guthrie, 19 Oct. 1957.

337 **"shirt of Nessus,"** RD, PI, 23 June 1982.

337 **leper**, RD, letter to Davenport, 19 Oct. 1957.

337 **"the whole buttock,"** "Works in Progress" notebook 17.

338 **one amazing week**, "False Birth Notice Furnished Examiner,"
Examiner 8 Feb. 1946: 9 and "Who Thinks This Is Funny?" edi-
torial, Examiner 9 Feb. 1946: 4. See also Conversations 37, and
RD, "This Country in the Morning," with Peter Gzowski, CBC
Radio, 27 Sept. 1973.

338 **"Theme: a false,"** "Works in Progress" notebook 10.

340 **recall or anticipate**, editorials, Examiner 31 Mar. 1949: 4, 19 Mar.
1955: 4, and 21 Nov. 1956: 4.

340 **certain antiquated**, one of these was "an old man named Klugh,"
see Rupert Davies, quoted in Arnold Edinborough, An
Autobiography (Toronto: Stoddart, 1991) 78.

340 **Peterborough's Mr. Kerr**, PI, 24 Oct. 1984.

341 **had unscrupulously**, Conversations 39 and PI, 21 Sept. 1983.

341 **"I think,"** Robertson, "Report on Manuscript [of the first third of
Leaven of Malice]."

342 **notes for Bevill**, "Works in Progress" notebook 16.

342 **"putting another,"** RD, letter to Robertson, [May 1954], CI,
McMaster.

343 **"the man of many,"** quoted in Alf and Dama Bell, PI, 9-10 May
1982.

343 **"'We Have With Us To-Night,'"** The Leacock Roundabout (New
York: Dodd, Mead, 1965) 343-355.

343 **"Its plot,"** J. K. Elliott, "Salterton Revived by Bearded Bard," 25
Sept. 1954: 26.

343 **"...it is,"** Jan Hilliard, "Canadian Novels," 2 Oct. 1954: 12.

343 **"The plot is,"** J. B. M. "The Book Corner," 2 Oct. 1954: 10.

343 **"There is little,"** Janet Lunn, "The Bookmark," 23 Oct. 1954: 4.

343 **"I cannot say,"** RD, letter to G. H. Clarke, 27 May 1952.

343 **"would have a,"** mentioned in Robertson, "Report on Manuscript
[of the first third of Leaven of Malice]."

344 **Nigel Nicolson**, "A Bride Invented—What a Row!" Daily Dispatch
18 Feb. 1955.

344 **Elizabeth Bowen**, "Mischief in Canada," Tatler 9 Mar. 1955.

344 **about 7,000**, the precise figure quoted in Willis Kingsley Wing, letter to RD, 6 June 1956, Columbia Box 32 #2, was 6,829.

344 **"but I think,"** quoted in PI, 4 May 1983.

344 **"far reaching"** and **"technique of correction,"** Shaw, London Music
as Heard by Corno di Bassetto (Later Known as Bernard Shaw)

with Some Further Autobiographical Particulars (London: Constable, 1937) 19.

344 **Huxley had claimed,** *Ends and Means: An Enquiry into the Nature of Ideals and into the Methods Employed for Their Realization* (London: Chatto & Windus, 1938) 223-24, 326.

344 **able to gather,** RD, "Medicine Marches On," editorial, *Examiner* 24 Mar. 1942: 4, and PI, 4 May 1983.

345 **"The neck free,"** quoted in Brenda Davies, PI, 7 May 1991.

346 **"interesting, practical,"** PI, 3 Nov. 1982.

346 **each wrote a testimonial,** letters from "B. D." and "R. D." quoted in Lulie Westfeldt, *F. Matthias Alexander: The Man and His Work* (1964; Longbeach, CA: Centreline, 1986), 117-20.

346 **In 1958, he,** Westfeldt 119-20.

347 **"Feet a little" and "Ah, your jaw's,"** *Frailties* 113-14; see also *Frailties* 156.

347 **"It's mostly your,"** *Wonders* 204.

348 **"Authors are attempting,"** *Voice* 307. Davies read the second edition of Bergler's book, which appeared in 1954. He may have read it that year but the first reference I find to it is in "The Incorruptible Savant," *SN* 15 Feb. 1958: 21.

349 **"for some better,"** *Conversations* 120. In addition to sources mentioned specifically in footnotes, this account of Davies' attitude toward Jung and Freud depends on: *Conversations* 77-78, 81-83; RD, rev. of *C. G. Jung: Letters, Vol I: 1906-1950*, ed. Gerhard Adler and Aniela Jaffe and *C. G. Jung* by Anthony Storr, *New York Times Book Review* 25 Feb. 1973: 31; RD, "His Own Ulysses," *Canadian Forum* June-July 1978: 24-25; *Enthusiasms* 234-37; RD, "History, Freud and a 'Symphonic Treatment' of Sexual Life," *Globe and Mail* 17 May 1986: D20; "The Art of Fiction" 54-57; and RD, "Jung and the Writer," Gothenburg Book Fair, Gothenburg, 7 Sept. 1989, ts. 1-5.

350 **"Compare what,"** RD, "A Forward Look," *SN* 21 Jan. 1956: 21.

350 **"as a therapeutic,"** "The Individual and the Mass" 26.

351 **"I am not,"** RD, Diary, as transcribed by RD for my use.

352 **"gross symptoms" and "splendidly at home,"** RD, letter to Roper, 23 Aug. 1972; see also PI, 14 June 1990.

353 **"It was most,"** *Memories, Dreams, Reflections* 189.

355 **"I do not go,"** RD, letter to Roper, 8 Feb. 1955.

355 **"Oh, come on,"** PI, 23 June 1982.

355 **"expanding in a way,"** RD, letter to Robertson, 18 June 1957, CI, McMaster.

356 "...I have run," RD, letter to Tyrone and Judith Guthrie, 19 Oct. 1957.

358 "When it was on," *Frailties* 354-55.

358 "If it were still," *Frailties* 269.

359 "And serve Ma," *Frailties* 369.

359 "quite an" and "That's where you're," *Frailties* 282.

359 "For in Ma," *Frailties* 303; see also *Murther* 232.

362 "other-worldliness," *Arts National.*

362 Their house, Davies also set "Three Gypsies" in this house (Cefn Bryntalch, Abermule, Montgomeryshire).

362 had seen musical, RD, interview, *Arts National.*

363 had taken note of, see Gray, *Peter Warlock* (London: Cape, 1934), master at Eton 37, Beecham and desire to conduct 129-37, *Sackbut* 205, Newman 207-8, right 211, cats etc. 254-55, feuds 288-89, flat 287 and 89, suicide 290. For a consideration of some links between Revelstoke and Gray's life of Heseltine see Michael Peterman, *Robertson Davies* (Boston: Twayne, 1986) 107-8.

363 "will be the best," RD, letter to Tyrone and Judith Guthrie, 19 Oct. 1957.

364 "Poetry and music," *Frailties* 154.

364 "...she was a little," *Frailties* 246.

364 "...she felt, stronger," *Frailties* 319; see also *Frailties* 173.

365 He too has been haunted, Travel 14 Feb. and 29 Sept. 1989, and PI, 15 May 1991. Compare the passage about the importance of "Hums" in *Lyre* 255.

365 "Is it perhaps," *Frailties* 372.

365 H. P. Blunt had introduced, RD, "As Others See Us," 10 May 1978, ts. 4-5.

365 Davies concluded, *Conversations* 83.

366 "...he is very aware," Brenda Davies, PI, 14 Apr. 1984.

366 "the metamorphosis of," *Frailties* 316.

366 "We dismiss...at," *Frailties* 377.

367 "*Water parted from*," *Frailties* 305.

367 "toward all the vast," *Frailties* 311.

367 which comes from, see RD, letter to Gloria Shephard, 5 Apr. 1961. Davies found the quotation from which the title is drawn in Logan Pearsall Smith, *A Treasury of English Aphorisms* (London: Constable, 1928) 85-86 (see RD, letter to George F. Weld, 17 Jan. 1989).

367 **A summary of,** statement attached to G. I. Clarke, letter to Willis
     Kingsley Wing, 10 Mar. 1958.

367 **Robertson remembered,** see pages 236 and 264 above.

368 **"The Author agrees,"** quoted in Willis Kingsley Wing, letter to
     RD, 13 Jan. 1958.

368 **"too much ribaldry"** and **"I think Mr. Davies,"** NRW, "Report on
     Manuscript [of *A Mixture of Frailties*]," 27 Feb. 1958, CI,
     McMaster.

369 **"You refer"** and **"My Dear Charles,"** quoted in PI, 16 June 1982.
     He told a slightly different version of this story in PI, 26 Oct.
     1983.

369 **"I think & hope,"** Travel 1 Sept. 1958.

Chapter 11—Playwright and Director: 1950-60

371 **"The pattern of work,"** *Frailties* 315.

372 **at the Brae Manor,** in early July 1951 *At My Heart's Core* (Davies
     directed, Brenda played Mrs. Stewart); from 20-23 Aug. 1952
     Olympia (Davies directed, Brenda played Princess and Davies
     Prince Plata-Ettingen); from 25-29 August 1953 *The White-
     Headed Boy* (Davies directed, Brenda played Aunt Ellen); and
     from 11-14 Aug. 1954 *The Late Christopher Bean* (Davies
     directed and Brenda played Gwenny).

372 **Straw Hat Players,** the dates for *Ten Nights* are 15-27 Aug. 1955
     and for *Visit to a Small Planet* 31 Aug.-5 Sept 1959.

372 **between 1955 and 1960,** *Two Gentlemen of Soho* (Little Theatre, 19
     Nov. 1955), *Mr. Bolfry* (Little Theatre, 24-25 Feb. and one of
     13, 14, 16 or 17 Mar. 1956), *Pinocchio* (skating club, Mar. 1955,
     Rosamond played Cleo), *The Emperor's New Clothes* (skating
     club, Mar. 1958, Davies wrote the script [see Archives 8.19] and
     Rosamond was in it), *Arms and the Man* (Cobourg Opera and
     Dramatic Guild, 20 and one of 26, 27 or 28 Nov. 1959), *At the
     Gates of the Righteous* (Eastern Ontario Drama League's work-
     shop, 30 Jan. 1960).

372 **repertory-standard presentations,** Jane Austen's *Pride and Prejudice*,
     Pinero's *Trelawny of the "Wells,"* Wilder's *The Matchmaker*, and
     Priestley's *When We Are Married*.

373 **"Some of the,"** Ralph Hancox, PI, 27 Oct. 1982.

374 **"good declamation,"** RD, introduction, *Aesop* v.

374 **"This was not only,"** letter to RD, 14 Feb. 1953.

374 **"I don't know,"** quoted in Alan G. A. Stephen, letter to RD, 5 May
     1952.

374 **"what about,"** RD, letter to Alan G. A. Stephen, 11 Sept. 1954, UCC.

375 **an editorial,** RD, "Peterborough a Festival City?" *Examiner* 23 June 1952: 4.

375 **observers like,** Herbert Whittaker, PI, 11 Oct. 1983.

375 **who let it be known,** RD, "The Festival Idea," editorial, *Examiner* 26 July 1952: 4.

375 **at Guthrie's urging,** Guthrie made the suggestion in a letter to Tom Patterson on 24 July 1952. James Forsyth (Guthrie's biographer) quoted this letter to me in a letter written 12 Oct. 1982.

375 **stepped down,** even after 1971, he served for a number of years on the archive and planning committees.

375 **bridging a gap,** Alf and Dama Bell, PI, 9-10 May 1982.

375 **Festival was broadened,** John Hayes, PI, 10 May 1982.

376 **influential reviews,** for a selection of these reviews and of those in the *Examiner*, see *Well-Tempered* 69-85, 87-96, 102-121.

376 **"A good production,"** Theatre 17 June 1963.

377 **"As Troilus,"** RD, "Stratford Festival 1963," *Examiner* 22 June 1963: 4.

377 **At intervals,** the articles appear in the programs for 1954, 55, 56, 57, 62 and 90; the seminar papers were given in 1960, 62, 68, 75 and 90 and the public lectures in 1982, 92 and 93. For the seminar papers see *Enthusiasms* 291-300, and RD, "Changing Fashions in Shakespearean Production," *Stratford Papers on Shakespeare 1962*, ed. B.W. Jackson (Toronto: Gage, 1963) 66-116, and Archives 30.15, 28.9, and "Lecture for the Stratford Shakespearean Festival," 10 June 1990, Archives 92/152; for the public lectures, see *Thirty Years at Stratford*.

377 **a Canadian version,** the following account depends largely on letters written by RD, Willis Kingsley Wing, Peter H. Bennett (Managing Director, Stratford Festival), A. M. Bell (Vice President, Stratford Festival), and Michael Langham (Artistic Director, Stratford Festival). For many of these, see Columbia Box 32 #1 and #2 and Box 1055.

377 **Working with a text,** see Archives 1.9-10.

378 **the resulting typescript,** Archives 1.11-13.

378 **sent the script,** "*Bartholomew Fair*: A Comedy by Ben Jonson: 1614: Freely Adapted by Robertson Davies: 1956: for The Stratford Festival," Archives 1.14.

379 **"some months"** and **not the right director,** Michael Langham, letter to RD, 25 November 1956.

379 **several directors**, Nicholas Goldschmidt in 1960, Mavor Moore in 1963, Douglas Campbell in 1966, Leon Major in 1968, Urjo Kareda in 1980.

379 **"The 'Lost' Scenes from** *The Merry Wives of Windsor*," see Archives 8.20.

380 **jokingly recommended** and **"Well, all,"** Alf and Dama Bell, PI, 9-10 May 1982.

380 **its own ghost**, RD, letter to Tanya Moiseiwitsch, 11 July 1961, and Tanya Moiseiwitsch, PI, 9 May 1982.

380 **"doubtless because,"** RD, letter to Tanya Moiseiwitsch, [June] 1962.

382 **set the Davises**, Donald Davis, PI, 15 Apr. 1983.

382 **on February 1, 1955**, the date is noted at the top of page [1] of Davies' yellow typescript draft, see Archives 4.4.

383 **except Nathan Cohen**, Nathan Cohen, *CJBC Views the Shows*, CJBC Radio, Toronto, 27 Nov. 1955.

383 **"shocked revulsion,"** quoted in Herbert Whittaker, "Showbusiness," *Globe and Mail* 1 Dec. 1955: 10.

384 **"an absolutely,"** PI, 19 Jan. 1983.

384 **"What an entrance,"** J. B. Priestley, introduction, *The Glass Cage* (Toronto: Kingswood, 1957) vii.

384 **"I wish you'd,"** quoted in PI, 19 Apr. 1983, and in slightly different words in PI, 19 Jan. 1983.

385 **"Jungian,"** according to RD, Diary, 23 May 1956, as transcribed by Davies for my use.

385 **by August 25** and **on September 13**, RD, Diary, as transcribed by Davies for my use.

385 **"cut the throat,"** Theatre 15 Mar. 1957.

385 **that August**, RD, Diary, 24 Aug. 1957, as transcribed for my use.

385 **copy of his scenario**, this was provisionally titled "A Comedy of Conscience," see Archives 2.9-12 where the fair copy is misdated 1958.

385 **in February 1958**, see RD, letter to Davenport, 4 Feb. 1958.

385 **in May**, see RD, letter to Willis Kingsley Wing, 28 Apr. 1958. Later Davies came to believe that he had written the play in 1956 (see RD, letter to Kathleen Griffin, 14 Mar. 1961, and "Author's Note" to *General Confession* in *Hunting* 197).

385 **"rejected"** and **"Box Office,"** RD, Diary, 1 June 1958, as transcribed by Davies for my use.

385 **title** *General Confession*, Davies first suggested this as a title in RD, letter to Kathleen Griffin, 14 Mar. 1961.

387 **Davies modified**, see Stone-Blackburn 140-41.

387 **"typical forms of,"** Jung 8: paragraph 435.

388 **The Anima**, John Keats, *Endymion: A Poetic Romance*, engravings by John Buckland-Wright (London: Golden Cockerel Press, [1947]) [35].

390 **Davies was well aware**, Marchbanks, *Examiner* 24 Feb. 1951: 4; RD, "The Fate of 'Tamburlaine,'" editorial, *Examiner* 3 Feb. 1956: 4; RD, "The Seventeenth Doll and Ourselves," editorial, *Examiner* 12 Feb. 1958: 4.

390 **"A Plan for Dramatizing,"** see Archives 13.1.

390 **a new outline**, RD, letter to Tyrone Guthrie, 13 Jan. 1959.

390 **"Leaven of Malice,"** see Archives 13.3.

392 **"lunatic keeper's,"** Travel 10 July 1959.

392 **"Things begin to,"** Travel 11 July 1959.

392 **"Malice Domestic,"** see Archives 13.6.

392 **In May**, the changes that produced the "resulting script" were first typed separately as "Leaven of Malice Changes in Script," Archives 13.8-9.

393 **"Tyrone Guthrie's production of *Leaven*,"** see Archives 13.12.

393 **"Tyrone Guthrie's production of *Love*,"** Archives 13.10.

393 **"father in,"** Theatre.

393 **"You know, we,"** quoted in PI, 13 Apr. 1983.

394 **and in public**, WD, *Star* 22 Oct. 1960: 30 and 19 Nov. 1960: 30.

394 **"Was desperately depressed,"** Theatre, and quoted in *Conversations* 29.

395 **"the way you,"** Amelia Hall, PI, 3 and 27 Jan. 1984.

395 **"Well, Jack,"** quoted in Jack Merigold, PI, 8 Aug. 1984.

395 **"My dear friends—,"** Amelia Hall Scrapbook 18, Metropolitan Toronto Reference Library, microfilm.

395 **"Love and Libel: Adapted from,"** Archives 13.17; the title page reads "Tyrone Guthrie's Production of *Leaven of Malice*: A Comedy adapted from the novel by Robertson Davies: New York Title: Love and Libel."

395 **"*of course*,"** Tyrone Guthrie, letter to RD, 26 Apr. 1960, as quoted in Theatre 5 June 1961.

Chapter 12—Master of Massey College: 1961-81

397 **"...our Guest Nights,"** *Angels* 167-68 (I have rearranged the order of these sentences).

399 "But...damn it all," *The Imperial Canadian* 5.

399 to feel strongly, this statement of Massey's views depends on Vincent Massey, letter to Eric Phillips, 14 Dec. 1959, quoted in *What's Past Is Prologue* 527-28, and on Claude Bissell, PI, 1 June 1983.

400 Davies the editorialist, RD, "Massey College," *Examiner* 19 Dec. 1959: 4.

401 an editorial urging, RD, "A Precedent Is Needed," *Examiner* 18 Jan. 1960: 4.

401 "good fun," Vincent Massey, Diary, 2 Nov. 1960, on deposit from Massey College in the U of Toronto Archives, Vincent Massey, B87-0082/315.

401 on CBC Radio, "Broadcast Talk on Stephen Leacock," ts., recorded 3 Feb. 1956, Archives 26.12.

401 in 1952, Davies' side of the "Trinity College Debate" is in Archives 32.11.

401 "enriching" four undergraduate, Roper, letter to RD, 24 May 1960.

402 "that solitary," RD, "Welcome to Newly Elected Fellows," appended to the "Minutes of the Meeting of the Master and Fellows of Massey College," 16 Sept. 1961.

402 "the old folks," Brenda Davies, PI, 3 May 1983. Davies made the same point in PI, 4 May 1983.

402 "Oh, you," Rupert Davies quoted in PI, 9 Dec. 1982.

403 The university had agreed, see "The Master and Fellows of Massey College Act," *Statutes of Ontario, 1960-61*, chapter 53.

403 Over the next few years, Davies has drawn several word portraits of Vincent Massey, most notably, RD, "The Twenty-Fifth Anniversary Ghost Story," Massey College, 10 Dec. 1988, ts. 18-22.

404 Hart...disliked Davies and Nor did he share, Claude Bissell, PI, 31 May 1983.

404 provided drama, Claude Bissell, PI, 31 May 1983.

405 "an astute," *The Imperial Canadian* 302.

405 "dignity," quoted in Ron Thom, "Massey College, Toronto, Canada," *Canadian Architect* 8.10 (1963): 48.

405 it should look inward, Ron Thom, PI, 28 May 1984.

405 "the 'Blood Bath,'" Vincent Massey, Diary, 2 July 1960. Massey used the phrase again 3 July 1960. See also 5 July 1960 and 15-16 Oct. 1960.

405 "to bring a whisper," *One Half* 85.

405 "Mimesis at Massey," *Enthusiasms* 298-303.

406 "I shd.," RD, Diary, 8 Dec. 1958 (as transcribed by Davies for my use).

406 "splendidly," Travel 25 Apr. 1961.

407 "Cherish," RD, "Welcome to Newly Elected Fellows," 16 Sept. 1961.

407 "Love God," RD, "Inaugural Address to the Faculty of Humanities," *CALUM* [Univ. of Calgary] 9.4 (1978): 7.

407 "To begin boldly," PI, 14 June 1990.

408 "Happiness is impossible," Davies found the passages in Logan Pearsall Smith, *Little Essays Drawn from the Writings of George Santayana* (1920; Freeport, N. Y.: Books for Libraries, 1967) 278, 280. He made a number of minor changes. The first sentence of the quotation figures in his story "Christmas Carol Reharmonized."

408 Shortly before noon, for descriptions of the ceremony see "A Royal Day at Massey College," *Varsity Graduate* [U of Toronto] 10.1: 61-70 and "Prince Lays Stone, 'Crasher' an Egg," *Telegram* [Toronto] 25 May 1962: 49.

409 "a really first," quoted in PI, 6 Feb. 1985.

409 "That's an absurd," quoted in PI, 1 Nov. 1983.

410 morning constitutional, for a detailed account by Davies of this walk, see RD, "Queen's Park," *Toronto Life* April 1982: 58, 81-82.

410 "task for," "seeking" and "I am rested," Travel 6 and 16 Aug. 1963.

411 On hearing that, Douglas Lochhead, PI, 3 May 1983.

412 female undergraduates picketed, "The Twenty-Fifth Anniversary Ghost Story" ts. 14.

413 "To have," RD, letter to Davenport, 6 Jan. [1962].

415 "But, Robert," quoted in Robert Finch, PI, 2 June 1983.

416 Montague Rhodes James, see *One Half* 235-36.

417 "Life is a," *Explorations*.

417 texts that contrasted, Ecclesiasticus 4 and 1 Corinthians 2.

417 a depiction of, *Spirits* 61 and 108.

417 Speaking at, quoted in "Chapel," *A Letter to the Members of the College Association* Oct. 1981: n.p.

418 "Well, of course," quoted in Giles Bryant, PI, 10 Oct. 1990. The following account is largely based on interviews with Gordon Wry's widow, Joyce (PI, 24 Oct. 1990), and with Giles Bryant.

419 "He's a very," Giles Bryant, PI, 10 Oct. 1990.

419 **met the predictable criticisms,** Davies summarized many of these in "The Twenty-Fifth Anniversary Ghost Story" ts. 10.

420 **"Heav'n has,"** an example cited in "The Massey Experiment," *Globe Magazine* [*Globe and Mail*] 13 Nov. 1965: 16, but quoted as it appears in *The Oxford Dictionary of Quotations.*

420 **picked the story up,** Arnold Rockman, "Life and the Arts," *Star* 5 Oct. 1963: 28; and "Fan Club Fame," *Varsity* [U of Toronto] 11 Oct. 1963: 3.

420 **"I always thought,"** quoted in Daniel Bratton, PI, 18 May 1983.

420 **"You will never,"** PI, 11 May 1983.

421 **But this issue divided,** my account of the sequence of events here depends on an interview with Hart Massey, PI, 23 Jan. 1990.

421 **"of his family's"** and **"well within,"** *The Imperial Canadian* 308.

421 **threats of suit,** PI, 11 May 1983, and RD, letter to Leigh M. Gossage, 7 Jan. 1970.

421 **"Have you ever tried,"** RD, letter to Davenport, 30 Dec. [1965].

422 **"...the Bursar and,"** Douglas Lochhead, PI, 3 May 1983.

423 **"The Pageant of,"** see Archives 9.2.

429 **"despite the fact,"** Ramsay Derry, PI, 5 Oct. 1983.

429 **drama survey at University,** "Option for Religious Knowledge in Honour Courses" (ten plays from *Oedipus Rex* to *Murder in the Cathedral*).

429 **two courses he taught,** I use the course titles assigned by the English Department. The Drama Centre used the title "Special Studies in Theatrical History and Style," for "Nineteenth-Century English Theatre and Drama." For two years (1976-78), the Shaw course had a narrower focus and was called "Edwardian Theatre."

429 **sparkling lecture** and **perceptions,** David Gardner, PI, 4 Feb. 1983 and Gardner's notes for "English Drama from 1800 to the Present," 25 Sept. 1973 and 12 Feb. 1974, contractions expanded.

430 **"airy fairy,"** Ian Alexander, PI, 12 Dec. 1983.

430 **"Are youse,"** quoted by Daniel Bratton, PI, 18 May 1983.

430 **formal complaints,** there was only one, for example, during Ann Saddlemyer's tenure as director of the Drama Centre 1972-77 (Ann Saddlemyer, PI, 30 Sept. 1983).

431 **"They're brilliant,"** quoted in Dusty Vineberg, "Devil's Advocate," *Montreal Star* 3 Feb. 1973: C7.

431 **"They are more,"** RD, "Robertson Davies: Part II," *Ontarion* 20 Feb. 1979: 21.

432 **"wars"** and **"to try to,"** *Conversations* 124, 123. See also RD,
     "Leacock the Humorist: Leacock the Teacher," *Monday Morning*
     Nov. 1969: 25.

432 **"Men reason,"** quoted in a letter to the author, from a woman who
     had taken one of Davies' courses and who asked not to be identi-
     fied.

432 **women chose**, Ann Saddlemyer, PI, 30 Sept. 1983.

432 **"they don't,"** Vineberg C7.

432 **"—PLEASE do not,"** RD, notes selected from the many on David
     Gardner's thesis, 1978-81. They are typical.

433 **prepared his own students**, RD, letter to Mr. Sharman, n. d. (the
     advice in this letter is consistent with what students report).

433 **"to just spread,"** Peter Brigg, PI, 25 Apr. 1983.

434 **Opinion began to**, J. R. de J. Jackson, PI, 15 Feb. 1983.

434 **"...the first of them,"** Nevill Coghill, "Drama Versus Literature,"
     University of Toronto, 7 Dec. 1964.

435 **"always"** and **"always,"** Ann Saddlemyer, PI, 30 Sept. 1983.

437 *The Diary*, to update the *Diary* Davies wrote a short introduction,
     made minor changes throughout and replaced 40 entries with
     pieces from columns of 1951-53 (37 of these were made in the
     revised typescript at the end of May 1965, and 3 more in
     January 1966 when he read proof).

437 *The Table Talk*, Davies made minor cuts to *Table Talk*, primarily of
     out-of-date material, but added nothing new, and had the type-
     script ready in January 1967.

437 **pulled the book into shape**, Davies integrated the almanack mater-
     ial that he had created in June 1953, cut entries that had been
     used for the *Diary* update, removed the playlets from Taurus and
     Aquarius and modernized some words and phrases (see Archives
     10.15-11.5).

438 **Virgo**, *Almanack* 99.

439 **"The fact of"** and **"his fits of,"** RD, letter to J. G. McClelland, 18
     Jan. 1968.

439 **Carleton University speech**, see RD, "Stephen Leacock," in *Our
     Living Tradition: Seven Canadians*, First Series, ed. Claude T.
     Bissell (Toronto: U of Toronto P, 1957) 128-49.

439 **"The good professor,"** *Stephen Leacock* 36 and in some copies 38.

440 **"The godlike"** and **"another kind of novel,"** *Stephen Leacock* 25
     and in some copies 27-28.

440 **"I am sending you,"** RD, letter to Anna Szigethy [of McClelland
     and Stewart], 2 Apr. 1970.

442   **fired...changed...published**, Anna Szigethy, letter to RD, 9 Apr. 1970.

442   **"...let all be peace,"** RD, letter to Anna Szigethy, 10 Apr. 1970.

442   **"I am sorry,"** RD, letter to Josephine Rogers, 13 Aug. 1971.

442   **"it should be,"** RD, letter to Alan G. A. Stephen, 5 June 1958, UCC.

444   **"a two-hour,"** Ron Evans, "A Centennial Bomb," *Telegram* [Toronto] 12 Jan. 1967: 68. See also Audrey M. Ashley, "Canada's Story on Stage May Take Another Century," *Ottawa Citizen* 12 Jan. 1967: 51; Herbert Whittaker, "Swinging Quebec Fares Best in Centennial Play," *Globe and Mail* [Toronto] 12 Jan. 1967: 11.

445   **"Some idiot of,"** quoted in John Fraser, "Davies and His Revenge Therapy," *Globe and Mail* 5 Mar. 1977: 37; for a slightly different version of this story see "Profile," *Quill and Quire* 6 Nov. 1970: 4.

445   **"They pay you nothing,"** RD, quoted in Fraser.

446   **"argues persuasively,"** Urjo Kareda, "Leaven of Malice an 'Ingeniously Sprung Trick-Box' on Stage," *Star* 13 Oct. 1973: F3.

446   **Written in the early,** this is a guess, based on the absence of references to the play in the many letters to Gordon Roper in 1972 and on the fact that *Brothers* must have been completed well before 30 July 1973 when the CBC began to film it (see the blue page at the beginning of the CBC television script, Archives 2.7).

446   **Drama Centre's production,** Debbie Nathan, "Excellent Interpretation of Ibsen's Peer Gynt," *Varsity* [University of Toronto] 21 Jan. 1974: 10.

447   **"By concentrating,"** John Fraser, "Cast Catches Noye's Fludde Grandeur," *Globe and Mail* 29 Nov. 1974: 17.

447   **between July 1 and August 27, 1974,** Davies wrote these dates on the title page of his first draft, see Archives 1.1.

448   **"a very grand"** and **"cool and bossily,"** Urjo Kareda, "Question Time Is a Grand Disaster," *Star* 26 Feb. 1975: E20.

448   **called forth,** see, for example, Scott Young, "Hero Gelding," *Globe and Mail* 28 Feb. 1975: 27; Louis K. Fleming, letter, *Star* 4 Mar. 1975: B5.

448   **pulling 80 percent houses,** RD, letter to Rota Lister, 6 Jan. 1976.

448   **a searing blast,** see Clives Barnes, "Theater: Canadian 'Leaven of Malice,'" *New York Times,* 9 June 1975: 43.

448   **moving Davies to observe,** Theatre 21 and 22 July 1975.

448   "quite marvellous," Martin Hunter, PI, 27 Mar. 1986.

448   "Brenda v. good," Theatre 22-31 Jan. 1976.

449   Davies set, it was Bryden who, in a letter to Davies, had suggested that Davies set his play during the court martial and that scenes from *Ponteach* be presented as evidence (Ronald Bryden, telephone interview, 7 Feb. 1991).

449   revised and revised, see Archives 5.15-17 and 6.1-4.

449   the critics delivered, see Bryan Johnson, "Pontiac Gets Lost in a Hopeless Muddle," *Globe and Mail* 27 Oct. 1977: 15, and Gina Mallet, "The Letdowns at Hart House Are Hurting," *Star* 7 Nov. 1977: D6.

449   "The newspapers," RD, letter to Davenport, 10 Nov. 1977.

449   a prologue, see Archives 8.26.

450   "Great Goldfish Caper," John Browne, "Five Years After, or How to Get a Fly-Whisk Named after You," *Massey College Bull* 2.4 (1973): 5 and Jeffrey M. Heath, PI, 29 Nov. 1983.

451   another occasion, see RD, Diary, 30 Apr. 1971; Colin Friesen, PI, 7 June 1983; Robert Finch, PI, 2 June 1983; and Douglas Lochhead, PI, 3 May 1983.

452   Lending a sympathetic ear, Iain Dobson, PI, 28 Jan. 1985; Robert Finch, PI, 2 June 1983; Peter Brigg, PI, 25 Apr. 1983; and many others.

452   disgruntlement with, Peter Brigg, PI, 25 Apr. 1983; Colin Friesen, PI, 7 June 1983; and many others.

452   Dobson continued to, Peter Brigg, PI, 25 Apr. 1983; Douglas Lochhead, PI, 3 May 1983.

452   "Night of the," "Five Years After" 5, and Iain Dobson, PI, 28 Jan. 1985.

452   "Oh, no no no no," quoted in PI, 12 Nov. 1986; Davies assigned Dobson slightly different words in PI, 15 Nov. 1983, but the gist is the same. Dobson's son Iain believes that his father did not want the Mastership; he had withdrawn from administrative duties at the time in order to concentrate on research.

453   "Finally, Dr.," "Special Meeting of the Common Room Club, December 15, 1972," *Massey College Bull* 2.3 (1973): 17.

454   They felt they, see "Whither Massey College?" *Massey College Bull* 2.4 (1973) 7-8. The junior Fellows had been concerned about the loss of residential places in the late 1960s, according to Peter Brigg, PI, 25 Apr. 1983.

454   "the Act and the Statutes," "The Female of the Species— Chronologically Speaking," *Massey College Bull* 4.1 (1974): 7.

454 **"Over my dead,"** quoted as apocryphal by William Stoneman, PI, 9 Nov. 1984.

454 **"If Balliol is,"** RD, letter to Christopher Hill, 18 Nov. 1971.

456 **published an interview,** Gordon Elliot, "A Conversation with Robertson Davies," *Massey College Bull* 3.1 (1973) 1, 4, 7.

456 **one of the senior,** an incident recounted by Christina McCall Newman, speech, launching party for *Trudeau and Our Times,* Massey College, 21 Oct. 1990.

456 **"Matters of concern,"** *A Letter to the Members of the College Association* Oct. 1976: n.p.

Chapter 13—The Deptford Trilogy: 1958-75

457 **"P.m. walk,"** Travel 10 Aug. 1965.

459 *A Voice,* in England, this book was titled *The Personal Art: Reading to Good Purpose.*

459 **"WRD grows v. old,"** Travel 24 July 1966.

459 **"for these partings,"** Travel 6 Aug. 1963.

460 **"one who discerns,"** Travel 18 Apr. 1961.

460 **"had never expected,"** Travel 18 July 1963.

461 **"As Jung explains,"** *One Half* 127-28.

463 **"The degree,"** *One Half* 133.

463 **a waking dream,** this probably belongs to 1964 or to 1967, years when Robertson urged ideas for books on him.

464 **"No, you must,"** PI, 13 July 1988.

464 **"A fine performance,"** *One Half* 145.

464 **"Alchemic symbolism,"** "Ben Jonson and Alchemy" 57-58.

465 **"myth and"** and **"we move,"** *One Half* 131.

465 **Early in 1959, in the,** *Explorations,* by 1960, however, the influence of Jung is evident: "The final product of a thorough Jungian analysis is the Individuated Man, controlled not by the Ego but the Self. And—this is important—this Self is an image of God" (WD, *Star* 4 June 1960: 34). For a later reflection about finding one's soul in solitude, see *Lyre* 380.

466-7 **"(a) This world"** and **"Marvellous morning,"** Travel 22 July 1967.

467 **"at the least,"** *One Half* 244.

467 **"the existence,"** *One Half* 264.

467 **"leaves Protestantism,"** from Jung's "Answer to Job," as quoted in WD, *Star* 11 July 1959: 28.

467 **"the bringing of,"** *Conversations* 138-39.

468 "...we must make," "Ben Jonson and Alchemy" 54.

468 "not the commonplace," *Conversations* 137-38.

468 In 1958, Davies places the appearance of this image in the years when Massey College was being planned. But, as he made his first notes for the novel no later than 1960 (see below), it must belong to the late 1950s.

468 "[It was] a, RD, "Shamanstvo," Jung Instititue of San Francisco, 16 Feb. 1979, ts. 18, Archives 35.4.

468 Subsequent accounts, PI, 7 Mar. 1984; the 1986 interview published as "Art of Fiction" 40-41; RD, "The Neil Gunn Lecture," Edinburgh, 27 May 1988, ts. 34, Archives 36.5; RD, "Jung and the Writer," Gothenburg Book Fair, Gothenburg, 7 Sept. 1989, ts. 19; and RD, "Literature and Moral Purpose," *First Things: A Monthly Journal of Religion and Public Life* Nov. 1990: 22.

469 "not later than," RD, "The Deptford Trilogy in Retrospect," Studies 7.

469 "The next time," RD, letter to Mrs. Julius Marmur, 21 Sept. 1959.

469 The notes begin, I quote from the notes themselves which are now in Archives 15.2. Davies edited them lightly and omitted much of his third page when quoting them in "The Deptford Trilogy in Retrospect" 7-8.

470 "guilt began," "Shamanstvo" ts. 20.

470 "My long pondered," "Works in Progress" notebook 71-72, Archives 23.9.

471 "There were heroes," "Shamanstvo" ts. 18-19. Davies told a different version of this story in PI, 7 Mar. 1984.

471 by September 1965, Travel 15 Sept. 1965.

472 "a psychological," *Fifth* 234.

472 "flashes of insight" and "a collaborator," *Fifth* 132 and 197. See also *Fifth* 147.

473 "It is autobiographical," RD, letter to Davenport, 10 May 1968.

474 draw a little, RD, letter to Ralph Hancox, 15 Nov. 1970.

474 "what future awaits," Travel 20 July 1963.

475 And the bearded, see, for example, Marchbanks, *Examiner* 13 Sept. 1941: 4, *Hunting* 193, and *Tempest-Tost* 363.

475 he had first become, Dusty Vineberg, "Devil's Advocate," *Montreal Star* 3 Feb. 1973: C7.

475 "Saints for Soldiers," *Examiner* 9 Oct. 1943: 4.

475 "must try," Travel 23 Aug. 1965.

476 "St Dunstan stood," Richard Harris Barham, "A Lay of St Dunstan," *The Ingoldsby Legends* (London: Dent, 1960) 44.

Davies now possesses eleven editions of this book.

477 "She did not know," *Fifth* 68-69.

478 "a *Last Supper*" and "inside the courtyard," Travel 20 Aug. and 19 Aug. 1968.

479 "swift-flowing" and "*Faust* had put me," Travel 9 Aug. 1965.

479 "I hoped to do," RD, letter to Davenport, 10 May 1968.

480 "Why don't you," *Fifth* 266.

480 at the time, PI, 6 Dec. 1989.

480 "and as I dreamed," RD, "The Wiegand Lecture," Dept. of History, U of Toronto, Toronto, 8 Nov. 1989, ts. 43, Archives 92/152.

481 several pages of queries, see Archives 15.11.

481 the publisher's editor, Ramsay Derry, PI, 5 Oct. 1983.

482 "we might well," KAM [Ken McVey], "Second Reading: *Fifth Business*," 18 Dec. 1969, Macmillan, McMaster.

482 "just knew," Ramsay Derry, interview, "Ideas," CBC Radio, 14 Nov. 1988.

482 Gray himself, JMG, "Report on *Fifth Business*," 30 Dec. 1969, Macmillan, McMaster.

482 "telegram from," Travel 31 Dec. 1969.

482 "Very fine—but," Ramsay Derry, PI, 5 Oct. 1983.

482 On March 15, this date is cited in G. Ashley Thomson, "The Publishing History of *Fifth Business*," an essay prepared for Dr. F. Halpenny, U of Toronto, Nov. 1971, ts. 7, Davis.

482 "What are all these," quoted in Ramsay Derry, PI, 5 Oct. 1983; and see also Thomson ts. 8.

482 Alan Maclean...was concerned, Thomson ts. 8 says that it was Gray who wanted the explanation, but Davies recollects that it was Maclean (RD, letter to the author, early Oct. 1993).

483 "in the interest of," RD, letter to Ramsay Derry, 26 Mar. 1970, Macmillan, McMaster.

483 "use the story," RD, letter to Sigmund Hoftun, 13 August 1979; Davies tells a broad version of this story in "Jung and the Writer" ts. 22-24.

483 "...in the beginning," "The Neil Gunn Lecture" ts. 37; see also Frank Rasky, "The Master Is Jubilant over New Popularity," *Star* 24 Feb. 1975: D12 and "The Deptford Trilogy in Retrospect" 8.

484 "A marvelously," Christopher Lehmann-Haupt, "A Magical Mystery Fiction," *New York Times* 23 Nov. 1970: 35.

484 "a mature, accomplished," L. J. Davis, "From Canada Comes a Master of the Novel," *Book World* [*Washington Post*] 13 Dec. 1970: 1.

484 **imaginative merchandising,** see Thomson ts. 15-16.

484 **"could only have,"** Patrick Scott, "Assignment," 18 June 1971.

484 **hardcover sold,** Patrick Scott, "Public Is Behind Robertson Davies Even If the Literary Mafia Is Not," *Star* 3 Feb. 1973: 81. Davies' New York agents, Curtis Brown, substantiate the 5,000 figure (Grace Wherry, letter to the author, 5 Oct. 1993).

485 **He represented,** CP, "Six Authors Win Governor-General Literary Awards," *Star* 5 Mar. 1971: 24 and Donald Cameron, "The Three People inside Dave Godfrey," *SN* Sept. 1971: 20-21.

485 **His novel—complex,** Robert Weaver, rev. of *The New Ancestors,* by Dave Godfrey, *Maclean's* Feb. 1971: 57-58 and Morris Wolfe, "Meeting the Past in Dark Movie Minds," rev. of *The New Ancestors,* by Dave Godfrey, *SN* Feb. 1971: 29.

485 **a close vote,** William French, "Books & Bookmen," *Globe Magazine* [*Globe and Mail*] 27 Mar. 1971: 34.

485 **Viking, decided,** "Authors & Editors," *Publishers' Weekly* 5 Apr. 1971: 21.

485 **tenth place,** James Atlas, "Making the List: How Some Books Get on the Best-Seller List—And How Some Don't," *Atlantic* Dec. 1983: 111.

485 **hardcover sales,** Wherry (note, however, that a "Viking Book Brief" on *The Papers of Samuel Marchbanks* in Viking's New York editorial files reports 19,120 as the cumulative hardcover sale).

485 **plus 10,000,** Thomson ts. 19.

485 **In Britain,** Wherry (Thomson ts. 17 reports 2,500).

485 **"I had meant,"** RD, letter to Corlies M. Smith, 15 June [1970].

485 **"but it will be ditch-digger's,"** RD, letter to Josephine Rogers, 5 May 1971.

486 **"1. Why I Went,"** "Works in Progress" notebook, loose page inserted between 110 and 111.

487 **"something of Wales,"** RD, letter to Dora Herbert-Jones, 1 June 1971.

487 **"the picture of,"** PI, 15 May 1991.

487 **"a beginning,"** RD, letter to Josephine Rogers, 5 May 1971.

487 **"well into the,"** RD, letter to Josephine Rogers, 14 May 1971.

487 **first section,** RD, letter to Corlies M. Smith, 11 June 1971.

487 **By August 28,** RD, letter to Margaret Laurence.

487 **before the end,** RD, letter to Corlies M. Smith, 17 Feb. 1972.

487 **"not a sequel"** and **"about Edward David,"** RD, letter to Corlies M. Smith, 15 June 1970.

487 "I feel impelled," RD, letter to Hugh MacLennan, 13 Jan. [1971]
       (This letter is misdated 1970, but internal evidence makes the
       actual year clear. It is with the Hugh MacLennan fonds, Special
       Collections, University of Calgary Library.)

489 But now that both, *Conversations* 101, 107.

490 "that things were," PI, 27 Mar. 1986.

490 "Realm of the Mothers," *Bred* 434.

492 "He who strives," RD, letter to Alan B. Beddoe, 11 Dec. 1962.

493 "Pay off," *Manticore* 214.

493 held 49 percent of, Fetherling 249-50.

493 now wholly owned, Fetherling 226.

494 By placing his confidence, compare Magnus Eisengrim's declara-
       tion: "Most men are much more partial to their grandfathers
       than to their fathers, just as they admire their grandsons but
       rarely their sons" (*Wonders* 310).

494 "the measure of," *Manticore* 40.

494 "markedly lost," Travel 21 June 1967.

495 "V. good crowd," Travel 22 June 1967.

495 "poachers, hostlers" and "What clothes!" Travel 25 June 1967.

496 "a hand lawnmower," *Murther* 313.

496 "composed of," RD, letter to Roper, 23 Aug. 1972.

497 Zurich Seminar 1925, see "Works in Progress" notebook 107 and
       108.

497 "not at all," Travel 16 Dec. 1970.

497 "splendidly at home," RD, letter to Roper, 23 Aug. 1972; see also
       PI, 14 June 1990.

498 "I would have said," quoted in PI, 11 Oct. 1982.

498 To make David's dreams, RD, letter to Josephine Rogers, 8 May
       1972.

498 One vision actually, PI, 7 Mar. 1984 and 7 June 1989.

498 "it had the body" and "a thing composed," "Wiegand" ts. 45.
       There are other accounts of this vision in *Conversations* 123 and
       "Jung and the Writer" ts. 28-29.

498 manticore as pictured, the card credits "a translation by T. H.
       White of *A Latin Bestiary*, Twelfth century A.D.," for the
       illustration, but White's *The Book of Beasts: Being a Translation
       from a Latin Bestiary of the Twelfth Century* gives the engraving
       the caption "The Mantichora" (Topsell's *Historie of Foure-Footed
       Beastes*, 1607).

499 "odd to find," Travel 17 Dec. 1970. The "pen-pic of J.C." figures

in *Bred* 332.

500 **serendipitous discovery,** for the information Davies used in *Manticore* 268-73, see Joseph Campbell, *The Masks of God: Primitive Mythology* (1959; Penguin, 1976) 339, 341.

501 **indeed, the case of the woman,** see RD, "Murder As It Looks to a Literary Man: A Talk to the Clarke Institute," Toronto, 28 Apr. 1983, ts. 10, Archives 35.13.

501 **"this turning of a case,"** Corlies M. Smith, letter to RD, 29 Mar. 1972.

501 **"a lucky and,"** RD, letter to Josephine Rogers, 12 Apr. 1972.

501 **counter-proposed,** RD, letters to Corlies M. Smith, 25 Apr. and 1 May 1972. Davies' recent accounts of the titling of this novel ("Jung and the Writer" ts. 29 and "Wiegand" ts. 45) differ considerably from the story told in the contemporary correspondence.

501 **"If I have,"** RD, letter to Corlies M. Smith, 17 Feb. 1972; see also RD, letter to Roper, 16 Aug. 1972.

502 **"are generally," "almost invariably"** and **"something so,"** *Conversations* 103, 108.

502 **"the feeling tone of"** and **"into a perfectly,"** June Singer, rev. of *Manticore, Psychology Today* Feb. 1973: 84; See also Lee Roloff, rev. of *Manticore, Transformation: The Bulletin of the Analytical Psychology Club of Chicago* Mar. 1973: 3-5.

502 **sales…in Canada,** Scott, "Public" 81 (Wherry substantiates the 6,500 figure).

502 **in the United States,** Wherry (the 8,000 figure reported in "Viking Book Brief" appears to be incorrect).

502 **in Britain,** Wherry.

503 **"the Spirit,"** RD, letter to Roper, 1 July 1972.

503 **"…the presence,"** RD, letter to Roper, 4 Aug. 1972.

504 **"The Hideous,"** RD, letter to Roper, 4 Aug. 1972.

505 **"to assert itself,"** RD, letter to Roper, 6 Nov. 1972.

505 **"'double' for Sir,"** "Works in Progress" notebook 124-25 (part of the entry dated Nov. 4: 1972).

505 **"complete the story"** and **"It was never,"** RD, letter to Roper, 6 Nov. 1972. Recently Davies has simplified the story of the evolution of the trilogy. See, for example, "Jung and the Writer" ts. 27-28.

506 **On July 2,** RD, letter to Arnold Edinborough, 27 June 1973.

506 **From Horace,** Davenport, inclusion in letter to RD, 16 Dec. 1972.

506 **questions about,** RD, letter to Andrew King, 27 Mar. 1973.

506 **"There used to,"** RD, "Ben Jonson and Alchemy" 59.

506 **side-show tent**, RD, letter to Andrew King, 27 Mar. 1973.

506 **From a passage**, Jean-Eugène Robert-Houdin, *Memoirs of Robert-Houdin*, trans. Lascelles Wraxall (1859; New York: Dover, 1964) 108-10. Davies owns a first edition.

506 **"kill a monkey,"** "Works in Progress" notebook 132.

508 **an interesting anecdote**, RD, editorial, *Examiner* 20 May 1944: 4.

508 *Dr. Jekyll and Mr. Hyde*, as he noted in his travel diary, Davies purchased a copy of this at Samuel French's in London on 8 June 1972 "as groundwork for my JMH bk."

508 **"quaint sight,"** *Wonders* 242.

508 **"Train call at,"** Theatre 6 Nov. 1960.

509 **"an interleaved,"** *Wonders* 211.

509 **when he wrote**, *Revels* 243 and the footnote on 252.

510 **interest in clocks and automata**, see *Table Talk* 184.

510 **"it was a figure,"** RD, letter to Mary Jo Morris, 16 Nov. 1983.

511 **"reflected,"** *Conversations* 153; see also "Jung and the Writer" ts. 28; and RD, letter to the author, 27 June 1992.

512 **"a seedy,"** *Wonders* 190.

513 **"the name of,"** *Wonders* 347.

513 **"It is obvious"**; with regard to **"so does Edward,"** note that at the end of *Manticore* it is hinted that Liesl is David Staunton's first sexual partner after analysis brings him to self-knowledge.

513 **"From buggery,"** *Wonders* 327.

513 **"the Loathly,"** *Wonders* 326.

514 **"get into a car,"** *Fifth* 284.

514 **"mythical elements"** and **"underlie,"** *Fifth* 47.

514 **"Was the story,"** *Fifth* 219.

514 **"The bee,"** *Manticore* 106.

515 **"if we are really,"** *Manticore* 278-79.

515 **"the man,"** *Wonders* 155.

515 **"It was a sense,"** *Wonders* 323.

515 **"We have educated,"** *Wonders* 324. Davies' source for the Magian World View was Joseph Campbell, *The Masks of God: Occidental Mythology* (1964; Penguin, 1976) 454.

516 **"romance and,"** *Fifth* 244.

516 **"great myths,"** *Manticore* 158.

516 **"such visions,"** *Fifth* 236.

516 **"A man who,"** *Wonders* 4.

517 **"A Bottle in the Smoke,"** RD, letter to Richard [Barber of Viking

in New York], 10 July 1974.

517 **"Merlin's Laugh,"** RD, letter to William G. Thompson, 14 July 1975.

517 **14,311 in Canada**, Wherry (Jo McNeill of Macmillan of Canada, letter to the author, 20 July 1993, reports 15,676).

517 **7,760 in the United States**, Wherry (a "Viking Book Brief" has 7,000).

517 **1,200 in Britain**, Wherry.

518 **50,000**, Rasky D12.

518 **145,000**, RD, unpublished letter to the editor of *Fanfare* ⌊*Globe and Mail*⌋, 13 Sept. 1977.

518 **"'Oooh, it's lovely,'"** "Backstage," *Globe and Mail* 11 June 1977: 33.

Chapter 14—*The Rebel Angels*: 1976-81

519 **"Enoch relates,"** Jung 11: paragraph 669.

520 **in 1972** Gordon Roper, "Robertson Davies' *Fifth Business* and 'That Old Fantastical Duke of Dark Corners, C. G. Jung,'" *Journal of Canadian Fiction* 1.1 (1972): 33-39 (a later version of Roper's article is reprinted in *An Appreciation* 81-95).

520 **Roper gave another**, "A Davies Log," *Journal of Canadian Studies* 12.1 (1977): 4-19.

521 **two collections**, *Enthusiasms* and *Well-Tempered*.

521 **a volume of articles**, see *Studies*.

521 **an annotated**, see Ryrie.

521 **and a special**, *Canadian Drama: L'Art dramatique canadien* 7:2 (1981).

521 **"Robertson Davies' contribution,"** Alan Hughes, rev. of *Theatrical Touring and Founding in North America*, ed. L. W. Conolly, *Theatre History in Canada* 5 (1984): 86. Davies wrote his paper for presentation at the Association for Canadian Theatre History Symposium, U of Toronto, 2 Aug. 1979.

522 **"The expression,"** RD, letter, *New Republic* 27 May 1978: 3; Oates' review of *One Half* appeared 15 Apr. 1978: 22-25 (rpt. in *An Appreciation*). For other attacks, see Gina Mallet, "Doesn't Robertson Davies Ever Stop Speechifying?" *Star* 15 Oct. 1977: D7; Iain McKellar, "Definitely Not His Better Half," *Ottawa Citizen* 12 Nov. 1977: 36.

524 **"a celebration,"** RD, letter to Roper, 16 June 1980.

524 **"a great paean,"** RD, letter to Davenport, 26 Feb. 1981.

524 **"the young come,"** *Angels* 186-87.

524 "A university," "Delusions of Literacy" 250 and compare *Angels* 62.

527 From the beginning, RD, letter to Sifton, [August 1976].

527 "murder of," PI, 2 May 1984.

527 only a few of them, see, for example, 5a, 13a, 40d, 57d, 76a, verso 90, 100b.

528 "long philosophical," RD, letter to Fr. H. Greenwood, 19 June 1985. For factual details about Pearson's life see the "Abstract" included in the prefatory pages of Pearson's U of Toronto doctoral thesis, "Scepticism and Action" and Muriel Lipsey, "Sceptics and Sextus," *Manitoban* [U of Manitoba] 26 Oct. 1948.

528 habits and characteristics, these are familiar to many who were at Massey College during Dobson's period: Dobson's supporters view many of them in a positive light.

528 only a couple, see 8a and 106a.

529 "anybody who had studied," I give the quotation as it appears in *Angels* 48, not in the slightly different forms Claude Bissell gave it in PI, 1 June 1983, and Vincent Bladen in *Bladen on Bladen: Memoirs of a Political Economist* (Toronto: Scarborough College, 1978) 143. As Dean of Arts and Science, Bladen had to deal with the difficulty of the assistants and of relieving Dobson of his chair.

530 "still presented," Norman J. Endicott, "Douglas Moerdyke Duncan: a Memoir," in Pierre Théberge's *Gift from the Douglas M. Duncan Collection and the Milne-Duncan Bequest* (Ottawa: National Gallery of Canada, 1971) 20.

530 "However remote," Jung 12, 2nd. ed.: paragraph 432.

532 From the beginning, see 2a, 2b, 12b, 20a, 48e, 53d.

532 stressed by Jung, see, for example, Jung 12: paragraphs 103, 421, 453-54, 485, 509; and 13: paragraphs 182 note 61, and 209.

532 "that this," RD, letter to Mrs. G. Kind, 2 Feb. 1988. See also RD, "The Wiegand Lecture," Dept. of History, U of Toronto, Toronto, 8 Nov. 1989, ts. 2, Archives 92/152. This is not the connection that Davies has Froats draw in *Angels* 105, however. For the quotation in *Angels*, see William Osler, *The Principles and Practice of Medicine* (New York, 1892) 388.

533 "physicians, alchemists," E. J. Holmyard, *Alchemy* (Harmondsworth: Penguin Books, 1957) 166.

533 "One of Mamusia's," see also 85d.

533 Hugo's, RD, letter to Sifton, 10 July 1978.

533 the beautiful Gypsy, Beverley Slopen, "U.S. Publisher to Promote

Davies' Novel," *Sunday Star* 8 Nov. 1981: B10.

533 **personal loss he had felt,** RD, "In the Name of Racial Purity," editorial, *Examiner* 2 Feb. 1945: 4.

534 **"perhaps the most,"** "Ben Jonson and Alchemy" 51.

534 **"The physician,"** these quotations are drawn from *Paracelsus: Selected Writings*, ed. Jolande Jacobi, trans. Norbert Guterman, Bollingen Series 28 (New York: Pantheon, 1951) 131, 133, 134-35.

534 **Also late,** see entries 85c, 88b, 108d, 109b and 110d.

535 **"it is a heresy,"** "Ben Jonson and Alchemy" 52.

536 **"chirping over,"** PI, 13 Apr. 1983 and compare *Angels* 169.

536 **For years he had,** see for example, Marchbanks, *Examiner* 23 Oct. 1946: 4; and WD, *Star* 18 Mar. 1961: 29.

536 **"uproarious big,"** PI, 2 May 1984.

536 **"Latinist an alchemist,"** these notes appear on the back of an Aug. 6, 1976, page of an appointment book stuck into Davies' old "Works in Progress" notebook between 154 and 155, Archives 23.9.

537 **Davies quickly realized,** see 21c, 48d, 55c.

537 **"They went to sea,"** Davenport, letter to RD, n.d. (but written after reading *World of Wonders*), Archives 23.6. For the use Davies made of the idea see *Angels* 52.

537 **The sights and,** three-ringed notebook for the Cornish trilogy 34c (Archives 37) and see *Angels* 134-36.

537 **he had previously envisioned,** three-ringed notebook 15c.

538 **"It is always,"** Archives 23.6.

538 **on April 13,** Davies noted the date at the top of the first page of his first draft (Archives 19.12).

538 **on June 30,** RD, letter to Sifton, 2 July 1980.

539 **"The room of a,"** *Angels* 11.

539 **"Rooting about,"** *Angels* 28.

540 **"can lead"** and **"alchemists and,"** *Angels* 37.

540 **"It's astonishingly,"** *Angels* 82.

540 **"the high,"** *Angels* 157.

540 **"the lifeblood,"** *Angels* 86.

541 **"if not an alchemist,"** *Angels* 92.

541 **"chirping over their,"** *Angels* 169.

542 **"the *phuri dai*"** and **"the Alma,"** *Angels* 319.

543 **The illustration,** Archives 19.13.

543 **add several pages,** see *Angels* 141-45 from "How odd are you?" to "I know him fairly well," and *Angels* 306-7 from "Where did

you get the idea I have no family?" to "Girls grow to be very like their mothers, you know."

543 **"write in the,"** I. M. Owen, "Dons and Rebels," *Books in Canada* October 1981: 13.

544 **so admires in Joyce,** see *Enthusiasms* 158-60.

544 **Horace Davenport,** Davenport, letter to the author, 1 Aug. 1988.

544 **"The scientific,"** RD, letter to Davenport, 26 Feb. 1981. There are similar comments in RD, letter to Davenport, 9 Nov. 1978 and RD, letter to Inge and Horace W. Davenport, 2 Oct. 1981.

544 **Frye's fictional categories,** for Frye's views on the novel, confession, anatomy and romance, see *Anatomy of Criticism: Four Essays* (Princeton, New Jersey: Princeton UP, 1957) 303-14.

545 **"eerie" and "a very,"** Douglas Gibson, letter to RD, 2 July 1981. Gibson described the events of the photography session in PI, 22 May 1984.

545 **"too narrowly bound" and "scenes which,"** Peter Stevens, "Hobgoblins in an Ivory Tower," *Windsor Star* 10 Oct. 1981: E11.

545 **"creaks under,"** Sam Solecki, "The Other Half of Robertson Davies," *Canadian Forum* Dec./Jan. 1981: 31.

545-6 **"will be recognized,"** John Kenneth Galbraith, "An Appreciation: The World of Wonders of Robertson Davies," *New York Times Book Review* 14 Feb. 1982: 30 (Galbraith's "Appreciation" is reprinted in *An Appreciation* 36-41).

546 **"Among Canadian,"** Anthony Burgess, "Maple-Leaf Rabelais," *Observer* 4 Apr. 1982: 33.

546 **he lobbied the,** see Ken Adachi, "Davies Shares his Sublime Sense of the Ridiculous," *Sunday Star* 17 Nov. 1985: G1.

546 **13,595 copies,** Grace Wherry of Curtis Brown, letter to the author, 5 Oct. 1993 (note that Jo McNeill of Macmillan of Canada, letter to the author, 20 July 1993, reports 12,887).

546 **12,101 in the United States,** Wherry (note that Peter Mayer, memo to Christine Pevitt, 4 Dec. 1987, Viking editorial files, has 13,200).

546 **2,959 in Britain,** Wherry.

546 **"a man who can,"** RD, letter to Davenport, 26 Feb. 1981.

547 **Brian Parker,** caricature of Davies in 1981, by fellow academic Brian Parker, from the invitation to the retirement dinner at Hart House.

548 **the college had spent,** J. N. Patterson Hume, PI, 19 Oct. 1984.

548 **he had felt warmly,** John Leyerle, PI, 4 Aug. 1984.

Chapter 15—*What's Bred in the Bone*: 1980-85

551 "*Monday Aug. 3*," Travel. I added the "s" to Veronese and "and London" to the title of the travel diary and corrected "Folly's mouth" to "Cupid's mouth."

553 "because I was," RD, letter to Sifton, 2 July 1980.

553 "forces itself," this quotation (together with others from his letters to her) was later integrated into the published version of the interview that Sifton conducted with Davies in 1986, see "Art of Fiction" 40.

553 "(1) the childhood" and "Getting these," RD, letter to Sifton, 6 Feb. 1982.

554 By April, PI, 14 Apr. 1982.

554 on July 8, see RD, letter to Sifton, 8 July 1982.

554 Right after his return, Davies had made substantial progress by 30 Mar. 1983, when he read the novel's opening section to me. The sequence appears to have been this—a false start in late February 1983, a draft of Part One, then another revision of the opening pages begun on 7 July 1983, Part Two begun on 18 July, Part Three on 19 Nov., Part Four on 21 Jan. 1984, Part Five on 1 Mar., Part Six on 5 July and the first draft completed on 9 Aug. 1984. (Davies noted the date he started writing each section at the top of its opening page, and the date he finished on his last page [Archives 20.17-20 and 21.1-2].)

554 "burnt itself" and "and he could," *One Half* 215.

554 "in my next," PI, 14 Apr. 1982.

554 "One of the," PI, 23 June 1982.

555 "...Davies is so," William French, "Magical Tweaks in an Uncumber World," *Globe Magazine* [*Globe and Mail*, Toronto] 7 Nov. 1970: 19.

555 in reviewing, *Enthusiasms* 161-65.

555 "anticipatory embalming," RD, letter to Sifton, 11 Jan. 1982.

555 "...I have been," RD, letter to Sifton, 8 July 1982.

556 the Lesser Zadkiel, Davies invented this angel after reading in Gustav Davidson's *A Dictionary of Angels Including the Fallen Angels* (New York: Free Press, 1967) about "Recording Angel," "Radueriel," "Angel of Memory" and "Zadkiel."

556 Maimas, was inspired primarily by the suggestive entry for "Genius" in *The Oxford English Dictionary.*

559 "I keep pushing," RD, letter to Sifton, 27 July 1983.

560 growing success, by the end of 1980 Penguin Books Canada had sold more than 77,000 copies of *Fifth Business*, more than

50,000 of *The Manticore* and almost 55,000 of *World of Wonders* since the firm had published the books in paperback in 1976 and 1977 (Peter J. Waldock, letter to RD, 20 Feb. 1981).

560 "very heavy," PI, 19 Oct. 1983.

561 "speak resonantly," RD, "Painting, Fiction and Faking," Metropolitan Museum, New York, 27 Apr. 1988, ts. 4, Archives 36.4.

561 "...I dearly love," RD, Speech to the Royal Canadian Academy of Arts, 17 Nov. 1973, ts. 2-3, Archives 33.25.

561 "plainly the work," Travel 14 June 1972.

561 Goldsmith's marvellous capacity, *Stage* 65.

562 deal of research, Charles Morgan's *The Writer and His World: Lectures and Essays* (London: Macmillan, 1960) 123 supplied the drawing test that Saraceni gives Francis in *Bred* 238, and Jacques Maroger's *The Secret Formulas and Techniques of the Masters* (New York: Studio Publications, 1948) was a source for some of the technical information about Renaissance painting.

562 "the Countess," Travel 18 Oct. 1981.

562 "in which," Travel 29 Sept 1983.

562 "boundless cruelty," Travel 1 Oct. 1983.

562 "I sympathise," Travel 7 Oct. 1983.

563 "the many sorts," *Bred* 87.

563 "Sun Pictures," see page 223 and note that in Archives 23.6, among the clippings, letters, articles and notes that Davies gathered as he conceived *What's Bred in the Bone*, there is a copy of an old-fashioned poem about photographs, which uses the term "sun-picture."

564 "The first was," RD, unpublished letter to the editor of the *Times* [London] 13 Apr. 1982.

565 "...to the Ntl," Travel 10 Feb. 1983; Davies presented this scene somewhat differently in "Painting, Fiction and Faking" ts. 14.

566 courtesy of Panofsky, see Erwin Panofsky, *Studies in Iconology* (1939; New York: Harper Torchbook, 1962) 84-91.

566 "Impressed as always," Travel 13 Oct. 1985.

566 has his own encounter, see *Bred* 278.

566 "a wistful, appealing," *Bred* 261.

567 reading up his iconography, Panofsky 195 note.

568 "with insight" and "On his best," Robert Fulford, "Notebook: Divine Comedies," *SN* Oct. 85: 8.

568 "to take the," PI, 18 Mar. 1987.

568 "art is a way," *Bred* 327.

569 As he explained, "Painting, Fiction and Faking" ts. 6-8, 19-20, 32-35. To some extent Davies was influenced by what Aniela Jaffé has to say about "Modern Art as an Expression of Inner Experience," in *The Myth of Meaning*, trans. R. F. C. Hall (New York: Putnam's, 1971) 61-68.

569 "The best of them," *Bred* 333-34.

570 "like that of," *Bred* 413.

570 "a Mannerist writer," RD, letter to the author, 27 June 1992.

570 "means something between," RD, letter to the author, 27 June 1992.

570 "is not a technical," "Painting, Fiction and Faking" ts. 18.

571 "the distortion" and "Italianate," *Bred* 389.

571 "The book, as," RD, letter to Douglas Gibson, 27 Aug. 1984.

572 "pretentious," Allan Gould, "Robertson Davies' New Book Little Reason for Critics to Rave," *Examiner* 12 Oct. 1985: 3A.

572 "interminable," Mark Feeney, "Bone-Worrying Determinism," *Boston Globe* 27 Nov. 1985: A15.

572 "too improbable," Isabel Raphael, "Living through Kith and Kin," *Times* [London] 27 Feb. 1986: 11.

572 "five brilliant," Sean French, "On a Level with the Angels," *Times Literary Supplement* 28 Feb. 1986: 215.

572 "Canada's cleverest," David Twiston Davies, "Recent Fiction," *Daily Telegraph* 28 Feb. 1986.

572 "one of the," Malcolm Bradbury, "The Restorative World," *Sunday Times* 9 Mar. 1986: 43.

573 21,795 in Canada, Grace Wherry of Curtis Brown, letter to the author, 5 Oct. 1993 (note that Jo McNeill of Macmillan of Canada, letter to the author, 20 July 1993, reports 20,777).

573 40,759, Wherry (note that Peter Mayer, memo to Christine Pevitt, 4 Dec. 1987, Viking editorial files, reports 44,800).

573 5,995 in Britain, Wherry.

574 "a book of warmed," RD, letter to Douglas Gibson, 16 Apr. 1982.

574 "I believe that," Douglas Gibson, letter to RD, 5 Aug. 1982.

575 "real academic," RD, letter to Davenport, 3 Feb. 1985.

Chapter 16—*The Lyre of Orpheus*: 1984-88

577 "...Giles' ring," *Frailties* 356.

578 "a dead set" and "Wd. once," Travel 10 Sept. 1986.

578 "I know it," Travel 15 Oct. 1986.

578   **"Try not to,"** Travel 24 Sept. 1986.

578   **"the Booker & the,"** Travel 26 Sept. 1986.

579   **"looked at the,"** Travel 2 Oct. 1986.

579   **"the most unremittingly,"** Travel 23 Oct. 1986.

579-80 **"laid the keel,"** Travel 5 Jan. 1985.

580   **"A week of,"** quoted in Rhoda Koenig, "At Play in the Fields of the Word: Alienation, Imagination, Feminism, and Foolishness at PEN," *New York* 3 Feb. 1986: 47. See also Jack Kapica, "Davies Shines at Topsy-Turvy PEN Session," *Globe and Mail* 16 Jan. 1986: C1.

580   **By January 1,** Davies typed the date at the top of the first page of his first draft, Archives 22.7.

580   **in 1989 he reported,** RD, "Opera as Related to Literature," Roy Thomson Hall, Toronto, 15 Mar. 1989, ts. 2.

580   **"Opera gives,"** "Canada's Man Of Letters Explains Opera's Appeal," *Globe and Mail* 9 Nov. 1990: C2.

581   **"Opera in,"** "Opera as Related to Literature" ts. 18-19; Davies also discussed opera on "Arts National" and in "Opera and Humour: The Prince of Hesse Memorial Lecture," Aldeburgh, 11 June 1991, Archives 92/152.

581   **"must above all,"** *Lyre* 137.

584   **"When you asked,"** the ellipsis in the last paragraph of this letter is Davies'.

586   **"Darcourt yearned,"** *Lyre* 105.

586   **"he was wholly,"** *Lyre* 190.

586   **"as a gifted,"** *Lyre* 109.

586   **"hums,"** *Lyre* 255.

587   **"without particularly,"** **"always having"** and **"had to find,"** PI, 26 Nov. 1987.

587   **"as a great,"** *Lyre* 431.

587   **"The autobiography,"** PI, 15 May 1991; the full title of Andersen's autobiography in Danish is *Mit Livs Eventyr* ("My Life's Adventure").

587   **Articles and reviews,** see Archives 23.7.

587   **"is crack-brained,"** *Lyre* 2.

588   **A little of,** see *Lyre* 375-76, 366, 435.

589   **"Shakespearean"** and **"gigantic,"** *Lyre* 110 and 111.

589   **"The piece is said,"** Theatre 30 Sept. and 1 Oct. 1960. Davies also reviewed *Camelot* ("World Premiere of Camelot Seen at Opening of Centre," *Examiner* 3 Oct. 1960: 9).

589 "a great dream," *One Half* 145 and see page 464.

589 "if I had," RD, letter to Corlies M. Smith, 15 June 1970, and see
       also *Spirits* 120.

590 the love lyric, see *Lyre* 315-16, and *The Lay of the Last Minstrel*
       Canto 5, 13.

590 much enjoys his verse, note that Humphrey Cobbler quotes
       Beddoes in *Tempest-Tost* 245, 246.

590 "This is perfect," Brenda Davies, quoted in PI, 12 Nov. 1986.

590 "with no interfering," *Lyre* 447.

591 "what that was" and "that nags me," PI, 12 Dec. 1984.

591 although he did anticipate, PI, 28 May 1987.

591 "It's been said," *Lyre* 146. In using the metaphor of the unchanging
       wax, Davies was influenced by lines 239-250 of Dryden's transla-
       tion of *Metamorphoses* 15 (see the cross reference in 182c of
       Davies' three-ringed notebook).

591 "amazing and," *Lyre* 240.

591 "A Man's life," *Lyre* 468; for the ideas in this paragraph, see also
       Lyre 171, 285, 300.

592 "take a hint" and "a destiny," *Lyre* 232.

592 "because we will," *Lyre* 248.

592 "in the grip," *Lyre* 268.

592 "Of course you," *Lyre* 472.

593 "there are not," *Lyre* 240.

593 "a good old," *Lyre* 146.

593 "Fifth Business," *Lyre* 147.

593 "an educated," *Lyre* 9.

596 Andrew Porter, Travel 16 June 1989.

597 31,943, Jo McNeill of Macmillan of Canada, letter to the author,
       20 July 1993.

597 53,916 and 6,609, Grace Wherry of Curtis Brown, letter to the
       author, 5 Oct. 1993.

598 "sign outside," Travel 30 Sept. 1988.

598 "abt. Free" and "go for a walk," Travel 9 Feb. 1989.

599 *Boston Globe* reported, Daniel Golden, "The Fiction Alchemist,"
       Boston Globe Magazine [*Boston Globe*] 15 Jan. 1989: 43.

599 had been cut, the suppressed passages were "Stalin and Mao" *Fifth*
       192; from "You Protestants, if you" to "the statues of Mary and
       those of St. John—" *Fifth* 199-201; from "He certainly won't be
       a Jew" to "Pretender" *Fifth* 206; from "No, better not" to
       "Canadian passport" *Fifth* 254; and from "Of course, that was a

meeting of brothers" to "that pertain to a senior" *Fifth* 293.

599 **not without commenting,** RD, letter to Krzysztof Karzecki, 23 June 1987.

600 **"Many thanks for,"** RD, letter to Celina Cardim Cavalcante, 2 July 1985. See *Fifth* 106.

600 **"Thank you for,"** RD, letter to Celina Cardim Cavalcante, 2 Oct. 1985. See *Angels* 102, and compare the explanation in *The Oxford Dictionary of Nursery Rhymes*, ed. Iona and Peter Opie (Oxford: Clarendon, 1952) 222-23.

601 **"...I like the narrative,"** RD, letter, 10 Jan. 1989.

Chapter 17—*Murther and Walking Spirits*: 1988-91

603 **"Mary Jones Gage,"** *Historical Records* 57. The Account of "Our Gage Family" is largely based on a paper prepared by John Pierce Langs for a reunion of the Gage-Westbrook family in 1909. Mills, who drew *Historical Records* together, marked material quoted directly from Pierce with quotation marks. Like several other patches scattered through this article, this passage does not have quotation marks.

603 **"Shortly after that,"** *Far-Off* 70-72.

605 **"Unwilling though,"** RD, "The Report of the Massey Commission," editorial, *Examiner* 5 June 1951: 4.

605 **"a nation of,"** *Well-Tempered* 65.

606 **"Our climate,"** *Well-Tempered* 214.

606 **"a favoured,"** *Well-Tempered* 229.

606 **"We are still apt,"** RD, "Speech to Honour Students Banquet," Stratford, Ont., 10 May 1962, ts. 13-14, Archives 32.21.

607 **he berated,** see *Well-Tempered* 234-37, 246 ff.

607 **a new metaphor for Canada,** see *Well-Tempered* 246, and RD, "Some Thoughts on the Present State of Canadian Literature," *Proceedings and Transactions of the Royal Society of Canada*, 23 vols., series 4 (Ottawa: Royal Society of Canada, 1971) 9: 263-64, and *One Half* 273-74.

607 **a protracted struggle,** *One Half* 278 ff.

607 **"may be a hero,"** *One Half* 286.

608 **several long articles and speeches,** see for example "Mixed Grill" (presented in 1979, published 1982), "Theatre in Canada" (1980); *Thirty Years at Stratford*; "Nineteenth-Century" (written 1982, published 1990); and RD, "But Why Do You Call It Canadian?" The Spencer Trask Lecture Series, Princeton

University, 16 April 1985, Archives 35.16.

608 **"psychological energy,"** RD, "The Evangeline Wilbour Blashfield Foundation Address," The American Academy and Institute of Arts and Letters, New York, 15 May 1985, ts. 5, Archives 35.15.

608 **"assumes that it must,"** "?Aca nada?" 1070.

608 **"established your national,"** "Blashfield" ts. 8-9.

608-9 **"psychological energy turns inward,"** "Blashfield" ts. 5.

609 **"feels no impulsion,"** "?Aca nada?" 1070.

609 **"It is not simply,"** "But Why Do You Call It Canadian?" ts. 19.

609 **thoughtlessly aping,** "Keeping Faith" 192.

609 **"No, if you,"** PI, 12 Dec. 1984.

610 **of the notebook,** Archives 92/152.

610 **before July 13,** see PI, 13 July 1988.

610 **before December 7,** PI, 7 Dec. 1988.

610 **"Forty days after,"** notebook for *Murther* 4.

611 **"Where All the,"** Travel 19 Aug. 1990.

611 **"Afterlife in,"** RD, letter to Janet Turnbull Irving, 24 Nov. 1990.

611 *Murther and Walking Spirits,* for Davies' epigraph and title see Samuel Butler, *Prose Observations,* ed. Hugh de Quehen (Oxford: Clarendon, 1979) 159.

611 **on November 20,** Davies typed the date at the top of his first draft, Archives 92/152.

611 **and was finished a little,** on 12 Dec. 1990 Davies told me that he had completed his new novel except for the final section and he would write that over the Christmas holidays.

611 **"how-to book,"** *Murther* 25.

613 **"death means,"** *Conversations* 157.

613 **"possibility," "blooming"** and **"it is absurd,"** *Conversations* 211 and compare *Conversations* 157-58 and *One Half* 246.

613 **and roots his own,** RD, "Easter: For the C.B.C. 'Stereo Morning,'" ts., 18 Mar. 1981, 1-5.

613 **by a patient,** see R. L. MacMillan and K. W. G. Brown, "Cardiac Arrest Remembered," Coronary Unit, Toronto General Hospital, Archives 23.6.

613 **C. G. Jung,** see *Memories, Dreams, Reflections* 289-90.

614 **"I haven't any,"** *Conversations* 158 and compare *Conversations* 211.

614 **"I thought at,"** *Conversations* 211-12 and compare *One Half* 247.

614 **"I believe in,"** *Spirits* 5.

614 **"It is wonderful,"** *Spirits* 5.

614 "something has been," *Spirits* 4.

614 "they are a manifestation," *One Half* 227.

615 In 1988, RD, "The Twenty-Fifth Anniversary Ghost Story," Massey College, 10 Dec. 1988; see also, "Christmas Carol Reharmonized" and "The Harper of the Stones: Ghost Story for Music," 8 Nov. 1986, Archives 9.7 (performed at the Young People's Theatre, Toronto, 11 May 1987).

615 "While I was Master," RD, speech, Party Honouring Donors to the Robertson Davies Library Fund, Massey College, 13 Mar. 1989, ts. 3.

615 "technically tricky," PI, 7 Dec. 1988.

615 variety of sources, Travel 16, 18, 21 Feb. 1989.

616 *The Tibetan Book of the Dead*, ed. W. Y. Evans-Wentz, trans. Kazi Dawa-Samdup, with a psychological commentary by C. G. Jung, 3rd ed. (1957: New York: OUP, 1960).

616 "picked up a pewter" and "about nine inches," *Spirits* 168.

617 "a strong charge," *Murther* 6.

617 "in so far," *Murther* 15.

617 "the Shakespearean," *Murther* 22.

617 cautious about the value, for Davies' views on eastern religious practices, see *Conversations* 140.

617 "geography and race," *Murther* 23.

617 "one's personal drama," *Murther* 268.

618 "I have...been," RD, "Literature and Technology," Fourth Annual Tuzo Wilson Lecture Series, Ontario Science Centre, Toronto, 26 Nov. 1989, ts. 36-37, Archives 92/152.

619 "bound to fact" and "the totality," PI, 15 May 1991.

620 "having to go," PI, 14 Apr. 1982.

621 A favourite story, PI, 11 Dec. 1991.

621 draw on notes, the idea arose in the course of a discussion about literary impostures. See Travel 10 and 15 May 1961, and Davies' "Works in Progress" notebook, 69, Archives 23.9. Some of the notes he made are now in Archives 92/152.

622 "a contractor," *Far-Off* 79.

622 a tavern, a local history supports this story. It records that by 1858 a William McKay owned a tract of land and a red brick hotel on the south side of Highway 2, across the road from the original Jacob Langs farm near Langford. This William McKay married twice, and in his second marriage produced two children, one of them also named William. The latter married a Lovina Langs and was a builder (Langford W. I., "McKay Tract—Madden,"

The Tweedsmuir History, ms., Archives of Ontario).

622 "opium-eater," PI, 12 Dec. 1984.

622 "the old devil," PI, 28 Apr. 1982.

623 "a gruesome," PI, 7 Apr. 1982.

623 "aids to beauty" and "had sometimes," "Harp" 377-78. In this article Davies says that his grandmother confided these secrets to
him, but to me he explained that they actually came to him
through his mother (PI, 21 Apr. 1982).

624 "And do you know," *Murther* 172-73.

624 a reunion, Davies' *Scrapbook Begun Christmas 1927* includes a
newspaper clipping titled "Family Reunion" [55] which describes
such a gathering of the Gage-Westbrook clan and there is a reference to another such gathering in *Historical Records* 55.

624 not be able to be fair, PI, 13 July 1988.

624 "whose travelling complaints," Travel 25 Aug. 1990.

625 "Malvina had been," *Murther* 205.

626 used details, see *Frailties* 63-65.

626 worked her way up, see *Murther* 198. Davies confuses the
Canadian Order of Foresters with the Independent Order of
Foresters, which was dominated by the Mohawk Indian, Doctor
Oronhyatekha, and had its head office in Toronto.

627 "Bespoke tailor," quoted in PI, 11 Dec. 1991.

627 "prayed them," PI, 14 Apr. 1982.

627 At a family gathering, PI, 14 Apr. 1982 and 6 Feb. 1985.

627 "My inner music," Travel 14 Feb. 1989.

628 "Both. Or" and "You don't love," *Murther* 302.

628 "like a family," *Murther* 302-3.

629 "Vengeance," *Murther* 338.

630 "the woman in," *Murther* 356.

630 "had healed," *Murther* 316.

630 "it is the Eternal," *Murther* 24.

630 "How people," quoted in Beverley Slopen, "Davies Follows Editor
to a New Publisher," *Star* 17 Mar. 1991: C8.

630 "Why has this," *Murther* 256.

631 "and an important," *Murther* 277-78.

631 "had rather," PI, 11 Dec. 1991.

632 "some people," PI, 11 Dec. 1991.

632 "Robertson Davies's theatrical," George Woodcock, "Atwood's
Dark Parables, Davies's Ballad of Bankruptcy," *Quill and Quire*
August 1991: 14.

632 **After the short list,** Marian Finlay, "'Whiff of Bile' Hangs over Booker Prize," *Star* 21 Oct. 1991: B6.

633 **"It seems almost churlish,"** John Melmoth, "When the Going Gets Tough," *Sunday Times* 6 Oct. 1991: sec. 7: 14.

633 **"It's hard to doubt,"** Valentine Cunningham, "Ancestral Movie Matinee," *Observer* [London] 29 Sept. 1991: 60.

633 **25,000,** Douglas M. Gibson, facsimile to Jane Cain of Penguin Books Canada, 12 July 1994.

633 **40,638,** Grace Wherry of Curtis Brown, telephone interview, 27 Apr. 1994.

633 **"Davies has said,"** Ross C6.

Chapter 18—Endings and Beginnings

635 **"My desire is to die,"** Marchbanks, *Examiner*: 4 and rpt. *Table Talk* 120-21.

635 **"By preparation for,"** rpt. *Conversations* 160-61.

636 **"a good beano,"** PI, 6 Feb. 1985.

636 **"Lord, let me know,"** this was edited by Giles Bryant and published under the title "Lord Let Me Know Mine End" as No. 1 in the *Massey College Series of 18th Century Verse Anthems* (Toronto: Leeds Music, 1967).

637 **"hay & broken,"** Travel 22 June 1972.

637 **"some miserable plot,"** PI, 6 Feb. 1985.

637 **"oblivion in this,"** *Conversations* 212.

638 **their primary effect,** Travel 31 Dec. 1984.

638 **Senex,** RD, "The Senex: For the C.B.C. 'Stereo Morning,'" 8 Dec. 1980, ts. 2-3.

638 **would himself select,** Travel 15 Sept. 1989 and RD, "Folksong: A Lost World of Archetypes," The Analytical Psychology Society of Ontario, Toronto, 5 May 1986, ts. 23-24, Archives 36.1.

638 **"old age...a,"** RD, introduction, *Vital Signs: International Stories on Aging,* ed. Dorothy Sennett with Anne Czarniecki (Saint Paul: Graywolf Press, 1991) xiii, rpt. RD, "You're Not Getting Older, You're Getting Nosier," *New York Times Book Review* 12 May 1991: 35.

639 **Annotations on,** Archives 92/152.

640 **In "Opera as,"** Roy Thomson Hall, Toronto, 15 Mar. 1989.

640 **"Everything flows,"** RD, "Opera and Humour: The Prince of Hesse Memorial Lecture," Aldeburgh, 11 June 1991, ts. 11, Archives 92/152.

641 "with one eye cocked" and "out of this feat," "Opera and Humour" 13.

641 a lecture in 1980, "Rhetoric" 195.

641 "the mysticism of," "Opera and Humour" 31.

641 "the sense of splendour," PI, 13 Mar. 1991.

641 at least since, his first published use of the phrase seems to have been in "*A Midsummer Night's Dream,*" *The Stratford Scene, 1958-1968,* ed. Peter Raby (Toronto: Clarke, Irwin, 1968) 182.

641 "the city of our youth," Travel 13 July 1990.

641 "B. & I go," Travel 3 June 1988.

641 In Edinburgh, Travel 26 May 1988.

641-2 At Balliol, Travel 14 Oct. 1985.

642 At Buxton, Travel 31 May 1988.

642 In London, Travel 8 Oct. 1989.

642 In Ireland, Travel 8-9 July 1990.

642 At the Theatre Museum, Travel 14 June 1988.

643 "How often have I," Theatre 4 Aug. 1985.

643 "I first saw," Theatre 4 Sept. 1985. I have corrected the Maurice Coleman of the "Notes" to Maurice Colbourne.

643 Dear Miss B., RD, letter to Domini Blythe, 29 Aug. 1983.

643 Then in 1959, the date was actually 1957.

643 the Stratford production, this was done in 1964.

644 all the important productions, there was at least one other—at the Royal Court Theatre in 1956 in which Joan Plowright made an outstanding success as Margery Pinchwife.

644 "strange sensation," Travel 14 June 1988.

644 "an ikon" and "Astonishing," Travel 7 Sept. 1988.

644 "Acclaimed," Travel 28 Feb. 1989.

644 "a very nervous-making," PI, 15 May 1991.

645 The day-long affair, PI, 20 Jan 1993.

646 interrupted the writing, the typescript is dated 5 Apr. 1990.

646 Old Testament story, see 1 Kings 16 and 21, and 2 Kings 9.

647 a warm reception, see, for example, Tamara Bernstein, "P. S. Too Bad You Missed Jezebel," *Globe and Mail* 5 June 1993: C5.

647 "Perhaps," RD, "Why I Do Not Intend to Write an Autobiography," Wang International Festival of Authors, Premiere Dance Theatre, Harbourfront, Toronto, 19 Oct. 1989, ts. 15.

647 "A man who," *Wonders* 4.

648 **There, in 1979**, RD, "Shamanstvo," Jung Instititute of San Francisco, 16 Feb. 1979, ts. 18, Archives 35.4.

649 **"It is here,"** RD, "The Wiegand Lecture," Dept. of History, U of Toronto, Toronto, 8 Nov. 1989, ts. 41, Archives 92/152.

649 **"to tie, to fasten"** and **"to consider,"** "Wiegand" 16-17.

649 **"the exploration,"** "Wiegand" 48; Davies also drew the distinction between *religare* and *religere* in "Keeping Faith" 187 and 192.

650 **It was made**, RD, letter to Andrew Hoyem, 16 Aug. 1989 (Archives 92/152).

651 **"we love in terms,"** RD, "The 1966 Stratford Lectures: Third Lecture: *Twelfth Night*," Extension Department, University of Toronto, 31 May 1966, ts. 7-8, Archives 28.1.

651 **"We lunch,"** Travel 1 Jan. 1971.

651 **"This has,"** Travel 26 May 1984.

652 **"mass of incident"** and **"to get them down,"** PI, 20 Jan. 1993.

652 **"the picture of"** and **"a thing which,"** PI, 15 May 1991.

653 **"Your name and college?"** quoted in PI, 22 Aug. 1986.

653 **"something of Wales,"** RD, letter to Dora Herbert-Jones, 1 June 1971.

653 **"if I were,"** PI, 15 May 1991.

653 **"sums up an enormous,"** PI, 12 Dec. 1984.

653 **"a reminder,"** RD, "Jung and Heraldry," *Book Forum* 5 (1980): 233.

Permissions

All material quoted and reproduced from the papers and the published works of Robertson Davies is used with his permission and, in the case of the Marchbanks columns, with that of the *Peterborough Examiner.*

All material quoted and reproduced from the files of Clarke, Irwin & Company is used with the permission of Stoddart Publishing Company Limited.

All material quoted from the files of Macmillan of Canada is used with permission.

The excerpt from W.B. Spears' letter to Robertson Davies is reprinted with the permission of The Toronto Star Syndicate.

"If You Can't Sing It (You'll Have To Swing It)—Mr. Paganini," Copyright © 1936 by Famous Music Corporation, Copyright renewed 1936 by Famous Music Corporation, is quoted with permission.

Excerpts from the *Peterborough Examiner* are reprinted with permission.

Photograph and Illustration Credits

Metropolitan Toronto Reference Library, 7.

Robertson and Brenda Davies, 13, 114, 252, 492.

R.W. B. Jackson Library, Ontario Institute for Studies in Education, 58.

Associated University Presses, 388.

Robertson and Brenda Davies, photograph section 1 [1, 2, 3, 4, 5 bottom, 7, 11, 13, 15], and 2 [1, 5, 7 top, 9, 14 bottom, 15].

Upper Canada College, photograph section 1 [8].

Eleanor A. Sweezey, 1 [9 bottom].

Michigan Historical Collections, Bentley Historical Library, University of Michigan, Aa/2 Davenport, Horace W., photograph section 1 [10 top].

Metropolitan Toronto Reference Library, photograph section 1 [12 bottom], and 2 [5, 8, 10].

National Archives of Canada/PA-191382, photograph section 1 [16].

Peterborough Museums and Archives Division (*Overlaid,* and *Man Who Married a Dumb Wife*), photograph section 2 [2, 3].

Agnes Etherington Art Centre, Queen's University, Kingston (a gift of the McLean Foundation), photograph section 2 [4 top].

The Estate of Grant Macdonald, photograph section 2 [4 top, 5].

Margaret Davies, photograph section 2 [6].

Diana Tremain 2 [13 bottom].

Every effort has been made to contact or trace all copyright holders. The publishers will be glad to make good any errors or omissions brought to our attention in future editions.

787

"**R**obertson Davies's skill and curiosity are as agile as ever, and his store of incidental knowledge is a constant pleasure. *Long may he continue to divert us.* — **The New York Times Book Review**

ROBERTSON DAVIES

✿ *THE* ✿
CUNNING MAN

"Once the word is out that a new book has been glimpsed in the bookshops, Davies devotees know that they must buy it and read it. The sooner, the better."
— *The Washington Post Book World*

In this perceptive and entertaining memoir of a doctor's life, we encounter at least one miraculous cure, a bad breath contest of Olympian standards, tales of cannibals and Tsarist bordellos, medical solutions to literary mysteries – and startling insights into the secrets of a doctor's consulting room.

"The sparkling history of [the] erudite and amusing Dr. Hullah, who knows the souls of his patients as well as he knows their bodies…Never fails to both enlighten and delight."
— *The London Free Press*

"…Davies is a good companion. Settling into **The Cunning Man** is like taking a comfortable chair opposite a favourite uncle who has seen and done everything."
— *Maclean's*

"…wonderfully funny, poignant, and never less than totally engrossing…" — *Publishers Weekly*